THE MIDDLE EAST TODAY

THE MIDDLE EAST TODAY

Fourth Edition

Don Peretz

PRAEGER

PRAEGER SPECIAL STUDIES • PRAEGER SCIENTIFIC

Library of Congress Cataloging in Publication Data

Peretz, Don, 1922–
  The Middle East today.

  Bibliography: p.
  Includes index.
  1. Near East—Politics and government. I. Title.
DS62.8.P45 1983   956   83-10887
ISBN 0-03-063347-8 (pbk.)

Published in 1983 by Praeger Publishers
CBS Educational and Professional Publishing
a division of CBS Inc.
521 Fifth Avenue, New York, NY 10175 USA

© 1983 by Praeger Publishers

3456789 052 98765432

Printed in the United States of America
on acid-free paper

Preface

This book is intended as an introduction to the Middle East today for those who have made little or no previous academic study of the region. In attempting to introduce the area as a whole and in treating each of the specific countries, I have tried to simplify many of the complicated background factors and to present them in a fashion that will be comprehensible to the uninitiated.

I have drawn my material from many original and secondary sources and from my own years of experience in the Middle East as a student, journalist, and researcher. Frequently I have borrowed ideas, opinions, and concepts from those who are outstanding scholars in their fields, views with which the novice to the area should become acquainted.

The book first presents some general observations about the area as a whole: how it acquired its specific designation, what some of the general characteristics are, and what remain some of its fundamental internal differences. The beginning chapters trace the Islamic and Ottoman backgrounds and influences common to most of the countries in the region. Each of the principal countries is then examined separately in an attempt to show how it acquired its contemporary image and to present that image as truly as possible.

The fourth edition has much new material added, including discussion of the 1982 war in Lebanon and its impact on the region, the Reagan peace plan, new political orientations within the PLO, and the extensive effects of the 1978 revolution in Iran, including the recent resurgence of Islam.

Since there is a variety of transliterations and spellings of Middle Eastern Arabic, Turkish, Persian, and Hebrew names, I have arbitrarily used spellings that either closely adhere to the original language or are those I think will be most convenient to the reader.

Don Peretz
Binghamton, New York
March 1983

Contents

List of Maps

xiii

What Is the Middle East?

THE IMPORTANCE OF THE MIDDLE EAST

Few regions of the world provoke more interest, controversy, or international crises than the Middle East. Although the region has only come to the fore of American consciousness since World War II, it has been an important arena of world events from the beginning of written history. In ancient times, Egyptian, Sumerian, Babylonian, and Assyrian civilizations flourished in the Middle East. Judaism, the first of the three great monotheistic religions, took form here during the 3000 years of the Old Testament era. From its seeds sprang Christianity and Islam, the two other world faiths born in the Middle East. The region was, successively, a part of the Persian, Greek, Roman, Arab, Mongol, Tatar, and Turkish empires, each contributing to a new fusion of culture and civilization there, fusions that at times reached high points in man's development. During medieval times, the European Crusaders wrested the eastern shores of the Mediterranean from the Muslims in their attempts to seize the Holy Land. The practical result was to open Asia to contact and a free flow of trade with Western Europe.

Napoleon began the era of modern history in the Middle East when he crossed the Mediterranean to reach the banks of the Nile and occupy parts of Palestine. He hoped to establish a base from which to demolish the British Indian empire. Throughout the nineteenth century the great powers, recognizing the strategic value of the Middle East as the gateway to Asia made attempts to neutralize it, or, if that was not possible, to seize for themselves an area of influence within its confines. Tsarist Russia periodically thrust southward in the attempt to expand into Turkey and Iran. Nineteenth-century European diplomacy was plagued by the Eastern Question—as the many problems created by the disintegration of the Ottoman Empire were called—culminating at mid-century in the Crimean War from 1853 to 1856. Thereafter, the rise of numerous Balkan nationalist movements, the opening of the Suez Canal in 1869, and the continuing dispute over the Turkish Straits resulted in several wars and major European diplomatic conferences. At the end of the century Kaiser Wilhelm II, considering the possibilities of the area as a bridge to vast German empire in the East, devoted a major part of his foreign policy to acquiring a foothold on this doorstep to Asia. During both World Wars I and II, the Middle East played a major role in the grand strategy of the major contestants. When the United States and the Soviet Union became allies in World War II, tanks, trucks, and other lend-lease supplies from America reached Russia via the Persian Gulf and Iran.

Before its direct involvement in World War II, the United States concern with the Middle East had been small. To most Americans it seemed as remote as the valleys of the moon. A few missionaries and educators had become involved in setting up churches, schools, and colleges there; archaeologists and students of ancient history knew of the rich heritage of the area; and some commercial interests, such as the American Tobacco Company, which obtained tobacco from Turkey, were drawn to the Middle East. The first American oil holdings were obtained during the 1920s and 1930s, but they did not begin to realize fantastic incomes until after World War II.

By the mid 1940s the oil resources of the Arab world and Iran had become the most important single reason for the strategic value of the region to the United States. Companies with concessions in the Middle East produced hundred-million-dollar incomes, becoming the most profitable of all overseas investments. Oil brought such profits to Western investors because it had become a chief source of energy for European industry. At least 80 to 90 percent of the oil used in most of the countries of Western Europe came from the Middle East. By 1960 Iran and the oil-endowed Arab states were producing nearly a quarter of the world's output and contained two thirds of the known reserves.

The importance of the region's oil and its strategic location on the air and sea routes between Europe and Africa, Southeast Asia, and the Far East involved the Middle East in the bipolar conflict between Communist and non-Communist regions that came to the surface a few months after the end of World War II. Both the Soviet Union and the major Western powers began their attempt to capture or influence the explosive nationalist movements that dominated the Middle Eastern scene in the late 1940s and early 1950s. The contemporary American could no longer consider the Middle East an obscure backwater area of importance only to a few scholars or those with specialized interests.

WHAT DOES "MIDDLE EAST" MEAN?

Both the "Middle East" and the "Near East," the older form of the term, are used daily in the press and even in diplomatic exchanges; yet there exists no general agreement concerning the boundaries of the area so described. Not even scholars who have specialized in the study of this area wholly agree upon what territory or populations should be included in the term. The concept of a "Near East" emerged in the Western world in the great Age of Discovery, which began in the fifteenth century with the explorations of the Portuguese to find a new route to the East. With increasing contact, the area farthest away from Europe came to be called the Far East, while the lands on the eastern shores of the Mediterranean that lay between Europe and the Far East became in common parlance the "Near East." The term was generally used to describe the lands that came to be ruled as part of the Ottoman Empire after 1453. The similar term "Levant," which is sometimes used for this area, merely comes from the French word meaning the "rising" of the sun, or the East.[1]

During World War II the British began officially to categorize as the "Middle East" those Asian and North African lands that lay west of India. One of the largest Allied organizations was the jointly managed British and American Middle East Supply Center set up to service the Arab world, Turkey, Iran, and other nearby countries. Allied military activities in the region were under the British Middle East Command. Countries within the scope of both organizations have continued to be referred to as the "Middle East" by many scholars and writers since the war. General acceptance of the term has been hampered by the tenacity of the previously established usage and by the lack of universally accepted geographical boundaries. "Near East" is increasingly being displaced by "Middle East," however, although the interchangeable terminology continues to create confusion. For example, until recently the National Geographic Society labeled its maps of the area "The Lands of the Near East," while the same region is studied by the Middle East Institute in Washington. The Department of State compromises by using the designation "Near and Middle East." Some definitions include all the territory from Morocco across Arab North Africa through western Pakistan up to the borders of India and from Turkey on the Black Sea southwards through Ethiopia and the Sudan.

Despite conflicting usage, these terms do emphasize that the area being described owes its regional character to other than indigenous factors. As diverse as the countries of Europe, these lands are included in a single term merely because they are "near to" or "in the middle of" other regions. Whatever unity does exist within the region today is largely functional: it is a unity in relation to the outside world rather than an inherent unity arising from similar geographical and social conditions or from a recent common history. Since "Near East" and "Middle East" are Western terms indicating the location of the region relative to Europe, they are often not used at all by Asians. Many Indians, for example, refer to this part of the world today as Southwest Asia.[2]

The Near East or Middle East will be used in this book to include Turkey, Iran, Israel, the Arab countries of Lebanon, Iraq, Jordan, Syria, Egypt, and the kingdoms, sheikhdoms, principalities, and other minor subdivisions of the Arabian heartland.

UNITY AND DIVERSITY IN THE MIDDLE EAST

Physical Geography

The prevailing Western image of the Middle East is a false one of vast desert lands inhabited by nomadic tribesmen mounted on camels or Arabian steeds and driving their flocks of goats and sheep from oasis to oasis. It is true that well over 90 percent of the region is arid and uncultivated because of climatic conditions. In much of the area the climate resembles that in southwestern United States: the Red Sea region is like the Gulf of California; the climate of Israel and Lebanon is similar to that of southern California; the Turkish coasts resemble northern California; and Syria and northern Arabia are arid like Arizona and New Mexico, both separated from a moist coast by a mountain screen. There is nothing in North America, however, as hot and dry as the great desert of central Arabia. However, the generally sparse rainfall, the scarcity of agricultural land, and the limited natural resources of the barren earth have burdened the Middle East with problems common to most arid lands.

Fortunately not all the region is desert wasteland. A fertile crescent stretches along the Levantine coast of the Mediterranean up to the foothills of the Taurus Mountains in Turkey and down again through the Tigris and Euphrates valleys in Syria and Iraq to the Persian Gulf. There are also the great alluvial strip in the Nile Valley, enclaves of fairly rich agricultural land in Iran, and fertile coastal regions in Yemen in southern Arabia and in eastern Turkey along the Mediterranean. Lofty mountain ranges like the Taurus in Turkey, the Elburz and the Zagros in Iran, and the highlands of Yemen cut the region into many isolated units. In the Elburz range the highest peak, Demavend, soars to over 18,900 feet and is snow-capped all year round.

Generally the region is poor in natural resources other than petroleum. Turkey has enough mineral diversity for a modest industrial development; but even its iron, coal, and copper deposits are national resources of secondary importance. Although the oil of Iran and some of the states of the Arabian peninsula is a major asset, its value depends on sales to world markets rather than internal use. Only in recent decades have oil profits been used extensively for national development of basic agricultural resources. Not all the region is "oil rich"; a majority of Middle Eastern countries produce no oil at all or only small quantities of it. Paradoxically, the countries with the greatest rate of economic development—Egypt, Syria, Turkey, and Israel—have only relatively small petroleum deposits, while those rich in this resource—such as Saudi Arabia, Kuwait, and Abu Dhabi have difficulty in absorbing hundreds of millions of dollars annually in constructive development projects. Iraq and Iran have made major efforts to use oil profits for building up the nation, but political and social obstacles have prevented real success.

Water is the scarcest and most valuable resource of the Middle East. While the total amount available is not inconsiderable, poor distribution creates the region's major problem. A greater part of the desert will always remain desert, for little can be done to alter the climatic conditions that have made most of the Middle East arid. The only hope for the better use of water is in improving irrigation facilities connected with the region's few rivers, or desalination of brackish water. At present about 5 percent of the total area is used for crops. About one fifth of the cultivated land requires additional water. To expand the cultivated area by as much as 1 or 2 percent a decade, with present methods of increasing irrigation and soil productivity, would require a massive effort. Meanwhile, population increases at over 2 percent a year, creating a lag of resources behind population growth. Cheap processes for desalting sea water may soon be available, but even if there were unlimited amounts of irrigation water from the ocean, the cost of pumping it into upland fields would be prohibitive. Consequently, most of the approximately three million square miles in the Middle East will remain permanently unproductive desert and mountain.

There are only two major river systems in the area covered by this book: the Nile, fed by sources in Ethiopia and Central Africa, and the Shatt el-Arab, fed by the Euphrates, Tigris, and Karun rivers. The only other river over 350 miles long is the Kizil Irmak (Red River) in Turkey. Parallel to the eastern Mediterranean shore, the Jordan, Litani, and Orontes rivers create small fertile areas in Lebanon, Israel, Jordan, and Syria. The largest of these, the Jordan itself, is only 85 miles long. The length of the Jordan Valley from the principal source of the river at Mount Hermon to the southern end of the stream at the Dead Sea is 110 miles.

Agricultural Produce and Livestock
The principal food crop grown throughout the area is wheat, which was probably first cultivated in the Middle East. Turkey is a large producer, although it is the mainstay of life in each of the countries we shall survey. Barley is the second most important food crop, known in the region since neolithic times. Its pattern of distribution, like wheat, is concentrated in the

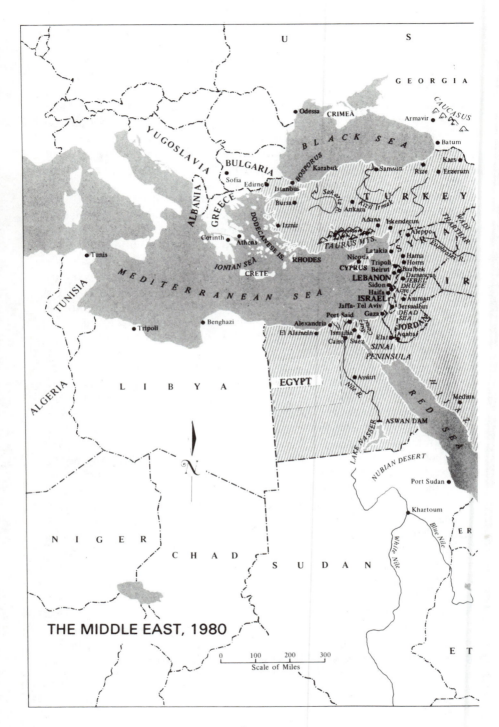

THE MIDDLE EAST, 1980

0   100   200   300
Scale of Miles

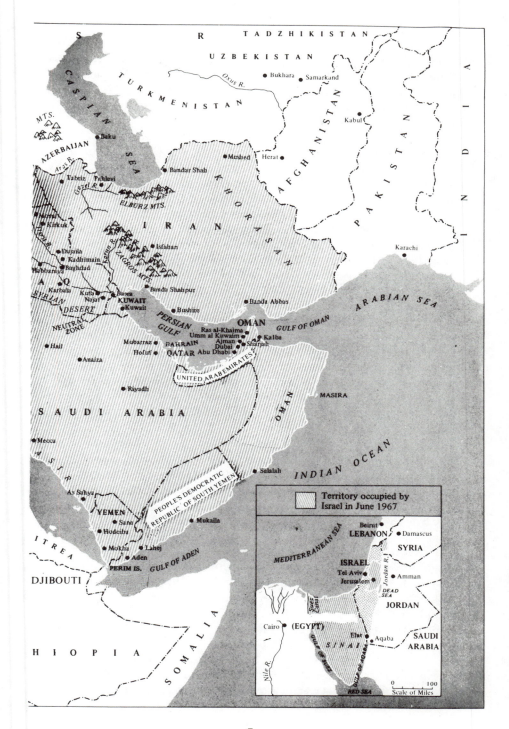

north, with crops becoming increasingly sparse as one moves toward southern Arabia. Most other grains like corn and rye and the drought-tolerant crops such as millets and sorghums are also grown. Rice is a favored crop, especially in the desert, and is grown with the aid of irrigation primarily in Egypt, Iran, and in the marsh lands of lower Iraq.

Despite the existence of such a widespread grain area, the Middle East as a whole does not produce enough to feed itself. It is a net importer of grain, although some barley and rice are exported. Turkey, Iraq, and Syria sometimes have a wheat surplus, while Iran, Israel, and Egypt commonly must import grain.

Principal Middle Eastern tree crops are olives, citrus fruits, and dates. The coastal regions of Turkey, Syria, Lebanon, and Israel produce olives; Iran is a minor producer. The citrus probably originated in the area and was introduced to Europe by the Crusaders in the eleventh century. Oranges, raised in the Levant, southern Turkey, and northern Iran, are the leading citrus crop. They are one of Israel's leading exports, having supplied more than half its foreign-currency earnings during the country's first decade. Dates, the chief diet item of the desert nomad, are the one important crop in which the Middle East leads. Three quarters of the world's supply are grown in one country—Iraq. The date has many uses. Not only is it a food staple, it is mashed and fermented to provide alcohol for the native drink *arak*; the pits are ground up as animal fodder; fibers of the date-tree trunk make excellent rope, and its wood is a source of fuel. Date palms occupy about 90 percent of most Arabian peninsula oases. Saudi Arabia and Iran follow Iraq as principal producers.

Many varieties of fruits and nuts are grown. Almonds, walnuts, hazelnuts, and pistachios are common. Lebanon's excellent apples are raised in its highlands; superior apricots and melons are grown in Iran; and Turkish figs are world famous. As in all Mediterranean lands, the production of grapes ranks high. Most grapes are dried and used as raisins, however, since the use of wine is prohibited by Islamic law.

The leading industrial crop is cotton. Egypt's long-fiber cotton is its most vital export, although the government has been attempting to diversify agricultural production to avoid overdependence on this single crop. Turkey follows Egypt in the production of cotton, but its total crop is far less. Syria, Iraq, Israel, and Iran have experimented with cotton, but they cannot compete with Egypt's long staple export. Flax, hemp, and silk are also grown in the fertile crescent region, but not in large enough quantities to become major exports.

Among other minor crops is coffee, cultivated on the mountain slopes of Yemen. In ancient times it was exported from Mocha, but the port is little used now. Small quantities of tea are grown in the north along Turkey's Black Sea coast and the Caspian shore of Iran. Both beet and sugar cane are also produced, primarily in Turkey. Near its Aegean Sea coast Turkey also raises tobacco and the crop is produced in small quantities along the Levant coast and in Iran.

Livestock is an important source of income for both the desert nomad and the settled cultivator. The camel is still the distinctive animal of the Middle East. Unsubstantiated estimates by the U.N. Food and Agricultural Organization suggest that the total number of camels today is under a million. Perhaps twice that number existed before the truck displaced the caravan. So important has the "ship of the desert" been, however, that there are a thousand Arabic terms for camels in various stages of growth. They still supply the desert nomad with transport, food, and wealth. He drinks their milk, eats their flesh, weaves their hair into tents and cloaks, burns their dung for fuel, uses their urine for medicine and hair tonic, measures a bride's dowry in camels, and uses the beast to turn his water wheel and pull his plow.

Both the sheep and goats are raised throughout the area. Their numbers are estimated in tens of millions. Unlike the camel, they can go without water only two or three days; therefore their grazing areas are limited to a few miles from a watering place. Goats, known as the poor man's cow, are notorious for their destructive way of eating grass down to the roots so that it cannot reproduce itself. Attempts at reforestation and land reclamation are doomed so long as goats are permitted to graze without restriction.

Cattle are small in size and few in number because of fodder shortages. Their milk yield is low, so most of them are used as draft animals. They are more commonly raised by settled farmers than by nomads, who prefer the more mobile sheep and goats. In areas inundated by water, like the marshlands of southern Iraq and the Nile Valley, the water buffalo replaces the cow as a draft animal.

Horses are becoming less common in the Middle East, the famous Arabian breeds being now only a luxury animal. More commonly used for riding is the donkey. Pigs are also relatively scarce, being raised only by the Christian minorities because of the Islamic prohibition on pork.

Ethnic Geography

Middle Eastern life has always been marked by its oasis character. Since time immemorial clusters of families have gathered around a spring or a river bank or in an area of greater rainfall. Within such more or less isolated geographic pockets a variety of peoples and cultures have developed, many having little knowledge of their neighbors, being cut off from them by natural barriers. Islands of culture have thus developed in many areas, each society consisting of limited, self-sustaining settlements isolated by the surrounding aridity. Until very modern times, the only links with the outside world that these "islanders" had were the occasional camel caravans passing through the barren wastes from one isolated settlement to another.

The largest island or oasis is that of the desert Arabs in Saudi Arabia, where, as it has been phrased by Philip Hitti, "ethnic purity is a reward...of ungrateful and isolated environment." In the highland plateaus of the Levant coast are found pockets of religious groups such as the Samaritans, Druses, Maronites, Metawilas, and Alawis. In Iran, the Bakhtiari and Kashgai tribes, if they have not kept themselves completely isolated, have at least maintained their cultural autonomy behind their mountain walls. In eastern Anatolia and northern Iran the Kurds, as an ethnic group, have preserved a distinctive identity within the protecting Taurus and Zagros ranges. In northern Iraq are the Kurds, the Yezidis, a religious faction, and the Circassians and Turcomens, tribes with their own distinctive languages.

The main peoples with which we will deal in our study of the modern Middle East are the Semitic, Turkish, and Iranian linguistic groups. These are broad classifications and within each there are numerous subdivisions. It is difficult, if not impossible, to divide them into precise, scientific categories. Terms such as race, nationality, and religion often have meanings in the Middle East that differ from those of the Western world. For this reason the following descriptions of the peoples of the Middle East, using these classifications, must be understood as approximations only.

The Semites. The largest group is the Semitic, whose principal living tongues are Arabic and Hebrew, the language of modern Israel. A few small remnants still use Chaldean and Syriac, but primarily for religious purposes. Our knowledge of Semitic languages begins with the written records left by the Akkadians, who were the forebears of the Babylonians and Assyrians. None of these civilizations has any existing direct linguistic or ethnic survivors except for the few users of Syriac.

The tiny group of people which today call themselves Assyrians do not speak that ancient language but a modern form of Syriac, which is a branch of Aramaic. During the time of Christ, Aramaic was the language of Palestine west of the Jordan and also that of Iraq. The Semitic peoples who adopted Christianity used Aramaic and its Syriac script. When the Arabs swept up out of Arabia into Syria and Iraq, the majority of the inhabitants in these regions were members of various Christian sects using variants of the Aramaic language and script. As the new conquerors established themselves, most of these peoples learned Arabic and became Muslims. Small, scattered pockets of Christians assimilated the Arabic language but retained their own religion. Today in Iraq there are still remnants of the Nestorians, formerly the principal Christian sect in the area. Larger early Christian groups remain unconverted in Syria, and in Lebanon nearly half the population today are Maronites (Eastern Uniates who are under the Church of Rome), Greek Orthodox,

Jacobites, and other sects who are unconverted descendants from the pre-Islamic era. Most of these sects continue to use Syriac as a ritual language, and in a few villages the language is still spoken.

The origin of both modern Arabic and Hebrew script can be traced to the Phoenicians, another ancient but now extinct Semitic people. Historians postulate that they migrated to the Levant coast from the shores of the Persian Gulf around the beginning of the Iron Age. Not only were the Phoenicians responsible for originating the Semitic alphabets, they also introduced many new techniques in craftsmanship and navigation. They explored the Mediterranean and opened the first sea-trade routes between the Middle East and Europe. Carthage, in North Africa, was originally a Phoenician traders' outpost. Although there are no Phoenicians today, the Arab sailors of Kuwait and Muscat and the traders of Lebanon dealing in global commerce may well be descendants of this ancient inventive and productive people.

The Arabs. Arabic was not originally the language of all this region. Its spread is a relatively new phenomenon in history. Two thousand years ago it was but one of many Semitic languages with its locus in central Arabia. Not until the Arab conquests following the birth of Islam in the seventh and eighth centuries did it reach a position of cultural dominance. Prior to that time the languages of North Africa and parts of Iran were not Semitic, and those of Palestine and Syria, although Semitic, were not Arabic.

In the area we will cover, nearly one hundred million inhabitants are called, or call themselves, Arabs. Although the Arabs have much in common, there is almost as much diversity in their language and way of life as there is among the Latin peoples on the other side of the Mediterranean. In some respects there is even greater variety.

The term Arab does not yet designate a formal nationality, for there is still no single Arab nation—although many Arab nationalists aspire to one. Arabs are today nationals of Egypt, the Kingdom of Saudi Arabia, the Hashemite Kingdom of Jordan, the Republic of Lebanon, the Republic of Iraq, the Syrian Arab Republic, or, until recently, if inhabitants of the Crown Colony of Aden or one of the Aden protectorates, which became the People's Democratic Republic of South Yemen, they may have traveled on British passports under the protection of the British sovereign.

Neither does the term indicate race in the modern, anthropological sense. Along the eastern coast of the Mediterranean there are whole towns full of blond, blue-eyed, light-skinned Arabs. Many of the leaders of the Arab world, in a mixed gathering of diplomats, would be indistinguishable from Germans or Swedes. But in the streets of almost any metropolis in the Arab world a traveler will pass some Arabs whose black skin, kinky hair, and Negroid facial features would not seem out of place in Ghana or Nigeria. Africa's contribution through migration and the slave trade to the racial types of the

Middle East is evident. So great is the variety in hues of skin color, head shape, facial features, type of hair, and body build throughout the Arab East that the term Arab cannot be understood to indicate race.

Frequently in discussions of Middle East problems we hear mention of "Jews and Arabs" in the area. This may result from wrongly interchanging the terms "Arab" and "Muslim," "Jew" and "Zionist." So common is this error that in an early United Nations debate on the Palestine problem, United States Representative Warren Austin called upon "Jews and Arabs" to settle their differences in a "Christian" manner. Apparently Mr. Austin, as so many non-Middle Easterners, failed to realize that not all Arabs are Muslim. Indeed, there are actually thousands of Arab Jews. Even larger—several million—are the numbers of Arab Christians. True, all Arab nations, except Lebanon, are predominantly Muslim, but Islam is the official religion in only a few. Most of these countries are Muslim only in the sense that the United States is Christian. In fact the Arabs constitute but a small minority of the world's Muslim population. Out of a world total of nearly a billion Muslims, less than a fifth are Arab. Obviously then, the term "Arab" does not indicate the religion of those who so classify themselves.

What does the term mean then if it does not indicate race, religion, or nationality? As other such ethnic terms, like that of Jew, it is easier to indicate what an Arab is not than what he is. Arab national leaders are more and more associating the term with language, with culture, and with a vague, intangible emotional identification with "the Arab cause." This is not an incontestable definition. There are many individuals and groups of people whose native tongue is Arabic but who would not consider themselves members of the Arab community. Professor H.A.R Gibb of Harvard maintained that all those are Arabs for whom the central fact of history is the mission of Muhammad and the memory of the Arab Empire and who in addition cherish the Arabic tongue and its cultural heritage as their common possession. For the sake of convenience, we will accept as a general rule that an Arab is one whose native language and culture is Arabic and who identifies with "Arab" problems, which will be discussed later.

Although we will deal only with the Arabic-speaking nations on the Asian continent and with Egypt, the other African countries that are Arab should be noted: Sudan, Libya, Morocco, Mauritania, Somalia, Djibouti, Tunisia, and Algeria. They, along with Egypt, Syria, Iraq, Lebanon, Jordan, Yemen, the People's Democratic Republic of Yemen, Kuwait, Saudi Arabia, Bahrain, Oman, Qatar, United Arab Emirates, and Palestine, are members of the League of Arab States. The official language of all is Arabic, and all consider themselves to be Arab nations. The single greatest factor of unity and common identity among them is language. An approximate comparison is the somewhat similar identity of the English-speaking countries—the United

States, Great Britain, and the British Commonwealth nations: Canada, Australia, and New Zealand.

But even accepting this generalization, one is likely to fall into oversimplification. Although the literate inhabitants of all the Arab nations read and write the same language, local dialects, of which there are dozens, are quite varied. Such dialects are often mixed with Persian, Turkish, English, French, or Berber words, depending on the speaker's origin. Carleton S. Coon in *Caravan* tells of the chagrin felt by a devout Arabian Muslim on his pilgrimage to Mecca when an Algerian Arab greeted him with *"Bonjour 'alaikum"* (with the Arabic meaning "unto you"). Colloquial Arabic is so imprecise that often the same terms have opposite meanings in different parts of the Arab world. For example, North Africans say *muzien* for "good," while in Iraq *mu-zen,* pronounced almost the same way, has the opposite meaning.

In general, there are five main groups of Arabic dialects within which exist dozens of subdivisions: Moroccan spoken west of Tunis; Egyptian divided from Syrian and Arabian dialects by the Sinai peninsula; Syrian spoken in western Jordan, Israel, Lebanon, and Syria; the speech of Iraq; and that considered to be most pure, spoken east of the Jordan and in Arabia.

The classical, or written, Arabic that is common to all literate Arabs, and to millions of other Muslims, is found in the Koran, Islam's Holy Book, which Muslims believe was revealed to the Prophet Muhammad by Allah, the Arabic word for God. Indeed, many devout Muslims in Pakistan, Iran, Turkey, and Indonesia cannot speak Arabic but can read it, and use it for worship.

In modern times, with the development of mass communications and diffusion of newspapers, radio broadcasts, and motion pictures, it has become increasingly necessary to fuse the classical and colloquial languages; to this end there is now emerging a popular newspaper Arabic in which the Egyptian and Syrian dialects are most influential.

The Jews. The only other large Semitic group in the Middle East are the Jews, now concentrated in Israel. Their language, Hebrew (not to be confused with Yiddish, an East European German dialect using many Hebrew expressions, as well as Hebrew script, and sometimes called "Jewish"), is derived from the same source as Arabic and is like a sister tongue because it is so similar in grammar, vocabulary, sentence structure, and script. Not only are the roots of many Arabic and Hebrew words identical, but actual terminology is so similar that a knowledge of either Hebrew or Arabic gives a student considerable advantage in learning the other.

Like "Arab," the term "Jew" is difficult to define and the subject of much controversy. It is, of course, not a nationality since there are not only Israeli but American, French, Russian, and even Arab Jews. Racially the Jews are as composite a people as the Arabs, if not more so. The racial types visible in the streets of Tel Aviv or Jerusalem today are literally gathered from the four corners of the earth. Fair-skinned "Nordics," Negroes, brown-skinned Indians, and even a few Chinese mix in the racial mélange.

Most controversial is the question of whether or not the designation "Jewish" indicates only religion or some broader classification, such as an ethnic group or a "people." In Israel and elsewhere there are many individuals who are not religious in any commonly accepted sense of the term, yet they consider themselves and are regarded by others as Jews. There are also a few Israeli Jews who have converted to Christianity but insist that they are still Jewish. Most Israeli Jews link being Jewish with nationality since, they maintain, Israel was established as a "Jewish State." When the issue was debated in the Knesset (the Israeli parliament) during 1960–1961, some members insisted that anyone choosing to call himself a Jew and to identify with Jewish problems and life should be accepted as Jewish. At the other extreme, orthodox religious members would exclude anyone whose mother was not a Jewess, or who had not gone through the conversion ritual prescribed by orthodox Jewish law and tradition. They would in fact have excluded thousands of Israelis who were accepted as Jews but were the offspring of non-Jewish mothers. To clarify the issue, Prime Minister Ben Gurion sent questionnaires to recognized Jewish scholars around the world requesting their opinions. So varied were the views that the matter has not yet been resolved.

Although the Jews are Semitic people by virtue of their historic and contemporary use of Hebrew, it is the native tongue of less than half of the population of Israel. Most inhabitants immigrated to the new state from other areas and had to learn the language upon arrival. Consequently, the Semitic Hebrew of modern Israel is a strange blend of accents. It is spoken with Polish, Russian, French, English, Arabic, and other nuances, although the Eastern European intonation is considered most acceptable because the original Jewish settlers in the country came from that part of the world.

The Turks. After the Semitic peoples, the next largest group in the Middle East is the Turks. They are descended from tribes which swept out of Central Asia in the eleventh and twelfth centuries. As the Turkish tribes moved west, they were converted to Islam, and the overwhelming majority of Turks today are Muslim. Indeed, the term "Turk" generally refers to a Muslim whose mother tongue is Turkish. In the contemporary Turkish Republic, although the constitution specifically separates the state and religion, it is the rare non-Muslim Turkish citizen who will claim he or she is a Turk.

The Turks are related to the tribes of Mongoloid peoples—of which the Huns were the first to achieve fame—that came out of the grasslands of

Mongolia to overrun most of Europe as well as the Middle East at one time. Their linguistic influence in Europe is still evident in Hungarian, which stems from the same origins as Turkish—the Ural-Altaic family of languages that includes both Finnish and Mongolian.

Turkish tribes began infiltrating the Middle East by way of Turkestan during the seventh century. After their conversion to Islam they invaded Asia Minor, where they set up the Seljuk Sultanate of Rum—at that time inhabited principally by Christian Greeks, Armenians, Syrians, and Muslim Kurds (see chapter 3). Since then most of these groups have been assimilated, although small clusters remain within modern Turkey.

The Turks were followed by the Mongols who, led by Genghis Khan (1162–1227), overran most of Iran in the thirteenth century. His grandson, Hulagu, destroyed Baghdad and laid waste the formerly fertile country by destroying the great irrigation works that controlled the flow of the Tigris-Euphrates river system. So terrible was the havoc they wrought that the memory of the Mongols is today still regarded with dread in Iraq. The Mongol dynasty disintegrated during the fourteenth century leaving behind it not much more than an ugly memory. A few thousand of their racially recognizable descendants can still be found in eastern Iran and western Afghanistan.

The greatest Turkish impact on the Middle East was through the Ottoman Empire. In the clashes between the Mongols and the Turks, the Seljuk Sultanate of Rum was toppled, and another tribe of Anatolian Turks, named after their leader Osman (Osmanli or Ottoman), began their steady ascent to power—a struggle that, within a few centuries, brought them the caliphate of Islam and control of the Middle East up to the gates of Iran (see chapter 3). For 400 years the Ottoman Empire dominated the Arab East, until the end of World War I, when it was carved up into a number of separate Arab states and the present Turkish republic.

Today the geographic boundaries of the Turkish republic overlap an area in which live over forty-five million people, or less than half of those who are Turkish speaking. In the Soviet Union there are over sixty million Turkish-speaking peoples, who inhabit the Central Asian and Caucasion areas bordering Turkey, Iran, and Afghanistan. They are the second most numerous ethnic minority in the USSR after the Slavs. At least six million Iranians exhibit elements of Turkish in their speech. In Afghanistan there are over a million and a half such Turkish-speaking people, and there are a few thousand others scattered throughout the Arab nations.

There are well over one hundred million people whose speech is strongly influenced by Turkish, more than half of whom are behind the "iron curtain." Aside from the millions of such people in the Soviet Union, there are several millions in Communist China and a very small number in Korea. Strong religious and linguistic ties bind them with their ethnic cousins in Turkey, as evidenced by the unqualified willingness of the Turkish republic to take in thousands of refugees whose spoken language is some Turkish dialect.

During the nineteenth and early twentieth centuries there were Pan-Turkish movements, but there is no strong sentiment in that direction today. No concept like the Arab passion for "unity," or the Zionist ideal of "ingathering" all Jews to Israel affected republican Turkey. The idea of unifying the Turkish world was cast aside by Ataturk after World War I and has never since been seriously revived.

The Iranians. The Persian-speaking Iranians, numbering over thirty million, are the third largest linguistic group of Middle Eastern peoples. They belong to the Indo-Europeans, who originated outside the Middle East and heavily influenced, as the name indicates, the languages of Europe. There were several Indo-European languages in ancient times. Other ethnic groups who today speak their own distinctive Indo-European languages are the Pathans, Kafirs, Armenians, Greeks, and the Sephardic Jews who use Ladino.

Linguistically related to the Iranians are the Kurds, who are scattered through eastern Turkey, Iraq, northern Syria, northeastern Iran, and Russia. Accurate statistics are unavailable and estimates concerning their numbers range from three and one half million to eleven million. Scholars generally accept the figure of eight and one half million to ten million, of whom over four million are in Turkey, three million in Iran, two million in Iraq, and one half million in Syria and Russian Transcaucasia. The Kurds have been able to maintain not only their common language and cultural characteristics but also the physical traits that tend to identify them because of their self-imposed isolation. In Turkey, Iraq, and Iran, they constitute such large minorities that they frequently cause complicated political problems. There has never been a really independent Kurdish nation, but rather a tradition of tribal autonomy. Yet a strong "national" sentiment does exist. Again, it is difficult to define in precise terms the bonds of Kurdish kinship, for like some other peoples we have been describing, the Kurds are not a race, they have no political state, and they possess no religion exclusively their own (nearly all are Sunni Muslims). Yet they are a characteristic "national" group in the Middle East. So strong is their national sentiment that in World War I the Allied nations promised to carve a national territory for the Kurds out of the fragments of the Ottoman Empire. But the Turkish republic refused to surrender this area and the plan failed (see sections on Kurds in chapters on Iraq and Iran).

HOW THE PEOPLES LIVE

Under 50 percent of Middle Easterners cultivate the soil; more than 45 percent are urban dwellers; and less than 5 percent are nomads. Although rural, urban, and nomad patterns of life have distinctive characteristics, they also differ, not only from country to country but even within each nation. Since 1970 there has been a rapid shift of population from the countryside to the cities.

Rural Life

The cultivators of the Middle East share many of the problems found in most underdeveloped and nonproductive regions. They include the unscientific use of soil and water; the possession of antiquated agricultural tools; poor health, which not only causes a high mortality but also restricts productive capacity; and illiteracy, which contributes to slowness in accepting such new ideas as modern technology and agronomy.

The average Middle Eastern peasant lives not on a farm, but in a village near or in the midst of his fields. For generations families have lived in the same village and tilled the same plot of land. Life follows a changeless pattern engraved by custom, religion, and the cycles of the agricultural seasons. When the peasant leaves his hut at sunrise, he goes out to work as his ancestors before him labored for centuries.

His tools are as ancient as his way of life. Those used by the Egyptian peasant are depicted in 2000-year-old Ptolemaic temples. They are a short-handled hoe, the long, pointed wooden plow, and the *shaduf,* a pole weighted at one end and attached at the other to a skin bag or pitcher, used to draw water from the irrigation canals. These tools are similar throughout the area, for only few farmers have access to mechanized methods of agriculture, although the number is growing. In areas like Egypt, some forms of agricultural mechanization would be uneconomical because of the large labor surplus available.

Although there are variations in architecture due to climatic conditions and available building materials, rural villages in the Middle East greatly resemble one another. In most, the one- or two-story dwellings are jammed together with little space between them. In mountain regions greater use is made of stone, while in the mud-rich river valleys, the one- or two-room sun-baked houses are made of crude mud bricks mixed with straw. In Egypt, village construction has changed little since the time of the Pharaohs. There the peasant makes his adobe brick, an ideal material for so rainless a country, by treading down the mud used as raw material with chopped straw. The adobe keeps out the heat so that indoor temperatures may be almost pleasantly cool while it may be over 100° F outside. However, in times of flood, the material melts away and whole villages or towns have disappeared when the Nile has overflowed.

Houses, mostly flat roofed, are generally built around a courtyard and face south to absorb the winter sun. Within the compact enclosure live dozens of people of all ages with their water buffalo, cattle, an ox or camel, an ass, and a few scrawny chickens. Furniture, if it exists at all, is sparse, and the average hut is furnished only with a crude grass mat or carpet to cover the earthen floor.

Bread is the staff of peasant life, supplemented by some vegetables. Occasionally, on festive days such as the Prophet's birthday, there are eggs, meat, and fruit. Clothing is of the most simple kind. In Egypt the male peasant wears a cotton nightgownlike garment called the *galabiya*. Elsewhere men wear coarse, loose cotton trousers drawn together at the waist and a cotton shirt. Most women are wrapped in long black garments, the style of which varies from country to country.

Disease, high birth and mortality rates, and illiteracy plague village life here as in most of Asia. Intestinal and eye diseases are prevalent. Even though there has been vast improvement in public health and available medical facilities, lack of sanitation and deficient nutrition make the peasant continuously susceptible to sickness. In some areas the use of narcotics to escape daily drudgery and pain is habitual. In Iran a quarter of the population is believed to be addicted to opium.

Most Middle Eastern farmers are share-cropping tenants who are bound to their native villages. Their only source of income is a portion of the crop they grow, which varies from 50 down to 20 percent depending on the services, such as seed, work animals, water, or tools, supplied by the land owners. In some rural regions powerful landlords own great tracts of the most fertile land, although agrarian reform has changed conditions of tenancy throughout the area since the Egyptian revolution in 1952. Until recently, Syrian agriculture was dominated by owners who lived in the cities and had little interest in farming. Until the 1958 revolution in Iraq great sheikhs and urban merchants controlled most of the holdings. Before 1952 half of Egypt's agricultural land was owned by wealthy farmers, many of whom actually lived on the soil and hired the laborers. Until Iran's agrarian reform, at least half the land was owned by absentee owners, a quarter by religious foundations, and 10 percent by the state and royal family, leaving about 15 percent in the hands of peasant cultivators.

The Townsman
The greatest diversity within the Middle East is in its towns and cities. They vary from the most modern "Western" centers like Haifa or Beirut to towns that are now emerging from the Middle Ages, like Mecca or Sana. Until the population explosion of the 1960s, only six cities had more than half a million inhabitants: Cairo, Alexandria, Istanbul, Beirut, Baghdad, and Tehran. Probably two dozen others had populations between 100,000 and 500,000. In recent years the number of large cities has increased with the inflow of present population and high birth rates. The area is dotted with several thousand towns of a few hundred people, and tens of thousands of villages with as few as a dozen families. The large cities, except for those in Iraq and Iran, are concentrated near the Mediterranean coast.

Urban centers are formed through numerous influences. Politics has shaped capitals such as Ankara and Riyadh. Jerusalem and Mecca were religious centers. Cairo, now one of the world's ten most populous cities, is a center of education, culture, and government. Beirut, Alexandria, and Haifa are large Mediterranean seaports. Isfahan and Meshed grew up around oases in arid regions. New centers in the Persian Gulf developed from the oil industry. Throughout the region there are hundreds of market towns and centers of production where semiskilled craftsmen turn out their products. Often cities are at the center of rich agricultural areas, from which the urban populations obtain their food.

Middle Eastern cities have traditionally been divided into quarters or sections inhabited by distinctive religious or ethnic groups or by specific crafts and trades—such as tinsmiths, brass workers, or money changers (in the manner of medieval cities in the West). Often members of specific religious or ethnic groups historically practiced or monopolized certain professions. Thus commerce was usually divided among non-Muslims and those who practiced commerce lived in one of the Christian or Jewish quarters, although in modern times these patterns have broken down.

Within some Middle Eastern cities can be found the remnants of ancient walls that once surrounded them for protection against marauding tribesmen or other enemies. But by the mid-nineteenth century when security conditions had improved, cities began to spread beyond these ancient barriers. Today most cities have suburbs as modern as those of any Western nation. Nearly all large towns and cities are rapidly growing due to population explosion resulting from improved health conditions and the influx of rural inhabitants attracted by new opportunities in commerce and industry. This urban growth is marked on the one hand by modern office buildings, apartment houses, and theatres and on the other by badly crowded slum dwellings that have grown up around the edges of many cities to house dislocated peasants and nomads who congregate there in their search for work.

Because most of the educated elite live in cities, such centers also become the focus of political action. It is in the cities that political parties are born and the leaders emerge who will form new governments, engage in parliamentary debates, and draft new constitutions. The mob demonstrations that can make or break a government take place in the cities. It is there that monarchies have become republics, there that our daily newspaper headlines are made, and there that international crises arise.

Because of their great mélange of religions, races, and political and social groups, it is impossible to generalize about Middle Eastern cities. They often contain nearly every racial type and political creed. Within urban centers exist the greatest extremes of poverty and affluence. While the most wealthy live in magnificent palaces in lavish splendor, the great mass of people dwell in miserable poverty. Only during the past few decades has there begun to emerge a large middle class. In general, living conditions of the city dweller are far worse than those of his rural cousins. City life disrupts the conservative family patterns established by ancient tradition in the rural areas. Political agitators who violate these patterns often succeed in arousing the towns to violent action. In rural areas poverty can be more easily endured because of the interdependence of large families. When they come to the cities and become part of the urban proletariat, however, the former countrymen become isolated from and lose their ties with their extended families.

Among the urban elite and newly forming middle class, there is a blending of Oriental and Western culture. New political and social ideologies have been brought into the country by the upper- and middle-class urban dweller from his studies in European and American universities. The bazaar merchant, the taxi driver, and the tinsmith all have their opinions about international affairs, opinions that would often be quite incomprehensible to the village farmer. With the advent of modern communications the city dweller is no longer isolated from the influence of the contemporary world. In response to his new environment he has developed a wide range of economic and political interests that differentiate him from the great peasant majority. The Middle Eastern city has thus become the frontier between centuries, the center where the untroubled past of the countryside meets the turbulent currents of modernity.

The Nomad

To many Westerners, the most familiar Middle Eastern figure is the nomad tribesman, roaming the desert. The nomad's way of life still plays an important role in most of the Middle East, but its importance is declining as thousands each year become settled agriculturalists or seek permanent urban employment. The process of making permanent settlers of the nomads has been hastened by the growth of more strongly centralized governments and the impact of Western technology, especially the development of communications which has ended the isolation of many areas inaccessible before the advent of the automobile, the airplane, and the radio.

But there are a few wandering tribes still searching for a livelihood in all Middle Eastern nations. In general they occupy semiarid lands between the barren desert and the fringes of cultivated areas. Two types of nomadism prevail: "horizontal" and "vertical." The "horizontal" nomads follow the rain across the desert. When during autumn and winter months fertile areas are extended by rainfall, their wanderings are fewer, for in these seasons their flocks and herds, the mainstay of their livelihood, have less trouble in finding grazing land. During the summer, however, the desert residents must search out camp sites near permanent water supplies. Their camels drink more frequently at this time because of the heat and lack of moisture in the fodder. In winter, when water is less scarce, nomads may also raise a few scattered grain crops if they are near a sufficiently fertile area.

"Vertical" nomads live in or near mountainous regions, such as those in western Iran. They winter on the plains and ascend the mountains in early summer. Month by month they follow the burgeoning vegetation to higher altitudes. In the fall, the journey is reversed and they follow the vegetation line down to the plains again.

The largest area of nomadism is still central Arabia, although there are also Arab tribes along the semiarid strips of land dividing settled regions from desert areas, as in Egypt's Western Desert, the Sinai peninsula, the Negev desert of Israel, and in Iraq, Syria, Lebanon, and Jordan. Most Turkish nomads are Kurds, while those in Iran include Arabs, Kurds, Bakhtiari, Kashgai, and Lurs.

Most nomad life is pastoral, based on raising sheep and goats and selling their by-products, milk, butter, cheese, and wool, to the towns. The type of nomad called *Bedouin* also breeds camels and horses. The wandering tribes virtually live on their flocks and herds. They dwell in black goat- or camel-hair tents, woven by the women. For the Bedouin, the one-humped camel, or dromedary, supplies milk and meat, clothing and housing, and transportation. Since they are so mobile, the nomads have few possessions. Their tents are furnished only with floor rugs or mats and the utensils needed for daily life.

The Arab, Kurd, and Persian nomadic tribes are all organized along similar lines. Their immediate families, extended families, clans, and tribes are all organized into federations ruled by elected or hereditary leaders called sheikhs by the Arabs and khans in Iran. In all nomad groups, loyalty to the tribe is supreme, rather than loyalty to some distant, often unsympathetic government. Because of this loyalty to none other than their own leaders and their unabating individualism, tribes have often become a law unto themselves, presenting great problems to central government authorities. They refuse to pay taxes, to recognize the laws of parliaments, to render military service, or to respect national frontiers.

Reluctance to obey constituted authority has frequently brought the tribes into conflict with national governments. With the establishment of immigration and custom regulations, and the growing importance of border security, governments have become increasingly reluctant to allow these traditional wanderers the free movement to which they have been accustomed for centuries. In recent years their perambulations have caused international border conflicts. For example, Israel's attempts to prevent the traditional cross-frontier wanderings of the Negev Bedouin once led to clashes with Egypt that eventually came before the United Nations. In Arabia, the Saudi, Iraq, and Kuwait governments attempted to deal with traditional Bedouin border crossings by establishing neutral zones into which the tribes could move freely between the nations without interference.

Some Western writers have romanticized Bedouin life because of their attraction to its apparent freedom and dignity. The social customs of the

Bedouin, for instance, are closely akin to those that were followed by the Prophet Muhammad and his followers, and their speech is the purest Arabic. Their hospitality and systems of dealing with slaves and enemies are still those prescribed in the Koran, the Holy Book of Islam.

Although within a generation or two the romantic picture of the Middle Eastern nomad will probably fade away, his contribution to the history of the region will continue to be important. Born in the heart of nomadic society, Islamic ideas, customs, and observances continue to reflect the social practices of tribal Arabia during the time of Muhammad. The Islamic concept of God, according to some scholars, is that of the paramount sheikh—powerful, just, gracious to his own tribesmen, yet with a streak of unpredictability. The interrelationships among Islamic communities, both between believers and between believers and outside groups, still reflect the pattern of Bedouin life.

From this brief description of the Middle East as a whole, we see, on the one hand, that the region has many common characteristics that can be attributed to both natural forces and history. On the other hand, so great is the diversity among and within these countries that variety is as much an intrinsic characteristic as are the unifying qualities and attributes. How then did the region become the "Middle East"? This appellation is more the result of history than of geography. The next chapter will trace the early historical forces that gave the "Middle East" its distinctive identity.

NOTES

1.   In this book the term "Levant" will be used to mean specifically the eastern coast of the Mediterranean and its hinterland.

2.   In his geography of the area, George B. Cressey also calls the region Southwest Asia. "If the term Middle East is to be used at all," he states, "its justification is to be found in the centrality which it implies, for the area is strategically located at the crossroads between Europe, Africa, and the bulk of Asia." *Crossroads,* Philadelphia, 1960, p. 10.

2   Islam: Past and Present

Islam, more than any other factor, has given the Middle East its distinctive identity. The social, cultural, and political life of every nation in the region, including Jewish Israel, bears the stamp of this latest of the world's three great monotheistic religions. After more than thirteen centuries the spiritual force of Islam is still vital, although the form in which it was first propagated by the Prophet Muhammad has undergone change. Today the original teachings have been diffused into a variety of traditions, practices, and customs. But Islam is still the one pattern that covers the whole Middle East.

THE PROPHET MUHAMMAD AND THE ORIGINS OF ISLAM

When the founder of Islam was born in the late sixth century A.D., his native Mecca was in great turmoil. For several decades Arabia had suffered an economic depression resulting from decline of the region's trade with Europe, the routes to the West having been cut off by the successive battles between the Eastern Roman Empire and its Iranian Sassanid neighbors. Widespread dissatisfaction existed both with the social order maintained by the important Meccan families and with the pagan rites over which those families officiated in the *Kaaba,* a sanctuary for many of the idols to which the Arabs of the region paid homage. Economic and social unrest made southern Arabia more receptive to those ideas promising change that began to find their way there both from the Christian Eastern Roman Empire and from Zoroastrian Persia (Iran) in the northeast.

Little is known about the life of Muhammad (Most Highly Praised) until he reached the age of about forty. The exact date of his birth is uncertain (between A.D. 570 and 580), but he was known to be a scion of the Meccan aristocracy and his grandfather had been a keeper of the Kaaba. His early career showed no special promise. Although there is no real proof concerning his early activities, according to tradition he was, as a youth, a trader who traveled northwards to Syria and Palestine. It is clear that Muhammad was influenced by Judaism and Christianity, although in what way he met with their teachings is still a matter of speculation. Unquestionably the Jewish Arab tribes who lived near Mecca were later to have considerable influence on his religious preachings.

Muhammad began to preach in Mecca when he was about forty years old after receiving his first revelations from the Angel Gabriel. His initial efforts in propagating the new faith—Islam (submission to the will of Allah, or God)—were singularly unsuccessful. In Mecca his monotheistic teachings were considered subversive of the status quo because they endangered the established idol worship at the Kaaba from which the town's merchant oligarchy earned great profits. Muhammad and his few dozen followers therefore slipped out of Mecca in the summer of 622 and moved to the town of Medina some 200 miles away. This *hijrah* (hegira, migration or exodus) was later designated as the beginning of the Muslim era because it was the turning point in the Prophet's career. In Medina, Muhammad became the town's leading warrior, legislator, judge, and civil administrator, planting the first seeds of the classic Muslim states that later caliphs (successors) established in Syria and Iraq. He was so strengthened by his success in Medina that he returned and conquered his home town. By the time of Muhammad's death in 632, most of the Arabian peninsula had been subjugated and forced to accept or to acknowledge the authority of the new faith.

During his lifetime the Prophet made comprehensible and acceptable to the Arabs of the peninsula a variety of beliefs and practices whose powerful attraction most local inhabitants found irresistible. Jewish and Christian monotheism appealed to the more sophisticated who had become discontented with the polytheism of the Kaaba. Emphasis on a community of belief rather than blood relationships brought peace to settlements torn by intrafamily feuds always threatening to disrupt the land. Islam did not appear as a foreign import or the esoteric belief of a small group; it had "mass appeal." It was distinctively Arab, retaining a reverence for such local symbols as the black meteoric rock in the Kaaba and continuing to emphasize the tribal traditions of treatment for friends, family, guests, and enemies.

The new faith sparked the first unity the Arabs had known, enabling them to overcome divisive local loyalties and to form an effective fighting force superior to any in the region. Once they had seen with what ease all local opposition was overcome, the Arabs undertook to carry their mission beyond local borders and began to probe the non-Arab territory to the north.

Muhammad's Successors

When Muhammad died, Islam was left without a leader, for the Prophet had designated no successor, or caliph. Instead, Abu Bakr, the Prophet's father-in-law, maneuvered into the position. He and his three immediate successors—subsequently known as the *Rashidun*—'Umar, 'Uthman, and 'Ali (the latter being the husband of Fatima, Muhammad's daughter), came to be accepted by most Muslims as Muhammad's legal heirs. By the time 'Ali was proclaimed caliph in 656, the Arabs had conquered nearly all the Middle East, including the region from the Egyptian frontier to the borders of present day Pakistan.

'Ali's succession to the caliphate brought the Arab governor of Syria, Mu'awiya, into open revolt. Mu'awiya was a cousin of 'Uthman and a member of the aristocratic Umayyad family. Among those who had supported the election of 'Ali to the caliphate were the men responsible for the assassination of 'Uthman. Armed clash between the two rival forces was suspended when both sides agreed to arbitration, and only after the assassination of 'Ali by one of his former supporters in 661 was Mu'awiya able to gain recognition as the sole caliph of the Muslim world. Damascus, the center of Mu'awiya's power, became the seat of government, and the Umayyad dynasty was born (661–750). Mu'awiya established the principle of hereditary succession to the caliphate when he named his son, Yazid, his successor. The beginning of Mu'awiya's reign marks the close of the orthodox period, and some later Arab historians, attempting to discredit the Umayyad dynasty, refer to the kingship, rather than caliphate, of Mu'awiya and his successors.

During the Umayyad era the Arab empire expanded to its maximum extent. It swept across North Africa and up into Spain and France; it reached the gates of Byzantine Constantinople; it spread into Central Asia beyond the Oxus River to the north and into the Indus Valley to the east. By 732 the Arab-ruled area extended from the Atlantic Ocean to the boundaries of India and China. Although the religious factor was important, the Umayyads laid greater stress on the political structure and economic aspects of government, attempting to organize and centralize their new empire. In administration it was less an Arab than a Persian and Byzantine succession state using Syrian Christians and Persian Zoroastrians as administrators. The Umayyads began to transform the empire from a theoretical Islamic theocracy to an Arab secular state in which Arabs dominated as a hereditary social caste that could be entered only by birth.

Although the Umayyad dynasty brought the Arabs to the apogee of their territorial expansion, it was marked by numerous internal weaknesses. Mu'awiya's successors abandoned the simplicity and piety for which the *Rashidun* had been esteemed by orthodox Muslims, and palace life degenerated into lavish orgies. Corruption spread to the army and civilian administration, resulting in excessive taxation, inter-Arab tribal conflicts, and hatred by the non-Arab minorities who resented Umayyad claims of racial superiority.

Open revolt against the regime broke out in 747, led by an Iranian at the head of a southern Arabian tribe. Soon they were joined by various disaffected elements: followers of 'Ali who had never accepted the caliphate of Mu'awiya or his successors; Iranians, Syrians, Iraqis, and other non-Arabs who protested Arab hegemony; non-Muslims; and Arab tribes who simply refused to accept Umayyad rule. They chose Muhammad Ibn 'Ali ibn al Abbas to lead them to victory. Replacement of the Umayyads by the Abbasids (750–1258) is evaluated by Bernard Lewis as more than a mere change of dynasty. "It was a revolution in the history of Islam, as important a turning point as the French and Russian Revolutions in the history of the West. It came about not as the result of a palace conspiracy or *coup d'état,* but by the action of an extensive and successful revolutionary propaganda and organization, representing and expressing the dissatisfactions of important elements of the populations with the previous regime and built up over a long period of time."[1]

A major consequence of the revolutionary change was transfer of the center of gravity in the Muslim empire from the Mediterranean province of

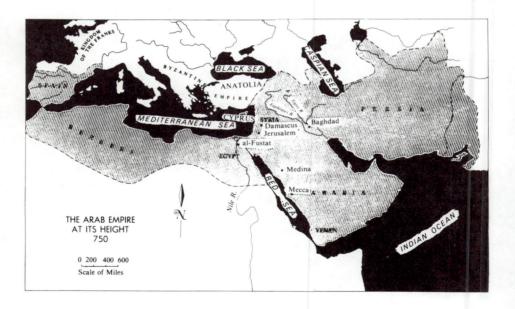

THE ARAB EMPIRE
AT ITS HEIGHT
750

0 200 400 600
Scale of Miles

Syria to the rich, river-irrigated Mesopotamian valley. It symbolized the change in the empire from a Byzantine successor state to an oriental autocracy ruled on the traditional Persian model. First Iranians and then Turks filtered in from Central Asia so that the Abbasid Caliphate became far less Arab than its Umayyad predecessor. Whereas during the Umayyad era the empire had spread to several times its original size, there was little military conquest under the Abbasids. Only Sicily, Sardinia, Crete, and a few lesser Mediterranean islands were conquered. The Abbasid dynasty was renowned less for its military prowess than for the myriad of administrative, cultural, and intellectual accomplishments that it made possible (described below in the section on "Medieval and Classic Islam").

The Arab Expansion

When the Arabs moved northward out of the peninsula, there were two major powers on the Middle Eastern scene, Christian Byzantium and the Zoroastrian Sassanid kingdom of Iran. For 300 years these two empires had contended with each other for the Middle East. The Byzantine Empire included the Balkans, Asia Minor, the Levantine coast, the Nile Valley, and North Africa as far west as Libya. The Iranians held the area from present day Pakistan west to Iraq, bordering on the Byzantine provinces (see chapter 17). Both powers were so weakened by their struggle that they were unable to resist the Arab force suddenly erupting from the southern deserts. Sassanid Persia (Iran) collapsed and Byzantium was driven north into Anatolia within twenty-five years. Arab success was due to the propelling force of its internal dynamism and military power, attracted onward by the wealth available in the decay of two once powerful empires.

At first the Arabs did not proselytize Islam in the conquered territory north of the peninsula. It was considered an Arab faith. Recognition was granted to a sect called the Sabians and to Judaism, Christianity, and Zoroastrianism, the religions from which Islam had borrowed, but Sabians, Jews, Christians, and Zoroastrians were permitted only a second-class status in the state. Pagans and members of other faiths were theoretically forced to submit to Islam or perish. Usually, however, they were permitted to live if they paid their taxes.

After occupying the Byzantine and Iranian lands, the Arabs found that they were ill-prepared to administer them. Consequently they borrowed both institutions and personnel from the conquered peoples. Public administration continued as it had for previous generations in many parts of the new empire. Arab military governors appointed Greek, Persian, Jewish, and Christian officials to the highest posts, and life initially continued much as it had before the conquest.

The conquerors at first separated themselves from the subject peoples in garrison towns scattered through the empire, thus maintaining their identity as a distinctive religious and ethnic group. These outposts were established in existing centers along the desert's edge, like Damascus, or in new ones, like Kufa and Basra in Iraq, and al-Fustat (later joined with Cairo) in Egypt. Although the Arabs were a minority in the conquered provinces as a whole, they constituted a majority in the important garrison towns.

Arabic and Islamic influences gradually spread from the garrison towns throughout most of the Middle East. The regions closest to Arabia became Arabic in language and culture, although many groups with more sophisticated and complex religions remained non-Muslim, retaining their distinctive cultural traits—such as Egyptian Copts, the Jews, and various Eastern rite Christian minorities.

Throughout a much more extensive area whole populations converted to Islam without absorbing the Arabic language and culture. The advantages of conversion were exemption from the taxes imposed on the Christians, Jews, and Zoroastrians in lieu of military service, a share in the spoils of the conquered regions, and the social prestige of identification with the ruling group. Others adopted Islam because it was more tolerant than fanatic Byzantine Christianity, which forcefully converted or killed all not of its persuasion. But since Islam was at first thought of as an Arab faith, newcomers could only join by becoming clients of an Arab tribe. Only later were non-Arabs completely integrated into Islam.

The non-Arab Islamic area included the present-day states of Turkey, Iran, and Pakistan. Muslim missionaries later converted millions in Indonesia, China, and as far from Arabia as the Philippines. Iran and Pakistan became Muslim although not Arab, the Arabs being driven from these countries after they had converted most of the population but before the language could take root. Later, converted Turkish tribes overran Anatolia and the Balkans, bringing the Muslim religion with them long after the decline of the Arab empire. Thus millions of Albanians, Yugoslavs, and Bulgars also became Muslims.

Arab expansion was a two-way process. On the one hand, subject peoples acquired in varying degrees the faith, culture, and language of the conquerors. On the other hand, the Arabs absorbed many of the social and cultural characteristics of the subject peoples. Arabic language, theology, philosophy, science, art, and literature became a mosaic of many regional influences, ranging from those of China under the Mongols in the East through Latin and French elements in the West.

As more subject peoples became Muslim, the religion became less "Arab," developing philosophies, sects, and subsects that reflected the character of the differing localities. Byzantine Christian Hellenism, Turkish elements from Central Asia, Zoroastrian philosophy from Iran, Hindu concepts from India, and Mongol influences from China all left their mark on the faith. Today, only the Wahabis of Saudi Arabia practice Islam as preached by the Prophet 1300 years ago.

THE ISLAMIC RELIGION

Central to the Islamic faith is monotheism. God (Allah) has no partner. While Allah is merciful and compassionate, like Jehova he is also fiercely jealous and omnipotent. Acceptance of the fundamental doctrine, "there is no god but Allah," is the essence of Islam. The second most important dogma of Islam is the affirmation that Muhammad is the messenger, or apostle, of God and the last or "seal of the prophets." Common articles of faith include belief in the last judgment, predestination, and in a hierarchy of evil and beneficent angels. Although Islam, like Christianity, has been rent by many schisms and sects, these fundamental tenets are accepted by all members of the faith.

Basic principles are recorded in the Koran (meaning "recitations") revealed to Muhammad during the latter part of his life by the Angel Gabriel. The Koran, the cornerstone of Islam, records the Prophet's views on God, religion, and life. Its 114 chapters (*suras*) were collected after Muhammad's death, for he had made no written record of them. They had been transcribed on parchment, carved on camels' shoulder blades, or memorized by his followers in the latter years of his life. According to tradition, the first caliph, Abu Bakr, ordered the compilation after a battle during which many Koran reciters were killed. But it was not until the tenth century that the present text was adopted from a number of different versions.

Many of the parables and stories of the Koran are taken from the Old and New Testaments and their associated literature, such as the Talmud, but often in an incomplete form revealing Muhammad's superficial impressions of Judaism and Christianity. There are stories of Adam, Noah, Abraham, Joseph, David, Solomon, Elijah, Job, Zachariah, John the Baptist, Mary, and Jesus. Several passages in the Koran are identical to those in the Old Testament. To the Westerner, many aspects of the Koran may seem naïve for its descriptions of the Day of Judgment and the Resurrection, Paradise and Hell, and angels and devils, all presented in a vivid language whose terms were especially meaningful to the desert Arab of Muhammad's time.

To true believers, the Koran is the final authority on all matters it treats. The Koran and its subsequent commentaries supply guidance, not only on God and prayer, but on the most intimate personal details and interrelationships. It contains the basis of the Islamic social system and a regimen for conduct from cradle to grave. Translation of the Koran was frowned on; therefore Arabic became a bond of educated Muslims everywhere, as did Hebrew for literate Jews and Latin for the Roman Catholics of the West. (Only in the 1920s did republican Turkey authorize its translation into Turkish). The Koran is still the basic text for students in mosque schools throughout the world. It is a style manual and grammar in the study of Arabic. In Muslim theological colleges, the Koran is the basis of the entire curriculum.

Muslim religious duties are divided into five categories, called "the pillars of Islam." The first is open profession of the belief that: "there is no god but Allah and Muhammad is the messenger of God." It is obligatory for all Muslims and the proclamation of this belief is sufficient to ensure acceptance into the faith.

Performance of worship or ritual prayer is the second duty, prescribed five times daily between daybreak and nightfall. Although group prayer in unison, if possible in a mosque, is preferable, the pious Muslim prays wherever he may be. At the prescribed hours throughout the Muslim world it is common to see men bowed toward Mecca, in their fields, at the intersection of crowded streets, on the decks of ships, or on building roofs. A common ritual of prayer positions including prostrations and genuflexions has evolved since Muhammad's day. Most mosques are equipped with fountains at which the devout religionist may purify himself by washing his arms to the elbow, his face, and his feet before prayer. Islam's desert heritage permits the use of sand in the absence of water.

Almsgiving as a manifestation of piety and love is the third pillar of Islam. Muhammad initiated the practice with a 2½ percent levy on the produce and income of his followers for the public treasury. The proceeds were distributed to the poor and used to erect public buildings and to defray government expenditure. When the state was no longer strong enough to impose this tax, almsgiving became an act of piety recorded in the Muslim's heavenly book of deeds.

Fasting during the Muslim month of Ramadan is a fourth duty. Between dawn and sunset during Ramadan no food, drink, medicine, or smoke may enter the lips of the pious. Bleeding and leech applications (once part of ordinary medical procedures) and sexual intercourse are also banned. Strictness of observance varies, although all Muslims acknowledge the fast. In Arabia, the obligation is legally enforced, while Tunisia's President Bourguiba created great controversy a few years ago when he advised his government employees not to fast lest observance interfere with the task of building up the nation.

Pilgrimage, the fifth pillar of Islam, is enjoined upon all able-bodied Muslims who can afford it, at least once in a lifetime. This institution, called the *haj*, was incorporated into Islamic practice by Muhammad from ancient Arabian rites. During the prescribed month of *haj*, Muslims converge from all the world to the Kaaba at Mecca. The Saudi Arabian government stated that 600,000 pilgrims attended in 1958, and the number has since increased. At the Kaaba, housing the ancient meteoric black stone upon which Abraham was to have sacrificed his son Isaac, the pilgrims go through a number of exercises and rituals similar to those in pre-Islamic times. Since Muhammad's death, non-Muslims are banned from Mecca, although a few have gained entry in disguise during the time of pilgrimage in order to write of their observations. Like the use of Arabic, the pilgrimage serves as a valuable unifying force in

Islam. At Mecca, Arabs, Iranians, Turks, Pakistanis, Chinese, Indonesians, Filipinos, and Soviet citizens of all races are bound together in a common ritual of brotherhood that transcends their differences.

After the Prophet's death, religious questions arose that were not answered in the Koran and further guidance was sought. For most but not all Muslims, the second most authoritative religious source after the Koran became the *Hadith,* or collected traditions of Muhammad. These are sayings or hearsay statements attributed to the Prophet by his contemporary and later followers. They are compiled in six collections that form the common law of Islam, or the *Sunna.* Not until two centuries after his death did the traditions of Muhammad's sayings come to be regarded as an authentic source of Muslim law. Those who observe its traditional interpretations are Sunnis, comprising about 90 percent of all Muslims today.

Even these traditions were inadequate to meet the growing legal needs of expanding Muslim society. Additional rules were devised by jurists who acted initially according to their own concept of right. But the opinion *(ra'y)* of individual judges was often too subjective or fallible a basis for interpretation of divine law. The individual's use of analogy *(qiyas)* by which it was possible to extend a rule in the Koran or Sunna to any local situation often seemed inappropriate. It was felt that if the great jurists acted collectively there would be less chance of error. Thus consensus *(ijm'a)* of the jurists representing the Islamic community emerged as a later manifestation of God's will. Classic Islamic jurisprudence recognized as the basis of law the Koran, the Sunna recorded in the Hadith, and the consensus *(ijm'a)* of the jurists with analogical deduction *(qiyas)* if it were based on consensus. Together this body of rules and theological interpretations builds the *Sharia,* or straight path of sacred law, and the religious courts that administer it are called Sharia courts. The compilations of legal interpretations cover all aspects of religious, political, civil, and family life, including marriage, divorce, inheritance, and adoption.

As Islam expanded through a score of countries, meeting new conditions and changing circumstances, various schools of Islamic thought and legal interpretation arose to cope with the variety of social systems ranging from the French along the Atlantic coast to the Indian in southern Asia. By the tenth century several schools of thought had crystalized, and the right of free interpretation *(ijtihad)* fell into abeyance. The "door of *ijtihad* was closed." Thereafter all jurists were obliged to accept the opinions of their predecessors and were deprived of exercising private judgment. While Muslim law and its various schools remained a principle discipline, Islamic theology became moribund, confining itself to the production of commentaries and secondary interpretations—most of which repeated the work of previous scholars.

Eventually four schools survived in Sunni Islam, each named for a particular jurist. While differing on numerous fine points, they recognized each other's orthodoxy. Nearly half of Sunnite Islam belongs to the *Hanafite* school, whose followers predominate in Muslim India and most of the former regions of the Ottoman Empire. The *Shafi'ites* prevail in southern Arabia, the East Indies, lower Egypt, Palestine, and East Africa. The more conservative *Malikites,* who attach importance to the Hadith second only to that of the Koran, are now found in North Africa from Suez to the Atlantic. The most rigid and orthodox school, the *Hanbalites,* exist today almost exclusively among the Wahabis of Saudi Arabia.

A mystic strain called *Sufism* began to develop in Islam during the eighth century, acquiring its name from the garment of wool (Arabic, *suf*) once worn by its adherents. The thrust of the movement was rebellion against the intellectualism and rigid legalism of conventional Islam. It drove its followers to seek a personal relationship with the deity, a concept not in keeping with Islam's transcendental conception of Allah. Sufi preoccupation with personal sin and disdain of hypocrisy led them to value the intention more than the act itself, obedience more than observance. This emphasis did not escape the criticism of canonists and theologians whose law provided for punishment of public sins only and had no weapon against religious hypocrisy. To achieve mystic union with the divine being, Sufis began to practice all-night vigils, long periods of contemplation, and self-induced religious ecstasies. Many became ascetics (hence their wool garments), and they periodically fasted. Some were Dervishes (from the Persian for "beggar"), wandering through the countryside practicing their Sufi rites.

As the movement spread throughout the Muslim world it absorbed concepts and practices from other religions. Monastic orders or brotherhoods resembling those of medieval Christianity emerged by the tenth century. Their devotees wore monklike cloaks, practiced celibacy, and sang litanies. They proclaimed a doctrine of brotherly love resembling New Testament teachings and revered their own saints. Buddhist influences were evident in the Sufi doctrine of "fina," a form of Nirvana, and in the belief that a traveler on his way to heaven must pass through a number of earthly "stations," or degrees of piety. After Aristotle's writings were translated into Arabic in the ninth century, Neoplatonic theology, especially the doctrine of Gnosis, became influential among a number of Sufi orders.

By the fifteenth century many Sufi orders forgot their pietist and mystic origins, degenerating into cults practicing bizarre rites, such as those of the whirling or dancing Dervishes—swallowing toads, eating glass, and inflicting wounds on themselves. While popular or folk Sufism became infused with superstition and charlatanism, however, the intellectual movement left a legacy of inspirational writings, especially Turkish and Persian poetry, the beauty of which has not been surpassed in Islamic literature.

During the decade of Muhammad's rule and for a generation or so after his death, mankind, according to the Muslim theologians, came as close as possible to perfection because of its nearness in time to the direct word of Allah. Thereafter a gap began to develop between the ideal and the practical, between the "word" of the sacred law and makeshift day-to-day decisions.

Gradually the government proclaimed by Allah, and that of his earthly representatives, grew farther apart, until the Muslim found himself faced with two laws: the eternal law applicable to him because of membership in the "true faith"; and a transient, revocable law devised to cope with life's complications and to check man's sinfulness. Therefore the purpose of God's law, believed the Islamic jurists, was to limit man's original liberty, which if unchecked would lead to self-destruction. All man's actions were consequently divided into those that were required, forbidden, recommended, disapproved, or merely permitted by God according to the Koran and Sunna.

"Islam is the community of Allah," writes Gustave E. von Grunebaum in *Medieval Islam*.[2]

> He is the living truth to which it owes its life. He is the center and the goal of its spiritual experience. But he is also the mundane head of his community which he not only rules but governs. He is the reason for the state's existence, he is the principle of unity... which both upholds and justifies the continuance of the commonwealth. This makes the Muslim army the "Army of Allah," the Muslim treasury, "the Treasury of Allah." What is more, it places the life of the community in its entirety as well as the private lives of the individual members under his direct legislative and supervisory power.

While creating an ideal human, Islam depersonalized the individual. Man was viewed as weak and insensitive, his precarious existence maintained only by God's will. Islam is obsessed with salvation or damnation of the individual. Only piety can raise a man to perfection.

Muhammad's proclamation of equality for all believers was negated by political considerations. It became necessary to grant some groups extensive economic concessions and recognize special social prestige to reconcile powerful antagonists and to forestall tribal disloyalty. The Arabs considered themselves the true Islamic aristocracy by virtue of their conquests and closeness to the Prophet. Originally great prestige was attached to kinship with the Prophet. This criterion, or an early date of conversion, determined a warrior's share of booty. As the Muslim social order evolved, however, the age-old determinants of wealth, influence, and power became the determining factors in Islamic aristocracy.

In the Muslim, as in the Latin and Greek Orthodox worlds, religion provided the institutional framework of life. The only justification for political power was to extend the faith. Citizenship, in so far as the concept existed, meant for the individual Muslim affiliation with the world of Islam, just as for the Catholic it was membership in Latin Christendom and for the Byzantine it was being part of the Greek Orthodox world. The idea of personal identification with one's particular political state was still unknown. This situation merely continued the earlier Mesopotamian and Hebrew concept of group identification that recognized no boundary between religion and political life.

Although Jews, Christians, Sabians, and Zoroastrians were accorded recognition as practitioners of God-fearing religions, they had no equality with Muslims. Islam's reputation for tolerance was based on its attitudes toward minorities as compared to those of European Christendom. When the West was forcibly converting or often even putting to death non-Christians, the Muslims were under no obligation to convert or exterminate other "peoples of the Book," or *dhimmi,* so called because they possessed a protective treaty or *dhimma* in which they renounced certain rights in exchange for permission to retain their own religion and customs. This continued an ancient pre-Islamic Arab tribal tradition granting protection to those who accepted client status.

Nevertheless, only those who followed Islam followed the right path toward ultimate truth. Only they were the elect of Allah and therefore superior to those who followed something less than the final truth, something outmoded and inferior. The Prophet enjoined his followers to eschew close contact with Jews and Christians. Jews were the "people of wrath," while the cross-adoring, trinitarian Christians were led astray by error. Because of their superiority, Muslims were the ones endowed with the sovereign right to rule.

Islamic Subdivisions and Sects

A major division developed within Islam as a result of non-Arab reaction to the Arab aristocracy, and the political struggle for succession to the caliphate. The initial split occurred when 'Ali, the fourth caliph, was assassinated in 661 and 'Ali's first son, Hasan, relinquished his claim to the caliphate in recognition of Mu'awiya. Mu'awiya's death and the elevation of his son to the caliphate, brought 'Ali's second son, Husain, out of retirement to claim the title of caliph. An armed clash resulted in the massacre of Husain and most of his followers at Karbala in Iraq in 680. From that moment, those who supported 'Ali's line of succession became a religious sect as well as a mere dissident political group. They are known as Shi'ites from the Arabic *shi'a* meaning party (the party of 'Ali). The partisans of 'Ali, or Shi'ites, absorbed not only many non-Arab followers, but Persian customs and traditions such as determining succession in a direct line from father to son and certain Persian mystical religious beliefs.

Because neither wealth, learning, nor political influence freed the newly converted Persians, Greeks, and Turks, from Arab contempt, it was easy to rally non-Arabs to the new movement. Since most partisans of 'Ali were in Iraq, the movement took on a coloration of local patriotism in opposition to the Umayyad Arabs in Syria. The dividing line between Arabs and non-Arabs gradually disappeared and today 90 percent of all Muslims are Sunni, mostly non-Arabs, while Shi'ites include many who are Arab. Most Muslims in Iran and Yemen, about half those in Iraq, and small pockets elsewhere in the Middle East and southern Asia, in all nearly 100 million, are Shi'ites.

Shi'ites attributed special rights to 'Ali and maintained that they were handed down to his successors in a line of *imams* (religious leaders) with unusual powers. Ultra-Shi'ites, who felt the need for some incarnate manifestation of God, even deified 'Ali and his sons with mystical ardor. The violent deaths of 'Ali and Husain brought them the status of martyrs and bound their followers in a blood pact. Until today, Husain's defeat at Karbala is commemorated annually by a passion play during which fanatic mourners flagellate themselves. Most Shi'ites believe that after 'Ali and his two sons there were nine more direct, infallible successors, or imams, and that the last of twelve disappeared in obscure circumstances. Eventually this "hidden" or "expected imam" will reappear as the *Mahdi* (Rightly Guided One) or savior of mankind. Until his coming, Islam is to be interpreted by scholars acting as the Mahdi's agents. This predominant group is known as Imami, Ithna Ashari, or Twelvers—Imam Shi'ites.

The Shi'ite revolutionists against Umayyad rule also produced counter-revolutionists after consolidating power in Iraq. Dissatisfied peasant groups and rebellions against the dominant Imami Shi'ites developed into religious schisms that subdivided the Shi'ites. "Whenever a grievance or a conflict of interests created a faction in Islam, its doctrines were a theology, its instrument a sect, its agent a missionary, its leader usually a Messiah or his representative."[3] In a society in which church and state were indistinguishably fused, religious controversy played the role that politics plays in the modern world, an outlet for economic and social discontent.

The Ismailis were such a group. They inherited the revolutionary character of the early Shi'ite movement and gathered the urban and rural disaffected into an offshoot of the Imamis. The dispute erupted over succession to the sixth imam. Next in line was Ismail, but the "Twelvers" bypassed him because of his addiction to wine. His followers, the Ismailis, or "Seveners," considered him not only the legal heir but the last visible or hidden and expected imam for whom the Shi'ites had been waiting. The contemporary Ismaili leader is the Agha Khan of Pakistan with followers throughout the Middle East and in Africa.

The Zaidis of Yemen left the main branch of Shi'ism in 731, also in a dispute over succession. They supported Zaid, 'Ali's great-grandson, in preference to Zaid's brother. Zaid was martyred in an uprising against the Umayyads in 740. The sect named after him became official in Yemen and is closer to the Sunni community than any other Shi'ite group.

The Assassins were a neo-Ismailite protest movement against Egypt's Ismaili rulers at the end of the eleventh century. Its leader, Hasan ibn al-Sabbah retreated to Abbasid Iran where he led fanatical devotees in terror and assassination campaigns against the princes of Islam. Branches of his movement flourished in the Syrian mountains under direction of a "grand master." The Crusaders gave the name Assassins to these zealots because of their self-sacrificers who were allegedly drugged with hashish (hence hash-ishin, Assassins, or users of hashish) in preparation for their suicide missions. One of the most notorious Assassin grand masters was known to the Crusaders as the "Old Man of the Mountain" because of his Syrian mountain redoubts.

Other surviving Ismaili offshoots with secret religious rites are the Druses, now in Syria, Lebanon, Jordan, and Israel, and the Nusayris or Alawis found in northern Syria and Lebanon. Both groups are discussed below in chapters 13 and 14 on Lebanon and Syria.

MEDIEVAL AND CLASSICAL ISLAM

The early Muslim conquests were nominally directed by a central power with headquarters first in Arabia, then in the Umayyad capital at Damascus, Syria, and after 762 in Abbasid Baghdad in Iraq. For five centuries after the Muslim empire reached the zenith of its western conquests in 732, it held its ground, receding only slowly in the West. During this era the over-all political structure of the Mediterranean remained remarkably stable despite constant wars and periodical exchanges of territory between the three great religious empires of the day: the Muslim, the Byzantine Greek Orthodox, and the Latin Catholic.

Each bloc tended to expand away from the center of power. The Latins pushed northward seizing the Baltic regions and converting the western Slavs. The Byzantines evangelized the Balkans and spread into Russia. Islam continued its expansion into east and central Asia and Africa. Occasionally there were incursions like the twelfth- and thirteenth-century Crusader bridgehead in the Levant, but they were successfully checked.

While religious ties remained strong within each of the three areas, political control disintegrated as each suffered similarly from poor communications, inadequate public finances, and a general decline in the prestige of their leaders, leaving each in approximately the same power relationship to the others as had obtained earlier. Boundaries between them were determined by religion. In each a person was first a Christian or a Muslim, next a subject of his local lord, and only last a Frenchman, Egyptian, or Greek.

Each of the three principal religious groups was convinced of its own superiority; each aspired to rule the civilized world. Byzantium continued to claim territory it had lost despite its growing weakness. Islam divided the world into regions where Islam prevailed called *dar al-Islam* (world of Islam) and those yet to be Islamicized or *dar al-Harb* (world of war). Between the two there could be no permanent peace, at best a long-term truce. The result was unceasing border warfare along the Muslim-Christian frontiers.

Hereditary groups of professional soldiers were established in military feudal estates along the borders in both the Muslim and Greek Orthodox regions. In both Muslim and Byzantine feudalism the fiefholder depended directly on his sovereign for his domain. They differed from Western feudalism, which was built on a hierarchy of fiefholders, each directly responsible to his immediate overlord.

Since Rome had ruled an extensive part of all three regions, Roman institutions strongly influenced their development. Latin was still the language of administration and education in the Latin and Greek zones. The Muslim bloc was also a legatee of Roman influences in its law, administration, finance, philosophy, literature, and architecture, largely as a result of its Byzantine heritage.

Although Islamic civilization reached the quintessence of its development in Baghdad between the eighth and tenth centuries, political control of the western provinces became progressively weaker as the Arab capital moved east. Spain became an autonomous Arab kingdom in 756, followed by Morocco in 788, Tunisia in 800, and Egypt in 868. Each country became virtually independent under its own local Muslim dynasty. By the mid-tenth century, the same process of political erosion began in the eastern region, until the Abbasid caliphs controlled only Iraq and parts of Syria. Although the region had disintegrated into numerous states, all were Muslim and all continued their resistance to incursions by other religious blocs. Similarly in Europe the Latin Catholic and Greek Orthodox blocs were fragmented into numerous kingdoms. But among all three blocs, religion fostered a cultural and spiritual unity that continued long after political fragmentation. Not until the Christian reconquest of Spain during the fifteenth century was there any considerable loss of Muslim territory. The Muslims who remained in Christian Spain became the first sizable Muslim minority group.

Even after the political fragmentation of the Islamic world, language and faith supported an intellectual unity that made the educated Muslim accepted as a fellow "citizen" anywhere Islam was recognized. The famous traveler, Ibn Battuta, a native of Tangier, became a judge in Delhi. Ibn Khaldun, the historian and statesman born in Tunis, served various North African princes and became a chief judge in Cairo.

The Umayyad dynasty tried to keep the traditional Arab government led by the *sayyid*, or tribal chieftain. The latter owed his office to personal prestige derived from his noble lineage, although this alone did not determine succession. Qualities of leadership and generosity were essential too. He was merely the first among equals, chosen democratically by the tribal council. His prerogatives did not infringe upon the essential equality of his followers. All had access to him for he was shrouded behind no elaborate ceremonial.

The tribal system of government became increasingly difficult to maintain as the empire expanded, and the Abbasids incorporated many of the traditions of their Iranian supporters including the concept of kingship. The Iranian king had ruled by divine right, which he inherited from a long line of previous rulers. Too close contact with the masses was thought to be defiling and to detract from the awe with which he should be regarded; therefore he was protected by an elaborate etiquette and ceremony. Under the Abbasids, the Iranian despot was merged with the Islamic theocratic representative of Allah, and the ancient Arab chief, although the attributes of a democratic chief were lost when the caliph became an outright autocrat.

Gradually the caliph became no less despotic than the Byzantine rulers. Like the Roman emperors, both Byzantine monarchs and Abbasid caliphs had unlimited power. Although theory supported the election of both emperor and caliph, practice worked in favor of heredity. The Byzantine emperor was also the titular head of the Greek Orthodox church, whereas the caliph was merely administrator of the Islamic state with no power to alter the body of religious law. In the latter years of the Abbasid Caliphate, after it had become prisoner of the Seljuk Turks, the caliphate lost all political or legal significance and was merely the symbol of Islamic unity.

Under the aegis of the sultan-caliph, an elaborate civil bureaucracy developed along Persian lines. It was headed by the *wazir* (Turkish, *vezir*), the caliph's helper who directed civil administration. He supervised the various bureau *(diwan)* heads such as the treasury, war office, and posts. Each province also had its own diwan, but around the year 900 they were incorporated into a central bureau with three main branches. Provincial governors had responsibility for local civil and military affairs including tax collection. They increasingly asserted their independence of Baghdad until many became autonomous, acknowledging to the caliph only a token fealty.

State income came from a number of sources: tribute from conquered lands; loot gained in battle; the alms tax, including the tithe paid on agricultural lands and products; taxes on non-Muslims; local imposts; money extorted from fallen officials or otherwise confiscated; and fees, tolls, and customs. Taxes were farmed out to the highest bidders and assessments imposed collectively on local communities. Until the tenth century the empire succeeded in raising adequate sums for its public expenses, such as frontier security, road maintenance, and payment of provincial officials. But by the tenth century expenditures began to exceed income due to diminishing sources caused by the contraction of the Abbasid territories. Corruption, nepotism, and inefficiency also undermined financial stability. Maladministration had become so prevalent that of some sixteen million dinars (the principal gold coin of the Muslims) collected in one year, only two million were used for public expenses. The rest was drained off to support the royal household and to pay exorbitant salaries to officials in the capital.

Parallel to the civil bureaucracy were the Islamic courts headed by *kadis,* or judges, who interpreted the Sharia law. In the early Abbasid era the caliphs themselves and their governors in the provinces assumed the kadi's function. By the eleventh century regular judges were left with little power; the civil bureaucracy had usurped their function.

Even though much of the able-bodied Muslim's life was spent under arms, and Arab and Iranian tradition both emphasized courage and soldierly qualities, the civilization was not military. While the military elite frequently ruled behind the scenes, there was formal civilian leadership and the wazir outranked the general. Between the seventh and ninth centuries the transformation of the caliph from a general to a chief administrator was completed.

Although official posts were not hereditary, most appointments were made from a small circle of families who possessed intimate knowledge of government operations, were familiar with conditions throughout the empire, and had the right connections. Not infrequently positions remained within the same family or group of families for generations.

The civil servant was trained in grammar, belles-lettres, and history. He sought facility and elegance in writing and mastery of etiquette and style. Judges and theologians had to master the science of Hadith, or traditions, canon law, and scholastic theology. Each civil servant wore a distinctive dress indicating his position.

The scholar was especially favored and considered practically omniscient. As time wore on, however, original thought and legal opinion were less acceptable than commentary on earlier achievements, and scholarly functions became limited to protecting religious law and lore. The ascetic or saint who became an authorized spokesman for the oppressed was closely related to the scholar. Although the saint and savant frequently expressed general criticism of society and its institutions, the idea of social progress was not widely accepted. The effectiveness of Muslim reformers was lessened by their concentration on specific abuses and on curing the evils of the day rather than on an attempt to alter the system.

Islamic Culture and Society

As the number of Arabic language scholars recruited from non-Arab peoples increased, the relatively poor Arabian culture gradually became a rich multiethnic Muslim civilization. Not only non-Arab but also non-Islamic elements were woven into the fabric of the cosmopolitan Abbasid civilization, unified, however, by the common use of the Arabic language and the prevailing practice of Islamic orthodoxy. The talents of the best minds from all the empire's various nationalities were thus combined, culminating in the Islamic Golden Age between 750 and 950.

Von Grunebaum traces five principal culture strains determining Islamic development.[4] At first Muhammad welded Judeo-Christian with Arabic ideas and values including much pre-Islamic pagan tradition. Later Hellenic-Greek thought was absorbed through translations from the Syriac. Greek dialectics and methods of allegorical interpretation and Christian asceticism were adopted to broaden Islam's base beyond the limitations of the Koran. Discussion of problems according to categories of formal logic, purely theoretical speculation, and a secular science independent of religious sectarianism was Greek in origin. The Persian tradition, itself earlier influenced by Hellenism, shaped the ethics of civic life. Ancient guilds, the Sassanid Persian financial system, and oriental religious despotism were all present. Indian medicine, pharmacology, mathematics, and possibly Indian mysticism and literary theory also left their imprint on Islamic learning.

Islam's originality consisted in adapting these imports to its own requirements and blending them within its civilization. Elements that might endanger its own religious foundation were eliminated or neutralized. From this synthesis of older classical cultures emerged the distinctive Islamic civilization with its own extensions and contributions in philosophy, medicine, mathematics, astronomy, science, geography, architecture, and, above all, in literature. "Islam," writes von Grunebaum, "can hardly be called creative in the sense that the Greeks were creative in the fifth and fourth centuries B.C. or the Western world since the Renaissance, but its flavor is unmistakable on whatever it touched; and, while very little of its conceptual and not too much of its emotional contribution is new or unique, its style of thought and range of feelings are without a real precedent."[5]

Nearly all the Hellenic and Hellenistic philosophies were translated from Greek into Arabic, becoming the basis for early Islamic philosophy. Five Islamic philosophers were of truly international status: al-Kindi, al-Farabi, Ibn Sina, al-Ghazali, and Ibn Rushd. All were strongly influenced by Neoplatonism. The earliest Arab philosopher was al-Kindi (Alkindius) born in Iraq during the ninth century. He blended philosophy and theology, holding the world of intelligence as supreme. He also wrote on medicine and astrology and was a prolific translator of Greek works. Immortality, he argued, resulted from the correct knowledge of God and the universe. He regarded mathematics as the basis of both scientific and philosophic investigations. In the next century, al-Farabi (Alpharabius), a Turk, combined the thought of Aristotle, Plato, and the Sufi Muslim mystics. He outlined his philosophy in a treatise describing a model city where happiness governed all. His belief that the world had no beginning shocked many Muslims—and influenced St. Thomas Aquinas. Al-Ghazali, born in 1059 in Persia, after studying the rationalist philosophers became a mystic convinced that ultimate truth could be attained only through revelation. While other philosophers claimed that God dealt only with universals, Ghazali's God was concerned with the most minute details. Perhaps best known to the Western World were Ibn Sina, known in Europe as Avicenna (980–1037), and Ibn Rushd (Averroes). Ibn Sina was an Ismaili Muslim born in Bukhara at the end of the tenth century. His numerous works, also rooted in Aristotle, greatly influenced medieval European philosophers such as Abelard, Albertus Magnus, and St. Thomas Aquinas. Ibn Rushd, born in 1126 in Spain, wrote about philosophy, mathematics, law, and theology, building upon his predecessors, al-Farabi and Ibn Sina. He was the last of the classical Muslim philosophers in Spain. Faith in the existence of human knowledge in all men marked his philosophy—which also had many similarities to that of Thomas Aquinas.

Throughout the era of medieval Islam most Muslim philosophers and scientists studied medicine and many were practicing physicians. These skills also were learned from the Greeks, Syrians, and Iranians by way of Greek works. Hospitals were imported from the Iranians by Harun al-Rashid and schools of pharmacy were established. The most outstanding physician was al-Razi (865–925), called Rhazes in the West. His writings greatly influenced European medical thought. He compiled the first medical encyclopedia (more than twenty volumes), giving a complete account of all Greek, Syriac, and Arabic medical knowledge at the time. Ibn Sina, the philosopher, produced the most famous Muslim medical works in the eleventh century. He recognized the contagious nature of some diseases and that they could be spread through water. His *Canon of Medicine (al-Kanun)* was the chief medical book of the Middle East and Western Europe from the twelfth to the seventeenth century. During the Black Death in the fourteenth century, two Muslim physicians in Granada, Spain, recognized its contagious nature. So skillful were the Muslim physicians that their services were eagerly sought by the Crusaders.

Building on Indian and Greek works, Islamic civilization greatly advanced the study of mathematics by transmitting and simplifying Greek arithmetic, introducing Arabic numerals (whose origin is still disputed) and the decimal system. Arab use of zero—a concept that probably originated with Indian scholars—and the digit to denote units of tens, hundreds, thousands, and so on made mathematics useful in everyday life. Algebra, geometry, and trigonometry were carried on to the West by the Arab mathematicians.

Arab astronomy also developed from Greek, Iranian, and Indian contributions. Through study of the planets, stars, and constellations, the Arabs determined the earth's diameter and circumference and measured the length of the Mediterranean. They gave Arabic names to many stars and constellations and contributed words such as *azimuth, nadir,* and *zenith.*

Arabic works on chemistry introduced words such as alkali, alcohol, and antimony into modern usage. In physics, theoretical and applied mechanics, experiments related in particular to irrigation and the flow of water were useful Arab contributions. Most significant in physics were experiments in optics proving faulty Euclid's and Ptolemy's theory that the eye emits visual rays and replacing it by the theory that vision comes from the impact of light rays.

From the original Arabian mosque plan—a square composed of palm-trunk rows surrounded by stone and brick walls and probably covered with a flimsy palm branch roof—developed the magnificent mosque architecture found throughout the Mediterranean region today. Muslim architecture borrowed extensively from Roman, Persian, and Byzantine models, developing the dome, arches, columns, and capitals into a new, characteristic Muslim design. The mosque minaret, probably developed from pre-Islamic lighthouses, became the model for the Christian bell tower. While many mosques are decorated with elaborate facades, the major emphasis is on the interior work where the arabesque can be seen in its greatest splendor. Since Islamic tradition hampered reproduction of living forms, Islamic art has been decorative using elaborate geometric forms.

Islamic civilization reached its apogee in the humanities. Whereas contributions in science, mathematics, music, art, and architecture were largely influenced by Greek, Persian, and Indian precedents, there was far greater originality and initiative in historiography, philology, and literature. While the roots of Muslim literary tradition were also Persian and Greek, the Arabic was the most influential. The most well-known medieval Muslim literature has been the colorful *Thousand and One Nights* or *Arabian Nights,* developed from numerous oriental folk tales in various sections of the Arabic-speaking world between 900 and 1500. Many stories originally of Jewish, Buddhist, or Hellenistic inspiration were absorbed into the Muslim tradition and recolored with Muslim mores and lore and, in turn, have influenced European literature. In historical writing, the long genealogies of the Arab tribes traced back the changes in political groupings, alliances, and Bedouin federations and confederations. The best known of the medieval Muslim historians was Ibn Khaldun (1332–1406). Although born in Tunisia, he was esteemed and held high positions in Granada in Spain, in Algeria, and in Cairo. Most renowned has been the first volume of his long history called the *Mukaddamah (Prolegomena),* outlining a philosophy of history based on a study of its interrelated social, economic, geographic, and cultural factors.

Islam's Decline

Islamic civilization reached its zenith when political fragmentation had already begun to erode the unity of the empire. When the era of cultural flowering began to wither away around 950, Baghdad, seat of the Abbasid Caliphate, had lost its authority. Thereafter Islamic cultural influence continued its general decline until it became almost insignificant compared to the new cultures and civilizations flourishing in Western Europe. By 1500 Europe had drained what there was to learn from the Muslim world. As medieval Europe emerged into the modern era, medieval Islam withdrew to the east side of the Mediterranean, where it remained a dormant force in world politics until the nineteenth century reawakening.

Much in medieval Islam and medieval Christianity was similar. The difference was that the Islamic Middle Age lasted longer whereas medieval Christianity ended when the Renaissance began. Von Grunebaum has criticized medieval Islam for never making a concerted effort to galvanize its strength and thereby ensure the progressive control of life's physical conditions. While accepting innovations in medicine, science, and education, medieval Islam did not use them to improve the life of the masses. Science and the humanities remained largely the property of a small intellectual elite. Critics of the social system never directed their discontent into a constructive political force.

> From the viewpoint of what it set out to do, Islam failed to make good its universalist claim, but it succeeded in providing the believer with a civilized and dignified form of life. Islam has not conquered the world. Muslim civilization grew through its tolerance of alien elements, but their variety defied complete integration and the intellectual basis of its Arab roots proved too slim to carry and unify the legacies of the many pasts which Islam found itself called upon to administer. In the light of the crudeness of its origin its achievement is extraordinary, and the tenacious vitality of this civilization, whose answers to the elemental questions besetting the human mind still satisfy about one-eighth of mankind, is indeed a cause for wonder.[6]

As for its impact on Europe, Islam was a transmitter of Greek and Roman thought, bringing back to the West what had been lost during the era of barbarian despoilation. Islam, so to speak, restored the continuity of Western civilization that had been broken when the Greek and Latin empires fell, rather than contributing original thought. But Western civilization was, nevertheless, enriched in nearly every area of life by Islam. The long catalog of contributions includes foods, drinks, drugs, armor, heraldry, industrial techniques, commerce, navigation, pure science, mathematics, and esthetics. The greatest medieval Christian theologians, poets, and philosophers were influenced by Islam.

Despite their common heritage, from the fourteenth century onward the two civilizations grew further apart. Political and commercial ties became fewer. As Europe regained its spiritual independence, and concentrated on itself in an effort to revive its classical past, Islamic civilization was no longer the teacher, but now became an object of study by the intellectual elite.

ISLAM TODAY

Since the medieval era, there has been no major development of new Islamic sects, doctrines, philosophy, or ritual. However, in the last century secular nationalism, modern technology, and European ideologies have fundamentally altered Islam's role in Middle Eastern society. Striking is the separation of church and state in Turkey and the attempt to circumscribe the influence of religion there. In other Middle Eastern countries there have been more recent trends toward separation of church and state, or subordination of Islam to the needs of the nation. In later chapters we will examine in detail instances of the relationship between Islam and modern Middle Eastern governments. However, before examining Islam in specific areas, let us briefly consider its historic role in the region as a whole, as a political system, a social force, and a religion, and its continued role in forming popular attitudes.

Two manifestations of Islamic influence in politics are Pan-Islam, the idea of creating a greater Muslim state, and Islam as related to individual national states. The Middle East was a Pan-Islamic entity for only a brief era. Original Islam was "Pan-Islamic," in the sense of envisioning an expanding community where bonds of religious loyalty would be the basis of group identification rather than the prevailing tribal or familial system. But this "ideal" Islamic empire never really extended beyond the Arabian peninsula. Under the Umayyads in Damascus, the first haphazard attempts were made to expand the basis of Islamic identity, but in reality, the Umayyad dynasty remained strictly Arab. After the collapse of the Umayyads during the eighth century, the Islamic community was far more hospitable to non-Arabs, but the fabric of the universal Muslim state was rent by Arab tribal rivalries and the revival of cultural, regional, and ethnic separatist sentiments among the conquered non-Arab peoples. The Islamic empire fragmented into numerous totally autonomous, if not actually independent, provinces.

Just as the Roman ideal of universal citizenship lingered on in the Byzantine Empire, so in the remnants of the Islamic state the caliph remained a symbol of a unity that no longer aroused great fervor. Once Islam displayed its inability to contain and overrule dynastic struggles and separatist loyalties, it permanently lost the possibility of becoming the galvanizing force in a far-flung political system. In the last century, the concept of Pan-Islam has been revived, but usually as a propaganda device to strengthen the position of such Muslim rulers as the Ottoman sultans over Islamic peoples.

Realization of Pan-Islam in the modern world would be difficult if not impossible because of the inherent obstacles faced today by any group of states with a special political and ideological system attempting to achieve a self-contained existence. From the seventh to the tenth centuries, when the Muslim world was more or less culturally and economically self-sustaining, it might have developed and maintained a religious state. But such an accomplishment is no longer possible in a world becoming increasingly interdependent, economically, culturally, and politically. Under the circumstances, it is impossible for any state or group of states characterized by a radically different political and social system to exist without coming into conflict with the rest of the world, as evidenced by the contemporary bipolar conflict. Only if each world could successfully isolate itself from the other would a form of coexistence be possible in which neither affected the other.

The problem is similar for the traditional Muslim state. Only remote areas such as Central Arabia can continue to maintain Islam as *the* only political force, and only so long as they succeed in escaping influences of the modern world. Even these regions have already felt the first tremors of those great changes that will soon alter their character as traditional Muslim states.

Some modern Muslim thinkers believe that achievement of an Islamic state is no longer possible. Dr. Shafik Ghorbal, one of Egypt's leading historians, has written that:

The period of 150 years which began with the French invasion of Egypt (1798) witnessed the emerging of our Islamic society into the world society of the present era. We, the members of the Islamic society, have not been fully aware of all the implications of the events of this period.... The influence has been so great that even when the Islamic people have regained their political independence they have found that a return to the traditional way of life was not possible—even if it were desirable. It needs to be emphasized that such a return is not deemed desirable even when lip service is paid to the glorious traditions of the past.[7]

A century ago, when religious institutions had not yet been replaced by secular institutions, the former were still the principal source of an educated elite. But with the growth of national secular educational systems and the increasing number of students who studied in Western universities, Muslim intellectual leadership in several countries lost its preponderant influence and ability to cope with the problems of the modern state.

In some countries the nontheological scope of Islamic institutions was sharply curtailed by law, particularly the Sharia courts, which used to be supreme. In the modern period, Sharia law is increasingly being limited to matters of personal status such as divorce and inheritance. Even in the area of personal status, the state has not hesitated to alter the law when national welfare seemed to demand it.

Islamic institutions, however, have not been altogether excised from political life. In nations such as Egypt and Iran after 1979, they were used by nationalists to further their own purposes. Often, faced with the necessity of creating a national "type" or "pattern," politicians—some of whom are openly cynical concerning Islam—have made the teaching of Islam in secular schools obligatory and have insisted that the state exercise control over the resulting religious curriculum. In North Africa some of the historic Muslim universities, such as Cairo's al-Azhar, are being turned into training centers for nationalist missionaries. Muslims brought to these institutions from central Africa, ostensibly to be trained in religious leadership, are actually inculcated with the spirit of nationalism. Upon completion of their education, they return to their home communities as political agitators as well as religious functionaries. Although secular-minded, President Gamal Nasser and the leadership of Egypt have used Islam as a device to attain a much sought after national homogeneity and to attract support from the Islamic world.

Attitudes toward authority, family life, and relationships of the individual to his fellow citizens are still determined by classic Muslim patterns throughout most of the Middle East. Egypt's revolutionary regime exploited this continued attachment to Islam by issuing government-prepared sermons to village prayer leaders on matters of concern to the state. In Iran the 1979 Revolution was led by Shi'ite clerics who adopted an Islamic constitution and established a Shi'ite Republic in 1979 (see chapter 17).

Turkey, under Kemal Ataturk, rejected the use of formal Islamic institutions when attempting to modernize society, turning instead to Western systems of law and government. German, French, Italian, and Swiss law codes were taken over to replace the existing Ottoman and Muslim legal systems. Ataturk made some tentative attempts to use mosques as political platforms when he ordered their preachers to deliver government-issued sermons. Recent Turkish governments have been more aware of the possibilities in using Islamic institutions. A government-sponsored modern Muslim theological seminary has been opened in Ankara to train clerics who will make more extensive use of Islam in winning over rural areas to government policies.

Following the Iranian revolution of 1979 and the ascent to power of Ayatollah Khomeini and the Shi'ite clergy of Iran, there was much discussion in the West of a worldwide "Islamic resurgence." Much of the rhetoric which emanated from Iran's revolutionary council, and the new regime's plans to institute an Islamic constitution and government strengthened Western perceptions of an Islamic revival. These perceptions were reinforced by an enthusiastic outburst of support for the Shi'ite radicals in Teheren by large numbers of Muslims, both Shi'ite and Sunni in many other of the forty or more nations with large numbers of Muslims. Attempts by the new Iranian revolutionary regime to impose a "purely" Islamic state on the country seemed to have grass roots support, not only in Iran but across the Muslim world. Many observers saw these events as a resurgence of Islam resulting from disillusionment with Western political institutions, the failure of imported parliamentary and party systems, and a century long attrition of social and economic life which had been modeled on or was strongly influenced by ideas imported from the West, including social democracy, communism and socialism. Other observers maintained that these mass outbursts were merely "the more or less normal conduct of people who are deeply religious, and who are leading a life founded upon a religious world vision."

In any event, the revolt of the Shi'ite clergy in Iran stirred a new awareness of Islam in the West, and aroused a fresh interest in their religious heritage among many ostensibly secular-minded intellectuals in the Middle East (see Chapter 17).

Islamic Theology

Historic Islam, like Christianity, developed a complete intellectual formulation of life. This was most enduringly embodied in classical Muslim theology, which has remained the intellectual reservoir for modern Muslim religious thought. However, the Muslim masses (like their Christian counterparts) have never been consciously theological and have not based their religious life on theological systems. The class that was theologically minded, the intellectual elite, is the very group that increasingly finds the operating principles of its life in modern science, sociology, and politics. Although there are indeed many "defenses of Islam" in modern literature, the very phrase, "defense," reveals what is happening. In the past, Muslim thought was the standard by which the thought and activities of man and his society were judged. Islam held the absolute truth, revealed by God, and formed the ultimate loyalty and criterion for all action.

So far no enduring liberal movement for reconsidering the relations between the Islamic intellectual heritage and the modern world has emerged in the Middle East. A generation ago there were a few scattered individual liberals, but they were too weak and dispersed to form a truly "liberal school" that could win popular attention or support. Moreover, Islamic intellectual liberalism has been largely a facade for modern science and philosophy and has not answered crucial theological questions satisfactorily.

The failure to provide a modern reinterpretation of, or substitute for, classical Muslim thought has implications that are more than religious. For if either the reality or the pertinency of the Muslim tradition disappears, the chaotic modern world of the Middle East will be left without any framework of alternate moral values. In the Western world, religious thought has been more successful in relating itself to modern trends. Moreover, together with the Christian tradition, Western civilization also absorbed the content of Greek humanism. For those to whom religious thought no longer has basic value, this humanistic tradition has become a valuable and enduring standard on which to base judgments concerning the evolution of modern institutions. Like the religious tradition, it is above and beyond modern science, politics, and culture, and thus provides certain absolute values.

But Islam never absorbed humanism. Although it utilized classical philosophy and found in Neoplatonic metaphysics and Aristotelian logic the intellectual implements for building its own theology, Islam never drank from the springs of the classical humanistic spirit to which the Western world is so deeply indebted. Consequently, few Muslims really grasp the humanistic spirit behind Western scientific thought and technology, even though they may understand the fruits of that thought. The decay and impotence of classical Muslim thought leaves a void in the soul of modern intellectualism in the Middle East.

In the future, nationalism may become an end in itself and the sole determinant of all values. If this happens, there will be no point from which Muslim leadership will be able to criticize the extremes of national hysteria or xenophobic emotions.

Residual Islamic Sentiment

The most difficult aspect of Islam to evaluate is the residual deposit of attitudes and unconscious reactions from the past that, in some sense, determine the way modern Muslims react to their world.

First there is the feeling that Islam creates for the Muslim that his community is the historic incarnation of the divine. The "straight way" in which the Muslim seeks to be guided is a way of social and political relationships. Muhammad did not establish merely a personal ethic or call, or method of personal conversion. He founded a community, governed by divine laws expressing God's will in history, a community that had primacy over the individual, family, or tribe.

The individualistic basis of Western democracy as found in the "social contract" theory of the social group does not exist in the Muslim attitude toward society. Even when Islamic society ceased to be religious and found its political and social patterns in modern secularism, the feeling about the supremacy of society over the individual persisted. This was well illustrated in an article that appeared in the Cairo newspaper *al-Ahram* in 1941. The author, writing of society and social conditions in Egypt, emphasized that the state is a single organism like the human body, and possesses a single soul. Consequently, any sign of malfunction or corruption in any one member causes pain and disability to the body as a whole. In conclusion, he exhorted his readers to "remember that you are a cell of that body." It is also interesting to note that nowhere in the article was there a reference to Islam or to religious faith in general. A similar outlook is seen in the Egyptian revolutionary government, which depends not so much on police power as on the feeling that the state is an entity to which the individual must adjust himself. It is also evident in the constant emphasis on national rights as distinct from individual rights, which are often overlooked when national independence has been attained. Thus various forms of authoritarian government are probably more at home in the Middle East than in the Western world, where they often clash with a sense of individual rights.

Since it came into existence, the Muslim community has been in active conflict with the Western world. It expanded through conquests of Western lands, and the returning tide of the Crusades perpetuated the conflict. Although religious differences between Islamic countries and those of the West are not so operative today, it would not be unfair to say that in most Muslim countries there is a certain inherent anti-Western feeling that grows out of the religious conflict of the past. This may in part account for the strong feelings of "positive neutralism" in many Muslim countries. Beneath the inherited religious hostility, there are remnants of the feeling that Islam has its own destiny and cannot depend on the fate of any outside, non-Islamic powers.

In most Middle Eastern countries, full national identity is either overtly or covertly identified with membership in the Islamic community. The non-Muslim, including native Christians and Jews whose families may have lived in the region for centuries, is never quite a first-class citizen in the eyes of the Muslim majority. This is true even in Turkey, where the state has repudiated its religious basis, although for different reasons than in the Arab countries. Perhaps the only exception was Lebanon, where the delicate balance of Christian and Muslim populations was such that each had to accept the other as fully Lebanese. But that acceptance was undermined in the recent civil wars.

While the enlightened modern Muslim is perfectly sincere in maintaining that he does not discriminate among his compatriots on a religious basis, most, in fact, have different attitudes toward their non-Muslim countrymen. No matter what guarantees of equality that state may give, this identification of "Muslimness" and nationality will probably long continue.

The tendency of the contemporary Middle East to accept "strong men" as leaders rather than attempt vigorously to make democracy function is another unconscious indication of the influence of Muslim attitudes. Many Middle Easterners would strenuously deny the validity of this observation. However, it is not far-fetched to reason that the authoritarian emphasis of Islam and its desire to identify the *status quo* power of the ruler with the predestining will of God makes it easy and natural to accept the roles of a Nasser, a Khomeini, or an Ataturk, and of the many other military men who have established firm one-man rule.

An additional unconscious Muslim attitude is the prevailing respect for religious—any religious—life. This is evident in the attitude of Muslims to the religiosity—or lack of it—in the foreign communities living among them. Even the nonpracticing Muslim has an innate respect for the non-Muslim who practices his own religion. Examples of such regard have been the respectful visits made by Presidents Neguib and Nasser to Jewish synagogues and Christian churches in Egypt, and the invitations extended to the chief rabbi and various Christian religious dignitaries to appear on public platforms in positions of honor at high state occasions. Even when Iraq and Egypt were at war with Israel, the formalities of respect for the official leaders of the Jewish communities in these Arab countries were maintained.

Despite the variations of Islamic practice and custom that have evolved throughout the Middle East during the past 1300 years, and regardless of the recent decline or revival in the overt importance of Muslim institutions, the Islamic heritage gives a distinct hue to the contemporary social and political life of the region. Distinctive social, political, and religious attitudes and outlooks derived from Islamic tradition set the Middle East apart from other regions and endow it with characteristics peculiar to itself.

NOTES

1. Bernard Lewis, *The Arabs in History,* London, 1956, p. 80.
2. Univ. of Chicago Press, 1946, p. 142.
3. Bernard Lewis, *op. cit.,* p. 99.
4. Von Grunebaum, *op. cit.,* p. 322ff.
5. *Ibid.,* p. 324.
6. *Ibid.,* pp. 345–346.
7. *Islam—The Straight Path,* ed. Kenneth W. Morgan, New York, 1958, p. 78.

3   Rise and Fall of the Ottomans

Throughout the contemporary Middle East Ottoman influences are second in importance only to those of the Arabs. All countries covered in this book, except Iran and those in southern Arabia, were part of the Ottoman Empire from the early sixteenth century until World War I. While Arab influences were largely cultural, the Ottoman imprint is visible on political, social, and economic institutions. Only Anatolia became Turkified, but Ottoman law still governs personal status, property, and minority rights in several Middle Eastern nations. Even in the most Westernized, Israel, Ottoman codes remain the basis of a large part of the legal system.

ORIGIN

The Ottomans were one of a large group of fierce Turkish warrior tribes whose ancestors pushed westward from the Far East and Central Asia. The Scythians, Huns, Mongols, and Tatars also originated in these Central and Eastern Asian grasslands. Through mastery of the horse and the bow, which gave them both great mobility and the advantage of offering attack from a relatively long distance instead of in hand-to-hand combat, the Turko-Mongol peoples became a great military force.

These Central Asian tribes were a racial mixture, some resembling the Chinese in skin color and facial characteristics, others being more like the Caucasians of southern Russia. All the Turko-Mongols had a similar social organization, culture, customs, and language structure. The tongues they spoke were of the Altaic family of languages—originating in Central Asia between the Ural and Altai mountain ranges. In addition to Turkish (also spoken by the Huns), Mongol, Tungus, and Samoyedic are also Altaic languages.

The ancestors of the Ottoman Turks began their westward trek several centuries after the Huns. During the seventh century one of the tribes, the Seljuks or Oghuz, began to penetrate the borders of the Middle East. Within 300 years they had gained control of the Turkestani grasslands, now in Soviet Central Asia. As their contacts became more intimate with the developed regions around Bukhara, the Seljuk nomads, like other Turkish tribes, embraced Islam.

The Abbasid dynasty (described in chapter 2) used many of the new converts as soldiers. Many of the Mamluks (lit., slave) were Turkish slaves originally trained by the Arabs and Iranians for military and administrative duties. When the Abbasid dynasty began to decline and it became increasingly difficult to recruit Arab troops, the Baghdad caliphs used whole armies of Turks.

While the Arabs lost strength, the Seljuks became more powerful until, in 1055, they took over the Abbasid capital at Baghdad. After conquering Iran and Iraq, the Turks defeated the Byzantines in 1071, driving the Eastern Christian empire from Anatolia and the Levant. After seizing Baghdad, the Seljuks—who, like the Arabs, were Sunni Muslims—permitted the Abbasid caliphs to retain their title. The real rulers, however, were the Seljuk grand sultans, for the caliphate was reduced to a mere shadow of its former authority.

Two centuries later the Seljuks were overthrown by successive waves of Mongols from Central Asia. In 1258 Baghdad fell to the Mongols, who murdered the caliph, slaughtered most of his entourage, and wreaked great destruction on the city. The Mongols also destroyed Iraq's irrigation system and slaughtered scores of Sunni Muslims—at the behest of their Shi'ite adviser.

The Crusaders still clung precariously to a few areas along the Levantine coast while a new Muslim dynasty, the Turco-Kurdish Ayyubid rulers based in Egypt, rose to power. Although Kurdish in origin, the Ayyubids were ruled by a Turkish military autocracy organized like the Seljuks. This Turkish autocracy became famous in history as the Mamluk dynasty of Egypt. It was these Mamluks who stopped the Mongols in 1260 from moving further west, and it was these same Mamluks who, shortly after defeating the Mongols, finally drove the Crusaders from the Middle East. The Mamluks ruled Egypt and controlled Syria with varying success until they lost both to the Ottomans in 1517.

The origin of the Ottomans is shrouded in myth. The leader of what was probably a fragment of a Turkish tribe displaced by the Mongol upheavals,

Ertogrul by name, was enfiefed in northwestern Anatolia by one of the last of the Seljuk sultans. In 1288 Ertogrul's son, Osman (from the Turkish pronunciation of the Arabic 'Uthman), began a policy of expansion at Byzantine expense. By 1326 Bursa in northwestern Anatolia had been captured and made the first Ottoman capital. Osman died shortly after the capture of Bursa, but his policy of expansion was carried on by his descendants. The Ottomans (the term is a European corruption of Osmanli), once established, remained imperial rulers for over 600 years, until 1922.

By 1366 the Ottmans not only had driven the Byzantines out of Anatolia but had secured sufficient control of the southern Balkans to make Edirne (Adrianople) their new capital. A few isolated political centers, including Constantinople, the Byzantine capital, managed to stave off capture by the Ottomans, although that outpost of European Christianity was outflanked for nearly a century. The imperial city finally fell May 29, 1453, to Sultan Fatih (the Conqueror) Mehmet II. It remained the capital of an empire, but now of the Turkish Muslim empire of the Ottomans.

From its Anatolian heartland, the Ottoman Empire spread over three continents, Asia, Europe, and Africa. In 1516–1517, the armies of Sultan Selim I captured Syria—including Palestine—and Egypt. His successor, Suleiman the Magnificent (1520–1566), expanded the empire through Iraq up to the present borders of Iran and, in the other direction, penetrated into central Europe, making Hungary part of his domains. Ottoman Turkey reached the zenith of its territorial conquests by 1683, when it stretched from the gates of Vienna to Iran and included parts of southern Russia. In the Arabian peninsula the conquests reached halfway down the western shore of the Persian Gulf and included the eastern Red Sea coast as far south as the Arabian Sea. North Africa as far west as Morocco was also within the empire. The Black Sea became an Ottoman lake and the Crimea, the bread basket for Istanbul (Constantinople).

Both Ottoman strength and the weakness of Ottoman adversaries accounted for these rapid conquests. When the expansion began, *ghazis,* warriors for the faith, were attracted in large numbers to Osman's forces, for he was struggling against Islam's chief enemy at the time—Byzantium. Although Osman's principality was among the smaller Turkish states, it acquired an exceptionally large and well-trained military striking force. After driving the Byzantines from Asia Minor, the ghazis insisted on extending the Islamic conquests across the Dardanelles where feeble non-Muslim Balkan kingdoms provided opportunities for glory and riches. The Byzantine Empire had been seriously weakened by conflict with Western Christendom and Balkan uprisings. The Orthodox Church had become so repressive that Christian peasants appealed for help from the Turkish conquerors. Indeed, the lot of the Greeks improved considerably immediately after the Ottoman conquest as anarchy and terror gave way to peace and security.

OTTOMAN GOVERNMENT AND SOCIETY

Within the sprawling Ottoman Empire lived a diversity of religious, national, and ethnic groups: Turks, Tatars, Arabs, Kurds, Turkomans, Berbers, Mamluks, Bosnians, Albanians, Greeks, Bulgarians, Hungarians, South Slavs, Rumanians, Armenians, Copts, Georgians, and Jews. Presiding over this mélange of peoples was the imperial Ottoman hierarchy or Ruling Institution.

The Ruling Institution

At the apex of the empire stood the sultan-caliph, who was both a secular ruler and religious symbol. Originally the sultan was a warrior nomad chief, an absolute lord whose strong hand led migrations, organized raids, and punished violators of tribal law. Tribal organization was strict and discipline severe, although willingly accepted.

The Ottoman Turks acquired the Arab title of caliph, or successor to the Prophet, when they conquered Egypt in 1517. (The surviving members of the Abbasid family had moved to Egypt after the Mongols killed the last Baghdad caliph in 1258.) Sultan Selim I induced the Abbasid successor to cede his hereditary rights and office to the Ottoman throne and dynasty, although according to Islamic theory the Ottoman sultan was unqualified to assume the title because it was reserved for descendants from the tribe of the Prophet. This requirement was overlooked, however, by an assembly of Muslim leaders which chose Sultan Selim I for the post because they considered him the greatest Muslim potentate of the age.

The imperial household or *seray* (palace) was at the center of the Ruling Institution. The seray became a training college for administrators and officers who governed the sultan's domains as well as the sultan's personal residence. In addition to the sultan's private quarters, a palace in itself, the seray included the throne and council chambers, the royal stables, kitchens, and baths, dormitories for palace functionaries, and an elite study group of future top administrators. Each of these divisions was housed in separate buildings, grouped in three courts according to importance, and the entire maze was surrounded by a high wall. This outer wall contained niches in which were displayed, from time to time, the severed heads of those officials who had either bungled their jobs or incurred royal displeasure. During the reign of Suleiman I (1520–1566), the *harem* (forbidden; sacred), exclusive quarters for the women in a Muslim household, was moved to the seray to form a fourth court. Despite their confinement, the women of the royal harem became so powerful that from 1578 until 1656 they virtually ruled the empire through male favorites whom they persuaded the sultans to appoint to high office. Even their eunuch guards became politically influential as a result of the strategic posts they occupied.

The Ruling Institution, an imperial Ottoman creation, was a centralized bureaucracy whose efficiency depended upon the personal character of the sultan or his chief deputy, the grand vezir. The grand vezir was, in effect, a kind of prime minister, but one responsible only to the sultan. How much of the sultan's authority he would exercise naturally depended on each sultan's decision to rule or merely to reign. As he could be dismissed at will by the sultan, there were obvious pitfalls for a strong, independent grand vezir who would agree to wield the sultan's authority. Since the majority of sultans after Suleiman I generally preferred the pleasures of the harem to worries over imperial administration, the grand vezirs' office grew in importance, if not commensurately in power. Opposition to his policies or jealous rivalry often brought about the dismissal of the chief minister, whom sultans made their scapegoat. This is the explanation for the sometimes bewilderingly rapid succession of grand vezirs, as many as three in one year and a total of thirteen in five years in the early reign of Mehmet IV (1648–1687).

In addition to the grand vezir, the top administration of the Ruling Institution included two *defterdars* (treasurers), one for Europe and one for Asia; a *nishanci* (secretary); two *kadiaskers* (judges with jurisdiction over most of the hierarchy's members), representing Europe and Asia, two *beylerbeys* (governors general of Europe and Asia); the *aga* (leader of the Janissaries; and the *kaptan pasha* (lord high admiral). Each of these highest ranking administrators presided over a complex bureaucracy. They held a *divan* (cabinet meeting) four times a week, at which the early sultans were generally present. Later, as many sultans shifted more administrative duties to the grand vezir, the chief minister held his own divan at his special residence, the Sublime Porte, while imperial divans were held only infrequently and often for purely ceremonial purposes.

The sultan's administrators were primarily concerned with the maintenance of internal security, the collection of taxes, and the expansion of the empire or, at the very least, the preservation of Ottoman frontiers. They were incidentally involved in assuring sufficient food supplies to the populace of Istanbul. They appointed provincial governors, tax officials, and assigned different sections of the army to various police duties.

One of the more extraordinary aspects of the imperial Ottoman administration was its military character. Every administrator in the Ruling Institution had undergone military training from an early age. Indeed, for centuries the ruling elite were obliged to ride to war under either sultan or grand vezir.

Originally, Osmanli administrators had been free-born Muslims. After the conquest of Istanbul, however, Fatih Mehmet elaborated a system of palace schools to which were assigned Christian boys from the ages of eight to eighteen. These boys were chosen either from among the captives of newly conquered Balkan territory or through a system of conscription called the *devshirme.* Every five years, or sometimes annually, depending on need, Ottoman officials toured the Balkans choosing the brightest and sturdiest Christian boys to be brought to Istanbul, tested again, and entered as students in the various palace schools. Originally these boys were trained to become the standing army of the empire: the sultan's personal bodyguard; the cavalry of the Porte; and the famous infantry, the Janissaries. Under Fatih Mehmet's expansion of the palace school system, all members of the Ruling Institution, except the two kadiaskers, were to be drawn from Christian captives or the devshirme.

Upon enrollment in the palace schools, the new students were converted to Islam, trained in the Sharia (Muslim law), Arabic, Persian, and Turkish grammar and literature. Mathematics, music, Turkish history, calligraphy, and vocational training were standard courses. The students were given increasingly strenuous physical exercise as well as rigorous military training. From the top palace school, housed in the imperial seray itself, emerged the elite of the administration. From the second-ranking school came the Janissaries, the artillerymen, the standing cavalry, and the sultan's elite guard; and from the lower palace schools the lesser bureaucratic positions in the Ruling Institution were filled. The bulk of these palace school graduates were paid a money salary by the sultan and owed their fortunes in life exclusively to him. Advancement was to be based on merit, and for over a century this seemed to be the general rule. Punishment tended to be quick and extreme, quite commonly being death.

In addition to the palace school elite, there existed a feudal cavalry corps, the *sipahi* (cavalrymen), who were granted land as a consequence of some meritorious action in battle. The sipahi were permitted to collect the revenues from their fiefs so long as they answered the call to arms accompanied by a number of armed men, depending on the extent of a fief's revenue. A fief could be enlarged as a reward for distinguished service in a campaign, but only the original fief would pass to the sipahi's son, who would have to earn any similar additions to it. The sipahi's duties also included maintenance of those roads lying closest to his fief and the duties of a rural policeman as well. He was prohibited from expelling any of his peasant tenants, be they Christian or Muslim. Unlike the paid palace school graduates, the sipahis were to a large degree free-born Muslims. The total land enfiefed to the sipahis, however, never represented a majority of all the land enfiefed for one purpose or another within the empire. And, as in theory, the sipahi controlled his land only on the sultan's sufferance and was not free to augment or dispose of it. He was therefore neither a political nor a military threat to the central government and, in this way, differed from the landed aristocracy in Europe.

It may be well to point out that although the Ottoman dynasty has usually been considered both Turkish and Muslim, this element in the population never constituted a majority throughout the more than 600-year history of the empire. Indeed, Muslims only constituted a majority of the empire's population in the last half of the nineteenth century.

All members of the Ruling Institution were considered the sultan's slaves, a misnomer in its English translation since these "slaves" were the ruling elite of an empire. In theory, since these "slaves" were now Muslim, none of their children were eligible for entry into the palace schools. By this means, Muslims by birth were to be excluded from the ruling elite of a Muslim empire. Quite clearly, pressure from Muslims for administrative participation in the ruling elite was bound to increase. Muslim pressure was ultimately successful by the end of the seventeenth century, when the devshirme was abolished. From then until the demise of the empire, native-born Muslims filled the palace schools.

The Janissaries. To Europeans, the best known graduates of the palace schools were the Janissaries. Indeed, the system of converting Christian boys to Islam and training them under the immediate supervision of the sultan was devised specifically for the Janissary corps sometime in the fourteenth century. These "new troops" were expected to undergo exacting training and endure severe punishments. Until the later part of the sixteenth century, they constituted between 10,000 and 15,000 men. They were forbidden to marry while on the active list, although they were free to do so upon being pensioned into retirement. In return for withstanding these rigors, they were granted special privileges. They were freed from taxation and had the right of trial only by the aga of the Janissaries.

For some two centuries their performances in battle were generally outstanding and more often than not determined a successful outcome. Perhaps their very successes helped to undermine the organization. Even at the beginning of the sixteenth century, the Janissaries were sufficiently conscious of their power to force the abdication of the reigning sultan for his younger and martial son. They also managed to impose upon the sultans the habit of presenting the corps with a cash donation upon each new succession to the throne. Although they might be the essential core of the sultans' military forces, few early sultans looked upon them with equanimity.

By the end of the sixteenth century, Murat III (1574–1595), in an attempt to weaken the corps through corruption, opened their ranks to untrained recruits who would pay for the honor, a disastrous decision. Also around this time, the stricture against marriage while on active duty was no longer enforced; consequently, fewer and fewer Janissaries occupied their barracks, naturally preferring the comforts of their homes. Further, the corps was permitted to enroll the sons of Janissaries. Only two more steps were needed to destroy the military effectiveness of this much-vaunted group. As the ranks had doubled and even tripled, the government was hard pressed to pay these additional men. It resolved the dilemma on the one hand, by debasing the coinage, and, on the other, by permitting the Janissaries to engage in trade. The Janissaries thereby struck deep roots among the artisan class of the cities, most of which included themselves on the rosters of the corps. All this did indeed weaken the corps militarily, but it also strengthened it immeasurably in real political power. For the sultans had now to deal not with a mere 15,000 crack troops, but with an unruly rabble in the large cities of the empire. In the capital itself more than one sultan was deposed and lost his life because he dared to restrain these ruffians. Annihilation of the institution was to be the only solution. It did not take place until 1826.

The Religious Institution

The Religious or Muslim Institution paralleled the Ruling Institution. At the top of its bureaucratic hierarchy stood the mufti of Istanbul or sheikhh ul Islam, as he was called from Suleiman I's reign to the expiration of the Ottoman Empire. In theory, the sheikh ul Islam held more power than the sultans since he was authorized to veto any decision by the sultans that was contrary to the Sharia. In fact, the sheikh ul Islam was appointed by the sultan and could be dismissed by him at any time. Even so, the sheikh ul Islam's *fetvas* (legal opinions) were generally always respected. No sultan could issue a *kanun* (law) before obtaining a fetva from the sheikh ul Islam stating that the intended kanun was compatible with the Sharia. The sheikh ul Islam was always a free-born Muslim, as indeed were all members of the Religious Institution.

The post of sheikh ul Islam was the highest to which a member of the ulema could attain in the Religious Institution. The *ulema,* or body of learned men, was made up of Muslim religious leaders concerned with administrating or teaching Muslim law. (They were called ulema because they possessed *'ilm* (Arabic: knowledge, especially of Islamic law). A Muslim was considered a member of the ulema once he had progressed from the *kuttab* (mosque school) to the *medresse* (college). From the ulema were drawn the two kadiaskers, the Religious Institution's only direct representation in the Ruling Institution. In addition, the poets, scholars, court historians, astrologers, mosque officials, teachers, and judges were members of the ulema.

All members of the Ruling Institution as well as all Ottoman Muslim citizens came under the jurisdiction of the Sharia. The Sharia was administered by *kadis* (judges). The more important kadis were generally appointed by the sheikh ul Islam. As we have seen, members of the Ruling Institution were judged by the two kadiaskers with the exception of the Janissaries who had the right to be tried by their aga. The kadiaskers were supported financially by the Ruling Institution. The kadis, on the other hand, gained their remuneration by charging litigants a fee. Non-Muslims came into contact with Muslim law only when involved in a dispute with a Muslim, and then the non-Muslim concerned was obliged to appear before a kadi for a decision in the case.

Revenue from a *vakif* (Arabic: *wakf;* endowment) went to pay the salaries of teachers and mosque officials. Vakifs might be set up by any Muslim and for a multitude of purposes. Mosques, medresses, libraries, soup kitchens for the poor, student dormitories, baths, fountains, and orphanages were among the most common vakifs. A Muslim might decide to set aside enough of his property to support a mosque and additional buildings. He might then choose an architect and supervise the construction, paying both the architect and construction fees from his pocket. Once completed, the mosque and its additional buildings might include a medresse, a soup kitchen, and a student dormitory. In order to pay the salaries of the teachers and mosque officials, the maintenance of the students, and the upkeep of the various buildings, the donor would have to set aside enough property the revenue of which would be sufficient for these purposes. Once a vakif was established, it and the property from which it derived its support were tax exempt forever. The sheikh ul Islam was then charged with the regulation and administration of most of the vakifs. The most splendid mosques in Istanbul today, for example, are vakifs left by some of the sultans and now administered by the Turkish republic's Ministry of Vakifs.

Since the value of the vakif generally determined its quality, there was naturally a wide difference between a modest medresse in Yugoslavia and a lavish one in Istanbul, or even between two different medresses in the capital city. This meant there would be considerable variety in the curriculum and in the quality of the teachers from one medresse to the next. Although an outstanding medresse like Al Azhar in Cairo might maintain fairly consistently a high level of scholarship over the centuries, the standards of most medresses fluctuated to a substantial degree. At the best medresses, through the centuries, students were taught Arabic, grammar, the Koran, metaphysics, mathematics, astronomy, medicine, the Sharia, and theology according to classical Muslim tradition.

When Muslims gained entry into the Ruling Institution, corruption began to subvert the vakif system, not because native Muslims were more susceptible to corruption than converted Muslims, but because native-born Muslims in the Ruling Institution wished to preserve their property from confiscation by the sultan. Converted Muslims had been brought up to accept this procedure. One means of maintaining much of their property intact was to set it up as vakif to be managed by members of the donor's family. This practice was not only a serious financial loss to the government, it also resulted in the negligence and deterioration of much property. Even more disastrous was the decline in educational quality suffered by most medresses.

The Millet System and the Capitulations. All Ottoman citizens were divided in *millets* (nations) on the basis of religion. Until the reign of Suleiman I, the Ottoman government recognized four millets, the Muslim, Greek Orthodox, Armenian Gregorian, and Jewish. The head of the Muslim millet was naturally the sheikh ul Islam, whose other functions we have already described. The leaders of the Greek Orthodox and Armenian millets were the patriarchs of their respective churches. The Armenian millet was also to include all those Christians who were not Greek Orthodox. The chief rabbi represented the Jewish millet. The millet system was regularized by Fatih Mehmet after the capture of Constantinople (Istanbul) in 1453. Each millet was permitted wide autonomy to develop its religious, cultural, and educational life. Each used its own language and was under the jurisdiction of its own legal system, except when a non-Muslim and a Muslim were concerned and the former had to appear before the latter's kadi for justice. As the Ottoman Empire proclaimed itself a Muslim empire, the Muslim millet understandably held a favorable position within the empire.

Dhimmis (non-Muslims) could not hold Imperial positions unless they converted to Islam. And dhimmis were required to pay a special tax called the *cizya* for the privilege of religious dissent. The patriarchs and the chief rabbi were responsible for the annual collection of the cizya from their respective millets and its remittance to the sultan. All three dhimmi leaders were required to reside in the capital, and it was largely through them that the Ottoman government conducted its relations with its dhimmis. The clergy of all three millets thereby acquired extensive temporal as well as religious power and assumed the attributes of kingship in many areas. When nationalism caught fire among the Balkan peoples in the nineteenth century, it might have seemed natural for the dhimmi leaders to exercise leadership of the independence movements. By and large, however, they did not do so because most of them were unwilling to give up the power and prestige they exercised under the sultan for an uncertain future position. Dhimmis were not expected to bear arms, and with few exceptions no non-Muslims helped expand the empire or defend it when it was attacked. The Greek Orthodox millet suffered or benefited, depending upon the viewpoint, in that the devshirme was culled only from its members.

The dhimmis were viewed as less than perfect, as persons occupying the halfway station to truth, since they had accepted only the initial revelations and not the final manifestations of God's truth as revealed by Muhammad. Dhimmis, then, were clearly inferior in intelligence to Muslims. Inferiority was not innate, since any dhimmi could attain superiority by converting to Islam. If a dhimmi converted to Islam, he left his previous millet and entered immediately the Muslim millet. A dhimmi converting from Gregorian (Armenian) to Greek Orthodox similarly changed his millet. In the Ottoman

Empire a man's "nation" status or "nationality" was determined by his religious affiliation. Muslims were generally enjoined from entering any of the dhimmi millets by conversion, and until the last half of the nineteenth century there was little reason for them to do so. The large measure of freedom in autonomy granted dhimmis in the Ottoman Empire contrasted quite favorably with Christian, particularly Catholic, Europe where tolerance of religious dissent, when it did exist, was extremely circumscribed.

During the reign of Suleiman I, a fifth millet was recognized. This millet was generally made up of Catholics, all of whom were non-Osmanli citizens. The fifth millet originated with the first treaty of capitulations signed between Suleiman I and Francis I of France in 1536. (The term "capitulations" comes from the Latin *capitula,* chapter of an agreement.) These capitulations granted reciprocity of treatment to French and Ottoman merchants selling goods and establishing residence in either area. French citizens traveling or making their residence in the Ottoman Empire for the purpose of commerce would be tax exempt and would not be subject to the Sharia or to the law of any of the other three Ottoman millets. In a similar manner, Ottoman subjects traveling or residing in France were not to be subjected to French law or taxes. The French ambassador was looked upon as the head of this fifth or foreign millet. By the end of the sixteenth century, England and Holland were also granted capitulary treaties, but the French ambassador remained chief of the millet until the advent of Napoleon, when the fifth millet was fractured into as many different parts as there were nations with capitulary treaties with the Ottoman government.

Although the capitulary treaties were reciprocal in the early years and were a manifestation of Ottoman power rather than weakness, the Ottomans rarely took advantage of this reciprocity. Failure to do so soon made Ottoman exports and imports the exclusive preserve of Europeans. The European takeover of this Ottoman export-import trade was coupled with a general decline in the power and efficiency of the Ottoman government; thus the capitulations actually became an instrument of European power and influence within the Ottoman Empire.

In taking advantage of the extraterritoriality clauses of the capitulations, European states set up consulates in various Ottoman cities, staffing them primarily with Ottoman citizens. Beginning in the eighteenth century, however, some of these Ottoman citizens were granted first French and then other European citizenships, thereby obtaining exemption from Ottoman taxation—a situation that might be considered desirable by any number of Ottomans. In the eighteenth century such action was infrequent, but in the nineteenth century competition for European citizenship became fierce, among the dhimmis in particular since Muslims still had a stake in the Ottoman government. More often than not, European citizenship was merely granted by the various European embassies to the highest bidder, an open perversion of the capitulations and, for Osmanli Muslims, a clear demonstration of Western power. In addition to the grant of citizenship, the European states proclaimed themselves "protectors" of various groups within the empire: among others, Russia claimed the Greek Orthodox; France, the Catholics; the United States, the Armenian Protestants. These "protectors" probably gave less real protection to their respective groups than any self-proclaimed defenders throughout history. The proclaimed interest in such groups, however, could be and was used at the diplomatic conference table to establish justification for international interference (see chapter 4).

The Decline of the Ottomans

The whole elaborate Osmanli governmental structure depended for its efficiency upon the character and determination of one man—the sultan. It is true that the grand vezir could assume many of the essential functions of the sultan, but only with the sultan's approval and wholehearted support. The sultan was the crown of the empire. What he did or failed to do influenced every group, not merely the governing hierarchy. Once a sultan accepted a money gift from some official, or permitted high officials themselves to accept such presents, it did not take long for this to become an established practice rather than a singular exception. So, too, once a sultan made an appointment of a high post based on favoritism rather than on merit, he upset the intricate functioning of the Ruling Institution. It did not take long, then, to pass from promotion by merit to promotion by bribery in the Religious Institution as well as in the Ruling Institution.

Succession to the throne proved a knotty problem, but not for lack of heirs as in Europe: the harem system insured that the Osmanli dynasty would endure. Until the seventeenth century, sons of a reigning sultan were given provincial government posts to acquaint them with the business of government. It was not unusual, however, for sons to compete with one another for the throne—and Selim I (1512–1520) deposed his own father, Beyazit II (1481–1512). Even before Fatih Mehmet published his kanun on fratricide in the fifteenth century, some sultans, upon attaining the throne, had killed their brothers. Fatih Mehmet's kanun not only made this action permissible, it proclaimed the idea desirable because it helped to avoid civil strive. Such a practice solved nothing, for it meant that a sultan's brothers must either emigrate or fight for their lives; competition between the sons of a reigning sultan merely became more deadly since in the end only one could be girded with the sword of Osman.

By the seventeenth century both the practice of fratricide and the appointment of the sultan's sons to governmental posts were abandoned. Instead, all the sons of the reigning sultan were kept in the palace, each in separate quarters called *kafes* (cage), and the succession was to go automatically to the oldest living male. This new system unfortunately ensured that no sultan from the seventeenth century on would have any knowledge of or training in government affairs until he came to the throne. As most of the companions during his confinement were the female members of his harem, many a new sultan found the temptation to spend the bulk of his time in the harem greater than the temptation to rule. The harem, therefore, came to exercise a great influence on government affairs, particularly in the appointment of officials.

Corruption in high officials infected their subordinates, spread to the Religious Institution, and wrecked the military system. Instead of a highly trained and disciplined force, the sultans from the seventeenth century on found themselves in peacetime with a large paper army that shrank in wartime to a motley assortment of undisciplined scavengers.

The first ten sultans had been larger than life. Under their rule the Ottoman Empire had spread throughout eastern Europe, Asia, and North Africa. The whole complex of Ottoman rulings and religious institutions that has just been described was created by the first ten sultans. The temptation to relax some of these very taxing burdens began with the tenth sultan, Suleiman I. Yet the very centralization of power and authority meant that any relaxation at the heart would seriously undermine control of the parts.

Many of the outlying provinces of the empire—such as Egypt, Yemen, the coastal provinces of the Arabian peninsula, the Kurdish provinces in eastern Turkey, and even Moldavia and Wallachia (part of modern Rumania) —had always been controlled lightly from Istanbul, for they had been allowed to retain pre-Ottoman ruling hierarchies provided only that requisite taxes were sent to the capital. With both relaxation and corruption at the center, many of these provinces became semi-independent, acknowledging the sultan's authority only when forced to do so by the military. Even the Druse amirs in the mountains of the Levant coast became virtually independent for a time during the seventeenth century (see also chapter 4). Fakhr ud-Din, establishing himself in Lebanon and northern Palestine between 1585 and 1635, made his own diplomatic agreements with European powers and invited in Christian missionaries to set up schools and European engineers to improve the area. In Egypt, the Mamluks had been permitted to retain their administrative functions under the nominal eye of an Osmanli pasha. More than once, some of the Mamluks had attempted the exercise of independent power. The native rulers of Moldavia and Wallachia were less successful, largely because the imperial government took care to keep and even to tighten its control over the European provinces, since it was through them that the European states traditionally attacked the empire.

The general decay of Ottoman governmental institutions coincided with the rise of more powerful European nation states. By the end of the seventeenth century, the Ottoman Empire was under concerted attack by the Europeans. Competition among the Europeans for Ottoman territory and for the exercise of power and influence over the empire helped to preserve the

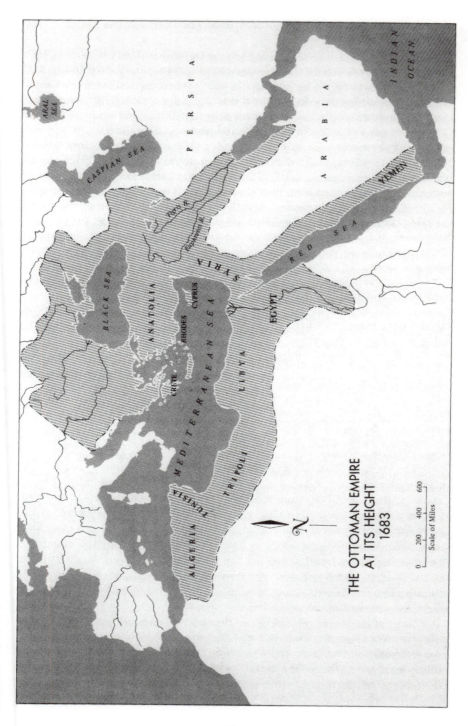

THE OTTOMAN EMPIRE
AT ITS HEIGHT
1683

Scale of Miles

0   200   400   600

Osmanlis since no European state wished to see its rival gain the ascendancy. It was generally deemed better to have the Ottoman Empire continue to exist than to allow the division of the territorial spoils that would occur once it fell.

Efforts were made to stem the tide throughout the Ottoman decline. Signs of recovery appeared on the eve of the first great territorial loss when, in 1656, Grand Vezir Mehmet Koprulu instituted a regime of honest and efficient government. During the five years of his vezirate, 30,000 officers, theologians, judges, and other officials were executed for undermining the state through corruption. In the next half century the Koprulu family rallied the empire, even expanding into Poland and the Ukraine. But by the end of the seventeenth century, however, the Koprulus resigned themselves to the orderly liquidation of territorial losses suffered to Austria, Poland, and Russia.

A second nonmilitary rally roused the empire between 1703 and 1730 when the Ottoman court attempted to emulate the styles of France. Houses, clothing, court etiquette, and the floral arrangements of the Versailles gardens were imitated in what came to be called the "tulip period." The imitation was even more successful than intended, for the "after us the deluge" spirit of Louis XV pervaded the era. Although little was accomplished to strengthen the empire, more positive aspects of the new European intellectual and scientific awakening began to have an impact on some members of the Ottoman educated elite, as was evident by the introduction of the first printing press with Arabic characters.

THE TANZIMAT

The modern reform era, called in Turkish the *Tanzimat,* began after a crushing defeat by Russia in 1774. Ottoman rulers then began to search in earnest for the means to stem the European onrush. They turned first to the use of those techniques, tactics, and tools with which the Europeans had defeated the empire. To the sultans Western strength seemed rooted in modern military prowess. Only by acquiring this technology too could they become strong enough to forestall the West from overwhelming Ottoman-Islamic society. They did not yet comprehend the need for the fundamental changes in society that would be necessary if they were to keep up with the growing power of the West.

Serious efforts at reform were initiated by Selim III (1789–1808), who became sultan shortly before the outbreak of the French Revolution in 1789. By reorganizing the imperial divan into a cabinet of twelve ministers, the sultan was able to reduce the authority of the grand vezir. Plans were laid for revitalizing education: printing plants were opened; Western authors were translated and circulated in the capital; and the permanent embassies were established in London, Paris, Vienna, and Berlin to acquire information about the West.

Selim III realized that unless he strengthened control over his army the provinces would remain beyond his influence. A Turk who had served in the Russian army was authorized to equip and modernize a new corps of some 600 men. Napoleon's ambassador to the Porte (see chapter 4 for a discussion of this period) offered to supply the army with French uniforms and with specialists in tactics and weapons. When the sultan attempted to introduce these modernization measures into the Janissary corps, that group staged a revolt and forced him to withdraw the order. This recalcitrant corps also rejected the gift of French artillery pieces sent in 1796, although these "Christian" devices were readily adopted by other army units. A final modernization attempt by Selim III in 1807 sparked an insurrection among the Janissaries that forced him to abdicate the following year. His innovations were temporarily abandoned, and other reformers in the court were slaughtered by reactionary military leaders.

Mahmud II

Selim's ineffectual nephew succeeded him for a few months, but was soon replaced by Selim's brother, Mahmud II, in July 1808. Mahmud's twenty-one-year regime has been compared to that of Peter the Great in Russia because of his efforts to revolutionize the Ottoman Empire without destroying its Ottoman character. Like his unfortunate older brother, he also began with military reforms, but he proceeded with more caution. Before attempting to impose new techniques on all army units, Mahmud built up a reservoir of support among influential officers. The loyalty of the grand vezir, the sheikh ul Islam, and the Janissary aga was cultivated, and a large complement of faithful and well-trained artillerymen was brought to the capital. When he felt sure of his strength, Mahmud struck, turning first to deal with the reactionary and undisciplined Janissary corps.

Orders were again given for the Janissaries to adopt European military drills, and again most of them revolted. In retaliation, the sultan surrounded their barracks with his loyal units, the sheikh ul Islam was called upon to pronounce the malediction against them, and the artillery was ordered to cut them down. Elsewhere in Istanbul and throughout the empire the Janissaries were hunted out and thousands killed; their banners and insignia were dragged through the mud, their mosques and cafés razed, and their Bektashi religious order (an offshoot of Sufism) was dissolved. All other troops suspected of sympathies with the Janissaries were liquidated. Thus, in one concentrated effort, the center of opposition to military reform was obliterated.

With the greatest obstacle to army reorganization removed, Mahmud proceeded to organize a new 40,000-man force. A group of Prussian officers was invited to Istanbul to train the military, and the younger Ottoman officers were sent to England for instruction. A national militia was organized in 1834 to set up military training in the outlying provinces, and military colleges were established with foreign assistance.

With his new military prowess, Mahmud reasserted authority over feudal lords in provinces beyond the capital where, for the past 200 years, the sultan's influence had been at best shadowy. The power of provincial governors was reduced, and they were now forbidden to carry out executions without central government approval. Abler men were recruited for the Ruling Institution at higher salaries, with a consequent lessening of the twin hazards of bribery and red tape. New roads, improved administrative techniques, and Western legal codes facilitated governmental efforts to stimulate trade. The postal system, introduced in 1832, made possible dependable communication throughout the empire.

In the new military and medical colleges hundreds of students learned French and German and were thereby exposed to the liberal ideas that were current in European literature. Presses in Istanbul and Izmir began to publish Western books. French newspapers began publication in Izmir during the 1820s, and the first Turkish newssheet was issued in the capital with official support in 1832. When the reactionary ulema, including the sheikh ul Islam, opposed these "Christian" innovations, they were overridden by Mahmud. Leaders of the Dervish orders (described in chapter 2), who attempted to sabotage the reform, were exiled.

Mahmud even attempted to change the outward appearance of Osmanli Muslims. The traditional turban was replaced by the red Venetian fez, then considered a stylish Western headgear. The frock coat, called the stambuli jacket, became standard dress in urban areas, and beards were shaven to conform with European standards.

Although the list of Mahmud's reforms seems impressive, they did not reach the masses of his Muslim subjects, being confined to Istanbul's governmental and social elite. Religious opposition, peasant conservatism, and failure to understand the roots of European social reform and technology prevented a really fundamental change in Ottoman society. Most reforms were superficially imitative rather than basic. French military uniforms, equipment, drills, and organization were adopted without training Ottoman soldiers how to service artillery pieces or to replace imperfect parts. The sudden change to modern techniques and tools was incomprehensible both to the average Ottoman officer and to the common soldier. Similarly, the precipitous transition from outdated Ottoman administrative practices to modern European governmental organizations was not understood by most members of the Ruling Institution, who had become conservative over the years.

The Ottoman Liberals

There was a dualism among Ottomans in their attitudes toward these early Westernizing reforms. The "idealists," strongly influenced by writings of the French Encyclopedists and the eighteenth-century American revolutionaries, were convinced that constitutional government was essential, that only European political institutions could cure Ottoman society of its ills. The "realists" were unconcerned about constitutionalism, civil liberties, and liberalism. They were sure that the empire's lost power and prestige could be recouped simply through the adoption of Western material techniques.

An early liberal was Reshid Pasha, who became familiar with the West while ambassador to England and France. The great political reforms in England during the early 1830s aroused his enthusiasm, and when he returned to Istanbul as foreign minister, he attempted to introduce similar changes. Reshid collaborated closely with Mahmud II in preparing the first great reform edict, the *Hatti Sherif of Gulhané* (noble rescript of the sultan's rose chamber), proclaimed in 1839. Issuance of the edict, only a few months after Mahmud's death from alcoholism, was probably also influenced by a desire to arouse English public opinion in support of a loan the Ottoman Empire was then seeking.

While the new decree strongly reflected European liberalism, it also considerably widened and strengthened the authority of the central government, following the example of Napoleon Bonaparte. Life and honor, it stated, were "the most precious gifts of mankind," which, when secured, would lead men to "contribute to the good of government" and of their brothers. The decree promised security of life and property to all Ottomans— Muslims, Christians, and Jews. The notorious *iltizam,* or tax-farming system, was to be replaced by an equitable levy based on income. Regularized military recruitment without discrimination between Muslim and non-Muslim was proposed. Service was to be reduced to four or five years, instead of the indefinite period of duty prevailing until 1839, a system that had undermined the development of agriculture by depopulating the countryside. Criminal trials were to be publicly judged in accordance with regular legal procedures and no one was to be put to death secretly or publicly without official authorization. All the ulema and the "grandees" of the empire were to be equally subject to the rule of the law. Rigorous measures were to be taken to punish those who attempted bribery. To end the practice of *baksheesh* (gratuities), government employees were promised higher salaries.

Reshid's attempts to implement the reform decree were aborted when he lost power in 1841 because of a dispute over a new commercial law code. The reformer's successor was a conservative who distrusted Christians and soon abandoned all efforts to change the government. Revolutionary outbreaks among the Christian Balkan principalities only intensified efforts to undo Reshid's work.

In 1845 Reshid returned as grand vezir and reinstituted the reform movement. Having learned from experience that considerable time was needed to overcome the influence of the religious conservatives, he attempted to adapt the movement to established Islamic practices and customs. Reshid had strong support from his close friend the British ambassador, Sir Stratford Canning (later Viscount de Redcliffe).

Educational reforms were introduced, and the colleges of medicine, agriculture, naval science, and government were combined in 1846 with the newly established University of Istanbul. Recommendations of a special council on educational problems resulted in the opening of six schools with universal, compulsory, free education. However, the drive to improve education collapsed after 1851 because of lack of funds and continued conservative fears of radical "Christian innovations."

In the provinces, Reshid attempted to set up local assemblies to advise the governors and to ratify their decisions. But only wealthy notables, who became guardians of the old order rather than advocates of the new, filled these assemblies. Within five years, Reshid's second attempt at reform also slowed to a halt. Reshid was so victimized by nepotism and maladministration that he lost the valuable friendship of Sir Stratford, who finally reported to Queen Victoria in 1851 that all hope for development of a modern Turkey seemed lost.

More penetrating than the paper reforms and administrative decrees was the spirit of the Tanzimat among Western-educated youth. Young Ottoman intellectuals were exposed to an increasing barrage of European periodicals and books. Ottoman works on politics, history, philosophy, and government also flourished. The liberal awakening of young Ottoman intellectuals, inspired by the French Enlightenment, did have its paradoxical side, however. The same spirit also aroused the Balkan non-Muslims—Greeks, Armenians, Bulgarians, Serbians, Rumanians, and others—and a tide of anti-Ottoman fervor swept over southeast Europe. These Christian revolts in turn stirred the embers of an exclusively Turkish nationalism, which sought to suppress the uprisings lest the empire be torn apart.

The Crimean War, between 1853 and 1856, accelerated the pace of the Tanzimat. Since one of its causes was dispute over the inequitable status of non-Muslim Ottoman subjects, the Ottoman Empire's Western allies pressured the sultan to hasten reform. Their intent was to weaken Russian assertions that the Greek Orthodox Ottoman citizens required foreign protection. By the mid-1850s the ideas of Western-educated youth were beginning to influence their more conservative elders and many Europeans in the capital, stationed there to help defend the empire, pressured the government to adopt reforms.

When the war was about to end in an Anglo-French–aided victory over Russia, the allies persuaded the sultan to issue a second major reform edict, the *Hatti-Humayun* (imperial rescript) of 1856. It proclaimed his desire to "renew and enlarge still more the new institutions," and to "effect the happiness of all" subjects regardless of nationality. In accord with these sentiments, the principal emphasis of the Hatti-Humayun was on the rights of non-Muslims. The millet system was modified so that patriarchs and millet leaders were appointed for life through selection by popular assemblies of the various religious groups. Forcible conversions to Islam were outlawed. Religious discrimination in government employment, the state civil and military schools, and in the army was banned, although non-Muslims were permitted to continue the practice of providing substitutes for, or buying exemption from, conscription. Mixed tribunals were to judge disputes in public hearings. The Sharia was thus no longer supreme, but merely placed on an equal level with other religious codes, at least in theory. Reform of the penal codes and prison system was proposed, including abolition of "everything that resembles torture." Again, tax reforms were promised, including replacement of tax farming by direct collections based on income. Banks and other financial institutions were called upon to assist in the reformation of the monetary and financial systems, and to help create investment funds. Obstacles to development of commerce and agriculture were abolished by decree, including the ban on sale of real estate to foreigners. To help implement the new legislation, the heads of each religious community were invited to participate in deliberations of the Supreme Justice Council.

The Hatti-Humayun, however, fared no better than the 1839 reform decree. Within several months all its stated objectives were forgotten and the traditional pattern of Ottoman administration again prevailed. The old oligarchy resented "Christian" practices with a hatred fanned by the overwhelming tide of Balkan Christian nationalism. Every effort was made by most of the Ottoman officials to evade rather than to implement the new decrees. One observer noted that the Hatti-Humayun left nothing to be desired but its execution. Perhaps this was too quick a judgment, however, for in the decades following 1839, modernization of government departments did begin, some of the grossest corruption and maladministration were eliminated, and influence of the royal court was lessened in favor of the modernized Ruling Institution.

The last great Tanzimat reformer was Midhat Pasha, father of the 1876 Ottoman constitution. In Bulgaria he had acquired a reputation for enlightenment while he was governor. He built roads, bridges, schools, hospitals, banks, cooperatives, and other public institutions, while ruthlessly crushing uprisings against the sultan. Midhat's harsh imposition of law and order was applied equally to Muslims and Christians. Following his Balkan assignment, Midhat served as governor of Iraq, and later, of Salonika, until temporary retirement in Istanbul.

During Midhat's absence from active government life, Sultan Abdul Aziz, notorious for his profligate spending, brought the empire to the verge of bankruptcy. Fearing another threat of foreign intervention, Midhat organized a coup that deposed the spendthrift in 1876. The sultan's successor had a nervous breakdown within three months and was replaced by a brother, Abdul Hamid II. The liberals had great expectations for Abdul Hamid II because he had been exposed to European ideas while visiting the continent. Their hopes were initially realized when the new sultan appointed Midhat as grand vezir and the two proclaimed a constitution.

The drafting committee shaped a constitutional monarchy with Belgium and France as models. All subjects were again declared free and equal, but Islam was still the acknowledged state religion. An innovation was a two-chamber parliament empowered to approve legislation initiated by the sultan's council of ministers. In case of deadlock between the ministers and parliament, the sultan could either call for elections or appoint a new ministerial council. In the provinces and municipal areas, councils were authorized to deal with strictly local matters, such as public utilities, communications, and agriculture. During national emergencies the sultan could suspend civil liberties and expel dangerous citizens.

Abdul Hamid II

Abdul Hamid II lost little time in exploiting his emergency powers. A year after promulgating the constitution, he suspended it under the pretext of crisis created by the Russo-Turkish war of 1877–1878. Midhat was summarily exiled and the new parliament prorogued. All the reformers were discharged and Abdul Hamid surrounded himself with sycophants. The sultan wreaked his vengeance on Midhat five years later when the former grand vezir and several of his liberal followers were strangled in their dungeons in far off Arabia. The struggle between Abdul Hamid and the reformers had been sparked by dispute over the sultan's powers. He refused to surrender control of the royal finances, to sanction abolition of the slave trade, or to permit mixed Christian-Muslim schools. Such innovations were far too radical for the sultan and the conservative court clique.

Abdul Hamid II did not completely abandon the idea of European innovation; instead, he shifted the emphasis from constitutionalism to military reforms. German officers were invited to train the army, a British colonel was engaged to reorganize the police, and British ships were ordered for the navy.

Debts to European bondholders, totaling nearly 200 million pounds and incurred in the last Russian war, forced the government into bankruptcy and brought about the establishment of the Ottoman National Debt Administration in 1881. Five of the seven members on the council of the Debt Administration represented European bondholders; one member, the Ottoman Bank, was jointly operated by British and French interests; and a single member was nominated by the sultan. All revenues from the government salt and tobacco monopolies; stamp taxes; tariffs on fish, spirits, and silk; and income from the administration of Bulgaria and Cyprus were all turned over to the administration to be used for debt liquidation. Although widely resented as a representative of the Christian imperialists, the administration, staffed mainly by Turks, was a noteworthy example of Ottoman administrative capabilities. In fact, the administration eventually restored Ottoman international credit, and European entrepreneurs were again encouraged to invest in large capital developments. As a result of the National Debt Administration's activities, roads and railways were constructed and modern industrial goods were distributed in many parts of the empire, accelerating the penetration of Western innovations and ideas.

Abdul Hamid II's belief in technological progress was inconsistent with his political ideology. All political progress was abandoned, all opposition ruthlessly hunted down, and all governmental power concentrated in his own hands. Extensive spy networks were spread through the empire in search of "subversives." Rigid press censorship, frequent suspension of newspapers, and the exile of editors who did not toe the official line undermined whatever literary progress had been made earlier in the century. Many liberal Ottoman writers became expatriates and published their works abroad, but their writings were then smuggled back into the country.

The sultan tried to divert public opinion and attention from his repressive measures by arousing nationalist sentiment through an Islamic revival. The title of caliph, which had fallen into disuse, was resurrected; and Abdul Hamid II sought to galvanize a pan-Islamic movement with himself as the central figure. This diversionary tactic was partially successful in stimulating Muslim fervor against the Christian nationalists within and without the empire, but it did not satisfy the growing unrest of the younger Ottoman intellectuals who had already tasted the fruits of European liberalism.

THE YOUNG TURK REVOLUTION

It was hardly possible to teach army officers, teachers, and technicians the latest European technological developments while isolating them from Western intellectual life. Liberalism slipped into the country despite the secret police, spies, *sub rosa* executions, and torture racks; and it spread through the army, the very institution upon which the sultan placed greatest hopes. Younger officers conspired with students in the medical college and the engineering and military-training schools to overthrow the despot. Many young Ottomans inside the empire were in contact with their exiled compatriots in Europe.

The group which staged the 1908 revolution was essentially Turkish, but other Muslim, Jewish, and Christian groups joined them. Various ideologies were represented among the revolutionaries. Profoundly religious Muslims opposed the sultan because they held him responsible for the Christian threat to Islam. They had little in common with the freethinking, atheistically inclined young men who led the Committee of Union and Progress (CUP), where leadership of the Young Turk movement was later concentrated.

Some revolutionaries favored "Ottomanism," that is, a multinational concept which viewed all subjects, regardless of race, nationality, or religion, as equal. The "Ottomanists" were influenced by liberal political ideology and the example of the multinational Austro-Hungarian Empire.

Pan-Turanists were infected with pseudo-racial nationalism inspired by concepts of blood and soil and searched far back into antiquity for their "pure" Turkish origins. The Ottoman Turks, they declared, were but a single offshoot of the great Turanian race which spread deep into Russia, Central Asia, and China. Ancient history, folklore, and the "original" Turkish language were the hallmarks of their ideology.

Opposition to the sultan was also divided between individuals who advocated a highly centralized government and the proponents of decentralization, who favored greater provincial autonomy, especially for the Balkan provinces.

Within the army Mustafa Kemal (later Kemal Ataturk) helped organize the secret revolutionary society *Vatan* (Fatherland). Many of its members were officers serving in Syria. The Ottoman Society of Liberty, established in Salonika (now in Greece), also included the leaders of the 1908 revolution: Talat Bey, Fethi Bey, and Colonel Jemal Bey. Later it joined forces with an offshoot of Mustafa Kemal's Vatan.

A secret student group established in Istanbul in 1889 later organized branches in Paris and Geneva called the Committees of Progress and Union, not to be confused with the CUP formed later. Its program denounced violence and the overthrow of the ruling dynasty, advocated Ottomanism and reform, and opposed all European intervention in the Ottoman Empire's internal affairs.

The various Ottoman revolutionary groups in Europe and within the empire convened in 1907 at a congress of Ottoman liberals in Paris, where they were even joined by an Armenian revolutionary society. Out of this meeting emerged the Society of Union and Progress, directed by the Committee of Union and Progress, the CUP. The new society vowed to oppose Abdul Hamid II's government in every possible way. To preserve secrecy, they patterned their activities and organization on the European freemason movement, which was closely identified with middle-class, liberal, and revolutionary nationalist sentiments.

Although its headquarters was in Paris, branches of the CUP sprang up throughout the Ottoman Empire, especially among army officers, government officials, and professional men. The CUP was forced into action in 1908, a year ahead of its schedule, when army units rose in protest against intolerable living conditions and arrears in pay. Although the central executive committee had not planned for a general uprising until 1909, its followers now seized most of Macedonia. Backed by army units in Edirne and Salonika, the CUP sent an ultimatum to Abdul Hamid II in July 1908 demanding restoration of the 1876 constitution.

Hoping to gain time by temporary capitulation, the sultan reconvened the old Ottoman parliament and appointed a new cabinet acceptable to the CUP. In Istanbul and other racially mixed cities, Muslims, Jews, and Christians fraternized in spontaneous street demonstrations of approval. It seemed to many that a new era of brotherhood had arrived and that freedom would be the order of the future.

Yet liberal hopes were soon to be frustrated. Although despotism was dead, democracy had not been born. The revolution merely transferred the Ottoman government from the sultan and his entourage to another small clique of CUP men dominated by the army.

In parliament three distinct groups emerged. The Liberal Unionists sought to cure the empire's ills through a loose federation of autonomous nationalist provinces. They were opposed by the Muslim Association, firm advocates of religious law and pan-Islam. Neither group could compete with the army-dominated CUP, which controlled all parliamentary and governmental proceedings. The CUP overwhelmed its opposition by force or political maneuvers on all issues of importance.

Within a few months, disenchantment with the CUP was almost as widespread as it had been with despotic Abdul Hamid. Liberal Unionists spoke out against the secretive and domineering ways of the CUP, accusing it of abandoning the principles of the revolution and creating a dictatorship. The hopes of Albanians, Armenians, Bulgarians, Greeks, Kurds, and Arabs for equality within a multinational Ottoman confederation foundered on the ultranationalist CUP program of Turkification. The ulema and their devout followers were shocked by the freethinking and atheistic views of some CUP leaders.

A counterrevolutionary movement to combat the "Godlessness" of the new regime was organized by the religious Muslim conservatives. They called their organization the League of Muhammad and chose Abdul Hamid II as their symbol of unity. With the sultan's backing, they succeeded in overthrowing the CUP government April 14, 1909. Ultra-Muslims stormed through Istanbul's streets shouting antirevolutionary slogans—down with the constitution, down with the CUP, long live the sacred law. But the eclipse of the CUP was only temporary. Within eleven days CUP forces reseized the capital and returned to power, deposed Sultan Abdul Hamid II, and brought his brother to the throne as Mehmet V. The CUP then proceeded to eliminate its chief antagonists, both liberal and conservative.

After successfully repressing the counterrevolution, the CUP gave up all pretense of liberalism and equal treatment for non-Turks. All power was concentrated in its central executive committee, which ruled the organization from headquarters in Salonika until it collapsed with the empire's defeat in World War I. During the five years after 1909, its Turkification program was intensified in reaction to successive Balkan uprisings. The empire began to lose its European provinces one by one. In North Africa, Tripoli (now Libya) was lost to Italy in 1912. There were Arab uprisings in Syria and Yemen. The concept of an ideal Osmanli community of free and equal citizens fell by the wayside and was replaced by pan-Turanism. The CUP was now determined to force all subjects, Arab, Armenian, Greek, to become Turks.

Following the disastrous defeats in the Balkan and North African wars during 1912, the CUP again lost power for a few months; but in January 1913, it returned through a third *coup d'état*. Until the end of World War I the CUP ruled the Ottoman Empire through a dictatorial triumvirate of Talat Bey, Enver Pasha, and Colonel Jemal Pasha. Both Talat and Enver were of lower-middle-class origin. Talat, minister of the interior, was a former telegraph operator who rose to leadership of the revolutionary movement in Salonika. Enver, minister of war, won fame for his heroic feats fighting the Italian invasion of Tripoli. Only Jemal, minister of marine, came from a background of wealth. This three-man dictatorship differed little from the despotism exercised by Abdul Hamid II. Secret police, imprisonment without trial, press censorship, and minority suppression once again became commonplace.

While the immediate political effect of Young Turk rule was not much different from that of previous attempts at reform, there were some efforts to change the social order. After the 1908 coup a few upper-class Turkish women discarded the veil and organized a club to encourage female participation in political life. Several of the CUP cabinet members introduced Western administrative and technical innovations into their departments. The finance minister solicited the aid of a French expert. An English official was hired to advise the customs bureau. Count Leon Ostorog, a French citizen born in Poland, was invited to suggest legal innovations that would not undermine the Sharia law.

But like all previous reformers, the Young Turks placed major emphasis on military changes. British admirals planned new tactics and weapons for the navy, and a Frenchman reorganized the gendarmerie. The most influential was the German military mission sent to reorganize the army. Enver especially had fallen under the spell of Prussian militarism when he had been an attaché in Berlin. His strong influence worked together with the traditional Ottoman antipathy to Russia to push the country into an alliance with Germany. Within a few weeks after the outbreak of World War I, the Ottoman Empire had become the ally of Germany, Austria-Hungary, and Bulgaria. By 1918 the Ottoman Empire was all but dead. The dying empire was occupied by the Allies and Enver and other prominent CUP members fled the country.

Ottoman reforms begun in the nineteenth century were too late to save the decaying institutions of the empire. Balkan nationalism could neither be checked nor thwarted by halfhearted attempts at structural changes in the governing institutions. Moreover, Christian nationalist leaders knew much more of Western techniques than did their Ottoman rulers. Anatolia, the most Turkish part of the Ottoman Empire was but a small base, and one of the more backward regions of the empire as well. The area of the empire where Turks were only a minority population far exceeded that of Anatolia.

When the Ottoman elite finally did comprehend that the empire could not be saved without reforms, their understanding of the Western methods they attempted to use was superficial. Many had obtained their knowledge of Western institutions only indirectly, from Western literature or from the "Westernized" Levantines of Istanbul. Often the would-be reformers merely emulated fads and fashions in clothing, food, and architecture, without understanding the need to master techniques of production, the efficient operation of mechanical apparatus, or the scientific basis of engineering. The scientific and philosophical foundations of Western culture were little understood, and therefore too often its superficial aspects were accepted as meaningful in themselves. There was overconcentration on modernizing the military machine, but even that was done without a real knowledge or understanding of the effective functioning of the Western soldier. A well-educated soldier elite and elaborate drills could not compensate for the abominable conditions of the Ottoman infantry, the arrears in salary, and the faulty equipment.

Plans to modernize the economy failed for similar reasons. Native Turkish crafts, such as pottery making and weaving, were permitted to decay without the development of new industries to take their place. Once the Muslim millet gained access to the Ruling Institution, Muslims tended to compete for positions in both the Ruling Institution and the Religious Institution, abandoning business activity to the dhimmis. Most economic life, therefore, remained in the hands of Greeks, Armenians, Jews, and, as a result of the capitulations, Europeans. Although foreigners in particular had a competitive lead because of assistance from the capitulations and the Ottoman National Debt Administration, few Muslims took advantage of opportunities to invest in productive enterprises, preferring to continue their primary concern—government.

The educated elite, concentrated almost exclusively in the capital, never attempted to bridge the chasm between themselves and the masses. Modernizing reforms introduced in Istanbul, therefore, seldom reached the peasant. The masses were shielded from these European, and therefore "Christian," innovations by their religious leaders, who remained overwhelmingly conservative. The ulema generally had become increasingly suspicious of non-Muslims, especially Christians. Their attitude became one of disdain and sometimes was openly hostile. This outlook was shared by many Ottoman officials, especially Turks who frequently looked upon Christians as enemies of the Ottoman Empire. And by the twentieth century, there were few Christians who wished for the preservation of the empire.

The attitude of a Turkish official, set forth in Sir Charles Eliot's *Turkey in Europe*,[1] illustrates the problems of the reformers. Sir Charles recounts the following conversation with a Turkish *vali,* a provincial governor:

> "Once," said the Vali..."I was a very young man, and went [for] a ride with my old father. I was foolish then, and my head was stuffed with silly notions and liberal ideas.... I told my father we ought to reform our constitution, systematise our administration, purify our family life, educate our women, introduce liberal ideas, and imitate Europeans. And my old father answered never a word. So we rode on along the banks of the Bosphorus. At last we came to a Christian village, and round the Christian village were many pigs. Then my father said to me, 'My son, what seest thou?' I replied, 'Pigs, my father.' 'My son,' he said, 'are they all similar in size and colour, or do they differ?' 'They differ, my father. There are big pigs and little pigs, white pigs and black pigs, brown pigs and mottled pigs.' 'But they are all of them swine, my son?' 'All, my father.' 'My son,' he said, 'it is with the Christians even as with the pigs. There are big Christians and little Christians, Russian Christians and English Christians, French Christians and German Christians; they are all of them swine, and he who wishes to imitate the Christians, wishes to wallow with the swine in the mire.'...I was very young then, and my brain was full of nonsense—so I thought my father was a fool. But now that my own beard is getting grey—by God, I think the old gentleman was right!"

NOTE

1. London, 1908, pp. 13–14.

4 The Middle East and the West before World War I

THE PRE-NAPOLEONIC ERA

The destinies of the Middle East and the Western world have been interwoven throughout modern history. Relations among the Western powers were often reflected in, or conditioned by, events in the Middle East, and the region has been vital to European imperial expansion. Contact with Europe has thoroughly transformed both East and West.

The Arabs wove a broad strand in the pattern of East-West relationships by their far-reaching conquests of the seventh and eighth centuries. In so doing they brought to Europe its first sense of Oriental civilization and ended the ancient Mediterranean cultural pattern that for centuries had been primarily Greco-Roman.

The Crusades

European desires for the material wealth, resources, and culture of the East were reawakened during the two-century endeavor of the Crusaders to replant the cross in the Levant. Although various attempts in the twelfth and thirteenth centuries to establish permanent Christian kingdoms in the Middle East failed, contact between the Christian West and Muslim East created significant changes in the life of medieval Europe.

From the Baltic to the Mediterranean, Christendom became aware of the rich complexity of Muslim culture. The Crusaders brought back an awareness of new horizons to their homelands, and eventually many Eastern luxuries became necessities in European life. Following the failure of their military exploits against the Muslims, the Christian nations embarked on an era of commercial relations with their former foes. From the ports of Europe merchant ships set out to fetch Eastern spices to facilitate food preservation, Eastern citrus fruit to vary monotonous diets, and Eastern fabrics to enrich the splendor of European courts and cathedrals. Silks from Damascus were introduced to the West, and from Mosul in Iraq the Christians first learned of muslin cotton goods.

Merchants from the city states of Florence, Pisa, Genoa, and Venice set the pace. They reshipped their Oriental commerce overland to all parts of Europe from the Italian peninsula. When large numbers of Italian business-men had penetrated the Middle East, they began to form semipermanent settlements from which they might operate their enterprises. Since many of these merchant-settlers stayed in their outposts for years at a time, they petitioned local rulers for privileges of limited self-government or legal extraterritoriality. Upon payment, many Middle Eastern princes granted the Italians the right to form semiautonomous settlements where, by mutual consent, the Europeans conducted their own lives free of Oriental custom and law.

The Portuguese

Italian monopoly of the Oriental trade was first challenged by Portugal in the fifteenth century. Prince Henry the Navigator (1394–1460) sought to by-pass the Mediterranean by dispatching expeditions around the coasts of Africa in search of another route to the East. The first great success was Bartholomew Diaz's journey around the Cape of Good Hope in 1488. A decade later, when Vasco da Gama opened up the new water route to India, his sovereign commemorated the event by assuming the title "Lord of the Conquest, Navigation, and Commerce of Ethiopia, Arabia, Persia, and India."

The Portuguese were motivated by more than commerce. They were eager to avenge the Muslim occupation of their country, which had been brought to an end only in the fourteenth century. Off the southern coast of Arabia, in the Indian Ocean they seized the strategic island of Socotra—from which they hoped to join forces with the mythical Prester John, believed to be the Christian negus of Ethiopia. With Christian Ethiopia's help, however, and with additional bases established in 1515 at Muscat, Hormuz, and Bahrain in the Persian Gulf, the Portuguese outflanked Islam both commercially and strategically.

The Venetian republic fought off Portuguese attempts to destroy their monopoly. They even assisted the Mamluk rulers of Egypt, offering them timber to build warships to drive Portugal from the Indian Ocean. In retaliation, the Portuguese admiral Alfonso de Albuquerque, based in Goa, threatened to deprive Egypt of its water supply by diverting the Upper Nile into the Red Sea. The Venetian-Mamluk alliance failed, and Lisbon displaced

Venice as the center of Europe's Oriental commerce. By the end of the sixteenth century, the sea route around the Cape was more frequently used than the trans-Mediterranean and overland routes to the East.

French Interests

France also joined the commercial competition with the Italian city states early in the sixteenth century, and for the next two and one half centuries, up to the time of the French Revolution, she developed extensive commercial and religious interests in the Ottoman Empire. Within a few years France became a dominant Mediterranean power and the most influential European nation at the Ottoman court. Like the Italians, the French also established semipermanent settlements in the East. In fact, agreements concerning European privileges in such settlements were usually modeled on the first treaty of capitulations signed in 1536 between Francis I and Suleiman I. As already noted in chapter 3, the treaty permitted Ottoman and French subjects to pursue freely their trading interests in each other's lands and provided that they be tried only by their own consuls or appointed representatives while in the territory of the other nation. Traders from the signatory states were also freed from customs duties and other taxation and were allowed to practice their own religion freely in each other's country. At first these capitulatory agreements were periodically renewable. In 1675, however, one was signed with England for an indefinite period (which lasted until the end of World War I), and an agreement in perpetuity was made with France in 1740.

When originally conceived, the capitulations served a mutually useful purpose by protecting travelers from foreign laws with which they were unfamiliar. Since most law was still religious, it would have been difficult for aliens to be answerable to both Christian and Muslim law. By the mid-nineteenth century, when European legal codes were replacing religious law in the Middle East, the capitulations no longer served their original function, becoming instead one of many devices used by Western powers to interfere in Ottoman affairs.

In areas where French commercial efforts were unsuccessful in establishing French influence, the Catholic Church became an instrument of French policy. After successive failures by the French East India Company to open up Iran to trade during the seventeenth century, France resorted to the Church. Cardinal Richelieu encouraged Capuchin, Jesuit, Carmelite, and Dominican missions to take up where the merchants had failed.

Both French commercial and missionary activities succeeded in giving France a position of importance in the Middle East. As early as the sixteenth century, Lebanon's Maronites (an Eastern sect that accepted Vatican authority during the Crusades and is distinguished by its use of Syriac, its own liturgy, and special religious customs that are not in conflict with those of the Roman Church) had been taken under the wing of France; and French commercial interests dominated the area until the defeat of Napoleon. On the eve of the French Revolution, Levantine trade with France was three times as great as with England. At the Ottoman court, France was recognized from the end of the sixteenth century as the guardian of all European Catholics within the sultan's realm. After 1639, even Ottoman Catholics were permitted to accept French protection.

Relations between France and the sultans generally reflected the European balance of power. French enemies became Ottoman enemies. While French armies fought the Hapsburgs in Spain during the sixteenth century, the Ottomans drove the Hapsburgs across Hungary back to the gates of Vienna. Of course, after the Ottoman Empire began its long spiral into decline at the end of the sixteenth century, the France-Ottoman alliance became an entirely one-sided affair, with the sultans in the role of junior partner. When Russia began to threaten the Ottoman Empire in the eighteenth century, French diplomats tried to ward off the blows and to prevent outright capture of Ottoman territory.

British Interests

English relations with the Ottomans originally developed with French assistance. But as England grew more powerful, London merchants tired of being mere clients of France. Increasing numbers of English ships were reaching Near Eastern ports and their owners coveted the same privileges as France. The first success was an agreement in 1553 between an enterprising merchant, Anthony Jenkinson, and Suleiman I. It permitted Jenkinson to bring English wares in English ships to Ottoman ports. But once within Ottoman jurisdiction, the English merchants were required to accept French jurisdiction.

Jenkinson never implemented his agreement with the sultan. Instead of accepting French protection, he decided to gain an independent footing in the Middle East through Iran. His tactic was to use the Moscovy Company, established in 1553, to search for a passage around northern Europe to the Far East. British merchants hoped to dispose of their surplus woolens in the Orient if they could reach its markets via this northern route. When it was learned that climatic conditions prevented opening a northeast passage, Jenkinson, commander of the Moscovy Company's fleet, abandoned his search for a direct sea passage and turned south intead, going overland until he reached the capital of Iran. It required six expeditions between 1562 and 1581 to establish trading privileges with Iran similar to those France had with the Ottoman Empire. The hazards along the route to the East by way of Russia, however, finally caused England to abandon the whole project.

Commerce with the Ottoman Empire on a sustained basis was inaugurated in 1581 by the new Levant Company of Merchants, which was less successful in business than in diplomacy. For two centuries and more it was custodian of British interests in the Ottoman lands. All British consular and diplomatic officials were its employees. When early in the nineteenth century the Levant Company began to achieve major commercial successes, Parliament, opposed to government ties with private business, dissolved it.

British interests in Iran, however, were not abandoned. Two brothers, Sir Anthony and Sir Robert Sherley, reopened the question of commercial operations with the shah in 1598, arriving at the court of Abbas the Great with a small band of their countrymen. The shah was quick to see that he might benefit from British ties. He hoped to use the British to force the Portuguese from the Persian Gulf in order to monopolize these markets for his own country's chief export, raw silk. Iran was also eagerly searching for European allies against the Osmanlis. The British East India Company took advantage of the shah's offer of capitulatory privileges in return for assistance.

The Portuguese failed to check the Anglo-Iranian alliance and were driven from their strategic base at Hormuz in 1622. Later the Iranians drove them from Bahrain too, and their final defeat was signaled by the loss of Muscat in 1650. British East India Company representatives took over most of the Portuguese bases, establishing factories (from factor, meaning agent) similar to the autonomous settlements of the French and the Italian city states. In addition to the Iranian factories, the English set up others at Mokha, for export of coffee from Yemen, and at Basra, as a center for river trade with Baghdad.

A by-product of the Anglo-Iranian victory over Portugal was the Dutch acquisition of capitulatory rights from the shah in 1623. The Dutch and English shared the Iranian trade for half a century, until Holland was also driven from the Persian Gulf by England during the seventeenth-century Anglo-Dutch wars.

In the turmoil of the eighteenth-century battles between Iran and Afghanistan, British trading headquarters were shifted to Basra in Iraq, then part of the Ottoman Empire. The new trading center served the British East India Company as a base for direct intervention in noncommercial affairs throughout the region: for example, the company lent the pasha of Baghdad six ships in 1766 to quell rebellious tribes; at various times it helped appoint and unseat governors; and on many occasions it arbitrated disputes among local chieftains. By the beginning of the nineteenth century, the whole Persian Gulf had, in effect, become a British lake.

Russian Interests

Russia was the third great European nation to stake out Middle Eastern claims in the pre-Napoleonic era. Russian success in becoming a major European power was partly at the expense of the declining Iranian and Ottoman empires: tsarist ambitions centering on the control of the Caspian and Black seas. Relentless Russian pressure pushed both shah and sultan farther and farther south into Asia. When the Safavid dynasty collapsed in Iran in 1722, there was a sharp diplomatic struggle between the Russians and Ottomans for Iranian territory. French mediation prevented an immediate outbreak of war and persuaded the tsar and sultan to divide the Iranian Transcaucasian and western provinces.

But the good offices of the French could not restrain dynamic Russia from overrunning the border provinces of the corrupt, effete Ottomans. The tsars were determined to establish themselves on the Black Sea and to dominate access to the rivers that flowed into it. For the next century and a half Russian endeavors to topple the Ottomans were a dominant concern of European diplomacy.

A landmark along the road to Russian mastery of the region was the 1774 treaty of Kuchuk Kainarji terminating a six-year war with the Ottomans. The document, which became the basis of Russo-Ottoman relations until World War I, ended the Ottoman's exclusive domination of the Black Sea. Russia now not only shared the shores of the Black Sea but was also assured of unrestricted commercial navigation through it, and through the Straits leading into the Mediterranean. From that time a major drive of Russian foreign policy became the complete domination of the Straits to gain unequivocal entrance into the Mediterranean.

The Kuchuk Kainarji treaty also gave Russia the same capitulatory privileges previously acquired by other European powers and extended tsarist protection over all Greek Orthodox Christians in the Ottoman Empire. The treaty was taken by England, whose Indian empire was expanding rapidly in the 1770s, as a warning of growing Russian might to the Middle East. For the first time Russian penetration of the region seemed to threaten the western overland approaches to India, particularly by way of Iran.

THE NAPOLEONIC ERA

The dramatic shifts in European patterns of power resulting from the French Revolution were reflected in the relationships between the Middle East and the West. England's war with the French revolutionaries had its Middle Eastern phase. Direct conflict in the eastern Mediterranean erupted in 1798 when the young French military genius Napoleon Bonaparte opened an offensive there. Only the year before he had abandoned his plans for a direct frontal attack on England by means of a cross-channel invasion. His position in the East, however, seemed far stronger. Victories in Austria and Italy, an alliance with Spain, and the withdrawal of the British fleet to the cover of Gibraltar all seemed to augur well for a major Mediterranean victory for the French.

For nearly a century France had not interfered in Egypt because of traditional friendship with the Ottomans. But the revolutionists were no respecters of ancient diplomatic tradition. The Mediterranean was open, and Ottoman authority in the Nile Valley was crumbling. Ostensibly, Napoleon undertook an expedition to suppress Mamluk revolution in Egypt, although the nominal Ottoman rulers had solicited no such aid. Napoleon drafted his own instructions to expel the British from all their Middle Eastern possessions, to destroy their Red Sea factories, to take Egypt, and to cut a canal through the isthmus of Suez, thus ensuring the French Republic exclusive control in the Red Sea.

When he arrived in Alexandria during July 1798, Napoleon proclaimed himself the liberator of Egypt from its Mamluk feudal lords, the protector of Islam, and the benefactor of the Egyptian people. The three-year French occupation was remarkable, not for its length, but for its political, social, and intellectual impact. European engineers, historians, archaeologists, architects, mathematicians, chemists, and Egyptologists who accompanied Napoleon's expedition gave Egypt its first awareness of European science and learning. They also made significant archaeological discoveries. The most important was the Rosetta stone, which later opened to modern researchers the meaning of ancient Pharaonic hieroglyphics. There was also an inrush of heady liberation concepts. Napoleon's proclamations, drafted in French revolutionary terminology, appealed to the "people" over the heads of their Ottoman and Mamluk rulers and the religious hierarchy. The appeals no doubt helped to inspire Muhammad 'Ali (Turkish, Mehmet Ali), the founder of modern Egypt, who arrived as a young officer in the Ottoman forces sent to recapture the country from France.

France's attack on Ottoman territory abruptly reversed the pattern of Eastern alliances and power relationships. Traditional Franco-Ottoman amity came to a violent end: with the same blow a century and a quarter of enmity between tsar and sultan was suspended. The two rulers quickly formed a defensive alliance. Russia, Napoleon's enemy, extended assurances that a dozen warships and an eighty-thousand-man army would be placed at the sultan's disposal. In return, the sultan agreed to the free passage of Russian warships through the Straits. By concurring in this agreement and joining in close alliance with the Ottomans, England also gave to the sultan the most extensive pledge of assistance it had ever granted the Ottomans.

The British regarded Napoleon's invasion of Egypt as a direct threat to India and immediately began to strengthen their strategic and diplomatic defenses between the Mediterranean and their Indian empire. They seized Perim, the tiny island at the straits between the Red Sea and the Gulf of Aden. Living conditions there were so intolerable, however, that the British forces moved over to Aden on the mainland by agreement with the sultan of Lahej.

Napoleon's attempt to outflank the British by agreements with the sultan of Oman in the Persian Gulf was quickly checked. Instead, the British East India Company induced the sultan to exclude all Frenchmen from his territories until the end of the war. The East India Company also exploited the opportunity to uproot the last vestiges of French influence in Iraq. In 1798 French consuls in Basra and Baghdad were arrested and their offices closed. By the time they were released, France had lost its influence in the area.

The network of agreements between England and the local chieftains was extended until most of the Persian Gulf and Red Sea principalities acknowledged diplomatic ties with the British. In return for British protection, nearly all these agreements provided for British control over foreign relations. Another British accomplishment was the suppression of predatory Arab pirates in the Persian Gulf. Punitive expeditions of the East India Company eventually culminated in a treaty between Great Britain and the sheikhs of the Omani, or Pirate, coast and the sheikh of Bahrain, entrusting Persian Gulf security to the British.

Napoleon did not accept defeat so easily. He attempted to compensate for the failure of his Egyptian campaign through a diplomatic offensive. His efforts were facilitated by the Anglo-French peace signed at Amiens in March 1802, re-establishing the prewar situation in the Ottoman Empire. France's capitulatory privileges were restored and French merchant vessels were permitted to trade freely in the Black Sea. Napoleon's astute diplomats not only disrupted the alliance between the Ottoman Empire, England, and Russia that had been signed in 1799, they even drew the Ottoman sultan into war with both Russia (1806–1812) and England (1807–1809).

Farther East, Napoleon tried to enlist the Iranian Kajar dynasty in his scheme to outflank the British and to invade India with both Ottoman and Iranian collaboration. But after concluding peace with Russia at Tilsit in 1807, Napoleon abandoned the East to tsarist ambitions. Russian armies immediately attacked Iran and accomplished the long-held goal of controlling the Caspian Sea. Only British concern about extended Russian ambitions saved the country. The shah again turned to a defensive alliance with England in 1814, in a treaty that became the basis for Anglo-Iranian relations for the next century.

Napoleon's collapse in 1814 brought to an end his temporary reversal of the British position in the Middle East and brought about still another phase of Middle Eastern relations with Europe. General European interest in the commercial possibilities and diplomatic importance of the Middle East was revived to a degree unsurpassed since the Crusades. Great Britain was now supreme in the Levant, the Persian Gulf, the Red Sea, and in southern Arabia. The British replaced France as the most influential power in the Ottoman court. British trade routes to India and the Far East again seemed secure. Only Russia, now strengthened by its participation in the defeat of Napoleon, seemed a possible threat to British supremacy. The earlier British indifference to the fate of the Ottomans consequently turned into a serious concern lest the Ottoman Empire lose its buffer role between Russia and the Indian hinterland.

In Egypt, Muhammad 'Ali's star was rising. He already had established a semiautonomous province under the sultan. So powerful was this new Ottoman pasha in Egypt that within a few years he, rather than the tsar, would be regarded as the principal threat to Ottoman existence. Throughout the Ottoman Empire, widened contacts with the West through military alliances, diplomatic intrigue, and expanded commercial intercourse introduced concepts that were later to bring about dramatic technological, political, and social change.

EUROPE IN THE MIDDLE EAST DURING THE NINETEENTH CENTURY

From the Congress of Vienna in 1814–1815 until the end of the nineteenth century, Western European fears of Russia's growing might dominated Middle Eastern policies. The tsars were determined to attain two objectives: control of the Asian lands south of Russia and a breakthrough of the land blockade cutting them off from any adequate warm-water port. Thus Iran, Central Asia, and the Ottoman Empire became focal points of diplomatic maneuvering and intrigue in the clash of European empires.

Russia did not always use frontal attacks in its Middle Eastern relations, preferring the fruits of a more subtle diplomacy. An opportunity for the latter arose in 1833, when Muhammad 'Ali (an Albanian and still the Osmanli governor of Egypt) undertook his first Syrian war and threatened to overrun the Ottoman Empire, depose the sultan, and establish his own dynasty at Istanbul. When the sultan appealed for aid in Austria, Great Britain, and France, they shortsightedly turned him down: France, because Muhammad 'Ali had become a French protégé; Great Britain, because her foreign policy was temporarily in the hands of isolationists; and Austria, because it hoped to receive a share in the spoils. Only the Ottoman Empire's traditional enemy, tsarist Russia, seemed interested in keeping out the Albanian intruder. Russia's concern was obvious. The tsar preferred to maintain a weak Osmanli sultan at the Straits rather than to replace him by the dynamic Albanian, especially since Muhammad 'Ali had formed such close ties with France. Tsarist troops were sent to the Straits to "protect" the Ottoman Empire, and a Russo-Ottoman defensive alliance was signed in July 1833 at Hunkiar Iskelesi. The other European powers, and England in particular, were aroused from their indifference by reports that circulated of a secret clause to close the Straits to all nations but Russia. Professing to fear that the pact would lead to armed Russian intervention in the Ottoman Empire's internal affairs, the British government warned that it would "hold itself at liberty to act upon such occasion, in any manner which the circumstances of the moment may appear to require."

Simultaneously, Great Britain and France pressed Muhammad 'Ali to withdraw his army from Anatolia. The Albanian was compensated by the sultan with the pashaliks of Syria, Palestine, and Cilicia. The anxiety of the British foreign secretary, Lord Palmerston, was aroused by the actions of all other parties to the intrigue: Russia obviously wanted to seize the Straits, and France, it seemed, was too close an ally of Muhammad 'Ali.

Tsar Nicholas I also was concerned because, to him, the brash Albanian represented a threat to European conservatism as well as to the fate of the Russo-Ottoman settlement. Hence direct intervention in Ottoman affairs seemed called for if necessary to prevent reoccurrence of such a direct threat. To fortify his position and guard against these incidents in the future, the tsar sought out a common policy with Austria's Prince Metternich, a leading opponent of European liberal movements. In 1833, two months after the Russo-Ottoman treaty had been concluded at Hunkiar Iskelesi, the two men secretly agreed at Müchengrätz to maintain the *status quo* in the Ottoman Empire.

When Muhammad 'Ali attempted a second Syrian war in 1838 to destroy the sultan, Great Britain moved before the Russians could take unilateral action. Her Majesty's ambassadors immediately called upon all the European powers to act in unison. France, now an inactive ally of the Albanian, stayed out of the fray. Great Britain, Austria, Prussia, and Russia, however, convened at London in 1840 to force a settlement. They ordered Muhammad 'Ali to evacuate Syria and to interpose "the desert between his troops and authorities of the sultan." An "equivalent advantage" was offered in the form of hereditary succession to Muhammad 'Ali's family in the governorship of Egypt. When the Albanian ignored the warning, he was driven back into Egypt by an Austrian and British blockade, and all the territory he had seized was returned to the sultan.

France returned to the European concert of powers in 1841 after the second Syrian war, joining a new treaty regularizing passage through the Straits. It disposed of any danger from secret agreements between the Ottoman Empire and Russia, for the sultan promised to abide by "the principle invariably established as the ancient rule of his empire," namely, that all foreign warships were banned from the Straits during peacetime. The 1841 London Straits Convention established the status of the waterway until World War I. It satisfied both Great Britain and Russia by keeping the warships of the latter out of the Mediterranean while, at the same time, closing the Straits and the Black Sea to other than Russian and Ottoman war vessels.

Fear of a revival of the French revolutionary spirit continued to plague the tsar. In an effort to end the threat of "radical" French interest in the Middle East once and for all, he went so far as to propose to divide the Ottoman Empire with Great Britain. An outline of this Russian scheme was submitted to the leaders of the British government in 1844. The division was to take effect only if the Ottoman Empire failed to be maintained "in its present state." Despite its favorable reception by some men then in command, the offer was never officially agreed upon. A revival of French "spiritual interest" in Palestine's holy places, in competition with similar Russian claims, served to allay Palmerston's fears that a Franco-Russian coalition might be effected to destroy the Ottoman Empire.

The Crimean War

Latin monks under French protection had attended the Palestinian shrines and holy places since the sixteenth century, a right that had been reconfirmed in the capitulations granted in perpetuity to France in 1740. The religious privileges, however, were allowed to lapse during the turbulent revolutionary era and the Napoleonic wars. Few Frenchmen betook themselves on pilgrimages, nor did the anticlerical revolutionary governments take an interest in protecting Christians. Astute Louis Napoleon, while still president of the French Republic, saw the political possibilities inherent in an Eastern religious revival, and hastened to seek reinstatement of the capitulations early in 1852. After being crowned emperor, he used concern about religion in the East as a rallying cry for French Catholics.

Tsar Nicholas I claimed that since the great majority of Christians were Greek or Eastern Orthodox, Russia, not France, was the true defender of Christianity in the East, the existence of such a "protectorate" having been spelled out some eighty years before in the treaty of Kuchuk Kainarji. Thousands of Orthodox pilgrims had flocked to the holy places when not a Frenchman was in sight. The tsar, the Orthodox Church, and pious Russians had made many generous gifts to holy land missions. When fire had destroyed the Church of the Holy Sepulchre in 1808, it had been rebuilt by the Orthodox, directed of course by the Greek patriarch at Istanbul, with funds collected from all Ottoman Orthodox Christians and supported by a generous gift from the sultan himself. The pro-Russian Greek patriarch of Jerusalem, who usually resided in Istanbul, set himself up in Jerusalem in 1843. To counterbalance his august presence, Pope Pius IX, an ally of Napoleon III, ordered the Latin patriarch of Jerusalem to move there from Rome for the first time in centuries.

The mounting tension broke into violence in Jerusalem where Latin Catholics and Greek Orthodox monks actually fought pitched battles. The incidents raged over such matters as theft of a silver star engraved with the arms of France which hung over the holy manger in Bethlehem, which door Latins should use when entering the sacred site, and who should repair the damaged cupola of the Holy Sepulchre in Jerusalem. At Christmas in 1847, Latin and Greek monks in Bethlehem battled with candlesticks and crosses over the birthplace of the Prince of Peace. To prevent Christian from killing Christian, the Ottoman governor, a Muslim, had to post sixty armed soldiers inside the Church of the Holy Sepulchre.

While fighting for position and prestige in the Holy Land, both sides also conducted diplomatic intrigues at the Ottoman court. French determination to re-establish a Middle Eastern empire revived Russian proposals for dividing the Ottoman lands. The tsar sounded out the British again, saying, "the Bear [the Ottoman Empire] is dying, you may give him musk, but even musk will not long keep him alive, and we can never allow such an event to take us by surprise. We must come to some understanding."[1] But the British still preferred a dying to a dead bear, and indicated that they would continue to do all in their power to keep him alive.

Since the British refused to be an accomplice in his plan, the tsar decided to go it alone. In 1853, a Russian ultimatum was delivered to the sultan that was virtually a demand for unconditional surrender; it required recognition of full Orthodox Christian rights in the Holy Land and the right of Russia to repair the Holy Sepulchre. The tsar also demanded a new treaty confirming Ottoman acknowledgment of Russia's right to protect the Greek Orthodox Christians; the placing of restrictions on other Christians who might interfere with Russian influence; and the conclusion of a new secret defensive alliance to "protect" the Ottoman Empire against the French. Only the first two demands were acknowledged by the sultan. Acceptance of the others would make of the Ottoman Empire a Russian vassal. Especially repugnant was the demand to protect between ten and twelve million Greek Orthodox inhabitants of the Ottoman Empire.

The tsar was not to be put off; he ordered his troops to occupy the Ottoman Danubian provinces of Moldavia and Wallachia. The result was war. After a few minor Ottoman victories, the Russians completely demolished the Ottoman Black Sea fleet. England and France sent a combined flotilla to rescue the Osmanlis from total disaster and informed the tsar that he must withdraw to the Crimea. His refusal ignited the Crimean War, which raged from 1853 to 1856, the bloodiest European conflict since the days of Napoleon I. Two years of fighting produced only a stalemate; Russia and the Allies (England, France, the Ottoman Empire, and Sardinia), therefore decided to accept an Austrian proposal that led to the peace concluded at Paris in 1856.

The Paris conference restored the prewar territorial status with modifications in the administration of some European Ottoman provinces. Serbia, Moldavia, Wallachia were promised autonomous regimes. Commissions were established to supervise free navigation on the Danube and in the Black Sea. The latter was neutralized and demilitarized except for police vessels, and the Straits were again closed to all warships. An internal consequence of the war, already described in chapter 3, was proclamation of the reform edict, the Hatti-Humayun, two months before the Paris conference.

Tsar Alexander II viewed the Crimean stalemate as only temporary and the Black Sea restrictions as a "blot on his reign," which he thereupon determined to remove. The opportunity came in 1870, during the Franco-Prussian War, when France was not in a position to help England to resist Russian demands. At the suggestion of Prussian chancellor Bismarck, the 1856 signatories of the Paris Convention compromised by lifting restrictions on Russia's Black Sea war fleet.

The Balkan Wars

The emergence of Slavic nationalism presented further opportunity for attacks on the Ottoman Empire during the 1870s. Russian agents actively propagated pan-Slavism and rallied local Orthodox Christians against the Muslims in Bulgaria, Herzegovina Serbia, Montenegro, and Rumania. Again Great Britain intervened when it became clear that the movement was being used as a device to extend tsarist influence. But British appeals for moderating and consultation among the powers were ignored by Russia. The tsar informed the other powers that his country's peace and security were jeopardized by the Balkan insurrections and the Ottoman reprisals and that, as protector of the Orthodox everywhere, he was compelled to intervene. None of the Western powers anticipated the disastrous results that followed the next Russo-Ottoman war, which ended in decisive Russian victory.

Russia imposed its terms at San Stefano in 1878. Kars, Ardahan, Batum, and much of the Armenian area of northeastern Anatolia were taken from the Ottomans. Serbia, Rumania, and Montenegro were given complete freedom in place of autonomy within the Ottoman Empire. Bulgaria was enlarged into an autonomous Orthodox state—virtually a Russian puppet—reaching from the Black Sea to the Aegean.

The major Western European states again felt threatened by Russia's expanding power, and another Crimean war threatened. The little Balkan states resented the new overgrown Bulgaria; Austria felt excluded from a settlement vital to its interests; in England, Prime Minister Disraeli warned Russia that the imperial lifelines of Great Britain would be endangered by Russian efforts to alter the status of the Straits. Anticipating a Russian move into the Mediterranean, Disraeli signed a defensive alliance (1878) with the sultan that included the right to occupy and administer the Ottoman island of Cyprus.

Bismarck, calling himself the "honest broker" of Europe, urged Western moderation and understanding of his Russian ally and convened the Congress of Berlin in 1878 to bring about peaceful revision of the treaty of San Stefano. The Berlin Treaty forestalled Russian penetration into the Balkans and the Ottoman Empire until World War I, and once again restored the balance of power in the Near East. Russian territorial gains were not returned to the Ottoman Empire but divided between the tsarist empire and Austria-Hungary, sacrificing local Balkan nationalisms to Bismarck's principle of "compensation" in order to preserve the European *status quo* at all costs.

"Big Bulgaria" was cut off from the Aegean and converted into a small autonomous Ottoman principality; what remained of Bulgaria in the south became Eastern Rumelia, with a Christian governor appointed by the sultan with consent of the European powers; Rumania, Serbia, and Montenegro became fully independent and acquired additional territory; Austria-Hungary was authorized to occupy Bosnia, Herzegovina, and Novibazar, although all were still theoretically Ottoman; constitutions were promised to other Ottoman provinces in Europe; a Danube Commission was given international supervision of that river; Greece was promised more Ottoman territory, which it acquired in 1881; Russia obtained Bessarabia from Rumania, and the latter was compensated with Dobruja; in Asia, Russia received Kars, Ardahan, and Batum, while parts of Armenia were returned to the Ottomans; minority rights (meaning non-Muslim) were once again guaranteed; and the previous agreements keeping warships from the Straits were reconfirmed.

Russia in Iran

From the time Empress Catherine the Great (1762–1796) extended Russian borders deep into Central Asia until the mid-nineteenth century, Russia and Iran were involved in continuous diplomatic maneuvers and at times war. During the Napoleonic era the shah had hoped for French assistance to hold off the tsar, but when Napoleon I abandoned his Middle East plans for a European empire, Iran lost its most powerful defender. Even before the Napoleonic wars had ended, Russian armies invaded the country; and in 1812 Iran was forced to surrender long-established rights in five Caucasian provinces and in all or parts of six others. As a result, Russia acquired almost complete control of the Caspian Sea.

Russia's victory drove Iran into the waiting arms of Great Britain. A defensive alliance, which had been pending for five years, was signed in 1814, establishing a pattern of relations between Great Britain and Iran that lasted until the Kajar dynasty collapsed in 1925. The treaty also opened an era of direct Anglo-Russian competition in Central Asia.

Neither Russians nor Iranians were satisfied with the conclusion of the 1812 war: Russia because it had not acquired enough Iranian territory, and the Iranians because the price they had paid for defeat was too costly. Continued boundary disputes between the two neighbors sparked still another war from 1826 to 1828. Iran lost two more provinces and Russia's exclusive right to navigate the Caspian Sea was reaffirmed. Russian subjects now obtained extraterritorial privileges, setting a pattern for other European capitulations.

Since any attempt to retake the lost territory from Russia seemed hopeless, the shah thought to balance his losses by turning against neighboring Afghanistan. In this he received encouragement from the Russians, but a warning from the British. Afghanistan, adjoining India, was too vital for the latter's security to permit Iranian intervention, so the British occupied parts of the remote kingdom and threatened to invade Iran if the shah attacked. The threat did not dissuade him and after a long wait the shah invaded his neighbor in 1856, but he was almost immediately forced out by British troops. Finally the shah abandoned his claims to Afghanistan and recognized its independence in 1857.

While the Russians were kept out of Iran by the threat of an attack by the British troops in Afghanistan, the tsars did not hesitate to round out their Central Asia territories during the mid-nineteenth century. One Asian tribal leader (khan) after another was defeated and his territory incorporated into Russia. Rapid tsarist territorial expansion north of Iran and shrewd diplomatic activity in Tehran intensified British attempts to gain every diplomatic and economic advantage possible in both Iran and Afghanistan. Baron Julius de Reuter, a British subject, acquired rights in Iran in 1872 to build a railroad, excavate mines, and establish a national bank. However, anti-European public opinion in Iran forced the shah to cancel the Reuter concession a few months after it had been given.

The Russians countered by gaining control over Iran's only effective military force, the Cossack Brigade, so called because it had been trained and commanded by tsarist officers under direct orders from St. Petersburg. Each time the British obtained a new economic concession, the Russians demanded its equivalent. When Reuter was granted a new concession for the Imperial Bank of Iran in 1889, the Russians also demanded and received a bank that was really a subsidiary of the tsarist Finance Ministry. Similarly, the English concession for a new railroad in 1890 was counterbalanced by the Russian demand for one of their own.

Anglo-French Rivalry

During the nine-year Egyptian occupation of Syria and Palestine (1831–1840), Muhammad 'Ali invited European experts to help develop the area under his rule. French Jesuits eagerly accepted his invitation and became most active using the opportunity to revive their order suspended there by the pope since 1773. Lebanese Maronites became special Jesuit protégés.

While France was furthering relations with the Maronites, the British befriended several Druse chiefs in southern Lebanon. In 1840 clashes between Maronites and Druses (heretics of Islam who formed a separate religious sect early in the eleventh century) were related to competition between France and Great Britain for influence in the Levant. Both powers induced the sultan to pacify the area in 1843 and to turn over affairs in the north to the French-supported Maronites and in the south to the British-backed Druses. The compromise lasted a decade until Maronite peasants, incited by their priests, rose against their landlords. In the north, where most estates were Maronite owned, the peasants seized the land and divided it. In the south, they refused to pay rent to the landlords, most of whom were Druse.

Maronite ecclesiastical leaders began preparations to drive the Druses from Lebanon with expectations of French support. The local Osmanli governor, who regarded both Druses and Maronites as troublemakers, fanned the fires, hoping that the two groups would destroy each other. In a massive Druse attack on the Maronites in 1860, nearly 14,000 of the latter were killed. Violence spread to Damascus where Druses, Kurds, and Syrian Muslims united to fall upon the Christian and Jewish communities, massacring 5000 people.

A new crusade to save the Lebanese Christians was proposed by France, and with the backing of Austria, Great Britain, Prussia, and Russia, French troops came to the rescue. By the time they arrived in the Levant during August 1860, the Ottomans had already restored order. But the French now refused to evacuate, arguing that their presence was required to prevent future massacres. The British insisted that the situation was well in hand and forced the French to withdraw nine months later. Instead of the French protectorate planned by Paris, an international commission established an autonomous status for Lebanon's Christian areas. The whole province was separated from Syria in 1864 and placed under an Osmanli Christian governor with a central administrative council to represent religious groups. Although Lebanon was lost to France as a protectorate, French interests flourished under the special compromise regime. Jesuits pursued their missionary and educational activities, and by 1914 nearly half the school children attended French Catholic institutions.

Within the rest of the Ottoman Empire, French commercial and cultural activities also flourished. The Ottoman Bank, opened in 1863 with a majority of French and some British capital, issued all banknotes and set up branches in every important town of the empire. While on a visit to Paris in 1867, the sultan was persuaded to enlarge the secular educational system and to initiate a public works and a communications program with French help. As a result, the first Ottoman secondary school admitting all Ottoman subjects, regardless of race or religion, was opened in 1868. In the same year, a railroad company whose major stockholders were French obtained a concession for lines connecting Istanbul and Salonika with railway systems along the Danube.

In Egypt the French had been active since Muhammad 'Ali. His fear of England led him to observe that "big fish eat up the little fish and since France was no longer a big fish, it was less to be feared than England." The Ottoman governor had employed many French technicians, educators, engineers, and military advisers. When Said, his son, became viceroy of Egypt in 1854, he also surrounded himself with Frenchmen, including Ferdinand de Lesseps, a former French consul general and the engineer who later built the Suez Canal.

The Suez Canal and Egypt. De Lesseps' vision of a waterway connecting the Mediterranean and Red seas was not original. Selim II's grand vezir, Mehmet Sokolli, had conceived of such a project back in the sixteenth century; Louis XIV had been enchanted with the possibility in the next century; it was a major goal of Napoleon's invasion a hundred years later; and it was again espoused by French enthusiasts in the 1820s and 1830s. Finally, in 1854, de Lesseps obtained a preliminary concession that was given definite status in 1856 when the *Compagnie Universelle du Canal Maritime de Suez* began work. But political, rather than engineering, difficulties caused major delays.

Lord Palmerston, British prime minister for most of the decade from 1855 to 1865, most vehemently objected. A large international waterway through Suez, he feared, would make Egypt a focal point for attack on British interests in the East. British maneuvers managed to delay construction of the canal so that fifteen years elapsed from the time de Lesseps obtained the concession until the waterway was opened in 1869. During this era British outposts between Egypt and India were strengthened as a safeguard against the time when the canal would become a fact. In 1854 the British outbid the French to acquire the Kuria Muria Islands in the Indian Ocean for a signal cable station; British troops reoccupied Perim Island off Aden in 1857; the French were prevailed upon to respect Oman's independence in 1862, although, in fact, the sultanate was dominated by the British Indian government; and in 1863 the harbors and docks of the Mediterranean island of Malta were expanded and military defenses strengthened. By the time shipping began to pass through the Suez Canal, British influence reached along the southern coast of Arabia from Aden eastwards. The chain of outposts was completed in 1876–1878, when the islands of Socrota and Cyprus became British protectorates.

British interests in Egypt were largely commercial, whereas France had cultivated cultural and political relations. The British textile industry was becoming increasingly dependent on Egyptian cotton, especially after the Civil War cut off the American supply. At the end of the Civil War, British trade with Egypt was larger than that of any other nation.

Since Palmerston's objections to the Suez Canal had prevented British investment in the waterway, it was largely French owned and operated, although by the mid 1870s more than two thirds of the shipping through it flew the Union Jack. One of Prime Minister Disraeli's first objectives after assuming office in 1874 was to rectify British complaints of discrimination against their merchantmen. The opportunity arose in 1875 when Khedive Ismail of Egypt, in great need of money, accepted Disraeli's offer to purchase 44 percent of the Suez Canel shares for 4 million pounds.

The sale failed to rescue Egypt and its khedive from financial disaster, however. Ismail, called the "Magnificent" because of his extravagance, increased his country's debts from 3 million pounds in 1863 to nearly 100 million by 1876, holding off his creditors for a decade by accepting loans at usurious rates from one European bank after another to pay his debts. The Europeans exploited his desperate situation by exacting up to forty percent in interest. The debacle came in April 1876 when Ismail was forced to turn the country's finances over to a joint international debt commission supervised by British and French controllers.

The debt controllers seemed unduly oppressive to the Egyptians, and Ismail tried to use this discontent to rid himself of the foreign interference. Finally, in 1879, the European creditors persuaded the Ottoman sultan to replace Ismail with his son Tewfik. Local hatred began to turn against not only the Europeans but also the Albanian dynasty itself, giving birth to the first Egyptian nationalist movement.

The nationalists, led by Colonel Ahmed Arabi, an Egyptian of peasant origin, forced the khedive to accept a government in which the nationalists were represented. When the English and French, fearing that the nationalist movement would destroy their influence, planned joint military intervention, the young Colonel sensed the danger and built up his army, placing political power in the hands of his officers. When he became minister for war in February 1882, England and France demanded that Arabi's supporters be dismissed from the government, backing up their demand by sending naval squadrons to Alexandria. Mobs in the port protesting the khedive's subservience to the Western powers caused nearly 200 deaths during the month of July. A British ultimatum ordering Arabi to cease work on the city's fortifications added to the tension. When the British failed to receive an answer, Her Majesty's fleet bombarded and destroyed the defenses; British troops landed, and by mid-September 1882 the nationalists were utterly crushed.

One of the first British acts after seizing Egypt was to inform Paris that French representatives in the former dual control were superfluous. Since the French had withdrawn their strength from the naval force a day before invasion was scheduled due to domestic political difficulties, Great Britain felt entitled to undertake unilateral action. British foreign secretary Granville announced his government's "temporary occupation" policy in January 1883. Since Her Majesty's government had suppressed "the military rebellion in Egypt" and restored peace and order without help, the resulting position "imposes upon them the duty of giving advice with the object of securing that the order of things to be established shall be of a satisfactory character, and possess the elements of stability and progress."[2] For the next twenty years, France periodically raised the question of Great Britain's "temporary occupation." Special negotiators sent from France to discuss the evacuation of British troops, commissions, and conferences all failed to convince Her Majesty's government that the time was opportune. Control of the Suez Canal, which was considered the most important link in the lifeline of the British Empire and had become one of the government's largest investments, could not be abandoned. In 1888, delegates from eight European powers met with representatives of the Ottoman Empire in Istanbul to draft an agreement establishing an international commission to safeguard passage through Suez. However, disagreement between Great Britain and France over implementation delayed British ratification until 1904 (see also chapter 8).

EVENTS AT THE TURN OF THE CENTURY

German Imperialism

German interests in the Middle East were minor until 1890 because of Bismarck's concentration on more pressing European problems. Except as interference or encouragement in Africa and Asia might gain a diplomatic advantage for his European policies, these areas were left to the British and French and the Balkans and Middle East to his Austrian and Russian allies. Nonetheless, there were German religious missions in Palestine and Syria; German officers were hired to train the Ottoman army; and German capitalists invested in Anatolian railways. But not until Kaiser Wilhelm II dismissed Bismarck in 1890 did Berlin take a major interest in the area.

The new kaiser assumed immediate command of German foreign policy, placing increasing emphasis upon a German role in the Middle East. More railway concessions were obtained; a direct steamship service was opened between Germany and the Ottoman Empire; and trade between the two powers increased several times over. At first, the British encouraged German ventures in the Middle East, regarding them as a foil to Russian and French competition. But a warning was sounded during the kaiser's visit to Jerusalem and Damascus in 1898, when that imperial monarch presented himself to the Eastern world as the protector of Islam. In the same year he accepted plans for a railroad to run between Berlin and the Persian Gulf. When he began to implement the scheme, the British had second thoughts about the potential threat raised by German interests in the Middle East.

The first clash came in 1900 when the kaiser tried to coerce the sheikh of Kuwait to accept a German technical mission. A secret agreement between the sheikh and the British government of India concluded in 1899 prohibited such action. The kaiser, however, was adamant. He demanded that the sultan send troops to enforce Ottoman authority on the recalcitrant sheikh. Use of force was forestalled by the presence of British warships in the Persian Gulf.

By 1903 plans for the Berlin to Baghdad railroad were completed, but more capital was needed to implement the project. Since sufficient funds could not be raised in Germany, both French and British capitalists were invited to participate. In England, opinion was divided. The Balfour government favored accepting the offer. But big business feared the continuing growth of German competition in foreign markets, especially in the Ottoman Empire. The British were still ahead in such competition, but between 1886 and 1910, German trade with the Ottoman Empire leaped from fifteenth to second place. German press comment became increasingly hostile to what was considered the British attempt to monopolize influence in the Middle East.

The Anglo-French Entente of 1904

Throughout the nineteenth century Queen Victoria's government had followed a policy of "splendid isolation," which meant forming close alliances with no one and intervening everywhere to preserve a balance of power. German colonial ambitions in Asia, Africa, and the Near East, the growth of German industrial might, increased German military expenditures, and the kaiser's aggressive diplomacy seriously worried the British. Relations with France did not strengthen England's position. Animosity between the two historical rivals brought them to the brink of war during the 1890s when both were striving to take over Africa: the British pushing southward by way of the Nile Valley, France cutting across the northern half of the continent from the Atlantic coast. During July 1898 a small French force reached Fashoda in southern Sudan while General Kitchener was leading British troops toward the same spot. After the two units met at the tiny outpost in September, Kitchener threatened to drive out the French, and a hastily arranged compromise prevented an armed clash.

The incident helped to dramatize to both Great Britain and France that their competition served only the advantage of their mutual rival Germany. An understanding not to fight over Fashoda opened the way to an accord in 1904: France agreed to cease obstructing British policy in Egypt with demands for a time limit for the "temporary" occupation and the British agreed to recognize a French sphere of influence in Morocco "to preserve order...and to provide assistance for...administrative, economic, financial, and military reforms." In addition, the British gave guarantees for the maintenance of certain French cultural prerogatives in Egypt, such as the right to maintain schools and to nominate the director general of Egyptian Antiquities. Other subsidiary agreements settled Anglo-French differences over a number of colonial outposts in Asia, Africa, and North America.

Anglo-Russian Agreement

British fears of Russian expansion in Asia were dispelled by the overwhelming power of Germany and the apparent decline in tsarist strength. When Russia was defeated by Japan in 1904–1905, it became obvious that the threat to British India was much less than had been feared. The opportunity seemed ripe to link the three major opponents of German expansion—France, Great Britain, and Russia—in a triple entente. France had already formed a semialliance with Russia in 1897. Now it remained for Great Britain and Russia to settle their differences. Defeat by Japan and revolutionary uprisings within the country had considerably softened Russia's resistance. By 1907 the two kingdoms were ready to agree on their outstanding colonial disputes, principally in Iran, Afghanistan, and Tibet. The 1907 treaty divided Iran into three zones. In the five northern provinces Russia was to have freedom to obtain concessions for railways, banks, telegraphs, roads, transport, insurance, and other economic interests. The southern part of Iran was to become a British sphere of influence, separated from the north by a neutral zone.

The tsar immediately sent troops to occupy the five northern provinces, which until World War I remained a virtual Russian colony. Early in that war, Osmanlis and Russians fought over the northwest corner of Iran, but when the Russian front collapsed after the Bolshevik revolution, the Red government renounced all previous tsarist claims and ended the Russian occupation.

The British were less heavy-handed in controlling their southern zone. Its potential economic importance had been underscored in 1901 by the acquisition of an oil concession there by William D'Arcy, an Australian financier. When the Anglo-Iranian Oil Company, formed in 1908 largely with British capital, became the major supplier of fuel for the British fleet, southern Iran became as important to British strategy as the Suez Canal. By the eve of World War I, the British had managed to bring the various tribes in their zone under control by payment of subsidies to their chiefs as well as by subtle political influence in Tehran, rather than by using direct military intervention.

The kaiser attempted to separate Tsar Nicholas II from his French and British allies at Potsdam in 1911, offering to recognize Russia's sphere of influence in northern Iran on condition that Germany receive permission to extend the Berlin to Baghdad railroad into the Russian zone. The tsar was not persuaded, however; the Triple Entente remained firm; and the German railroad never reached Iran.

THE MIDDLE EAST ON THE EVE OF WORLD WAR I

Throughout the nineteenth century Great Britain had pursued a policy of preventing any nation from becoming strong enough to dominate the

Ottoman Empire, lest this foothold endanger British possessions in India and the East. In support of its diplomacy, the British had acquired outposts from Malta all the way to the borders of India. No other power had such an elaborate or extensive defense system or controlled so vast a territory between the Mediterranean and India. Russia no longer seemed so great a threat, and differences with France had been settled amicably. Germany now loomed as the sole potential menace, not only to Great Britain, however, but to France and Russia also.

Extensive German economic and political penetration seemed to be undermining British policy in the Ottoman Empire. The Young Turks, admirers of Prussian militarism, had formed an alliance with the kaiser causing Russia to fear that her dream of controlling the Straits and absorbing northern Iran would never be realized; France resented its loss of predominant cultural and commercial influence in the Ottoman Empire; and the British were concerned about their network of bases between the Mediterranean and India.

Only Austria-Hungary seemed to be a reliable German ally. The Austrians hoped to accomplish the century-old goal of making the Balkan region an Austrian-dominated hinterland. Russia had replaced the Ottomans as the Hapsburgs' principal competitor, and both powers were competing to gain control over the European remnants of Ottoman territory. Thus the animosity between Austria and Russia committed each more strongly to the support of their respective allies.

A few months before the outbreak of World War I there seemed to be a growing awareness of the impending doom. Efforts were made by the British and Germans to compromise their commercial conflict in the Ottoman Empire. In exchange for acknowledging German rights to operate a Berlin-Baghdad railway, two British directors were appointed to its board of directors. Germany recognized the supremacy of British interests in Kuwait, along the Persian Gulf, and in the Anglo-Iranian oil concession. A supplementary agreement reorganized the Turkish Petroleum Company established in 1911. Three competing groups—the Deutsche Bank, the Anglo-Iranian Oil Company, and the Anglo-Saxon Oil Company (a subsidiary of the British- and Dutch-owned Royal-Dutch Shell Company)—were invited to join the concession hunt. It was too late for the commercial truce to have any effect on the general world political situation, however, and within a few weeks war broke out.

The international conflict found the Middle East divided into four principal areas: the Ottoman Empire, with the exception of Egypt, had shifted into the German sphere of influence: Egypt, theoretically still an autonomous province of the Ottoman Empire, was in reality a British protectorate; the southern and Persian Gulf coasts of the Arabian peninsula were completely dominated by Great Britain; and Iran was divided between British and Russian zones of influence.

Western ideas of nationalism had begun to take root in the region; Western cultural influences on government and society were beginning to be evident in parliaments, in governments, in the attitudes of the intellectual elite, and in new concepts of the role of women; Western techniques in industry, communications, health, agriculture, education, and military affairs were being emulated, though still only superficially. Islam's capacity to deal with these many new perplexing problems was being questioned for the first time. Like the rest of Asia, the Middle East was on the verge of events that would not only change its political relations with Europe but would also alter its own traditional society.

NOTES

1. J.C. Hurewitz, *Diplomacy in the Near and Middle East,* Princeton, 1956, vol. I, p. 141.
2. *Ibid.,* p. 197.

5   The Middle East and the West since World War I

THE WAR AND THE EAST

Shortly after the Ottoman Empire joined the Central Powers (Germany, Austria-Hungary, and Bulgaria) in World War I, their armies took the offensive against Russia in the Caucasian region and unsuccessfully tried to drive the British from Suez. The only really successful Ottoman military action, however, was the defense of the Dardanelles against the Allied invasion at Gallipoli during 1915–1916. At the end of the war, Ottoman troops were retreating on all fronts: they had been driven back into Palestine by the British from their Suez base and they had been forced to retreat in Iraq by British forces pushing up the Tigris and Euphrates rivers beyond Baghdad; only in the north had they been spared a Russian offensive by the Revolution of 1917.

More important than any military activity were the secret political arrangements made to divide the Ottoman territories among the victorious Allies. Great Britain, France, Russia, and Italy schemed to carve up the Ottoman Empire in four principal sets of agreements. The Constantinople Agreement—a series of diplomatic exchanges between England, France, and Russia during March and April 1915—completely reversed the traditional Western policy on the Straits, promising British and French support for the Russian annexation of the waterway and the areas surrounding it, provided only the tsar make Istanbul (Constantinople) a free port and guarantee free commercial navigation through the Straits. Arabia, including the Muslim holy places, would be taken from Ottoman control and placed under Arab rule. Most of the "neutral zone" in Iran between the Russian and British

100

spheres of influence would be attached to the latter. Russia would keep the north. A later agreement defined British and French rights in the Asiatic provinces of the Ottoman Empire.

Italy was bribed into the war by promises of Austrian and Ottoman territory in the secret Treaty of London signed in April 1915. England, France, and Russia recognized Italian interest in the Mediterranean and agreed that the monarchy receive a share in the region adjacent to the province of Adalia (Antalya), where Italy had already acquired some rights. Italy was to receive full sovereignty over the Dodecanese Islands, which she had been occupying since 1912. In Libya, which had been wrested from the Ottomans in 1912, rights and privileges still retained by the sultan were to be transferred to Italy. Territory was to be added to the Italian colonies of Eritrea, Somaliland, and Libya if England and France increased their African colonial empires.

After satisfying Italian and Russian demands, Great Britain and France agreed on their own mutual claims to the Ottoman possessions. The French were eager to hasten a settlement because they knew of British negotiations with Arab nationalist leaders concerning the territory in question. A series of notes exchanged by the British, French, and Russian governments during 1915 and 1916, called the Sykes-Picot Agreement, became the key to the future of Ottoman Arab lands. Northeastern Anatolia was originally promised to Russia, but this provision was invalidated by the 1917 revolution. France was to obtain outright possession of the Syrian coastal strip north of the city of Tyre, the Ottoman province of Adana, and a large part of Cilicia. Syria and northern Iraq, including Mosul's oil fields, would become an independent Arab zone under French protection. Iraq, from Baghdad to the Persian Gulf, and the city of Acre, with a surrounding enclave in Palestine, would become British spheres. An autonomous Arab zone under British protection would be established between the cities of Kirkuk in Iraq and Aqaba in southern Palestine, extending from the Mediterranean all the way to the Persian Gulf. Alexandretta (Iskenderun) on the Levant coast was to be proclaimed a free port. Russia insisted on the internationalization of Palestine west of the Jordan River between the cities of Gaza and Tyre (excluding the British enclave around Acre) because of its many Orthodox religious establishments.

The Italians now feared that French claims in southwestern Anatolia would conflict with their own ambitions and demanded that the matter be clarified in still another agreement. At first, Italy rejected a British compromise plan dividing Anatolian territory equally between themselves and France. The dispute was settled at St. Jean de Maurienne in April 1917 by turning over western Anatolia north of the already reserved Italian possession of Antalya. This additional territory included the important city of Izmir (Smyrna). This agreement conflicted with an earlier promise to Greece, which had lapsed when King Constantine refused to declare war on Germany. When the king later reversed his neutral policy and joined the Allies, Greece revived claims to the Izmir area as well as to Cyprus, which England had changed from a protectorate to a colony after declaring war on the Ottoman Empire in 1914.

In addition to the various secret agreements among the Allies, there were conflicting British commitments to the Zionists and the Arab nationalists. The sheikh of Kuwait was promised independence from the Ottoman Empire in November 1914 if he cooperated in a campaign against the Ottomans in Iraq. Amir Ibn Saud's independence from the Ottoman sultan was recognized in a treaty of friendship in December 1915. He was promised protection by the British Indian government and an annual subsidy in return for benevolent neutrality. Though he did not become an active British ally, Ibn Saud did fight the powerful pro-Ottoman Rashid clan in northern Arabia and rejected the sultan's appeal for a holy war. Qatar became a veiled British protectorate in November 1916 when its sheikh signed an agreement to suppress the slave trade, grant economic privileges to British nationals, and permit a British resident to manage his foreign affairs.

Ambiguities in British policy were created by conflict between the British Indian government and the Foreign Office. The former was primarily concerned with interests in the Persian Gulf and Iraq, while the Foreign Office concentrated on making fruitful contacts with Arab nationalists in the Arabian Hijaz and the Levant. Foreign Office representatives in Cairo schemed to involve the notable Hashimite family in the British cause with enticements of an independent Arab state. Negotiations were carried on through correspondence between Sherif Husein, keeper of the holy places in Mecca, and Sir Henry McMahon, British high commissioner in Egypt (see chapter 6). Although British promises to the Arabs were somewhat vague, they led to active nationalist support for the Allies. Uncertainty was caused not only by substance of the Husein-McMahon correspondence, but by the apparent conflict with other British commitments: India Office support of Husein's antagonist, Ibn Saud; the Sykes-Picot Agreement; and the Zionist claim to part of the holy land on the basis of the Balfour Declaration of November 1917.

The Balfour Declaration was proclaimed to win worldwide Jewish backing for the war effort at a time when Great Britain urgently needed every possible source of support. Because of the 1917 revolution, Russia had dropped out of the war. Since many leaders of the new antiwar leftist Soviet government were Jewish, it was feared that their coreligionists would support the revolutionary cause rather than the anti-Semitic tsarist regime whom the Allies backed. Many influential American Jewish leaders were also pro-Zionist, and their backing was an important asset. If an alliance could be contracted with worldwide Zionist interests, it might strengthen the pro-Allied sentiments of many influential Jews. Some British leaders even hoped to win German Jewish support away from the kaiser. Later, in 1936, wartime Prime Minister David Lloyd George revealed that the Zionists had promised to rally Jewish pro-Allied sentiment if they received a commitment for establishing a Jewish national home in Palestine. They were helpful, he commented in the House of Commons, both in America and in Russia, which at the time was walking out and leaving England alone.

The declaration took the form of a public letter from Alfred Balfour, the British foreign minister, to Lord Rothschild, a prominent English Jewish leader. It stated that

> His Majesty's Government view with favour the establishment in Palestine of a national home for the Jewish people, and will use their best endeavours to facilitate the achievement of this object, it being clearly understood that nothing shall be done which may prejudice the civil and religious rights of existing non-Jewish communities in Palestine, or the rights and political status enjoyed by Jews in any other country.[1] (See chapter 10.)

To mollify Arab concern about the statement, Commander D.G. Hogarth was sent to reassure Sherif Husein that Great Britain's promise to the Zionists would be implemented only in so far as it did not conflict with the freedom of the population in Palestine.

WORLD WAR I PEACE SETTLEMENTS

The war destroyed the Ottoman Empire, ending Ottoman sovereignty over all areas beyond Anatolia and a corner of Thrace in Europe. Turkish nationalists were to put the *coup de grâce* to the Osmanli dynasty altogether. When the fighting stopped, Great Britain controlled most of the Arab regions; an Allied Control Commission sat in Istanbul; and British, French, and Italian troops began occupying much of southwestern Anatolia. There was immediate competition among the three Allies and Greece to seize what territory they could. All Russian claims had been renounced by the Revolutionary government. Only the United States, insisting on President Wilson's policy of "no spoils to the victors," seemed interested in an open and just peace settlement.

The Ottoman Peace Settlement

The European Allies at first tried to impose their colonial ambitions on the defeated Ottoman government in the 1920 Treaty of Sèvres. The document cut the Ottoman provinces into a crazy-quilt pattern. All the Arab provinces were placed under British and French control. The dreams of Greek prime minister Venizelos to establish an empire around the Aegean were temporarily realized by acquiring Ottoman territory in Europe to within twenty miles of Istanbul. Athens was also given Izmir to administer for five years, when a plebiscite was to determine whether the region would finally become Greek. Italy annexed the Dodecanese Islands. A state of Armenia was carved out of northeastern provinces in Anatolia and was proclaimed independent. Southeastern Anatolia, to be called Kurdistan, was granted autonomy within the Turkish state with the promise of future independence. The Straits were demilitarized and put under international supervision. The armed forces and finances of what was left of Ottoman territory, and now called Turkey, were placed under the Allies. The hated capitulations, hallmark of foreign domination and unilaterally abolished by the Young Turks in 1914, were reinstated. Non-Muslims in the new Turkey stripped of all its extensive empire, received rights and privileges the Turks found humiliating.

This degrading document was intended to emasculate Turkish power for all time; it was reluctantly signed by representatives of the nearly impotent Ottoman government, but was never ratified thereafter. All its provisions, except those affecting the Arab provinces, remained a dead letter. Instead, a strong Turkish nationalist movement led by Mustafa Kemal (later Ataturk) swept out of the Anatolian mountains and drove the Allies (principally represented by Greek troops) from all parts of the country except Istanbul, which the nationalists now abandoned as their capital in favor of Ankara. What was left of the old Ottoman government was dismissed in November 1922. The country became a republic, strong and unified, capable, as it turned out, of resisting the many and varied Western schemes to carve it up.

Since the Sèvres treaty could not be enforced, a new peace conference was convened at Lausanne, Switzerland, where parleys dragged on for eight months as the adamant Turks resisted all attempts to limit their sovereignty. Ataturk's revolutionary government insisted that it would sign no document that did not recognize Turkish national dignity. Finally, in July 1923, a settlement was agreed upon: Anatolia was to remain intact and free of any foreign interference. Only the Aegean Islands, except for Tenedos and Imbros, were lost permanently to Greece, who had occupied them since 1913. The Turks recognized the British annexation of Cyprus and the Italian possession of the Dodecanese Islands. All other Greek, Italian, and French interests in Anatolia were voided. Independent Armenia and autonomous Kurdistan were forgotten. Mosul's future was left to be determined in the future because of Iraqi border disagreements between Turkey and England. The only military restriction accepted by the new state was a thirty-kilometer-wide demilitarized zone along the Turkish western frontier in Europe. All Allied economic controls were abandoned and no reparations demanded.

Turkey agreed to accept a token group of neutrals to observe its judicial system in lieu of capitulations. Minorities (non-Muslims) were to receive no separate treatment, meaning an end of the millet system. To help make their populations homogeneous, Greece and Turkey exchanged half a million Turkish-speaking Muslim Greek subjects for one and one half million Greek-speaking Christian residents of Turkey according to details worked out in a subsidiary agreement (see also chapter 7).

The only meaningful restriction on Turkish sovereignty was the international commission in charge of the Straits. But even this body was headed by a Turkish citizen and supervised by the League of Nations. Four zones along the waterway and the islands in the Sea of Marmara were demilitarized, and the Turkish garrison in Istanbul was limited to 12,000 men.

European failure to partition Turkey was due to Ataturk's debilitating campaign against the invaders after they had gone through an exhausting war. There was little stomach for the invasion in England, France, or Italy, although many Greeks became enthusiastic by visions of enhanced power at Turkey's expense. All the Allies were suffering from war weariness, exhausted military resources, and political dissent on their home fronts. To overthrow the new republican government would have meant a long costly campaign. Under the circumstances, the best course was graceful retreat via Lausanne.

The Arabs and the Peace

The former Arab provinces of the Ottoman Empire were less fortunate than Turkey for they were unable to resist successfully Allied plans for their future, and they became pawns in the great power struggle for war spoils. Thus, until after World War II, the history of the Arab world was determined less by the wishes of the native populations than by the decisions of Western politicians.

The 1918 armistice found most of the Arab East under British occupation. At the Paris Peace Conference in 1919, President Wilson tried to modify the Allied wartime agreements. In his view they violated publicized war aims stating that future governments in the area would be based on the self-determination of the local populations.

In spite of his British and French allies, Wilson sent the American members of an Interallied Commission to the Middle East to investigate the wishes of the local inhabitants. The two American commissioners, Charles R. Crane and Henry C. King, reported that independence was most fervently desired. If political restriction was required, the population would prefer an American mandate, although the British were acceptable as second best. Under no circumstances was France welcome.

Wilson's illness caused him to withdraw from the Paris conference and led to complete American inactivity. Great Britain and France utterly disregarded his recommendations, dividing the Arab East to suit their own

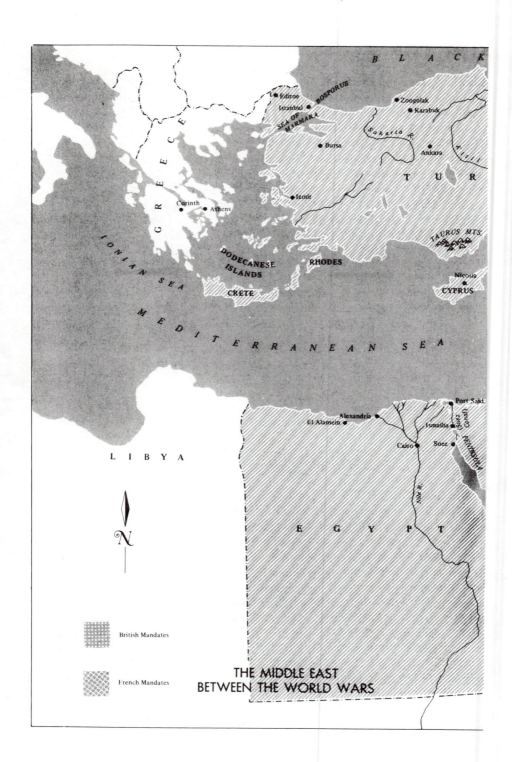

THE MIDDLE EAST
BETWEEN THE WORLD WARS

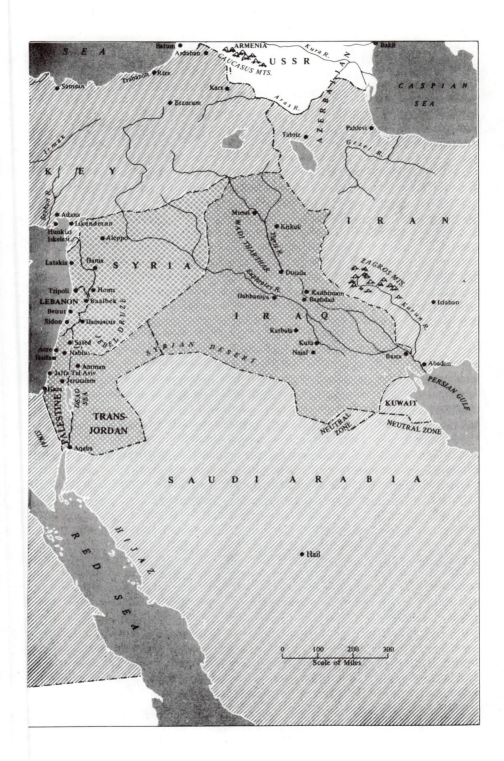

mutual convenience at San Remo in April 1920, where various modifications of the Sykes-Picot Agreement were agreed upon. France forfeited claims to Mosul in exchange for a quarter interest in the Turkish Petroleum Company (later the Iraq Petroleum Company), which formerly belonged to the German Deutsche Bank. Paris agreed to permit oil from the Mosul fields to pass through French-controlled Syria. American companies later obtained a share in the Iraq Petroleum Company after objections raised by the State Department to British and French discrimination against the United States. The protest was based on the premise that all the Allied powers were entitled to equal economic rights in the mandated territories. (See chapter 6:)

Syria and Lebanon. Immediately after victory, the British permitted Amir Faisal, son of Sherif Husein, to become military governor of Damascus. When French general Henri Gouraud's troops replaced British forces along the Syrian coast late in 1919, they had no authority as yet to interfere with Faisal's nationalist government. The nationalists declared Syria independent and proclaimed Faisal king in March 1920. When the Allied decisions at the San Remo Conference, held in April, to create a French mandate were made known, General Gouraud sent Faisal an ultimatum to surrender. He then captured Damascus and deposed the new king (see also chapter 14). Although the British had been sympathetic to Faisal, they were unwilling to intercede on his behalf lest they jeopardize their relations with France.

The mandate over Syria and Lebanon was confirmd by the League of Nations in 1922. Since France could not annex Syria and Lebanon outright, the mandate was her best possible compromise, for it re-established France in the Levant as a Middle East power and implemented much of the Sykes-Picot Agreement, while ostensibly realizing Wilson's goal of founding a regime in the best interests of the local population. (See chapters 13 and 14.)

Iraq. British officials were divided about the future of Iraq. The India Office was skeptical about the ability of the local population to govern itself, arguing that Arab regions along the Persian Gulf and in Iraq should be closely supervised by British officials. In fact, these regions were treated as appendages of the British Indian Empire. At the same time, individual Britons with long experience in the Middle East, like T.E. Lawrence and Gertrude Bell, were more sympathetic to Arab nationalism, favoring partial independence with British administrative and political advice. Initially, Iraq was turned over to administrators who agreed with the Indian Office. But their policies created widespread unrest and a nationalist revolution in 1920. Thereafter, the views of the Cairo "Arabists" were given much more serious consideration.

Overall British Middle East policy was thrashed out at a conference convened in Cairo by Colonial Secretary Winston Churchill during March

1921. Churchill and his colleagues decided to compensate Faisal for his loss of a Syrian kingdom by offering him the crown of the new kingdom of Iraq. Conflicting views of the pro-Arab nationalists and the imperialists were reconciled in the 1922 Anglo-Iraqi Treaty of Alliance. While recognizing Iraq's formal independence, the treaty authorized Great Britain to appoint advisers to the new government, to supervise its army, to protect foreigners, and to make recommendations on financial matters and foreign policy. Later protocols and modifications reduced the period and scope of British controls. Since Iraq was now "independent" by mutual agreement between Great Britain and the native population, the League of Nations was not formally required to assign the mandate, although officially the League maintained its jurisdiction over the British-Iraqi relationship.

Formal recognition of full independence came in 1930 after continued nationalist pressure. A new twenty-five year Anglo-Iraqi alliance replaced the 1922 treaty. Ostensibly, foreign controls were ended, and Great Britain promised to support Iraq's application for membership in the League of Nations. The British high commissioner was replaced by an ambassador, who was to have permanent seniority in the diplomatic corps. The two countries agreed to "full and frank consultation" of foreign policy and not to adopt policies that were "inconsistent with the alliance" or "might create difficulties for the other party." The agreement permitted the British to keep air bases at Basra and near Baghdad for the "defense of Iraq." In return, Iraq was required to provide "all facilities and assistance."

From 1932, when Iraq became a member of the League of Nations, until the end of World War II, its petroleum resources and military air bases made it a vital link in the British chain of Middle East outposts. During this era few policies not approved in London could be successfully adopted in Baghdad. (See chapter 15.)

Transjordan. Transjordan was also the creation of the 1921 British Middle East conference in Cairo. Because it was sparsely settled and its population undeveloped and politically unsophisticated, Transjordan resembled a British semicolony more than an autonomous nation. Creation of the country in the first place was due more to political circumstance than to geographic, ethnic, or nationalist factors. Between 1918 and 1920, its remote deserts had been divided between Faisal's Syrian kingdom and the Kingdom of Hijaz ruled by his father, Husein. British military authorities took it over in 1920, including it within the Palestine mandate. At the Cairo conference, British officials decided to bestow the territory on Faisal's brother, Abdullah, as an inducement not to avenge Faisal's defeat in Syria. Arab nationalist leaders in Syria and Iraq had previously indicated that Abdullah was their choice for the Iraqi crown, but the Cairo conference now decided to bestow it as compensation upon Faisal. Still another throne was needed, therefore, to compensate Abdullah. Transjordan was cut off from the Palestine mandate and converted into an amirate, a status somewhat lower than a kingdom. British military officers and civilian administrators managed all the country's affairs, theoretically in consultations with the amir. In practice, until 1928 the British high commissioner in Palestine was also the chief executive in Transjordan. More formal autonomy was conceded in an agreement in 1928, although the country continued to be run much like the British protectorates in the Persian Gulf. (See chapter 12.)

Palestine. Palestine was an anomaly. Its Jewish and Arab populations were among the most politically sophisticated and culturally developed in the area. Conflict between Jewish and Arab nationalisms, however, frustrated all British attempts to encourage local self-government. Arab nationalists considered Palestine part of the Arab heartland and refused to surrender any of their rights or claims. The Zionists, on the other hand, envisaged Palestine as a Jewish national homeland and were determined to realize their aspirations. Efforts to strengthen their hold on the country only intensified the Arab nationalists' fears of the Jewish minority and led to armed conflict between the two communities. Throughout the interwar mandatory era, therefore, Palestine was also ruled like a British colony; and relationships between the British administrators and the local inhabitants resembled those between native inhabitants and rulers in other colonies.

The League of Nations Palestine mandate conferred upon Great Britain in 1922 did nothing to resolve the dilemma. Whereas other mandates directed Great Britain and France "to facilitate... progressive development" toward independence, there was no such requirement called for in Palestine. There Great Britain was vested with "full powers of legislation and of administration." The Balfour Declaration, which was incorporated into the preamble of the mandate, presented a constant dilemma. Could the provision for "the establishment in Palestine of a national home for the Jewish people" in fact be implemented without "prejudice [to] the civil and religious rights of the existing non-Jewish communities"? By the outbreak of World War II the dilemma was still unresolved and the Palestine problem remained one of the thorniest confronting British policymakers (see also chapter 10).

Egypt. World War I ended the last shadowy vestiges of Ottoman suzerainty over Egypt and all pretense of Great Britain's "temporary" status in the country. A few weeks after the Ottoman Empire declared war on the German side, Great Britain proclaimed the country a British protectorate and deposed its pro-Ottoman khedive, Abbas Hilmi II. A loud nationalist outcry arose by the end of the war in response to growing discontent within the country and the hopes raised by the self-determination principle articulated by President Wilson. Saad Zaghlul, leader of the new "Egypt for the

Egyptians" movement, attempted to present its demands to the Paris peace conference, but never received a formal hearing. When he returned to Egypt, the British arrested and deported him. There was official recognition of the intense nationalist fervor sweeping through the country, however, and a British mission headed by Lord Milner was sent out to investigate. In December 1920, the Milner mission recommended that an independent Egypt, allied with Great Britain, replace the protectorate. Protracted negotiations between Egypt and Great Britain led nowhere until Lord Allenby, the British high commissioner, warned London in 1922 that if Egyptian hopes were again frustrated, he despaired of any future for the country, which would relapse into a state of alternating outbreaks and repression. Allenby's warning and threat to resign induced London to accept the essence of Milner's recommendations in 1922. Since the nationalists refused to sign any document that did not grant them complete, unqualified independence, Great Britain's proclamation of Egyptian independence was unilateral. Four points were "absolutely reserved to the discretion of His Majesty's Government." Until mutual agreement could be reached, Great Britain was to retain control of communications vital to the Empire, defense against foreign aggression or interference, foreign interests and minority rights in Egypt, and the Sudan.

The declaration of independence did little to diminish British influence in Egypt and nationalist agitation continued to smolder. The assassination of the British commander-in-chief of the Egyptian army and governor general of the Sudan, Sir Lee Stack, in November 1924 brought relations between rulers and subjects to a showdown. High Commissioner Lord Allenby delivered a sharp ultimatum to the Egyptian government demanding punishment of the killers, an apology, an indemnity of half a million Egyptian pounds, a ban on all political demonstrations, and evacuation of Egyptian troops from the Sudan. British advisers were to be imposed on the Ministries of France, Justice, and the European Department of the Ministry of Interior. The waters of the Blue Nile were diverted from Egyptian use to irrigate British-run cotton plantations in the Sudan. British troops took over the customs at Alexandria as a down payment on fulfillment of the ultimatum. Its effect was to make Egypt again a British protectorate and the Sudan a British colony. Later the British government relented the severity of the measures, but their attempts at partial compromise with the Egyptians continually failed until 1936.

The world situation in the 1930s, which contained a new and larger threat to international peace, began to have a mitigating effect on Anglo-Egyptian relations. Italian Dictator Mussolini's invasion of Ethiopia during 1935 enveloped British interests in the eastern Mediterranean and in the Red Sea area; and it was an object lesson to the Egyptians. Moderate nationalists preferred a compromise with Great Britain to the danger of Italian fascism, especially after reports about Mussolini's treatment of the Ethiopians.

Cordial Anglo-Egyptian negotiations produced a twenty-year defensive alliance in August 1936. All British troops were to be evacuated from Egypt except from the naval base at Alexandria and the Suez Canal zone. British police personnel were to be replaced by a military mission to advise the Egyptian army. Foreign training for Egyptian officers would be restricted to Great Britain. The ban of Egyptian immigration into the Sudan or the presence of Egyptian troops there was lifted. A British ambassador with permanent diplomatic seniority replaced the high commissioner. Great Britain also promised to support Egypt's application for membership in the League of Nations and abolition of the old capitulations. In return for a British commitment to defend the country, Egypt would turn over its communication facilities to Great Britain in wartime.

When Egypt joined the League in 1937, all nations with capitulatory privileges in the country agreed to terminate them. Only mixed courts (with both European and Egyptian judges) remained by agreement until 1949. Egypt now had more freedom than ever before; nationalist fervor was temporarily satisfied: and vital British communications in Egypt and the Sudan were still safeguarded (see also chapter 8).

The Arabian Peninsula. There was little increase in Western influence in the Arabian peninsula during the interwar period. Great Britain maintained its holdings along the southern coast and in the Persian Gulf. Mutually beneficial agreements were made with King Ibn Saud, who expanded his desert principality into the largest and most powerful state in the peninsula. After a clash with Sherif Husein, Ibn Saud took over Mecca and Medina and finally, in 1927, was proclaimed king of the Hijaz and Nejd. Ibn Saud's desire for an overland link with Syria would have separated Transjordan from Iraq. Since the British insisted that the land bridge between the two Hashemite kingdoms be maintained, Ibn Saud agreed to entrust the region temporarily to Abdullah in exchange for recognition of his "complete and absolute independence." The Arabian king also acknowledged Great Britain's special position in Bahrain and the Persian Gulf sheikhdoms.

Relations with Yemen remained unsettled because of disputes over the Aden frontier. The Royal Air Force continued to drive out Yemeni raiders until a treaty of friendship and cooperation, signed in 1934, calmed things temporarily in that disputed territory (see chapter 16).

Events in Iran

Following the collapse of the tsarist regime, Russia suspended its intervention in Iran's internal affairs, leaving the country completely under British control. British troops, stationed throughout Iran during the war, now used it as a base of operations against Soviet armies in the Caucasus and in Transcaucasia. The temptation was great to hold Iran because of its strategic position in the chain of British-controlled territories between the Mediterranean and India. When Iran sought to be admitted to the Paris peace conference, Great Britain persuaded the Allies to turn down the request. A virtual British protectorate seemed to be established as a result of the 1919 Anglo-Iranian treaty until strong nationalist sentiment caused the Iranian parliament to reject the document. Public opinion in England was not then in a mood to back still another military expedition; consequently, in 1921 British forces were withdrawn from both Iran and Soviet Central Asia.

Throughout the 1920s constant bickering over economic matters caused one crisis after another in Anglo-Iranian relations. Dispute over oil rich Bahrain in 1927 was caused by Great Britain's refusal to consider Iranian claims to the islands. In retaliation, the shah denounced the capitulations and withdrew British rights to fly over the Persian Gulf on the way to India. There were constant accusations by the shah that British agents were inciting the Kashgai, Bakhtiyari, Lur, and Kurdish tribes against his government. The accusations were temporarily suspended in 1928 when Iran and Great Britain signed a treaty granting certain safeguards to British subjects in lieu of the capitulations.

From the eve of World War I down to the present, Anglo-Iranian relations have been overshadowed by the Anglo-Iranian Oil Company, in which the British government was the principal shareholder. To the Iranians, the company loomed as an overpowering colossus. Its commercial and political contacts reached into every corner of the land. Reza Shah Pahlavi, who had seized control of the Iranian government in 1921, was jealous of the company's extensive visible and invisible power, and resented the large profits it was exporting. Since the British government controlled the company, its activities were regarded as more political than economic, and they offered a constant excuse for renewal of British intervention in Iran's domestic affairs. In 1932 Reza Shah decided to end this threat to his own supremacy once and for all by doing what all Iranians would applaud, nationalizing the company.

British protests and display of force in the form of warships sent to the Persian Gulf did not dissuade the shah. When it became evident that threats would not remedy the situation, Great Britain referred the dispute to the Council of the League of Nations. A new sixty-year concession was obtained that gave Iran substantially higher royalties and committed the company to increase gradually its Iranian employees.

In contrast to its conflicts with Great Britain, Iran's relationship with Soviet Russia was initially cordial. At a conference of the "Peoples of the East" in Baku during 1920, the new Red government proclaimed its friendship for all colonial peoples and renounced all imperialist privileges and concessions. A Soviet-Iranian treaty of friendship followed in 1921, reconfirming Soviet renunciation of all special privileges and concessions—which were turned over to Iran as compensation for losses due to the tsarist occupation—

and abrogating the 1828 treaty forbidding Iranian vessels to sail the Caspian Sea. One clause in the treaty was the root of future trouble, however: it forbade each signatory to permit any groups, organizations, or forces to use its territory for hostile acts against the other. A corollary provision permitted the Soviet government to send troops into Iran should the country be in danger of occupation by a power hostile to Russia. In World War II the Soviet Union justified its occupation of Iran on the basis of this agreement and, after the war, used it as justification for subsequent acts of intervention.

Although Soviet-Iranian relations had an auspicious beginning, they soon resumed their classic Russian form. Soviet agents infiltrated the country, stirring up rebellion in Azerbaijan and Khorasan. When British and American companies negotiated with Iran for concessions in the north, Russia protested that they violated the 1921 treaty forbidding Iran to turn over former tsarist concessions to any third party. Periodically, Russia closed its frontier with Iran in the hope that the resulting loss of trade would bring that country into line. Moscow's Ambassador Petrovsky in Tehran candidly outlined Soviet policy:

> What counts in Persia is North Persia only and the latter is fully dependent on Russia. All North Persian products that must be exported can find their only market in Russia. If we Russians stop buying them, Persia is bankrupt in one month. This is Russia's strength which has no equivalent on the British side.[2]

To counterbalance British and Russian pressures, Reza Shah began to cultivate closer ties with Germany in 1928. Within a decade Germans had become Iran's principal advisers on communications, industry, building, hospitals, and agriculture. More than 2000 German technicians, traders, tourists, and other visitors were in the country by 1939, and over 40 percent of Iran's foreign trade was with Germany. Hitler astutely phrased propaganda directed to Iran in terms emphasizing their "common Aryan background," and Reza Shah extolled the virtues of the Nazi regime as a bulwark against communism (see also chapter 17).

THE MIDDLE EAST ON THE EVE OF WORLD WAR II

By the eve of World War II, the Middle East was still dominated by Europeans. Only Turkey had real independence in domestic and foreign affairs and remained free from foreign interference. The mandated territories and Egypt were still occupied and their national policies still subject to the dictates of France and Britain. Although Great Britain and France had introduced Western parliamentary institutions and administrative apparatus in their respective territories, the basic pattern of life for the Middle Eastern masses had not changed. Only the small elite at the apex of society was affected by these innovations.

In the political realm, Great Britain had emerged as the most influential foreign power, with direct control over the greatest amount of territory. By 1939 British policies controlled Egypt, Iraq, Palestine, Transjordan, and the sheikhdoms of the Arabian peninsula; but an undercurrent of nationalism was already swirling about with greater violence than ever before, threatening to swamp British oil interests, military bases, and communication centers. Despite fervent nationalist protests, France managed to hold its own in Syria and Lebanon, but inflexible colonial policies had created such deep animosity that its imperial tenure was ever more precarious.

The Soviet Union was active only in Iran during the interwar period, although there were small and ineffectual Communist movements in Palestine and the neighboring Arab countries. Russian ambitions to control the Straits were temporarily suspended, though not abandoned. The 1936 Montreaux Convention gave Russia a slight advantage by reducing the tonnage of vessels belonging to nonriparian states permitted on the Black Sea. At the same time, it also terminated the International Straits Commission established by the Lausanne Treaty and permitted Turkey to remilitarize the area.

As a result of insistence by the United States government, a commercial open-door policy was accepted by the British; and several American companies obtained a major interest in the Iraq Petroleum Company. Other powerful American firms negotiated valuable petroleum concessions in Saudi Arabia, also contributing to the beginnings of a direct United States interest in the Middle East.

By 1939 Western interests were directly threatened by Hitler and Mussolini. British and Russian influence in Iran was rapidly being replaced by Germany. The latter established close economic ties with Turkey, receiving nearly half its exports. From the port of Bari the Italians broadcast inflammatory Arabic programs to incite the nationalists of Syria, Iraq, Palestine, and Egypt. German and Italian propaganda found willing listeners among local populations throughout the Middle East. Both nations waged a cultural offensive and enticed to their universities hundreds of impressionable young students from Turkey, Iran, and the Arab world.

THE MIDDLE EAST AND WORLD WAR II

The Middle East again became involved in international affairs when Europe entered World War II. There was little actual combat in the area itself, although it was a target of a vast German pincer movement pressing toward its center from the Balkans, the Caucasus, and across the deserts of North Africa.

The German force that came closest to achieving victory was finally turned back in November 1942 at the battle of el-Alamein in the Western Desert close to the border of Egypt. The region continued to be significant more because of its diplomatic rather than its military role in the war.

Turkey

In the last peaceful prewar months France turned to Turkey as a possible Mediterranean ally. Relations between the two had remained cordial ever since France became the first Western European power to recognize Ataturk's new national regime. Part of the Franklin-Bouillon Agreement establishing relations between the two republics in 1921 provided for a special administration in Syria's Alexandretta (Iskenderun) province, which the Turks had reluctantly relinquished. Both Syrians and Turks claimed that their respective countrymen were the predominant population in Iskenderun. In 1936 when it seemed likely that the French would conclude a treaty granting independence to Syria, Turkey objected to the inclusion of Iskenderun in Syrian territory. To avoid loss of Turkish friendship, which was considered far more valuable to France than that of Syria, Paris temporized. France next proposed autonomy for the province, but this settlement did not satisfy the Turks; fighting broke out in the province in 1938. France permitted Turkish troops to share police duties with the French forces already there, and a Franco-Turkish condominium was set up providing for the election of a local assembly. The voting, which took place in August 1938, gave the Turks a majority of twenty-two out of forty seats. The legislature was not long in declaring themselves the autonomous Republic of Hatay. Within a year Iskenderun voted to join Turkey, and with acceptance of this act on the part of Paris, France and Turkey formally became allies. Great Britain joined the Franco-Turkish entente in November 1939, extending financial assistance to Ankara.

Turkey had been shocked into a departure from Ataturk's traditional policy of avoiding entangling alliances by the Nazi-Soviet pact of August 1939, which openly assigned large parts of the Middle East to a Russian sphere of influence. The close ties between its traditional enemy and so formidable a revisionist power as Germany was enough to drive the Turks to the cover of the 1939 defensive alliance with the Western Allies.

After France fell in June 1940, the Balkans became the principal theatre of war operations. By 1941 Axis troops had occupied Bulgaria, seized Greece, Crete, and Yugoslavia, and camped along the Turkish frontier. Hitler's armies crept through the Caucasus, and by November 1943 they reached a point within fifty miles of the Caspian Sea. A pro-Axis coup in Iraq during 1941 had almost thrown that country into the Axis camp, but its fall was averted by a British invasion in May that year. On the southern fronts, Ethiopia and Italian East Africa became Axis bases. Libya was the taking-off point for invasion of Egypt and the Suez Canal by the German general Rommel, until he was defeated by British general Montgomery at el Alamein.

The German pincer movement closing in on the Middle East, together with the fall of France, caused second thoughts in Ankara about the Western alliance. Under the circumstances, a policy of friendly neutrality toward both Allies and Axis seemed most prudent. When the tide began to turn against Germany in 1944, however, Turkey again altered its policy, severing economic and diplomatic relations with Hitler. Since support for the allied cause was required for charter membership in the newly formed United Nations, Turkey declared war on Germany in February 1945.

Iran

The outbreak of the war found Iran trying to counterbalance British and Russian pressures by cultivating a relationship with Nazi Germany. Consequently, Reza Shah rejected Soviet and British requests in the summer of 1941 to use his territory for a supply route. Since this was their only viable route to Russia after the Nazi invasion of that country in June 1941, the Allies resorted to force. When the shah rejected an ultimatum demanding expulsion of a German fifth column and the establishment of Allied transit facilities, British and Russian troops invaded, dividing the country approximately along the lines of the 1907 Anglo-Russian agreement. The USSR occupied Iran's five northern provinces, and Great Britain the rest of the country. The capital, Tehran, became a neutral enclave. Reza Shah was deposed and exiled by the British, with Russian assent, and his twenty-year old son—the last shah—placed on the throne; a pro-Allied cabinet was thereupon installed. In January 1942 Iran, Great Britain, and the USSR signed a tripartite Treaty of Alliance giving the Allies use of transit and communications facilities. Special point was made of emphasizing that the country was not "occupied" and that its independence was to be respected. Within six months of the defeat of the Axis, the treaty avowed, Allied troops were to be withdrawn. The United States became a partner to the "nonoccupation" in 1942 when 30,000 American troops attached to the Persian Gulf Command moved in to operate a route for lend-lease supplies to Russia.

Within months after the occupation, Russia began to use its troops as a political lever. The Communist Tudeh party received their support, and a strong Communist press was established. The British attempted to undermine this Communist activity, but with little success. While the United States supplied both economic and technical assistance to the Tehran government, it could do little to prevent the USSR from completely dominating the north.

The Levant

In the Levant, France cancelled all self-government experiments and reasserted its authority when war broke out by re-establishing direct control over Syria and once again dividing the Druse and Latakia districts from the rest of the country into separate regimes. In both Syria and Lebanon, the high commissioner suspended the constitution and dissolved parliament. These heavy-handed tactics, in addition to the surrender of Iskenderun to Turkey, aroused nationalist ire and turned most of the population against the Allied cause.

When France surrendered to Germany, the Vichy regime sent its officials to administer the Levant, and Axis influence was widespread. Numerous German and Italian officers came to the region, turning it into a base for anti-Allied activities. After the Vichy high commissioner announced it would permit German planes to use Syrian airfields when they arrived to assist the anti-Hashemite revolt in Iraq, the British decided to act. In July 1941, a month after the Iraqi uprising, British and Free French troops dislodged the Vichy forces with little fighting, interning the Germans and Italians. The Free French, however, had grave suspicions about British intentions in Syria and demanded assurances that they would recover the area after victory. British minister of state for the Middle East, Oliver Lyttleton, promised General Charles de Gaulle in August 1941 that His Majesty's government was interested only in winning the war. After defeating the Axis, he promised that France would have the predominant position over any other European power in Syria and Lebanon.

Iraq

In the Arab world, Axis propaganda had been most successful in Iraq, where strong nationalist forces led by Rashid Ali al-Gilani became influential. While Britain was fighting alone for its life after the fall of France, Rashid Ali and a shadow cabinet of Palestinian nationalist zealots—who had fled to Iraq where they were cordially received by Arab nationalist leaders—plotted to obtain Axis support for their independence. The opportunity seemed inviting in April 1941 during the invasion of Greece. After a successful coup, the nationalists hesitated, for the loudly promised German aid was in fact sent to other battle areas. British troops were landed in the south of Iraq, and Rashid Ali demanded their evacuation. When they refused to leave, Rashid Ali's forces attacked the British air base at Habbaniya and seized the Iraq Petroleum Company's oil-pumping installations. But the Iraqis were unable to cope with the situation. Their appeals to Hitler were unanswered because of German involvements elsewhere. British and Transjordanian troops took over the country. Rashid Ali and his followers decamped in haste, and a pro-British government was reinstated for the remainder of the war. (See chapter 15.)

Palestine and Transjordan

Palestine was remarkably quiet during the war years. The Arab rebellion, which had erupted in 1936, petered out by 1939, and the Zionists called a halt to their major political maneuvers against the British. When war broke out, one of the first moves of the Zionist leadership was to pledge all-out assistance to the Allies against Nazi Germany. Throughout the war, however, they did continue attempts to rescue persecuted Jews from Europe by smuggling them into Palestine against the wishes of the Arab majority and the British authorities. British restrictions on immigration caused a rift among the Jewish underground forces, and one small terrorist fragment led by Abraham Stern kept up its militant activities against Great Britain. The rest of the Jewish community participated fully in the war effort, through economic cooperation and large-scale military recruitment.

Transjordan, Palestine's neighbor, and its ruler Amir Abdullah remained loyal British allies. There were no nationalist outbreaks in his amirate. On the contrary, the Transjordanian Arab Legion actively assisted the British forces to put down the Rashid Ali revolt in Iraq. (See chapters 10 and 12.)

Egypt

Egypt was the center of Allied Middle East wartime activity. The British Middle East Command, the office of Minister of State for the Middle East, and the Middle East Supply Center were located in Cairo. Over half a million British, Indian, Australian, New Zealand, South African, Polish, Greek, Czechoslovak, Yugoslav, and American soldiers passed through the country on their way to various battle fronts. The historic 1943 conference between United States president Roosevelt, British prime minister Churchill, Chinese general Chiang Kai-Shek, and Turkish president Inonu was held in the shadow of the pyramids.

Egyptian sympathies were divided. Some nationalists, including several of the younger officers who were later to lead the 1952 revolution under Nasser, joined former chief-of-staff General Aziz al-Misri in an unsuccessful attempt to collaborate with the Nazis. Cabinet ministers and some members of the royal court, who had personal attachments with the Italian royal family, could hardly disguise their Axis sympathies. On the other side, leaders of the social-democratic Wafd party backed the British war effort.

At first, Great Britain did not expect an Egyptian war declaration, only benevolent neutrality. When Italy attacked France in June 1940, however, the British ambassador demanded that Prime Minister Ali Maher join the Allies. When the latter refused, Great Britain insisted that the king dismiss him and appoint a pro-Allied Wafdist government under Nahas Pasha. To enforce their ultimatum, British armored units surrounded the king's palace and threatened to deport him unless Nahas was immediately appointed. To many nationalists, the incident seemed to turn the clock back to 1882. It was a major factor in the subsequent unpopularity of the king and the Wafd among the younger nationalist army officers.

When Allied victory was within reach in February 1945, Egypt declared war on Germany, thus becoming eligible to participate in the San Francisco conference to establish the United Nations. (See chapter 8.)

Arabia

The sovereign Arab state most friendly to the Allies was Saudia Arabia, although it remained neutral until March 1945, when Ibn Saud also declared war on Germany to become eligible for United Nations membership. When the war began, Great Britain dominated the peninsula. Although American oil companies had been operating in eastern Arabia since 1933, the United States government had remained officially aloof. There was not even a United States consular office in Jidda, Saudi Arabia's diplomatic outpost. The country's deteriorating economy soon changed the situation. By 1941 King Ibn Saud's exchequer was nearly drained because of the collapse in pilgrim traffic to Mecca and the wartime curtailment of American oil operations. The king was now forced to seek aid from the United States and British governments and a subsidy from the oil company. Representatives of the latter, unable to assist, appealed to President Roosevelt on the king's behalf. But, Roosevelt explained, the grant of unilateral help would seem to be interfering in an area of exclusive British influence. Washington, therefore, requested Great Britain to share with Saudi Arabia some of the funds from a 425-million-dollar American loan.

The indirect American aid was supplemented by direct lend-lease to Saudi Arabia in 1943, and an American air base was set up at Dhahran to link the route with the Far East. Relations became so cordial that in 1945 King Ibn Saud was invited to visit President Roosevelt when the latter returned from Yalta by way of the Suez Canal. (See chapter 16.)

THE MIDDLE EAST AND THE WEST SINCE WORLD WAR II

When the war ended in 1945, Great Britain was still the paramount Western power in the East. Egypt, Palestine, Transjordan, Iraq, southern Arabia, and the Persian Gulf were fully within British control, while Russia had reasserted its influence in northern Iran. In Syria and Lebanon, the French had been displaced. American interests were just beginning to develop, and Russia had re-established its control over northern Iran. Within months after the Allied victory, the signs of a new Middle East power relationship began to appear. The region had acquired renewed importance and was soon to become a major center of tensions and clashes between the West and Russia.

French Departure from the Levant

Weakened by defeat in 1940, France was no longer able to contain the nationalist tide in Syria and Lebanon. When British and Free French forces had occupied the Levant in 1941, they had recognized the independence of the two Arab states. Pro-French governments in both were replaced by nationalist regimes which resisted the 1943 attempts by the de Gaulle Free French forces to reimpose the colonial administration. The British intervened, then and again in 1945, to protect the nationalists in their demand for complete independence. Both Syrian and Lebanese nationalist governments brought charges before the United Nations Security Council in 1946 claiming the continued presence of French and British troops to be unlawful. An American draft resolution calling on all four parties to negotiate the immediate evacuation of foreign troops was vetoed by Russia on the grounds that it was "ineffective." Nevertheless, Great Britain and France continued withdrawing their forces. By the end of 1946 the last foreign soldiers were gone, and Syria and Lebanon were completely free. The dominant position enjoyed by France for nearly four centuries had ended, although French cultural influences, especially in Lebanon, remained strong. (See chapters 13 and 14.)

Decline of British Interests

Great Britain withdrew from the Middle East, less precipitously than France. The first area abandoned was Palestine. Intensified hatred between the Palestinian Arabs, the Jews, and the British after the war made the latter's position untenable. After an unsuccessful attempt by the 1946 Anglo-American Committee of Inquiry to find a compromise, Great Britain handed over the dilemma to the United Nations. In November 1947 the General Assembly accepted the recommendations of its Special Committee on Palestine, which proposed the division of Palestine into an Arab and a Jewish state and the creation of an international zone in Jerusalem. Palestine's Arab majority and their supporters in the neighboring nations rejected the plan, and their protests gave birth to riots that grew into the Arab-Israeli war in 1948 (see also chapter 11). Great Britain evacuated its troops and officials from the country in the midst of these hostilities, abandoning the framework of government to whatever Arab or Jewish forces managed to effect a takeover. The thirty-year British occupation thus ended in shambles. With the British retreat, the Palestine war was brought to an end by armistice agreements between Israel and Egypt, Lebanon, Transjordan, and Syria. Palestine was thereupon divided into three segments: the new republic of Israel, the Gaza strip in southern Palestine occupied by Egypt, and about a quarter of the former eastern part of Palestine incorporated into the Hashemite Kingdom of Jordan (formerly Transjordan).

Nationalist pressures in Egypt reopened unsuccessful negotiations with the British for evacuation of both the Suez Canal zone and the Sudan. In 1947 Egypt tried to bring Great Britain before the U.N. Security Council, but neither side won sufficient votes to support its case. In the next phase, during 1950 Egypt unilaterally denounced the 1936 Anglo-Egyptian Treaty of Alliance, Great Britain refusing to acknowledge the act. A final settlement was at last reached after the 1952 Egyptian revolution. The young revolutionists accepted an agreement with England in February 1953 leading to Sudanese independence. Military evacuation of the canal zone and abrogation of the 1936 treaty was agreed on in October 1954. The new agreement provided that in case of attack on a member of the Arab League (created in Cairo in March 1945, see chapter 6) or on Turkey, British troops or those of England's allies were authorized to return to the canal zone; free navigation through the Suez Canal as specified in the 1888 Constantinople Convention was guaranteed. The Union Jack was at last lowered over the canal zone in June 1956, terminating seventy-four years of British military occupation (see also chapter 9).

Abdullah of Transjordan was rewarded for loyalty to the Allied cause with fuller control over his country at the end of the war, and his status raised from amir to king. Neither Arab nationalists in that country nor the Soviet Union acknowledged the change in title. When Transjordan applied for membership in the United Nations, Russia temporarily blocked its acceptance by arguing that the country was still a British vassal state (see chapter 12). Transjordan's fellow Arab League members (see chapter 6) also were critical of the kingdom's twenty-five–year preferential alliance with Great Britain signed in 1946. Despite a new document in 1948 granting Transjordan nominal independence, its deteriorating economic situation made it even more dependent upon British subsidies. After the Arab-Israeli war, Transjordan absorbed those parts of Palestine not conquered by the Israelis, and the resulting state was named in 1949 the Hashemite Kingdom of Jordan. The population increase by nearly one million Palestinians, one third of them refugees, was financially unabsorbable and deepened the dependence of Jordan upon British economic aid. Nationalists ignored the country's dependence on foreign economic aid, demanding an end of all ties with Great Britain. They temporarily succeeded in ending the three-decade-long relationship by forcing the ouster of General John Bagot Glubb and other British officers in 1956 in the uproar that followed the British effort to enlist Jordan in the Baghdad Pact. The last British troops departed in 1957 after the annulment of the 1948 Anglo-Transjordan Agreement, although a few economic ties with Britain remained (see also chapter 12).

The last former mandate from which British forces departed was Iraq. After the end of World War II only a few British officers remained at two royal air force bases in that country. Relationships between the two countries were redefined in the proposed Treaty of Portsmouth, signed in January 1948 but never ratified because of nationalist opposition. Instead, the arrangements in the 1930 Anglo-Iraqi treaty permitting Great Britain to use Iraqi bases continued until they were replaced by the Baghdad Pact in 1953. The pact recognized both nations as equals, but nationalists regarded it as yet another disguise for continued British control of Iraqi foreign policy. Continued British influence in the country and the pact were the principal targets of the revolutionists who overthrew the British-backed Hashemite monarchy in

1958. A few months later, the last small British units left their two air bases, the Baghdad Pact was denounced, and Iraq terminated some thirty years of alliance with Great Britain (see also chapter 15).

Even in South Arabia and in the Persian Gulf, areas of traditional British hegemony, the spread of nationalism undermined Western influences. During the 1960s radical Arab independence movements in Aden spread to the adjoining protectorates, principalities, sheikhdoms, and amirates. London at first attempted to shift its control gradually to local rulers organized in a South Arabian Federation, but revolutionary violence increased at such a rapid rate that Great Britain finally turned over its authority to the most radical nationalists who in 1967 created the leftist People's Republic of South Yemen. Similar problems faced the British in the Persian Gulf where conflict between traditional leaders who had been British protégés and radical Arab nationalists threatened to erupt after Great Britain's departure from all areas east of Suez in 1971 (see also chapter 16).

Great Britain and France made an abortive attempt to re-establish their Middle Eastern roles in 1956 when they joined Israel in attacking Egypt. France was eager to end Egyptian assistance to the Algerian nationalist movement engaging its forces in North Africa; Israel feared the growing strength of Arab nationalism symbolized by Egypt's President Nasser; both Great Britain and France were angered by Nasser's nationalization of the Suez Canal Company. President Nasser had taken over control of the waterway as a retaliatory act against withdrawal of American and British offers of assistance in constructing a new high Aswan Dam urgently needed to increase Egypt's productivity. After his seizure of the Suez Canal Company, England and France were determined to topple Nasser, by force if necessary, for his act had severely wounded their national pride and they considered him a potential future threat to the whole Middle East. They were largely held in check by American hopes for a negotiated settlement. But after three months, their patience was at an end and they attacked. The simultaneous Israeli invasion was occasioned by the rapid growth of Egyptian military strength resulting from large-scale acquisition of arms from the Soviet Union and the increase of Palestinian Arab harassment of the Israeli border.

The United Nations ordered the aggressors to evacuate their forces from Egypt immediately. Voting in the United Nations was marked by the concurrence of the United States, the Soviet Union, and several British Commonwealth members, producing an overwhelming majority. Russian threats to use rockets and to send volunteers to fight the aggressors added to the potential danger of the situation. Furthermore, large segments of public opinion in Great Britain strongly opposed the invasion of Egypt. By the end of 1956, British and French forces had retreated, and the last Israeli troops withdrew from the Gaza strip early in 1957.

In 1958 Great Britain again brought its power to bear in the Arab world. Following the overthrow of the Hashemite dynasty of Iraq in July 1958,

British troops were rushed to neighboring Jordan at the request of its ruler to help that nation prevent the revolution from spreading. Four months later King Husain felt sufficiently strong to permit the withdrawal of these forces.

By the end of the 1960s the British government had decided to cut back on all of its international obligations because of their great costs, especially the cost of maintaining military and naval forces in Asia. The Labour cabinet announced that all British troops in countries east of Suez would be withdrawn by 1971 and that other strategies would be sought to protect England's interests. This decline in the Empire tended to increase Soviet-American competition to replace the British in Asia, including the Middle East and the Persian Gulf.

After the 1967 Arab-Israeli war, France attempted to reassert some of its traditional influence, but there was little prospect that it would again become a major force in the region. Rather, the French government, by supplying arms to some Arab countries and diplomatic support, attained a more favorable public image in several Arab capitals.

American Middle East Interests and the Cold War

American interests in the area had been neither political nor strategic until World War II made involvement inevitable as part of the Allied grand strategy. American air bases were then established in Saudi Arabia and Egypt; in Iran, the Persian Gulf Command linked Russia with the lend-lease supply route; United States aid subsidized the Saudi Arabian government; and as a cosponsor of the Middle East Supply Center, the United States helped replan the region's economy.

Immediately after the war, most American interests were jettisoned. When Great Britain's financial situation became critical, however, and it was forced to abandon its self-imposed role as arbiter in the Middle East, the United States felt obliged to return and to assume many of the British commitments lest the area fall under Soviet influence.

The Soviet Union took advantage of victory over the Axis and the decline in British power to press historical Russian ambitions in Turkey and Iran. Even before the end of the war, the USSR began to accuse Turkey of prolonging the struggle by protecting the German flank in the Balkans through a policy of neutrality. Two months before the Nazi collapse, the Soviet government unilaterally denounced its 1925 pact of friendship and nonaggression with Turkey. Only if Ankara would return Kars and Ardahan, permit Soviet bases in the Straits, revise the 1936 Straits Convention in Russia's favor, and turn over part of Thrace to Communist Bulgaria would Moscow consider renewal of the friendship agreement. By the spring of 1947, many Turks feared possible Soviet armed intervention. Neighboring Greece was also in danger of losing its independence to Communist guerrilla forces inside the country. To prevent the impending disaster, President Truman asked Congress in March 1947 to approve a massive economic and military aid program to the beleaguered nations. A 400-million-dollar bill was approved in May and 100 million dollars immediately allocated to Turkey. The Truman Doctrine became part of America's policy to contain Russia and was its first major peacetime Middle East commitment, an initial step toward United States acceptance of what had been the historic British role throughout the region.

By 1949 Turkey had become a major American responsibility and was included among the sixteen recipients of assistance from the European Cooperation Administration. Turkish military assistance in the Korean War from 1950 on made it a valued ally in the Western defense system. Eagerness to participate on the Western side made Turkey the Middle Eastern cornerstone against Soviet expansion. Massive economic, technical, and military assistance programs soon resulted in an influx of American missions to help the country build a modern army and modern highway, railroad, and communication systems. After 1952 the Eisenhower administration encouraged Turkey to ally itself with the West in NATO and with Iraq, Iran, Pakistan, and Great Britain in the Baghdad Pact for defense of the Middle East.

The vacuum created by British evacuation from Iran after the war also attracted Soviet intervention. In the north, Russian troops had already moved in to back a Communist seizure of Azerbaijan province during 1945 and the establishment of a Soviet-type Kurdish Republic in Mahabad. Troops sent by the shah to repress these revolts were kept out by the Red army. Iran's appeal to the United Nations was of little direct help. Russia finally agreed to pull out of Iran in April 1946 as a result of international opinion, diplomatic counterpressures, and, perhaps most importantly, an agreement on the part of Iranian prime minister Ahmad Qavam to establish a Soviet-Iranian company to exploit the oil in the north and to appoint three pro-Communists as cabinet ministers. Russian troops finally left Iran in May 1946, two months after the deadline stipulated in the wartime agreement of 1942. With Russian pressure removed, the Iranian parliament felt free to reject Qavam's oil agreement and passed legislation banning concessions to any foreign power. After the departure of Soviet troops, the shah's forces reoccupied Azerbaijan and the Kurdish areas.

A torrent of Communist propaganda flooded Iran in retaliation for parliament's action. Tensions reached a breaking point in the spring of 1949 when Russian intervention again seemed imminent. To deter Moscow, the United States immediately increased the small-scale aid initiated under the Truman Doctrine. Iranians, however, complained that the assistance was inadequate. American reluctance to increase it substantially was caused by awareness of extensive corruption and malpractice within the Iranian government.

Iranian nationalists led by Muhammad Mosaddeq pressed parliament in March 1951 to nationalize the Anglo-Iranian Oil Company. The "victory over imperialism" so enhanced Mosaddeq's popularity that the shah was forced to appoint him prime minister within a few weeks. For the next three years, the nationalist government devoted most of its efforts to fighting the oil company. The shah himself was forced to leave the country. Intervention by the United Nations and the International Court failed to end the dispute. Nor did American conciliation, requested by both sides, calm the nationalists. President Truman's personal ambassador, W. Averell Harriman, was unable to reopen negotiations between the company and the Iranians. As the controversy dragged on, Western-controlled oil companies organized a boycott of Iranian oil and gradually replaced it with supplies from elsewhere. There seemed little hope for other than a pyrrhic victory, and the loss of revenue began to have a telling effect on the national economy; Mosaddeq's intransigence in the end cost him the loss of political power. Thus, despite Mosaddeq's popularity with the average Iranian, the army, with support and assistance from the United States Central Intelligence Agency, replaced him with a government favorable to the shah, who was now able to return and renewed negotiations.

The dispute was settled early in 1954 by forming a consortium of major Middle Eastern oil-producing companies. The Anglo-Iranian Oil Company (renamed British Petroleum in 1954) retained the largest share of 40 percent; Royal Dutch Shell obtained 14 percent; the California Standard, Gulf, New Jersey Standard, Socony-Vacuum (Socony Mobil), the Texas oil companies, 8 percent each (later reduced to 7 percent each to provide shares for independent American firms); and the French Petroleum Company, 6 percent. The consortium was to extract, refine, and market the oil for the National Iranian Oil Company, which would receive half the profits. Compensation would be paid to the Anglo-Iranian Oil Company by the government from its profits in the company. The consortium also agreed to employment of a number of Iranians in important positions in the company, a concession that helped mollify Iranian feelings.

Relations between the shah's government and the West steadily improved after the consortium agreement; American economic, technical, and military aid was renewed; and Iran was invited to join the Baghdad Pact in October 1955. Foreign troops were no longer present; British influence had been replaced by American; and Iran was now supported in resisting its traditional enemy, Russia, by an alliance within the Western defense system. To counterbalance growing American influence in Iran, the shah sought closer ties with the USSR, including mutually beneficial trading and technical agreements, air service between Tehran and Moscow, negotiations for Soviet oil exploration, and even Russian arms supplies. When prospects of British departure from the Persian Gulf became increasingly evident in the late 1960s, the shah asserted Iran's claims to the Gulf and openly voiced his aspirations to "fill the vacuum" left by Western departure (see also chapter 17).

The United States also replaced Great Britain in most of the Arab world after World War II. However, the strong support received by the Zionist cause from both the American government and the American public in the Palestine dispute seriously compromised United States standing with the Arabs. President Truman's immediate recognition of Israel in May 1948, and the massive technical and economic aid rendered to the new country, embittered the Arab nationalists. Their suspicions were not allayed by the continued United States alliance with France and Great Britain, the two most mistrusted Western nations. Although the Soviet Union also was among the first nations to recognize Israel, its friendly attitude toward the Zionists soon changed, and Soviet policy gave full backing to Arab nationalist aspirations, aware that this move would prove a source of embarrassment to the West.

Until 1952, little attention had been given in the United States to the strategic importance of the Arab world. The Eisenhower administration attempted to alter the trend when Secretary of State Dulles went to the Middle East to lay the groundwork for an Allied Middle East Command. The plan was intended as part of the global strategy to contain the spread of communism. There was little receptivity to the containment policy in the Arab world. Instead, a strong undercurrent of neutralism flowed through the region. Nationalist leaders felt that their interests were at cross purposes with the principal members of the Western defense system—the United States, Great Britain, France, and Turkey. These nations all seemed more favorably disposed to Israel than to the Arabs; indeed, all seemed hostile to the interests of Arab nationalism in the Middle East.

Egypt, which was to have been the cornerstone of a Middle Eastern defense plan, turned down the Dulles proposals because its leaders felt that by joining a Middle East defense organization they would be compromising their own freedom of action. Furthermore, neutralism was beginning to gain wide popularity among Arab nationalists, just as it was among Asian nationalists who believed that too close an identification with either one of the great power blocs would undermine their national sovereignty. Because of this turn of events, Dulles conceived the "northern tier" scheme. Turkey, Pakistan, Iraq, and Iran would become the defensive bulwark against communism. They were joined by Great Britain in the Baghdad Pact in 1955, with headquarters at that Iraqi capital. Iraq's membership in the Baghdad Pact was significant because it was the only Arab nation to join the "northern tier" organization and because of its strategic location, between Turkey and Iran, only a few miles below Russia's southern border. The success of Secretary of State Dulles in persuading the Iraqi government to cooperate could be attributed to the influence of Nuri Said, Iraq's strongly pro-Western political leader, who since the 1920s had committed himself to a policy of solidarity with Great Britain in maintaining the British Empire as a bulwark of stability in the Middle East.

While the United States fully backed the pact members with political and material assistance and was affiliated with several of its subcommittees, it refrained from full membership lest it antagonize other Arab nations, principally Egypt, Iraq's main rival. After Iraq withdrew from the pact following the revolution in 1958, the organization's headquarters were shifted to Turkey and its name changed to Central Treaty Organization (CENTO). Within a few years the organization lost any effectiveness and disappeared from the Middle East scene as a significant factor.

The American position improved somewhat after 1952 because of Washington's mediation in settling Anglo-Egyptian differences. But there was little stability in United States-Arab relations. They constantly fluctuated between hot and cold. When Egypt's revolutionary government failed to obtain weapons from the United States in 1954–1955, the Egyptians negotiated an arms agreement with Communist Czechoslovakia. Extensive military and economic assistance began to flow into Egypt from several Communist countries. Even Syria, which had at first been reluctant to take any foreign assistance, now accepted massive aid from the Soviet Union. Fears of the close ties between Egypt and the Communists so embittered Secretary of State Dulles that he precipitously cancelled negotiations with Egypt for American assistance in Egypt.

After the British, French, and Israeli invasion of Egypt in November 1956, the United States took a strong position in opposition to them at the United Nations, demanding their withdrawal. Early in 1957 President Eisenhower called upon the United States Congress to make available additional funds for special military and economic assistance to Middle Eastern nations threatened by "international communism." He was given sanction to spend up to 200 million dollars in already appropriated foreign aid funds for this purpose, and American aid was promised to any nations in the area that sought help because they were so threatened. This so-called Eisenhower Doctrine did little to win Arab sympathy, however, since most Arab nationalists regarded it as merely another device to extend "American imperialism," and especially because it made no reference to a threat from either Israel or any Western "imperialist" power.

Arab bitterness at the West—because of its support for Israel, because of long memories of the British and French administration of their Middle East mandates as though they were colonies, and because of the recent Anglo-French-Israeli attack on Egypt—facilitated Soviet advances. Moscow used every opportunity to press its cause. At the United Nations, Moscow backed the Arab position on major Middle Eastern issues concerned with Palestine, colonialism, and evacuation of foreign troops. Additional economic and military aid was pumped into Egypt and Syria in large quantities, and in smaller amounts into Yemen.

By 1958 anti-Western sentiment and the spread of Arab nationalist fervor symbolized by President Nasser brought a new series of crises. When Egypt and Syria were joined in the United Arab Republic in February of that year, enthusiasm in the neighboring Arab countries was overwhelming. Lebanese Arab nationalists were stirred to revolution against their pro-Western government. In Jordan and Iraq nationalist plots were undertaken to destroy the Hashemite regimes that were thought to be dominated by politicians who were "tools of Western imperialism." The antimonarchists succeeded in July in overthrowing Iraq's pro-Western regime and in replacing it with a republic. American troops sent to Lebanon—at the request of that country's President Chamoun under the terms of the Eisenhower Doctrine—and British forces flown into Jordan at that king's request—stymied nationalist coups in those two nations (see chapters 12 and 13). The foreign troops remained until the end of 1958, when relative stability returned to both Jordan and Lebanon. Communist influence in Iraq infiltrated the government, giving the Arab world its first direct experience with Soviet penetration. Until 1958 there had been direct contact only with British, French, and American "imperialism"; thus there had been little concern about Soviet influence even among most conservative leaders. The experience in Iraq developed the first strong Arab antipathy to Soviet maneuvers and aroused the first sentiment for a genuinely neutral foreign policy. Gradually Egypt, Syria, and Iraq shifted their pro-Soviet policies toward alliance with neutralist nations such as India, Indonesia, and Yugoslavia. By 1962 Nasser was again seriously considering approaching the United States for economic assistance. But Arab-American relations never reached an even keel. Complicated by continued American support for Israel, by the growing leftist tendencies of Arab nationalism, and by increased demands for an independent Arab role in foreign affairs, relations between the United States, the UAR, and other Arab radical regimes slowly deteriorated. These relations were dealt their most severe blow by Arab defeat in the Six-Day War of June 1967 when the armies of Egypt, Jordan, and Syria were crushed by Israel. As Israel's friend, the United States was held responsible, in large measure, for the defeat, although it played no direct or active role in the fighting. Arab defeat failed to produce peace or security for Israel. On the contrary, it stimulated the birth of a Palestine Arab guerrilla movement whose activities soon escalated into renewed fighting along all of Israel's expanded frontiers. Within months of the war, the Soviet Union replaced most of the war material lost by Egypt. Thousands of Soviet military advisers and technicians also came to Egypt's assistance with the result that the United States found itself, as Israel's chief supplier of war planes, moving toward confrontation with the Soviet Union. After the June 1967 war, Moscow not only stepped up its military assistance to the UAR, but greatly expanded its Mediterranean fleet and acquired special privileges for its naval operations in several Arab ports. The buildup of Soviet strength in the area was in reality, not a new "intrusion," but a forceful reassertion of centuries-old Russian interests in an area considered vital to Russian security and commerce. As seen from the West, the Soviet buildup threatened the eastern wing of NATO and was evidence of growing militancy. The buildup, either directly by the USSR, or by proxy on the part of the United States through Israel, was an integral aspect of the bipolar competition between the two superpowers for spheres of influence. Soviet buildup in the Mediterranean and Arab East was seen by some as a challenge to American intervention in Southeast Asia, especially since it occurred at a time when American policy in Indo-China was being subjected to critical evaluation both at home and abroad.

The dangers of a superpower confrontation in the Middle East became apparent as escalation of fighting along the Suez Canal between Israel and the UAR threatened to involve Russia and the United States in support of their respective clients. In August 1970 both powers persuaded Israel and the UAR to renew the 1967 cease-fire and to enter peace negotiations through the United Nations. Although Israel and the United States accused the UAR and Russia of violating the renewed cease-fire agreement by installing Soviet anti-aircraft missiles in the Suez Canal cease-fire zone, negotiations continued through the superpowers to "rectify" the violations and to prevent another dangerous outbreak of Arab-Israeli conflict.

The tenuous cease-fire lasted until October 1973 when the fourth Arab-Israeli war broke out. In their surprise attack on Israel, Egypt and Syria hoped to reverse the ignominious defeat of 1967 and to regain the Arab lands lost then. The war lasted longer than expected, nearly three weeks, and ended with Israel on the offensive. For the first time Arab armies successfully drove the Israelis back from their front-line positions along the Suez Canal and in the Syrian Golan Heights. When the war was brought to a halt by American and Russian intervention, the Israelis had driven wedges into the Arab lines, recapturing some of the territory they had lost. Egypt and Syria considered their advances a great victory, but the Israelis did not regard the outcome as a defeat even though their casualties were prohibitive, with some 3,000 dead. The costs of the war reached tens of billions of dollars. The three weeks of combat used the equivalent of about one year's GNP for each of the contestants. Battles fought were larger than any since World War II, destroying thousands of tanks and planes, more than were in the arsenals of any NATO country other than the United States.

As the battles raged back and forth in Sinai and Golan the United States and Russia each supplied their respective clients through massive airlifts. Neither Arabs nor Israelis would have been able to continue the struggle without their big-power supplier. Once again the war brought Soviet-American relations to a precarious balance. When Moscow threatened to intervene in Egypt's behalf to prevent a disastrous defeat, Washington issued an alert that sparked world attention and apprehension. Russia did not directly intervene and the two superpowers imposed another cease-fire in the region through the United Nations.

In the aftermath of the war they convened a Middle East Peace Conference at Geneva in December 1973. But it met only two days, then deferred further action for several years. Through the intercession of U.S. secretary of state Henry Kissinger disengagement agreements were signed between Israel and Egypt and Syria. As a result of the two-phased disengagement with Egypt, one agreement signed in 1974 and a second in 1975, Israel withdrew from substantial parts of Sinai. This made it possible for Egypt to reopen the Suez Canal which had been closed since 1967. In exchange for Israel's withdrawal, Egypt permitted shipment of cargoes to Israel on non-Israeli ships. Both Israel and Egypt received large amounts of economic assistance from the United States and Israel was guaranteed several billion dollars in American military assistance. A separate disengagement agreement was signed under Secretary Kissinger's auspices between Israel and Syria, calling for the former's withdrawal from small areas in the Golan.

After the Kissinger "shuttle" diplomacy from one Middle East capital to another during 1974–1975, relations between the United States and the major Arab states greatly improved. Diplomatic relations were restored between the United States and Egypt and Syria, and the presidents of these nations visited each other. The credibility of the United States as "honest broker" in the Arab-Israel conflict was restored.

Saudi Arabia was brought directly into the negotiations because of its large scale economic assistance to Egypt and Syria. Without Saudi oil revenues, it would have been impossible for the two Arab confrontation states to finance the purchase of Soviet weapons with which they fought the October war. Furthermore, Saudi Arabia, as the world's major oil exporter, called the tune in use of petroleum as a weapon during the October war. The weapon was used as a double-edged sword; it financed the war for the Arabs, and an Arab oil boycott against Western countries sympathetic to Israel was a major factor in altering diplomatic positions of several European countries.

As relations improved between the United States and Egypt, they deteriorated between Egypt and Russia. Egypt's President Sadat charged that after the October war the Soviet Union reneged on promises of aid, refusing to resupply his country with parts and equipment lost in the fighting. Soviet technicians were withdrawn in larger numbers from Egypt, as the two former friends exchanged acrimonious charges. Deterioration of relations between Moscow and Cairo also affected relations between Egypt and Syria, and the strong alliance that gave them so great an advantage in October 1973 was weakened. The situation was saved by Saudi Arabia in 1976 when it used its financial clout to halt the inter-Arab fight.

Changes in the Middle East balance of power were accentuated by Egyptian president Anwar Sadat's peace initiatives in 1977. After a dramatic and surprise visit to Jerusalem during November 1977, Sadat opened direct peace negotiations with Israel, establishing the first direct Arab contact with the Jewish state since it was established in 1948. Lengthy discussions between Egypt and Israel facilitated by the United States as a third partner led to the Egyptian-Israeli peace treaty signed at Washington, D.C. in March 1979. The treaty was followed by Israel's return to Egypt of all the Sinai peninsula seized in the 1967 war and by normalization of diplomatic relations between the two countries. Embassies were opened in each other's capitals; trade, commercial, cultural, and tourist exchanges were initiated as Egypt became the first Arab country to end the thirty-year boycott and blockade of the Jewish State.

The basis for negotiations between Egypt and Israel was provided by U.S. president Jimmy Carter at the presidential retreat in Camp David near Washington during 1978. The Camp David agreements included a proposal submitted by Israel's prime minister, Menachem Begin, for Arab autonomy in Gaza and the West Bank, which were among the territories seized by Israel in the 1967 war. Despite successful conclusion of the peace treaty, negotiations for autonomy were long and arduous, frequently causing acrimonious tensions between Israel and Egypt and the U.S. Egypt perceived autonomy as a step toward self-government by the Arab inhabitants of the occupied territories, whereas the Begin government vowed that Gaza and the West Bank (Judea and Samaria) would become integral parts of the Jewish state because of their historic ties with Israel.

Relations between Egypt and the rest of the Arab world were also strained because of the peace treaty. Egypt was expelled from the Arab League in 1979 and its members were divided among moderate and fervent critics of Sadat. After his assassination in 1981, several Arab governments began to relax their boycott of Egypt, but the diplomatic balance was thrown askew in 1982 by Israel's invasion of Lebanon. The invasion was aimed at destruction of the Palestine Liberation Organization and its bases in Lebanon. Notable was the lack of any strenuous Soviet or Arab action to counteract Israel's military activity or to assist the PLO, despite nearly universal diplomatic condemnation of the invasion.

U.S. president Ronald Reagan used the occasion of the Palestinian defeat and PLO departure from Beirut to announce a more decisive and clear-cut American policy in the Arab-Israeli dispute. He called for a cessation of further Israeli settlement in the West Bank and Gaza, establishment of "full autonomy" under Jordanian supervision for the Arab inhabitants rather than an independent Palestinian state, and negotiations for an "undivided" Jerusalem.

While the Begin government categorically rejected the plan, it received the sympathetic attention of several Arab governments and some PLO leaders. Even the leaders of Israel's Labor opposition expressed willingness to discuss Reagan's plan as a basis for peace. If Reagan could back up his proposals with concrete actions, it seemed that he might re-establish some of the American credibility lost as a result of deterioration in the U.S. diplomatic position following the 1979 revolution in Iran and the political upheaval in the Arab world caused by the Egyptian-Israeli peace treaty and the invasion of Lebanon.

Use of the oil weapon in 1973 was a major turn in relations between the Middle East and the West. For the first time, contrary to expectations of most Westerners, the Arab states were able to unite. By combining the military prowess of non-oil producing states such as Egypt and Syria, with the economic power of the oil producers including Saudi Arabia, Kuwait, and the United Arab Emirates, political influence flowed from the Middle East toward the West. Iran, a non-Arab state, neutral in the Arab-Israel conflict, used the occasion to raise oil prices.

Convergence of oil shortages caused by the boycott with a five-fold price increase seemed to restore some of the political balance in favor of the Middle Eastern countries. The price increase seriously jeopardized development efforts in many Third World countries, which became increasingly dependent on the Middle East. Repercussions of these events were felt inside the region and the world at large. Internally, extensive development projects costing billions of dollars were initiated in the oil producing countries. Both Iran and Saudi Arabia stepped up their armament programs, acquiring billions of dollars' worth of new weapons. To balance the outflow of capital from Western countries, they sent the latest, most sophisticated weapons to the Middle East, starting a dangerous arms race in the area. Convergence of all these events gave the Middle East a new and central importance in world politics.

There were 400 years of unbroken contact between the Western world and the Middle East by the 1980s, going back to the first commercial contacts between the Ottoman Empire and European merchants. Initially, relations were on an equal footing, but as Ottoman power declined, the West used commerce as an entering wedge for political domination of the region. At the end of the Napoleonic wars, Ottoman weakness was so great that only Western fear of Russian expansion kept the empire alive as a buffer region. For the next century and a half, Great Britain was the dominant power within the region, striving to uphold the *status quo*. Russia, a dynamic and expanding new power, constantly sought to break into the area through Turkey and Iran. France, Austria-Hungary, Germany, and Italy played lesser roles down to World War I, at which time the German and Austrian defeat and the Russian Revolution caused these former great powers to lose their Middle Eastern interests and holdings. By the end of World War II, Great Britain and France were also no longer in a position to retain strong imperial outposts in the Middle East because of their loss of military and political power and their postwar economic problems. Only a revived Communist Russia remained as a significant force, and only a strong America was capable of preventing the region from becoming Communist dominated.

A new third force, modern nationalism, became an equally significant factor by the 1950s. By nature it was volatile and unpredictable, at times forming alliances with the Soviet Union and native Communists, at other times combating Soviet influences with the same tenacity with which it had struggled against Western imperialism. The new third force was a reaction against Western dominance as well as a new awakening to the value of indigenous cultures.

Until the eighteenth century, Middle Easterners had viewed Westerners as inferior beings. Living upon the memories of the Arab and Ottoman conquests, they had regarded Islam as the superior civilization. The Ottomans first awakened to their own inner weaknesses in the century following their defeat at Vienna in 1683. When the Ottomans were humiliated by Russia in the great war of 1768–1774, Ottoman rulers began to re-evaluate their own civilization: "Till then," observes Arnold Toynbee, "the Turks had thought of the Russians as country cousins of the Turks' own despised Eastern Orthodox Christian Greek and Bulgarian subjects; and now the Turks had suffered a crushing defeat at these rustic Russians' hands because the Russians had mastered the Western military technique."[3]

Throughout the nineteenth and early twentieth centuries, attempts were made to "catch up" with the West, but progress was only superficial. Middle Eastern leaders assumed great interest in Western parliamentary institutions, legal codes, political systems, and even the Western way of life, but never succeeded in more than copying external forms. Only the very top of the social pyramid was affected. The great mass of peasants in the Middle East lived as they had for centuries, unaffected by contact with the West. Only after the first tremors of modern nationalism, with its broad popular base, began to shake Middle East societies was there anything like a genuine mass awakening. During the 1950s and 1960s education from the lower levels up through university became available to larger numbers of people. Expanding educational systems sensitized millions of people to international political affairs, opening the region to a political mobilization that set in motion fundamental changes in society. By the 1970s, the "oil revolution" was also beginning to undermine the old order. In the major cities of the oil-producing countries class distinctions between rich and poor, the politically powerful and the impoverished, were becoming intensified as they never had before. Oil money, a new fourth force, threatened to bring not only technological change, but social and economic upheaval such as the countries of the region had never seen.

NOTES

1. J.C. Hurewitz, *Diplomacy in the Near and Middle East,* vol. II, p. 26.
2. George Lenczowski, *The Middle East in World Affairs,* Ithaca, 1952, p. 165.
3. Arnold Toynbee, *The World and the West,* New York, 1953, p. 20.

6   Arab Nationalism

Hans Kohn, the historian of modern nationalism, observed that the Middle East was entering

> an epoch in which nationalism is the highest and most vitally symbolic social and intellectual form and sets its stamp upon the whole era. A few years back religion was the determining factor in the East. Nationalism is not ousting religion, but more or less rapidly it is taking a place beside it, frequently fortifying it, beginning to transform and impair it. National symbols are acquiring religious authority and sacramental inviolability. The truth which men will defend with their lives is no longer exclusively religious, on occasion even it is no longer religious at all, but in increasing measure national.[1]

Until the late nineteenth century, communal identity in the East had little to do with territorial boundaries, but was religious under the Ottoman millet system in which members of each faith belonged to a socioreligious community. Loyalties transcending religion were unknown. Thus Muslims, Christians, and Jews often lived side by side within a single town, each group under the jurisdiction of its own clerical hierarchy, each governed by its own religious law. Muslims owed allegiance to the sultan-caliph; Jews to the grand rabbi; and Christians to their respective patriarchs. Non-Muslim community leaders were responsible to the sultan or his duly constituted representatives. Since communal and religious loyalty were indivisible there was little concern about loyalty to the state. An Ottoman subject was regarded abroad and by his fellow Ottoman subjects as a Christian from the Levant, a Jew from Salonika, or a Sunni from Tripoli, hardly ever as an Ottoman citizen.

The symbols of group identity were religious—the cross, the Koran, the Torah, some holy site, the tomb of a martyr, a saint, a patriarch, or the scene of some ancient religious event that had become part of the folklore. Sometimes group identification was, as in medieval Europe, with a village, town, or city. Religious groups or tribes would contend for control of local areas, or even a large region of a country. "Religious-national" loyalty was as fierce as modern "territorial nationalism," frequently flaring into bitter warfare among neighboring groups of different faith. Feuds might continue for centuries, often lasting well into the modern era, long after the point under dispute had been forgotten.

Modern nationalism still incorporates many religious symbols, as Professor Kohn has indicated, but it has often used them for its own purposes; thus their original significance is often lost. In part, modern Middle Eastern nationalism was a reaction of the Muslim world to its own political degeneration, an awakening to its own weakness, an attempt to remedy its shortcomings by use of the latest imported Western ideologies.

ARAB NATIONALISM AND THE LITERARY REVIVAL

Of the four or five principal examples of Middle Eastern nationalism flourishing at mid-twentieth century—Turkish, Israeli, Iranian, Kurdish, and Arab—the latter is most extensive, volatile, and dynamic, covering a larger part of the area than the others because of the greater spread of Arab culture throughout the region.

During the four centuries of Ottoman domination, Turkish and Arab civilizations blended many institutions. Beneath the surface of Turkish administration, Arab culture and language continued to exist. Arabs and their language played important roles in the Ottoman administration. Arabic was the language of the Koran and the mosque. The backbone of Ottoman government was the sacred Sharia law which could not be mastered without a thorough knowledge of Arabic. Al-Azhar University, founded during the tenth century in Cairo, and the Sunni religious schools at Damascus, Tripoli, and Aleppo—where many of the ulema were trained—were still Arab during the Ottoman period. The religious and legal officials appointed by the Ottoman government throughout the empire were mostly Arabs. In the capital, the highest religious dignitary, the sheikh ul Islam, was usually an Arab. So important was his office that its sanction was required to remove the sultan. Arab troops and high ranking officers distinguished themselves in battles for the Ottoman Empire. Arabs became prime ministers, generals, and governors; they were in all ranks of the state services. They generally shared with the Turks the rights and responsibilities of government without any racial distinction.

Ottoman control over the Arab provinces of the empire varied in form and intensity throughout the four-century Ottoman era. When local sheikhs and amirs became fully autonomous, paying only formal homage to the Ottoman (often Turkish) pashas sent to govern them, the sultan's suzerainty became no more than a shadow. In Lebanon, Palestine, and Iraq, local Arab rulers carved nearly independent principalities for themselves. When Ibrahim, son of Muhammad 'Ali, the Albanian ruler of Egypt during the first half of the nineteenth century, conquered Syria, he introduced reforms regarded as the beginning of the country's modern age. Ibrahim has been called by some admirers the founder of modern Arabism. His emphasis on education contributed substantially to the Arab revival. In 1831 he permitted French Jesuits, who had departed during the French revolutionary era, to return and open a number of schools; later, in 1875, they founded the Université de St. Joseph, which attained a rank second only to that of the famed American University of Beirut. The American Presbyterian mission that arrived in 1820 imported its own Arabic press as an aid to educational activities. By 1860 they operated thirty-three schools with a thousand students; and in 1866 they opened the Syrian Protestant College, which subsequently became the American University of Beirut.

Introduction of Arabic printing presses was vital to the nationalist movement in stimulating intellectual activities, reawakening interest in the Arab classics and medieval Arab intellectual accomplishments. Only after Arab presses began to turn out modern literary and scientific works in Istanbul in 1816 and in Cairo in 1822 was there a real Arabic literary revival.

Ibrahim succeeded where Napoleon failed because he was not regarded as an outsider. He was a Muslim and an Easterner whom the people regarded as one of themselves. While commanding his father's armies in Arabia, Ibrahim concluded that the empire he and his father dreamed of could be more solidly supported by a regenerated Arab people. Ibrahim's army proclamations frequently reminded his troops of ancient Arab glories. The victories of his military forces, largely recruited from poor rural families, were a great source of pride to the masses, because hitherto the downtrodden peasants had come to regard themselves without self-respect.

Muhammad 'Ali's dreams of empire were frustrated by the European powers in 1840 before mass sentiment could be rallied to support the idea of a nation. The concept of nationalism was still beyond the comprehension of the poverty-stricken villagers and townsmen. Their emphasis was still on religion, and all true believers were considered equal members of the great confraternity. Although Ibrahim failed to arouse general enthusiasm, his interest in education sparked the intellectual awakening that gave birth to the first genuine Arab nationalist movement.

By mid-century, there were three centers of Arab intellectualism—Cairo, Beirut, and Damascus. The Arab renaissance in Beirut was mostly Christian led, working in close association with American missionaries there. The latter helped Nasif Yazeji and Butrus Bustani, both Christians, to form the first Arab Society of Arts and Sciences in 1847, where papers were read on learned subjects. Following the American precedent, the Jesuits established the Oriental Society in 1850. The greatest obstacle to forming genuinely Arab associations was Druse and Muslim suspicion of Christian missionary ties with these first groups. An attempt to overcome this handicap resulted in the Syrian Scientific Society founded in 1857. Its activities received a temporary setback at the time of the intercommunal massacres in 1860 (see chapter 4), but the group was reconstituted and received Ottoman recognition eight years later. The society became the first established as an "Arab" group without any religious associations. In an environment in which nearly all community associations and activities were based on religion, this secular organization was indeed a radical departure. It was probably the first group that truly manifested an "Arab" consciousness in modern times and the first group in which non-Muslims were truly on a level equal to followers of the Prophet.

Simultaneously, a number of intellectuals influenced by Jamal al-Din al-Afghani in Cairo during the 1870s worked for an Islamic revival. Although born in Iran, al-Afghani had acquired his name from youthful residence in Afghanistan. Subsequently he was active as a leader in Iranian, Turkish, and Egyptian political movements. At first the rulers of these areas warmly welcomed him, but they each came to reject him when they began to fear his influence and popularity. Al-Afghani wanted to revive Islam and introduce modern concepts into it, in other words to free it from the influences of ulema who refused to accept the social changes of the nineteenth century. He preached that freed from the stultifying ideas of the ulema, Islam could make the Muslim world great once again. Islamic beliefs did not in themselves inspire rejection of modern science, he contended. On the contrary, if understood and used constructively, they would inspire progress. Without intellectual freedom, however, progress was stymied. Subjugation to the West was a principal cause of the Islamic degeneration. Once freed from foreign domination, the whole Islamic world should unite under a caliph who would have sufficient power to be master in his own house, whether he be a Turk, an Egyptian, an Afghan, or an Iranian.

Al-Afghani's ideas strongly influenced other Arab intellectuals such as the Egyptian Islamic reformer and nationalist, Muhammad Abdu, and Abdal Rahman al-Kawakibi, a native of Aleppo who, during the 1880s, fled Abdul Hamid's tyranny to the freer intellectual climate then prevailing in British-controlled Cairo. In *The Nature of Despotism* he analyzed the ruinous effects of tyranny on the people. It corrupted morals; frustrated love of country, friends, and family; and replaced mutual confidence with fear and repression. Because national resources were squandered, misery became the lot of the masses. Religion had been reduced to an opiate that diverted attention from the evils of the day to dreams of an unrealistic future life. Only in intellectual darkness could despotism survive. If rulers were to be restrained from misuse of their power, they would have to be constantly subjected to public scrutiny.

Public education could train the people to resist tyranny, and a mild form of socialism could bring them together by helping the weak.

In another major work, much discussed by later nineteenth-century Arab intellectuals, *The Mother of Towns,* al-Kawakibi wrote an imaginary dialogue among pilgrims gathered in Mecca from all parts of the Islamic world. Concerned by religious, political, and intellectual degeneration throughout the Muslim society, they discussed ways in which a revival and reformation might save the faith. The Arabs, al-Kawakibi believed, had a special role in the Islamic revival because of their historic connection with the religion. While all Muslims should be united under the caliph, the title should belong to an Arab resident of Mecca born to the Prophet's family.

Muhammad Abdu was also exiled, from Egypt, because of his support for the nationalist movement (see chapter 8). He joined al-Afghani in Paris where they edited an influential pan-Islamic journal. Later, after being permitted to return to Egypt, he became grand mufti until his death in 1905. As an Islamic reformer, Muhammed Abdu called for independent judgment in interpreting the Sharia and for introducing more scientific curriculum at al-Azhar University. Although a modernist who also called for renovating the Arabic language, he rejected most Western influences as superficial and corrupting. Rather, Islam should reform by returning to its early and purest dogma. Politically, he called for liberation of Muslim peoples from both Oriental despotism and from European domination. However, rather than through revolution, national liberation and Islamic reform could best be attained by a gradual process, through reason and pragmatic accommodation.

POLITICAL NATIONALISM

No leading Muslim advocated Arab separation from the Ottoman Empire before the end of the nineteenth century. The emphasis was rather on decentralization, on autonomy within a multinational "Ottoman Commonwealth of Nations." The separatists were principally Maronite, Greek Orthodox, or Protestant Arabs, many of whom studied at the American University of Beirut. They were little concerned with an Islamic revival. Instead, they harked back to the language forms and culture of pre-Islamic Arabs. Since the Christians looked to European assistance, their Muslim associates mistrusted them. Several Christian nationalists in Beirut organized the first Arab nationalist secret society in 1875. They surreptitiously distributed revolutionary pamphlets and plastered posters in prominent places. When they realized that Muslim support was essential, leading members of the society joined the nonreligious masonic lodge, where they hoped to contact influential Muslims. The few Muslim notables who also joined the lodge never agreed with their Christian friends, however, and the secret society suspended its activities after only a few years of existence.

George Antonious, historian of the Arab nationalist movement, attaches relatively little importance to this early era. He writes:

> In the main, the period of 'Abdul-Hamid's reign was for the Arab national consciousness one of slow and almost imperceptible growth. Only on two occasions had the infant movement reared its head: once, at the beginning of the reign, with the campaign of the Bairut secret society; and once, in its closing years, when al-Kawakebi had stirred up eddies of agitation. Except for those two manifestations, the movement had lain prone as though in sleep, held down by 'Abdul-Hamid's tyranny and drugged with the opiates of his Arab policy.[2]

When the Committee of Union and Progress (CUP) took over the Ottoman government in 1908 (see chapter 3), the Arabs, and other nationalities as well, believed in their promised era of progress and equality; but by World War I, the Turks had so alienated the non-Turks that they were instrumental in creating fervent nationalist movements. During the first flush of the Young Turk victory over Abdul Hamid II, an Ottoman Arab fraternity was formed in Istanbul calling for unity of all races in loyalty to the sultan. Its purpose was to promote the welfare of the Arab provinces, foster Arabic education, and encourage Arab culture. As a measure of their sincerity, the Young Turks even insisted that the sultan appoint the Arab noble Sherif Husein governor of Hijaz, keeper of the holy places, and prince of Mecca.

Within weeks, however, the era of "fraternity" received its first jolt. Through manipulation of electoral machinery and gerrymandering of districts, the Turks assured themselves control of the new parliament, although they were outnumbered by the Arab population in a ratio of 3 to 2. When the new Chamber of Deputies was constituted, the 60 Arab members were confronted by 150 Turks. In the 40-man Senate, only 3 were Arabs.

The CUP threw to the wind all thoughts of toleration and cooperation after crushing a counterrevolution in 1909. They now expected all groups to become Turkified within a homogeneous Ottoman state. An initial step was to ban all non-Turkish societies, including the Ottoman Arab fraternity.

The Young Turk government, directed by the CUP, reached out for power over the diverse national groups in the empire by stripping local officials of their authority. Some CUP radicals even wanted to abolish Arabic and translate the Koran into Turkish. When the ulema protested, Islam itself was attacked. The more extreme Turanists started a pre-Islamic movement, eulogizing ancient Mongol and Tatar heroes as a weapon against "degenerate Arabism."

At least ten groups opposed to the Turkification program sprang up among Arabs in Istanbul, Damascus, Beirut, Aleppo, Baghdad, and other Arab cities. Some were secret and others were public; all probably worked in some degree of harmony.

The earliest nonsecret society was the Literary Club, established in Istanbul in 1909 as a meeting place for Arab officials, deputies, writers, students, and visitors. The club produced no new ideas, but was rather a clearing house where Arabs from all the empire could meet in a free atmosphere to discuss their mutual problems. Its political influence was acknowledged when the Young Turks turned to its leaders as intermediaries in their disputes with the Arabs.

The best organized and most widely known of the Arab groups was the Ottoman Decentralization party established in Cairo during 1912. Its program called for a multinational, multiracial empire rallied about the Ottoman throne. Each Ottoman province would control its own internal affairs through locally elected representative bodies; Turkish and the language of each local population both would be official; and education would be offered in the local tongue. The society built an elaborate machinery with branches throughout Iraq and Syria and set up close connections with other groups, both secret and public.

An important secret organization was the Young Arab Society, al-Fatat, organized by seven Muslim students in Paris before World War I. No other society, according to Antonius, played as determining a part in the history of the national movement. The members strove for Arab independence within a biracial Turko-Arab Ottoman Empire, along the lines of the Austro-Hungarian dual monarchy. It sought to raise the Arab social and technological level to that of the West. On the eve of the war, the society moved first to Beirut and then to Damascus.

In Beirut in 1913, the interfaith Committee of Reform roused sentiment for Arab autonomy. Public meetings cheered it in Damascus, Aleppo, Acre, Nablus, Baghdad, and Basra. Later in the year when the Young Turks began to suppress the committee and arrested several of its leaders for disloyalty, Beirut shops and offices closed and the press went on strike. Agitation became so great that the government released the leaders and announced acceptance of the committee's proposals, including increasing powers for provincial bodies. But the government's acceptance fell so short of the Reform Committee's expectations that the nationalists suspected merely another drive to strengthen Turkish control.

The first Arab congress of nationalist groups was convened in Paris during June 1913 by al-Fatat. Denial of Arab rights was leading the non-Turkish provinces toward chaos and the danger of foreign intervention, complained two dozen delegates, half of whom were Muslim and half Christian, mostly from Syria, Only two came from Iraq, and three others represented Arab communities in the United States. Besides delegates from al-Fatat, the Ottoman Decentralization party and the Beirut Committee of Reform sent representatives. There was no talk of succession, only of implementing the reforms demanded by the Cairo and Beirut organizations.

The stated objective was an Ottoman government that was neither wholly Turkish nor wholly Arab, one in which all citizens would have equal rights and obligations, whether they were Arab, Turk, Armenian, Kurd, Muslim, Christian, Jew, or Druse.

When Ottoman authorities failed to persuade the French government to ban the congress, the Porte decided to negotiate with it. An accord was reached stipulating extensive reforms, but an imperial decree published in August 1913 modified these promises to a considerable degree. Arabic could be used in both primary and secondary schools, but the latter were also required to teach Turkish. No mention was made of using Arabic as an official language or of giving influential positions in the central government to Arabs.

Most nationalists considered the decree a betrayal, although a few, like Hamid al-Zahrawi, who had presided over the Paris congress, were still willing to compromise. Al-Zahrawi was rewarded for his moderation with a seat in the Ottoman senate. He explained his acceptance as a tactical move that would place him in a position from which to persuade the CUP to liberalize its policies.

One of the most colorful Arab nationalists was the Egyptian officer Aziz al-Masri. Early in his career he sympathized with the Young Turks, but he became disillusioned with their overemphasis on Turkish nationalism and therefore joined the Arab movement. Al-Masri was a commander of the Ottoman forces which fought the Italian invasion of Libya in 1912. When his affiliation with Arab underground societies was revealed, the Ottoman authorities sentenced him to execution at a trial for treason carried out during the Libyan campaign. He had become such a popular hero that mass demonstrations and the intervention of prominent figures forced the government to commute his sentence and later to pardon him. At the instigation of the London *Times,* even the British Foreign Office intervened. One of the *Times* editorials warned that "...should the injustice which has already been done to the gallant Arab officer be followed by what would be neither more nor less than a judicial murder, the relations between the Ottoman Government and Egypt would be seriously affected, and probably not only the relations between Turkey and Egypt."[3]

Aziz al-Masri represented a generation of conservative individualists who desired to revive past Arab glories without succumbing to Western influences. The secret group of which he was a prominent member, al-Kahtaniya (named after a legendary Arab hero), advocated a dual Ottoman monarchy. The Arab provinces would become one kingdom with its own parliament, government, and Arab institutions; the Ottoman sultan in Istanbul would rule the other, in addition to wearing the crown of the Arab kingdom, just as the Hapsburg emperor in Vienna ruled both Austria and Hungary. When the Turkification attempts of the CUP ended hopes of this program, al-Masri organized a new secret society, al-Ahd (the Covenant), with similar objectives. Most of its members were Arab officers in the Ottoman army, principally Iraqis.

After the pardon for treason, al-Masri settled in Egypt, later becoming chief of staff in King Farouk's army. (During World War II he collaborated with the group of younger Egyptian officers who later overthrew the monarchy.)

Arab Nationalism during World War I

From the mid-nineteenth century until the Young Turk revolution, only Christian Arabs aspired to independence; the Muslims desired reforms and greater Arab autonomy. The militant Turkification program of the CUP after 1909, however, also made Muslim Arabs aware of their distinctive character within the Ottoman Empire.

During World War I, the various Arab nationalist trends converged into a single independence movement. Many of the leaders were initially conscious-stricken about deserting their fellow Muslims in the Ottoman Empire who supported the Central Powers to join the Christians on the Allied side. Al-Fatat's Higher Committee, for example, promised to assist Turkey in resisting "foreign penetration of whatever kind or form," even though it continued to demand Arab freedom. Aziz al-Masri warned fellow al-Ahd members against the temptations of joining the Europeans. The fear was that insurrection within the empire would lead to foreign conquest.

Most other Arab nationalists, however, broke with the Ottoman government, and leadership of the nationalist movement shifted to Sherif Husein and his sons in Arabia. Months before the outbreak of war, Husein's son Abdullah informed the British consul general in Cairo, Lord Kitchener, that strained relations between the sherif and the sultan were reaching a crisis. If the sultan deposed Husein, Abdullah informed Kitchener, there would certainly be revolution in the Hijaz against the Ottoman Empire because of the sherif's popularity. When Kitchener was appointed secretary of state for war soon after the outbreak of the struggle, he recalled the conversation; Ronald Storrs, British oriental secretary in Egypt, was thereupon instructed to reopen contacts with the Hashemites.

Negotiations between the Arab nationalists and the Allies were conducted through an exchange of letters during 1915 and 1916 between the sherif and Sir Henry McMahon, British high commissioner for Egypt. The Husein-McMahon Agreement formed a military alliance on the basis of a fairly ambiguous political understanding. To prevent delay in an Arab uprising against the Ottomans details were left to be ironed out in the future. Great Britain agreed to support Arab independence in all regions demanded by Sherif Husein, comprising the Ottoman Arab provinces south of Anatolia, including the Arabian peninsula and the regions from the Mediterranean and the Red Sea eastward to Iran and the Persian Gulf. Husein acknowledged

British supremacy in Aden, but questioned McMahon's exclusion of the "two districts of Mersina and Alexandretta and portions of Syria lying to the west of the districts of Damascus, Homs, Hama, and Aleppo [which] cannot be said to be purely Arab...."[4] The sherif insisted that the excluded area was purely Arab since Christian and Muslim Arabs were "both descendants of one forefather." These "minor details" were later to cause much bitterness between the Arab nationalists and the British and figured prominently in the subsequent Palestine dispute.

Husein established contact with the secret al-Fatat and al-Ahd societies through his sons before concluding negotiations with the British. Both secret societies, despite their earlier support of the Turks, were drawn into military action against the Ottomans on the basis of the agreement with McMahon.

The ruthlessness of Jemal Pasha, Turkish-Ottoman governor and commander in chief of Syria, helped goad the Arabs into support of the Allies. At first Jemal Pasha tried to win them over with promises of a program for Arab welfare "more comprehensive than anything you can imagine." Turks and Arabs were to be united as separate nations, under the caliph. "Turkish and Arab ideals do not conflict," he declared. "They were brothers in their national strivings, and perhaps their efforts are complementary...." With this exhortation, Jemal Pasha called the Arabs to a *jihad* (holy war) to defend Islam.

But Turkish promises came too late. Arab national consciousness had gained too much momentum to be deterred by vague offers of freedom or calls to Muslim patriotism. Jemal therefore decided to strike with all his vigor at the Arab leaders. His frenzy was intensified by defeat of an expedition he had sent against the British in the Suez Canal zone during 1915. Treason trials were held at which thirty-four nationalists (twenty-seven of them Muslims) were condemned to death as "traitors" who desired to "sell their country to the foreigner." Hundreds of others were deported to remote parts of Anatolia, and a severe police regime was imposed.

The largest group of Arab "traitors" was executed May 6, 1916, in the public squares of Damascus and Beirut. According to a semiofficial British view: "The effect of Ahmed Djemal Pasha's 'reign of terror' was not only to deprive Syria of almost all possible leaders of revolt, but to increase in the people the spirit of revolt. It crowned seven years of Ottomanising efforts by making Ottomanism impossible for the Arabs."[5]

While Jemal Pasha was executing nationalists in Syria, the Ottomans also decided to reinforce their position in Arabia. Arrival in Yemen of an elite Ottoman brigade under German officers alarmed Sherif Husein, who feared that they would be used against the local population. The threat of military repression in Arabia and the executions in Syria set off the military phase of the Arab revolt. There has been considerable controversy about the effectiveness of this revolt and about the role played in it by Colonel T.E. Lawrence. After the war, Lord Wavell offered the following evaluation:

Its value to the British commander was great, since it diverted considerable Turkish reinforcements and supplies to the Hijaz, and protected the right flank of the British armies in their advance through Palestine. Further, it put an end to German propaganda in south-western Arabia and removed any danger of the establishment of a German submarine base on the Red Sea. These were important services, and worth the subsidies in gold and munitions expended on the Arab forces.[6]

The Arab revolt was by no means a mass movement. There was no widespread civil unrest against Ottoman authority, due partly to Ottoman repression and partly to lack of encouragement from the government of British India. British Indian army officers who occupied Iraq were skeptical of the Arabs' ability to win independence. The viceroy of India regarded the Arab revolt as "a displeasing surprise whose collapse would be far less prejudicial to us than would our military intervention in support of it."[7] Arab independence, he feared, would disrupt plans of the British Indian government to annex lower Iraq and might create unrest among the ninety million Muslims in India who had a sentimental attachment to the Ottoman caliphate.

Post-World War I Arab Nationalism

By the end of World War I, the Arab nationalist movement was divided into diverse currents. Egyptians, deeply involved in their own struggle with Great Britain, did not yet identify with neighboring movements. The Arabian peninsula was divided among numerous sheikhs, amirs, and other tribal leaders, none of whom had significant power. Within the following decade, however, Ibn Saud emerged as the dominant force in Arabia and his Saudi kingdom became the largest and most powerful one there. He defeated Yemen in 1934, but permitted it to retain its independence. Only the threat of British intervention prevented him from attacking other principalities along the Arabian Sea and the Persian Gulf coasts. A separate nationalist movement emerged in Iraq. It had closer ties with the Syrian nationalists than did the Egyptians, but it too remained apart. The heart of the Arab nationalist sentiment and successor to the prewar movements was that of greater Syria— Syria, Palestine, and Lebanon.

Several former secret societies now became political parties. The former Decentralization party became the Syrian Union party, demanding an independent Syria. Al-Fatat changed its name to the Arab Independence party, campaigning for Arab unity. It was supported by Husein's son Faisal, who attempted to direct its activities within an orderly constitutional framework.

A pall of disillusionment fell over all the Arab movements when they discovered that the promises of freedom made during the war were now to be sacrificed to European political claims in the region. President Wilson attempted to modify British and French plans to carve up the area by sending a commission to determine the wishes of the people. Since the other Allies boycotted the commission's activities, Wilson alone sent his two American representatives, from whose names came its title, the King-Crane Commission (see chapter 5).

The arrival of these Americans in Syria in June 1919 encouraged the nationalists, led by former al-Fatat members, to convene a General Syrian Congress in Damascus. It demanded a United Syrian constitutional monarchy under King Faisal to include the area from the Taurus Mountains to the borders of Arabia and from the Mediterranean to Iraq. In support of these nationalists, the commission reported that: "The territory concerned is too limited, the population too small, and the economic, geographic, racial and language unity too manifest, to make the setting up of independent states within its boundaries desirable, if such division can possibly be avoided. The country is very largely Arab in language, culture, traditions, and customs." It also agreed with the congress that Iraq should receive complete independence and that no commercial barriers should be erected between the two Arab nations.[8]

When it became plain in March 1920 that the Paris Peace Conference would reject the King-Crane proposals, the Syrian General Congress transformed itself into a constituent assembly, declared Syria (including Lebanon and Palestine) independent, endorsed a decentralized government, and demanded evacuation of British and French troops. Iraq's independence was also proclaimed, with political and economic union between the two states set as a goal. Within a month the San Remo conference met and completely disregarded the Arab congress decisions, dividing the region into French and British mandates. When King Faisal's Syrian government in the interior refused to cooperate, the French army crushed the nationalists and drove Faisal from the country (see chapter 5).

French and British Policies toward the Nationalists

France followed a divide-and-rule policy by encouraging the separatist aspirations of minorities living in more or less compact geographical blocs. The policy split the Levant into several autonomous regions based on religious differences. Sunni Muslim Arabs comprised about 53 percent of the total Levant population; groups of Christian Maronites lived in the Mount Lebanon region; a somewhat smaller number of Muslim Alawis were settled along the northern Mediterranean (Latakia) shore; Druses held the Jebel (Mount) Druse region of southern Lebanon; Kurds, the Gezira of northeast Syria; and other smaller groups were scattered throughout the whole area. Lebanon was tripled in size during 1920, expanding from the old autonomous Christian province to a state that included predominantly Muslim Beirut, Tripoli, and Sidon; southern Lebanon to the Palestine frontier, with a predominantly Shi'ite population; and the fertile Biqa Valley with mixed

Muslim and Greek Orthodox citizens. In old Lebanon, the Christians had constituted a large majority; in the new state they made up just a little more than half the population and were therefore the more dependent on French protection from political encroachment by the large Muslim minority. The Jebel Druse and Alawi autonomous states were carved out of Syria in 1921 and 1922 respectively. The rest of the country was divided into the autonomous states of Damascus and Aleppo in 1920, but were then reunited five years later.

French efforts to repress or fragment the nationalist movement were less successful than they had hoped. Periodically there were armed uprisings. The 1925 Druse revolt in Syria spread to all the neighboring cities before it was crushed, and Damascus was twice shelled with over a thousand deaths resulting (see also chapters 13 and 14).

The British had to suppress a costly rebellion in Iraq against the San Remo decisions, and Palestine also became a center of nationalist unrest. Protests against the terms of the Palestine mandate, calling for establishment of a Jewish homeland, grew into riots, and between 1936 and 1939, into a full-fledged Arab rebellion. The Palestine and Syrian movements were originally united in local Muslim-Christian associations affiliated with the Syrian General Congress. But when the French destroyed Faisal's independent Syria, the Palestine Arabs formed their own nationalist groups (see chapter 10).

After the demise of the Syrian General Congress, there was little unity among the various Arab nationalists movements. Within each of the European-dominated countries, Arab leaders emphasized local problems, giving little thought to an over-all policy. Not until the eve of World War II, when concerted action was planned on the Palestine problem, were there any joint endeavors worthy of mention. Until then there were no social or economic programs and no success in enlisting mass support for the various political groups formed around individuals. Aside from their personality orientation, the only common denominator of the various movements was their desire to rid the region of Great Britain and France. In Lebanon, some Christian groups were less hostile to French guidance, but they were a minority. Differences among the various leaders had less to do with doctrine or philosophy than with the tactics of timing and methods that they espoused to get rid of the foreigners.

BEGINNINGS OF ARAB UNITY

The Palestine Arab revolt in 1936 fused nationalist policies together in a common front for the first time since the end of World War I. Both Amir Abdullah of Transjordan and the Iraqi foreign minister, General Nuri al-Said, intervened with the British as friends of the Palestine Arab nationalists. Later in 1936, the rulers of Iraq, Saudi Arabia, Transjordan, and Yemen attempted to find a face-saving device for the Palestine rebels. Committees for the Defense of Palestine were organized in various Arab cities. The Damascus committee sponsored a conference of its sister groups at Bludan in Syria during September 1937, and in the summer of 1938 the Parliamentary Defense Committees in Egypt and Syria joined with other groups to form a World Interparliamentary Congress of Arab and Muslim Countries for the Defense of Palestine. Some 2500 participants attended its meetings in Cairo during October 1938. Great Britain signified its recognition of the Arab interests in the Palestine problem when it invited Egypt, Transjordan, Yemen, Iraq, and Saudi Arabia to participate in the 1939 London conferences convened in a last futile prewar effort to reconcile Arab and Jewish differences.

During World War II, rather vague proposals for a "Greater Syria" and for unity of the "fertile crescent" were discussed by Iraqi, Syrian, and Transjordanian leaders. Both plans envisaged some form of Syrian federation or a United Arab State with details left for the future. Iraq's prime minister, Nuri al-Said, spoke of an "Arab League" federating his country with a United Syria. Other Arab nations were not included in the plan, but provisions were made for their future participation.

Unrest also stimulated the abortive wartime coups of Rashid Ali al-Gilani in Iraq and General Aziz al-Masri in Egypt. Although both attempts failed, they made British officials acutely aware of the strong undercurrents of nationalist dissatisfaction. Recognition of this growing nationalist fervor stimulated Foreign Minister Anthony Eden to announce in May 1941 that Great Britain realized that

> many Arab thinkers desire for the Arab peoples a greater degree of unity than they now enjoy. In reaching out towards this unity they hope for our support. No such appeal from our friends should go unanswered. It seems to me both natural and right that the cultural and economic ties between the Arab countries, and the political ties too, should be strengthened. His Majesty's Government for their part will give their full support to any scheme that commands general approval.[9]

The Egyptian government followed Eden's lead in parleys with other Arab governments leading to formation of the League of Arab States in 1945. The Arab League was a loose federation of Egypt, Syria, Lebanon, Iraq, Transjordan, Saudi Arabia, and Yemen. Like the Pan-American Union, it was not a supranational organization; members surrendered none of their sovereignty nor could they be forced to any action except on the unlikely basis of unanimity. Although the organization was less a vehicle for implementing decisions than a platform for discussion of mutual Arab problems, it roused a new common Arab consciousness. Its purposes, according to the League pact, were to strengthen relations among member states; to coordinate policies and effect cooperation to safeguard independence and sovereignty; and to consider, in a general way, affairs of mutual interest. The stated areas of activity included economic and financial affairs, communications, cultural matters, nationality and extradition, social affairs, and health problems. Since the organization was founded, Sudan, Libya, Tunisia, Algeria, Morocco, Kuwait, the People's Democratic Republic of South Yemen, Bahrain, Mauritania, Oman, Qatar, Djibouti, Somalia, United Arab Emirates, and Palestine have also joined.

The British approach to economic policy during World War II helped accelerate inter-Arab cooperation by opening the channels of mutual planning. The Middle East Supply Center was created in 1941 to organize planning of regional economic affairs in cooperation with the several Arab governments. After the war, regional economic, social, and cultural cooperation continued to be maintained on a modest scale through the Arab League. Nonetheless, the initial failure of the League to organize its membership effectively to oppose the Zionists during the Palestine war was a setback from which the League never fully recuperated. Since 1948 it has been discredited in the eyes of many Arab nationalists, and the more aggressive moves toward Arab unity have originated outside the League. For example, the League played no role in the formation of the UAR, a notable attempt in this direction, whatever its fate.

A period of self-analysis by Arab intellectuals followed the loss of their position in Palestine. The Arab defeat by meagre, though well-trained, Jewish forces seemed to many youthful nationalists to point out clearly the ineffectualness of the methods used by the older generation and quite fundamental defects within Arab society. In this way, within a decade after the war, the Zionist victory contributed indirectly to nationalist revolutions in Egypt, Jordan, Syria, Lebanon, and Iraq.

The most radical and pervasive social changes occurred in Egypt where the old regime was totally demolished. Under the leadership of Colonel Gamal Abdel Nasser, intensive efforts were begun in 1956 to reconstruct Arab society along lines never before attempted. Consequently Nasser and the Egyptian revolution came to symbolize a "new nationalism," whose ideology spread throughout the whole Arab East. To some, Egypt's revolution seemed to be the first Arab application of Ataturk's successful principles. Nasser's actions and ideas appealed to the youth who had come into contact with the more radical Western ideologies as students in Europe or America, or who had learned of them from Western periodicals and pamphlets obtained at home. The grand old men of Arab nationalism—such as Mustafa al-Nahas in Egypt, Nuri al-Said in Iraq. Bishara al-Khuri in Lebanon, and Shukri al-Kuwatly in Syria—were no longer respected, for they had lost touch with the new generation. Only the revolutionary regime in Egypt seemed capable of understanding and implementing the appealing new revolutionary doctrines. Nasser's popularity was intense because his government was the first to overthrow a monarchy, one considered the symbol of the old regimes with their social and economic ills. It was the first to attempt extensive reforms that hit directly at the powerful propertied classes; it was the first to propagate the slogans and symbols of socialism and popular democracy and to attack the "exploiting capitalists." When the revolutionary government broke all precedents by purchasing arms from Communist Czechoslovakia in 1955, its popularity grew by leaps and bounds throughout the Arab world. The action was interpreted as the first time an Arab nation had successfully thwarted the Western "imperialists."

During the Afro-Asian conference at Bandung earlier in 1955. Nasser had been raised to leadership with men such as Nehru and Mao Tse-tung. After Bandung, his frequent parleys with Marshall Tito of Yugoslavia, with Prime Minister Nehru of India, and with various African leaders all signified that the Arabs had become important in world affairs because of their own active role rather than merely as someone else's steppingstone to empire. Nationalization of the Suez Canal Company in July 1956 was the climax in Nasser's ascent to leadership, serving even to dwarf the poor military showing Egypt then made when attacked by Israel, Great Britain, and France late in October 1956 (see chapters 5 and 9). Egypt's military defeats in the Sinai peninsula and at Suez were turned to diplomatic victories by the revolutionists. The subsequent technical skill with which the Egyptian Canal Authority operated the waterway was looked upon with pride even by those Arab leaders who disagreed with Nasser's ambitions.

Nasser made extensive use of propaganda, secret agents, and sabotage, but his aggressive stance in foreign affairs proved to be the catalyst that rallied younger Arab nationalists to his revolutionary cause. The slogans of the new Arab nationalism are also those of the Egyptian revolution: republicanism, neutralism, socialism, and Arab unity. Today there are few Arab political parties which do not espouse similar slogans. Since the end of World War II, at least a dozen such groups claim to be socialist, or use the slogans of socialism. They included the Arab Socialist Renaissance (Ba'ath) party, and the Corporative Socialist party in Syria; the Nationalist Socialist and Ba'ath parties in Jordan; the Socialist Party of the Nation and the National Democratic party in Iraq; and the Progressive Socialist and Syrian Nationalist parties in Lebanon, in addition to various Communist movements. In later chapters these new forces on the political scene will be examined in each country separately.

The defeat of Egypt, Jordan, and Syria in the 1967 war with Israel, while a stunning blow to Arab pride, awakened widespread national consciousness, especially among the Palestinians. The anti-Israel virus spread from the Arab East across all North Africa, and ardent Arab nationalists throughout the Middle East and North Africa joined in support of the Palestinian guerrilla movements. Although the guerrilla movements were underground, they soon became a major competitor with UAR president Nasser for the support of national zealots. Their strength increased within two years to a point where they were able to seize control of border areas in Lebanon and what remained of Jordan. However, by 1970 they still had not succeeded in inflicting severe damage on Israel. Their greatest significance was the enthusiasm they aroused among young nationalists from Morocco to Kuwait.

The spread of pan-Arab consciousness was evident in the fervent emotion stirred by plans for unification of the Arab world. The first step was the fusion of Egypt and Syria in the United Arab Republic (UAR) in 1958. Although establishment of the UAR with Nasser as president raised the hopes of all Arab nationalists, the union failed when Syria withdrew in 1961 because of bitter disagreements with the Egyptians who dominated the new state. Talks between Egypt, Syria, and Iraq for a new form of union were revived in the 1960s but produced no practical results. Again, in 1970, after Nasser's death, another attempt was made to federate Egypt (which kept the name of UAR until 1971) with neighboring Libya and Sudan. The latter two nations had joined the war against Israel and had overthrown their old regimes to become "socialist" republics. Despite great differences between the three Arab-African nations in population, resources, and living styles, the federation was viewed as a framework for a larger entity which would eventually include other Arab countries as well. Indeed, soon after the three neighbors formed the new federation, Syria also applied for and was accepted as an associate. (See chapters 9 and 14.)

The greatest weakness of the new Arab nationalism is the failure of most leaders to understand the concepts and slogans they have borrowed from the West. Adoption of "socialism" and "democracy" has been superficial. Egypt's president Nasser told the American Socialist leader Norman Thomas in 1957 that democracy must be established "not in parliaments and slogans," but "in the life of the people." Egyptians, Nasser believed, were not yet ready for the Western democracy that the old regime had "corrupted into a parody of freedom." He insisted that his country would need a long transition period before the people could be trusted with parliamentary institutions as they are used in the West.

Arab nationalist thought is still inchoate and difficult to define. Despite the general trends indicated above, variations in interpretation and objective differences in economic, cultural, and social levels make impossible the attainment of a cohesive Arab national ideology and a unified movement in the near future.

PALESTINIAN NATIONALISM

After the 1967 war Palestine became the focus of Arab nationalism; according to some, the issue of Palestine was the cement which bound it together. Arab defeat sparked interest in the dispute with Israel across the whole Arab world, from Morocco to the Gulf. In the aftermath of Israel's attack on Egypt, Syria, and Jordan, mobs rioted as far away as Algiers and Tunis in North Africa. For the first time in years, there were anti-Jewish manifestations in countries like Morocco and Tunisia, whose leaders were regarded as protectors of Jewish minorities. It was evident that the feelings about Palestine were deep. During the next decade, every Arab Summit Conference, Arab League Assembly, or Third World meeting where the Arabs were represented discussed Palestine. The question was the cause of differences, as well as one which bound the Arabs together.

The Palestinians themselves experienced a new awakening after 1967. The younger generation was disillusioned with their own traditional leaders and the Arab chiefs, movements, and political ideologies in which many of them had placed their confidence after 1948. During the generation after the Arab flight from Palestine in 1948, most Palestinians identified their national aspirations with Nasser, the Baathists, the Arab National Movement, or some other pan-Arab figure or organization. After the defeat in 1967, they turned inward and began to establish their own organizations.

At first there were dozens of separate groups, mostly paramilitary, with the single goal of "liberating the Palestinian homeland." By the late 1960s the Palestinian organizations were reduced to half a dozen of importance. They were generally divided into those organizations whose primary goal was to liberate Palestine and those with larger political and social goals in which Palestine was a part. The largest was *Fatah,* headed by Yassir Arafat, who was also chosen as president of the covering Palestine Liberation Organization (PLO). Fatah's tendencies were at first conservative, with no focus on economic and social goals. Like most of the commando groups in PLO, *Fatah* later moved leftward in its ideology.

Other principal commando groups affiliated with the PLO included the Popular Front for the Liberation of Palestine, led by Dr. George Habash, a Christian Arab who had been a founder of the Arab Nationalist Movement. The PFLP sought not only the liberation of Palestine, but overthrow of most Arab regimes, considering them reactionary and antiquated. Two other Marxist, or quasi-Marxist offshoots of the Habash movement were the Democratic Popular Front for the Liberation of Palestine and the PFLP—General Command. Saiqa (Vanguard of the Popular Liberation War) was established under Syrian patronage and followed the political line of Damascus. The Arab Liberation Front was a similar Palestinian commando group under Iraqi patronage.

Differences among the various commando organizations were not always ideological. Often personal animosities or disagreement over tactics caused splits. At times they clashed in military confrontations as during the Lebanese civil war in 1975–1976.

The PLO was established in 1964 at the first Arab Summit Meeting in Cairo. Originally it was manipulated by the various Arab governments, but after 1967 when Yassir Arafat, leader of *Fatah* became PLO president, it followed a more independent course, frequently at odds with the Arab League States. The PLO became the equivalent of a Palestine government in exile. Its roots were the Palestine National Assembly which convened periodically, usually in Cairo or Damascas, to make general policy for the Palestinian movement. In addition to the commando groups, a variety of other Palestinian organizations were affiliated with the PNC. They included organizations of women, academicians, physicians, lawyers, and workers. The PNC, despite the radical rhetoric of its proclamations, represented bourgeois interests and outlooks rather than those of Palestinian workers and peasants. By 1977 the PLO had achieved international recognition as the vehicle for Palestinian nationalism and the movement had become the major focus of Arab nationalism.

While Arab nationalism is the most pervasive, the most volatile, and the most significant of Middle Eastern nationalisms for the West, other national movements in the Middle East are also important. Those in Turkey, Israel, and Iran will be examined in later chapters (7, 10, and 17).

COMPARISONS OF ARAB AND OTHER
MIDDLE EAST NATIONALISMS

A major aspiration of nearly all nationalist movements in the Middle East is to purify the nation of foreign influences, to create a homogeneous "national type" of Arab, Turk, or Israeli. But before such homogeneity can be attained, there is the need to rid the nation of "imperialists." Ataturk first fought to rid his republic of Greek and other European invaders; the Arabs struggled against France and Great Britain, and today they continue the battle against the Israeli Jews; both Russia and England, and, more recently, the United States, have been the enemy in Iran.

Nearly all Middle Eastern nationalist leaders claim territory from some neighbor. The desire to unite all "national territory" within the borders of a single state and to unify all Arabs, Turks, Israelis, or Iranians under a single flag—so that all may participate in national life and be more effectively controlled by national leaders—creates irredentism. Additional territory and population also add to national prestige and strength. Examples of "Arabia irredentia" are today Iskenderun and Israel. Many Israelis hoped to "redeem" the Hashemite Kingdom of Jordan, Gaza, and the Sinai peninsula; and, indeed, most of these areas were occupied by Israel in June 1967. Iran disputes Iraq for control of the river Shatt al-Arab and claims Bahrain, while Iraq for several years insisted that it owned Kuwait.

Until World War II, the new nationalism had only a middle-class base. In Iran and the Arab world, there were no mass nationalist movements, although street mobs could be worked into frenzied antiforeign riots and uprisings against authority. There were no organizations for mass involvement: no strong labor or peasant movements, no nationwide cooperatives, and really few effective professional, youth, or women's organizations. Leadership of Arab and Iranian nationalist movements was largely controlled by small oligarchies. Ataturk had been somewhat more successful in rallying the masses, due in part to his emphasis on social action. Although Zionist nationalism had strong social motivation, the movement before the growth of Nazism in Germany was relatively small and without the support of world Jewry it later obtained. Hans Kohn writes:

> Nationalism was the intellectual form assumed by the needs of incipient capitalism and the youthful middle class.... In the East nationalism still, or already—according to whether we regard the situation from the standpoint of Europe to-day or of the East in the recent past—meets social and economic needs. Capitalist forms of industry are making their way into the East, money economy and industrialization are taking their place beside barter and agriculture, and a youthful middle class is arising, becoming conscious of its mission and task, and entering upon a struggle against the feudal nobility. In doing so it feels itself to stand not for its own interests alone, but for the whole people, who are beginning to acquire national consciousness. The forms assumed by this economic transformation and social upward trend are similar to those which are familiar in European history; here, too, the middle class speaks the language of nationalism and democracy.[10]

Emerging middle-class interests, such as those of native businessmen and industrialists, frequently clashed with the economic policies of the foreign rulers. The "open door" in the British and French mandates was an invitation to Western economic interests to flood the region with the goods of their already developed industries, thus discouraging the development of nascent local industry. In Egypt, British, French, Italian, Greek, and other Christian and Jewish minorities dominated commerce and industry. Greeks and Armenians in Turkey controlled the economy until the Young Turk Revolution.

The ability of "foreigners" to manipulate politics through pervasive control of the national economy made them the target of the new middle-class opposition. Educated youth, unable to find employment, turned against the "foreigners" and minorities, like the Copts in Egypt, to whom historical circumstance and special relations with occupying powers had given positions of great power and affluence.

Minorities were identified with the *status quo* regimes against which the rising middle class was battling. Not only were minorities an economically privileged group, but they were also sometimes a Trojan Horse used by the imperial power to interfere in domestic affairs, as the Copts were at one time used by the British in Egypt, the Maronites by the French in Lebanon, and the Orthodox Church by Russia.

Thus Middle Eastern nationalism is ambivalent in its treatment of minorities. During World War II, the Turkish government gave official sanction to its bias when it imposed a ruinous capital levy on non-Muslim businessmen. International pressure forced the government to cancel the tax, but only after one of its purposes was accomplished: many sectors of the economy still dominated by non-Muslims finally fell into the hands of either the government or "Turkish Turks." Although there is at present no overt legal discrimination against Jewish and Christian Turkish citizens, only a Muslim is truly regarded as a "Turkish Turk" (see also chapter 7).

Israel makes no pretenses about being other than a "Jewish state," although it has both Christian and Muslim citizens. The United Nations November 1947 partition resolution, Israel's "birth certificate," called it a "Jewish state" and so do the proclamations of its leaders and the prevailing national sentiment. Israel's nationality legislation makes it possible for Jews to become citizens automatically, while non-Jews must be naturalized. Other legislation, without explicitly stated differences between Jews and non-Jews, discriminates against the country's Arab minority. The land of several thousand Israeli citizens was confiscated for "security reasons," that is, because they were Arabs, during and after the Palestine war in 1948.

Before 1952, religious distinctions were less sharply drawn in Egypt. Muslims as well as some Copts and Jews were active in the national resistance to the British. Although there has been an increasing trend toward secularization since the 1952 revolution, non-Muslims are less secure. Life became uncomfortable for Jews during the Palestine war because of the tendency to regard them as sympathetic to Egypt's enemy, the "Jewish state." Many individual Jews in Egypt were closely associated with the British, French, Italian, Greek, and other foreign communities. When nationalist sentiment became inflamed against Israel and the West, it also rose against the Jewish community, finally bringing about a mass exodus after the British, French, and Israeli invasion late in 1956. Within two years, more than 90 percent of the Jews resident in Egypt had left the country and only a tiny remnant remained by 1970.

The position of the approximately two to three million Copts of Egypt also became increasingly insecure after 1956. Although many Copts had been active in the national movement against the British, popular feeling turned against them for the same reasons that it turned against other non-Muslim groups: many had been used by Great Britain in the past; many had attained great affluence and prestige—far beyond their proportion in the population— in the nation's economic life; and many were reluctant to identify with the nationalist revival emphasizing Arab unity and revival of ancient Arab glories.

Religion thus continues to play an important role in Middle East nationalism—much more than it has done in Western movements—for several reasons. Islam is still identified with determined resistance to the invading "Christian" West. The English, French, and Americans are still regarded as part of one great Christian group to be resisted at all costs, just as the Christian West was opposed at the time of the Crusades. Preservation of the Muslim way of life has inspired nationalist groups like the Muslim Brotherhood in the Arab world and the Devotees of Islam (*Fidaiyan-i Islam*) in Iran. In Israel, the Mizrachi party, also adamantly insisted that national life be based on religious conformity.

Even secular nationalists use the symbols of religion. The Arab-Resurrection-Socialist party, which opposes a preferential role for Islam in the modern state, is nevertheless inspired by the desire to return to the Islamic Golden Age. Even secular-minded Israeli nationalists are quite likely to recall the glories of the Old Testament heroes, David and Solomon, and the rise and fall of the ancient Hebrew kingdoms. Street names, army ranks, and other official nomenclature are taken directly from the Bible. Symbols on coins and other national pageantry reproduce Biblical symbolism. Israel's antireligious, leftist Zionist parties extol the Old Testament, using its folklore and heroes to instill Jewish national consciousness. Even atheistic Zionist leaders do not hesitate to base their claim to Palestine on the Biblical accounts of the ancient Hebrews. The national holidays and heroes of secular Israel are mostly of Biblical origin.

While trimming the power of the Muslim hierarchy, Egyptian President Nasser used Islam to enhance the prestige of his revolution. The ulema and institutions such as al-Azhar served the new government well. In *The Philosophy of the Revolution,* President Nasser tells of his

> belief in the possibility of extending the effectiveness of the Pilgrimage [to Mecca], building upon the strength of the Islamic tie that binds all Muslims.... Our view of the Pilgrimage must change. It should not be regarded as only a ticket of admission into Paradise.... It should become an institution of great political power and significance.... When I consider these hundreds of millions [of Muslims] united by a single creed, I emerge with a sense of the tremendous possibilities which we might realize through the cooperation of all these Muslims...enabling them and their brothers in faith to wield power wisely and without limit.[11]

Ataturk attempted to sever his nation's Islamic roots and replace them with a distinctive Turkish past complete with unique symbols, heroes, and history unconnected with those of the Arabs and Islam. A thesis was advanced that the greatest ancient peoples were either Turks or raised from their natural brutishness by Turkish civilization. The new history of the "Hun-Turks" cited Sumerians, Hittites, Huns, and Scythians as direct lineal ancestors. This specious heritage is still recalled in such government institutions at the Eti (Hittite) and Sumer (Sumerian) banks. When the vogue was at its height, infants were given central Asian names like Genghiz, Attila, and Oguz in preference to the Muslim Mehmet, Ahmet, or Ismail.

Revival of ancient, and creation of new, linguistic forms and literature is another device. Ataturk attempted to divorce the Turkish language from its Arab and Iranian roots by purging the language of "foreign" words and replacing Arabic with Latin script. A Turkish linguistic society was formed in 1932 to produce a glossary of "genuine Turkish" terms. Finding it impossible to "purify" the language, the "Sun-Language" theory was improvised "proving" that not only Arabic and Iranian but also many other languages were really of Turkish origin. Since Arabic and Iranian words were thus really Turkish, they would not have to be abolished.

Israeli nationalism strongly emphasizes the revival of Hebrew. Use of the language for other than religious purposes was considered sacrilegious by many Jews until several decades ago. During the late nineteenth and early twentieth centuries, it again became the native language of Palestine's Jews, spoken in schools, offices, and the streets of the country. Today there are airplane tickets, true romance and crime magazines, existentialist poetry, and law books, all in Hebrew.

Revival of Arabic was essential to modern Arab nationalism. The movement grew out of the formation of literary groups intended to bring the classics to popular attention. When the idea took hold, Arab writers began to write their own modern poetry, drama, criticism, and history. A century and a half ago there was no Arabic newspaper. Today there are hundreds of dailies, weeklies, and monthlies and an ever expanding literature on every imaginable subject.

When modern Middle Eastern nationalism was largely a middle-class movement, social action was less emphasized than the revival of history, language, and religion. The situation has radically changed since the 1952 Egyptian revolution. Now the slogans of socialism are increasingly used. The social gospel preached by a few small Arab leftist parties after World War II has been woven into the new nationalism. Possibilities for social mobility are rapidly increasing as individuals from all stations in life ascend the ranks to political power. The effective power, influence, and prestige of the small affluent cliques of notable families is disappearing, and formerly politically inactive rural populations are also becoming involved in nationalism.

The broadened base of Arab nationalism is due in part to the increased political activism of the military. Unlike Israel, where there are a multitude of political, social, labor, women's, youth, and other organizations facilitating popular participation in national life, political organization in the Arab world has been limited to the few. Only the army was a broad-based organization. Until the recent revolutions its top command was held by members of influential families or palace favorites; its junior officers were largely of peasant or lower-middle-class origin. Until the end of World War II, however, these armies were not free agents; they were still under the control of Great

Britain and France. They relied on these Europeans for equipment, training, and leadership. Only since the early 1950s have they become truly free of foreign domination.

Now the Arab military officer has become the effective spokesman for a changing environment. Frustrated by the perversion of parliamentary procedures, he has turned to the *coup d'état*. In Turkey the army also played a significant role. The first two leaders of the Republic, Ataturk and Ismet Inonu, were generals. While both strongly emphasized the civilian nature of their regimes, the army was always a significant factor in the background. Adnan Menderes' dictatorial regime would never have been toppled in 1960 had the army not taken the initiative.

With military men in strategic positions, the struggle to attain armed might becomes another manifestation of the new nationalism. Possession of powerful armies, navies, and air forces becomes a goal in itself, since these are thought of as symbols of prestige and keys to international political power. Even when attainment of the latest supersonic aircraft, heavy artillery, and rockets jeopardizes the national economy, they must be had because of their symbolic importance and the emotional fervor they stir among the street masses. As already noted, when President Nasser successfully concluded the 1955 arms agreement with Communist Czechoslovakia, his prestige rose to an all time high with the masses throughout the Arab world.

Even though hostile to the West, many Middle Eastern nationalists strive to emulate its techniques in industry, public relations, government administration, and other vital aspects of the modern state. By incorporating Western techniques in Eastern society, they hope to acquire the strength that enabled the "Christian" powers to subjugate them. Rapid industrialization with emphasis on heavy prestige plants such as iron and steel are common. Ataturk's huge steel combine at Karabuk modeled on Europe's most modern plants during the 1930s is a classic example. The plant never functioned at more than a fraction of its productive capacity because it lacked ancillary services, skilled workmen, technicians, and managers. Today both Israel and Egypt are likewise spending huge amounts of capital to create steel plants, armament industries, and aircraft factories in their race for prestige.

The large broadcasting stations, public information divisions, and other propaganda services of governments such as Egypt and Israel emulate Western techniques in reaching local populations, compatriots in irredentist territory, and beyond. Radio Cairo has been one of the most effective instruments in spreading the revolutionary nationalism that has caught fire among so many of the neighboring Arab and colonial peoples in Africa south of the Sahara.

Great wealth acquired by Iran and several Arab countries from increased oil production and escalating prices contributed greatly to national self-awareness. Western European, Japanese, and American dependence on Middle East oil gave the region a new centrality, power, and consciousness it had not had since the rise of Islam. With about half the world's petroleum productive capacity and 60 percent of the proven reserves, the Middle East held the key to Western prosperity. Formation of the Organization of Petroleum Exporting Countries (OPEC) in 1960 by Saudi Arabia, Venezuela, Iran, Iraq, and Kuwait made it possible for the producing countries to attain higher prices. (Later Algeria, Ecuador, Gabon, Indonesia, Libya, Nigeria, Qatar, and the United Arab Emirates also joined.) Through OPEC the Middle East producing countries were able to drive the Western oil companies onto the defensive, eventually taking over most of their holdings in the region. The oil-producing countries rather than the Western companies now set prices and policies for production and sales. In 1968 the Arab countries formed the Organization of Arab Petroleum Exporting Countries (OAPEC) which overlapped with OPEC. Its members, Algeria, Bahrain, Egypt, Kuwait, Libya, Qatar, Saudi Arabia, Syria, and the United Arab Emirates, decided to use Arab oil to obtain international political goals. During 1973 and 1974 they successfully pressured several European countries into policies more favorable to the Arab alliance in the dispute with Israel. Oil became a weapon with which countries like Saudi Arabia and Kuwait achieved international status and political influence. We shall now examine Middle Eastern nationalism as it has affected the individual states in the region.

NOTES

1.   Hans Kohn, *Nationalism and Imperialism in the Hither East,* London, 1932, p. 19.

2.   George Antonius, *The Arab Awakening,* London, 1945, p. 99.

3.   *Ibid.,* p. 120.

4.   J.C. Hurewitz, *Diplomacy in the Near and Middle East,* vol. II, p. 15.

5.   This and the above quotes from Jemal Pasha are cited in Zeine E. Zeine, *Arab-Turkish Relations and the Emergence of Arab Nationalism,* Beirut, 1958, pp. 101 and 114.

6.   Cited in George E. Kirk, *A Short History of the Middle East,* 5th ed., New York, 1959, p. 127.

7.   *Ibid.,* pp. 127–128.

8.   Hurewitz, *op. cit.,* p. 67.

9.   Cited in George Kirk, *The Middle East in the War,* London, 1954, p. 334.

10.   Hans Kohn, *op. cit.,* pp. 19–20.

11.   Gamal Abdel Nasser, *Egypt's Liberation, The Philosophy of the Revolution,* Washington, D.C., 1955, pp. 111–114.

7   Modern Turkey

SOCIAL AND ECONOMIC BACKGROUND

By the end of World War II the social and economic systems inherited by the Turkish republic had not changed for hundreds of years. The population was still primarily agricultural, living from crops it produced by methods centuries old. Cities and towns lived off the immediate countryside. The only transport of any reasonable quality was along the coastal regions. The few railways that existed had been constructed less for economic than for strategic or political reasons. Of the 15,000 miles of road in 1949, less than 600 were hard surfaced.

Even after World War II, Max Thornburg writes: "Within the political boundaries of Turkey are a hundred 'little Turkeys,' each economically isolated from the rest and usually producing a fractional part—one third to one tenth—of its potential."[1] Without linking these "little Turkeys" the country could never develop its potential economic strength; it would be unable to produce a surplus in national wealth with which to develop local industries; and it would be unable to expand purchasing power to make it possible to diversify and increase consumption. Yet these were true prerequisites for raising living standards.

However, unlike other Middle Eastern peasants, those of Turkey are not the victims of a landed aristocracy. In 1945, about two thirds of the peasantry owned land, partly due to the postrevolution redistribution of vakif properties and those of the former Osmanli dynasty as well. Nearly three quarters of

Turkey's farms were owner operated. A further distribution of government land between 1945 and 1955 resulted in land ownership by 93 percent as sharecroppers, a far different situation from that prevailing in Iran and the Arab world. Not until the mid-1950s did the question of land shortages arise, and then only as a potential threat caused by the beginning of a large growth of population.

NATIONALISM

In chapter 3 we saw how the failure of the Young Turks to achieve national homogeneity in the multinational Ottoman Empire contributed to its demise. The centrifugal force of Balkan and Arab nationalist movements helped to fragment the Ottoman Empire into numerous states, and defeat by the Allies in 1918 resulted in separating Turkish Anatolia from both non-Muslim– and non-Turkish–speaking parts of the former empire.

The first genuine nationalist sentiment among the masses developed during the Turko-Greek war between 1919 and 1922. Until then, Turkish nationalism was a sentiment expressed almost exclusively by intellectuals and professionals of the small Ottoman ruling class, men who had little direct contact with the peasant.

After World War I, nationalism became the most potent force in Turkey. On the one hand, it was used as an avenue to a new national culture, one freed from the failures of the Ottoman past; on the other, it was used as a shield against the new and unorthodox by pious conservatives who held to the old ideas and customs. In this way conservatives felt that they could devote themselves just as wholeheartedly and without reservation to Turkish nationalism as they had dedicated themselves to Islam in the past. To many Turks, nationalism became an outlet for bitterness at the decline of the empire and loss of prestige among the major powers. Even after the era of modernization opened Turkey's doors to Western techniques and innovations, distrust of the West continued, expressed in the slogan: "We resemble none but ourselves."

Ataturk's 1922 victory over the invading Allies helped to arouse a national sentiment of an intensity that had never before existed among the Turkish masses. The strong national solidarity created by the Turko-Greek war was an essential prerequisite to implementing the comprehensive program of reforms in education, law, the status of women, economic organization, and government that was to come later.

The initial rallying cry of the nationalists, "Turkey for the Turks," was realized by victory in the 1919–1922 war. The Lausanne Treaty of 1923, ending the capitulations and the millet system, removing the last foreign troops from

Turkish soil, and terminating most restrictions on Turkish sovereignty except with regard to the Straits, confirmed Allied recognition of Turkish independence. The treaty rudely shocked Turkey's minorities, such as the Kurds, Armenians, and Greeks, who had expected the country to be partitioned into Kurdish, Armenian, and Greek areas. The Lausanne Treaty also helped to create homogeneity by providing for an exchange of the Muslim minority in Greece and the Greek Orthodox minority in Anatolia (see also chapter 6). As a result of the Lausanne settlement, the population of the new Turkish republic is over 95 percent Muslim, of whom the overwhelming majority are Turkish speaking.

Ziya Gokalp

The ideological basis of modern Turkish nationalism came from the works of Ziya Gokalp (1875–1924), a writer and sociologist who had been strongly influenced by Western thought. National sentiment, Gokalp wrote, was based on race, geography, political affinity, and chiefly, culture—a culture made up of a common language, religion, system of ethics, and art. Gokalp believed that Islam was an intrinsic ingredient of Turkish nationalism, but that it should be separated from the state and modernized so as to rid it of backward oriental characteristics. In his view, Muslim law and the authority of the ulema in government and education were anachronistic.

Gokalp's political ideas were influenced by the collectivist philosophy of the French sociologist Émile Durkheim; they also drew upon the German writers of the Romantic era who idealized the virtues of a collective society and considered the growth of individualism as a sign of social decadence. Gokalp substituted the Turkish nation for Durkheim's ultimate society as the highest stage of human development, and like Mazzini, he rationalized as morally good all that the nation did. The individual self would find its social personality in collective enthusiasm, an aspect of Gokalp's theory that coincided with Islam's tradition of fraternity and equality among believers. In Turkish society, the supreme moral authority of Islam was the source of all constructive ideas. An obvious by-product of this theory was the absolute denial of internationalism.

An intellectual elite would lead society, helping the masses to express their long dormant "true native" values through development of a folk culture that united the nation in a linguistic group with a common education, religion, morality, and esthetic ideal. Civilization, as distinct from culture, was material and practical. The Turks, according to Gokalp, had a rich indigenous culture, but were poor in civilization. While rejecting European culture, Turkey should, he believed, accept its civilization.

The national economic structure was to fuse the best aspects of socialism and capitalism. The capitalist class system, of whose dangers Marx had warned, would be replaced by occupational unions and guilds bound together by national solidarity. To achieve economic progress, however, local industry would have to be supported against foreign competition; foreign advice and such controls as the capitulations and National Debt Commission would have to be abolished; and Islamic restrictions on and interference with capital investment (such as the tithe, the vakif, and the ban on interest) would have to end.

Although he accepted much of Gokalp's nationalist theory, Ataturk's practical efforts to create a "national type" were sometimes based on such historical perversions as the "Sun-Language" theory and the rewriting of history to identify Turks with heroic ancient peoples (see chapter 6). Adoption of surnames with historical meaning was another practical device to implement nationalist theories. Thus Mustafa Kemal became Kemal Ataturk (Father of the Turks). His close friend and second in command, Ismet, became Ismet Inonu, commemorating victory over the Greeks at Inonu in 1921. Transferring the capital from "effete," "degenerate" Istanbul to "pure" Turkish Ankara in the Anatolian highlands was intended to remove the republican government from "foreign" influences, from "cosmopolitanism," and from stagnating influence of the old Ottoman sultanate and its conservative entourage. Many towns were renamed in modern Turkish: Angora became Ankara; Smyrna, Izmir; and Adrianople, Edirne. After 1932, letters addressed with the old names were not delivered.

Although Ataturk was basically a secularist, nationalism was increasingly identified in the popular consciousness with Islam. This was true from the time of the Turko-Greek war against the "Christian infidels" when Ataturk was proclaimed Ghazi (Champion of Islam) by the Turkish parliament. Only a Muslim is considered a "Turkish Turk," although there are a few thousand Christian and Jewish citizens in the republic. The relatively small number of non-Muslims, although equal under law, are discriminated against in most spheres of public life. None has ever achieved high government office or top rank in the army. Preference for Muslims was indicated in the post–World War I population exchanges when the basis for uprooting Greeks was not culture or language, but religion. Only Christians were forced to move from the country, whereas the few Greek-speaking Muslims were permitted to remain; and only Muslims were permitted to "return," even though many could not speak Turkish. Since the end of World War II, Turkey has also agreed to accept Muslim refugees from Communist-dominated nations.

Recent Ideological Trends

Until World War II, the intellectual elite's interpretation of the nationalist movement was secularist, and Islamic identification was more popular than official. Since 1945, however, larger numbers of intellectuals have abandoned this secular emphasis and have begun to express nationalism in religious terms. This shift has represented, in part, a rightist reaction to the rapid, world wide growth of leftist ideologies. Within the new trend there are tendencies toward religious fundamentalism, xenophobia, and pan-Turanism.

Turkish nationalist ideology has been free from racism. Even during the Ottoman era, the cream of the Ottoman elite was a Balkan ethnic mixture, and within the empire, Ottoman Turks were a minority among a potpourri of national groups. Of the 214 Ottoman grand vezirs, a mere 79 had been Turks, and only a fraction of the ancestors of the Osmanli dynasty had been Turkish because of extensive intermarriage. Only during the Young Turk era, when leaders such as Enver Pasha emphasized pan-Turanism, did racialism find any official support. Both racialism and pan-Turanism were rejected by Ataturk and his followers.

During World War II, German attempts to arouse pan-Turanism as a weapon against the Soviet Union failed. Pan-Turanists in Turkey were encouraged and supported by the Germans; but when the war turned against Germany in 1944, the republican government crushed the pan-Turanists and arrested several of their leaders. Today, the racialists are an isolated lunatic fringe, and their views are considered by most intellectuals as lacking any relationship to political reality.

Ironically, Turkish identification with Islam creates no special bond with other Muslim states. Modern, "reformed" Turkish Islam is considered superior to that practiced among the more "primitive" neighbors. Although Islam has, in varying degrees, influenced the policies of other predominantly Muslim states in such matters as their relationship with Israel, such is not the case in Turkey.

In 1960, after a decade of political domination, the Democratic party was toppled in a revolution that was followed by emergence of a diverse range of Turkish political thought. In the new atmosphere, many ideas blossomed, although most of them found few followers. At one end of the political spectrum were the conservative, elitist nationalists strongly emphasizing the Turanist and racist aspects of Turkish nationalism. Through revival of pan-Turkism they sought ties among all peoples with Turkic roots speaking the Turkish language, and of the Turkic "race." The great mass of Turks living in the Asian lands east of Turkey, extending to the Sea of Japan, were referred to as the "outside" Turks who were "enslaved" by their foreign rulers and whom they once hoped to unify in one nation, the Turan. Now, instead of reviving the old slogans of unity in one Turkish country, the pan-Turanists played up to the theme of liberation for the twenty-five to thirty million Turkish-speaking peoples in the Soviet Union and in Communist China. The goal of the new pan-Turanists was to associate these "outside" Turks with the greater Turkish Republic. Many of these ideas were the basis of the National Action Party (see below). However, all Turkish governments since the time of Ataturk have continued to reject the idea of forming close associations or of dealing with the Turkic groups living in the Soviet Union, China, or elsewhere outside Republican Turkey for fear of antagonizing their neighbors and of creating dangerous international complications.

Another newly formed ideological group, the Labor party of Turkey, was established by a small number of trade unionists in 1961. While the leadership of the party was Marxist and consisted mostly of urban intellectuals, they carefully avoided any identification with communism or with the Soviet Union, recalling the centuries-long animosity that has pervaded relationships between Russia and Turkey. The party adopted a program calling for democratic and free parliamentary elections striving toward the traditional goals of Marxian socialists such as nationalization of all means of production, distribution of land to landless peasants, and of ending "the system of exploitation of man by man...to make Turkey a country where people rely on each other as brothers, cooperate in freedom and equality, and live in an advanced civilization of culture, in full independence in the service of humanity, peace and democracy."[2] These goals have not attracted a numerous following in Turkey. Few workers joined the party, and it won only a small fraction of votes in any of the elections in which it participated. In the 1969 election the party won less than 3 percent of the votes. The party was dissolved after the 1971 military coup, but reemerged as the rallying point for many leftists disenchanted with other groups. It was dissolved again after the 1980 coup. Its effect has been far more significant as an intellectual stimulus than as a political force, gathering most of its following among university professors, students, and other intellectuals. The Labor party may be said to exercise more influence than its numbers would warrant, since other political groups such as the PRP have put more emphasis on the rights of labor and labor unions following its emergence.

The Kurdish Minority Problem

The single barrier to national homogeneity has been the Kurdish minority of approximately 10 to 20 percent. Unlike the Greeks, Armenians, and Jews, the Kurds are a linguistic minority who, like the Turkish majority, are Sunni Muslims. The nature of the Kurdish problem has been more one of social than political adjustment. The government has attempted to settle permanently a once nomadic people who, for centuries, were free to move across the Anatolian borders into Syria, Iran, and Iraq. The Kurdish tribal chiefs rebelled against the republic's new ways and its interference with their autonomous, highly mobile life. Many Kurds resented Ataturk's "godlessness" and his restrictions on public religious observance. The government resorted to force in 1925 to suppress a Kurdish revolt in the eastern provinces. Military rule was not lifted and civil administration restored in the Kurdish areas until after 1946, when the deportees were finally permitted to return.

During the 1950s Prime Minister Menderes attempted to win support from the religious and conservatively oriented Kurdish regions by restoring limited local autonomy and political power to Kurdish village and tribal leaders, or agas. Renewed local autonomy against the background of an upsurge of Kurdish nationalist fervor during the 1950s and 1960s in neighboring Iraq resulted in renewed government restrictions after the overthrow of Menderes in 1960. The army, fearing an upsurge of local national sentiment in eastern Anatolia, used its special emergency powers for maintaining national security to exile several agas in 1961.

There is only little evidence of a Kurdish nationalist movement in Turkey today. The power of the agas, or tribal chiefs, has been destroyed, and tribal formations have been broken up. It is rare to meet young men in most Kurdish sections who are not bilingual; even the women are beginning to learn Turkish. The single real barrier to Kurdish assimilation—language—is rapidly diminishing, and the group is moving toward complete integration into modern Turkish society. For the problems they raise for Syria and Iraq, see chapters 14 and 15.

The Cyprus Problem

Nationalist consciousness was inflamed in Turkey during the late 1950s and 1960s by eruption of the Cyprus problem. Although Turks were fewer than 20 percent of the island's approximately 600,000 people, national pride in Anatolia was deeply affected by developments on the island after World War II. Cyprus has been part of the Ottoman Empire since the time of its conquest from the Venetians during the sixteenth century until it was placed under British control in 1878. With the rise of a strong religiously oriented Greek nationalist movement on the island during the 1950s its Turkish residents and their compatriots on the mainland began to have apprehensions about the future. During the struggle between Cypriot Greeks and British armed forces after 1955 the Turks played a passive role if not one sympathetic to the British.

After Cyprus became independent in 1960, the Turkish minority was regarded by the Greek majority as a disloyal element. Tensions between the Cypriot Greek and Turkish communities were intensified by differences in religion—the Turks being Muslim and Greeks being Cypriot Orthodox—language, and disparity in social and economic conditions. The Greeks had a far higher standard of living and were more politically, culturally, and economically sophisticated, tending to look down on the Turks. Against the background of traditional Turkish-Greek animosities and centuries of warfare between the two peoples culminating in the Turko-Greek War of the 1920s the virus of nationalism spread to the Greek and Turkish mainlands. The Turks felt it necessary to come to the defense of their coreligionists on Cyprus as a matter of national pride. Greeks also sided with their countrymen on the island. The situation threatened to spark a major conflict between the two nations and to undermine the eastern wing of NATO in which they were the principal pillars of support.

Both Athens and Ankara threatened to intervene with troops. In Turkey the question became a major political one, each political party vying with the next in support of Turkish nationalism on the island. While Cypriot Greeks and their supporters on the mainland called for reunion or *Enosis* of Cyprus with Greece, the Turks counterreplied with a plan to partition the island as the only acceptable solution. Conflict was temporarily dampened through U.N. intervention in 1964, acceptance by all parties of a United Nations peace force on the island, and recognition of the integrity and independence of Cyprus. However, continuing incidents have led Turkish nationalists to call for intervention to prevent "genocide," while Athens countered with threats to send troops. President Inonu's attempts at moderation placed him in a precarious position, as evidenced by the close 200 to 194 vote of confidence supporting his Cyprus policy in the National Assembly during June 1964.

At this time Greece secretly sent volunteers to help the armed Greek Cypriot forces. In retaliation the Turkish air force strafed the northern coast of Cyprus where Turkish Cypriots were hard pressed during August 1964. The Greek president of the island, Archbishop Makarios, escalated the conflict with an economic blockade on various Turkish sections of the island until he was forced to desist through U.N. intervention.

The Cyprus question also had a direct impact upon Turkey's relations with the United States and the Soviet Union. Fearing a Turkish invasion of the island, President Johnson sent a personal letter to President Inonu in 1964, pointing out the dangers of possible Soviet intervention and warning Inonu that in such an event Turkey could not expect NATO protection. As a result of the Johnson letter and the ambiguous position of the United States on the Cyprus question, anti-American feeling spread through Turkey. This feeling was heightened by resentments growing out of the large number of American bases in the country and growing neutralist trends among Turkish intellectuals. Since 1964 there have been increasing pressures by both right- and left-wing nationalists to curtail or remove the large number of American weapons and bases in the country. Student demonstrations against America and against visits by the Sixth Fleet to Istanbul are evidence of the growing feeling among many Turks that they cannot rely on the United States as an unconditional ally. As a result, in 1964 the Turkish government initiated negotiations with the Soviet Union on trade and agricultural exchanges and other large-scale Russian economic assistance. The negotiations were accompanied by exchanges of parliamentary delegations, foreign ministers, and chiefs of state between 1964 and 1967, resulting in a more neutral Soviet position on the dispute.

A military coup in July 1974 by right wing Greek Cypriots against Archbishop Makarios precipitated unilateral Turkish military intervention. The rightists were believed to be collaborating with the ruling military junta of the Greek government. The immediate Turkish objective was to prevent

Enosis and to protect the Turkish population. United Nations Peace-Keeping Forces on the island were unable to halt the fighting or the Turkish advance. Conflict between local Turks and Greeks spread, accompanied by massacres and other atrocities. Each community attempted to "purify" itself of the opposing ethnic group, with the result that an ethnic partition occurred, with tens of thousands of refugees. Most Greeks were driven from those parts of the island occupied by Turkey, and nearly all Turks fled or were driven from the Greek sectors. When the fighting ended, Turkey held the northern 40 percent of the island, with about 18 percent of the population, mostly Turks. President Makarios was restored to power late in 1974, as head of the largely Greek government in the southern 60 percent of the island. With tens of thousands of refugees from the north and a breakdown in communications, transportation, and trade, the island faced serious economic difficulties. Turkey refused to permit the return of large numbers of Greeks to their homes, businesses, and farms in the north. Instead, Greek holdings were turned over to Turkish Cypriots and settlers from mainland Turkey.

Shortly after the coup and Turkish invasion of 1974, a new democratic government came to power in Athens. Negotiations were again opened between all the parties to the conflict—Greece, Turkey, Cypriot Greeks, and Cypriot Turks, but no compromise could be found. The Turkish Cypriots, backed by Ankara, insisted on establishment of an autonomous government in the north; the Greek Cypriots, supported by Athens, wanted to restore the pre-1974 arrangements but conceded greater self-government for the Turks. In effect, the island was divided into two separate states—the former Cyprus Republic in the south, now largely Greek, and a new autonomous Turkish government in the north closely tied to the mainland, and occupied by its troops. The division was reinforced by establishment of the Turkish Federated State of Cyprus (TFSC) in 1975 and formation of a Turkish government that assumed most civil functions. There was little or no contact between the two parts of the island. Even mail service was cut, so that letters to Turkish Cyprus were sent via Adrine. After the death of Archbishop Makarios in 1977 prospects for a Cyprus settlement seemed even more remote. The Cypriot Turkish leaders proclaimed that they would never recognize Makarios' successor as president of all Cyprus, but only as leader of the Greek community.

Cyprus became a major issue in Turkish domestic politics. As a result, Bulent Ecevit, leader of the PRP who was prime minister during the invasion, became a national hero. The Cyprus question was crucial because the National Salvation party, a small group which both major parties required in their government coalitions, adamantly opposed Turkish departure from northern Cyprus.

The major effects of the Cyprus problem on Turkey were renewal of zealous Turkish nationalism, which won support of all political parties, deterioration of relations between Greece and Turkey with consequent weakening of the eastern wing of NATO, improvement of relationships between Turkey and the Soviet Union, and cooling of Turkish-American relations. This was evident in the renegotiation during 1969 of the Turkish-American Defense Pact replacing some 50 post–World War II agreements. The new agreements emphasized Turkish sovereignty over American bases and a Turkish voice in determining the number of American troops and weapons in the country. In general, it may be said that Turkey has moved from the position of a staunch defender of Western interests in the eastern Mediterranean to a more neutral stance seeking to maintain close ties and associations with the West through membership in the Common Market and in an increasingly less important NATO, on the one hand. On the other hand, relationships have improved with the Soviet Union to balance American aid, which was cut to pressure Turkey into compromise.

SECULARISM

Initial efforts to circumscribe the authority of Islam began during the nineteenth-century Tanzimat era, described in chapter 3. Such attempts included the 1839 Hatti Sherif of Gulhané, the 1856 Hatti-Humayun, the 1876 constitution, and the administrative reforms of the Young Turks. Ataturk greatly intensified these efforts. Republican leaders viewed the religiopolitical structure and organization of Islam as medieval, even foreign. First, they disestablished the religion and curtailed its political, social, and economic power, changing it from a state creed to a private faith. Secondly, they desired to reform the private faith to free it from "degenerative" Arab influences that barred the way to progress.

The first step was abolition of the caliphate in March 1924 (the sultanate had been abolished in 1922) and banishment of the former Osmanli dynasty. Ataturk indicated his disapproval of this Islamic institution by rejecting the title of caliph when it was offered him by parliament. Clerical control of education was terminated, and simultaneously, all schools were placed under a Ministry of Public Instruction. Unification of the whole school system under the state ended the practice whereby the educational institutions of the various millets were permitted to exist alongside secular institutions. Islam's official status was terminated when the Ministry of Religious Affairs and the Sharia was abolished. Vakifs were placed under a special Department of Endowments within the prime minister's office; a few weeks later Sharia courts were abolished and their jurisdiction taken over by secular courts. Public appearance in clerical garb was forbidden to all but mosque officials. Muslim monastic orders were abolished and the shrines and tombs of holy men were closed. By removing these symbols of the "old Islam" from public view, Ataturk hoped to wipe them from public consciousness.

These initial measures aroused widespread opposition among conservatives and traditionalists. Some religious dissidents joined the short-lived Progressive party, formed in 1924, to combat Ataturk's program. Conservative attachment to the new party, originally intended as a genuine liberal movement, so stigmatized the Progressives that they failed within a year and their party was disbanded. Loyal Ataturk supporters charged that the Progressive party was surreptitiously linked with the Kurdish uprising, which had also been partly instigated by outraged religious sentiment.

Ataturk took little notice of popular opposition to his secularization program and pressed it with even greater vigor. The most startling of his innovations to many Turks was a 1925 law forbidding men to wear the fez (the red hat introduced a century earlier as a "Western" innovation, see chapter 3) and ordering that all headgear be equipped with a brim or visor. This act was intended to symbolize the modernization of Turkey; in fact, it aroused much wider criticism than the more fundamental reform legislation. Villagers protested that the new visored headgear interfered with performance of religious duties. The visor made it impossible to touch their forehead to the ground during prayers. To wear such a hat had always been considered symbolic of apostasy, or entering the service of a foreign power. Wearing a straw panama, Ataturk personally inaugurated the new style in a tour of villages, and photographs of him so hatted appeared in the press. The armed services were also outfitted and paraded in Western military caps. But opposition to the "infidel" innovation was so violent in Rize on the Black Sea, that a cruiser was sent there to suppress disorders and several local religious leaders were hanged for preaching against the hat law.

A measure of Ataturk's great influence over his country, however, is that today, in many remote Turkish villages, the only visible symbol of the revolution is the wearing of the visored cap similar to that worn by the European working class. Even conservative Muslims who have not abandoned their traditional ways wear the cap, but they wear it backwards during prayers so that their foreheads may touch the ground.

The veiling of women was also attacked by Ataturk, although it was never outlawed. Only in the large cosmopolitan cities were efforts to discourage it successful. In smaller towns and in the older sections of the new capital today, many women still either wear a veil or hide their faces in a shawl when strangers approach. Despite the sexual gulf Turkey has one of the highest percentages of university educated women in the Middle East and the number of women professionals—lawyers, physicians, professors, bankers—is larger than in any other Muslim country, putting Turkey ahead of some European countries.

The Gregorian calendar replaced the Islamic calendar on New Year's Day 1926, when the year 1342 officially became 1926, although religious holidays and Ramazan (Arabic: Ramadan) are still calculated by the Islamic method. The country also began to use the international designations for time, instead of the traditional Muslim method of calculating the hours of the day from sunset.

Legal Changes

The most pervasive revolutionary change occurred when Sharia law was supplanted by Western legal codes in 1926. Until then, the various Christian and Jewish millets were governed by their own religious laws. In 1925 Jewish and Armenian religious leaders were persuaded to renounce their privileges, guaranteed in the Lausanne Treaty, and to submit to national civil jurisdiction. Early in 1926, the Greek Christians who remained in the country also followed suit, and the last vestiges of the millet system disappeared. For the first time all groups were subject to the same law.

Swiss civil legislation, Italian penal laws, and German commercial codes replaced all religious law. But the transition was not easy to accomplish in practice. The country was unprepared for the sudden adoption of French, German, and Italian laws. There were shortages of competent jurists and lawyers, difficulties in introducing new court procedures, and problems in persuading the public that such foreign innovations could be useful to them. Not until a few months before the reform was decreed, in November 1925, had a law school been established to train personnel in these European systems. Even today many villagers settle disputes among themselves by traditional Sharia law, rather than bring cases to the "infidel" courts.

The Sharia had commanded the pious throughout their daily lives; its abolition deprived them not only of a familiar legal system but also of those ties that had traditionally bound man to God. Polygamy, inheritance, marital relations, diet, and animal slaughter had been regulated by the Sharia. The drastic changes made in the legal codes meant that Turkey was no longer bound by Islamic convention.

Adoption of the Swiss civil code revolutionized the role of women in Turkish society. Polygamy was banned and wives attained the same legal rights as their husbands in divorce proceedings. Although only civil marriage was officially sanctioned, villagers supplemented it with traditional Muslim customs and ceremonies. Gradually women began to take part in public life. In 1930 they were permitted to vote in local elections, and their political emancipation was completed four years later when they were allowed to vote for delegates to the National Assembly and were permitted to run for office, a privilege that led to the election of 17 women in the 399-member parliament. Even though women have received full legal rights and have become university graduates, members of parliament, and high government officials, there is an ambivalence about Turkish attitudes toward their emancipation.

Many are still closely guarded, and severe penalties are imposed on transgressors of a rigid moral code resembling more the attitudes of the mid-Victorian era than the mid–twentieth century.

By 1928 secularization had progressed so far that Ataturk no longer felt obliged to render even token homage to Islam. The last religious formalities were abandoned when the constitution was amended to eliminate all mention of Islam. The state was no longer officially Islamic, and Assembly members were now required to swear allegiance on their honor rather than before God. In a still further effort at formal secularization, the Muslim day of prayer, Friday, was ignored when a new weekly rest period was established from one o'clock Saturday afternoon through Sunday. Alphabet and language reform was another measure partially intended to undermine old Islamic traditions. Attack on the traditional linguistic forms began in 1924 at a conference of Soviet Turkish Peoples that decided to replace the traditional Arabic script with Latin letters because the Arabic alphabet lacked many vowels essential in Turkish word formation. Often Turkish, written in Arabic script, would be incomprehensible without some previous knowledge of the text. Ataturk followed the Soviet Turkish example by appointing a special commission in 1928 to produce a new phonetic alphabet and to revise the prevailing system of writing numbers.

By simplifying the writing and reading of Turkish, the new alphabet was to aid the fight to combat illiteracy. Literacy would no longer be the gift of an elite, particularly in rural areas where only the conservative ulema had had access to the written word. Extensive literacy would make it possible for the revolutionary government to reach a broad cross-section of the population and thus undermine clerical control. Linguistic reform was also intended to weaken the Turkish attachment to Islamic literature. Since only Turkish translations of the Koran were printed in the country, it would be difficult to obtain Arabic versions of the Holy Book. The effect is evident among modern Turkish intellectuals, few of whom have any knowledge of traditional Islamic literature or any attachment of the religious customs and practices of the "backward Arabs" (see also chapter 6).

Ataturk also personally introduced the linguistic changes. He conducted classes in the Latin alphabet for the nation's leaders; then he toured the countryside armed with a blackboard and chalk. In village after village he assembled the peasants, requiring them to show their reading skills. By such means Kemal Ataturk became a living legend. Local officials were intimidated by the president's fiery temper and scathing tongue and were terrified lest they blunder in his presence.

Three months after the new alphabet was introduced, parliament decreed a halt in publication of all books in Arabic by January 1929. From that date, all books, public signs, newspapers, and other printed material had to be in the new script. All Assembly members hastened to learn their lessons lest they be barred from office by the constitutional provision excluding illiterates.

To effect the reform, new texts had to be published for all schools in every subject, new presses had to be imported, and an army of officials was required to travel through the land giving lessons. Within a decade, the government claimed that the rate of illiteracy had dropped from 80 to approximately 50 percent. Books and newspapers multiplied and were avidly read. So successfully was the Arabic script uprooted that it is difficult to find a young Turk who can read it today. The literacy campaign also spawned a massive investment in primary schools and adult education which contributed to rapid decline in illiteracy.

Attempts to cleanse the Turkish language of "degenerate" Arabic and Iranian vocabulary and grammatical forms have already been described in chapter 6. The intent was to restore the "people's" language, which had fallen into disuse among the elite during the Ottoman era when an elaborate, highly Iranianized and Arabized language developed, unique to governing circles. To become fully accepted in the Ottoman ruling group, one had to have been a Sunni Muslim and to have spoken and lived according to the "Ottoman way"; thus the "true Ottoman" becasme easily distinguished from the simple Anatolian peasant by his speech. Ataturk adopted Ziya Gokalp's theory of propagating folk culture and eliminating the class distinctions represented by the cultural distance that existed between the elite and the peasantry. He ordered the Turkish Linguistic Society, founded in 1932, to devise a "genuine Turkish" from the simple language of the Anatolian peasant. Since "purification" of Turkish soon proved to be impossible, the "Sun-Language" theory (described in chapter 6) was invented, tracing the origin of all modern tongues to ancient Turkish, the linguistic "sun" around which other languages revolved. The society did succeed in eliminating use of the elaborate Arabic polite form, while introducing such European terms as *telefon* and *telegraf*.

EFFECTS OF SECULARIZATION

Three strands run through Ataturk's secularization efforts. One was the separation of religion from politics; another was the isolation of religion as much as possible from social life; the third was the Turkification of Islam, ridding it of Arab influences. The first was accomplished through the various decrees described above, but there was less success in achieving the latter two. Turkey's intellectual elite—university students and professors, high ranking army officers, and government officials—were profoundly affected by secularization, but the strong emotional ties of the peasantry to their religious faith remained. Nor did the ban on the use of Arabic in mosques and translation of the Koran into Turkish curb the popular longing for the language as a religious form, for Turkish translations of the Holy Book had lost much of the literary quality and the music of the Arabic chant that was familiar to Muslims the world over. The villages, small towns, and even the poorer quarters of the urban centers still maintain their "folk" attachment to Islam and continue to observe its traditions and beliefs.

Today, however, religious institutions have far less influence in Turkish life than they did previously. The authority of the village imam or prayer leader as teacher and legal expert has been replaced by young government teachers educated in the nonreligious, if not antireligious, atmosphere of the metropolitan colleges. Formal justice is administered by the courts and police authorities under civil, not Sharia, law. Healing is no longer a matter of religious superstition, but a function of private or government physicians. In the old regime, the youth could leave the village for urban life only by becoming part of the ulema. Now they can enter the free state educational system. They are subject to universal military service and have opportunities for work that bring them to the cities without any religious obligations.

The attitudes of village leaders, however, are often indecisive. Few of them understand the purpose of secularization, and they often attempt to evade official restrictions on Islam. While enforcing the ban on the fez, they maintain their traditional attitudes toward women and the age-old customs of daily life. For many of them, Islam is still the all-embracing and unalterable system of ritual and moral conduct within which the peasant's whole physical and social life exists. When asked for explanations about natural phenomena such as floods, earthquakes, and the like, the peasant will often answer, "It is in our Book!"

A Western student of Turkish peasant life, Paul Stirling, has observed that: "What the villagers believe to be the divinely guaranteed order is what they in fact do and experience at present, and this argument is always to hand against any innovations not obviously desirable." While they may overlook the Koranic injunction against interest and pay modest fees on credit from the Agricultural Bank because of the great benefit thus offered them, many continue their objections to youthful government-trained school masters who teach their children the "infidel script." They "still largely see their world and their way of life, their rulers, their wives, even their illnesses, as sent by Allah.... The Western notion of 'progress' is totally lacking." There are still itinerant exorcisers who play on folk superstitions, preachers who still oppose "modernity" and inveigh against stylish or short-sleeved women's dresses. Stirling concludes that: "The ideology underlying the new social order can replace the traditional Islamic view of life only piecemeal in the course of generations, and since this ideology is itself changing and confused, there will always be inconsistencies."[3]

Village isolation also helps perpetuate conservative attitudes. Residents of communities that are hours by foot or oxcart from the nearest town are unlikely to be easily convinced of the advantages in unveiling their women or in the equity of secular law. They are reluctant to accept views likely to disturb neighbors, friends, and elder relatives. Rural isolation and conservativism have therefore widened the gap between the rural village and the city and between the peasant and the urban intellectual, who merely arouses suspicion by his efforts to end ignorance and bigotry.

To help overcome the gap between town and country—and also as a reaction to postwar leftist agitation—the Democratic party (see below) began to alter secularization policies during the 1950s. Debate on secularization started in 1946 after the government had begun to liberalize its policies. Conservatives argued that religion filled a spiritual need required for the framework of an educational system. Moderates considered religion a matter of individual choice. The convinced secularists maintained firm opposition to removal of any restrictions on religion, lest Islamic influences subvert the advances of the previous decades. The secularists were not successful in this debate because many intellectuals were now becoming interested in Islam as a source of personal religious inspiration and as an added defense against the increasingly powerful materialist philosophies. New political parties, formed in 1946, urged modifications in the official restrictions on Islam. Even the Peoples' Republican party (PRP) abandoned its rigid attitude and recognized the growing need for a new policy. The first retreat from its traditional policy was a proposal by the party council in 1947 to authorize private individuals, under government supervision, to teach Islam in the Latin script outside the school system and to open schools for imams. One new religious-education law authorized the reopening of schools for Muslim clergy. The justification for this law was that villages bereft of religious guidance were reverting to ancient superstitions. In 1949 a divinity faculty was established at the University of Ankara, replacing the defunct theological school at Istanbul University that was closed in 1933 for lack of students. The new religious institutions were not confined to the study of Islam, but included modern secular subjects as well. Immediately there was a large enrollment and graduates were much sought after as teachers, army chaplains, and to staff government agencies such as the Evkaf (plural of vakif) Administration and the presidency of Religious Affairs.

Conservatism, symbolized by an outbreak of fez wearing in the eastern provinces, broke to the surface in 1950 after the Democratic party replaced the PRP in office. Many hoped that the Democrats would not only end restrictions on Islam, but would even lead an Islamic revival. The expectations of the ardent Islamicists, however, were not fulfilled. Although the Democrats modified a number of restrictions, they also cracked down on religious extremists. An initial measure ended the ban on the Arabic call to prayer and sponsored Koran readings over the state radio. While the official ban on Arabic remains, religious slogans and symbols using it are on the open market and are widely displayed in taxis, homes, and shops. Under the Democrats, government funds were allocated for the upkeep and construction of village mosques, and foreign currency was made available for the pilgrimage to Mecca. The tombs of the sultans, closed to public view in 1925, were reopened, and former members of the royal family were permitted to visit Turkey.

The experiment of the fervent secularists failed. Ataturk's religious reforms never received genuine popular support. Nor, for that matter, did they ever succeed in retaining their hold over the intellectual elite. Beneath the surface of Turkish life attachment to Islam remains one of the binding social forces. Indeed, many intellectuals have now come to feel that a reformed and modified Islam fills a vital need in their nation. Islam has returned, not as the state religion, but as the religion of the state's people, and it is again acknowledged as such by the government.

DEMOCRACY AND THE REPUBLIC

The republic's first political organizations—the Congress of Sivas, the Congress of Erzerum, the Assembly to Defend the Rights and Interests of the Provinces of Anatolia and Rumelia, and the Eastern Provinces Society for the Defense of National Rights—were patriotic groups with wide popular support. Established during 1919 and 1920 as emergency committees to prevent national collapse, they gave birth to a National Assembly in 1920, synthesizing their doctrines in the National Pact, and to the Peoples Republican party. Most other political parties formed since the beginning of the republic have been offshoots of the PRP.

While Ataturk was organizing the nationalist movement in the hinterlands during 1919 and 1920, the Ottoman government also continued to function in Istanbul under Allied control. When the Ottoman authorities realized how strong the nationalists were, the sultan convened a parliament in which he asked Ataturk's followers to participate. However, when the nationalists began to act independently of him, the sultan dissolved the parliament. Several of the nationalist leaders were seized by the Allies and deported to Malta. Ataturk, who had forewarned his colleagues of just such a danger, retaliated by establishing a rival capital on the central Anatolian plateau at the town of Angora (renamed Ankara), where he convened the Grand National Assembly.

The fundamental pattern of organization and the general principles upon which the new government was based were legalized in January 1921 in the Provisional Law of Fundamental Organization. The new decree was really a series of amendments to the 1876 and 1908 Ottoman constitutions, giving a certain continuity with the previous regimes. The principles on which the provisional law was conceived were taken from the writings of Ziya Gokalp: sovereignty belongs unconditionally to the nation; all executive and legislative powers and authorities were to be concentrated in the Grand National Assembly, "the sole representative of the Nation"; and members were to be elected by direct popular ballot.

Initially, several revolutionary and conservative groups formed the new parliament. But after the Greek invasion, all dissenting opinions were silenced. In April 1921, after a serious defeat, Ataturk was called upon to lead the Nationalist armies in the field. He made his acceptance conditional on receiving the legislative powers of the National Assembly for the duration of the emergency. Immediately after becoming commander in chief, he imposed a series of draconic laws, confiscating many civilian goods, and established independent tribunals vested with summary powers, authorized to impose the commander's orders.

Once victory was in his hands, Ataturk did not surrender his extraordinary authority, but directed it instead toward peaceful "national" ends. He, or his followers, controlled all elections until the end of World War II. Ataturk's concept of democracy was formulated from Ziya Gokalp's collectivist view of society in which the individual is subordinated to the nation. Therefore, although Ataturk held absolute power, he nonetheless conceived of himself as representing the popular will. He prevailed upon the National Assembly, in October 1923, to declare Turkey a republic, to appoint him as its first president, and to make his friend, former general Ismet Pasha (Ismet Inonu), prime minister. Since the president presided over the cabinet and the Assembly, and since Ataturk controlled most members of the new parliament, he was now guaranteed total power. The last major obstacle to this policies was removed in March 1924 by abolishing the caliphate and expelling the caliph and the rest of the Osmanli dynasty.

The last vestiges of Ottoman rule were terminated in April 1924 by adoption of a constitution that continued until the 1960 revolution. The new constitution concentrated all power in the hands of the chief executive. Ataturk avoided the stigma of despotism by working through the PRP, formed in 1923 from the League for Defense of Rights, one of the revolutionary patriotic groups. The party itself agreed to surrender its authority to its leader, who manipulated the organization through an original group of 260 members. At first, an opposition group of some 40 members objected to Ataturk's exclusive power, fearing that the sultan's despotism would merely be replaced by Ataturk's military autocracy. But Ataturk's popularity was so immense that all members of the second group lost their Assembly seats in the 1923 elections.

Opposition Parties

Periodically, there were outbursts against Ataturk's secularist reforms and the poor economic conditions that prevailed throughout the country. A wave of unrest during 1924 led to numerous resignations from the PRP and bitter attacks on the prime minister and other associates of the president. Because of his extreme popularity and the strict control of the PRP, Ataturk himself remained above criticism. Several dissidents formed a new political group, the Progressive Republican party, which opposed the concentration of power in the National Assembly. Only four days after it was formed, the new group forced Inonu's resignation and replaced him with one of their own leaders.

Since a major claim of the Progressives was that they had come to protect religion against the government, they aroused Ataturk's suspicions. Using special emergency legislation intended to "establish order" during the 1925 Kurdish revolt, he abolished the party because of its "collusion with the rebels."

For the next five years, Ataturk ruled with no formal opposition, although eddies of discontent swirled beneath the surface of the reform movement. By 1930, popular unrest began to be a source of serious concern to the president. Complaints from all parts of the country arose over the mismanagement of transportation facilities, lack of credit facilities for farmers, unemployment among villagers, exorbitant taxes, and the growing number of bureaucrats. Ataturk decided to create an outlet for the discontent by permitting an old associate, Fethi Okyar, to establish a Liberal party in August 1930 and encouraged many of his acquaintances, including his sister, to join. Fethi campaigned for a free press, reduced taxes, less state control of business, improved administrative procedures, and a war on corruption.

The public, however, was not prepared for free criticism of the government and Fethi's supporters got out of hand in September 1930, when a mob of Fethi enthusiasts rioted in Izmir. Police fired on the crowd and harassed the town's Liberals.

Fethi never had a real chance of election because the PRP controlled the electoral machinery. Dissension between Fethi's followers and the PRP culminated in accusations that he was a disguised reactionary. Throughout the campaign, Ataturk had professed neutrality, but now the PRP solicited his aid to condemn the Liberals. Faced with opposition from the national leader himself, the Liberals abandoned all their efforts in November 1930. They and all other minor parties were banned after another mob, in the town of Menemen, incited by a fanatic Dervish, beheaded an army officer.

THE CORPORATE STATE

Following the failure of the second experiment in multiparty democracy, a new political trend developed, placing more emphasis on social and economic developments within the nation. Advocates of the new trend expressed their views in the magazine *Kadro,* widely read in official circles.

Kadro wrote that the Turkish revolution was part of the worldwide struggle against capitalism and imperialism, and that leadership in the fight for national economic liberation should be entrusted to a cadre of progressives. Class struggle could by obviated in Turkey by investing government funds in the national economy; the nation's principal problem was not reconciliation of varied class interests, but creation of a modern technology that could revamp the economy. The state should organize society and be free to interfere in all activities to further economic development. Although the group dissolved after it was accused of leftist leanings, its ideas subsequently became influential in formulating policy among younger intellectuals.

PRP secretary general Recep Peker's approach to reform resembled to a great extent the trend then developing in Italy and Germany. Even in its administrative organization, the PRP emulated Fascist party organization. A vast bureaucracy, all of whose members were PRP members, was entrenched in official positions throughout Turkey. In 1935 the secretary general of the party became minister of the interior, with control of the police; heads of the local party organizations became provincial governors. The whole nation was now considered an integral part of the PRP, and Ataturk, the party leader, was also the national leader.

These corporate-state techniques of organization were reflected in subsequent legislation. A 1936 law, modeled on that of Fascist Italy, denied laborers the right to organize and to strike. A law aimed at masonic lodges in 1938 banned all organizations other than those approved by the PRP. Police officials were authorized to arrest and hold indefinitely without a warrant anyone they considered dangerous. Government officials were freed from accountability for their acts before all but the highest authorities. A Press Union was formed to control and rigidly supervise all publications. When Ismet Inonu succeeded Ataturk after the latter's death in November 1938, the rightist trend was intensified. The chief of state and other leaders of the country were placed above all criticism and lionized as personifications, or symbols, of the nation.

World War II provided the government with an opportunity to consolidate its power further. A particularly discriminatory act was the capital levy (*varlik vergisi*) of November 1942, which was enforced against non-Muslims. Tax payments were determined by local officials according to their own estimates, without recourse by the taxpayer to higher appeal. The property of individuals who could not raise their assessments was sold at public auction, and if the sale failed to produce the required amount, the owners were sent to forced labor camps run by the Ministry of Public Works. Two tax lists were drawn up in each district, one for Muslims and one for non-Muslims. The latter were taxed up to ten times more than the Muslims. Special consideration was given to the Donmes, a group belonging to a Muslim sect with Jewish antecedents. They were merely required to pay double the amount collected from ordinary Muslims. One critic characterized the law as the last manifestation of the "vampire-mentality" of extortion. Allied çensure and Germany's military collapse led the government to abandon the *varlik vergisi,* but not before nearly fifty-five million dollars was raised from confiscated property. This unfair tax created such a feeling of insecurity among non-Muslims that today most of them still feel they are not fully integrated Turkish citizens.

PEACEFUL REVOLUTION

Allied victory in 1945 completely discredited fascism and corporate-state ideologies. At the same time there was renewal of popular discontent with the government's policies: liberals resented censorship of the press and other communications media; the commercial class, enriched by war gains, sought escape from economic controls in the hope of profitably investing their accumulated capital; labor grew restive under a strike ban and the spiraling inflation that rapidly depreciated the value of their wages; minority groups had not yet been able to recover from the fleecing of the *varlik vergisi;* and religious conservatives still longed to undo the secularist reforms of the previous two decades. Many government officials had serious second thoughts about the value of totalitarianism and the use of personal dictatorship as a device to create a new society.

Both official and unofficial trends toward liberalism began soon after Germany was defeated. A first step was re-establishment of the Supreme Administrative Court in which a citizen could sue the government for damages. For the first time in years, speeches critical of the government were heard in the National Assembly. Party spokesmen no longer talked of popular dictatorship, but of popular sovereignty and democracy; and in parliament, a group of seven deputies broke party discipline by voting against a government bill. A new opposition within the PRP galvanized around the veteran leaders, Celal Bayar, Adnan Menderes, Fuad Koprulu, and Refik Koraltan. In June of 1945 they submitted the "Proposal of the Four" to the PRP parliamentary delegation, calling for an end to war restrictions, restoration of the powers of the National Assembly, individual liberties, and a multiparty system. Although President Inonu declared that he favored limited democracy—so long as it did not threaten the party—the four dissidents were forced to leave the PRP. They received support from Turkey's respected senior journalist, Ahmet Emin Yalman, editor of *Vatan.*

The PRP leaders gave token recognition to the trend by authorizing Nuri Demirag, a rich industrialist, to form an opposition group called the National Recovery party in 1945. Its free-enterprise program rallied little support, and the party rapidly faded away. The four PRP dissidents previously mentioned also formed an opposition party in January 1946, called the Democratic party, with far greater success. Like nearly all previous political opposition, it grew from a splinter of the PRP. Most original Democratic party members were former PRP members who had become dissatisfied with the parent party. Because of its close identity with the PRP, the Democratic party initially had little popular backing. Skeptics regarded it, like the Liberal party in 1930, as a device created by the PRP to give the appearance of an opposition.

Indeed, relations between the PRP and the Democrats were initially quite cordial. The PRP leadership even encouraged Bayar and his followers to develop a program of their own. But when the Democrats began to form a genuine opposition, gathering support in towns and villages, relations between the two groups cooled. Even though Bayar's group had no clear-cut program, the fact that it really began to oppose the government won wide support and sufficient followers to organize numerous local branches.

Democratic success in winning a popular following soon began to worry the PRP leadership, who had never anticipated that their encouragement would lead to such results. President Inonu attempted to forestall the new party's advance by pushing the national elections ahead by one year in the hope that the opposition would be unable to organize effectively in so short a time. The first real test of free elections occurred during the May 1946 municipal election when a number of non-PRP candidates were elected for the first time.

The government responded to the obvious current of discontent by cancelling several laws, such as those imposing price restrictions and enforcing emergency work levies. Authority to close newspapers was transferred from civil to judicial officials. Universities received greater autonomy. The ban on forming associations was eased.

By the eve of the July 1946 national elections, the Democrats had established organizations in forty-one of the country's sixty-three provinces. One of their greatest coups was winning the support of Fevzi Cakmak, Turkey's only living marshal who had been a close associate of Ataturk in the War of Liberation. The old hero's backing was particularly valuable because of the high esteem in which he was held by many religious conservatives.

The Democratic "march against despotism" was symbolized in posters showing a raised hand emblazoned with the slogan: "artik yeter!" (Enough!). Their campaign promises included encouragement of free enterprise, greater religious freedom, and the reduction of the executive powers. The PRP ran a gamut of charges against the Democrats, including everything from leftist leanings to reactionary use of religious propaganda. Popular interest was so stimulated that PRP candidates, who normally seldom visited their constituencies, now campaigned forcefully. Electioneering was easier for the Democrats, since they had only to play on the many themes of popular discontent and had no record to defend. Several leading newspapers came to their support, and a number of new ones were formed to oppose the PRP.

The 1946 election results were a disappointment for the Democrats, for they won only 62 of the 465 seats in parliament (they ran 273 candidates). When it became clear that the PRP victory was a result of widespread interference with voting, intimidation, and ballot box stuffing, however, the public became even more antigovernment. *Vatan* commented: "the Democratic party did not win the election; the Republic party lost it." Within the PRP itself, dissent was growing among younger liberals, who demanded that promises of free elections be fulfilled. As a result of internal and outside pressures, an election law satisfactory to all parties was passed for the 1950 election. It provided for a secret ballot, public vote counting, equal radio time for all parties, and judicial supervision of elections.

Three major groups ran for office in 1950, the first time that there was a truly free Turkish election: the PRP, the Democrats, and an offshoot of the latter, the Nation party founded in 1948. Many members of the Nation party, including Marshal Fevzi Cakmak, originally supported the Democrats but were disillusioned with its failure to undo the work of the "Godless Republic." The Marshal, leader of the Nation party, charged that both PRP and Democrats were too bound by Kemalist principles. Besides emphasizing a return to religion, the Marshal's backers advocated free enterprise.

Despite the split in the Democratic party, its victory in the May 1950 election was so overpowering that with justification it could be called a bloodless revolution. The party swept into power with 408 seats, leaving only 69 to the PRP, 1 for the Nation party, and 9 independents. Because of the electoral system, the landslide did not accurately reflect the balloting. To capture a district, a party had only to win a simple majority. Thus by winning 51 percent of the votes in every electoral district, it could gain all seats in the National Assembly. The Democrats topped their victory by electing Celal Bayar president of the republic and choosing Adnan Menderes prime minister.

The victory was unexpected in the outside world. Few observers thought that the PRP would permit its own defeat, especially since it controlled the army and all the civil administration. President Inonu could readily have forestalled a fair election by imposing emergency powers, using as a pretext the threat of a Soviet attack. However, Inonu and his followers withdrew gracefully, permitting a peaceful transition to a multiparty system.

The Democratic Era
The Democrats made few immediate changes after assuming office. Since they had not yet built up a cadre of party professionals and technicians, they were forced to retain many of the old officials. Among their first reforms were

those lifting the ban on criticism of the government. Restrictions on the press and freedom to form organizations were modified. The initial effect of the "bloodless revolution" profoundly affected public attitudes. The number of periodicals circulated increased considerably, after remaining almost static between 1928 and 1956. High government officials, who had remained aloof from the masses, surrendered their privileges—such as private railroad coaches—and engaged in public discussion of government policies. Both urban and rural police authority was curbed. Gendarmes, the "masters of the villages," were transferred from military to civil authority and deprived of their coercive powers. For the first time bureaucrats could be hailed before civil courts for offenses committed against the public, and the government even requested the public to complain to higher authorities of improper treatment. After 1950, high army posts were no longer the exclusive preserve of the PRP.

The era of new democracy was short lived, however. Within two years after assuming office, Bayar's party began to impose restrictions on its opponents, eventually placing Democratic leaders and policies above criticism. Not only were all the old PRP restrictions restored, but new ones were added. Suspension of the Nation party in 1953, on the charge that it advocated an Islamic state, restitution of the Arabic script, the fez, and the veil, was the first blow to free parliamentary government. In January 1954, the party was banned altogether and its leaders given token prison terms and fines. Even the PRP protested the ban as an attempt to subvert the impending elections.

Prime Minister Menderes used every opportunity to whip up sentiment against opposition to his policies in an effort to destroy free criticism. All PRP property was confiscated late in 1953 on the charge that the party's leaders had embezzled large sums while in power—despite the fact that many Democratic bosses had previously also been PRP leaders. The daily newspaper, *Ulus,* established by Ataturk in 1920, was confiscated; 200 PRP branch offices were closed; and the Democrats threatened to treat former President Inonu's protests as treason. A 1954 press law sought to silence criticism of Menderes's reckless economic policies by increasing penalties for spreading "inaccurate information" calculated to endanger the political and economic stability of Turkey. The decree was followed by imprisonment of scores of leading Turkish writers who dared voice their opposition. Even the dean of Turkish journalism, Ahmet Emin Yalman of *Vatan,* who had originally backed the Democrats, was jailed and later banished to a remote village.

During the 1954 and 1957 national elections, the Democrats won overwhelming victories because of wide peasant support. Victory was attributed to a temporary economic improvement and liberalization of religious restrictions. The restrictions on political criticism imposed by Menderes had not affected most rural inhabitants, but had interfered chiefly with the free expression of intellectuals and professionals. With only 58 percent of the popular vote, the Democrats won 503 of the Assembly's 541 seats in 1954.

Menderes seemed bent on wiping out all political criticism, as well as all opposition to his economic policies. By using anti-Communist ordinances, he was able to suppress university professors who deviated from the government line. Coalitions against his party were banned, and opposition speakers were kept off the state radio. New legislation authorized him to force retirement of judges after twenty-five years' service and to discharge undesirable civil servants, including university professors.

Arrests mounted for such crimes as "insults to the nation," "impugning the moral personality of the National Assembly," and "attacking the personality of the prime minister." The wave of totalitarianism disgusted many who had been original members of Menderes's own party but who now resigned to form the new Freedom party in 1955. Although supported by university professors, journalists, and other professionals, the group fared so badly in the 1957 elections (winning only four seats) that its members remerged with the PRP in November 1958. Other Democratic dissidents and former Nation party members formed the Republican National party during 1954 to restore freedom of speech and of the press. Winning only four seats in 1957, they subsequently merged with the small Peasant party, which became the ineffectual Republican Peasant National party.

THE 1960 REVOLUTION AND AFTER

Menderes toppled over his own regime when he attempted to involve the armed forces in politics by using them to impose his dictates on opposition parties. The crisis erupted in the spring of 1960 when the army was ordered to hinder the movements of former President Inonu and other PRP leaders. The threat to their national hero brought thousands of university students and cadets out into street demonstrations against Menderes. Urban unrest so threatened public order that a group of younger officers led by General Cemal Gursel seized the government and deposed Menderes and his entire regime on May 27, 1960. More than 600 Democrats and Democratic government appointees, including most of the parliamentary delegation, President Bayar, and Menderes, were imprisoned on an island near Istanbul to await trial for abuse of public funds and confidence. After a trial lasting almost a year, Menderes and two other former cabinet ministers were hanged. Nearly 500 other members of the Menderes regime received sentences of one year to life imprisonment. Former President Bayar's death sentence was commuted to life imprisonment.

The new twenty-three–man junta, calling itself the Committee of National Unity, promised to revamp the whole political structure of the

Nation along truly democratic lines. The junta governed alone until January 1961 when, establishing itself as a Constituent Assembly, it created itself a twenty-three-member Senate and also set up a 272-member House of Representatives. In the latter, some members were appointed and others were elected by provincial organizations, political parties, labor unions, teachers' associations, the judiciary, press syndicates, and similar organizations in order to obtain a cross section of professional representation in parliament. Preparatory to holding elections, announced for October 1961, a committee was appointed to draft a new constitution; political parties were permitted to re-form, provided they did not use the name "Democratic." Final power, however, remained in the hands of the military junta dominated by General Gursel, who continued to promise restoration of full civil government when he should decide that the time was opportune.

In July 1961, a referendum was held in which 47 percent of the electorate approved a new constitution to replace the one in force since 1924. The new constitutional system set up a series of checks and balances to offset the concentration of power in the executive. A bicameral legislature replaced the former single-chamber parliament. The new Grand National Assembly was composed of a 450-member National Assembly, in which any Turkish citizen thirty years old or more could stand for election, and a 150-member Republican Senate whose members had to be over forty years of age with a high level of education. Both chambers were to be elected by popular vote; fifteen additional senators were appointed by the president, to include the members of the military junta. Political power was concentrated in the Assembly with the Senate serving a secondary role. A fifteen-member Constitutional Court was established to pass on the legality of proposed legislation. An Assembly of High Judges composed of eighteen jurists was appointed to maintain the independent status of judges.

The new constitution contained a number of provisions for the social security of the citizen and for the protection of basic rights and civil liberties. Eighteen of the document's articles outlined the responsibility of the state toward the individual. It was clearly the aim of the new constitutional system to decentralize and depersonalize power as far as possible and thus obviate the reoccurrence of the kind of one-man rule imposed upon Turkey by Adnan Menderes.

In September 1961, Turkey's new political parties were permitted to start campaigning for the October elections. The junta authorized four parties to participate: two of them, the PRP and the Nation—renamed the Republican Peasants National—party, had existed before the 1960 revolution; the other two, the New Turkey and the Justice parties, were formed in 1961. The New Turkey party was formed by ex-members of the Freedom party, which had been established in 1955 by opponents of Menderes who had rebelled against his one-man rule of the Democratic party. The Justice party was founded by a retired general, Regip Gumuspala, and was supported almost entirely by rank-and-file members of the former Democratic party. Efforts to unite the Justice and New Turkey parties failed because of personal antagonisms between the leaders.

The PRP, led by former president Ismet Inonu, polled the largest number (between 40 and 42 percent) of the ten million votes cast, a proportion no higher than it received in the 1957 elections when it lost to Menderes's Democratic party. The large number of votes received by the Justice party for both the Senate and Assembly indicated that, as successor to the former Democrats, it had a wide peasant following. While the PRP captured the lead in most urban centers except Istanbul, the Justice party led in primarily rural districts where there had been strong support for Menderes.

The nature of the voting seemed to indicate that voters who desired a change from the policies of the former Democrats voted for the Nation or the New Turkey rather than for the PRP, although neither of the smaller parties made a strong showing. Since no party received a majority of the votes or a majority of representatives in either chamber, it became necessary to form a coalition government headed by former president Inonu, who now became prime minister under the new president, General Gursel. But within six months the parliamentary regime was torn by dissention, and the coalition collapsed. On the right, the conservative peasants, who had idolized Menderes and were now supporting the Justice party, opposed the efforts of Inonu to work out an equitable tax system and to introduce more planning of the national economy. On the other side of the political spectrum were the urban intellectuals, younger army officers, and labor leaders, who felt that the prime minister's reform program was moving too slowly. They demanded a greater amount of land reform, more housing programs, and speedier industrialization. So restive did some of the younger officers become that a group of them unsuccessfully tried to seize the government in emulation of radical officers' coups in the neighboring Arab countries. However, General Gursel crushed their attempt. By the end of 1962, although a new coalition headed by Inonu had been formed, both right and left were still dissatisfied with the government in power.

Despite Menderes's totalitarian policies, certain fundamental changes had occurred in his regime which in themselves tended to help democratize Turkish society. Until the post–World War II era, clear-cut class lines divided the peasants from the gentry—army officers, government officials, journalists, and intellectuals. The gentry, comprising 10 to 15 percent of the population, lived mostly in towns and large cities having little contact with either the urban working class or the peasants. They were descendants of the liberal Ottoman reformers, the Young Turks, and the leaders in the War of Liberation. Many of their traditions and attitudes, such as contempt for manual labor, were inherited from the Ottoman era. Under Ataturk it was they who rammed through unpopular reforms, and until recently they led the country. Few peasants or laborers have been represented in the power elite. The only exception occurred after failure of the Liberal party in 1930 when Ataturk handpicked a few working-class men and small shopkeepers for the PRP election lists. Of the 250 Democratic candidates for the Assembly in 1954, 52 were lawyers, 41 landowners, 40 doctors, 39 businessmen, 15 retired generals, 14 engineers, 13 teachers, and the rest from other professions. Most PRP candidates were retired officers, political personalities, high government officials, and a few professionals.

Menderes's appeals to the Turkish farmer now made the village an important factor in politics. All politicians began to consider the peasant, and both urban and rural lower classes came to feel a closer identity with the mainstream of Turkish political, economic, and social life, so much so that no party could hope to win without rural support. The trend was so evident during the Menderes regime that the urban middle class began to interpret these political appeals to the village as representative of deterioration of national values that threatened to undermine development of centers of higher culture. Menderes's anti-intellectualism, attacks made by small town politicians on the big city universities, and dismissals of politically active or outspoken professors seemed to bear out these fears. The problem became quite evident after the May 1960 revolution, for the military junta found that while its aims were understood in urban areas, the villagers could not really grasp the significance of Menderes's misuse of power.

The growing influence of the rural sector of the electorate was reflected during the 1960s, on the one hand by decline of the PRP, and on the other by the rapid rise in influence, popularity, and legitimation of the Justice party. Although the Justice party was formed by a handful of ambitious men, it successfully captured the votes of a larger and diverse number of ex-Democrats who were left partyless after the 1960 revolution.

During the first five years after the 1960 revolution, the PRP under the leadership of Inonu was unable to recapture its power base in the government administration or in the various regions of Anatolia. In Turkey's western provinces the Justice party successfully held onto most of the old Democratic provincial organizations. In central Anatolia the Republican Peasants National party, long a bastion of rural anticapitalist conservatism held sway. In eastern Turkey the New Turkey party, former dissidents from Menderes's Democratic party captured the party organizations. Unable to control a parliamentary majority, Prime Minister Inonu during this period formed three different coalition governments. At the same time, the Justice party was building a broad base of support which would in 1965 lead it to become the majority party.

The broadest base of the Justice party support came from smallholder peasants, a new class of farmers that came into existence as a result of improvements in the country's agricultural organization. The peasants were allied with other major economic groups including small- and middle-range commercial and industrial entrepreneurs, urban labor groups recently arrived from the countryside, and many wealthy farmers. Even the urban working-class support built up by the Justice party had a rural base, since it followed voting patterns established in the countryside.

In rural Turkey, voting still follows kinship lines, with most peasants following patterns established by family elders. However, active political participation in rural areas was left largely to the literate, educated, wealthy, and frequently younger middle class such as doctors and lawyers who assumed leadership roles in local party organizations. Since many of these younger men had only recently risen from the village proletariat, they were excluded from the elitist groups which formed the leadership of the PRP, finding their first political opportunities with the Democratic party and its successor, the Justice party. In the city much of the new urban lower class was composed of peasants who maintained ties with their home villages, consequently maintaining former village voting patterns.

During the 1960s the Justice party outbid the Labor party, the PRP, and other groups, to win lower-class votes. Villagers arriving in the growing urban centers gravitated toward districts populated by other villagers from the same region. Local Justice party officials greatly helped in aiding villagers to find themselves, to make contact with the authorities, to locate employment, and to cope with innumerable problems arising in the rapidly growing and increasingly overcrowded areas. Frequently the Justice party representative resided in the urban slums, whereas other party representatives were outsiders unable to establish personal contact with the new arrivals.

The Justice party did not fail to appeal to the religious bias of the peasantry. It responded to their widespread desire to tone down the anti-religious zealotry of the PRP reformers. With Justice party encouragement, hundreds of new mosques were built, prayers rendered with increasing frequency in the traditional Arabic, and religious instruction again permitted in schools. This permissive attitude toward religion and genuine concern for the peasants, as evident in extension of rural highways, water, and education services, as well as generous government support of agricultural prices, added to the image of the Justice party as the party of the peasant.

The significance of the Justice party and what it represented was perhaps best personified by the party's leader, Suleymen Demirel. Unlike the country's former charismatic leaders—Kemal Ataturk, Ismet Inonu, and Adnan Menderes—Demirel was an unglamorous technocrat of peasant origin. He rose from the village to become a leading water expert, serving as an adviser to former prime minister Menderes. The American-educated politician was known as a pragmatic executive rather than as a fiery political leader.

By 1965 the Justice party had established its roots so deeply in the country that it won an electoral victory, enabling it to take over the reins of government on its own, without forming a coalition. The party won 53 percent of the popular votes and 240 of the 450 seats in the National Assembly. The smashing victory was marked by further decline of the PRP, which barely won a third of the seats. The balance of votes were won by a wide spectrum of smaller parties, all of which developed from dissenting factions of either the PRP or the former Democratic party. At one end of the spectrum was the conservative and highly nationalist Peasant Republican National party, and at the other, the newly formed Marxist but non-Communist Turkish Labor party, neither of which succeeded in obtaining as much as 3 percent of the votes.

Demirel's Justice party administration proved to be so successful that the party again won an even larger majority in the 1969 election, 259 of the 450 seats. Demirel's renewed success was due to continued improvement of conditions among the middle- and lower-income rural classes. During these years the percent of people in professions, trades, services and other skilled jobs was increasing, drawing a larger number of their personnel from the new prosperous agricultural regions. As a result of the influx of peasants who still retain close ties with the countryside, the number of cities with populations of over 100,000 rose from about a dozen to nearly thirty between 1955 and 1970.

Political instability characterized Turkey during the 1970s. Convergence of serious economic problems, social unrest, dissatisfaction of students and intellectuals, land shortages in rural areas, and overpopulation in the cities undermined government authority. On university campuses students split into sharply polarized factions of right and left. Their use of firearms and bombs led to army intervention and the shutdown of many schools. Rival trade unions also clashed and strikes spread among public employees. Anti-Americanism led to bomb attacks on American property and kidnapping of U.S. citizens by leftists. In 1971 Kurds, inspired by the insurrection in Iraq, started a separatist movement, and the Arabs of Hatay province were reportedly urged by Syria to rebel.

The Justice party was unable to cope with the situation since it lost its majority shortly after the 1969 election when several of Demirel's right wing opponents left to form a new Democratic party. In the National Assembly factions and splits played havoc with the party system. A new rightist group with Islamic pretensions called the National Order party was formed by professor Necmettin Erbakan.

In March 1971 the army once again intervened, charging the parliament and the government had driven the country "into anarchy, fratricidal strife and social and economic unrest; made the public lose all hope of reaching a level of contemporary civilization...and placed the future of the Turkish republic in grave danger." Under the threat of an army takeover, Demirel resigned.

His replacement by a non-party prime minister failed to subdue the violence despite his promises of sweeping reforms in taxes, the land system, education, and the economy. Terrorism continued as the underground

Turkish People's Liberation Army attacked both foreign and domestic enemies. After martial law was proclaimed during April 1971 in several regions, newspapers were suppressed, strikes banned, and hundreds of leftists arrested. Both the right wing National Order party and the leftist Turkish Labor party were dissolved. The new prime minster, Dr. Nihat Erim, used the occasion to introduce constitutional amendments giving the government sweeping powers with the support of the army. With his new authority, the prime minister suspended civil rights, and autonomy of the universities, radio and television. Restrictions were clamped on the press and labor unions. It seemed that Turkey was about to return to the authoritarian era which had brought on the 1960 revolution.

Unable to obtain parliamentary support for his programs, Dr. Erim resigned in April after a year in office. He was replaced by a coalition of the PRP, Justice, and National Reliance parties, headed by Ferit Melen, leader of the Reliance party. It was a conservative group formed in 1967 after breaking with the PRP because of PRP increasing "radicalism."

PRP's move to the left began after Bulent Ecevit, a journalist and intellectual, whom some called the "poet-politician," became secretary general in 1966. Gradually he assumed leadership of the party; as its traditional chief, Ismet Inonu, now an octogenarian, turned over day-to-day operations. Borrowing many doctrines from the social-democratic movements of Western Europe, Ecevit advocated prolabor policies and greater government involvement in the country's social and economic life. Conservatives in PRP accused him of leading the party into "dangerous leftist adventures," causing the 1967 split when fifty PRP senators and representatives resigned in protest. Initially Inonu supported Ecevit, asserting that his proposed reforms would take the wind out of the sails of other leftist movements. When Ecevit protested against the repressive measures taken by the army in 1972 to suppress leftist groups and terrorism, twenty-six more senators and deputies resigned, including Ismet Inonu. Joining with earlier dissidents from the Reliance party, several of them formed the Republican Reliance party in 1973. With its right wing gone, Ecevit led the PRP into opposition against the government which he considered to be dominated by the military.

Another constitutional crisis came when President Sunay's term expired in March 1973. A new candidate with miltary backing, the army chief-of-staff, was opposed by most of the major political parties. They finally agreed on the retired commander-in-chief of the navy, Fahri Koruturk, who was then an elderly senator unaffiliated with any political faction. Many army officers now agreed that the time had come to return to their barracks. Political unrest seemed to decline and martial law was gradually lifted, coming to an end in September 1973. The new chief-of-staff, General Sancar, used his power to retire nearly 200 senior officers, many of whom had been involved in politics.

An interim government, organized to manage affairs until the October 1973 election, introduced several reforms demanded by advocates of social change. Eight million acres of land were redistributed to some 500,00 peasants and greater restrictions were placed on foreign investments in the mining and oil industries.

The PRP staged a political comeback in the 1973 national elections, emerging as the largest party with 185 of the 450 seats in the National Assembly and the prime minister's office. Loss of the PRP's large conservative constituency in parliament gave Ecevit an opportunity to campaign as a left-of-center social democrat, attracting votes from the Turkish Labor party, still banned because of its leftist orientation. Demirel's Justice party declined to 149 deputies at the expense of the Republican and National Salvation parties. The latter was established by Professor Erbakan in 1973 to replace his National Order party. It became the third largest group in the Assembly.

It was difficult for Ecevit to find compatible partners for a coalition government, required because he failed to obtain a majority. After three months of bargaining, a government was formed from the unlikely combination of PRP, with Ecevit as prime minister, and the National Salvationists, with Erbakan as deputy prime minister. Ecevit had to tread delicately, balancing his "radical" ideology with the traditionalist views of Erbakan. During this period Erbakan succeeded in having Turkey represented at an Islamic Summit Conference for the first time. Ecevit traded off concessions to national and religious feeling, in exchange for liberalization measures including removal of many security restrictions imposed during the martial law of 1972. He won over many farmers and simultaneously appealed to anti-Americanism by rescinding the ban on opium production which had been introduced under U.S. pressure.

In its initial phases Ecevit's regime was popular because of several balancing actions. In May 1972, 50,000 prisoners, both political and criminal, were granted amnesty, an act supported by both left and right. The left was gratified when permission was granted to organize a new Turkish Socialist Worker's party from ex-members of the outlawed Turkish Labor movement. Permission to use "socialist" was considered a radical departure from established precedent because the word, to conservative Turks, was identical to "communist." The regime reached the peak of its popularity during the invasion of Cyprus during the summer of 1974. All the nation from right to left rallied to this "sacred" cause. Ecevit decided to test his popularity by resigning in September 1974 and calling for new elections.

Instead an interim government was formed, unrest and street demonstration erupted, and in March 1975 Demirel was again called on to form a government. He had to form an even broader coalition of four parties. In addition to his Justice party and the National Salvationists, it included the Republican Reliance and National Action parties. The National Action party is called neo-fascist because of its militant nationalist doctrines. Its chief, Alparslan Turkes, was once leader of the country's pan-Turanist movement calling for unity of all Turks in the Middle East. The party is secular, in contrast to the Salvationists, but supports free enterprise and "scientific" national development.

In this unsteady coalition, Demirel was unable to deal with the complex domestic problems—unemployment, inflation, and widespread dissent. Presence of militant pan-Islamists and pan-Turks in the cabinet also blocked movement on the Cyprus conflict.

The 1977 election, resulting in a PRP plurality of 213 seats, failed to resolve any of these problems. Ecevit once again became prime minister, but he was unable to rally enough votes in parliament to support his government, and after only ten days Demirel again replaced him with a precarious three-party coalition. The game of musical chairs between the leaders of the country's two largest parties continued through 1980 with Ecevit and Demirel successively in the prime ministry. In 1980 Demirel became prime minister for the fourth time in a dozen years by forging another right-of-center coalition with Erbakan's National Salvationists and Turkes' National Action party, unlikely partners in a government with Ecevit, now identified as a liberal, left-of-center social democrat. Although the PRP and Justice party managed to retain their mass following, neither was able to capture enough votes from the left, right, or independent factions, which stubbornly resisted absorption into the two mass parties.

The steadily deteriorating economy, the growing social and political unrest that culminated in widespread terrorism and collapse of civil authority in dozens of places across Turkey brought the country to one of its worst crises. Turkish pride in the post–World War II transition from authoritarianism to political democracy was threatened by a complex of seemingly insoluble problems. With per capita income only a fourth of that in Western Europe, Turkey was the world's poorest democracy except for India. The burden of maintaining a massive military establishment with nearly 500,000 men under arms, the largest standing army among Europe's NATO members, further drained the economy. Both internal and external factors conspired to bring economic growth almost to a halt, down from one of the highest rates among developing countries.

Industrial development had altered the urban-rural balance between 1945 and 1975 from 25 percent to 50 percent of the population living in cities. However, urban infrastructure lagged far behind the explosive population expansion, with millions crowded into the festering *gecekondu* settlements surrounding cities like Istanbul, Ankara, and Izmir. The *gecekondu,* from the Turkish to "build overnight," were hastily, often illegally erected shack towns thrown up by migrants from rural areas in search of a better life in metropolitan Turkey. But a growing number of urban dwellers were bereft of opportunity for self-improvement in this critical era of declining industrial production, closing factories and growth of unemployment from 20 to 25 percent by the late 1970s.

These conditions became the breeding ground for militantly radical political factions of both right and left in the *gecekondus,* on university campuses, in rural areas where latent disaffection erupted, among the Kurds in the east, among the Shi'ite minority in central Turkey, and among those whose hopes were frustrated all over the country. Dozens of new Marxist, neo-Marxist, Islamic, and outright fascist factions appeared, many of them committed to overthrow of established law and order through use of terrorist tactics.

By 1979–1980 the number of terrorist victims was in the hundreds each month; some estimates were that there was a daily average of ten political assassinations. The victims were in all political factions and from every sector of society. They included high police officials, university professors, journalists, government employees, and finally former prime minister Erim.

Attempts to deal with the situation through parliamentary means were frustrated by the bitter recriminations between the PRP and Justice party leaders, each of whom used the liberal provisions of the 1961 constitution to stymie actions or policies of the other. Parliament was frequently thrown into disarray, and instability increased as the minority factions and independents threw their support first to Demirel, then to Ecevit. Attempts to form a broad-based interparty coalition to face the crisis failed when each major group renounced cooperation with the other. When out of power, Ecevit attacked suggestions for imposition of martial law by Demirel as an infringement on civil liberty. And when Ecevit imposed martial law in 13 of Turkey's 67 provinces during 1978, Justice MPs accused him of not demonstrating sufficient strength or determination.

The slaughter of over 100 Shi'ite Alevis and 1,000 other casualties in the town of Karamanmaras (Maras) in December 1978 finally induced Ecevit to declare martial law. After 1970 sectarian hostilities ended centuries of relatively peaceful relations between the Sunni majority and Alevis (a Shi'ite sect) and hatred intensified into violence between majority and minority. The Alevis, a group of between three and five million at the lower end of the social scale, tended to support the PRP because of Ecevit's greater emphasis on social programs and welfare support for the disadvantaged, whereas the Sunnis in rural areas were more inclined to back Demirel. Sectarian strife also spread to eastern Anatolia where a dozen Kurdish nationalist groups were exposed, ranging from those calling for cultural recognition to those demanding an independent Kurdistan.

Characteristic of the noncooperation between PRP and the Justice party was the impasse in parliament over selection of a successor to President Koroturk, whose seven-year term ended in 1980. There were more than 100 votes in the Assembly before it was decided to appoint an acting president to fill the post because the two major parties were so uncompromising.

After Ecevit's fall and Demirel's return to power following still another parliamentary crisis in October 1979, the army warned the two leaders that growing political violence and parliamentary instability were threatening to undermine the whole state. As army pressure increased on Demirel he stepped up law-and-order measures, dismissing some 1,700 elected mayors and city councils in September 1980. The Constitutional Court also ordered the Marxist Workers party to disband because of its insistence on support for Kurdish language schools, a violation of traditional emphasis on the country's "Turkish character."

On September 12, 1980, a six-man military junta of five army generals and an admiral, lead by general Kenan Evren, leader of the National Security Council, took over the government. Their stated objective was to combat and prevent anarchy and terrorism: to "repair a democracy which has been spoiled." Harkening back to the traditions of Kemal Ataturk, their proclamations asserted that the operation was necessary "to defend and protect the republic." The new National Security Council immediately clamped down on terrorism and imposed a number of restrictive measures. Parliament was suspended; some 30,000 suspected political dissidents were arrested, as well as leaders of all major parties, including Demirel and Ecevit; strikes and protest demonstrations were banned; political party activities were curtailed; and stricter press censorship was imposed. Certain martial law actions that led to charges of human rights violations and torture by Amnesty International and several Western European governments, resulted in Turkey's exclusion from a number of European Community activities.

A new 27-member cabinet of nonpolitical "experts," which included seven other retired officers, was headed by a retired admiral as prime minister. A few weeks later all 16 political parties were dissolved and their property confiscated. Plans for a totally new, strongly centralized government were put forward and a 160-member Advisory Assembly was appointed to draft a new constitution and to prepare the way for national elections.

Within a year both security and economic conditions greatly improved. Deaths from terror declined from 200 to less than 30 a month; both Demirel and Ecevit were released from prison, although Ecevit was later reincarcerated; inflation dropped from its all time high of 120 to 40 percent; and there was even a 3 percent decline in unemployment.

By mid-1982 the Consultative Assembly completed its constitutional draft, and plans were announced for a constitutional referendum. The new document was lengthy and detailed, with over 200 articles. It replaced the balance of power in the 1961 constitution with a strong president, elected for seven years by a new single-chamber, 400-member Grand National Assembly (elected for five years). Many presidential powers resembled those acquired by Charles de Gaulle when he became president of the fifth French republic. The president could appoint and dismiss the prime minister and cabinet, could dissolve parliament and order new elections after a government crisis of more than 30 days, could rule by decree after declaring a state of emergency, and could make many high level appointments including the appointment of senior judges. New political parties would be permitted except for those which were class based, Communist or Fascist, or advocated a religious state. Strict new controls were imposed on labor unions and the press. It was obvious that the drafters were attempting to exclude from political life militant factions of both right and left, to ban both Marxists and Islamic militants by returning to the political ideology of Ataturk.

While the National Security Council stated that the new constitution would end abuses of the 1961 document, many members of the Consultative Council, university faculties, and former social democratic parties charged that the president and public authorities in the new system were being given too much power and control over the mass media, trade unions, and human rights. Despite this criticism, the new constitution was approved in a referendum held during 1982 by 90 percent of the 20 million Turkish voters who participated. At the same time they elected General Evren president of the country for a seven-year term, assuring continued control by the junta in the years ahead.

ECONOMIC REFORM

As nonagricultural unemployment increased with the failure of small local industries late in the Ottoman era, popular resentment was fanned against foreign capital and the "Christian" middle class. The Young Turks attempted unsuccessfully to free the economy from foreign domination and to induce Muslims to take over the minority-controlled finance and commerce. During World War I, the government abolished the capitulations, established a national bank to finance "Turkish" enterprises, and encouraged cooperatives. Boards of directors were required to include Turkish citizens, and government-instigated boycotts were aimed at minority-owned enterprises in order to boost purely Turkish enterprises.

But industry continued to suffer from the effects of the capitulations, which had encouraged the influx of cheap European goods. Manufactured products, most of which were imported, were paid for by specialized exports grown near the coast, such as tobacco, nuts, raisins, and figs. Only handicraft industries, like rugs, were of local importance.

Étatism

The measures taken to further economic development during World War I set the tone for Ataturk's economic policies after the capitulations were abolished and the millet system ended in 1924. Although Turkey lacked investment capital, nationalist leaders were still suspicious of foreign funds, constantly emphasizing self-sufficiency. Against this background "étatism," or state direction of the economy, developed. Its purpose was to create an independent economy liberated from non-Turkish capital. "We shall create," declared Ataturk, "every industry, great or small, for which there are in our land the economic conditions necessary to its work and development."

The Ish (Business) Bank was established in 1924 to organize and finance local business. Although *pro forma* a private institution, its board of directors were Assembly deputies, Ataturk personally underwriting several shares. The Industrial and Mining, later Sumer, Bank was established in 1925 to run state industries, which were intended to supplement, not replace, private enterprise. To help overcome conservative attitudes that slowed down progress, the Assembly made state lands available at low prices, revived the Agricultural Bank, reduced taxes and freight charges, and modified import duties. A government statistical department was organized, and professional men were released from the military to join industrial establishments. Foreign employment was greatly restricted to encourage native Turkish talent. Gradually, the government purchased foreign-owned railroads and built new ones.

When the world depression struck in 1929, little had been accomplished in raising living standards, and the progress that did exist was set back. After a four-year hiatus, the government plunged fully into the economy, declaring outright étatism. A new, large-scale economic program was initiated with Soviet assistance in grants, machinery, technical aid and advice, and training for Turkish workmen. The Russians helped draft a five-year plan and provided machinery for the Sumer Bank's huge textile plant at Kayseri. A similar agreement was signed with Nazi Germany, resulting by 1936 in a shift of half of Turkey's exports to the Third Reich.

After the étatists established the Eti Bank in 1935, it acquired an empire of power stations and transmission lines; took over the country's coal, iron, chrome, copper, lignite, and sulphur mines; and in addition acquired shares in the Ankara Insurance Company and the People's Bank.

A Turkish government agricultural agency bought, sold, and stored surpluses, imported and exported foodstuffs, and operated flour mills and bakeries. Agricultural cooperatives established in the mid-1930s were only slightly successful, enlisting fewer than 100,000 members by the end of the war. Efforts of the Ministry of Agriculture to improve rural conditions through an extensive research program, an agricultural college, several schools, an extension service, and a forestry program also affected only a fraction of the peasantry.

Industry

Throughout the history of the republic, the government has controlled directly or indirectly most industry, commerce, and finance. The list of state enterprises includes: farms; forestry establishments; mining companies; steel, cement, leather, paper, textile, tobacco, and alcohol plants; companies distributing agricultural, gas, and coal products and controlling utilities; ice factories; slaughter houses; beach resorts; restaurants; and sports stadia.

One prime minister defined Ataturk's étatist program as an "advanced type of socialism." Celal Bayar, however, who was prime minister when the program began early in the 1930s, believed its purpose was to advance private initiative. Individual enterprise was encouraged in theory, but government economic activities actually left little room for private competition. Until 1950, political considerations outweighed economic objectives. Emphasis was placed on heavy prestige industries, even when they became an economic burden. "Ataturk's minarets," the slender smoking chimneys of modern plants, appeared among the mosque minarets of large cities. But their high-speed, chromium-plated, and cellophane-wrapped products, writes Thornburg, were "in many cases as alien to the life and the most elementary needs of the Turks as are the smoking 'Ataturk minarets' to the Mosque of Sulaiman the Magnificent."[4]

While the most modern steel plants were being imported, there were no commercial foundries of any importance manufacturing basic farm tools. The gap between primitive handicrafts and the most advanced and complicated productive facilities was never bridged. A notorious example was the gigantic steel plant at Karabuk, planned so inefficiently that its "waste of capital would be serious for any country; to Turkey it represents a tragic diversion of scanty resources." When it was built, continues Thornburg, "the Turks were under the spell of the Soviet passion for the magnificent planning and construction of heavy industries which had incurred Lenin's criticism of 'gigantomania.'"[5]

The government failed to develop social services, regulations to protect labor, unemployment agencies, or insurance, social security, and compensation programs until after World War II. Unions were banned, and in some parts of the country labor was auctioned to the highest bidder by middlemen who then kept the difference between wages paid to the peasant and the amount received from employers.

Discontent with the PRP's program rose to the surface after World War II. Farmers and low income groups resented industrialization at their expense, and merchants who had accumulated large war profits sought less government controls. Criticism came to a head when wartime prosperity ended and Turkish goods lost their world markets. Étatism was increasingly attacked by those who desired a free market. The program had attained its objective, they argued, and Turkey had won economic independence; étatism was now obsolete. When the United States initiated its massive economic assistance program, American advisers also pressured for an end of state controls.

After its 1950 victory the Democratic party, sponsoring free enterprise, attempted to persuade private capital to take over government businesses. But it was easier to attract foreign than local capital. Turkish investors were far too wary of possible reversals in government attitudes. They needed not only legal but also psychological guarantees for the future. Since early Ottoman times, the state had played the dominant role in all phases of the economy. Thus it was difficult to change the prevailing outlook about the relationship between private capital and government. Private entrepreneurs still depended on the government to secure foreign exchange, to raise protective barriers against foreign competition, to correct incompetence, and to provide numerous social services. Instead of diminishing, state enterprise increased under the Menderes regime. New state sugar plants were opened, and government investment in heavy industries expanded.

Under Menderes a vast industrialization program was initiated. His attempts to develop industry at a rapid pace soon led the country into escalating debt and inflation. The failure to offset the heavy import of industrial goods and machinery by expanded exports produced major foreign trade deficits and acute shortages of foreign exchange. At the time of Menderes's massive economic expansion, Turkey was maintaining the third largest army in the non-Communist world, which absorbed nearly 40 percent of the national budget. Despite large-scale American economic assistance, Menderes was unable to stem the rapid escalation of inflation and high prices. In the decade between 1953 and 1963 the cost of living increased by nearly 150 percent. Although tight controls were placed on credit, foreign trade, and industrial profit margins, the inflation continued, with rapid devaluation of the Turkish lira. Criticism of Menderes's economic policies led to his increased sensitivity at press commentary, which in turn resulted in the unrest leading to the 1960 revolution.

Since the 1960 revolution, and especially since the period of Justice party government in 1965, more emphasis has been placed upon the private sector, which now accounts for some 70 percent of Turkish industry. But even the Justice party found it difficult to decentralize the large state industries, many of which are controlled through the government-owned companies such as Sumer and Eti banks. Legislation has been introduced to encourage investments of foreign private capital in the country, but because of inflation, foreign capital has been reluctant. State monopolies still control the manufacture and marketing of tobacco, liquors, beer, salt, and tea.

The Democrats' Farm Program

While failing to end industrial étatism, the Democrats, backed by American economic and technical assistance, wrought an economic transformation in many rural areas, winning the confidence of the Turkish peasant. They undertook extensive rural mechanization programs, made agricultural credit easier, and subsidized farm prices on a level far above those on the world market. Between 1947 and 1955 the number of tractors increased from 3000 to over 40,000. An American program expanded the network of all-weather roads by more than twenty times, opening new areas to cultivation and linking hundreds of formerly isolated villages with urban markets. For a few years Turkey changed from a net importer of wheat to one of the world's leading exporters. An extensive sugar-refining industry grew up, fed by new beet-growing regions in which there was widespread mechanization.

Many villages, until recently primitive backwaters, have now become equipped with radios, electric lights, and buses that bring the farmers to urban centers where they purchase modern agricultural equipment, learn the latest political gossip, and acquire new ideas about farming and village industry. Peasants have begun to imitate city manners, habits, and customs. Smaller villages fuse with larger ones as the rural population grows. Immigration to the cities between 1945 and 1955 led to a decline in peasant population from 83 to 71 percent of the nation. Domination of the old landed families is no longer a feature of rural life since younger men have assumed local power.

With two-thirds of its population still dependent on the land for their living, and a rapidly increasing birth rate approaching 3 percent a year, Turkey's planners have begun to be concerned about land availability. The population increased by some 10 million to over 34 million in the 15-year period between 1955 and 1970. This increase undercut the annual economic growth rate, which during the decade of the 1960s was sustained at about 7 percent a year.

Despite government assistance to small- and medium-size landowners and large U.S. credits contributed to agricultural development, critics of the agricultural system maintain that a major agricultural reformation is needed to change the pattern of land ownership which made it possible for 10 percent of the owners to obtain more than 50 percent of national farm income. Although nearly three-fourths of the peasants own their own land, less than one out of four reaps the profits from about 70 percent of the land. Estimates in the 1960s were that nearly a third of the agricultural families did not own sufficient land to maintain themselves. Attempts to remedy the situation during the 1950s by distribution of government lands were strongly opposed by landowners in both major political parties.

Land reform programs urged by the PRP in the late 1960s failed to carry a wide appeal. Much more popular was the agricultural program of the conservative Justice party which exempted farmers from any substantial taxation. The *laissez-faire* policies of the Justice party, while winning wide approval from a large number of rural peasantry, tended to postpone for the future many of the more urgent problems of economic development facing the country at the end of the 1960s.

The party's extensive appeals to the rural sector also aroused wide opposition to the government among urban workers' groups, students, the city middle class, and leftist intellectuals. Students, intellectuals, and labor leaders were resentful of being excluded from power. The paradoxes of Turkey's economic situation would create serious complications for any government. Despite the large number of students, the official illiteracy rate was almost 40 percent, and the universities produced thousands of graduates who could not find jobs. The country's astronomical birthrate vastly increased the number of secondary school candidates for higher education, but in 1975 only 20 percent of the 300,000 applicants could find a place and of these a mere 5 percent went to the school of their choice.

Industrial development was largely dependent on imported raw materials, capital goods, and technology in an era when many of these items, especially oil and machinery, were escalating in price, while Turkey's own agricultural exports were declining on world markets. In 1976, for example, the country's three auto plants depended on import of over half their parts, but none of the cars produced were exported to earn the hard currency required to pay for their imported components. Furthermore, Turkey was short of high level technical skills and capital required to develop an efficient and profitable industrial plant. Advisors recommended a shift from industry dependent on capital imports to export of manufactures that would utilize the country's rich supply of raw materials and food.

Just when the need for and shortages of foreign capital shot upward, the economic recession in Western Europe slowed the import of foreign currency remittances from the several million Turkish workers in Western Europe (over one million in Germany alone). The world economic crisis was intensified in Turkey where inflation suddenly shot up from 50 percent to over 100 percent during 1979–1980. Only 40 percent of industrial capacity was being used by the end of 1980. Development plans for eastern Turkey, where only 10 percent of the villages had electricity and a mere seven percent of the cultivated land was irrigated, were suspended or never initiated.

Only a small number of Turkey's 40,000 villages have been swept into the modernization era. Those in the east and in remote mountain regions have not yet been affected. There the wooden plow is still the most commonly used agricultural implement, and age-old custom and superstition continue to dominate the routine of peasant life. Although Turkey will continue for decades to be more a part of the Orient than of the West, the ferment of progress has stimulated the beginnings of drastic change throughout society. Turkey is a nation with great undeveloped human and natural resources, with great moral fiber and intense national consciousness. Its future will be determined by the ability of its leaders to galvanize these assets into a major effort required to complete the transformation begun by Ataturk in the early days of the republic.

NOTES

1. Cited in Max Thornburg, Graham Spry, and George Soule, *Turkey and Economic Appraisal,* New York, 1949, p. 76.

2.   Kemal Karpat, *Political and Social Thought in the Contemporary Middle East,* New York, 1968, p. 360.

3.   Paul Stirling, "Religious Change in Republican Turkey," *The Middle East Journal,* vol. 12, no. 4, autumn 1958, pp. 395–408.

4.   Thornburg, *et al., op. cit.,* p. 106.

5.   *Ibid.,* pp. 108, 109.

8 Origins of Modern Egypt

THE NAPOLEONIC IMPACT

Egypt was a decaying appendage of the Ottoman Empire when Napoleon occupied it in July 1798. Conditions had changed little since the Ottoman conquest in 1517 (see chapter 3). The country remained a loosely held province subject to the avarice of some two dozen quarreling Mamluk elite. According to a description in the 1780s, it was a land of "ruined villages, revolting nakedness, hideous rags, smoke-blackened shacks where the talk is of nothing but extortion, beatings and murders...[with] a government indifferent to everybody's property or safety, a coarse and licentious soldiery which leaves the peasants just enough to prevent them from dying.... Under the barbarous rule of ignorant despotism, there can be no tomorrow."[1]

Napoleon presented himself as Egypt's great liberator from Mamluk thralldom. An early admiration for Islam and the teachings of Muhammad enabled Napoleon to cloak his policy in a Muslim guise that was compatible with his and the Egyptians' conception of the state. He set up a divan, or council, of nine al-Azhar sheikhs charged with appointing police, supply, and other administrative officials. They and similar provincial councils assisting the French military governors all swore allegiance to the French Republic. Mamluks were replaced in top government posts by Egyptians. A regular government system of tax collection was established to replace the predatory tax farmers. French schools and libraries opened by Napoleon introduced contemporary Western ideas and helped sow the seeds of Egypt's intellectual reawakening. The country received its first printing press with Arabic type;

the library of the Egyptian Institute (established 1798–1801) introduced many Egyptians to the French writings on science. French became the second language of the middle class.

Despite his attempts to found a "progressive" Muslim state, Napoleon was regarded as a Christian infidel by the masses and was twice forced to suppress uprisings. When Cairo mobs attacked the French barracks, Napoleon shelled al-Azhar mosque, the rebel stronghold. Quartering French troops there considerably cooled his formerly cordial relations with the sheikhs. In the end the French occupation left as bitter a memory as the depredations of the other conquerors.

MUHAMMAD 'ALI

Muhammad 'Ali might never have had the opportunity to establish modern Egypt had the French never invaded that country. Born in 1769 to a middle-class Albanian family living at Kavalla in Macedonia, Muhammad 'Ali became a tobacco merchant. He left commerce to join the Ottoman force sent to fight Napoleon in 1799. In Egypt his abilities enabled him to rise quickly from junior officer rank to general. In 1803, after the French and British evacuation of Egypt, Muhammad 'Ali became governor, or pasha, of the province; and by 1805 clever divide-and-rule tactics and cultivation of influential opinion in Cairo had made him Egypt's strongest political figure.

The sultan realized that Muhammed 'Ali was a threat to Ottoman suzerainty in Egypt, but he failed to recognize the pasha's real strength and unsuccessfully attempted to overthrow him with Mamluk help. Despite the abortive Ottoman attempt to get rid of him, Muhammad 'Ali offered his services to the sultan during the second phase of the Napoleonic wars when France became an Ottoman ally and the English, now the enemy of the sultan, attempted to invade Egypt. No military effort was actually required to repulse the British, however, for they suddenly withdrew their forces after becoming reallied with the sultan in 1807. Muhammad 'Ali was left master of the country.

Thereafter the Albanian concentrated on strengthening his own position by centralizing the regime in Cairo. The Mamluk threat was removed in 1811 when 300 of their chiefs were invited to a parley in the capital and massacred. The pasha was no Islamic enthusiast, and he had no objections to using qualified local Armenians, Greeks, and Copts in high state positions. The pattern of religious toleration set up at this time continued throughout the course of Egyptian politics down to the 1956 invasion by Israel, Great Britain, and France (see chapter 9).

After Muhammad 'Ali's select Albanian force failed at the beginning of the 1811–1818 campaign against the rebellious Wahabis of central Arabia, he dissolved their units and drafted fresh troops from the peasants, or fellahin, who had not before been used for military service. Trained with European weapons and tactics by a former French captain, the peasant army proved its effectiveness in Arabia (see chapter 16), against the Greeks in 1824–1825, in the Sudan, and against the Ottoman Empire itself in the 1832–1833 and 1839–1841 Syrian expeditions (see chapter 6).

The early victories so whetted Muhammad 'Ali's appetite for military prowess that he engaged additional French and Italian officers to open academies for infantry, cavalry, naval, and staff officers. A music school was even established to ensure that his forces would march to appropriate military airs. By 1839, the Western trained and equipped Egyptian army of 200,000 could compare favorably with forces in Europe.

However, efforts to arouse a widespread Egyptian patriotism in the conscript army failed miserably. To evade service, peasants maimed themselves or fled their homes. Despite the smart uniforms, relatively high and regular pay, and extra rewards for meritorious service, intelligent Egyptians often tried to become al-Azhar students to obtain exemption. Still, those who became junior officers acquired a measure of social status, for they rose from backward villages to obtain education, position, and security. The junior-officer elite was later to become an influential political factor, as will be seen below by their roles in the 1880s and 1950s.

Realizing that he could not create an effective Western military machine without native technicians, engineers, doctors, teachers, and other craftsmen, Muhammed 'Ali set out to train them. But European experts were required to educate his Egyptian apprentices. Since Westerners were reluctant to settle without their families, educational and health facilities had to be built for their use. Consequently, foreign military advisers arrived with their own teachers and physicians. The European hospitals were then opened to Egyptians.

Because the existing religious institutions were inadequate for a modern education, a parallel school system, run on modern French lines, was established. Secular and religious systems of education continued to exist side by side until after the 1952 revolution. Most Egyptians continued to receive religious schooling, however, secular institutions being suspected by the common people because of their foreign origins.

Under French medical supervision, the decimating annual cholera and bubonic plagues were brought under control. In Alexandria, foreign consuls became members of a Sanitation Board, enforcing rigid quarantines. Such controls, however, eventually created a problem as well as solving one, for by the end of the century, they helped foster the great population explosion that is so critical in Egypt today.

Muhammad 'Ali's modernization attempts were financed by a crude form of statism. All land on which there were tax arrears and that either belonged to enemies of the state or was part of the wakfs system (see chapter 3) was seized for distribution to Muhammad 'Ali's relatives and followers, making his family the largest landowners in Egypt. Some small plots (between three and five acres) were distributed to the fellahin, although theoretically all land belonged to the Ottoman sultan. Land use and the distribution of its profits were determined by Muhammad 'Ali. Local governors, who fixed the areas to be tilled and amount of crops to be grown, supplied the peasants with farm implements, animals, and seed. After all the prescribed taxes and imposts had been deducted, however, the peasant was usually left with only one sixth of his produce. Harvests were stored in government warehouses and disposed of when local or foreign markets provided the best opportunities. Muhammad 'Ali, like the ancient Pharoahs, actually controlled all the country's resources and was the sole distributor of the necessities of daily life. Even the brutality of his methods of enforcement resembled the callous methods of antiquity. The corvée, or forced labor system, was imposed. Discipline was backed by the use of the *courbash,* a whip made of hippopotamus hide, and unruly peasants were in danger of being hanged, buried alive, beaten, or loaded with chains. Yet the farmer became economically more secure than he was in Mamluk times. Agricultural conditions had been so bad in the decade before 1808 that crop cultivation was said to have declined by two thirds. By the end of Muhammad 'Ali's reign, land under the plow had increased to a third, to nearly four million acres.

The successful planting of long staple cotton by the French engineer Jumel in 1820 revolutionized Egyptian agriculture. By 1835, production of "Jumel's cotton" increased from about 50 tons to some 12,000 tons. High prices paid by Europe soon made long staple cotton the backbone of Egypt's economic and financial system, and all agriculture was adapted to its cultivation. The Mahmudia Canal was built in 1819 to transport cotton from the Nile Valley to Alexandria, and a barrier across the Nile was begun to dam up a water supply in the Delta region for use during the dry summers. River banks were raised and strengthened for flood protection, and the Delta canals were deepened to ensure a year-round water supply.

Until these Nile barriers were constructed, irrigation in Upper Egypt had always utilized the basin system. Once a year, when the river rose, over 200 basins, averaging some 7000 acres each, were filled with slimy water for thirty to forty days. When the water drained away, winter seed was sown in the moist mud, producing a single yearly harvest. Storing the summer flow of the Nile behind barriers facilitated water distribution throughout the year and made possible the cultivation of several summer crops, such as cotton and sesame, thus more than doubling Egypt's agricultural output.

Industrialization Efforts

Muhammad 'Ali also initiated a program of local industry to free Egypt from prolonged dependence on European arms, uniforms, and other supplies.

But the country was hardly ready for advanced technology. Local handicraft had begun to decline with the influx of cheap European goods with which the Egyptians, without modern production techniques, could not successfully compete. The pasha did not believe that private enterprise could succeed until the Egyptian overcame his reluctance to invest in risky and long-term investments. He therefore considered it necessary for the government to lead the way by embarking on a large-scale economic development program. Muhammad 'Ali planned to use foreign experts and advisers in his state monopolies until they could be replaced by Egyptians who had mastered Western techniques.

Beginning in 1816, he was able to establish iron foundaries, a sugar refinery, a glass factory, munitions plants, and a shipyard. The first cotton spinning and weaving mills opened in 1821; seven years later they were able to absorb a quarter of Egypt's cotton production. Within the decade, local factories were responsible for the total domestic supply of cheap cottons. A foundry established in Cairo in 1820 attempted to provide castings for machinery, looms, spinning machines, arsenal parts, and steam-engine repairs. During the Egyptian occupation of the Levant, industrialization efforts were also carried into Syria, where Muhammad 'Ali's son Ibrahim set up textile plants and exploited local mineral deposits.

Muhammad 'Ali's efforts to emulate the West failed to have long-lasting effects because few Egyptians were capable of dealing with the details of running such factories. Ignorant or careless management left machinery unoiled; instead of utilizing the waterpower of the Nile, the traditional oxen were put to use. Fellahin were unaccustomed to the discipline of regular factory work, and beating them, as was done with recalcitrant army conscripts, did not solve the problem of keeping the factories adequately supplied with workers. Similarly, there was a dearth of skilled managers to run the factories.

Foreign merchants were not particularly helpful in supporting this program. England protested that Egyptian state monopolies constituted unfair competition to British commerce, and Lord Palmerston insisted that such state-sponsored Egyptian competition with British industry would undermine his country's free trade policy. After the pasha was defeated by the European powers in 1840, they forced him to abolish most of his government monopolies and to submit to the special privileges granted by the capitulations to the Western merchant. Within a few years little was left of Egypt's first industrial revolution except factory ruins and rusted machinery.

In government administration and organization, Muhammad 'Ali's efforts were more durable. Egypt was unified administratively under a strong central authority in Cairo for the first time since the sixteenth century. A network of provincial governors *(mudirs)* reported directly to the pasha on the affairs of each village under their jurisdiction. The central government organized departments of war, navy, cultivation, finance, commerce, education, police, and foreign affairs; and a council was established in 1819 to give legislative advice. At the capital, the Sharia courts were supplemented with a system of civil law using the Code Napoléon, and this system was eventually extended to the provinces. Minorities, who for centuries had been required to wear degrading symbols or special clothing, were no longer so required and were now free to practice their religions and to build churches, convents, or synagogues. They played an important role in helping to develop the country. Armenians were active in government, Jews in finance, and European-educated Syrian Christians as middle men in business.

Muhammad 'Ali is often called the father of modern Egypt. During his regime the country developed from a backward outpost of the Ottoman Empire into a powerful autonomous province owing only nominal allegiance to the sultan. A distinctive Egyptian national character and national consciousness were encouraged. Significantly, the first seeds of twentieth-century nationalism were thus planted in the traditions of the junior ranks of the army and the middle class. Most important of all for this initial stage, Europe also began to regard Egypt as a separate political entity, with its own policies independent of and separate from those of Istanbul.

MUHAMMAD 'ALI'S SUCCESSORS

Between 1840 and his death in 1849, Muhammad 'Ali turned over the reins of government, first to his son Ibrahim, and then to his grandson Abbas. Neither Abbas nor his successor in 1854, Said, inherited the dynamism of the founder of modern Egypt, and gradually the government, economy, and social life sank into a torpor and corruption that led to national bankruptcy, international economic control, and, finally, to the British occupation of 1882.

Ismail the Magnificent

The most illustrious of Muhammad 'Ali's successors was his grandson Ismail, who governed from 1863 to 1879. Like his grandfather, Ismail strove to purify the nation, but he also chose to exploit it as a private estate for his own benefit. Ismail finally took over one fifth of the cultivable area, which he worked with forced labor and imported machinery. He was particularly fortunate when he came to power to be able to take advantage of a world cotton shortage caused by the American Civil War. The demand for Egypt's long-staple product soon exceeded the supply, prices skyrocketed, and

Egypt's landowners profited. The inflated cotton prices brought on a period of wild financial speculation and uncontrolled, irresponsible spending.

Ismail himself set the example for his courtiers. "Everyone," he exclaimed, "has a mania for something—mine is for stone and mortar." His palaces and public works were the envy of modern monarches. "Even what Louis XIV had achieved for Paris could not surpass what Ismail achieved for Cairo and Alexandria," writes M. Rifaat Bey. "Go wherever you like in Cairo, you are sure to have your eye attracted by some grand building, garden or statue, avenue, fountain or road, or a whole quarter planned and executed by Ismail the Magnificent."[2] Ismail's construction mania converted the insignificant desert village of Helwan into Cairo's favorite aristocratic suburb, full of mansions, hotels, and watering places.

Ismail's public works also included gas and water facilities for Cairo and Alexandria and a railway system linking the whole Nile Valley southward into the Sudan. Over 8000 miles of new canals and river-barrier improvements greatly expanded the area for profitable cultivation. Telegraph lines were extended from a mere 350 to more than 5200 miles, also reaching deep into the Sudan. The post office was purchased from its Italian concessionaires and converted into a government department. Alexandria's port was developed into one of the best in the Mediterranean. Egypt's mercantile fleet, which had begun with only seven ships, became so profitable that Ismail bought all the shares and converted the company into the government-owned Khedivial Mail Line. By 1873 the line had sixteen ships plying the Mediterranean and nine on the Red Sea and was on the way to making Egypt one of the leading nations in Mediterranean maritime commerce.

Realizing that stone and mortar alone could not create a modern nation, Ismail also turned his efforts to education. His interest was broader than his grandfather's had been. He divorced the system from the war department— where its primary function had been the teaching of Western military techniques—and placed it under leading British and Swiss educationalists. A new law in 1868 established primary, secondary, and higher educational institutions in which religion was de-emphasized. Ismail's wife opened the first girls' school in 1873, and teacher-training institutes were established. Government-sponsored printing presses and a new paper factory helped increase the number of newspapers and books that could be published. By the end of Ismail's regime, the number of state schools had increased from 185 to nearly 5000. Nearly 100,000 of Egypt's 2,500,000 males were in school, a larger proportion than in many mid-nineteenth–century European nations.

After the Suez Canal was opened in 1869, Egypt became a focal point of European diplomacy. The country was in constant danger of foreign intervention. Instead of using military force to keep his province autonomous, Ismail used flattery, gold, and silver. He cultivated his relations with the Ottoman sultan through increased annual tribute and military assistance during the Cretan uprising (1866–1868). In return, during 1867 he obtained the right to issue independent decrees on all matters except foreign affairs and received the grandiloquent ancient Iranian title of khedive, or prince, which carried far more prestige than pasha, vali, viceroy, or governor general. In 1873, the sultan authorized Ismail to take over the Sudan, to contract freely any loans and commercial treaties he might desire from foreign nations, and to expand his military forces. The only remaining restrictions were a maximum placed on the annual budget, a restriction that foreign diplomatic appointments be approved by the Porte, and a restriction against building of armored warships without prior imperial consent. The symbols of Ottoman sovereignty, such as the imperial flag and system of coinage, also remained. The essence of the 1873 decree made Egypt legally an autonomous province within the Ottoman Empire similar to the autonomous Danubian principalities (see chapter 3).

During the 1870s, Ismail's outstanding diplomat, the Armenian Nubar Pasha, negotiated modifications in the capitulatory system imposed on Egypt by the West after 1840. Under the prevailing system, for a crime committed in Egypt, a Frenchman might be tried only in Marseilles, an Italian only in Ancona, or a Greek only in Athens. The capitulations were so abused that few who sought their consul's support were refused. Nubar gained support for a mixed-court system in civil cases independent of both government and foreign consuls. Under the reorganization, three courts were established with seventeen foreign and twelve Egyptian judges. The mixed-court system was to last from 1875 until 1949.

The khedive's colonial ambitions took Egyptian troops deep into Africa as far as Ethiopia, modern-day Kenya, and the Congo on great "geographical and anti-slavery" expeditions. In the 1860s and 1870s, to help subjugate the Sudan, the khedive enlisted the aid of European explorers and soldiers like Sir Samuel Baker and General Charles ("Chinese") Gordon. After a dispute with Gordon, the Khedive turned to a number of American Civil War veterans, among whom was Charles Chaille[1]-Long, one of the first explorers of the headwaters of the Nile. Conquest of the Sudan, however, did not ensure control of the Nile. That objective led Egypt into a disastrous war with Ethiopia and brought to an end the Khedive's African expansion. The Americans in charge were blamed for the defeat and discharged shortly afterward.

EGYPT FACES BANKRUPTCY

Only Egypt's small upper class of landowners benefited from Ismail's extravagant schemes. The fellah had little access to the schools, hospitals, railways, telegraph lines, and other paraphernalia imported from the West.

His lot worsened considerably at the end of the Civil War when the cotton bubble burst and Egypt again had to face American competition in world markets. Not only did prices fall, but intensive use had depleted the soil, huge state debts had accumulated, and taxes accordingly spiralled.

Attempts to supplement cotton with sugar only served to worsen the situation. Ismail's investments in imported European sugar factories were lost because of poor management, corruption, and wasted materials. To pay for these cotton and sugar failures, the Egyptian population was taxed for its land, date palms, and new houses. Fees were raised on patents, licenses, servants, and tradesmen. These and other imposts, however, could not stave off financial disaster. Another direct fund-raising measure was the *mukabala* loan made compulsory in 1874. It was a payment that amounted to six times the annual land tax, in return for which the taxpayer received a 50 percent tax reduction in perpetuity. The effect, of course, was merely to sacrifice half the future land revenue for the sake of a relatively small immediate lump sum. A small amount of debt relief came from the sale of the khedive's Suez Canal shares to Great Britain in 1875 for some four million pounds.

But none of these measures could in any way solve Ismail's financial problems. Between 1863 and 1876 his extravagances had multiplied the foreign debt more than thirty times, while the domestic one increased by a factor of ten. Foreign bankers, agents, concessionaires, and other profit seekers did not hesitate to involve Egypt in the treadmill of usurious loans, worthless concessions, and unfulfilled contracts. In 1875 Egypt received only thirty-five million pounds from foreign loans negotiated in the amount of over fifty-five million. The balance was deducted in advance for interest and fees. Finally, in 1876, Ismail declared himself bankrupt, ceased payment of interest on all debts, withheld government salaries, and doubled the fellah head tax.

When it became obvious that the khedive could not pay foreign debts, the European powers intervened directly. An English financial expert, Stephen Cave, reported after investigating the situation in 1875 that, "Egypt suffers from the ignorance, dishonesty, waste, and extravagance of the East, and at the same time, from the vast expenses caused by hasty, inconsiderate endeavours to adopt the civilization of the West. Immense sums are expended on unproductive works, or on productive works carried out in the wrong way or too soon."[3] Cave's recommendations led to an agreement between Egypt and its English and French creditors to fund the sums owed over a period of sixty-three years. Under an International Debt Commission established in 1876 to represent England, France, Italy, Austria, and Russia, an English controller general was appointed to head the Revenue Office and a Frenchman to run the Audit Office. The commission was authorized to collect the country's most important revenues and to make equitable payments against debts.

Ismail hoped to mitigate the effects of foreign intervention by sharing his responsibilities with a cabinet and an assembly of notables, which he had established in 1866 and convened in the crisis of 1878. His first prime minister, Nubar Pasha, proposed an Englishman as finance minister and a Frenchman as minister of public works. Relations in the cabinet flared into angry outbursts as Ismail jealously sought to fend off the British and French curtailment of his personal power. His appeals for support from the assembly of notables called them to defend the "national honor." They succeeded in rallying Egyptian sentiment against the foreigners and finally demanded the resignation of the English and French cabinet ministers.

Recalcitrance only stiffened European demands. Led by Chancellor Bismarck, the European powers demanded that the Ottoman sultan replace Ismail with a khedive more amenable to their dictates. Thereupon Ismail's weak son Tewfik was chosen in 1879 to succeed his father, and Ismail went into exile.

THE FIRST NATIONAL UPRISING

Four Egyptian political groups now emerged: a small group of wealthy landowners favorable to foreign intervention as a means of protecting their vested interests; a vigorous Islamic modernist movement opposed to the foreigners, led by Muhammad Abduh (a disciple of Jamal al-Din al-Afghani, discussed in chapter 6); another group of wealthy landowners who desired independence; and an army clique of antiforeign junior officers who believed that the khedive was merely a tool of his Osmanli courtiers and of the Europeans around him. The division resembled the situation that came to prevail in Egypt between 1920 and 1950, when the royal court alternated between support for the nationalists and reliance on the British (see below).

The junior officers at the forefront of this first nationalist movement were led by Colonel Ahmad Arabi. He like many officers from peasant families had found that the only opportunity for self-advancement lay in the army. Peasant origins made these officers resentful of the prominent role played in government by large landowners. Economies imposed on the army and plans to reduce the number of native officers embittered them. Court favoritism toward Turkish and Circassian staff officers also aroused the jealousy of the Egyptians.

Between 1879 and 1882, the junior officers became powerful enough to force the dismissal of Prime Minister Nubar, whom they regarded as an English puppet (1879); to exile the Turkish war minister, Osman Rifki (1881); and to form a nationalist government headed by a civilian sympathizer, who made Colonel Arabi war minister (1882). To support their aims, they endorsed a liberal constitution and reconvened the assembly of notables, now filled with nationalists.

In France and England, it was feared that dangerous radicals were taking over Egypt. Afraid lest they lose their financial control over Egypt, the two powers sought a pretext to crush the nationalist movement. The opportunity arose when Great Britain and France sent a joint fleet to demonstrate before Alexandria as a warning to the nationalists against any harm that might come to Europeans. The demonstration, however, only made the situation more tense, resulting in savage attacks on foreigners by Egyptian mobs. To protect Egypt against intervention by the great powers, Arabi began to fortify Alexandria. When he ignored a British ultimatum to cease work on these defenses, the city was bombarded by the British fleet. British troops were landed in July 1882, and within a few weeks the country had become, for all practical purposes, a British protectorate.

The officers' rebellion and the nationalist movement proved symptomatic of new developments that were to characterize Egyptian politics into the next century. The Egyptian army, which was largely of rural origin, became an important link between the peasantry and the top echelons of society, especially since officers from peasant families could rise to fairly high ranks. A national awareness thus began to emerge in rural as well as urban areas as such army officers, imbued with patriotism, brought an "Egyptian" consciousness back to their native villages. The need for compromises between Islam and the modern world was increasingly acknowledged by these young Muslim officers who had received a Western education. Even Lord Cromer, British "viceroy" in Egypt after 1882, conceded that most peasants were sympathetic to Colonel Arabi's cause and that: "They look to him to deliver them from the usurer and the Pasha."

LORD CROMER AND THE BRITISH OCCUPATION

Under the British occupation Egypt was still theoretically an Ottoman province administered by the Khedive. Egyptians were Ottoman subjects who ostensibly paid their taxes to the sultan. The national flag and the system of coinage remained Osmanli. Without the sultan's approval, no Egyptian territory could be ceded and no foreign political treaties signed. All Egyptian army appointments above the rank of colonel had to be approved in Istanbul, with the result that the highest officers were usually Turkish or Circassian, except the British *sirdar,* or commander in chief.

The actual ruler, however, was the British agent and consul general. Between 1883 and 1907 Sir Evelyn Baring (made Lord Cromer in 1892) held the post. When he was thirty-six, Cromer—an army officer—was Britain's representative on the Debt Commission for a year. Five years later, in 1882, he returned from a tour of duty in India to become the real ruler of Egypt. Legally he had no more power to impose his suggestion than any other foreign diplomat. But Cromer actually stood in the same relation to the khedive that British residents came to assume toward the native princes of India. A suggestion from the British resident had the force of the British army behind it. Cromer and his British staff thus, in effect, took over the running of finances, trade, agriculture, communications, irrigation, health, foreign affairs, and the military establishment. No policies could be executed or originated without their approval.

In Cromer's view, British troops had not been sent to annex Egypt, but to make sure that the khedive did the "right thing." His mission, he believed, was "to save Egyptian society." Theoretically, England was exercising equal rights with other powers to rescue the country from cruel, inept, barbarian adventurers. Again theoretically, the Ottoman sultan was still the country's monarch and the khedive his representative on the spot. English occupation was considered by the sultan a temporary expedient to restore normal conditions. The British, however, let it be known who was in charge. In his initial task, to prevent bankruptcy, Cromer was successful. Increased cotton production after 1888 (at the expense of the wheat crop) and a rise of cotton prices in the world market saved the country from financial disaster. Adequate taxes were collected from the landowners, and the financial administration was centralized and simplified. Standardized accounting systems, regularized government salaries, public bids for contracts, and better civil service recruiting under British supervision greatly diminished corruption and improved local attitudes toward government administration.

Financial solvency enabled Cromer to finance construction of new dams and river barriers that expanded the irrigated areas and greatly increased production. In 1902 a dam was completed at Aswan (the predecessor of the newest high dam there) and its height was raised between 1907 and 1910. River barriers constructed at Assiut and Esna gave water to Upper Egypt. These and other devices enabled Egypt to increase its cultivated area by 20 percent before World War I.

British policies encouraged small landowners by extending the area under cultivation, abolishing restrictions on ownership, dividing up the 280,000 acres in the khedivial estates, forming companies to reclaim land to be sold to the peasants, and expanding credit facilities. These measures, and enforced subdivision of land among heirs, more than doubled the number of landowners by 1914. However, the greatest beneficiaries of the land redistribution were favorites of the royal court, who received the largest estates and the best land. The peasant's lot was greatly alleviated by the ban on slavery, forced labor, and the use of the whip. Prisons were reformed and effective medical and sanitation services greatly cut down the mortality rate. All these reforms, in Cromer's view, "required the singular political adaptability of Englishmen to execute them."

State railways were more than doubled in mileage during the British occupation; but development of river commerce was neglected. To divert traffic to the railways, tolls, and licences were devised and bridges and irrigation canals built without considering the equally vital needs of the river craft, such as locks, ports, and landing facilities. The British may have intended this policy to isolate the Sudan from Egypt and divert Sudanese commerce from Alexandria to the new Port Sudan.

The Constitutional System

As has been noted, when the British arrived in 1882 the country had recently become a constitutional principality in which the formerly all-powerful khedive was assisted by an assembly of notables and cabinet. The system was formalized by the British constitutional specialist Lord Dufferin in an Organic Law under which the country was governed from 1883 to 1913. It provided a two-chamber parliament with only advisory powers. The government could enact legislation over the opposition of the two chambers and was required only to explain its actions, not obtain parliamentary support for them. The only authority possessed by the eighty-two member assembly was to approve new direct taxes. The Organic Law also established provincial councils headed by Cairo-appointed governors, each of whom was supplied with a British adviser. They were charged with local problems such as roads, canals, and markets. This phantom constitutional system lasted until 1913 when Lord Kitchener combined the two chambers into one Legislative Assembly with somewhat broader powers. Although it was to be a little more democratic in scope, it met for only a single session before it was suspended because of the outbreak of World War I.

The judicial system was a hodgepodge of codes, which the British did not reform. International tribunals, or mixed courts (described above), tried civil cases between Europeans and Egyptians and between foreigners. With no specific legal precedents to guide them, the European and Egyptian judges in practice improvised law to fit their needs. Native tribunals dealt with criminal and civil cases involving Egyptians. European consuls retained exclusive jurisdiction over criminal cases involving their nationals.

The International Debt Commission, representing half a dozen nations, further complicated British civil administration because that multinational body was authorized to cancel any loan and to sue the government before the mixed courts. Foreigners other than the British were also represented in the railway administration and the management of half a million acres of Ismail's personal property held in escrow for debt payment.

British Shortcomings

Cromer distinguished between reforms that could be implemented by administrative fiat and those that would require a social revolution, concentrating his efforts on the former and discouraging the latter. Therefore few fundamental social changes occurred during the British occupation. The Turkish and Circassian landowners in particular benefited from the improvement in agriculture and the breakup of large estates. From the time of Muhammad 'Ali they had occupied a privileged position because of their intimate connections with the court. Throughout the first half of the nineteenth century Turks and Circassians were employed to staff the higher ranks of the army and civilian administration, rather than local Egyptians; the former were more trusted and considered better trained in military and administrative skills than the Egyptians. Copts were not only retained in their traditional posts, but were even given greater authority and prestige by the British because they had received a better education in their Christian schools than the local Muslims had and because, as Christians, they were more trusted by the British. Although the lot of the fellah improved materially, the political and social institutions that directly affected him—the Sharia courts, the schools, the wakf system, and the status of women—remained unchanged. In the cities the middle class—lawyers, doctors, journalists, teachers, and minor officials—was still excluded from top governmental positions and from the social life of the conservative upper-class elite.

Government educational expenditures under Cromer were less than those of Ismail; Cromer never used more than 3 percent of the budget for education. The British goal was to spread a simple form of schooling, emphasizing the elementary arithmetic and reading required to fill clerical jobs, not to create a truly educated people. Not until 1908 did Arabic replace English as the principal language of instruction. Previously established technical schools were maintained, but not expanded. The first secular university was established in 1908 with private, not government, initiative and funds. Not only did the occupation government fail to expand the educational system, but the number of students relative to the growing population decreased.

Industry also stagnated under Cromer because he believed that its development would be detrimental to both England and Egypt. In his view, the revenue from customs on imported cotton goods was more valuable than developing local textile factories. It was certainly better for Great Britain to have Egypt supply raw cotton to its Lancashire mills, which could then sell their cotton cloth to the Egyptians.

Nearly all local industry and commerce was in the hands of non-Muslims, partly because of the Islamic prohibition on profit-bearing investment. According to the 1905 Annual Government Report, "Boot-mending, as well as boot-making, is almost entirely in the hands of Greeks and Armenians. The drapery trade is controlled by Jews, Syrians, and Europeans, the tailoring trade by Jews."[4] Jews controlled finance, Syrian Christians provided officials, writers, traders, and village moneylenders, and Armenians were skilled artisans. From 1836 to 1907, the number of foreigners (mostly European and Levantines) in Egypt grew from 3000 to 147,000.

MUSTAFA KAMIL (1874–1908)

At the end of his service in Egypt even Cromer acknowledged the failure of a "full stomach" policy. "We were popular," he paraphrased another colleague, "as long as we bandaged wounds. Nothing can prevail against the fact that we are not Muslims, and that we neither eat, nor drink, nor marry as they do."

Such religious and social differences, as well as growing discontent among the middle classes, the students, and the workers, reactivated the nationalist movement, which had been dormant since Arabi's defeat in 1882. An armed uprising against the British was triggered in June 1906 when British officers accidentally shot a woman in Dinshawai while pigeon hunting. The indignant peasants fell on the hunters and killed one. Cromer ordered the culprits condemned. Four were publicly hanged and seventeen flogged and imprisoned. The consequent storm of protest in Europe and in Parliament in Great Britain provided a major *cause célèbre* for the nationalists and led to the replacement of Cromer by Sir Eldon Gorst within a year.

Cromer had so little respect for the nationalists that he made no attempt to silence their press. All such "upstarts" were the same, in his opinion. "Young Turkey has proved a complete failure. So has Young Persia. So has Young Egypt. And Young China does not appear to have been much more successful." The development of representative institutions in such countries, "if it ever takes place at all, will probably be the work, not of generations, but of centuries."[5]

The founder of a revitalized nationalist movement was Mustafa Kamil, a French-educated Egyptian lawyer. Khedive Abbas, who had succeeded his father Tewfik in 1892, used Kamil's al-Watani (Fatherland) party as a foil against the British in the 1890s to divert attention from his own foibles. The party's initial program was antireligious and zealously nationalistic. It emphasized constitutionalism, education, and a literary revival. Mustafa Kamil, like many of his contemporaries, failed to recognize the need for dealing with economic and social problems and concentrated his attacks on the British occupation. Until 1904 he had hoped for French support, but the possibility disappeared after the Anglo-French entente was reached in 1904. Al-Watani, unlike the nationalist movement of 1880 had little contact with the army, but it did keep in touch with the khedive despite quarrels. Nearly all of its active members were from the middle class. Few appeals were made to, nor did direct support come from, the rural or urban masses.

BRITISH POLICIES AFTER CROMER

Sir Eldon Gorst, who replaced Cromer in 1907, hoped to salvage Great Britain's position in the Nile Valley by cultivating nationalist sympathy by means of greater authority for the national and provincial legislative bodies. Although he won support from the moderate Umma (Popular) party, which represented a liberal group of landowners, Mustafa Kamil's al-Watani party protested that Gorst's policies were inadequate. At a national congress of over 1000 representatives during December 1907, al-Watani demanded that Egyptians take over immediately and propagandized their new slogan, "Egypt for the Egyptians!" A year later, Mustafa Kamil died. After World War I, al-Watani was completely overshadowed by the Wafd and only a remnant of its pre–World War I organization remained until the abolition of all political parties in January 1953 (see chapter 9).

Nationalism was not altogether submerged. The era was ripe for new ideas, and Egyptians were eager to emulate the example set by Iran and the Young Turks. When in 1911 Gorst's successor, Lord Kitchener attempted to revive Cromer's more autocratic system, nationalism again flared up. In his general outlook, Kitchener, the former commander in chief of the Egyptian army, greatly resembled Cromer. His methods were highhanded, prejudiced, and abrupt; he was filled with a sense of mission to improve the country's material standards, but bent upon keeping the nationalists in their place. After an attempt on his life by students in 1912, he so ruthlessly suppressed the nationalist movement that it dared not raise its head until after World War I.

Kitchener's "Five Feddan Law," or Homestead Exemption Act, introduced to save the peasant from the growing danger of economic ruin, was a major contribution to stability, although there was no improvement in the peasant's dismal living conditions, caused by the growing population pressure on the country's limited resources (for brief descriptions of the peasant's life, see chapters 1 and 9). The law prevented seizure for debt of farms under five acres. It also required that the farmer be left with at least two of his farm animals, his home, and tools.

Kitchener's "good works" were vitiated by his arbitrary treatment of the nationalists. After he had insulted Saad Zaghlul, the Egyptian minister of education and considered to be a moderate, Zaghlul resigned his appointed post in the administration to become the elected president of the Legislative Assembly.

With the outbreak of World War I, the government concentrated on military activities and paid little attention to further development of the civil administration. For Egypt, the war meant the disappearance of the last shadowy vestiges of Ottoman rule and the establishment of a formal British protectorate in 1914. The pro-Ottoman khedive, Abbas, was replaced by his uncle Husain Kamil, who was then vested by the British with the title of sultan. Sir Henry McMahon (of the Husain-McMahon correspondence) a former Anglo-Indian official, became high commissioner and actual ruler.

McMahon absorbed Egypt completely in the war effort and unilaterally terminated what remained of local autonomy. The Legislative Assembly was suspended, the press muzzled, and forced labor reimposed. Local officials were again authorized to raise the quotas of workers for the government by all means, including terror. Forced "contributions" were collected for the Red Cross; grain, mules, and camels were commandeered by the Allies.

The drastic war measures so aroused the peasants that they too became active in the anti-British movement. Now all classes were embittered by the imposed British levies. Landowners protested cotton restrictions and government resale of confiscated crops at huge profits. The urban middle class was hit by inflation caused by high prices paid for local commodities by thousands of foreign troops in the towns. For the first time skilled workmen began to organize in the new spinning mills, tobacco plants, and sugar refineries established to meet war needs. The old distinction among the ruling Turco-Circassian class, the middle class of Coptic and Syrian merchants, professionals, and government employees, and the Nile Valley peasantry of Arab and Nubian stock crumbled, to be replaced by the conventional Western class divisions of society—wealthy, well-to-do, and workers.

SAAD ZAGHLUL AND POST-WORLD WAR I NATIONALISM

By 1918 a strong nationalist movement was smouldering beneath the British occupation. Its new leader was Saad Zaghlul, whom Kitchener drove from the government. Zaghlul, son of a peasant family, had been an al-Azhar student of Jamal ad-Din al-Afgani and Muhammad Abduh, had participated in Arabi's movement, and then had become "Westernized" through his study of French law. As a result of his marriage to the daughter of a high government official who was friendly to the British, Zaghlul rapidly rose to the top of the civil administration. When the Umma party was formed in 1907 as a foil to Mustafa Kamil's al-Watani party, Zaghlul was one of its leaders. But Kitchener's insults and Britain's war policies converted him into an embittered nationalist by 1918.

Two days after the armistice, Zaghlul presented the British high commissioner with a demand for independence, Zaghlul and his followers, called the Egyptian Delegation (Wafd al-Misri), requested permission to present their case in Great Britain. From this group developed the Wafd party that was to dominate Egyptian politics for the next three decades.

The high commissioner, Sir Reginald Wingate, sympathized with the nationalists, recommending that they be permitted to travel abroad. When Downing Street rebuffed them, Wafd leaders organized mass meetings and threatened the Egyptian sultan violence if he collaborated with the British occupation. British military authorities retaliated in March 1919 by deporting Zaghlul and three of his followers to Malta. The arrests sparked a mass insurrection, led by university students. Strikes, riots, and sabotage spread to all parts of the country. In Cairo and other towns, pitched battles were fought between British troops and the nationalists. A nationalist solidarity between Copts and Muslims, between rich and poor, was the order of the day. Only a tiny group of landlords refrained from full participation in the movement, fearing that it might turn into a social as well as a political revolution.

The insurrection did convince British Prime Minister David Lloyd George to release the prisoners and permit them to attend the Paris Peace Conference, but their visit failed. No country at the conference recognized that they represented a strong popular movement, and even President Wilson acknowledged the British protectorate over Egypt. Lloyd George, however, did send a commission headed by Lord Milner to investigate and make recommendations for a new constitution. The nationalists considered Milner's proposals for "the progressive development of self-governing institutions" far too meager and refused even to consult with British experts sent to establish a new constitutional system. Even the peasants turned their backs.

The British attempt to outmaneuver Zaghlul in 1921 by negotiations with a delegation representing the palace and the aristocracy of Turkish ancestry only produced new riots for which Zaghlul was blamed and again deported. Lord Allenby, who became the new high commissioner, warned that the protectorate must end and urged London to recognize Egyptian independence. On his recommendation, the protectorate was terminated in March 1922. Egypt became a monarchy, Sultan Ahmed Fuad (who had succeeded his brother Husain upon the latter's death in 1917) became its king, and Zaghlul in September 1923 was once more permitted to return from exile.

To the nationalists, the unilateral declaration of independence was a chimera cloaking Britain's continued occupation in a more liberal guise. British troops still occupied the country and the high commissioner retained the nearly absolute power of his predecessors. To make the situation more palatable, Allenby prodded King Fuad to appoint a commission to draft a new constitution. This document, produced in 1923 and modeled on the 1831 Belgian constitution, granted extensive power to the king while maintaining a parliamentary facade. Only a two-thirds vote of the members of parliament could override the king's veto on all legislation. In case of disagreement with parliament, the king could dissolve it and rule by decree. Although ministers were responsible to parliament, they were appointed and could be dismissed by the monarch. The elected Chamber of Deputies was balanced by a Senate in which two-fifths of the members and the president were appointed by the king. The rest of the senators were elected indirectly. All had to be men of considerable property or of high position.

In the first elections under this constitution, the Wafd party won 188 of the 215 seats in the Chamber of Deputies. When it convened in January 1924, it chose Zaghlul, president of the Wafd, as prime minister, beginning what was to become a three-way power struggle between the Wafd, the palace, and the British. Alliances between these conflicting elements shifted constantly, so that each found itself pitted against the other two at one time or another during the next quarter century.

The king formed his own Ittihad (Union) party to block the Wafdists, but it had no mass support and was composed solely of the king's friends. So obvious were its attachments that it was popularly known as *hizb al-Malik* (the King's party). Another group of elder politicians, many descended from the old Ottoman aristocracy, formed the Liberal Constitutionalists to limit the king's power.

THE WAFD PARTY

The only party with mass support and local branches was the Wafd. Its leaders acquired Mustafa Kamil's mantle, although remnants of the al-Watani still existed. The Wafd was essentially middle class and anti-British, with a following of students, merchants, new industrialists, and landlords who encouraged their peasants to vote Wafd. The country's leaders preferred mass support for the Wafd to a genuinely leftist group advocating violent social change. Jean and Simonne Lacouture describe the Wafd as

> the expression of the entire people, of which in the fullest sense it was the *delegate*. Any attempt at defining it would involve a complete description of Egypt. It contained all the generosity, intellectual muddle, good nature, contradictions and mythomania of its millions of supporters. It united the unlimited poverty of some and the insultingly bloated fortunes of others, the demand for change and the demand for conservatism, reaction and movement. There was something spongy, lax and warm about it which is typical of Egypt.[6]

During the three decades after 1922, the Wafd held power for only ninety months, but nothing can change the fact that Egyptians saw themselves reflected in the party. All knew it would be "more virtuous in opposition than in power, quicker to accuse its opponents than to clean up its own corruption, and that the more absolute the power invested in it by public confidence, the less it would be inclined to take action. But the masses remained faithful to it."[7]

The British at times supported the Wafd because its leaders knew when to compromise and could persuade the masses to accept agreements that others could not even have proposed while remaining in power. Both Zaghlul and Mustafa Nahas, who succeeded Zaghlul after his death in 1927, were of fellah background; both knew the techniques of appealing to and inciting the masses; the personalities of both were attuned to the Egyptian masses. After all, they proposed no fundamentally radical economic or social programs; they drew their principal support from the conservative peasantry, not the Cairo street mobs.

The party was free of religious or racial discrimination and Zaghlul ardently fought Muslim fanaticism, urging the Copts to play an active role in the nationalist movement. Copts held the key Ministries of Foreign Affairs and Finance, and another cabinet post was held by a Jew. The presence of Christian and Jewish professionals was much appreciated by the party chiefs, who were usually lawyers and landowners. Party policies were largely formulated by its upper-middle-class members, a fact that prevented the Wafd from developing a strong social conscience or program until the years immediately before its demise in 1952. Not until 1936 did any influential Egyptian recognize the need for basic social reform, and the first effort made in this direction was the organization of the Bureau of Intellectual Unemployment. The government banned trade unions until 1942. The first Wafdist-supported cooperative movement was launched in 1950, and Wafd party leaders offered the initial proposals put forward for a modest agrarian reform in 1951. When "socialism" became the vogue after World War II, the Wafd also adopted its slogans, but it did nothing to implement them. There was little debate in parliament on the need for social change and no significant social legislation. Nearly all nationalist energies were devoted to the conflict with the king and the British.

The first overt clash between the Egyptian nationalists and the British after independence followed the assassination of Sir Lee Stack, governor general of the Sudan. Zaghlul rejected Lord Allenby's ultimatum to punish the killers, pay an indemnity, and remove Egyptian troops from the Sudan (see chapter 5). Reprisals, which had the effect of again converting Egypt into a British protectorate, caused Zaghlul to resign. His initial showdown with King Fuad occurred after the Wafd defeat in the 1924 elections by a coalition of Constitutional Liberals, Unionists, and independents. Despite the defeat, the Chamber of Deputies elected Zaghlul its president, whereupon the king dissolved parliament. Zaghlul retaliated by forming a rump parliament in a nearby hotel. This time British High Commissioner Lord Lloyd backed the nationalists because he feared a popular uprising. In the 1926 elections the Wafd won a sweeping victory, but Lord Lloyd now convinced Zaghlul to compromise by turning the prime ministry over to the middle of the road Liberal Constitutionalists.

Throughout the interwar era, Egypt and Great Britain continued to negotiate the exact nature of Egypt's status. On several occasions they came close to agreement, but internal disquiet always sabotaged a final settlement. This failure brought about a turning point in Wafdist fortunes in 1929, resulting in the temporary dictatorship of Prime Minister Ismail Sidki and his Shaab (People's) party. He suspended the 1923 constitution and forced the Wafd party from parliament. In 1933, the illness of both the king and Sidki created a political vacuum, during which one of the king's private counselors tried to build up his own power; a popular outcry finally forced the king to restore the 1923 constitution and to abrogate the electoral law that excluded the Wafd from power.

An era of lessened hostility to Great Britain followed the death of King Fuad and the Italian invasion of Ethiopia in 1936. Palace attempts to pit one party against the other now ended. Mussolini's threat to Africa caused both the British and the Egyptians to put aside their sixteen-year-old feud, at least temporarily. Fuad was succeeded by his younger son Farouk, widely regarded as sympathetic to the nationalist aspirations. Soon after, a new election gave the Wafd its usual large majority and the government reopened negotiations with Great Britain to determine future relations between the two countries. This time the parlays were successful, and Egypt received more independence than it had ever had since the time of Muhammad 'Ali.

British meddling in domestic politics was curtailed considerably by the abolishing of the high commissioner's office, and the British troops were to be kept in the Suez Canal zone. A date was fixed for terminating the capitulations, the mixed courts were to take over criminal cases as well as civil ones for another twelve years, until 1949, and consular courts were abolished. Egypt now had its own nearly independent judicial system, and non-Egyptians were subject to the country's laws, taxes, and financial regulations.

The era of good feeling between the nationalists, the king, and the British was short-lived. When King Farouk came of age in 1937, he followed in his father's footsteps, forcing the Wafd from power for five years. British popularity also declined within a year after British troops had been cheered in the streets. After Mussolini's war scare subsided, politics returned to the traditional anti-British slogans. To demonstrate its renewed patriotism, the Wafd organized a "Blue Shirt" youth group, which again raised a clamor against the "occupiers."

Farouk ruled with the support of dissident Wafdists, who formed the Saadist party in 1937 (named after Saad Zaghlul). Although they had a good case against growing corruption in the Wafd and its domination by Nahas, they could not compete with the great machine built by the parent organization. The Saadists never became popular and were forced into the position of serving the king as the only justification for their existence.

WORLD WAR II AND THE REVOLUTION

The Egyptian independence established by the 1936 Anglo-European Treaty was put to the test within three years. Immediately after the outbreak of World War II, Great Britain converted Egypt to a major base. The king was forced to sever relations with Germany, and censorship was imposed. Industry was vastly expanded to supply Allied troops. At one time, Allied expenditure represented a quarter of the national income. About 200,000 Egyptians were employed in British workshops and camps. Small local industries were encouraged to develop to produce such products as textiles, preserved foods, chemicals, glass, leather, cement, building materials, petroleum, and machinery. War profits increased bank deposits from 45 million pounds in 1940 to 120 million by 1943, and the country's 50 millionaires became 400. Prosperity made Egypt a creditor nation to the extent of some 300 million pounds.

However, the apparent prosperity was deceiving. Only a relatively few Egyptians grew richer while the masses became more impoverished than ever. Wartime inflation caused prices to spiral upwards until by 1944 they were nearly three times those of 1939. Nearly 1,200,000 farmers had to seek tax exemption in 1942 because of poverty. Most hard hit were the unskilled urban and rural workers and the salaried middle class, who suffered severe privation. Expansion of the industrial proletariat by 35 to 40 percent created major urban problems. In Cairo when starved mobs attacked wheat shipments in 1942, a Wafdist leader commented that, "On the eve of the French Revolution the people of Paris shouted, 'We want bread.' The people of Cairo have done just the same thing.... The situation in this country can be described as revolutionary." Despite the 300 million sterling credits, the country was left with nearly a quarter million urban unemployed when the Allies withdrew after the war.

Obviously the Egyptians felt they had little if anything to gain from the war, and this attitude was evident throughout the fighting. From September 1939 to June 1940, Prime Minister Ali Maher was as favorable to the Axis as the Anglo-Egyptian Treaty would permit. After the fall of France, he was removed by British pressure because of his close ties with the Italians. His successors, Hasan Sabri and later Husain Siri, tried to be sympathetically neutral to Great Britain. But when Siri broke off relations with the Vichy French in 1941, Farouk dismissed him. At once the British decided to brook no more pro-Axis sentiments or maneuvers. Ali Maher was arrested for espionage, the royal palace was barricaded by British tanks, and Farouk was forced at pistol point to turn the government over to Nahas. All pro-Axis sympathizers who could be found were weeded out of the government and replaced with officials sympathetic to the Allies. Although the British coup saved Egypt from the Nazis, it aroused the spleen of nationalists against the king and the Wafd for surrendering to the occupiers. By the end of the war, smouldering political and economic discontent made Egypt ripe for a variety of radical protest movements.

Communists and Socialists

Until 1942 the Egyptian Communists were little more than factionalized groups of intellectuals, consisting mostly of Greeks, Armenians, Jews, and other non-Muslims. Their plaintive pleas for "international solidarity" meant little to the Arabic-speaking nationalists. However, tactics changed after the Soviet Union became embroiled in the war, and minorities and "foreigners" were relegated to less obtrusive positions in the Egyptian Communist party. By 1946 the movement had thus become "Egyptianized" and revitalized. Both domestic and international conditions favored the Communists, and their leaders were active in organizing a spate of strikes to demonstrate their new power. Textile and transport workers, police and hospital employees rebelled against the deterioration in postwar conditions. While full party membership was never more than 7000, Communist leaders in various labor groups controlled about 60,000 workers. The movement remained urban centered, in front organizations like the Workers' Committee for National Liberation and the National Committee of Students and Workers. Although "Egyptianized," leadership was still in the hands of intellectuals and petite bourgeoisie, who never succeeded in making it into a really effective threat to the government.

Ahmed Husain, founder and leader of the prewar Fascist "Greenshirts" or Young Egypt party (Misr al-Fatat) organized a bogus socialist group. His youthful followers, who had been enamored of Fascist and Nazi successes, changed ideologies, like their shirts, after the Nazi eclipse in 1945. At first they became the Islamic Nationalist party; but when socialism became the vogue in the postwar era, they took up its slogans. In the 1950 parliamentary elections they even captured one seat. Although they changed their slogans and shirts, they continued to employ the same terroristic tactics. The demented appeals of their leaders and their threats of assassination of the royal family aroused far more fear than respect, although the party was never regarded as a serious political group.

The Muslim Brotherhood

Next to the Wafd, the Muslim Brotherhood was Egypt's most effective political organization. Established about 1928 by Hasan al-Bana, an obscure teacher of the Koran, the Brotherhood grew until, according to some estimates, it had a million members. Al-Bana's disarmingly simple program to revive Islam by combating secularization through social justice had wide appeal for the urban proletariat, impoverished students, and the fellahin. If

Muslims would follow the Brotherhood exhortation, "The Koran is our Constitution," there would be no need for the government apparatus of Western society. Despite the simplicity of the Brotherhood appeals, the organization and its leaders were imbued with a social idealism that could attract those most disaffected by the increasingly complex economic pressures of modern society. To the peasant, the organization offered a program of more equitable taxes and a social service system based on Islamic cooperatives. The lower-middle class was roused by promises to rid Egypt of the hundreds of thousands of foreigners (meaning, to Muslim zealots, non-Muslims) dominating commercial and financial activity. Fervent nationalism incited students and intellectuals, who faced the problem of white-collar unemployment in an underdeveloped economy.

What was social justice according to al-Bana's followers? A living wage, education, and social services for all. Elections, public-utility legislation, and labor laws would be based on the Koran. Banking would be nationalized and usury outlawed in accordance with Muslim practice. The Muslim "system" would borrow the best ideas from all others—democracy, monarchy, communism, and socialism. When the Islamic era was reinstituted, the leaders would again be bound by the *ijm'a* principle, or consensus of the citizenry, and would decide whether to establish a monarchy or a republic.

Various political trends, from far left to far right, formed pressure groups within the Brotherhood. Its activists were not above using assassination to rid the country of "unpatriotic traitors" who did not heed the Brotherhood's advice or warnings. Brotherhood cells, organized throughout Egypt, were controlled by an elite, often operating clandestinely. Because they were banned much of the time, there was never an accurate estimate of membership, although up to one-third of university youth and many junior police and army officers joined or cooperated with the organization.

After 1936 the Brotherhood gained so much momentum that several leading politicians hoped to use it for their own ends. Wartime conditions gave it greater impetus, and it spread throughout Egypt. During the postwar turmoil, the group reached the zenith of its power through the organization of violent strikes and demonstrations. Its political murders, student riots, and bombings of public places so terrorized Egyptian politicians that they listened seriously to Brotherhood demands.

Brotherhood armed units joined the battle against Zionism even before the Egyptian government sent its troops into Palestine in 1948. To the Muslim zealots, the struggle was against "imperialists" and "infidels" who were bringing their foreign way of life into the Muslim heartland. Farouk was another principal target of the Brotherhood, especially after reports that his "Iron Guard" had killed Hasan al-Bana as a birthday present to the king in 1949. Thereafter, the Brotherhood urged establishment of an Islamic republic, which they claimed was envisaged by Muhammad.

After 1950, the Brotherhood was reorganized by Hasan al-Hodeiby, a well-known judge, who was said to have agreed with the king to refrain from resort to violence. When he became its leader, the group was again permitted to operate publicly and played a leading role in the guerrilla fighting against the British in the Suez Canal zone during 1951.

None of Egypt's political parties or acknowledged leaders seemed capable of running an orderly or effective government administration by the end of World War II, despite the development of all the paraphernalia of a modern political organization. Neither the country's administrative set-up nor its elected government with its parliament, its political-party system, and its constitution, seemed capable of coping with the problems that modern society had brought. A fundamental weakness was the inability of the diverse political parties to cooperate either to run the government or to effect social and economic reform. The result, as we shall see in the next chapter, was the threat of chaos.

NOTES

1. C.F. Volney, cited in Jean and Simonne Lacouture, *Egypt in Transition,* New York, 1958, p. 42.

2. M. Rifaat Bey, *The Awakening of Modern Egypt,* London, 1947, p. 106.

3. *Ibid.,* p. 157.

4. Charles Issawi, *Egypt at Mid-Century,* London, 1954, pp. 42–43.

5. *Ibid.,* p. 44.

6. J. and S. Lacouture, *op. cit.,* p. 91.

7. *Ibid.,* p. 92.

9   Revolutionary Egypt

SOCIOPOLITICAL BACKGROUND

The small, but growing, Egyptian middle class was becoming increasingly dissatisfied with the country's political and social conditions after World War II. The middle class particularly resented concentration of power in the hands of the king and a few large landowners who, by virtue of their extensive agricultural holdings, continued to dominate Egyptian economic, social, and political life. This small group of landowners, representing less than one half of 1 percent (some 12,000) of the proprietors, owned 37 percent of the arable land—more than two million acres. They led the country's principal political parties, controlled parliament, determined what legislation would be enacted, and decided upon the government's domestic and foreign policies. Political power in Egypt (as in most underdeveloped areas) was equated with land holdings, and nearly all leading politicians were among the 0.4 percent of the population who owned more than 50 acres. The more conservative a politician, the larger his estates were likely to be. Those with over 200 acres were usually closely associated with the king. Moderates like the Constitutional Liberals, Shaabists, and Saadists were not quite so land wealthy, but even most Wafd leaders, although of middle-class origin, had also acquired enough property to be among the upper 0.4 percent in this respect. Prerevolutionary parliaments almost always represented primarily landlord interests.

By 1950 the failure of large-landowner policies was leading rapidly toward a national crisis. In foreign affairs the landed upper class had failed to satisfy the ardent nationalists, who demanded the complete withdrawal of the British from Egypt and the Sudan, and these leaders had led the country to defeat in the 1948 Palestine war, fought to prevent the establishment of Israel. Within the country the number of urban unemployed was increasing, the poverty of the peasants was becoming greater in the face of increased population growth and a stagnant economy, and extensive graft and corruption was rampant within the top echelons of government. Few of the country's leading politicians seemed capable of, or even interested in, taking the radical action required to cope with these pressing problems. They were primarily interested in protecting their own privileged position.

Most of the upper class lived in the large cities, having little contact with the problems of rural Egypt, where some 80 percent of the population lived. Their ostentatious mode of life, which for centuries had been more or less philosophically accepted by those less favored as the "will of God," was now beginning to excite more invidious reactions among the urban middle and lower classes, to such an extent that the government felt the need to establish a special commission to probe the postwar growth of communism. The investigators reported that a principal reason for increased radical activity was smouldering resentment againt the conspicuous consumption of the upper class. Most blatant in its display of ostentation was the royal family. King Farouk, who came to symbolize to many of his countrymen all the evils of the old regime, set an example in profligate living of such proportions that he acquired international notoriety. The king was accused of draining millions of pounds from the nation's income to satisfy his gargantuan appetite for food, women, yachts, lavish parties, rare postage stamps, jewels, and bizarre gadgets. Some observers stated that Farouk was encouraged by politicians who, remembering the difficulties they had encountered with his strong-willed father, hoped to dissipate the son's energies and gain domination of the royal court so that they could manipulate its political decisions.

At the same time, Egypt's peasants were among the world's most poverty-stricken, with an annual per capita income of $55 to $65. They lived in disease, filth, and on the verge of starvation. Doreen Warriner writes:

> To speak of housing conditions is to exaggerate.... The fellaheen inhabit mud huts, built by making a framework of sticks, usually cotton sticks, and plastering it with mud. The hut is in a small enclosed yard, where the family and the buffalo live together, with a small inner room with a roof but no window and a sleeping roof where chickens, rabbits, and goats are kept.[1]

Possessions were limited to some reed floor mats, a few simple cooking utensils, and a garment or two per person. Food was cooked over dung fires whose smoke irritated the eyes, usually already infected with trachoma. Most of the rural population was infected by the liver fluke, bilharzia, whose parasites weakened its victims, making them easy to prey to dysentery, malaria, and tuberculosis. Most peasants were old at forty, and nearly 80 percent of those of military draft age had to be rejected for service. Disease was spread by use of the filthy Nile water for drinking and washing. Unskilled workers earned the equivalent of about five cents for a twelve-hour day; and real income had actually declined since World War I. This was indicated by the decline in the total consumption of tobacco, coffee, meat, textiles, and cereals, despite a 25 percent increase in population.

The principal cause for poverty in an overall sense was the increase of population at a rate of more than half a million a year—an increase far greater than the country's natural resources could sustain at a reasonable standard. Only 4 percent of Egypt's 385,000 square miles was cultivable, and even if potentially cultivable areas were developed, 94 percent of the country would remain a desert. Most of the twenty-five million Egyptians had to find their livelihood within this limited area along the banks of the Nile. From the time of the British occupation in 1882, the agricultural area had increased by about one third, but—with improvement in sanitation and hygiene—the population had quadrupled, with the result that ever more people were pressing on the country's limited agricultural land. Today there are more than 1500 people per square mile of agricultural land, at least one-third of them constituting surplus labor. This is one of the worst man/land ratios in the world.

By the end of the war, Egypt's leading political party, the Wafd (see chapter 8), had lost its vitality and cohesiveness. The great *élan* of Zaghlul's days was dissipated, and the party had lost much of its popularity. It was resented by many nationalists because it had collaborated with the British during the war. Several Wafdist leaders, including Zaghlul's successor Nahas, had become involved in unlawful financial manipulations: many had enriched themselves by dipping into the public purse or by misusing confidential economic information.

The efforts of a small group of young reformers—representing a minority of the Wafdist parliamentary delegation—to convince their leaders of the urgency of long term social planning were only partially successful. This minority succeeded in pushing through a sketchy reform program, however—one that was to be greatly expanded after the 1952 revolution. A 1944 law outlined a plan to set up health centers for each 15,000 inhabitants, to institute programs for the eradication of infectious diseases, to increase the number of town hospitals, and to drain malaria breeding spots. But by the eve of the 1952 revolution all these problems had grown in magnitude. A number of liberal Wafdists also raised the question of land reform in parliamentary debates. Nahas admitted to parliament in 1944 that concentration of nearly all profits from the agrarian system in a few hands had been a major cause of a famine in Aswan province.

Most political leaders, however, concentrated their efforts on attempts to dislodge Great Britain from its remaining bases in Egypt. By the end of World War II in 1945 the Wafd, in an effort to regain its lost prestige, renewed its political struggle against England. The opportunity was ripe because of increased frustrations and discontent caused by wartime British activities. The country had been under total military occupation for seven years. The arbitrary policies of the British commanders and the sense of superiority manifested by many of their troops in their relations with the "natives" had antagonized the Egyptians and had nourished xenophobia; all national ills were now blamed on the Allies.

An outbreak of rioting in Cairo during February 1946 led to renewed negotiations for revising the 1936 Anglo-Egyptian treaty (see chapter 5). The tentative agreement reached between Egyptian prime minister Ismail Sidki and British foreign minister Ernest Bevin was not ratified, however, mainly because the Wafd did not feel that it offered sufficient protection against Great Britain's gaining a permanent foothold in the Sudan and thereby control over the Nile River, Egypt's principal source of irrigation. When the issue was brought before the United Nations in 1947, action was deferred by the Security Council on the grounds that all diplomatic efforts had not yet been examined and that in fact Great Britain was already withdrawing its troops from the rest of Egypt to an enclave within the Suez Canal zone.

The Palestine War (see chapter 11) also contributed to middle-class xenophobia (see also chapter 6) and dissatisfaction with the existing regime. Egyptian volunteers joined the fray soon after the 1947 United Nations resolution partitioning Palestine between Jews and Arabs. The Egyptian troops failed to defeat the Jewish forces, and the government signed an armistice agreement with Israel in 1949. Later it was revealed that the troops had been under the disadvantage of faulty arms purchased by the government from various European countries. Resentment of Western support for the new state of Israel and wounded national pride became so intense that Egypt turned against the West completely, becoming a declared neutral in the "cold war."

The Wafd, which had been out of office since the end of the war, rode to power once again on this wave of anti-Western feeling in 1950 and reopened secret parlays on the 1936 Anglo-European Treaty. Encouraged by the intransigence of Iran's prime minister Mosaddeq in his negotiations with Great Britain over nationalization of the Anglo-Iranian Oil Company, the Wafd raised its own demands. After taking office again, its leaders continued the negotiations with England, but again they failed, and street rioting once more disrupted Cairo.

Nahas attempted to distract attention from the failures of his party by emphasizing extremist nationalist slogans and demands. In October 1951, shortly after two Wafdist cabinet ministers resigned in protest against government corruption and mismanagement, Nahas unilaterally abrogated the 1936 treaty and the Anglo-Egyptian Condominium over the Sudan and proclaimed Farouk king of "Egypt and Sudan." The government now encouraged guerrilla fighting to harrass the British in the canal zone. Cairo ordered some 25,000 Egyptian laborers to abandon British outposts; each side blockaded the other, and an Egyptian campaign of anti-British terror was instigated. The British retaliated by seizing Egyptian villages in the zone and placing them under martial law. By December 1951 battles between British troops and Egyptian auxiliary police had resulted in the destruction of a village and in the death of forty-three policemen in the province of Ismailia.

In Cairo a mass protest meeting against the Ismailia slaughter on "Black Saturday," January 26, 1952, turned into such an outbreak of mob violence that large parts of the capital were left in charred ruins. Nearly 500 shops and businesses were destroyed—including such landmarks as the Turf Club and the famous Shepheard's Hotel. The demonstrators began by methodically ravishing luxury installations such as liquor warehouses, cinemas, and department stores. By evening, most of Cairo's business center was destroyed, to say nothing of the incalculable harm done to commercial credit, currency exchange, and tourism. No accurate tabulation was ever made of the deaths and casualties that occurred, but almost 12,000 families were left homeless. Subsequent investigations of the riot indicated that it had been well planned, probably by Ahmed Husain's pseudo-socialists and the Muslim Brotherhood (see chapter 8). Some maintain that Farouk was forewarned, but that he had hoped to exploit the demonstrations to his own advantage before they got out of hand.

The king did use the occasion to replace Nahas with Ali Maher, who promised to create a national front of all parties and to form a youth army to fight for the country's nationalist aspirations. No agreement was to be made with Great Britain that did not include removal of all British forces from the Nile Valley. Ali Maher's promises appeased the extreme nationalists and peace returned to the canal zone and to Cairo. However, the wily old politician seemed too strong politically for Farouk, and he was forced from office within a few weeks. Neguib al-Hilali, his successor, was also a forceful politician, who had resigned from the Wafd in protest against corruption, but he immediately encountered difficulties when he opened a campaign against graft and championed a purge of government offices. Because imminent economic collapse worsened his position, he was defeated in parliament by June 1952. Eighteen days after his resignation he was recalled, only to become involved in a dispute with Farouk over appointment of a minister for war and marine. The king favored his own brother-in-law, Colonel Ismail Sherin, for the post, but the young courtier was so inept that the proposed appointment aroused the wrath of the army.

BACKGROUND OF THE MILITARY COUP

Communist, socialist, and Muslim Brotherhood revolutionary ferment was too disorganized and lacked sufficient force for a political showdown in

1952; and as we have seen, the Wafd, Egypt's only other significant political organization, was ill prepared to cope with the country's problems. The only group capable of effective action against the old regime was the army.

Until 1936 the commander-in-chief of the army had been an Englishman; the army was British trained and it was supplied with British equipment. Merit was rarely a criterion for promotion to the highest ranks, which were reserved for court favorites. On the general staff, there was neither imagination nor initiative, and almost no concern for the "national cause." Many youngsters from lower-class families joined the army, for the educational opportunities that were unavailable to them elsewhere. Graduation from the military academy offered some of Egypt's best minds opportunities for useful service with a modest reward and a certain amount of security. They were far better off than graduates of the civilian universities, who because of their great number frequently found it difficult to obtain employment. The resentments and frustrations of these educated civilians often made them among the most active participants in the extremist movements that constantly threatened civil disorder.

The young officers first met at the Military Academy established by the British to create competent indigenous leadership. They found among their fellow officers often their first opportunity to discuss long-harbored secret resentments against the British occupation, the landed aristocracy, and dismal village life. At the academy these young men forged their grievances into a strong, potentially revolutionary force. A deep social chasm separated Egyptian junior officers from their superiors. Of the young men who were to lead the July 23 *coup d'état,* only one was from a family wealthy by Egyptian standards. The others were sons of small landowners, minor government officials, petty merchants, and commercial agents. Nasser's father, for example, was a postal clerk in Upper Egypt.

A few months after graduation from the Military Academy in 1938, a group of young officers led by Gamal Abdel Nasser began to plan for future ways of meeting the problems they saw facing Egypt. By 1942 Nasser's central committee had set up a society with numerous cells throughout the army. When Winston Churchill decided in 1942 that all Egyptian resources had to be utilized in the British war effort, resentment against arbitrary authority of the Allies turned many officers to favor the Axis powers who were fighting the British. Several plots were organized to join forces with the Nazis, but all of them failed. Contact was made with other clandestine groups and with individuals who were known to be anti-British, such as the Muslim Brothers and the mufti of Jerusalem. While the army officers admired Hasan al-Bana, founder of the Muslim Brotherhood, for what they believed to be his austere virtues contrasted to the corruption in the government, they also criticized him for opening his doors to both good and bad elements. After a considerable period of cooperation, relations cooled between the officers' secret society and the Brotherhood because the former accused al-Bana of placing the interests of his own organization above those of the nation. His movement, they said, seemed to have lost sight of the original idealistic aims and to have become perverted by a mystique of violence.

The unsuccessful war in which they failed to prevent the establishment of Israel in 1947–1948 kindled new fervor among the young Egyptian officers, who were now joined in a secret Free Officers Society of several hundred members. They saw the establishment of Israel as a last divisive effort by the Western imperialists to undermine Arab nationalist movements in the Middle East. To them, therefore, the Palestine war was a question of self-defense; it was a bitter blow to have the Palestine venture end in defeat. Resentment turned more against the politicians in Cairo than against the Jewish enemy, however. Evidence of corruption and the deliberate purchase of faulty arms drew the officers closer together against their superiors. "We were fighting in Palestine," wrote Nasser, "but all our thoughts were concentrated on Egypt... left an easy prey to hungry wolves.... We have been duped—pushed into a battle for which we were unprepared. Vile ambitions, insidious intrigues and inordinate lusts are toying with our destinies, and we are here left under fire unarmed."[2] When they returned from the front, the officers were provoked by a passionate desire to overthrow a regime which had once again demonstrated its complete impotence.

By 1950 the young army officers realized that a respected senior commander was needed to win public confidence. Their first choice was the former chief of staff General Aziz al-Misri, who had become a popular hero because of his years of nationalist activity. When he refused because of age, the choice fell on General Muhammad Neguib, who had an excellent war record and was known to have quarreled with his superiors about the misconduct of army affairs.

THE JULY 23 UPRISING

When it became evident that the king had learned of their clandestine activities and intended to destroy their organization, the Free Officers Society secretly decided to overthrow the government. Their coup on July 23, 1952 was almost bloodless. There was almost no resistance throughout the country and fewer than half a dozen casualties.

Youth was a distinguishing characteristic of the revolutionary group. The oldest member, General Neguib, was fifty-one; the youngest, twenty-nine; and the average age, thirty-four. Only two had any definitive political attachments. Yusuf Sadiq was a member of a Communist group, and Khaled Mohi ed-Din was sympathetic to the extreme left. Because of their extreme points of view, both were forced off the revolutionary executive committee within two years. Among the members of the Free Officers Society were some who were also members of the Muslim Brotherhood and a few Communist sympathizers, but the majority were independent nationalists with no clear-cut political or social views.

Lack of political orientation and of administrative and executive experience created confusion about the initial aims of the military coup. At first its stated purpose was to force a return to constitutional life and to purge the army of corrupt elements. The army itself, stated the leaders of the revolution, had no intention of interfering in political affairs. Nonetheless, the military gradually took over all positions of authority.

An almost immediate decision concerned the fate of King Farouk. After a heated debate, those who favored exile over execution won out, and the monarch was escorted from Egypt on July 26. A three-man regency council, which was given no authority, took the king's place until the monarchy was abolished the following June 18, 1953. Nearly all groups—including the Wafd, the Liberal Constitutionalists, nationalists, socialists, Communists, and members of the Muslim Brotherhood—supported the "Blessed Event," as the revolution was called, and Farouk's subsequent dethronement.

For the first few weeks after the coup, the revolutionists permitted civil authorities to fill the top posts of government, although all major decisions were taken by the Revolutionary Command Council (RCC), established in July 1952 as the new executive committee of the Free Officers Society. Ex-prime minister Ali Maher was again chosen to take that post because of his nationalist views. He and the civilians he chose for his cabinet, however, soon proved far too conservative for the RCC. The revolutionaries quickly became impatient with the old civilian politicians. Impatience became suspicion, then turned into bitterness against nearly all civilian authorities, for they seemed to be stalling on the vital changes needed by the country.

In fact, cooperation between civilians and the RCC ended soon. Within two weeks of the coup all parties were ordered to purge themselves and remove "corrupt elements." A week later General Neguib warned that a dictatorship would be established because "the most evil elements, extending to the very top, still remain untouched." Seven purge commissions were appointed to investigate past scandals, such as the purchase of faulty arms, the manipulation of the cotton market, the illicit sale of state lands, and the widespread income tax evasion. By August 1953, the commissions had removed 800 civilians and 100 military and police officers from their posts. The bureaucrats who survived were "compelled to do a full day's work... something a good many... had never done before."[3]

Ali Maher was replaced by General Neguib in September 1952 because the former chief of government seemed to drag his feet on agrarian reform. Ali Maher had protested that confiscation of land under the agrarian reform was unconstitutional; he and several of his colleagues were thereupon discharged. For the first time, well-known nationalists were appointed to the cabinet. Sheikh Hassan al-Bakkouri, a former Muslim Brotherhood leader, became minister of wakfs and Fathi Radwan, formerly of the Nationalist party, became minister of information. Until the break with Ali Maher, the army worked behind the scenes of government; now the RCC put its men into cabinet posts. Dozens of men from the Free Officers Society were assigned offices in the various ministries. Every department had its corp of some thirty young army officers who were to provide a "progressive administrative element," meaning supervision and control of government activities. Because civil service veterans resented the arbitrary and abrupt manner of these young officers and their lack of administrative and personnel experience, these military watchdogs aroused both fear and suspicion among their civilian underlings. Impatient to accomplish great tasks, the youthful revolutionaries failed to grasp the difficulties that seemed to beset the "slothful" bureaucracy. Lack of any clear reorganizational or administrativer plans—or of any revolutionary blueprint or yardstick for measuring success or failure—also complicated their problems.

NASSER'S "GUIDED DEMOCRACY"

Soon after the RCC took over the government, it was faced with the problem of setting forth its revolutionary aims. Was this to be simply a military coup as had occurred in other Arab countries where small groups of officers had seized power but made no fundamental changes in society? The answer was complicated by Nasser's mistrust of the masses. Soon after the 1952 revolution, he wrote in the *Philosophy of the Revolution:*

> The masses did come. But how different is fiction from facts!...They came struggling in scattered groups. The Holy March to the Great Goal was halted.... It was only then that I realized, with an embittered heart torn with grief, that the vanguard's [RCC] mission did not end at that hour.... We were in need of discipline, but found nothing but anarchy. We were in need of unity, but found nothing but disunity. We were in need of work, but found nothing but indolence and inactivity. Hence the Motto of the Revolution—Discipline, Unity, and Work.[4]

Nasser took the position that democracy must be established not just in parliaments and slogans, but in the life of the people, and that the Egyptians are in fact not yet ready for the Western parliamentary institutions that the old regime had introduced only to pervert for its own ends. Before the revolution, he contended, the so-called democratic institutions, such as political parties and the parliament, were centers of political corruption and degradation. A transition period was therefore necessary, a period in which Egyptians could be educated to understand and use effectively such institutions. Rather than political freedom, accordingly, the revolutionary leaders in Egypt chose to emphasize "social democracy," by which they meant destroying the class distinctions of wealth and privilege.

Since its takeover, the revolutionary government closely guarded against political dissidence, but its police methods were not as brutal as those in many other totalitarian regimes. There have been few executions for political reasons, no mass imprisonments on the Communist or Fascist scale, and the exile or flight of relatively few Egyptian citizens who disagreed with the regime. Those of the inner circle who disagreed with the official point of view have not been liquidated, but rather given some honorific position, such as an ambassadorship, the editing of a government-backed publication, or membership on a committee not too close to the source of power.

Press freedom has gone through a variety of stages in Egypt. Formal censorship of domestic and foreign publications and correspondents has been imposed and removed several times since 1952. Government control of some domestic press was obtained gradually through the acquisition of shares in leading publications, state control of import licenses, domination of the Press Syndicate to which all local journalists must belong, and finally, by outright nationalization of the press in 1960. The reason for nationalization, Nasser explained, was the need to curb the irresponsibility and sensationalism he allegedly found in domestic publications. Under government control, runs this argument, they could be kept more easily to the socially useful task of educating the people.

The 1960 press law stated that newspapers must have a "mission" rather than be commodities for profit. After 1964 the Egptian press was owned, according to law, by the Arab Socialist Union. Press groups were run by boards which included journalists. Profits were divided, with half for reinvestment, and half for distribution to all the staff, including workers. Although under indirect government control through the Arab Socialist Union, the Egyptian Press frequently indulged in criticism of matters related to mismanagement by government in education, finance, and other similar matters which were also discussed in the National Assembly.

After Nasser's death in 1970, his successor, President Anwar Sadat, initiated a variety of liberalization measures including relaxation of press controls. Several prominent journalists who had been discharged, exiled, or imprisoned during the Nasser regime were reinstated. The liberalization tended to favor the right, permitting return of editors such as Mustafa and Ali Amin, formerly charged with collaboration with the United States. In 1975 Sadat created a Higher Press Board headed by the first secretary of the Arab

Socialist Union Central Committee. Its task was to draft a "charter" to regulate activities of Egyptian journalists and to authorize new publications. The decree also set the way for turning over 49 percent of shares in the country's publishing houses to their employees. Censorship on foreign journalists was lifted in September 1974, and also on international telephone communications. During Sadat's "de-Nasserization" era, there was more open discussion and debate than in the previous 25 years. But many subjects were still taboo. Open criticism of the president, his family, or the correctness of his basic policies was not tolerated. One British journalist was expelled for critical stories about Mrs. Sadat. During September 1981 after his crackdown on dissidents, Sadat had many journalists who were critical of his family arrested and imposed more restrictive controls on the press. While the Egyptian press reflected diverse political tendencies, from right to left, self-censorship remained strong and the authorities still issued directives to editorial boards on occasion. Technically, the leading newspapers remained government-owned and their editors were appointed by the state, despite a 1978 announcement that "state supervision of the information media had come to an end."

Nasser-Neguib Conflict

As the Free Officers Society strengthened its hold on the country, the question of democracy became an issue within the RCC. In 1953 General Neguib opposed militarizing the cabinet and questioned removing the civilian ministers from government. Later he called for elections and a new constitution. As titular leader of the Egyptian revolution, General Neguib felt that his opinions were entitled to more respect and authority than those of other RCC members, while his junior associates looked upon him primarily as the RCC figurehead. The essence of disagreement between Neguib and Nasser was the question of whether the country would merely institute reform of its existing institutions or create instead a totally new society. Neguib was the liberal who desired to preserve existing parliamentary institutions by reforming them; Nasser, the revolutionary who favored an all-pervasive social, political, and economic revolution that would totally transform Egyptian society. The outcome of the dispute was foreshadowed in the early weeks of the revolution when the king was deposed and the great estates broken up to destroy the power of the landlords.

A showdown between Neguib and Nasser occurred in February 1954, and the general was forced by the RCC to resign. It was still too early to dispense with the aura of respect and the popularity that Neguib gave the revolution, however, so he was recalled within a few days to assume the honorific presidency of the republic. Nasser took over as prime minister and restored the controls Neguib had seen fit to dispense with. Censorship was renewed; the universities, centers of pro-Neguib sentiment, were put under trusted army officers to curb student "political extremism"; several dozen "politically undesirable" professors were dismissed; and a number of officers were tried for helping Neguib to "incite mutiny" in the armed forces.

By the end of 1954, all opposition to Nasser and the RCC had been liquidated. Political parties had been banned, and after it had made an unsuccessful attempt on Nasser's life, the Muslim Brotherhood was broken up, scores of its members being imprisoned and the organization itself outlawed. Its leaders had turned on the RCC when the officers failed to follow Brotherhood proposals for reforming the country. Neguib, the government now charged, had collaborated with these reactionaries; therefore he was finally removed from the presidency and placed under permanent house detention.

Promises made by the RCC at the height of the Nasser-Neguib battle—to remove censorship, end the ban on political parties, transfer power to an elected constituent assembly, and withdraw the army from politics—were now ignored, and all major decisions came from the RCC, which increasingly came under the domination of Nasser. The only concession made to parliamentary procedure was the creation of a National Advisory Assembly, established to discuss, but not vote on, vital issues.

During 1953, all attempts to reform political parties or to amend the 1923 constitution were abandoned. Instead, the constitution, parliament, and all political parties were abolished, and a three-year "transition period" was proclaimed during which there would be preparation for a return to democratic institutions. During the three-year interval, the "Leader of the Revolution," meaning the head of the RCC, would also be chief of state with full powers to issue decrees free of judicial restrictions. A committee representing various political groups, professions, and religious communities was appointed to draft an entirely new constitution, but its work was abandoned after a few months when it produced but another version of the 1923 constitution; the task was then turned over to a group of RCC officers.

To fill the void created by abolishing political parties, the RCC established a "Liberation Rally" in January 1953. Managed and directed by the RCC, the rally was to "organize" the people and coordinate workers' efforts. In the past, Nasser proclaimed, the parties had formed a "limited company for theft and robbery in which the people had had no shares." Unlike the old parties, which had divided the country in its struggle against British imperialism, the Liberation Rally would unify the people. Actually, the Liberation Rally became an organization through which the RCC controlled labor, students, and other special groups.

At the end of the three-year transition period in January 1956, Nasser presented his new constitution. Some of the provisions and phrasing seemed to be influenced by the American Constitution (its proclamation begins in the name of "We, the Egyptian people"). The document proclaimed an RCC program aimed at abolishing imperialism, feudalism, and monopoly, and at the control of capitalist influence by the establishment of a strong army, social justice, and a democratic society. A bill of rights protected Egyptians from loss of citizenship; discrimination because of sex, race, language, or religion; banishment; property confiscation; and arbitrary arrest and imprisonment. The new one-chamber National Assembly was to have little control over the strong chief executive. The ban on political parties was to continue and the Liberation Rally would be replaced by a National Union, which would organize all political activity. All candidates to the new 350-member National Assembly would be nominated by the National Union, headed by Nasser and three other RCC officers who were authorized to veto the membership of any individual.

Of the 5,500,000 votes cast in the June 1956 plebiscite, Nasser won 99.9 percent of the votes for president and the new constitution was adopted by a 99.8 percent vote. Balloting was compulsory for men and permissible for women, both for the first time.

Elections for members in the new National Assembly originally slated for November 1956 had to be deferred until July 1957 because of the Suez attack (see chapter 5 and 6). During the election campaign, the army officers who directed the National Union eliminated nearly half the announced candidates as "undesirable" and "unworthy." Nevertheless, some political differences among the candidates remained. Some advocated socialism; others, free enterprise. All, however, were pledged to support the revolution, Nasser, and the constitution. The National Assembly lasted only a few months; in February 1958 the creation of the United Arab Republic brought it to an end (see below). The Assembly's negative votes had been ignored by the government, anyway, and Nasser had continued to rule without the Assembly's advice or consent.

After the July 1957 election, attempts were made to draw more Egyptians into political life by enlarging membership and participation in the National Union. All Egyptians approved by local committees of the National Union were entitled to membership. Nasser's purpose in expanding the organization was to gain popular support for the ruling military elite, which he believed had too little direct contact with the urban and rural masses. The National Union's predecessor, the Liberation Rally, had never succeeded in organizing a wide participation of Egyptians in the revolutionary movement.

The National Union's supreme executive committee, headed by Nasser, retained power to nominate all National Assembly candidates. Under the supreme executive, there was a general assembly chosen from local, area, provincial, and national committees. The proclaimed program of the

National Union, like that of the revolution, was to create a socialist, democratic, cooperative society, free from political, social, and economic exploitation.

The United Arab Republic (UAR)

The union between Egypt and Syria created in February 1958 (for details, see chapter 14) required a new system that would encompass the governmental structure and organization of both nations. A simultaneous plebiscite was arranged in Egypt and Syria to approve the union and Nasser as its president. This time there were fewer than 300 negative Egyptian votes out of a total of over 6,000,000; in Syria, 99.8 percent voted in favor of both the union and Nasser.

The new UAR constitution, proclaimed by Nasser in March 1958, superseded the two-year-old Egyptian constitution. The decision to adopt a new constitution was taken by the president without reference to any representative body. The only specific individual rights guaranteed in the new document were safeguards for private property and an assurance of equality of all citizens before the law regardless of race, origin, language, religion, or creed. The president, who was to determine the composition of the new National Assembly, was all powerful, and no provision was made for his election. He was authorized to convene and close the National Assembly, which could meet only at his summons. Laws were to be initiated and promulgated by the president. Those he disapproved, he could veto. Two thirds of the assembly could override a presidential veto, but this was an unlikely possibility since the members were to be chosen with presidential approval. Weak as the powers of the National Assembly were, the president could dispense with it altogether during a national emergency.

Parliament was not actually convened until July 1960, to commemorate the eighth anniversary of the Egyptian revolution. Of its 600 delegates, 400 were Egyptian and 200 Syrian. Half of each group had been selected from the previous Egyptian and Syrian parliaments. All those who were not former members of either the Syrian or Egyptian National Assemblies at the time of the 1958 merger were selected from the National Union, the only authorized political body in both the Northern (Syrian) and Southern (Egyptian) regions of the UAR. The only genuine function of the National Assembly was to discuss and approve government measures approved by the president.

After the Syrian revolution against Egypt and Syria's separation from the UAR in September 1961 (see chapter 14), Nasser dissolved the National Assembly and announced that a new body would be created representing peasants, workers, businessmen, and professionals. Despite the Syrian breakaway, Egypt's official name remained the United Arab Republic until 1971, when it was changed to the Arab Republic of Egypt.

The National Union also convened its first general congress in July 1960. It had been reorganized in Egypt and Syria on the basis of village council elections during the previous year. Village council members picked delegates to provincial councils, which then sent representatives to regional assemblies. They chose delegates to the general congress whose Supreme Executive Committee was in turn dominated by cabinet members, all former RCC officers. The philosophy of guided or controlled democracy underlying the organization of the National Union is that the government should gradually extend popular participation in national life. Initially, efforts were to be made at the village level. When there was successful participation in village councils, then the peasants would be permitted to participate directly in higher bodies such as provincial and regional assemblies.

Selection of National Union and Assembly members on the basis of vocations and professions was emphasized by Nasser to obtain a representative cross section of national life. In local elections and the subsequent secondary selection of representatives, lawyers, teachers, farmers, tradesmen, army officers, landowners, and others were chosen in representative numbers. Initially after the 1958 merger of Egypt and Syria, a few Syrians were invited to participate in the central UAR government in Cairo. But most of them were soon dispensed with and union soon came to mean Egyptian domination, with Nasser supreme in both countries.

After Syria's breakaway from the UAR in September 1961, attempts were renewed in Egypt to expand mass participation in the National Union and to revise the country's constitutional system once more. A Preparatory Committee of 250 was chosen to make plans for the new constitutional era and to arrange for a National Congress of Popular Forces. The Preparatory Committee, heavily weighted by professionals, was permitted to engage in a certain amount of free public discussion, resulting for a few days in the first open criticism of government restrictions on free speech and other civil liberties. The committee determined who would be qualified to run for the congress and who would be entitled to vote, setting up categories of "isolated" individuals who were to be banned from all political activity. They included, in addition to convicted criminals, those who had lost land as a result of agrarian reform legislation and many from whom property had been sequestered. However, "politically isolated" individuals could be "unisolated" by an appeal procedure. Voting for the National Congress of Popular Forces was to be organized through organizations representing farmers, workers, women, professionals, students, and other such categories. Since only a small proportion of the population actually belonged to such groups, only a relatively small number were thereby authorized to participate in the election. Representation in the congress was divided approximately into: peasants, 25 percent; workers, 20 percent; national capitalists, 10 percent; trade unionists,

15 percent; unorganized wage-earners, 9 percent; university teachers, 7 percent; students, 7 percent; and women's organizations, 7 percent. In all, some 1500 members were to be elected; together with the members of the government-chosen Preparatory Committee, they were to constitute a 1750-member congress.

The work of the National Congress, which met in May 1962, was to approve a national charter defining in very general terms the "model Arab state" that was to be guided by "Arab socialism." The national charter also represented the broad outlines of a new constitution and a General Congress of the National Union, which, Nasser declared, would be called the Arab Socialist Union. Eventually, according to government plans, members of the Arab Socialist Union, which was to become the only political party, would vote for a national assembly in which farmers and industrial workers would hold 50 percent of the seats.

The purpose of this circumscribed system of elections and approach to new constitutional structure was to involve the people in government gradually through a series of steps, each of which would extend popular participation in the law-making process. The procedure was in accord with Nasser's belief that Egypt was not yet ready for a Western-type parliamentary democratic system, but that his country required a long process of training and experience in government before it would be ready for democracy as known in the West. According to the president, there could be no free voting while there was mass poverty, for votes would be bought from those with nothing to eat.

From the Arab Socialist Union
to Limited Multiparty-Democracy

In an attempt to broaden the base of popular participation in the political process, membership in the newly created Arab Socialist Union was broadened in 1962 and opened to nearly everyone. More than five million Egyptians, the major part of the adult male population, were enlisted. As a result of the massive influx the organization attempted to terminate all new recruitment early in 1963. By 1968 it was estimated that five of every seven Egyptians qualified to vote were members of the ASU. The goal of a 50 percent worker and peasant membership was attained, and approximately 5 percent were women. There were four levels in the new mass membership organization. At the base were approximately 7000 units in villages, factories, schools, and urban quarters. These were organized into district units, which in turn formed units within each of the twenty-five governorates or provinces which were under the direction of the provincial ASU Congress and committees. At the top of this organizational pyramid stood the General National Congress of some seventeen hundred members. Since the National Congress met only every two years or during national emergencies, it in turn elected a General Central Committee of 150 plus fifty alternate members to convene at least twice a year. The real center of power was the Supreme Executive Committee, a ten member body, headed by the ASU President, controlling decisions at the top. Members of the Supreme Executive Committee were leading personalities in the Egyptian regime who had exceptionally broad powers, including management of day-to-day decisions and responsibility for over-all guidance of the ASU. Political power and decisions of importance, therefore, flowed from the top of the pyramid to the broad base composed of hundreds of units throughout Egypt.

By 1964 it became evident to the Nasser regime that mass participation in the newly formed ASU was in reality not much more successful than in the Liberation Rally, or the National Union. To stimulate the political process, the regime decided to create a new cadre of ASU militants. Members of the elite cadre would be carefully selected by leadership of the organization from "sincere revolutionary youth" of the country who would receive special political training and be sent to work at the village level throughout Egypt under ASU guidance. Membership in this political vanguard was to remain secret. In 1965 an Institute of Socialist Studies was opened to train the young political leaders for their work at the local level. Within a year it was claimed that some twenty thousand young men and women had been trained and graduated. But in 1968 the Institute was disbanded, and ASU leaders acknowledged that the experiment in creating new leadership had been unsuccessful.

During 1965 the two principal Communist parties of the UAR, one pro-Soviet and one Maoist—both of which were illegal—dissolved, and members were invited to join the ASU. In its attempt to concentrate political power, the ASU, rather than suppressing dissidence, attempted to absorb within its ranks many opponents of the regime. Subsequently many former leftists acquired positions of influence within the ASU and other administrative organs of the regime, especially in the press and publishing houses.

Since creation of the ASU in 1964 there was increasing convergence of the governmental and party hierarchies. While there was also increasing emphasis on civilian participation in ASU leadership, the Supreme Executive, which dominated the organization, was strongly influenced by membership of military officers close to President Nasser who were in significant governmental posts. Certain government agencies headed by former officers related to mass mobilization such as ministries of Local Administration, Labor, and Youth had closer interrelationships with the ASU than other civilian headed ministries.

ASU leadership was not free from criticism by the Egyptian press. Several prominent journalists charged that leadership of the organization was dominated by "political careerism," and that there was lack of popular participation in selecting leadership or determining policies at the top. Lack of popular interest and enthusiasm in the organization was evident during May 1968, when only 40 percent of ASU members had paid their dues; most of these were workers and peasants whose payments were automatic payroll deductions. Among those for whom there were no automatic deductions, such as agricultural workers or employees of small firms, only 2 to 3 percent had contributed to the organization.

While the charter of the ASU called for both "criticism of the establishment and self criticism," organization of opposition through class interests was considered subversive. Instead, society would be organized as a whole against the "reactionary forces" that had been excluded from participation in the political process. Differences within the "legitimate" national sectors were seen merely as family differences to be settled through group discussion rather than in the streets or in politically disruptive bodies. In this way, according to the ASU charter, a consensus of "the collectivity" would be achieved.

After defeat of the UAR in the third Arab-Israel War during June 1967, ASU members played an important role in convincing President Nasser to withdraw his resignation, which was tendered immediately after the war. The organization also played an important role in rallying public opinion and in attempting to recover from the deep psychological depression following Egypt's defeat by Israel.

When President Nasser died in September 1970, the ASU designated vice-president Anwar al-Sadat, one of the ten Supreme Executive Committee members, as the single candidate in the national referendum for Nasser's successor. Sadat, a former army officer and a close associate to the ex-president who had also served as speaker of the National Assembly, head of the Egyptian-dominated Islamic Congress, and in other trouble-shooting tasks, was proposed by the ASU Central Committee to the National Assembly as the party's candidate. He received over 90 percent of the more than 7,000,000 votes cast.

Sadat divided the roles of president, prime minister, and ASU chief, all of which had been held by Nasser. To assist him in his role as president he chose as prime minister Mahmud Fauzi, an elderly but respected civil servant and former diplomat, one of the few civilian holdovers from the prerevolutionary era. Other top posts were filled by former army officers, technicians who rose through the bureaucracy, and ASU leaders. Power was still concentrated in a few hands, but by individuals who had risen through government service, the army, or the ASU. Thus, unlike the situation in other Arab revolutionary states, succession to the founder of the regime was orderly and legitimized by institutions created by Nasser and a popular consensus, with the ASU playing a significant role.

Having placed Sadat in power, leaders of the ASU believed initially that they could manipulate him and shape his policies. Sadat, on the other hand, thought that the ASU should be directly controlled by the president and be the "popular foundation" for the executive power. When the ASU secretary general attempted to concentrate power in the hands of the party, there was a political confrontation. Lines were drawn in the struggle between Sadat, representing a moderate position in foreign and domestic affairs, and a group of ASU leftists, led by Vice-President Ali Sabri. Outnumbered in the ASU Executive Committee and in the Central Committee, Sadat preempted his opponents in May 1971. Within a few hours he concentrated power in his own hands by arresting several party officials. Those arrested included Vice-President Ali Sabri, known as a close friend of the USSR, the minister of the interior, who was notorious as one of Nasser's hatchet men, and the secretary general of the ASU. The President of the National or People's Assembly resigned and was arrested. In the following days the whole government and party administration were purged. Sadat revealed that his opponents had mounted a plot against the regime through a "secret organization" inside the ASU. His victory was facilitated by cooperation of the army chief of staff, known for anti-Soviet views. A few months later Sadat moved to keep the army in its place by firing several top officers who he believed were excessively anti-Soviet.

Two themes ran through these early efforts to consolidate Sadat's position—the question of presidential power and the question of relations with the Soviet Union. The question of presidential power was resolved in his favor as he ascended to a position nearly as autocratic as Nasser's and removed nearly all political competitors. Sadat's most pro-Soviet competitors were removed, but the power of the most militant rightists was also clipped. Ironically, two months after removing the rightists, Sadat made a brusque about-face and expelled several thousand Soviet experts from Egypt.

With consolidation of the president's power, the importance of the ASU declined. However, Sadat determined that the party would remain the framework for public discussion of the various trends in political ideology that emerged after Nasser's death. While concentrating ex-president Nasser's power in his own hands, Sadat also introduced a series of "liberalization" measures intended to balance the strong reaction to the former president's authoritarian policies. A new "Permanent Constitution," the first since the 1952 revolution, was approved in a national referendum during September 1971. Much of it was based on the 1964 "Interim Constitution," with far greater emphasis on individual civil and property rights. Membership in the ASU was no longer mandatory for holders of government or trade union posts. Instead emphasis was placed on voluntary association. Declining importance of the ASU did not mean that Sadat encouraged other centers of power. He still opposed independent parties which were considered a threat to national unity. His concept of "single party theory" was that the ASU would become an alliance of peasants, workers, soldiers, and national capitalists.

This modification emphasized "plurality of tendencies" or tribunes within the ASU. In Sadat's words, the ASU does not hold political power: its role is to "faithfully express the opinion of the popular base."

The purge of ASU leaders and former Nasser associates during May 1971 and adoption of the new liberal constitution in September marked the beginning of a new political phase in revolutionary Egypt, later called by Sadat, the "Corrective Revolution." The term implied an attempt to weed out those aspects of Nasserism that infringed on civil rights, led to over-bureaucratization, and impeded economic development because of their emphasis on doctrinaire socialism. On the other hand, socialism would not be abandoned, Sadat promised, but curtailed so as not to infringe upon "constructive" development in the private sector. Many aspects of the "Corrective Revolution" were symbolic, such as changing the name of the National Assembly (parliament) to the People's Assembly. Others, like returning many private enterprises to former owners and lifting restrictions on foreign and domestic investment were substantive. Measures to encourage the private sectors, both local and foreign, were later termed the *"infatah"* (opening) to capital investment.

Throughout Sadat's 11 years as president, until his assassination in 1981, his policies fluctuated between liberalization of Nasser's restrictions on both business and the individual, and defensive measures against his critics. He appealed to popular consciousness by holding periodic national referenda to win approval of sudden policy changes such as the peace arrangements with Israel, the crackdown on "enemies" of the regime, or new revisions of the constitution and the party system. Recognizing the underlying power of Islam in Egyptian society, Sadat cloaked many of his pronouncements and new policy directives in religious references, hoping to deflect criticism from illicit but powerful Muslim organizations.

A Committee for Sounding Opinions was formed in 1975 to prepare the ASU for establishment of diverse permanent tribunes. They were Sadat's answer to those who asked for return to a multiparty system as part of the de-Nasserization and liberalization trend. At the third national congress of the ASU in 1975 establishment of tribunes was formalized as a party principle, provided members pledge to "respect the basic principles of the July 23 revolution, to preserve national unity, not to belong to a political organization other than the ASU, and to yield to majority decisions after free and organized discussion."

In this framework of democratic centralism the number of tribunes increased to more than thirty-five, covering a gamut of ideologies from right to left. Fearful that the army would be drawn into the new political discussion, Sadat formed a special committee of 100 members of the ASU and the National or Popular Assembly to organize and formalize the tribunes into three distinct organizations. They were called: the Arab Socialist Organization of Egypt representing the center; the Liberal Socialist Organization representing the right; and the Alliance of National Progressive Unionists on the left. The maneuver was an attempt to neutralize both right and left by legitimizing them, while strengthening the strongest group in the center. By virtue of its quasi-official status, the center emerged as the predominant tribune, and was headed by prime minister Mamduh Salem.

In November 1976 President Sadat decided to allow the three ASU tribunes to become independent, similar to, but not quite, political parties. The new task of the ASU would be to supervise their activities and to oversee their financial resources. ASU would continue its ownership of the press, but mass organizations attached to it other than the Youth and Women's organizations would be disbanded. The new "parties" would be given authority to publish their own newspapers. Local units of the ASU in towns and other administrative districts were dissolved and their buildings turned over to the parties. ASU power was further curtailed in 1977 when additional parties were authorized outside its jurisdiction; and in 1978 its status as an umbrella institution over political parties was terminated. The Central Committee of the abolished ASU would be converted to a consultative council to meet annually on the anniversary of the 1952 revolution.

The center Arab Socialist Organization (later the NDP) of Egypt headed by the prime minister became the governmental party and the other two, the opposition. Neither the right nor left parties fared well nor did they rally substantial following. The Liberal Socialist Organization, or party of the right, had a program conflicting with its title: to cancel the socialist measures taken since 1952, to limit the public sector and to give the private sector a dominant role in national economy. The leftist alliance of National Progressive Unionists had many members who were former Communists and representatives of the Nasserite left.

Mass riots and demonstrations against inflation, rising food prices, and suspension of government subsidies on basic necessities in January 1977 were the most severe since the revolution. Egyptian police estimated that the riots caused 79 dead, 800 wounded, and over a billion dollars in damage. The January riots gave the government second thoughts about the new tribune or party system. Had it been too liberal too soon? Deterioration of living conditions for the working classes in Egypt's largest cities was a major factor in the riots, but the government blamed four illegal leftist groups: the Egyptian Communist party, the Revolutionary Tide, the Eighth of January Organization, and the Egyptian Communist Workers party. Over 1,200 people, mostly leftist, were arrested, including several leaders of the new but legally recognized National Progressive Unionist Alliance. The other two legal parties took the occasion to attack the leftists and the government threatened its legal status. In a referendum during February, President Sadat procured 99.42 percent of the votes approving his measures against the leftists.

Hardening of the regime's stance and the apparent retreat from liberalization led to protests by intellectuals both in Egypt and abroad.

Parallel with attempts to rally popular participation in support of the government was the introduction of the new "Interim Constitution" in March 1964. The document established a legislative body, the National Assembly. Under the new constitution the National Assembly nominated, and a national referendum subsequently elected, the president.

The National Assembly was supposedly the legislative body established to enact broad policies laid down by Egypt's one political party, the Arab Socialist Union. The Assembly was guided by the 1964 constitution and the National Charter of the Arab Socialist Union which defined the national ideology. Both were supposedly "revolutionary" bodies although the conservative instincts of Egyptians prevented any genuine revolutionary legislation from passing the Assembly. One attempt to reduce individual landholdings to no more than ten acres was rejected by the Assembly as contrary to the spirit of the National Charter. In 1971 Sadat changed the name to People's Assembly and in a 1979 referendum a measure was passed reserving 50 percent of membership in all organizations for workers and peasants. The Assembly membership was increased to 392 with 30 seats reserved for women.

As a consequence of new membership qualifications for the National Assembly a fairly large number of working-class people were brought into the governing process at the highest level for the first time in the country's history. The 75 accredited workers in the new 1964 Assembly included a bus driver, a weaver, craftsmen, and 35 trade unionists, one fifth of them from the textile union. However, genuine manual workers are still scarce in parliament. While there was an increase in the number of working-class people, President Nasser complained in May 1968 that too many large farmers, landlords, national capitalists, and employees got elected under the 50 percent rule. He proposed that the "worker" definition should bar all those who were graduates of universities and members of professional associations, and that "farmer" should apply only to those whose sole occupation was agriculture and who owned no more than ten acres. These more precise but limiting definitions were adopted in time for the January 1969 National Assembly elections. As a result, the number of workers rose to 119, a third of the Assembly, but the total number of registered peasants fell to 64.

In addition to the categories of "peasants" and "workers," other sectors under the ASU charter were the "army," the "intellectuals," and the "national capitalists." "Intellectuals" included physicians, journalists, university professors, lawyers, and technicians; "national capitalists" were small businessmen who are in "social constructive" enterprises.

As in most modern parliamentary systems, legislation originated with the government, but the Assembly frequently provided opportunity for debate and criticism of the bureaucracy. Complaints have included overly high prices, shortages of schools, hospitals, and paved roads, and faulty construction of buildings. There has even been criticism of the army for its interference in the transport authority and in consumer cooperatives and of the peace treaty with Israel. A major outlet for expression of discontent is opportunity provided for Assembly members to question government ministers or their representatives in parliament. Increasingly the Assembly made use of its numerous committees to make inquiries or to raise questions about extravagance in government expenditures, inflation of budgets in public organizations, and shortages of consumer goods. Investigations by the Assembly and its committee have led to changes in government personnel and shakeups in various branches of government.

Throughout the period between 1962 and 1970 the National Assembly as well as the Arab Socialist Union was dominated at the apex by close associates of President Nasser, mostly officers who were in the original group of 1952 revolutionaries. The 1967 cabinet of 29 members included 19 military officers, but after defeat in the 1967 war the number declined to 13 officers in the 1968 cabinet of 33 members. Army officers continue to play an important role in other sectors of Egyptian public life. A survey of managers by the Cairo National Institute of Management Developmenet showed in the late 1960s that 30 percent of 3000 top posts were former army officers, 20 percent were from the Civil Service, 36 percent were from private enterprise, and 15 percent from universities.

Both Nasser and Sadat used the Assembly to legitimize their programs and to sound out currents of Egyptian opinion. Its members represented the different regions of Egypt and its diverse interests and class groups. But their differences were frequently obscured because most candidates ran as members of the ASU and, after its dissolution, of the NDP, the government party. In elections to the Assembly, the most deviant views were screened out; thus criticism of the government in the Assembly was moderate. During the October 1976 elections more than 1,600 candidates registered for the 342 Assembly seats (eight were directly chosen by the president). In an animated electoral battle, candidates had an opportunity to express their opinions openly. However, in the elections the center party won 81.8 percent, the right 3.6, and the left, a mere 0.6 percent. Fourteen percent of those elected were independent. As a result of the election, the center or government obtained all posts in the government. Differences between the right and the left made a very weak opposition, guaranteeing the prime minister very wide freedom of action. In effect the cabinet and government were the administrative arm of the presidency, carrying out its policies with little interference from any organized opposition.

During 1978 the government permitted the Wafd party to reenter the political arena as the New Wafd party, but its representatives disbanded after four months in protest against a new internal security law severely restricting party activities. Indicative of Sadat's departure from Nasserism with its strong socialist orientation was his conversion of the government party or tribune, the Arab Socialist Organization, into the National Democratic party in 1978. Most deputies in the Assembly who were former ASO members now joined Sadat's new NDP, which, as the government party, dominated the political scene. Rather than emphasizing the socialist themes of Nasserism, the NDP harkened back to the nationalist rhetoric of Mustafa Kamil's Watani party (see chapter 8).

Members of the moderate left in the former ASU reorganized themselves in 1978 as a "loyal and constructive opposition" to the NDP in a new Socialist Labor party. Its democratic socialist program called for a more equitable distribution of national wealth between urban and rural areas.

Neither a revised party structure nor frequent elections reflected the growing unrest in Egypt resulting from rapid economic deterioration and disappointment with the Israeli-Egyptian peace treaty signed in 1979. Sadat had raised unrealistic expectations that peace with Israel would bring prosperity to Egypt. Instead peace resulted in Egypt's isolation in the Arab world, a substantial increase in the burden of military expenditures, continued erosion of the economic infrastructure, and bickering with Israel over implementation of the accords, especially those having to do with the future of Israel occupied Gaza and the West Bank.

In parliamentary elections during 1979 Sadat's NDP all but demolished the three opposition parties. The election was the first multiparty parliamentary contest since the 1952 revolution. The NDP captured 330 of the 392 seats, leaving the SLP, the main opposition faction, with only 29. The right-oriented Liberal Socialists won only 3 seats, while the Leftist National Progressive Unionists lost their 2 seats.

However, much of the discontent was concentrated among clandestine political factions outlawed by the government. They included several communist and Marxist groups and Islamic fundamentalists. Both the militant right and left opposed the peace treaty although their hostility to Sadat was intensified as much by his ostentatious and grandiose life style as by his economic and political policies. Attempts to repress the Muslim fundamentalists seemed only to breed a larger opposition. There were harbingers of the future in 1977 and after when hundreds of members of Islamic factions were imprisoned for political assassinations, protest riots, and attacks on Coptic citizens. Prominent among the factions were *Takfir wal-Hegira* (Repentance and Flight from Sin), and *al-Jihad* (the Holy Struggle), both of which were involved in terrorism.

In an attempt to stem the tide of dissidence and to consolidate his power, Sadat assumed the post of prime minister in addition to the presidency in May 1980. A national referendum was staged to approve a series of amendments to the 1971 constitution, one allowing the president more than two successive

6-year terms, which would have enabled Sadat to continue in office after 1982 (he was assassinated in 1981). In deference to the mounting Islamic resurgence, another amendment made the Sharia or Islamic religious code, "*the* principal" instead of "*a* principal" source of legislation. Sadat again won a massive 98.96 percent of the vote. While attempting to appease Islamic sentiment, the measure alienated Egypt's Coptic hierarchy, who protested by curtailing Easter celebrations and publicizing complaints of Muslim harassment.

Sadat's promises that 1980 would be "the year of prosperity" were frustrated by rising inflation and growing inequities in income distribution. On assuming the prime ministry he increased the minimum wage from $22 to $30 a month; reduced prices on basic foods, textiles, and other consumer items; and increased government subsidies on these basics. With 10 percent of the GNP already being spent to subsidize food staples, there was serious question about the sources to finance these new measures intended to capture public opinion.

As increasing numbers of prominent personalities, including most remaining members of the 1952 RCC, former cabinet members, leading journalists, and academicians openly expressed disappointment with Sadat's policies, especially with results of the Egyptian-Israeli peace treaty, he reacted with growing vehemence, a resumption of controls on the media, and appeals for public support through a series of national referenda intended to demonstrate mass approval. Although successful in obtaining votes of 98 or 99 percent in his favor, he found it necessary to enact various measures to prevent open criticism. In April 1980 the People's Assembly passed the "Law of Shame," a new code of ethics to punish various forms of "antisocial" behavior such as propagating antireligious philosophies, inciting opposition to the state economic, political and social system, and spreading false rumors.

During September 1981, in a final effort to contain dissidence, Sadat's government conducted the largest internal security operation since the revolution. Over 1,500 suspects were arrested from across the political spectrum, from Muslim zealots to the Coptic pope. More than a dozen Muslim and Coptic organizations were dissolved and seven periodicals were banned, including the newspaper of the opposition SLP. Hinting that public unrest was communist instigated, Sadat used the occasion to expel the Soviet ambassador and six of his staff. All these measures were approved by a vote of 99.45 percent in still another referendum. A month later Sadat was assassinated in a plot organized by Muslim zealots, who were later tried and executed or imprisoned.

Sadat was succeeded by his vice-president, Hosni Mubarak, a former commander of Egypt's air force. Mubarak was selected by the People's Assembly, which was controlled by the NDP, and its selection was ratified in a popular referendum with another massive vote.

Changes in the regime and its policies under Mubarak were gradual and unostentatious. The major change was in style. Whereas Sadat lavishly displayed the trappings of office and pugnaciously challenged his opponents at home and in the Arab world, Mubarak was low keyed, conciliatory to critics, seeming to search for accommodation with them. In an early gesture to the opposition, he released several prominent journalists and others arrested in Sadat's September roundup. Most importantly Mubarak pledged to retain fundamental policies such as keeping intact state ownership of the public sector and Egypt's peace commitments to Israel. However, economic problems continued to plague Egypt; Mubarak was no more successful than Sadat in coping with them because of the country's economic and social infrastructure, including problems of bureaucracy and the impact on Egypt of the general world economic recession.

CREATING A NATIONAL CHARACTER AND IDEOLOGY

When the RCC seized power in 1952, there was little positive identification by most Egyptians with the state. For centuries, the peasants had identified central authority with tyranny and had accordingly viewed it with suspicion. Primary loyalties were to the family, to the village, to Islam—not to the nation-state. In urban centers, society was divided by different educational systems, economic and social classes, and minority viewpoints. There was no homogeneous national ideology or national loyalty.

Nasser discussed the problem of national loyalty in *Philosophy of the Revolution,* describing the divisions he saw within Egyptian society. He presented the following description as typical for the average Egyptian family:

> The father, for example, is a turbaned fellah—a thoroughbred country-fellow. The mother is a lady of Turkish descent. The sons and daughters attend schools respectively following the French and English educational systems—all this in an atmosphere in which the thirteenth century spirit and twentieth century manifestations intermingle and interact.[5]

This portrait of an "average Egyptian family," however, is much less characteristic of rural than of urban Egypt. The peasants (over half the population) create no such problem, for they are a homogeneous group with their own distinctive characteristics. Peasant roots penetrate deep and their history reaches back to Pharaonic times. They therefore have a deep attachment to the soil of Egypt, if not to its government. Nasser's problem of creating a homogeneous Egyptian national type with strong national loyalty was more likely to arise in the great urban centers—in Cairo, Alexandria, Tanta, Assiut, Port Said, and Suez, the centers of the country's literature, press, politics, commerce, business, industry, and social thought. In the past, many of these activities had been dominated by groups which were not even considered "true Egyptians" by the majority of the population. The essence of the problem of creating a national ideology is that those in the capital most responsible for directing the mainstream of national life are remote from its realities.

As described in chapter 8, extensive foreign influences in Egyptian economic, social, and cultural life had begun more than a century ago when Egypt was still part of the Ottoman Empire. Because of the capitulations, the small non-Muslim group under European protection had obtained control of the economy. Non-Muslim (mostly foreign) businesses tended to hire Jews and Christians who were usually better educated and more adapted to the ways of the West, and the special position acquired by non-Muslims by virtue of their superior education continued. By the twentieth century, the white-collar labor market was flooded with "native" Egyptian graduates of the universities and secondary schools who, unable to find employment, resented the "privileges" that these minorities had acquired. Nationalist leaders increasingly demanded the creation of "Egyptian," that is, Muslim, banks, industries, and commerce and called for more legislation like the 1947 company law requiring the employment of specific percentages of native "Egyptians."

The revolutionary government continued to "Egyptianize" commerce and industry at a moderate rate, until the 1956 attack by England, France, and Israel. This became the occasion for telescoping within a few brief weeks the process of "Egyptianization," which was to have occurred over a number of years. For the first time many Christians, including Copts, were deprived of their employment. Egypt's Jewish community had already been the victim of national ferment. For nearly a decade Jews had been leaving Egypt in fairly large numbers because they feared the resentment against them stirred by the Palestine conflict. Until 1946 the Jewish community, like other minority groups, had enjoyed the luxuries and privileges of identity with the "foreigners." Indeed, many in the minority communities held foreign passports. The majority of the country's Jewish residents were of French, British, Italian, Greek, and other European nationalities. During the Palestine war in 1948 they suffered their first blow; many Jewish properties were confiscated and employment opportunities became difficult to find, resulting in the exodus of nearly a third (some 20,000) of the Jewish community. After Israel attacked Egypt in October–November 1956, repercussions were even more disastrous, resulting in the departure of all but about 5,000. By the time the Egyptian-Israeli peace treaty was signed in 1979 only a few hundred, mostly older Jews, remained.

Muslim resentment, fear, and suspicion of all non-Muslim groups intensified after the 1956 attack, though the Jewish community bore the brunt of the hostility. Large numbers of Italians and most of the Greek community, whose families had lived in Egypt for generations, began a hasty exodus; and even some younger Copts searched for a more congenial life abroad. Specific "official" acts against the Christians are difficult to isolate, but there was little doubt that they were facing increasing difficulties in obtaining employment in government, commerce, and industry. Copt university professors and government employees alleged that advancement was delayed. Many Copts who had formerly supported the revolution became disillusioned with the regime.

During 1981, religious tensions were heightened by growing disaffection among Muslim zealots. Antigovernment demonstrations in Cairo and in other parts of Egypt erupted into clashes between Copts and Muslims, with scores of deaths resulting from the fray. President Sadat accused Muslim "fanatics" as well as leaders of the Coptic church of "sectarian sedition," and in September 1981 the Coptic pope was arrested with several other officials of the church during the crackdown on dissidents. Sadat replaced the pope with a committee of five government selected bishops who were controlled by the president.

National Images—What Is an Egyptian?

Like Ataturk, Nasser used the past to help create national sentiment. In literature, popular drama, and the cinema, the exploits of folk heroes, such as those who resisted Napoleon, are glorified. Even postage stamps are decorated with slogans to arouse patriotic ferver. After the 1956 invasion, a popular postal issue warned: "Egypt—Grave of the Aggressor." Techniques of arousing national sentiment are directed by officers or ex-officers in a number of organizations such as the Higher Council for Arts and Letters and the Ministry of National Guidance.

The 1956 Suez attack was used to create "national homogeneity" in much the same way that Ataturk used the Greek invasion of 1919. Several mythical heroic incidents during the struggle became part of the official revolutionary history. Although the 1956 invasion was a military disaster, revolutionary Egypt made of it a symbol of sacrifice to be endured on the road to victory; it became for the revolutionists what Valley Forge became for American patriots.

The October 1973 war became an even more powerful symbol of national identity. It was the first time Egyptian forces were able to inflict severe losses on the Israelis and to seize substantial territory from the enemy. In crossing the Suez Canal Egyptians and all Arabs perceived a great victory that boosted their pride and compensated in part for previous defeats. The "Crossing" became a slogan and symbol of Egypt's new unity and accomplishment. It became a term applied in several contexts: The "Crossing" in industrial achievement, in agriculture, and in science and technology. Of course, these attainments were exaggerated, as was the importance of the canal crossing itself. But its psychological impact on Egyptian society should be not underestimated.

Arabism is another concept put forward to strengthen national pride. Until the 1955 Bandung Conference, Egyptians thought of the national type as primarily Egyptian, not Arab. Until then, nationalist leaders had concentrated on "unity of the Nile Valley," rather than on "Arab unity." Few Egyptians were emotionally stirred by the "Arab cause," despite great efforts of Arab nationalists in the Levant and Palestine to involve them. Even the Palestine war was primarily *against* "Western imperialism" rather than *for* "Arabism." In the midst of combat, the Free Officers Society was more bitter about the corrupt Cairo politicians than about Israel.

There was a reason, however, for active Egyptian participation in the Arab movement. Long before Nasser, Cairo had been the cultural and religious center of the Arab East. The thousand-year-old Azhar was headquarters for higher Islamic studies, attracting not only Arabs but Muslims from all over the world long before the revolution. Egyptian music, drama, and literature have been known throughout the Arab East since the nineteenth century. The Egyptian press was more widely read in Damascus, Beirut, and Amman than were the local newspapers. Radio Cairo was more listened to, more powerful, and more influential than local radio stations. Therefore it had not been difficult for Egyptians to identify with the Arab world or for the Arab world to identify with Egypt since the 1952 revolution. As Egypt's President Nasser became increasingly identified with the new revolutionary nationalism, and as this identification was strengthened by increasing political successes at the Bandung Conference, in the 1956 Suez Canal crisis, and by the president's close associations with leading third-world political figures, he acquired a charismatic role throughout most of the Arab East. As Egypt became increasingly identified with Arab world political leadership, Egyptians identified themselves as Arabs. Nasser and the Egyptian press and government radio placed increasing emphasis on the country's role in the greater Arab destiny. Perhaps the greatest impetus to this identification was Egypt's partnership with other Arab countries in the struggle against Israel. With each successive military defeat, it seems that greater emphasis was placed on association with the Arab world.

Cairo repeatedly was the center of inter-Arab conferences and meetings of chiefs of state. President Nasser, despite military setbacks, was called upon by other Arab nations to mediate their disputes. As leader of the Arab Socialist Revolution, Egypt came to the assistance of the Republic of Yemen in 1962 in its war against the monarchy. Only after Egypt's defeat in the 1967 war against Israel did President Nasser agree to withdraw from the unsuccessful operation in Yemen. During 1969 when Palestine Arab commandos clashed with the Lebanese army, the government of Lebanon called upon President Nasser to mediate. The confidence which other Arab governments placed in Egypt was evident in the establishment of an Arab military command whose chief of staff was an Egyptian general. The paradox of Egypt's identification as an Arab country is that the more serious the defeats suffered in the war with Israel, the more intense seems to become the desire by Egyptians for an Arab identification.

As a result of the defeat by Israel in June 1967, Egypt lost control of the Sinai Peninsula up to and including most of the eastern bank of the Suez Canal. Egypt, therefore, had a vested interest in association with other Arab nations who also were defeated and whose lands continued to be occupied. Israel also strengthened the image of Nasser as the leader of Arab nationalism, since Israelis maintained that peace with the Arab states was possible only after it had been concluded with Egypt.

The 1952 Revolution and Islam

In Egypt, Islamic consciousness is so deeply instilled that most citizens still equate a true fellow countryman with his acceptance of Islam. A major difference between the Turkish and Egyptian revolutions is that Ataturk attempted to separate Islam completely from politics and from as much of the social life as possible. Nasser attempted to use the religion and to reformulate it to suit the needs of the revolution.

The revolutionary leaders have emphasized that Egypt is a Muslim country. Although certain Muslim institutions such as the Sharia courts have been abolished and the influence of the Muslim clergy has been diminished, most of the population and many of the revolutionary leaders still have a strong attachment to Islam. The government has made good use of the political appeal of Islamic loyalty and Egypt as a Muslim community. All schools are required to teach the principles of Islam and official correspondence is prefaced by the opening verse of the Koran: "In the name of Allah the Beneficent, the Merciful."

As has already been noted, when the Free Officers Society seized power in 1952, it had close connections with the Muslim Brotherhood and several of the officers were members of the Brotherhood. Three cabinet posts were offered to Muslim Brothers, but the organization was finally liquidated when it sought to capture the revolution.

Since then, Nasser and his associates gradually imposed their own ideas on, and control of, the country's Islamic institutions. The Ministry of Wakfs was used to establish domination over the Muslim religious leaders. Their Friday speeches were prepared by the government, and prayer leaders throughout the Nile Valley preached state-supplied sermons on health, education, foreign affairs, and matters about which the government desired to educate the peasantry.

Abolition of all religious courts in 1956 was a major step toward secularization, although removing marriage, divorce, and other personal-status matters from religious jurisdiction deeply antagonized non-Muslim leaders, especially Christians, who felt that the loss of control over personal status threatened their hold over their flocks. Since the religious courts were closed, their functions have been taken over by civil courts, which apply religious law in personal status matters. Christians complain that this is not harmful to Muslims because most civil judges are Muslims, but that the latter are not qualified to interpret Christian ecclesiastical jurisprudence.

The government has used Islam widely to rally support for Egypt throughout Africa and in other Muslim countries. Young theological students from Indonesia, Burma, Ethiopia, and West Africa are encouraged to attend al-Azhar, where they are imbued not only with Islamic teachings but also with the ideas of the 1952 revolution, such as anti-imperialism, nationalism, and socialism. Radio Cairo's broadcasts to Africa strongly emphasize the role of Islam in combating the Western imperialists. To further pan-Islamic activities and to propagate the message of Islam in Africa and Asia, the RCC organized an Islamic Congress in 1954 to hold periodic conferences—at which more political than theological subjects are discussed.

After Egypt was expelled from the Arab League and the International Islamic Conference because of the peace agreement with Israel, Sadat formed a new League of Islamic and Arab peoples in 1980. Only Sudan and a few Afghan emigres openly supported the new organization; thus it failed to achieve any international significance.

Egypt's orthodox Muslim constituency generally distrusted Sadat's lip service to Islam and his gestures to win Muslim support, such as changing the motto of the state in 1979 to "knowledge and faith," or adoption of the Sharia as the primary source of the country's legislation. These gestures were overshadowed by Muslim disapproval of Sadat's grandiose lifestyle and his overtures to Israel.

Socialist Ideology

The post-World War II attraction of many newly emerging Asian and African nations to socialism was also characteristic of the Egyptian revolution. At first, the officers who led the revolution had no identifiable ideology. They came to power with no program for extensive social and economic change, but only with the desire to instill an honest and efficient government. Soon, however, they realized that their initial slogan—discipline, unity, work—was not enough, and by 1955 a new revolutionary slogan was proclaimed—to make Egypt a "democratic, socialist, cooperative society."

An initial socialist measure was the 1952 land reform, although many did not regard it as such. Extensive socialization of the economy resulted from the seizing of the property of foreigners following the 1956 attack. The initial purpose was not to socialize, but to Egyptianize the economy. At first, the government proposed that private Egyptian capital take over the hundreds of millions of dollars worth of British, French, and Jewish property. But private interests did not step in. Instead, the revolutionary government formed its own Economic Organization to manage the seized property. Some holdings were later returned but many remain in government hands. Not only were so-called enemy firms sequestered, dozens of other foreign businesses were ordered to Egyptianize within five years or also face confiscation.

By the end of 1957, the Economic Organization was managing dozens of these seized firms and announced plans to establish additional government owned and operated industrial, agricultural, commercial, and financial concerns whose profits could be used to develop the economy. Within a year and a half, the Economic Organization announced that it had liberated the most important sectors of national economy from foreign domination, and that it was now capable of directing the movement of finance, facilitating credit, and encouraging investments and savings. Upon union with Syria, this organization set about expanding its activities to the Northern Region of the UAR.

The Economic Organization thus formed was a pragmatic attempt to deal with an immediate situation—the sudden acquisition of large foreign properties. It was not formed as the result of a preconceived plan or an ideological or theoretical approach to the problems of national economy; it was established almost overnight as a result of the surprise attack in October 1956. Had it not been for the attack, the revolutionary leaders would probably have experimented for several years before devising a program for industrial and commercial development.

Between 1956 and 1961, Nasser seemed to become influenced by the socialist theories of Yugoslavia's President Tito, with whom he exchanged visits. The Titoist influence culminated in a number of radical decrees containing very wide nationalization measures, published in July 1961 on the ninth anniversary of the Free Officers Society coup. The decrees were aimed at assisting the country to double its national income within ten years and to redistribute further its national income, 50 percent of which had been in the hands of 1.5 percent of the population before the revolution. Implementation of these decrees would make the UAR economy resemble that of Yugoslavia more than that of any Western European country.

The measures nationalized 82 percent of business and industry in Egypt and Syria. Complete government control was ordered for all important cotton and textile, iron and steel, fertilizer, shipbuilding, and construction industries. All banks, insurance companies, and public utilities were taken over by the government. Left to the private sector were a few relatively unimportant industries such as beer, wine, retail outlets, and some small-scale enterprises.

But not even these businesses were completely exempt from government control, which was exercised by limiting the amount of stock any individual could hold to 10,000 Egyptian pounds (approximately equal to $28,000 U.S. currency) and by taking over as much as 50 percent of the stock in some cases.

Annual salaries were restricted to 5000 Egyptian pounds and all income above 10,000 Egyptian pounds was to be taxed 90 percent. At least 25 percent of all corporation profits were to be reserved for workers' bonuses, housing, schools, and medical care, and workers were to be represented on all corporate boards of directors.

A related decree, intended to force companies to hire additional workers, reduced the working day to seven hours and set a maximum work week of forty-two hours. No one was to hold more than one job, a restriction that would affect in particular those in the lower-middle class, many of whom supplemented their income by holding more than one position.

Private land holdings, which had been limited to 200 acres under the 1952 agrarian reform, were limited to 100 acres and again, to 50 acres in 1969. Payments required of the peasants in 1952 for their newly acquired holdings were to be cut in half. In all cases of confiscation by the government, former property owners were to be compensated in 15-year government bonds bearing 4-percent interest.

The 1964 constitution strongly emphasized the socialist character of the UAR. "Socialist solidarity," it stated, "is the basis of Egyptian society. The family is the foundation of society." Egypt's economy was to be based upon the socialist system with the entire national economy to be guided by development plans published by the state. Natural wealth in the subsoil belongs to the state. The people are to control means of production and dispose of surplus production according to the national development plan.

The constitution recognized three forms of ownership: (a) state ownership of property belonging to the people, (b) cooperative ownership of property belonging to those participating in cooperative societies, and (c) private ownership, whose social function is to be stipulated by law, but which is protected from expropriation except for public interest. All Egyptians were entitled to free public education through the university level. A unique feature of the constitution was its stipulation that at least half of the members of the National Assembly should be workers and farmers. Farmers or peasants are defined as those who own not over twenty-five fedans of land, and workers are almost anyone employed for a wage or salary.

The revolutionary government's policies toward capital and labor also developed from circumstance rather than doctrine. Initially, the proclaimed policy was to cooperate with "progressive" capitalists, but their "recalcitrance" to invest in approved enterprises soon created friction, and the officers increasingly found it necessary to "guide" them. Among the revolutionary leaders, there was deep suspicion of capitalists. They were viewed as mere "speculators," who, according to President Nasser, were only interested in exorbitant profits, not in helping the masses. The government soon justified the need to guide business, stating that its intention was to promote the public interest by preventing capitalism from exploiting the individual and society.

Labor unions, which were strictly controlled and supervised by the government even before the revolution, became army dominated, through the National Union. Their principal activities are political, not economic or social. In 1957, some 250,000 members of the loosely constituted movement were organized into a government-created federation under the direct supervision of Colonel Husein Shafei, then minister of social welfare. The stated objective of the federation was to protect the "principles and philosophy of the revolution."

In 1959 there were 1300 separate unions, of which 120 were in the textile industry organized separately in each factory. Hundreds of unions were consolidated, and a new national industrial wage structure was established in 1962, ranging from a minimum of 60 Egyptian pounds a year for adolescent apprentices to 1800 pounds a year for departmental managers. With increasing government control over industry and establishment of government standards in wages, working conditions, and management practices, opportunities have decreased for independent action by workers. While the government maintains that the right to strike exists, most officials would regard the subject as "irrelevant." In recent years there have been strikes among Alexandria doctors, taxi drivers, and industrial workers acting independently of their unions, but the strikes are usually kept quiet, with little if any reference to them in the press. The government would regard such actions as contrary to the spirit of the National Charter. Instead, the trade union movement has increasingly put emphasis on activities such as development of "labor culture," including classes for illiterates, vocational training, and ideological orientation.

Between July 1961 and 1965 most industry and commerce, except small retailing, was taken over by the government. The new nationalized industries were grouped into nine major General Organizations and distributed among various ministries. For example, General Organizations under the Ministry of Light Industry included food, spinning and weaving, and engineering. Those under the Ministry of Heavy Industry included chemical industries, construction, petroleum, mining, and metal industries. This resulted in development of a large state bureaucracy. Simultaneously, higher education has rapidly developed; the number of university graduates has increased several times. However, despite increasing opportunities in the new bureaucracy for university graduates, their numbers have grown so rapidly that many are unemployed.

Expansion of the government sector of the economy and development of the new bureaucracy have had two effects according to Malcolm Kerr.[6]

> First, it has undercut the potential for the development of sources of power and influence in society independent of the state, since the latter is now the predominant employer, entrepreneur, organizer, and dispenser of ideas. Second, however, the new demand of the state for professionally qualified personnel has brought together an ever-growing group of well-educated men whose talents and horizons cause them to become highly critical of the stultifying mediocrity of the bureaucratic life into which they have been thrust, and of the personal faults of those in authority over them. For the run-of-the-mill employees who fill the ranks of the government and its enterprises, such tendencies are no doubt vastly outweighed by the consideration of the security of livelihood that their jobs provide; but among those upon whose superior professional abilities the system really depends for its operation, a certain level of alienation is inescapable. Thus there is a tension between their dependence upon the system and their resentment of its failings. This may be only latent under normal circumstances when things are going tolerably well; these men, like others, have certainly been in sympathy with much that the regime has stood for and, as already mentioned, could feel that they had a stake in its reforms. Their reaction to major failures on the part of the regime, such as the military disaster of 1967 or perhaps even the mounting economic problems of the two preceding years, however, is a different matter. Although they lack the political or personal base from which to oppose or criticize the government openly, any sharp decline in their morale can only bode ill for both the effectiveness of the revolution's programs through the emigration of some of them to other countries and a drop in the performance of those who remain. Should an alternative to the present regime come clearly into view, it may find among these men a ready and waiting source of support.

> The bureaucracy is cumbersome and inefficient, and the attachment of its members to job security and routine procedure has attracted public complaint and ridicule for many years. Although this is obviously an obstacle to many of the regime's reforms, the bureaucracy is in some ways a political asset. It enables the business of the country to proceed without more vigorous political activity, and it facilitates the extensive organization of Egyptian society in a manner that keeps initiative out of hands other than those of the regime, enabling the regime to assert a tangible authority over all questions of public concern. Furthermore, although most things are apt to be done poorly, the availability of so much trained manpower and organizational framework means that at any given time the regime possesses the means to accomplish a few top-priority tasks very well indeed: the management of the Suez Canal, the construction of the High Dam, the supervision of banking and currency, and—not least of all—the maintenance of a vigorous internal security service.* Also, whether they are done

well or not, some administratively complex undertakings such as land reform and the nationalization of private properties and businesses, which are important to the regime for their political effect, are at least made possible by the existence of the bureaucracy.

   *If this is so, one might ask, why not also the armed forces? But the armed forces are too large to benefit dramatically from the assigning of special priority. Unlike the other cases, authority over the army is bound to be widely delegated and redelegated.

THE REVOLUTION AND REFORM

The clandestine tracts published by the Free Officers Society before the revolution made little reference to Egypt's economic and social problems. Primarily they emphasized changing the political structure to end the malfeasance in government that was sapping army strength. Only after the RCC seized power and was faced with the need to improve Egyptian life did reform become a primary objective.

Agrarian Reform
The 1952 agrarian reform soon became one of the revolution's proudest achievements. It was impatience with opposition to this first major social change that broke the short-lived partnership between the old civilian politicians and the young military revolutionists. Indeed, many reformers came to view the breaking up of the large estates in Egypt as the panacea for all of that country's ills, failing to realize that in fact there was not enough land to cope with the growing population. Communists, the Muslim Brothers, and even Nahas had suggested some form of land division in the prerevolutionary era. World War II German propaganda had exploited the issue and, during the battle of el Alamein, had stirred peasants in one village to subdivide their landlord's property. (It was returned to the landlords before the end of the war.) By the war's end, it was evident that there was a strong popular demand for land reform, but none of the bills introduced in parliament were ever passed.

   Land reform became the first dramatic social measure seized on by the RCC after coming to power, perhaps because it was the most obvious need. In the first weeks of the revolution, the RCC thought of land reform as one way of destroying the political power of the large landlords. Another objective of land reform was to divert investment from land speculation to much needed industry. Traditionally, investors preferred the safe and immediate returns from farm investment. However, this prevented creation of new wealth by concentrating capital in existing hands.

The greatest effect of the 1952 land reform law was to reduce the power of some 2000 individuals, who owned estates of over 200 acres. All land in estates of over 200 acres was requisitioned and subdivided among landless peasants or farmers with less than 5 acres per family. Former owners would be compensated over a period of twenty years with government bonds. The direct effect was far less dramatic than the country had expected. About 10 percent of the cultivated area actually changed hands, and less than 6 percent of the farmers (fewer than one million) received new holdings. Only one in five of those who were without property received any, and the idea of creating a strong small-peasant class soon disappeared. There was simply not enough land to keep up with the explosive rate of population increase. The most important political significance of the legislation perhaps was to lessen the power of some 2000 individuals from whom land was requisitioned.

One consequence of the agrarian reform was expansion of the cooperative movement that had begun in Europe before World War I. By the eve of the revolution, there were some 2000 societies with nearly 750,000 members. As a result of legislation requiring every peasant who received land from the government to join a cooperative, more than 270 new societies, constituting an additional 80,000 members, were added. When they were first formed, the peasants were suspicious of the government cooperatives, but within months they were eager to take advantage of the cooperative cultivation, land development, and crop-marketing services.

The agrarian reform was also supposed to reduce the exorbitant rents that existed on about two-thirds of the cultivated area, but land scarcity created such a great demand for property that high "black market" rents continued to prevail. The minimum wages for agricultural laborers specified in the law were to have raised the incomes of about one-third of the agricultural population. But again, implementation was short-circuited by Egypt's labor surplus, and black market labor continued to be available at rates far below the legal minimum. Even the formation of agrarian trade unions did not prevent the black marketing of farm labor.

The second land reform limiting individual ownership to 100 acres was undertaken in 1961. In 1969 the limit was set at 50 acres. These reforms affected about one fifth of the arable land. Thus the basic structure of land ownership remained unaffected. After redistribution of land among farmers without agricultural property, just over 5 percent of the owners continue to hold about half of the farms in the country, while some 95 percent of the owners share the other half. Average ownership among the 5 percent group is about 18 acres while the national average is still about 2 acres. This indicates that the overall problem is not one of distribution but scarcity of land. By June 1966 more than 300,000 families or one and a half million people had been settled on small holdings and organized into 500 land reform cooperatives.

A major effect of the land reform was to create two rural peasant classes. One relatively small group of landowners owning 3 to 5 acres belonged to the cooperative system. They were supplied with government funds and technical assistance through the cooperatives, and provided most peasant members of the Arab Socialist Union. The other, much larger, group was part of traditional Egypt and was not active in ASU politics. Radicals in the ASU unsuccessfully continued to press for further limitations of landholdings to 50, or to as few as 10 acres, to eliminate from the agrarian structure the "kulaks," who they believed were a major obstacle to truly socialist reform.

The greatest effect of the land reform on the peasant was psychological. The harsh agents of the absentee landlords no longer controlled the village police, the local tax collectors, or the municipal authorities, nor could they continue to manipulate local elections. Today, employees of the government's agrarian reform department have replaced the agents of the former owners, and the peasants no longer live in fear of being dispossessed from their farms.

A major problem faced by the revolutionary officers was the lack of professionally trained, experienced technicians to implement major economic programs. This often caused them to improvise plans without adequate preparation and to impose them without consulting informed specialists. The experiment in Liberation Province, intended to reclaim some 50,000 acres of desert west of the Nile Delta, was a serious case of poor planning. Liberation Province was to form a model cooperative for agrarian living in which all phases of life were strictly controlled and regimented. Families settled in the experimental cooperative were hand picked. None had more than one wife or more than three children; all were between twenty-three and thirty years old; all had an elementary knowledge of reading and writing; and all came from overpopulated regions. Members of the collective even did their morning calisthenics together, and wore identical clothing. Soon the officers discovered that the Egyptian peasant could not adapt to the rigid routine prescribed for Liberation Province dwellers. Financial and administrative mismanagement raised costs of the project far above those planned for and created a national scandal, so that the project as originally conceived was abandoned and the province became an ordinary development area.

The establishment of regional rural centers to help raise the level of village life was also a disappointment. Before the revolution, the first rural centers had been tried by a quasi-private organization on a pilot scale in two villages. Success of the pilot projects stimulated the government to expand the program in 1941 and to involve various ministries in carrying it out. But by 1952 the rural improvement program was still far from adequate to meet the country's needs. The revolutionary government decided that some 860 centers would be necessary if every village were to be within convenient range of a health unit, a school, a cooperative society, and social welfare services.

However, not only buildings and equipment but also physicians, nurses, veterinarians, sanitary and medical technicians, social workers, agricultural and irrigation engineers, and economists were necessary to operate the regional units. Although Egypt has far more of these specialists than any other Arab nation, the number is still insufficient to meet the needs of the 14,000 Nile villages. In addition, individuals trained for these tasks are often reluctant to leave the large urban centers because they regard life in remote villages as exile. Even those of rural origin often reject the idea of returning to a rural existence after receiving a university education. Furthermore, by the 1970s, many with these skills found employment in other developing Arab countries far more lucrative, with the result that thousands of Egyptians were employed in North Africa and the Gulf while hundreds of Nile villages were bereft of skilled technicians and professionals.

Increasing National Productivity

After initiating agrarian, health, and educational reforms, the revolutionary leaders realized that increased social services would not enable Egypt to cope with its pressing problem of population increase. Even more important than improving peasant living standards is the problem of increasing agricultural and industrial productivity. A Permanent Council for National Production was created in 1953 to devise first a five-year, then a ten-year integrated economic development program. Although the number of industrial workers has more than doubled since 1952, they still represent only about 10 percent of the total working force. The value of industrial produce has nearly doubled since 1952 and now almost equals that of agricultural produce. Together they provide two-thirds of the national income. Nasser's ten-year plan called for increasing the proportion of national income that derives from industry to about a third by 1970, while agriculture, despite its increased productivity and output, was expected to provide only a quarter of the national income. As part of the effort to expand industrial output and increase self-sufficiency, a number of new industries, including a steel mill and factories producing electric light bulbs, radios, automobiles, and pharmaceuticals, were begun after 1956.

The largest project was the Aswan High Nile Dam. So great was the enthusiasm for this construction that many Egyptians regarded it as the key to their national revival and the acid test of revolutionary progress. The decision to build the dam was announced in 1954, but extensive work was delayed until 1959 because of difficulties in obtaining international economic assistance (see chapter 5) and failure to reach agreement with the Sudan on the division of Nile waters. In 1959 the Soviet Union agreed to extend Egypt a 300-million dollar loan to build the dam, and Sudan and Egypt finally agreed on their use of the Nile waters. When completed, after fifteen years of work, the dam cost over two billion dollars. The planners hoped that it would enable the country to expand agricultural productivity by about one third by extending the cultivated area and by increasing irrigation in areas already cultivated. The cheap production of electricity would increase its availability for industry and communications more than tenfold and make possible electrification of all towns and villages in the country.

Within ten years of its completion the dam became a focus of political, economic, and ecological controversy. Many of the lofty goals for the project seemed unattainable. Only a third of the electric power envisioned was produced and a fraction of new lands were irrigated. Lake Nasser, the huge water storage area in southern Egypt and northern Sudan, was collecting the rich Nile silt and filling up. This deprived downstream lands of vital soil deposits. It also affected the fishing industry because the silt no longer flowed into the Mediterranean to the sardine feeding grounds, the basis of a formerly lucrative fishing industry. Lake Nasser and its irrigation canals became breeding grounds for tough and dense weeds which choked off water supplies. There was serious danger that waterlogging in the semi-stagnant canals would cause a sharp rise in soil salinity and spread the debilitating snail-borne disease, bilharzia. These shortcomings had to be balanced against the double and triple crops produced in fields that formerly were less productive. Even though the total acreage increase was much less than expected, double and triple cropping nearly doubled Egypt's total food production. The rapid rise in population consumed the food increase, making impossible much of a diet improvement, but without the dam the situation would have been far worse. The dam also saved Egypt from one of the most severe droughts to strike the Middle East, during 1972–1973. Part of the United States aid program included organization of a joint Egyptian-American research team of 100 scientists to answer the ecological questions.

According to one economist, by 1963 "it looked as if Egypt had entered upon the road of sustained growth." Aggregate output was increasing at about 6 percent a year over a six-year period. "The level of investments and the expansion of education and health services gave good promise that the economy should be able to continue at this rate of growth."[7] Expansion in industry was at a rate of 8.5 percent a year. Until 1967 vigorous expansion of Suez Canal traffic contributed to a rapid rise in the growth rate of transport and communications. Growth in the modern sectors of the economy compared very favorably with the low rate in agriculture, a mere 3.3 percent.

By the end of the 1960s industrial expansion had increased to the proportion of national income, about one quarter, sought by President Nasser at the beginning of the ten-year plan. However, only about 15 percent of the gross national product derived from what might be called modern industry, such as cement and fertilizer manufacturing, petroleum, and textiles. The largest expansion was in handicrafts and small-scale industries. Although population employed in the industrial labor force had grown, it was approximately the same percent as it had been at the beginning of the revolution because of overall population increase. By far the greatest industrial expansion occurred in the government sector, which had developed more than 40 general organizations controlling over 500 public enterprises in addition to 15 older authorities such as the Suez Canal.

Shortly after becoming President, Sadat initiated the first in a series of economic liberalization measures. His intent was to "open up" the economy by encouraging private Egyptian and foreign capital in the hope that they would expand the industrial sector. At first several smaller businesses were returned to their foreign owners. In 1974 Egypt's highest appeals court ruled that confiscation of private citizens' property during the Nasser era had been illegal and must be rescinded. Several of the companies nationalized in 1961 were returned to private ownership. To counteract the weakness of Egypt's currency many of the strict foreign money controls were relaxed for Egyptian and foreign investors, and Egyptian businessmen were authorized to keep most of their foreign currency earnings. Sadat traveled to several of the oil-producing countries in the Gulf to raise funds for investment in Egypt after the 1973 war, persuading them to form the Gulf Organization for Development in Egypt. American investors, too, were encouraged to help in the industrial expansion. These efforts included reconstruction of the Suez Canal Zone, devastated in the 1967 and 1973 wars, and turning it into a free zone, exempted from the network of government import restrictions and controls woven into the economy since the revolution.

Slogans and symbols of socialism were still retained, and the provisions of the 1971 constitution defining Egypt as a socialist country were never abrogated. But Sadat's critics on the left charged that his liberalization measures failed to strengthen the economy. Instead, they were tantamount to de-Nasserization or desocialization. A new wealthy bourgeois class was being created. The "new pashas," some 500 new millionaires, were mostly speculators in real estate and commerce, rather than in basic or productive enterprises.

Egypt's involvement in the Yemen War between 1962 and 1967 and the wars with Israel in 1967 and 1973 were both serious drains on national productivity. Soaring defense expenditures, which were between 20 and 25 percent of the gross national product, threw the economy out of balance and slowed down development. The value of military equipment lost in each of the wars was estimated at about two billion dollars, almost equal to investment in the High Nile Dam. While much military equipment was contributed by the Soviet Union, the scale of loss seriously drained the total economy.

A major setback resulting from the 1967 war was closure of the Suez

Canal. Much time, effort, and money were invested in expanding and improving the canal prior to 1967. As a result of its closure, Egyptian losses in foreign currency were estimated at between 200 and 300 million dollars a year, equal to nearly a quarter of the country's foreign currency earnings in normal times. When the canal was opened after the 1973 war, it again became a major source of government income. Losses resulting from the wars were partially recompensated for by contributions of economic aid from Saudi Arabia, Kuwait, and Libya. Large oil resources discovered along the Red Sea coast and in the Western Desert also provided a large income, helping to make up for war losses and defense expenditures. Two other principal sources of foreign currency were earnings from tourism and remittances sent home to Egypt by the several million workers in the other Arab countries.

Some critics of the High Nile Dam project maintained that population growth during the period of construction would leave the ratio of Egyptians to cultivated land in the early 1970s approximately the same as it was when construction began. However, this criticism overlooked the fact that no other alternative had been proposed by Egyptians or outside authorities for increasing agricultural and industrial productivity in so short a time and without even greater expenditures of effort and money. In addition to providing more land for irrigation, more efficient methods of agriculture, and increasing electrical power for industrial purposes, the dam made possible electrification of large numbers of villages and cities in Upper Egypt, thus greatly enhancing possibilities of modernization in these once lesser-developed regions of the Nile Valley.

In the first year of the revolution the power of the old conservative elite was demolished. A decade later only shadowy remnants of its former grandeur remained. The revolution had been a political and psychological success. Its slogans and its leaders had captured the imagination of the whole Arab world, and Nasser had a wide personal following among intellectuals throughout the Arab East. But in Egypt itself there had been little material improvement in the lives of the urban working class of the peasantry.

Since World War II, revolutionary ideas had infiltrated the Egyptian village through the coffeehouse radio and the presence of government technicians and social workers, but change was still regarded by the peasants with suspicion. Only with difficulty were they convinced of the benefits of the radical new government programs. From Alexandria to Aswan, great numbers of new schools and welfare centers have sprung up, and a traveler cannot go more than a few miles along the Nile now without finding some new government structure. While many of the centers are filled with peasants waiting for medical treatment, schooling, or agricultural advice, others are empty shells—some with a small staff awaiting villagers, some without even a staff. By 1962 Nasser felt a need to intensify the revolution, since it had done little to improve the life of the peasant majority. The pace of socialism was therefore stepped up, resulting in measures to liquidate the middle class.

Like a number of other third world countries, the UAR has sought to combine rapid development with expanding welfare, under the official slogan of "sufficiency and justice." The patterns of capital formation through mass deprivation characterizing the European industrial revolution and the Stalinist era in the USSR are explicitly excluded as morally unjust and politically unworkable......

In the past thirty years, many thousands of Egyptians have risen to a social status superior to that into which they were born. They live in a psychological proximity to the way of life they left behind, and in awareness of the vulnerability of their present status. To a large measure it is people of this category to whom the revolution carries its most effective appeal. The fact that they have risen from the bog and must fear that they or their children may be sucked back into it has inevitably had a moderating effect on their responsiveness to revolutionary reforms and ideological propositions. Expropriation can only seem invidious because of their uncertain implications. Thus insecurity breeds its own brand of tolerance, and creates great distaste for the prospect that violence, vengefulness, or forceful deprivation might be exercised even against groups other than one's own.[8]

Not until the country's population problem could be solved, however, would there be a really revolutionary change in the lives of its people. Neither the socialization measures nor the ten-year plans for increasing national productivity through expanding industrial and agricultural output could keep pace with the rate of population increase. Because of the imbalance between population growth and food production, it was necessary for Egypt to import about 60 percent of its food in the early 1980s. With the loss of cultivable land to urban expansion production was further diminished. Despite an increase of 4 percent in production between 1978 and 1980 consumption grew by 7 percent. At best, the successful implementation of the revolutionary government's long-term plans would just barely keep pace with the rate of natural population increase.

Until recently, a significant omission from the public plans and statements of the country's leaders has been reference to the population explosion or ways of limiting it. Some maintained that Nasser was giving serious consideration to family planning, but felt that it was still too early to publicize them. There are no Islamic religious prohibitions against birth control. Only a few years ago one of the country's highest religious dignitaries stated that the practice did not conflict with Islam. Family planning, however, enters an area traditionally sacrosanct in Eastern life. Any inquiries about, to say nothing of interference with, family intimacies are deeply resented. The average Egyptian is still far too conservative to acquiesce in public direction of his reproductive functions. Despite the strongly centralized revolutionary government and its growing control over all aspects of national life, those who know public opinion assert that until Nasser's mention of the problem before the Congress of Popular Forces in May 1962 no one could raise the issue of birth control in public. There is great doubt about the extent to which such advice can be absorbed by the public. As yet, methods of contraception are far too complex to be used effectively by the average villagers. Now, however, the Egyptian Medical Association is working in cooperation with local pharmaceutical firms to develop an oral contraceptive that may contribute toward greater control of the number of births.

By 1980 Egypt's population was more than 40 million, an increase of over 100 percent since the beginning of the revolution in 1952. With population growing at the rate of over one million a year, the increase alone was equal to a third of the population in neighboring Israel. By the end of the century the population would double with the present rate of increase. After the 1967 war the birth rate declined but rose again following the successful 1973 war. Most of the increase was in rural areas and among uneducated peasants, although in parts of Cairo there were 250,000 people per square mile. The population dilemma is compounded by the country's limited cultivable area. Although Egypt is twice the area of California, only 3.5 percent is inhabited, the rest being desert. Limiting the population increase is made more difficult by the high illiteracy rate. Between 1966 and 1976 functional literacy increased from a quarter to half the population, but still, only 25 percent could read and write. Illiteracy was highest, over 70 percent, among women, for whom most birth control programs were designed. It was still difficult to propagate these programs to farmers who desired large families to assist in agricultural work. In rural areas the average woman had ten pregnancies, of which eight produced live children. Fewer than five children lived beyond five years.

Despite government publicity only about 300,000 women visited, monthly, the few family planning centers, a number far too small to make any remedial impact. To help alleviate the problem, the government began in the late 1960s to authorize emigration in large numbers. By 1970 hundreds of Egyptians, mostly young men, were crowding emigration offices. Every week about a thousand requested emigration to the United States. Most were college graduates looking for economic opportunity abroad. Many professionals were also seeking opportunities abroad because of low salaries paid in Egypt. Whereas in an earlier period the government had opposed emigration of professionals, by 1970 it even initiated measures to assist the movement and simplify the bureaucratic procedures for exodus from the country. The government also organized a department of emigration to help find opportunities for Egyptian employment and emigration in countries of Africa such as the Sudan.

NOTES

1. Warriner, *Land and Poverty in the Middle East,* London, 1948, p. 43.
2. Gamal Abdel Nasser, *The Philosophy of the Revolution,* Cairo, n.d., pp. 14–15.

3. Muhammad Neguib, *Egypt's Destiny,* London, 1955, p. 155.

4. Nasser, *op. cit.,* p. 22.

5. *Ibid.,* p. 43.

6. Malcolm Kerr, *The United Arab Republic: The Domestic, Political, and Economic Background of Foreign Policy,* The RAND Corporation, Santa Monica, Calif., 1969, pp. 25–27. This paper appears in, and is reprinted by permission of, American Elsevier Publishing Company and The RAND Corporation from *Political Dynamics in the Middle East,* edited by Paul Y. Hammond and Sidney S. Alexander.

7. B. Hansen, *Economic Development in Egypt,* The RAND Corporation, Santa Monica, California, 1969, p. 3.

8. Kerr, *op. cit.,* pp. 27–28, 30–31.

Zionism

ISRAEL'S ORIGINS

Americans are more familiar with Israel than with most of its immediate neighbors for a variety of reasons. Many American Jews are personally concerned with Israeli activities. The religious and cultural heritage of Judaism is, of course, much better known in the Western world than is Islam. Israel's relatively high living standard and its Western outlook strike a familar and sympathetic chord among Americans. All these factors help to make Israel more well known in the United States than any other Middle Eastern country.

Israel is an anomaly in the Middle East. Demographically, the country differs from its neighbors because a large percentage of its citizens were born beyond its borders; only a little more than half of Israel's Jews are natives. Israel is the world's only Jewish state; most of its customs and traditions are Jewish and its official language is Hebrew. There are strong economic, religious, cultural, and emotional ties between Israel and Jewish communities throughout the world, although not all Jews identify themselves with the country.

Large-scale Jewish immigration to Israel after World War II left the country dependent upon foreign economic assistance; the resources of the country were inadequate to provide for the absorption of this massive influx. Thus without foreign aid the rapid immigration rate would not have been possible and Israel's population would have remained considerably smaller. Partly as a result of its financial dependence, particularly on the United States, and because of its strong Western political orientation, no other Middle East nation is so strongly identified with the Western world. Today, the majority of the population is of Asian and African origin, but the outlook and attitudes of most leaders and the emphasis of cultural life remain much more European than Middle Eastern.

These characteristics divide as well as distinguish Israel from its Arab neighbors. Israel's uniqueness explains much of its progress, but it also had a good deal to do with the hostility of the neighboring Arab states. Today, Israel is isolated in the Middle East in spite of the peace treaty with Egypt; the countries surrounding it in the Middle East are more remote economically, politically, and culturally than is Europe or America.

To understand how and why Israel is so different it is necessary to trace its origins back several decades before it became an independent nation on May 14, 1948. Although the first modern Israeli government was established on that day, the Jewish state had really been on the way for generations.

The European Beginnings

Modern Zionism, the movement for a Jewish return to the homeland, is inspired by the ancient land of Israel of the Old Testament. Zionism was a direct product of the economic, political, and social conditions of nineteenth-century European Jews and, indirectly, of the many centuries of Jewish history that followed the dispersion of the Palestine Jewish community after conquest by Rome during the first century A.D. From the Holy Land, Jews emigrated or were transported mainly to Europe, where they usually lived together in separate communities whose life was based on the laws, traditions, and customs of ancient Israel. In the Byzantine, Catholic, and Protestant realms recognizing a state religion, Jews could not participate in the mainstream of national life. They were not permitted to hold public office or to own land, and they were usually excluded from the dominant social life. Not only were Jews isolated from the community at large, but frequently they were expelled altogether. Nearly every major European nation—Spain, France, England, Poland, Rumania, and Germany—exiled its Jewish community at one time or another.

It is not surprising, therefore, that Jews did not really become Frenchmen, Englishmen, Poles, or Germans. They thought of themselves and were thought of by those around them primarily as Jews, and their national history and sentiment rested on historic memories of past glories in the Holy Land. Jews and non-Jews (Gentiles) came to regard each other with suspicion, the latter because they saw the Jewish community as a "foreign" element in their society and the former because they believed the Gentiles desired to persecute if not destroy them utterly.

Judaism as a religion was intimately linked with Palestine. Jewish rabbinical law favored the settler in the ancient homeland. Literature of the rabbinate echoed with such sayings as: "It is better to dwell in the deserts of Palestine than in palaces abroad"; "whoever lives in Palestine, lives sinless"; and "the air of Palestine makes one wise." Jewish attachment to the Holy Land was not only to the spiritual, but also to the physical land of Zion. Holidays and fasts commemorated events such as Moses' flight across the Sinai to Palestine, destruction of Solomon's temple, and the harvest season, not of Russia, Poland, or France, but of Palestine. The annual Passover festival memorializing the exodus from Egypt ended with the hopeful prayer, "next year in Jerusalem." There was a mystique about Palestine among Jews, especially while they were segregated into ghettos, and a great many felt a close personal identity with the land, though they had no physical contact with it. Jewish identification with Palestine, heightened by the conditions of their "exile," was far more intense and pervasive than that of the average Muslim or Christian.

In the wake of the French Revolution and the Napoleonic conquests developed our modern concepts of the nation state and the role of the citizen. Most important for the Jew was the destruction of the ghetto walls in Western Europe and his growing acceptance as an equal citizen without the compromise of his beliefs. By the mid-nineteenth century, the Western Jew was permitted, in varying degrees depending on country, to own property, to practice law, and to teach in universities. He acquired the vote along with his fellow citizens, often could stand for office, and even entered military service.

The Napoleonic concept of full equality for all citizens, regardless of religion, did not reach tsarist-controlled Europe at all. There the Jew became the butt of conservative reaction against the French revolutionary era. The Russian government actually imposed new restrictions on Jewish movement, places of habitation, and employment. Sporadic Jewish pogroms reached such intensity that by the 1880s waves of emigrants were fleeing Russia for Western Europe and the United States. The pogroms also led to the organization of the first social movements in Eastern Europe directed to the amelioration of the Jewish plight.

In the vanguard of these movements was the *Hoveve Zion* (Lovers of Zion), first established in Russia during the early 1880s. This group advocated Jewish settlement in Palestine as a practical measure of relief, rather than as a religious ideal. Many Jewish youths in Russia, disillusioned with the liberal ideas of political and social reform and enlightenment that in no way alleviated the plight of the Jews in that country, turned, like other nationalists, to the concept of self-determination. Their philosophy was expressed in Leo Pinsker's *Auto-Emancipation,* published in 1882. Legal emancipation, even out of humanitarian motives, he argued, was useless. Only a "land of our own," whether it be on the banks of the Jordan or the Mississippi, was a true solution.

It was easy for idealistic Jewish youths in Russia to become aroused by visions of a land offering hope of a better life. One such student group traveled through Russia recruiting some 500 fellow enthusiasts, who became the "Bilu"—from the Hebrew initials of their rallying call in Isaiah, "O house of Jacob, come, let us go forth." A few of them managed to settle in Palestine, where they established the small town of Rishon le-Zion (First in Zion) in 1882. Within the decade, other Russian and Polish Jewish youths set up a few similar small settlements. Economic difficulties and problems of adjustment to the arduous pioneer life stunted the new colonies so that they never developed significantly.

Only a handful of the first Zionists went to Palestine, whereas millions of Jews immigrated from Russia to America and Western Europe. Many who never contemplated emigration to the Middle East, including many who had settled in America and Western Europe, became ardent Zionists, however, deriving emotional satisfaction from identification with this "homeland" movement.

As in other nationalist movements of the day, various Zionist trends emerged reflecting the complexity of ideologies prevalent in mid-nineteenth-century Europe. Socialism, both Marxian and non-Marxian, was most influential. It strongly colored early Zionism with egalitarianism and a prolabor viewpoint that came to dominate the movement. The socialist emphasis also underscored the Zionist theory that Jews were concentrated in nonproductive occupations everywhere. Because, in the past, Jews had been excluded from land ownership and other "Christian" occupations, such as law, the army, government service, and the like, they had gravitated to money-lending, banking, and similar service professions. The Zionists as a group professed a desire to return to the land, not only in the national sense, but as farmers. But it was not easy for the lower-middle-class Jews, unaccustomed to such toil, to go to Palestine to work the soil, and their early failures were many. Many Bilu settlements, once they were actually set up, preferred to hire Arab labor rather than to dig the earth with their own hands.

THEODOR HERZL AND POLITICAL ZIONISM

A decade after the first Russian Jewish settlers landed in Palestine, the various Zionist groups coalesced into a single, large movement. Its founder was not from Poland or Russia, but was a Westerner who had had little to do with things Jewish—Theodor Herzl, born in Budapest in 1860. While a correspondent for an influential Viennese newspaper, Herzl attended the trial in Paris of Captain Alfred Dreyfus, a French Jew falsely accused of selling military secrets to Germany. Dreyfus was sentenced to imprisonment on Devil's Island and his trial stirred both a humanitarian protest and an answering wave of anti-Semitism. Herzl was deeply moved by such virulent expressions of hatred as the cry "Death to the Jews" that rose over the parade grounds during the captain's degradation.

Although Dreyfus was later exonerated and restored to rank, Herzl was disillusioned about the possibilities of full and equal Jewish participation or integration into European life. "Let the sovereignty be granted us over a portion of the globe large enough to satisfy the rightful requirements of a nation," he wrote, "and the rest we shall arrange ourselves."[1] This was the germ of his book, *Der Judenstaat (The Jewish State)*, written in 1895. Herzl was not the first to publish such views, but he had never read either Leo Pinsker's *Auto-Emancipation* or *Rome and Jerusalem* by Moses Hess, published in 1862. Herzl's writing became the essence of the Zionist cause, capturing the imagination of Eastern European Jewry.

The Jews, Herzl wrote, would always be persecuted no matter how useful or patriotic they were. Nowhere was their integration into national life possible, for the Jewish problem, the hatred of the Jewish minority by the non-Jewish majority, existed wherever there were Jews. Even immigration to hopefully safe places did not exempt Jews from eventual anti-Semitism. Perhaps, he conceded, if not persecuted or discriminated against for two generations, Jews might become part of a new liberal society, but it seemed unlikely that they would be free from persecution for such a long time. The Jewish problem was not religious or social, he concluded, but national: the Jews were a "nation without a land." Therefore they should be granted a territory by the world powers to fulfill the needs of a nation.

In his book, Herzl envisaged a "society of Jews" to organize the Jewish masses for emigration and to negotiate the acquisition of a national territory with the European powers. A Jewish company would raise the necessary funds and deal with economic and financial matters. Because he himself was not closely involved with the formal religious practice or observance of the Jewish faith, Herzl did not have the deep emotional ties to Palestine that his followers had. He suggested that either Palestine or Argentina—the latter because of its rich undeveloped territories—were possible choices for a new Jewish homeland. But Jewish public opinion and the Society of Jews would be the final judges.

The Jewish State stimulated fervent debates on the Jewish problem. Most Jewish leaders in Western Europe and America believed the program unrealistic and one that would jeopardize their possibilities of becoming fully integrated citizens. Orthodox extremists attacked it as blaspheming the "Mission of Israel" and the Messianic doctrine. Liberals opposed adding still another national movement to the already multiplying nineteenth-century nationalisms because they preferred to look forward to a new internationalism.

But most Eastern European Jewry lionized Herzl as a new Moses. Jewish enthusiasm was so great in Russia and Poland that Herzl successfully convened the First World Zionist Congress in Basel, Switzerland, in August 1897. As Sir Isaiah Berlin put it: "But for the character and needs of the eastern European Jews there would have been no Israel."[2] Over 200 delegates came to the congress from all over the world, representing Orthodoxy and Reform, Eastern and Oriental Jews, socialists, the middle class, and the wealthy.

The Congress's two principal accomplishments were establishment of the Zionist Organization, thereafter the principal organizer of Jewish nationalism, and formulation of the Basel program, which became the cornerstone of all Zionist groups. This program stated that: "The aim of Zionism is to create for the Jewish people a home in Palestine secured by public law." To attain this objective, all Jewry was to be organized to promote the systematic settlement of Jewish farmers, artisans, and craftsmen in Palestine. Jewish sentiment and awareness of nationalism was to be strengthened, and efforts were to be made to raise the necessary funds for achieving the Zionist objective. Thereafter, a Zionist was defined as a dues-paying supporter of the Basle program.

Shortly after the congress, Herzl wrote in his diary:

If I were to sum up the Basle Congress in one word—which I shall not do openly—it would be this: at Basle I founded the Jewish State. If I were to say this today, I would be met by universal laughter. In five years, perhaps, and certainly in fifty [1947], everyone will see it. The State is already founded, in essence, in the will of the people of the State.[3]

Eventually a worldwide Zionist movement grew out of this congress. Despite many controversies around and within the movement, it became the single most unifying force of world Jewry. In addition to the opposition of most Western European Jewish leaders, there were also violent disagreements among the Zionists themselves. Those who believed in emphasizing a cultural approach sought to revive Hebrew as a modern tongue, to establish a university, and to make Palestine the spiritual center of Jewish cultural revival rather than a political state for millions of people. The "politicals" emphasized the immediate need for a physical refuge and a territorial solution of the Jewish problem. Some were willing to accept any territory where large numbers of Jews could be settled, but most would accept no area other than the Holy Land. The offer of Uganda by the British government in 1902 stirred vehement controversy between those who urged acceptance and those, mostly from Eastern Europe, who because of religious ties insisted that only Palestine was acceptable. Even Herzl, greatly loved though he was as their leader, fell

victim to sharp attacks that forced him to declare that he had considered
Uganda as a temporary shelter only. A year after the Uganda quarrel, in July
1904, Herzl died at the age of forty-four.

By the outbreak of World War I, Zionism had grown from Herzl's
visionary idea to a strong, organized, worldwide movement. The Society of
Jews became the World Zionist Organization, with considerable finances
under its control. The Jewish Colonial Trust and the Jewish National Fund
(JNF) were set up to purchase land in Palestine. In Russia, where half of the
world's Jews lived, five of the fourteen Jews in the first Duma (the Russian
parliament) in 1905 were elected on the basis of Zionist platforms. In Austria,
four Zionists were chosen for parliament in 1907. Despite the strong
organization, backed by a widespread popular Jewish sentiment, little had
been done to obtain any political commitment from any powerful government
concerning the Holy Land. No government had been willing to approach the
Ottoman sultan on behalf of the Jews, and the Osmanlis were unwilling to
surrender any of their authority over Palestine or to permit large numbers of
outsiders to settle there.

THE SITUATION IN PALESTINE

One difficulty was that a political entity called Palestine did not exist. It
was merely a vague geographic designation indicating the general area where
the ancient Philistines and later the Jews had lived. After the Ottoman
conquest in 1517, the land had been divided and redivided into several
provinces until, in 1864, geographic Palestine was partitioned between the two
Ottoman *vilayets* (provinces) of Beirut and Syria and the smaller *sanjak*
(administrative subdivision) of Jerusalem. The latter was not attached to any
larger province because of its special status, guaranteed by the European
Christian powers when they intervened in the Levant to protect Christians
during the 1860s.

No accurate population estimates for Palestine existed. In 1914, there
were some 600,000 Arabs and 85,000 Jews. The Arabs had not as yet
developed a strong nationalist feeling. Their loyalty was to Islam, or to some
Christian millet, not to the state. Not until World War I was there a distinctive
Arab, and later a Palestine, nationalist movement. The Osmanlis had only a
shadowy control over many parts of Palestine, and roaming Bedouin
periodically raided the settled villages in the hill country or the northern plains.

Since the time of the Roman dispersion, small numbers of Jews had lived
in Palestine; there were only 5000 when Napoleon invaded the area. By
mid-century their numbers had doubled, and they doubled again by the 1880s.
Between 1882 and 1914, the number grew from 24,000 to 85,000. Most of these
were the pious elderly who, coming to die in one of the four holy cities,

Jerusalem, Hebron, Safed, or Tiberias, lived off charitable donations sent from abroad. About 12,000 Jews came to live in one or another of the forty-three Zionist agricultural settlements established by 1914. Only 10 percent of Palestine's total Jewish population were Ottoman subjects.

From the late 1880s until 1914, the greatest Zionist activity took place among the Russian and Polish Jewry, who found in the movement a great spiritual hope and community rallying point. Even the first Zionist self-government experiments were not in Palestine but in Odessa during the 1880s and 1890s, where Menachem Usishkin unsuccessfully tried to organize a *Kenessiyah* or elected assembly.

Unfortunately, the Jewish national movement had little contact with the Palestine Arabs. Relations between the scattered Jewish settlements in the country and their communities in the towns with the nearby Arabs were for the most part casual, and often cordial. No deep political schism emerged until World War I, and the occasional raids of Arab marauders on Jewish settlements were strictly for loot, rather than an expression of competing nationalisms.

Diaspora Jewry imagined the Holy Land as described in the Bible or, in the words of Herzl, as a land without a people awaiting a people without a land. Ahad Haam (One of the People) observed in 1891 that:

> We abroad have a way of thinking that Palestine to-day is almost desert, uncultivated wilderness, and that anyone who wishes to buy land there can do so to his heart's content. But that is not in fact the case. It is difficult to find any uncultivated land anywhere in the country.... We abroad have a way of thinking that the Arabs are all savages, on a level with the animals, and blind to what goes on around them. But that is quite mistaken. The Arabs, especially the townsmen, see through our activities in their country, and our aims, but they keep silence and make no sign, because for the present they anticipate no danger to their own future from what we are about. But if the time should ever come when our people have so far developed their life in Palestine that the indigenous population should feel more or less cramped, then they will not readily make way for us....[4]

The Balfour Declaration

Immediately after the outbreak of World War I, the Osmanlis clamped rigid restrictions on Palestine and the surrounding area. Added to their harsh treatment was a famine caused by widespread drought and a locust plague. Foreign minorities fared worse than others at the hands of the Ottoman government because they had lost the protection of the capitulations, abolished by the Osmanlis in 1914. Since many Jews were still subjects of the Ottoman enemy, Russia, they either fled or were deported. The Zionist movement itself was charged by the Osmanlis with being a subversive element aimed at carving up the Ottoman Empire, and a number of local Jewish leaders in Palestine were imprisoned or hanged. Zionist institutions like the Anglo-Palestine Bank were banned, and public use of Hebrew was forbidden in the streets of the new Jewish town, Tel Aviv. By the time British General Allenby entered the country in 1917, the Jewish population had been reduced by nearly a third to only 55,000.

The war fragmented the Zionist movement into three parts—one was in Allied-controlled countries, another remained under the Central Powers, and the third existed in neutral territory. To facilitate contact among them, neutral Copenhagen became the Zionist liaison center.

Jewish leaders in Allied capitals found the time expedient to press their claims to a homeland in Palestine and organized military units to help fight for that land. Joseph Trumpeldor gathered 900 men in the Zion Mule Corps, which saw service in Gallipoli. Later another Russian Zionist, Vladimir Jabotinsky, headed a campaign for a fighting unit that led to the formation of the Judeans, two battalions of Russian, British, American, and other Jewish volunteers. Still another battalion was added, bringing the Jewish combat strength in Allenby's Palestine armies to about 5000.

More significant were the political maneuvers of Dr. Chaim Weizmann, a chemistry lecturer at Manchester University and a prominent Zionist leader. Before becoming a British citizen, Dr. Weizmann had been a Jewish leader in Russia, his birthplace. He contributed to the Allied cause by developing a process to produce acetone, an essential ingredient for manufacturing the cordite required in artillery shells. Scientific discoveries brought Weizmann into intimate contact with British war leaders, whom he persuaded to favor the Zionist cause. They were especially amenable because they were searching for a dramatic appeal to rally world Jewry to their side at a time when the Allied position was doing badly. Perhaps American Jewish backing could be won and the Austrian and German Jews could be weaned away from their governments. Russia was already out of the war. An appeal to Jewish leaders in the new antiwar Bolshevik government, formed in 1917, might have a dramatic effect in winning their favor.

In the United States, Supreme Court Justice Louis D. Brandeis and Rabbi Stephen Wise, both prominent American Jewish leaders, persuaded President Wilson to back British support of Zionist aims in 1917. Negotiations finally culminated in the Balfour Declaration, published on November 2, 1917 (see chapter 5).

The Zionist formula was watered down in deference to non-Zionists so that the declaration called for establishment of "*a* national home" in Palestine in lieu of defining the country as "*the* national home of the Jewish people." This intervention by influential British Jews therefore resulted in a very vaguely worded document, subject to a variety of interpretations and containing a pledge that the rights of non-Jews in Palestine and Jews elsewhere would be protected.

The British information ministry followed through by creating a special Jewish department for liaison, propaganda, and research. It prepared leaflets containing the Balfour Declaration, which were dropped over enemy territory. To counteract Allied support for Zionism, the Central Powers made similarly vague statements of sympathy. Germany especially played up its concern for what had been the plight of Russian Jews under the tsars.

As a result of the Balfour and other conflicting Allied Statements, Palestine soon became a focal point of international disagreement. Actually none of the Allied wartime promises and agreements among themselves concerning the Holy Land carried any authority in international law since they were made while this territory was still part of the Ottoman Empire (see chapter 5).

THE BRITISH MANDATE

The conflicting British responsibilities became obvious immediately after General Allenby's conquest of Palestine. Zionist leaders demanded and received from Great Britain permission for a Zionist Commission of Allied Jews to visit the occupied areas, while the Arabs were already beginning to ask the British embarrassing questions about Jewish activities.

The Zionist Commission was supposed to represent both Palestinian and world Jewish interests in an advisory capacity to British authorities in the Holy Land. When meetings of the World Zionist Congress were resumed in 1921, the commission's functions were absorbed by the Zionist Executive. Locally, Palestine Jewry attempted to organize its own representative bodies. When the British took Jerusalem in 1917, the Jews organized a city council and, later, a country-wide temporary council to prepare the way for an elected Jewish constituent assembly they hoped the British would authorize. When the whole country was finally freed from Osmanli rule in 1918, a national conference representing several Jewish settlements chose Weizmann and a Russian Jewish colleague, Nahum Sokolow, to represent them at the Paris peace talks. But British military authorities blocked Jewish self-governing institutions as premature. Not until Palestine was turned over to civil authorities in 1920 did the British permit election of a Jewish constituent assembly.

Major decisions for the Yishuv (the historic name for the Palestine Jewish community) were made by European Zionist leaders such as Weizmann. The Yishuv was merely the "vanguard of world Jewry," hopefully laying the groundwork for the future immigration of most of the world's Jews. Jews abroad, the Zionists believed, were obligated to back this national home with financial contributions and political support.

Dr. Weizmann, not a Palestinian Jew, was called upon by the Yishuv and world Zionists to work for an amicable agreement with the Arabs. In an attempt to mollify growing Arab concern about Zionist aspirations,

Weizmann conducted several parleys with Syria's King Faisal, first at Aqaba in southern Palestine during 1918 and later in London. In January 1919, the two statesmen agreed on the need for Arab-Jewish cooperation. Faisal recognized the Balfour Declaration and encouraged Jewish immigration, provided Arab rights were not jeopardized. In return, Weizmann promised Zionist assistance in Arab economic development. Both Weizmann and Faisal agreed that the British were to arbitrate disputes between the two parties. Faisal, however, insisted that if Arab nationalist aspirations were not fully realized, he would "not then be bound by a single word of the present Agreement which shall be deemed void and of no account or validity, and I shall not be answerable in any way whatsoever."[5]

At Paris, it soon became clear that Faisal did not represent Arab feelings about Palestine. The head of the Syrian delegation warned that Palestine was incontestably the southern portion of his country. Although the Zionists claimed it, the Arabs had endured too much suffering like that of the Jews to throw open the door of Palestine. He would let the Jews settle in Palestine, but in an autonomous Palestine, connected with Syria by the sole bond of federation.

The Zionists urged the Paris conferees to turn Palestine over to the new League of Nations and ultimately to make the country an autonomous Jewish commonwealth. No decisions concerning Palestine's fate, they argued, should be made without consulting world Jewry. In return, they promised full religious freedom to Muslims and Christians.

Palestine's fate was determined by neither Zionists nor Arabs, however. The imperial needs of Great Britain and France were the decisive factors. Compromises made to reconcile British and French claims resulted in a northward extension of the frontier into an area originally claimed by France and southward to the Gulf of Aqaba, into a zone promised to the Arabs. Since the country had no historical or international frontier until after World War I, the British felt free to divide it in 1921 into Transjordan and western Palestine. The former was turned over to Faisal's brother Abdullah as a political reward. Both sections were governed by a British high commissioner under the Colonial Office. But Transjordan was thereafter excluded from commitments relating to establishment of a Jewish national home.

When the frontiers were agreed on with France at San Remo in 1920, Palestine received its first civilian high commissioner, Sir Herbert Samuel, an English Jew who had played an important role in framing the Balfour Declaration. Zionists were at first enthusiastic about the appointment, regarding it as official recognition of their aspirations.

Self-Government Failures

Sir Herbert had to cope with not only Zionists, but with the Arab nationalist movement that was then emerging (see discussion below), and the needs of Great Britain as well. The conflict of interests erupted into violence shortly after he became high commissioner when Bedouin attacked northern Jewish settlements. Violence in Jaffa and Jerusalem during April 1920 claimed still more victims, making it clear that Palestine Arab nationalists would not passively accept British or Jewish control. The Arabs insisted that they, the majority of the population, were being denied their rights to rule Palestine because of the 10 percent Jewish minority. The King-Crane Commission (see chapter 5), commenting on Arab fears, reported that "the Zionists looked forward to a practically complete dispossession of the present non-Jewish inhabitants of Palestine, by various forms of purchase."[6] There was nothing upon which the Palestine Arabs were more agreed than their opposition to the entire Zionist program, according to the members of the commission. More than 72 percent of all petitions received by the commission throughout Syria protested the Zionist program. No British officer consulted by the commissioners believed that Zionist aspirations could be implemented without military force.

Under the circumstances, Sir Herbert was compelled to maintain many features of a military government and to pattern his administration on that of a British crown colony. The high commissioner had final discretion in all matters. He was assisted by an Executive Council consisting of government department heads and district commissioners, all of whom were British, although some were British Jews, and by a twenty-two-member Advisory Council, of whom ten (four Muslims, three Christians, and three Jews) represented local populations. Preservation of the Ottoman millet system, dividing the population into religious communities, further encouraged Palestinians to form political groups along religious lines.

Arab nationalist unrest within and beyond the borders of Palestine forced the British to clarify their position in Winston Churchill's White Paper of July 1922. It recognized that Arab fears were caused by "exaggerated interpretations" of the Balfour Declaration and "unauthorized statements" that Palestine would become wholly Jewish. Weizmann's view that "Palestine is to become as Jewish as England is English," was rejected. Churchill warned the Zionists that Great Britain regarded any such hope as impracticable and had no such aim in view. The statement drew attention to the fact that the Balfour Declaration did not contemplate "that Palestine as a whole should be converted into a Jewish national home, but that such a home should be founded *in Palestine*." All citizens of the country were Palestinian, and none were entitled to any special juridical status.

However, to allay Jewish apprehensions, Churchill affirmed that the Balfour promises would not be abandoned. He explained that the Balfour Declaration did not mean imposition of Jewish nationality on all the country's inhabitants, but rather the continued political and economic development of the existing Jewish community with the help of world Jewry. Thereby Palestine could become a center "in which the Jewish people as a whole may take, on grounds of religion and race, an interest and a pride.... The Jewish people... should know that it is in Palestine as of right and not on sufferance." Jewish immigration would be continued up to the economic absorptive capacity of the country so that new immigrants would "not be a burden upon the people of Palestine as a whole."[7]

Even though Palestine was not included in the territory promised to the Arabs in the Husein-McMahon exchanges, Great Britain would foster "a full measure of self-government," but would do so gradually, step by step, according to a plan included in the memorandum calling first for a nominated Advisory Council and then for a partly nominated and a partly elected Legislative Council.

Great Britain's *de jure* position in Palestine was confirmed by the Lausanne peace Treaty with Turkey in 1923, although the League of Nations had already assigned the Palestine mandate in July 1922. It differed from other Middle East mandates, which called for the "progressive development" of independent states. In Palestine, the British were vested with "full powers of legislation and of administration, save as they may be limited by the terms of this Mandate." It barely mentioned the Arab community. An important exception, however, was recognition of Arabic as one of the three official languages; the others were English and Hebrew. The mandate included the provisions of the Balfour Declaration and specified that "an appropriate Jewish agency" was to work with the Palestine administration on matters affecting the Jewish national home. The Zionist Organization became the "appropriate" agency and was authorized to enlist cooperation of all Jews "willing to assist."

The mandate also authorized Jewish immigration and "close settlement" on the land. Jews who desired to establish permanent residence would be assisted in attaining Palestine citizenship. Jewish community leaders were authorized to construct and operate public works, services, and utilities not directly undertaken by the mandatory administration.

While the mandate recognized special Jewish rights, Great Britain was obligated to protect the religious institutions and interests, including religious courts, of all existing communities in Palestine. No citizen of a League member was to be discriminated against in taxation, commerce, industry, or exercise of professions. Each year the mandatory government was required to submit a report to the League Council on implementation of the mandate.

Both Jewish and Arab communities complained that the British mandatory authorities discriminated against them. Both protested any measure intended to lead toward self-government; the Arabs because it was not enough, the Jews because it favored the Arabs. The first effort was the plan for a twenty-three–member Legislative Council in 1922. Of the twelve-member elected majority, eight were to be Muslim, two Jewish, and two Christian. Another ten would be appointed by the high commissioner, who would act as council head. The Arabs rejected the plan because they feared that the two

Jews would vote with the high commissioner and the ten government-appointed council members to form an anti-Arab majority. The Jews, although willing to accept the proposal, were unenthusiastic because they would have only two of the twenty-three representatives. The Arabs attacked Sir Herbert as an "ardent Zionist," and the Zionists belabored him for "bending over backwards" to appease the Arabs. He finally cast aside all self-government plans and reconstituted the old Advisory Council. Even that was too much for the Arab nationalists, who compelled most members of their community to resign.

In still another effort, a year later, Sir Herbert encouraged the Arabs to develop their own self-governing institutions in the form of an Arab Agency similar to the Jewish Agency (described below). But again he was rebuffed, the nationalists arguing that this would mean recognizing the mandate and those of its terms providing for a Jewish national home.

Since no locally acceptable constitutional system could be worked out, Palestine was governed by an order-in-council issued by Great Britain in 1922. The order-in-council defined the legislative, administrative, executive, and judicial functions of the Palestine government and powers of its officials. Final authority remained with the high commissioner, who could be overridden only by London.

Torn between Arab and Jewish demands, the mandatory officials attempted to balance one side against the other. Some Britishers felt that implementation of the mandate was impossible and would jeopardize Great Britain's friendship with other Muslim nations by antagonizing the Arabs. Others regarded the Jewish community as a progressive element that could serve as an example to revitalize the whole Middle East. Thus policy fluctuated on all levels according to the whims and prejudices of local officials. In this environment, the antagonists became increasingly bitter toward each other and toward the mandatory power, until the gaps became unbridgeable. Each community went its own way, developing its separate institutions in violent conflict with those of the other. Despite formal existence of Palestine citizenship, a Palestine government, and Palestine officialdom, there was really no Palestine community—only British officialdom, with its own social life in the framework of the military and administrative organization; an Arab community, whose growing national movement fused the Muslim and various Christian millets under the control of the leading families; and the Yishuv, with its own self-governing institutions, which often supplemented the functions of the British mandatory government.

THE PALESTINE ARAB COMMUNITY

About 90 percent of the Arabs scattered through some 850 Palestine villages on the eve of World War I were Muslim, mostly Sunni. Most were illiterate and downtrodden peasants rooted in their ancestral soil, constantly at the mercy of absentee landlords and avaricious Osmanli tax collectors. Like other Ottoman subjects, the Palestine Arabs were divided into a Muslim millet and various Christian millets, with relatively little contact between them. A deep chasm separated the Arab gentry from the fellah, or peasant. Northern Palestine was controlled by a few landowners, most of whom lived in Beirut and Damascus. The southern half of the area was a barren desert peopled by Bedouin who belonged to tribal confederations in the Sinai peninsula or across the Jordan River. The largest towns were Jaffa and Jerusalem. Most Palestine Arabs did not think of themselves as Palestinians, but as related to Syrian or Lebanese centers.

Repressive Ottoman war measures and Allied promises of self-determination had sparked an Arab nationalist awakening by 1918, especially in the middle class. At first the Palestinians thought of themselves as part of Faisal's greater Syria and sent delegations to the nationalist congresses held at Damascus in 1919 and 1920. Associations of Christian and Muslim notables formed in several towns and induced the Syrian congresses to adopt anti-Zionist platforms.

Leadership of the Palestine Arabs was taken over by the Husayni family, notables who had obtained large land tracts in southern Palestine during the nineteenth century. Six of Jerusalem's thirteen mayors had been Husaynis in the fifty years preceding World War I. The British sought to maintain the existing social structure by supporting their leadership after 1918. Only after Husaynis had made their intense hostility clear were the British compelled to replace the mayor of Jerusalem, Musa Kazim al-Husayni, with Reghib Nashashibi, a leading member of the second most powerful Palestine Arab family group.

Because of their extensive family ties throughout the villages of Palestine, the Husaynis were able to control the anti-Zionist Muslim-Christian associations that had now been formed. By 1920, the Husaynis had shifted the emphasis of the nationalist movement from unity with Syria to independence for Palestine, both because they desired a province in which their control would be supreme and because Palestine was by then cut off from the Levant, under French mandatory control.

Mandatory relations with the Palestine Arab community were inconsistent. On the one hand, the Husaynis violently opposed any collaboration with Great Britain: on the other hand, Husayni influence and prestige was considerably enhanced by British recognition of their leading position. A most decisive step in this recognition was Sir Herbert's appointment of Haj Amin al-Husayni to the post of mufti of Jerusalem, the prestige of which helped him to become president of the Supreme Muslim Council. Sir Herbert's tactics were thus to counterbalance the appointment of the rival Nashashibis to the Jerusalem mayoralty.

Haj Amin al-Husayni's posts as mufti and Supreme Muslim Council president made him chief of Palestine's Muslim community and, thereby, leader of the Muslim Arab nationalist movement. As president of the Supreme Muslim Council, he was the successor, in Palestine, of the former Osmanli sheikh ul-Islam, with authority to appoint judges (*kadis*) in Muslim Sharia courts; to administer wakf funds for the maintenance of mosques, shrines, and schools; and to appoint and dismiss all officials in this extensive system. His religious power and wide family connections gave Haj Amin al-Husayni nearly complete control over Palestine's Muslims.

The rival Nashashibi family began to organize against the Husaynis during the 1920s, and by 1929 had nearly succeeded in persuading the British mandatory authorities to limit the mufti's exclusive powers. However, a plan to trim the mufti's authority was shelved soon thereafter because of nationalist outbreaks. The Nashashibis organized National Muslim Societies as a counterweight to the Husayni-controlled Muslim-Christian Associations (see above). While both groups were unwilling to compromise with Zionism, the Nashashibis were a little less vehement in opposing the British.

An attempt was made to unify the nationalist movement at an Arab Congress in Jerusalem during 1928, when an executive of thirty-six Muslims and twelve Christians was chosen as official spokesman for the Arab community. But the two leading factions would not be reconciled, and the congress executive disappeared after the death of Musa Kazim Husayni in 1934.

Failures at unification did not discourage the younger Arab intelligentsia, who were dissatisfied with the conservatives of both factions, and they decided to organize independently of the Husaynis and the Nashashibis. Between 1932 and 1935, six different groups formed, bringing the Arab nationalist movement into a new phase. The chief objective of these younger Arab leaders was to take over the nationalist movement. Little, if any, emphasis was placed on social or economic problems by these leaders. Differences between the groups were based largely on personalities and the extent to which they would, or would not, cooperate with the mandatory government. Membership was limited to male adults, mostly from influential families and the urban intelligentsia. There were no party elections or caucuses, and conferences were irregular, called only by the leaders to issue orders. Most parties were popularly known by the names of their Muslim leaders.

The most influential party remained that of the mufti, the Palestine Arab party, formed in 1935 from the Councilites (the mufti's supporters on the Supreme Muslim Council). To win Christian support, Alfred Roch, a prominent Catholic layman, was appointed by the mufti as vice president. Jerusalem and Haifa leaders of the Palestine Arab Workers' Society also were allied to this group, and an illegal quasi-military youth group, called the al-Futuwwah (Chivalry), was formed. The Palestine Arab party platform, called the National Pact, demanded that Great Britain repudiate the Balfour Declaration and end the mandate, that Jewish immigration and sale of land to Jews cease, and that Palestine immediately become an independent Arab state. The party used the mufti's position to persuade Arabs to sell land to the Supreme Muslim Council as a religious endowment of the Arab people in Palestine. Muslims who sold land to Jews were threatened with religious reprisals. An Arab National Fund unsuccessfully attempted to follow the example of the Jewish National Fund in acquiring, for the Arab nationalist cause, lands that the Jews tried to purchase.

The Nashashibis had formed the rival National Defense party in 1934, supported by the majority of Palestine's Arab mayors, who opposed the mufti. This group obtained Christian support from the Greek Orthodox vice mayor of Jerusalem, while labor collaboration was provided by the Jaffa leader of the Palestine Arab Workers' Society. Since the Nashashibis maintained close relations with Amir Abdullah of Transjordan, they were inclined to be less hostile to Great Britain.

Less significant groups included the Reform party, founded at Ramallah in 1935 by Dr. Husayn Fakhri al-Khalidi, a former Nashashibi man. Dr. Khalidi won the Jerusalem mayoralty from Raghib Nashashibi in 1934. Muslims in Nablus, Tulkarem, and Jaffa were appealed to by Abdel Latif Salah's National Bloc party, established in 1935. In the same year, the Arab Youth Congress party was formed in Haifa by leaders of an Arab Youth Congress that had been convened by young business and professional men in 1932.

Only the Istiqlal (Independence) party, formed at Haifa in 1932, had a program that strongly emphasized an ideology based on Arab unity. It was an offshoot of an organization formed in Damascus during 1919 to back Faisal for leadership of a greater Arab state. Several older Palestinians, who had been active in the prewar beginnings of the Arab nationalist movement, were the core of the Istiqlal. While they still favored the unity of all Arab countries, they now gave priority to the independence of each separate nation. This program attracted young progressive-minded doctors, lawyers, teachers, and government officials.

The common denominator of all the Arab parties was unqualified opposition to Zionism. All Arab nationalists denied that historical claims were a valid basis for establishing a Jewish national home in Palestine. They denied that local Arabs benefited to any appreciable extent from Zionist activities. They claimed that only the Syrian and Lebanese absentee owners who sold their land to Jews stood to gain. The local peasantry was being displaced from its ancestral home. True, the Arab leaders conceded, their followers were economically better off under the mandate than in Ottoman times, but this advantage, they held, was partially offset by the exorbitant taxes required to maintain the extensive British mandatory bureaucracy, by high tariffs protecting new Jewish industry, and by high prices paid for the products of Jewish commerce. The selection by Great Britain and the Western powers of Palestine, a land these nationalists now claimed had a nationally conscious people, as a refuge for persecuted Jews seemed to them misguided humanitarianism. The Arabs had already helped persecuted Jews by permitting an influx of hundreds of thousands. Furthermore, they asserted, the claim that Great Britain was supporting Zionism for purely humanitarian reasons was mere window dressing, for creating a Jewish state would destroy the national and cultural community of the Palestine Arabs. No more Jews could be taken in without displacing Arabs, and it was already becoming difficult to cope with the country's rapidly growing natural population increase.

This line of argument was propagated by the Arab press, in Friday mosque sermons, and throughout the Arab public school system. From headquarters in Jerusalem, the national movement rallied all the Arab regions, winning support not only from the middle and upper classes, but from peasants and city workers as well. The influx of Jewish refugees from Nazi Germany after 1933 sounded a warning knell to the growing Arab urban middle class, already frustrated by its inability to acquire power and influence. The addition of large numbers of educated European Jews would only increase the keen competition for desirable positions in government, such as lawyers, accountants, administrators, high-level clerks, and other middle-class occupations. Arab nationalists in Palestine also found inspiration in the rise of nationalist movements in neighboring Syria, Lebanon, and Iraq. The only differences among the Palestine Arab leaders were tactical. Moderates believed that through a measure of cooperation, they could win over the British. Extremists were for all out warfare—military, political, and economic —against both British and Jews.

When the parties failed to achieve unity, even during the year of the greatest Jewish prewar immigration in 1935, they became the butt of press attacks charging all leaders with sacrificing their cause to personal ambitions. Public pressure forced a loose federation of all Arab nationalist groups but the Istiqlal, which, because it refused even to negotiate with the British, refrained from cooperation with the other nationalists.

THE JEWISH QUASI GOVERNMENT

During the mandatory era the Yishuv, motivated by the nearly unanimous desire of its members to make Palestine the Jewish homeland, developed a political system, a civil administration, and police and security forces. Within half a century, Zionist nationalism had established a territorial base, complete with the institutions of a nation and a distinctive ethos far more sophisticated than any existing in the neighboring countries.

Immigration

The majority of the Yishuv were Jewish immigrants from Eastern Europe, primarily Poland and Russia, although smaller groups also came from Rumania, Bulgaria, and Hungary. In addition, there was a small group which had come from elsewhere in the Middle East, mainly from Yemen. After Hitler's rise, a new wave of immigration started from Germany. Only after World War II did substantial numbers come from other areas, such as North Africa, and even a few from Asian areas, such as India, Singapore, Hong Kong, and Cochin China. Never more than a handful of Jews immigrated from the United States, Great Britain, or France.

Each of the five successive waves of immigration was called *Aliya* (ascent), since the arrivals were "going up" to the Holy Land. The first Aliya comprised the small groups of Bilu from Russia who established the first Jewish colonies in the 1880s. Failure of the 1905 Russian revolution produced a somewhat larger second Aliya of young workers and socialists who had abandoned hope of freedom under the tsars. From this second group have come many of contemporary Israel's leaders, such as the first prime minister. David Ben Gurion, who helped establish the original collective settlements (*kibbutzim*) that came to symbolize Zionist activity. Between 1920 and 1922, the third Aliya came from Poland and other Eastern and Central European nations, where economic pressures on the lower-middle-class Jewish communities were becoming unbearable. When Poland's finance minister clamped discriminatory measures on the Jews in 1924, many of them made up the fourth Aliya. There were no really large immigration figures until Hitler's advent in 1933 precipitated the fifth, one of the largest Aliyas. Nazi repression completely changed the demographic structure of the Yishuv from a largely Eastern European community to one tempered with the ideas, techniques, and outlooks of Western Europe. German Jewry, with its distinctively middle-class liberal viewpoints, now mixed with the working-class socialists who had arrived earlier from Poland and Russia. By the time the British mandate came to an end, a multifold population increase, largely the result of immigration, had raised the Jewish population to about 650,000 (a number that still left them a third of Palestine's population). Less than a third of the local Jewish population was native born.

Social Structure

The Jewish community differed radically from the Arab one. Although Arab and Jewish settlements often stood side by side, they were literally separated by centuries. Jewish society as then constituted was nearly classless, marked by strong egalitarian tendencies. Few had immigrated to the Yishuv with great wealth. Whereas affluence was almost a prerequisite for political and social influence in the Arab community, it was frequently a handicap among Jewish settlers in this era. To prevent the formation of a large landowning class, the Zionists had created the Jewish National Fund, which became the largest purchaser and holder of property. A land shortage and the threats of Arab nationalists against those who sold property to the Jews had the effect of greatly inflating land values. Consequently, only the Jewish National Fund could afford the high prices that had to be paid for most real estate. Private Jewish landowners thus were few, and the holdings of those who had land were small compared to the land held by the Jewish National Fund or by private Arab landowners.

Jewish egalitarianism was also the product of early immigrant ideology that had borrowed heavily from European socialist doctrines. The result was to make the collective settlement a symbol of Zionist idealism, although the number of people living in such settlements was only a small fraction of the total Jewish population. Such settlements became to world Zionism the kind of symbol that the frontier was in American history. Through the powerful General Federation of Labor, or Histadrut, socialist influences became dominant in urban areas also. The Histadrut was not just an ordinary trade union; it was also a principal investor in all sectors of the economy, the publisher of the most widely read daily newspaper among Palestine Jews, and the chief supporter of numerous educational, social service (including medical care), and cultural activities.

High literacy rates and intense political consciousness in the Jewish community created fertile ground for development of excellent self-governing institutions. Long before the state of Israel was established, the Yishuv was a functioning democracy.

Political Institutions

The most important Jewish representative body in Palestine was the National Council (*Vaad Leumi*), established in 1920 under provisions of the British mandatory regulations that authorized each religious community in the country to establish its own institutions, a policy the British adopted from the Osmanlis. The council was chosen by the Elected Assembly (*Asafat ha-Nivharim*) of some 300 representatives nationally elected by Knesset Israel. Membership in Knesset Israel (the organized Jewish community) was obtained merely by paying a tax for its support. All significant organized Jewish groups belonged to Knesset Israel except the intensely orthodox Aguda, which declined to join because of its opposition to Zionist policies. They insisted that only by the hand of God, not man, could Israel truly be restored.

The mandatory government entrusted responsibility for Jewish communal affairs to the National Council as the representative body of Palestine

Jewry. By 1936, the council had taken over Jewish health services and education, as well as the clandestine recruitment and military training of Jewish youth. Several members of the National Council Executive (*Hanhalat Vaad ha-Leumi*) later became Israeli cabinet ministers, and their departments were subsequently absorbed by the Israeli government in 1948.

The interests of world Jewry in creating a homeland were represented at first by the World Zionist Organization and, later, by the Jewish Agency for Palestine (see below). By the eve of World War II, the Zionist Organization had grown into a massive enterprise with branches in some fifty nations and with approximately a million members. A biennial Zionist Congress, which decided on general policy, chose the Zionist General Council, which met every few months. Day-to-day decisions were taken by the Zionist Executive and the president of the World Zionist Organization on the basis of policy laid down at the biennial congresses.

By 1929 Zionist president Chaim Weizmann felt the need for the support of non-Zionist Jews in building up the Jewish national home. Hence the Jewish Agency for Palestine was created to include Jews who were sympathetic to the idea of a national home but not ideologically committed to Zionism. This agency took over the activities for building the national home that concerned Jews everywhere, such as raising funds and maintaining a liaison with foreign governments. It conducted negotiations with the Palestine mandatory government, the United Kingdom, and the League of Nations; its attempts to negotiate with the Arabs were unsuccessful. The most important offices of the Jewish Agency, including the presidency and the political, finance, labor, trade, industry, and statistical departments were in the hands of Zionists. Only those offices concerned with agricultural settlement and the problems of the German Jewish immigrants were directed by non-Zionist members of the Jewish Agency. Both Zionists and non-Zionists shared direction of the important immigration department.

By the late 1930s, the difference between Zionists and non-Zionists in these agencies was no longer significant and in no way affected policy. Palestinian Jews outnumbered representatives from other countries in the Zionist and Jewish Agency executives and in most of their component departments by the mid-1930s. For all practical purposes, all affairs of importance concerning the national Jewish home were in the hands of those who lived in the proposed homeland. Participation in the National Council, the Jewish Agency, the World Zionist Organization, and the various departments of the British-run mandatory government gave thousands of Palestine Jews a wealth of administrative experience that contributed greatly to the creation of a cadre of experienced officials for the future Jewish state. Such men obtained a rich background in the theoretical and practical problems of government and were supported by a core of well-trained civil servants, many of whom merely continued their administrative functions when they became part of the government of Israel in 1948.

Israel's defense system was also forged in the prestate era from the military arm of this quasi government. During the mandatory regime under the direction of the National Council and the Jewish Agency, the Haganah (meaning defense) was expanded as a secret and illegal body. By 1936, it had some 10,000 well-trained and relatively well-equipped members.

Most important of all in developing a national consciousness was the role of education. Whereas in the Arab community Palestine's Arab character was constantly emphasized, the Zionists referred only to its Jewishness. Thus the Jewish and Arab communities developed their own national consciousness, each with little regard for the aspirations of the other. A British Royal Commission observed in 1936 that from the educational "melting pot," emerged a national self-consciousness of unusual intensity.

Popular participation in Jewish communal activities was encouraged through a myriad of youth groups, sports organizations, labor activities, and political parties. By the 1930s, an elaborate multiparty system had developed, unique because of the large number of parties that existed in so small a community and because of their connections with related Jewish parties abroad. They were local because they were represented in the National Council and international by virtue of representation in the World Zionist Organization and Congress. Several had branches in many different countries, including the United States and Great Britain. Some were members of international federations or confederations; others maintained only loose ties of amity with their foreign associates (see chapter 11).

There were many opportunities for participation in elections. Yishuv members took part, as a section of the international Jewish community, in the biennial elections to the World Zionist Organization. Elections to the Elected Assembly, which chose the National Council, were irregular. Voting was by proportional representation. Candidates represented and were chosen by the whole Yishuv, not by separate districts. When casting a ballot, the voter chose a list of candidates representing a party, not just an individual candidate. Candidates were put on the ballot by the party leaders, rather than by primaries or in open caucus. When all the returns were in, the number of votes required to elect a candidate was obtained by dividing the total valid ballots cast by the number of offices to be filled. Replacements after an election were chosen by the party, not in a by-election. This system reflected a fairly accurate cross-section of public sympathies. Because of the great variety of political points of view in the Yishuv, representing many shades of opinion from various parts of Europe, the system of strict proportional representation produced an unusually large number of parties.

Because they were so small, parties became narrow in outlook, with carefully formulated and rigidly upheld programs. All but the very small Communist groups were founded on the principle of the eventual establishment of a Jewish national home in Palestine; all owed allegiance to the Zionist movement; and all were part of the Jewish quasi government. Differences concerned the nature of that home: would it be theocratic, socialist, capitalist, an independent unitary state, an autonomous province in a larger political entity, or a binational Jewish-Arab state? Because of their small number, members were required to support fully their party program. No halfhearted party identification was sanctioned.

Palestine Jewish heterogeneity in national origin, social viewpoint, and even religious observance fostered political diversity. Eastern European Jewry tended to drift toward the socialist left. The newer German arrivals were likely to be associated with the center. Some Jews from Yemen, Syria, and Iraq also formed their own groups, although most of them were politically inactive and remained unorganized. Older, established Jewish settlers who owned their own farms and industrial plants formed the right. No group ever attained a majority in community elections. The various Jewish political institutions were therefore run by loose coalitions, with the secular socialist groups usually acquiring an upper hand. Much of the socialists' power was exercised through the Histadrut, which became the most powerful single economic force, controlling many of the agricultural, industrial, commercial, and cooperative sectors of the country. This political system produced constant flux and change in political alliances. By 1936 there were ten main parties, each uniting two or more subgroups. They divided along four principal lines—labor, centrist, theocratic, and rightist.

CLASH BETWEEN JEWS AND ARABS

Even when Palestine's Jewish population grew from 10 percent to a third, there was little contact with the Arabs. Each community conducted its own social, political, economic, cultural, commercial, and other aspects of life with little regard for the other. Only in mixed areas, like Jerusalem and Haifa or rural lands where Jewish and Arab settlements adjoined, was there a direct intercommunity relationship. A rare exception in Jewish-Arab cooperation was citrus marketing, carried on by a joint board of private owners that each year sought the most favorable foreign markets.

As Jewish and Arab nationalisms grew in strength, numbers, and influence the ultimate objective of each became control of the whole of Palestine. Fewer and fewer Jews, Arabs, or British thought in terms of bridging the growing intercommunity gap. Two distinct communities, one Jewish and one Arab, emerged.

Demands for independence became more insistent among Muslim and Christian Arabs who felt that they were no less qualified to govern themselves than were their neighbors in Egypt, Iraq, and Syria. Indeed, their qualifications for self-rule seemed if anything more valid since their literacy rate was higher and their political sophistication greater. The Arab nationalist movement was also encouraged by Nazi Germany and Fascist Italy in the late

1930s by means of radio broadcasts, illicit arms shipments, and official backing that took advantage of this opportunity to embarrass the mandatory powers, Great Britain and France.

Nazi Germany, paradoxically, was also responsible for the dramatic spread of Jewish nationalism in the 1930s. Victims of Hitlerism flooded into Palestine when they could find no other refuge. In 1935, as many Jews arrived (over 61,000) as had come during the first five years of the mandate. During the first four years of Hitler's rule, the Jewish population in Palestine nearly doubled.

Arab nationalists were terrified by this rapidly growing number of Jews. Frenetic appeals were made to Great Britain to halt Jewish immigration, to restrict the sale of Arab land to Jews, and to grant the area immediate independence. Rifts were healed between squabbling political groups and Palestinewide committees sprang up throughout that area's Arab communities, finally coalescing to form the Arab Higher Committee. Militant tactics were adopted, such as a general strike in 1936, refusal of many to pay taxes to the mandatory, and violent attacks on both Jews and British. When the British retaliated by arresting nationalist leaders and imposing curfews and military control in Arab areas, Arab officials in the mandatory government formally protested. In June 1936, 137 senior Palestine government Arab officials and judges informed the British high commissioner in a memorandum that the disturbances were caused by the "profound sense of injustice" done to the Arabs. Because they had been so ignored, they were "driven into a state of verging on despair; and the present unrest is no more than an expression of that despair."[8]

Arab violence, beginning on a large scale in 1936, led to Jewish counterviolence, and the whole country became an arsenal of armed camps. A few solitary Jewish voices urged rapprochement with the Arabs, but they did little to influence the general direction of Jewish nationalism or to persuade the Arabs to compromise. The most significant calls for moderation came from Dr. Judah Magnes, first president of the Jerusalem Hebrew University, and from the Brit Shalom (Covenant of Peace), formed in 1920. Later many of its members joined other isolated Jewish seekers of peace in the League for Arab-Jewish Rapprochement and Cooperation, an organization to further creation of a binational (Arab-Jewish) state, rather than a Jewish or an Arab nation. Similarly, only a few isolated Arabs sympathized with the binationalists, and they dared not voice their opinions publicly lest they be cut down by Arab assassins.

INVESTIGATION COMMITTEES

Throughout the mandatory era it seemed that Palestine was the constant subject of investigating commissions, committees, and inquiries, beginning in

1921 with the survey headed by Sir Thomas Haycraft, Palestine's chief justice. He reported that riots in 1921 resulted from Arab concern with Jewish immigration and "their conception of Zionist policy as derived from Jewish exponents." During 1929, the Shaw Commission probed Arab-Jewish riots over the Wailing Wall in Jerusalem. Within the preceding ten years, the commission reported, there had been serious attacks by Arabs on Jews, although in the previous eighty none had been recorded. Until the war "Jews and Arabs lived side by side if not in amity, at least with tolerance, a quality which today is almost unknown in Palestine." Again, the cause was Arab fears that they would become a minority because of Jewish immigration and Zionist economic and political growth. Even during the slow years of Jewish immigration from 1925 to 1927, the rate of Jewish entrance to Palestine was higher than immigration into any other country. While Zionism had benefited the country economically, the lot of the average fellah had not appreciably improved, the commission observed.

Sharp protests by the League of Nations Permanent Mandates Commission against British efforts to curb Jewish immigration led to the economic investigation of Sir John Hope-Simpson in 1930. His report emphasized what he estimated to be Palestine's limited economic capacity and warned that the Arabs might face a land shortage if Jewish ownership continued to expand. This conclusion became the basis for the 1930 Passfield White Paper limiting immigration to "economic absorptive capacity" and reserving government areas for landless Arabs rather than for the Jews. So vehement was the reaction of world Zionist leadership that Prime Minister Ramsey MacDonald attempted to explain away the White Paper restrictions in a letter to Dr. Weizmann during 1931. Jewish immigration would be continued, MacDonald promised, and only those Arabs who surrendered property to Jews would receive government lands. The Arabs called MacDonald's note the "Black Paper" and used the opportunity to intensify their anti-British and anti-Zionist propaganda.

Most surveys were made during 1930–1931 by Lewis French on agricultural development and land settlement, by Inspector General Dowbiggin on police reorganization, by D.F. Strickland on Arab cooperatives, and by Sir Samuel O'Donnell and H. Brittain on reorganization of Palestine's administration. The League of Nations also sent out its own International Commission to determine Jewish and Arab rights at the Wailing Wall in 1930.

The state of investigations finally culminated in the Royal Commission of Inquiry under Earl Peel (former secretary of state for India), sent by Parliament following the 1936 Arab revolt. Only friendly intervention from neighboring rulers persuaded the Arab Higher Committee to talk with Peel. The commission came to the conclusion that no common ground existed between Palestine's 1,000,000 Arabs and 400,000 Jews.

The Arab community is predominantly Asiatic in character, the Jewish community predominantly European. They differ in religion and in language. Their cultural and social life, their ways of thought and conduct, are as incompatible as their national aspirations. These last are the greatest bar to peace.... The war [World War I] and its sequel have inspired all Arabs with the hope of reviving in a free and united Arab world the traditions of the Arab golden age. The Jews similarly are inspired by their historic past.... In the Arab picture the Jews could only occupy the place they occupied in Arab Egypt or [in] Arab Spain. The Arabs would be as much outside the Jewish picture as the Canaanites in the old land of Israel. The National Home...cannot be half-national.... This conflict was inherent in the situation from the outset. The terms of the Mandate tended to confirm it [and] the conflict has grown steadily more bitter.... In the earlier period hostility to the Jews was not widespread among the fellaheen. It is now general.... The intensification of the conflict will continue...[and] it seems probable that the situation, bad as it now is, will grow worse. The conflict will go on, the gulf between Arabs and Jews will widen.[9]

The Royal Commission proposed partition of Palestine into: a tiny Jewish state populated by 285,000 Jews and 225,000 Arabs; an international enclave from the coast to and including Jerusalem; and an Arab state including most of the country. Sir Herbert Samuel observed in 1937: "The Commission seemed to have picked out all the most awkward provisions of the Peace Treaties of Versailles, and to have put a Saar, a Polish Corridor and a half dozen Danzigs and Memels into a country the size of Wales."[10]

While certain Zionist leaders found the plan acceptable, the Twentieth Zionist Congress, meeting in 1937, rejected it. The organization demanded continuation of the mandate, increased Jewish immigration, the creation of a Jewish state, and a peaceful settlement with the Arabs. Arab moderates countered with a proposal for treaty relations similar to those that then existed between Egypt and Great Britain and maintenance of the existing Arab-Jewish Population ratio.

Arab rejection of the partition proposal was accompanied by increased violence. In a final effort to suppress revolt, the government banned the Arab Higher Committee and all other Palestinewide Arab committees, arrested and deported six Arab leaders, and deprived the mufti of his principal source of funds, the wakf.

The Palestine Partition (Woodhead) Commission sent to investigate ways of implementing the Peel plan in 1938 found unanimously that partition would be unworkable because the proposed Jewish state was too small and the likelihood of Arab resistance too great. Instead, Great Britain announced that an Anglo-Jewish-Arab conference would convene in London during February and March 1939 to discuss the future of Palestine. However, the

Arab-Jewish deadlock could not be broken. The antagonists would not even meet face to face.

In a final prewar White Paper, Great Britain promised Palestine self-government within a decade. Jewish immigration would be permitted for five years until Jews constituted a third of the population. Further immigration would depend on Arab acquiescence, and Jewish land purchases would be restricted to a small area of the country.

Arab moderates considered the 1939 White Paper a modest victory, although the mufti's followers continued to insist adamantly on immediate independence. A pall of disappointment fell over the Jewish community. In Palestine, Jewish demonstrators sacked government offices, stoned British police, and looted shops. At the Twenty-first Zionist Congress, Weizmann charged regretfully that Great Britain "has gone back on its promises....I must raise my voice in the strongest possible protest. We have not deserved this treatment."[11]

The League's Permanent Mandates Commission questioned the legality of the British White Paper because it violated the terms under which Great Britain had taken the Palestine mandate. But by August 1939 Palestine and its problems had faded into the background of world affairs in the wake of Germany's sweep into Poland. Not until the end of the war was the country's future to be decided.

NOTES

1. Cited in William Polk, D. Stamler, and E. Asfour, *Backdrop to Tragedy*, Boston, 1957, p. 149.

2. "The Origins of Israel," *The Middle East in Transition*, Walter Z. Laqueur, ed., New York, 1958, p. 208.

3. Israel Cohen, *The Zionist Movement*, New York, 1946, p. 78.

4. Cited in Hans Kohn, *Nationalism and Imperialism in the Hither East*, New York, 1932, pp. 291–292.

5. Cited in George Antonius, *The Arab Awakening*, p. 439.

6. Hurewitz, *Diplomacy in the Near and Middle East*, vol. II, p. 70.

7. Cited in Cohen, *op. cit.*, pp. 150–151.

8. Cited in Polk, Stamler, and Asfour, *Backdrop to Tragedy*, p. 193.

9. Cmd 5479, pp. 370–372, cited in *Ibid.*, p. 95.

10. *Foreign Affairs Quarterly*, XVI (1937), p. 152, cited in *Ibid.*, p. 97.

11. Cohen, *op. cit.*, p. 232.

11   The State of Israel

Despite bitterness created by the 1939 White Paper, the Yishuv and world Zionist leaders had no alternative but to support Allied war efforts against the Nazis who were persecuting European Jews. Before terminating the 1939 Zionist Congress, Weizmann informed Prime Minister Neville Chamberlain that the Jews "stand by Great Britain and will fight on the side of the democracies."

The National Council of Palestine's Jewish community initiated full-scale mobilization in 1939, enlisting some 135,000 volunteers for military and other services by the war's end. At first, Great Britain looked askance at an exclusively Jewish combat unit, enlisting equal numbers of Jewish and Arab volunteers for auxiliary work. When Italy joined the Nazis in 1940, Palestinians were accepted for combat in seven Arab and seven Jewish companies. For the Jews, an Allied victory over Hitler was a question of life or death; hence their enlistments were nearly three times those of the Arabs. A Jewish Rural Special Police unit was also formed in 1942 as a kind of home guard under the British Middle East commander-in-chief. Continued pressure throughout the war from world Jewry on the British government forced the gradual enlargement of Palestinian combat units, and finally the creation of a Jewish Brigade in 1944.

In Palestine during the war, the Jewish Agency channeled all material and technical resources of the Yishuv into the war effort. A fleet of 850 trucks equipped with drivers and mechanics was organized; agriculture and industry were mobilized; hundreds of Jewish shops turned out metal, electrical, timber, textile, leather, cement, and chemical supplies.

Palestine's political climate was considerably calmer than it had been in decades. The most fervent Arab nationalists had left, and most of the organized Jewish community called off their anti-British campaigns. The Jewish Agency, however, did not cease the underground rescue of Hitler's victims. Throughout the conflict, the agency continued to smuggle illegal immigrants into Palestine on rickety, leaking vessels. Those Jews who were caught by the British sea patrols were transferred to some British colony. Conflict over immigration cooled Zionist enthusiasm for cooperation with Great Britain. Palestine Jews regarded British policy as heartless politics aimed at Arab appeasement, while the British believed that the Zionist underground was motivated less by humanitarian than by political objectives. Zionist purposes, the British asserted, were to force England's hand on Jewish immigration and to sabotage the 1939 White Paper. Relations almost came to a breaking point when Palestine Jewish leaders were charged with illegally procuring weapons from British military depots at two public trials in Jerusalem. Jewish Agency chairman, David Ben Gurion, retorted that this was still another attempt to discredit the Yishuv and enforce the hated White Paper.

One tiny band of Jewish terrorists, the Stern group, kept up a private war against the British. The leader, Abraham Stern, and a handful of followers broke away from the IZL, the Irgun Zvai Leumi (National Military Organization), when that illegal parent group suspended its anti-British activities. Relations between the Zionists and Great Britain reached a crisis in November 1944 when two Sternists assassinated Lord Moyne, British minister resident in the Middle East. Weizmann now wrote to Churchill of his "deep moral indignation and horror," and pledged that the Yishuv would "go to the utmost limit of its power to cut out, root and branch, this evil from its midst."[1]

During the war, Zionist leaders restated their political objectives in the Biltmore Program, so called because of their meeting at the Biltmore Hotel in New York City during May 1942. The Biltmore Program demanded control by the Jewish Agency over immigration into Palestine and establishment of the country as a Jewish Commonwealth. Only a small group of binationalists, favoring a Jewish-Arab state, who were part of the left-wing Hashomer Hatzair (a predecessor of the Mapam party, discussed below), and followers of Dr. Judah Magnes opposed the new program.

PALESTINE BECOMES AN INTERNATIONAL CONCERN

World Jewry was horror struck at the war's end when it discovered that, in all, Hitler had liquidated at least six million of their coreligionists—nearly one in three of the world's Jewish population. Jewish communities everywhere were now organized in strenuous efforts to obtain Palestine as a refuge for the remnants of European Jewry. Political pressure was applied on the British and American governments. Illegal immigration was increased, and by 1946 Jewish terrorism against British troops in Palestine had been renewed.

Both British and American politicians found it expedient to capitalize on Jewish concern about Hitler's victims. The British Labor party not only fully supported Zionist demands, it went further and in December 1944 called for the transfer of Palestine Arabs to neighboring countries. In the 1944 American presidential election campaign, both Republican and Democratic leaders called for the removal of restrictions on Jewish immigration to Palestine and land purchases there.

Because of the great Jewish interest in and concern about the Palestine problem, it became an issue in American domestic politics and President Truman decided to join Great Britain in attempting to reach a solution. A joint Anglo-American Committee was sent to Europe and the Middle East in 1946 to make recommendations concerning Jewish immigration to Palestine and the country's future. The committee recommended a trusteeship in lieu of either an Arab or Jewish state; termination of the 1939 White Paper restrictions on the sale of land; and immediate admission of 100,000 refugees from European Displaced Persons camps. The Jewish ban on Arab employment in enterprises financed by the Jewish Agency and the use of violence by both sides was condemned by the commission. It urged the Jewish Agency to assist the mandatory government in suppressing both terrorism and illegal immigration.

During the 1948 election campaign, President Truman announced support for admission to Palestine of 100,000 refugees, but he made no mention of the other Anglo-American Committee recommendations. London notified him that this would force the British government to dispatch still another division of troops to Palestine, already overrun with armed forces. Only if the illegal Jewish units were disbanded and disarmed would Great Britain permit resumption of large-scale immigration.

The Yishuv answered Great Britain with an intensive military campaign waged by the Haganah, the Irgun, and the Sternists against the British authorities in Palestine. The latter retaliated by arresting several key Jewish Agency executives in June 1946 and by conducting widespread searches for arms hidden in the Jewish settlements.

In London, meanwhile, British and American officials consulted on still another partition proposal, the Morrison-Grady scheme, dividing Palestine into a British zone and Jewish and Arab autonomous provinces. But both protagonists continued to demand all the country. One last compromise proposal combined trusteeship and provincial autonomy, but that too was rejected by both Jews and Arabs.

　　　　Continued civil war in Palestine, American political pressures, and the desire to end the financial and administrative burdens of the mandate, led Great Britain to place the problem before the United Nations in April 1947. A special session of the General Assembly dispatched the United Nations Special Committee on Palestine (UNSCOP) to the region to find a solution. After retracing the steps of previous investigations, the UNSCOP majority also concluded that Arab-Jewish cooperation was unlikely.

　　　　The Special Committee's Indian, Iranian, and Yugoslav minority proposed a federal state as a last effort to prevent rupture of Arab-Jewish relations and to avoid the creation of dangerous irredentism, "the inevitable consequences of partition in whatever form." The UNSCOP majority of eight (Australia, Canada, Czechoslovakia, Guatemala, the Netherlands, Peru, Sweden, and Uruguay) recommended partition as soon as possible.

　　　　After intensive behind-the-scenes lobbying, the United Nations adopted the partition plan by 33 votes to 13, with 10 abstentions, on November 29, 1947. Palestine was divided into three Arab and three Jewish areas, forming an Arab and a Jewish state, while Jerusalem and its environs were set up as an international zone. The proposal placed a Jewish minority of 1.5 percent of the total population in the Arab state, and an Arab minority totaling 45 percent of the population in the Jewish state. Equal numbers of Jews and Arabs were to populate the international zone. Because of their economic interdependence, however, the seven parts were to be linked in an economic union.

The First Palestine War

　　　　The whole Arab world rose in protest against the United Nations partition resolution because it denied self-determination to Palestine's Arab majority, Palestinewide communities, like those formed by Palestine Arab leaders in 1936, were again formed to meet the crisis. Throughout the Arab East, angry demonstrations erupted against all those responsible for partition. The Yishuv and Zionists throughout the world, on the other hand, were overjoyed at the U.N. recommendation. Jewish youth in Tel Aviv and Jerusalem danced in the streets and openly fraternized with British troops. The public elation of Palestine's Jewish community was such as had not been displayed for decades. Zionist leaders made plans to establish a Jewish government. Great Britain refused to have anything to do with the U.N. proposals because only one, not both, sides approved them. Anticipating armed conflict between Jews and Arabs, British forces were withdrawn to security zones pending their evacuation. British mandatory authorities made no attempt to devise an orderly transfer of government authority and functions to either Jews or Arabs. As a result, when the British evacuated an area, Jews and Arabs fought to obtain control of it.

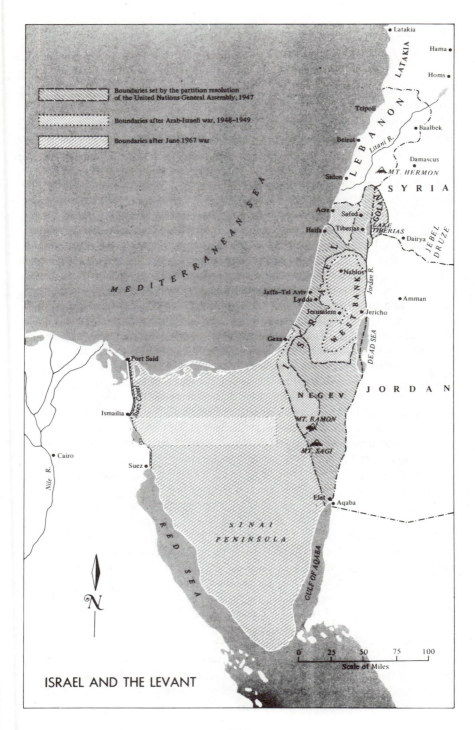

Legend:

- Boundaries set by the partition resolution of the United Nations General Assembly, 1947
- Boundaries after Arab-Israeli war, 1948–1949
- Boundaries after June 1967 war

Latakia

LATAKIA

Hama

Homs

Tripoli

SYRIA

Baalbek

Beirut

Litani R.

Damascus

MT. HERMON

Sidon

GOLAN

Acre

Safed

LAKE TIBERIAS

Haifa

Tiberias

Dairya

JEBEL DRUZE

MEDITERRANEAN SEA

I S R A E L

Nablus

Jordan R.

Jaffa–Tel Aviv

Lydda

Amman

Jerusalem

WEST BANK

Jericho

Gaza

DEAD SEA

Port Said

Suez Canal

N E G E V

J O R D A N

Ismailia

MT. RAMON

Nile R.

Cairo

MT. SAGI

Suez

Elat

Aqaba

S I N A I
P E N I N S U L A

RED SEA

GULF OF AQABA

0   25   50   75   100

Scale of Miles

ISRAEL AND THE LEVANT

Fervently enthusiastic celebrations by one side in the midst of bitter protests by the other made violence inevitable. Where Jews and Arabs lived side by side, as in Jerusalem, Arab demonstrators attacked Jewish shops and counterretaliations soon followed. Within hours, the whole country was torn by large-scale intercommunal warfare. There was no more room now for the few moderates who had urged compromise. It was to be a fight for complete Arab or Jewish victory.

Because Arab efforts to raise military forces and collect military equipment were poorly organized, with no really strong central authority, their numerical superiority and the assistance they received from foreign volunteers was of little advantage. Although a small volunteer force of Palestine Arab guerrilla fighters was organized, Arab villagers were not conscripted. In the larger cities, such as Jaffa, Jerusalem, and Haifa, Arab manpower was recruited for home guard duty. But most rural inhabitants were uninvolved until the fighting swept down on them and they were forced to flee for safety. Initial combat was carried out by small guerrilla cadres, many veterans of the 1936–1939 civil war.

The much smaller Jewish community was far more efficient. Every aspect of life was quickly organized for a full-scale war—food, medicine, transport, communications, and all other vital services. Not only did it have many combat veterans of Europe's World War II armies, it could also call upon Western-trained administrators to organize the community on a wartime footing. Most important was the great *élan* uniting the Yishuv, men, women, and children, as it had never been united before.

As the civil war spread, atrocities mounted on both sides and the struggle increasingly became a matter of life or death for everyone involved. The most notorious atrocity perpetrated was the Irgun massacre, in April 1948, of men, women, and children in Deir Yassin, near Jerusalem. The Haganah and the Jewish Agency strongly condemned it, but word of this brutal attack spread like wildfire through Arab towns and villages. Fear gave way to panic, and by the end of May, most Arab villagers and townsmen had fled to the neighboring Arab countries. The first Arab departures had occurred in December and January, when many of the wealthier families took "temporary" refuge in neighboring countries. As the conflict steadily grew more desperate, thousands of Arabs, then hundreds of thousands, fled for safety, so that by the end of the fighting, early in 1949, there were nearly 750,000 Palestine Arab refugees in Lebanon, Syria, Jordan, and the Egyptian-occupied Gaza strip in southern Palestine.

Differences in the organization of the Arab and Jewish communities accounted for differing reactions to the war. When the fighting began, the Jewish quasi government already had taken over many areas. Even a Jewish postal service, issuing its own stamps, was serving several communities before the British left. Law and order continued in the Jewish occupied zones and public morale was high as a consequence of the Yishuv's excellent leadership and organization.

The Arab community had no such leadership or administrative apparatus. Nearly all important government functions had been left to the direct control of British mandate officials. Shortly after most of the Arab leaders left the country, early in 1948, the British administrators also departed, leaving no effective body to manage essential services or maintain communal morale. All normal governmental functions necessary to preserve law, order, and well-being disintegrated—water, electricity, posts, police, education, health, and even sanitation. With no effective leaders left to guide them and the nearly complete collapse of government in most Palestine Arab communities, Arab hysteria rose with every Jewish military victory.

As long as the British remained in the country, until the middle of May 1948, the Arab-Jewish conflict was a civil war between Jewish and Arab Palestinians. On May 14, 1948, when the mandate formally came to an end, the last British units departed and the State of Israel was proclaimed. Armies from Egypt, Syria, Lebanon, Jordan, and Iraq poured across the frontiers to assist the Palestine Arabs. For the Israelis it now became a "War of Liberation." Despite their numbers the Arabs were too disorganized to wage an effective campaign, and soon the Israelis were on the offensive.

Efforts by the United Nations to halt the fighting, by bringing about truces or cease fires and by appointing Count Folke Bernadotte as a mediator, all failed. Finally in 1949, Dr. Ralph Bunche, after the assassination of Bernadotte by Israeli terrorists, successfully arranged armistice agreements between Israel and all the Arab combatants except Iraq. By successful military operations, Israel had gained nearly a third more territory than the amount allocated to it by the U.N. partition resolution.

THE GOVERNMENT OF ISRAEL

The provisional government of Israel, formed on May 14, 1948, was new in name only, for it had begun *de facto* functioning several months earlier. Shortly after voting for partition, the United Nations had sent a Palestine Commission to effect a transfer from the mandatory to the two proposed states. Since neither the Arabs nor the British were willing to cooperate with it, the commission worked exclusively with the Jewish community through the National Council and Jewish Agency to establish a Jewish government. As early as March 1948, a Jewish Provisional Council, chosen from National Council and Jewish Agency executive members, assumed control in many areas. The Provisional Council also reserved places for Jewish groups not members of the quasi government. On May 14, the new provisional government was formed from members of the Provisional Council and the Jewish Agency.

Numerous urgent problems had plagued the provisional government. The primary one was the ability of the Yishuv to resist the onslaught of five Arab armies. It was also feared that the great powers at the last moment would impose some alternative to partition. Such a possibility became a genuine threat early in the spring of 1948 when Count Bernadotte arrived with various alternatives to independence to end the war. At the United Nations, the Americans began to have second thoughts about partition and now proposed renewed discussion of a trusteeship plan. Lest their hopes now be thwarted, the Zionist leaders decided to ignore all urgent pleas to defer the formation of a Jewish state; on May 14, therefore, they issued Israel's proclamation of independence. Other initial acts repealed the British mandatory restrictions on immigration and the sale of land and converted the formerly illegal Haganah into the Defense Army of Israel.

The chief body of the provisional government was the thirty-eight-member State Council, representing a dozen political parties. The Mapai party, holding twelve of the thirty-eight seats, dominated government proceedings. The only non-Zionists were two Aguda members and a single Communist. The State Council acted in lieu of a parliament, since it was impossible to hold elections in the midst of a raging war. A provisional government, a cabinet of thirteen ministers representing seven of the parties, was chosen by the State Council from its members. The effective head of government was the prime minister appointed by the president from the various party leaders. While he was titular chief of state, the president, who was also elected by the State Council, had little effective power; he was to be primarily a figurehead. David Ben Gurion, former Jewish Agency chairman, became Israel's first prime minister, and Dr. Chaim Weizmann, former president of the World Zionist Organization, was chosen as the first president of Israel.

All the administrative functions that had been undertaken by the National Council, the British mandatory regime, and the Jewish Agency were now taken over by the new Israeli government. Upon these three principal pillars, therefore, the new administrative apparatus was built. The last functions that remained to the National Council, its educational duties, were turned over to the new Ministry of Education in September 1948. Then all government members resigned from the Jewish Agency except the finance minister, who retained his Jewish Agency post as a link between the Israeli government and world Jewry.

Many of the fundamental acts and legislative procedures adopted by the provisional government later became part of the constitutional system that emerged. The Supreme Court, for example, organized within six weeks of independence, became a permanent fixture. Methods of parliamentary procedure were borrowed from Great Britain, such as the opening of legislative sessions with questions from members and replies from ministers, the British system of debate, and the appointment of standing committees to examine draft laws and conduct hearings. Most of the laws that existed under the mandatory regime were taken over with no change and only gradually repealed, amended, or replaced by new codes. Many Israeli court decisions still draw heavily upon the precedents of English common law, and are even recorded in the original English. Along with English law, Israel continued to use a large body of Ottoman legislation that the British had retained after their conquest.

POLITICAL DIVERSITY

Israeli democracy is characterized by a wide diversity of political and social viewpoints given free expression in political parties, newspapers, and a variety of social, religious, cultural, and other organizations. Numerous minority and splinter factions freely criticize the government. The most notable example is the New Communist, or Rakah party, which, despite the provocation of its support for Arab positions in most recent international disputes, continues to be legally recognized and to send members to Israel's parliament. The New Communists are also represented in local government and in the trade-union movement.

The roots of political diversity can be found in the European origin of nearly all parties represented in parliament. Most parties are lineal descendants or offshoots of Zionist groups established early in the twentieth century. Eight of the thirteen parties which won seats in the Ninth Knesset during the 1977 elections originated in Europe and in 1981 eight of the ten parties elected were Zionist. Until today most Israeli political parties are associated with Zionist groups in Western Europe, South Africa, and North America.

The first Israeli national elections were held in January 1949. The electoral system and most of the political parties were identical to those in the Jewish community during the mandatory period. Members of parliament were chosen by proportional representation from a single constituency of the country as a whole rather than from smaller electoral districts. Each party received a number of seats in proportion to the number of nationwide votes it obtained. Twenty-one parties contested the 120 seats in the first Knesset, but only nine polled sufficient votes to elect at least one candidate. No political party won sufficient votes to command a majority in parliament from the first Knesset in 1949 until the tenth in 1981. Israel was thus governed by broad coalition governments dominated by the Mapai wing of the labor movement until 1977. During this era, Israel's political parties were transformed through numerous mergers, subdivisions, and remergers. However there was little substantial change in the political structure, since most parties retained their fundamental Zionist ideologies diversified by differing socioeconomic outlook and personality clashes.

Until the 1977 national election the country's parties could be classified into three principal blocs: Labor, Center-Right, and Religious. Within each bloc there were several parties, sometimes amalgamating into a single Knesset list, often splitting into separate and competing factions. At times splinters from one ideological bloc would join with a group in another. Despite the constant shifting of party factions and individuals from one Knesset list to another, the system maintained a remarkable stability until 1977. Until then Labor won every national election in the sense that it acquired a plurality, or more votes than any other list. Since no party won a majority every government was a coalition formed by the leaders of the Labor party from factions with enough votes to give the government a majority in the 120-member Knesset.

Before the 1977 election a new list was formed by an ex-general and was composed of prominent individuals representing diverse, often conflicting political views. Some came from Labor, others from the Center-Right, while still others had not been active in politics. The common denominator holding the new list together was a demand for change in the country's political system. Called the Democratic Movement for Change (DMC), it represented the feelings of widespread discontent with the establishment that swept through the country in the wake of the 1973 war. Surprisingly, DMC won sufficient votes to become Israel's third largest party by drawing much of its strength from the Labor party, thus causing Labor's first major defeat. It could be classified somewhere between the Labor and Center-Rightists; perhaps closest to a new liberal bloc.

THE LABOR BLOC

During Israel's first twenty-nine years the labor movement, with its various parties, unions, and other organizations commanded support of nearly half the Israeli electorate. In the Knesset the Labor Alignment was an amalgam of the Labor party and the Mapam party. Mapam insisted on preserving its distinctive identity, refusing to merge into the Labor party; thus the Labor list ran as an Alignment rather than a party. The Labor-Mapam Alignment was formed as a single list in 1969. The Labor party, also a new creation, was established in 1968 from Mapai and Ahdut Avoda, two of the older labor groups in the country. Rafi, a faction that had split from Mapai in 1965, reunited with its parent group and Ahdut Avoda in the Labor party during 1968.

The Mapai wing dominated the Labor bloc until 1973. Most party leaders, the most important cabinet posts, and most influential positions in the various labor organizations were controlled by Mapai. At its inception Mapai was strongly influenced by Marxian socialism, being the product of two previously established socialist factions which established the Histadrut (General Confederation of Labor) in 1920. Both labor groups strongly emphasized in their ideology use of Jewish labor to develop the Jewish homeland. One group, Ahdut Avoda (Labor Unity), represented the fusion between Poale Zion (Zion Workers) and small factions of other workers. The other group, Hapoel Hatzair (The Young Worker), was motivated by the ideology of Aaron David Gordon, father of the "religion of labor." Jewish nationalism meant to him regeneration of the people through hard physical labor and acceptance of social responsibility. The main struggle in society, he preached, was not between capitalists and workers, but between "creation and parasitism." Diaspora Jews had become parasites by losing a sense of the sanctity of labor, the basis of national and individual dignity. Thus only through labor could Israel be redeemed.

Gordon's non-Marxist idealization of physical labor was synthesized with the Marxian doctrine of Poale Zion preached by Ber Borochov, who believed that all social problems stemmed from conflict between those who controlled the forces of production, such as capital, machinery, and factories, and the workers struggling to improve their conditions by obtaining a larger share of the profits of their production. Most Jews, forced to compete with non-Jewish laborers in the struggle to obtain a larger share of the profits, were discriminated against just because they were a minority. The only solution for Jews was to concentrate their working-class proletariat in a single country and there develop its powers unhampered by competition with non-Jewish workers. Borochov's initial followers were mostly his fellow Jews from the depressed working class in Russia.

Gradually the followers of Gordon and Borochov absorbed the other labor factions representing the spectrum of revolutionary socialist ideologies: Marxism, social democracy, syndicalism, anarchism, and Tolstoyanism. Hapoel Hatzair and Ahdut Avoda established the Histadrut (Federation of Labor) in 1920, and continued their separate political ways for another nine years. After fusion into Mapai (Israel Worker's Party) during 1929, they retained much of their original leftist terminology, continued to identify Jewish national interests with those of labor, and accused other groups of purely selfish motives.

Control of the Histadrut gave Mapai an advantage over all other parties. While other groups were later represented in this labor organization, the majority of its elected offices were held by the Mapai founders. The Histadrut dominated not only labor unions, but also large sectors of the rural and urban economy. Originally, the Histadrut pioneered investment in enterprises that private capital found unrewarding. Because of its control over labor and large investment funds and its close connections with the government, the organization later exercised a considerable advantage over private industry. The Histadrut also controlled the Yishuv's large newspaper, *Davar,* a number of publishing houses, many cultural activities such as the theatre, and the best health and medical services available. In a country whose people were characterized by strong social motivations, it was inevitable that the party controlling the Histadrut would be supreme.

Domination of the Histadrut placed Mapai in a favorable position to capture a large share of the vote by means of their control of the labor exchanges and their processing of new arrivals as they entered the country. Control of labor exchanges gave Mapai direct access to those who were seeking jobs, and its initial contacts with new immigrants, enabled the party to indoctrinate them with its own ideology. So broad are Histadrut activities that

> a member...could spend his whole life within the framework of the organization. He wakes up in a house built by a Histadrut society, goes to work in a bus operated by a cooperative, spends his day in a factory owned by the Histadrut, sends his children to what used to be labour movement schools, goes to a Kupat Holim [the Histadrut health service] for medical treatment, spends his vacation at a Histadrut rest home, and finds entertainment in workers' clubs and theatres. It needs no big stretch of the imagination to say the same of the Mapai member who can, if he wishes, move exclusively within this huge, largely self-contained organization.[2]

Mapai became one of the strongest world Jewish groups through its posts in the World Zionist Organization and the Jewish Agency. Party leader Ben Gurion was Jewish Agency chairman, Moshe Sharett (formerly Shertok) was codirector of the Agency Political Department before he became Israel's first foreign minister; and Agency Treasurer Eliezer Kaplan became the first finance minister. From their key positions in the Jewish Agency, World Zionist Organization, National Council, Histadrut, trade unions, and Haganah, Mapai leaders continued to control most of the top positions in the state.

Control of the Mapai party was largely in the hands of the early Russian and Polish immigrants, although later, their children, such as Moshe Dayan and Shimon Peres, also received top posts. A large proportion were members of the collective and cooperative agricultural settlements established in the pioneer era. A 1956 survey showed that only 15 percent of the veteran leaders were university graduates, although a third had attended university. Only half had been to secondary school.

From its early days until the mid-1960s Mapai was dominated by David Ben Gurion, Israel's first prime minister. Ben Gurion led Israel through its birth pains during the first Arab-Israeli War of 1948, through the second war with Egypt in 1956, and through the critical period of early growth. Ben Gurion—or "the old man," as he was affectionately called—filled the role of tribal leader and father image during this era. He might be compared to the patriarchal figure of de Gaulle in France, Nehru in India, or Nasser in Egypt. However, after his retirement in 1966, Ben Gurion became a controversial figure, losing much of the prestige that he had earned when he had led Israel to its early military and political victories.

Between 1965 and 1968 Ben Gurion led a number of more militant Mapai leaders out of the party into a new political faction called Rafi (the Israel Labor List). Its leadership included the former Israeli chief of staff, Moshe Dayan, and others who believed that Mapai's stand was not militant enough on matters of national security or in relationships with neighboring Arab states. In 1969 Rafi rejoined the parent Mapai party, along with two other labor groups, to form the Alignment for the Unity of Israel's Workers. The three groups then remerged into the new Israel Labor party. They were joined by a fourth labor group, Mapam, with less binding ties. The four labor factions ran as a single list in the 1969 elections, winning just over 46 percent of the votes, still fewer than required to form a government majority.

Mapam

The core of Mapam is Hashomer Hatzair (Young Guard), a revolutionary socialist group founded in 1927. Because its Marxist ideology is too doctrinaire for most Israelis, it has had only a fraction of Mapai's strength. On the eve of Israel's creation, Hashomer Hatzair fused with Ahdut Avoda (Labor Unity) and a small splinter group, Paole Zion Smole (Left Zion Workers) to form Mapam (United Workers party). Besides being more ardent socialists, these groups favored a binational state and differed with Mapai over the Biltmore Program. Ahdut Avoda had been part of Mapai between 1920 and 1944, but had always been discontented with moderate policies. The small Left Zion faction had been out of the Zionist movement altogether for several years because it considered socialism more important than Zionism. Now that a Jewish state was about to be formed, the three groups felt that their mutual radical socialism was a basis of common interest on which to build effective opposition to the larger Mapai socialist party. Out of this common cause came Mapam.

Mapam members considered themselves an integral part of the world proletariat striving to replace "the capitalist system with its profits and exploitation of the many for the good of the few" by a new economic and social order in which class distinctions would disappear. Party leadership came largely from the left wing of the collective settlement movement. While Mapam could capture nearly half the votes of the collectives (with some 3 percent of the total votes) it remained weak in urban areas.

Since Mapam's core was rural, the party continually emphasized the ideology of Jewish labor on the land. Its numerous agricultural settlements have contributed remarkably to development of frontier areas and to idealization of the pioneer spirit. But the strong emphasis on rural development led Mapam to overlook the importance of the urban proletariat and the development of industry. Because few of its members have played a leading role in industry, Mapam was unable to compete with Mapai in placing directors in the nonagricultural sectors of the economy.

Mapam criticized Mapai governments because they were not militantly socialist. Its leaders urged larger income taxes for upper-bracket wealth, greater imposts on luxury imports, and higher inheritance levies. Until 1954, when there was an outbreak of anti-Jewish measures in Communist nations, Mapam favored closer ties with the USSR. Later, Mapam urged that Israel follow a neutralist foreign policy, make more strenuous efforts to achieve peace with the Arabs, and maintain closer ties with "uncommitted" nations such as Yugoslavia and India.

Bitter controversy over the implications of Communist anti-Jewish measures caused serious rifts in Mapam between 1952 and 1954, especially when Communists in Eastern Europe labeled Zionism as criminal and dangerous to the Soviet Union. A small pro-Soviet faction split off in 1953 to form the Left Front, which thereafter joined the Israel Communist party. Most Soviet critics were former Ahdut Avoda members, who left Mapam to reform their own party. The Hashomer Hatzair group remained the core of Mapam, urging the party to come to an understanding with the Soviet Union that would not compromise its Zionism. It also has been more willing to compromise in a peace settlement with the Arabs. After joining the Labor Alignment in 1969 Mapam continued to lose its distinctive identity, although there were enough members who felt that the party should remain intact.

Ahdut Avoda

When it separated from Mapam in 1953, Ahdut Avoda was stronger than the parent party, but it began to decline after Mapam abandoned its pro-Soviet orientation. Later, both parties urged a similar neutralist foreign policy. However, Ahdut Avoda was militantly activist in its approach to Israel's Arab neighbors. Mapam opposed the 1956 Israeli attack on Egypt; Ahdut Avoda gave it its blessing, although both parties gave their full support to the 1967 war. In 1965 Ahdut Avoda once again returned to join Mapai in formation of the Labor Alignment, and later fused with Mapai and Rafi in the new Labor Party, many of whose most prominent leaders formerly belonged to Ahdut Avoda.

LABOR'S DECLINE

The Labor bloc reached its zenith in 1959 when the various parties acquired 68 seats in parliament: Mapai—47, Ahdut Avoda—7, Mapam—9, and Arab lists affiliated with Mapai—5. Because the three major Labor parties were not then united, a coalition government was formed by Mapai. Since 1965 the number of Labor voters has steadily diminished at the expense of the right.

The elections in 1973 were held only two months after the October war which ended in neither victory nor defeat for Israel. But the Labor government then led by Prime Minister Golda Meir was held accountable for the large number of Israeli casualties, the diplomatic setback, and the nearly ruinous costs of the war. An impartial investigation commission exculpated the country's political leaders, but several high ranking army officers were blamed. Dissatisfied with these results, public opinion forced major changes in the government, including the resignation of Golda Meir, Defense Minister Moshe Dayan, and Foreign Minister Abba Eban. In April 1974 a new government was headed by Itzhak Rabin, the country's first sabra, or native born prime minister. Rabin, a former chief of staff and hero of the 1967 war, was not involved in the 1973 disaster because he was then serving as Israel's ambassador to the United States. After Rabin became prime minister, many of the old Mapai leaders retired or withdrew from government. His government was in effect a triumvirate in which he, Defense Minister Shimon Peres, formerly of Rafi, and Foreign Minister Yigal Allon of Ahdut Avoda shared power.

Gradually the old idealism of the Labor movement was dissipated as the party attempted to become all things to all voters. As its urban base expanded, less emphasis was placed on the mystique of the land. Demands of powerful labor unions had to be balanced against those of middle class voters whom the party wanted to attract. It had to be cautious not to offend orthodox Jews by too secular an emphasis lest it lose the religious vote. It was ambivalent about terms of a peace settlement with the Arabs and about policy in the occupied West Bank and Gaza. Fearing to alienate the nationalists, the government waffled on its position regarding new Jewish settlements in the occupied territories and the return of land captured in the 1967 war.

Within the Labor party there were conflicting views on most of the significant issues facing the country: Shimon Peres took the position that all land in Palestine should be open to Jewish settlement and opposed establishment of an Arab state in the West Bank. He was regarded as a technocrat on social and economic issues, not overly sympathetic to demands of the labor unions. On the other hand, Allon was perceived as a "dove" who was more willing to compromise with the Arabs. He accused Peres of "lacking labor values" when it came to domestic issues. Rabin's position seemed unclear, somewhere between his two colleagues in the triumvirate.

By 1977 rapidly escalating defense costs created an inflation of over 30 percent, the beginning of unemployment, and oppressive taxes. Government indecision on these vital issues occurred against a background of spreading corruption involving the highest officials. Rabin had to withdraw appointment of his designee for Director of the Bank of Israel and a Labor cabinet minister committed suicide when faced with charges of misuse of funds. Finally in 1977 Rabin and his wife were charged with failure to declare ownership of bank accounts in the United States, a serious financial misdemeanor, and he temporarily withdrew from the prime ministry.

The convergence of all these mishaps and Israel's increasingly serious economic and political situation led to the downfall of the Labor Alignment in the 1977 election. Because of the steady declining trend, many had forecast a loss of votes for Labor, but few had been able to predict the size of its defeat. For the first time Labor was not the winner. It lost 19 of its 54 Knesset seats, mostly to the new DMC. The election results were less a victory for the opposition Likud which increased its Knesset representation by four, than a major defeat for Labor which had to surrender its thirty-year control.

A NEW LIBERAL BLOC

Decline of the Labor Alignment was sharply at the expense of the Democratic Movement for Change established a few months before the 1977 election. Led by Yigal Yadin, former Israeli army general and since 1948 an academician who became noted for his work in archaeology, DMC was a coalition of hawks and doves, zealous and moderate nationalists, conservatives, and liberals. The common theme uniting them was a demand for "change" in the political environment and alteration of the system they believed responsible for the decline of national morale and morality.

The new list soon attracted a wide spectrum of known personalities, from Likud to the Labor Alignment. It absorbed the Free Center Movement which had once been part of the nationalist Herut (Freedom) party, several ex-leaders of the Labor party and Histadrut chiefs who had become disenchanted with the Labor old guard, and many middle-class professionals and intellectuals who had traditionally supported Labor. It too was a coalition of diverse forces and often contradictory political and social perspectives. Yadin's partner in forming the new group was the leader of *Shinui* (Change), an organization formed shortly after the 1973 war to protest the various national ailments.

DMC's platform placed major emphasis on electoral reform, an issue that was not rated in public opinion polls as a high national priority. By replacing the existing system of one national constituency with several electoral districts, DMC hoped to break the power of the traditional leaders and their parties. Election reform, they argued, would bring new blood into government and stimulate new ideas. It also would facilitate formation of a stable two- or three-party system in which leadership would no longer be forced to assemble a coalition of diverse, even conflicting programs.

On other issues, including peace, Israel's policy in the occupied territories, and economic problems, there were few major differences between DMC and Labor.

The election results in 1977 indicated that the voters balloted against Labor rather than for anything in particular. Labor lost one in five of its votes to DMC in the collective settlements, usually considered the mainstay of its support. Many middle-class professionals, professors, and government employees changed their allegiance to DMC during 1977. After the election a major question was, could DMC hold together and continue as a new middle-class party once the mood of protest had passed? With only 15 of the 120 Knesset seats it would be unable to carry out its principal objective, electoral reform. No other party supported the goal of new elections within two years to reconstitute the system.

DMC lived a short life. After joining Begin's new right wing coalition government in 1977, DMC began to fragment into quarreling factions. Finally on the eve of the 1981 election Yigal Yadin disbanded the party and withdrew from politics. Only the small *Shinui* faction remained with two seats in the Tenth Knesset.

THE CENTER-RIGHT

The *Likud* (Unity) bloc became Israel's major political opposition in the 1973 elections, and its largest party when it won 43 Knesset seats in 1977 and 48 in 1981. It too represented a wide spectrum of social and political views and factions. Likud was formed in 1973 as a national movement whose goal was to keep the territorial gains acquired by Israel in the 1967 war. Its followers adamantly opposed surrender of the West Bank or Gaza to Arab control. These areas were considered integral parts of historic Eretz Israel and the patrimony of the Jewish people. While the Likud list included factions that split from the Labor movement, its social and economic program has been antisocialist, favoring free enterprise and an unrestricted economy.

When it was established, Likud was a coalition of Gahal (Herut-Liberal bloc); the Free Center which had split from Herut earlier; the State party, a nationalist remnant of Rafi; and the Land of Israel or Greater Israel Movement. Policies on national security, foreign policy, and Israel's relations with the Arabs were largely determined by Herut and its leader, Menachem Begin. Economic and social policies came from the Liberal party leaders. In the 1977 elections Likud won support from younger voters, those of Oriental

Jewish background, and from blue collar workers despite the party's conservative approach to bread-and-butter issues.

Liberal Party

The Liberal party, formed a few months before the 1961 Knesset elections, represents an amalgamation of two middle-of-the-road Zionist groups: the General Zionists and the Progressives. Being less committed to any specific social ideology, the Liberals might be compared to American political parties. The worldwide General Zionist movement has attracted Western nonsocialist Jews who supported Zionism without any other specific ideological orientation. In the beginning, General Zionism was synonymous with Zionism itself. When different economic and social outlooks began to emerge, those who sought to overcome partisanship adopted the name General Zionists to stress nonpartisan fund raising, political and diplomatic negotiation, and the economic building up of the homeland.

In the wake of the socialist tide that swept over the Yishuv during the mandate, a specific middle-class outlook also began to emerge and, like the socialists, it soon was fragmented into right, left, and center: the Revisionists (later Herut), Progressives, and General Zionists, respectively. The center, or General Zionist party, was closely allied with the conservative Farmers Federation, representing private landholders and the Palestine (later Israel) Manufacturers Association. Relative to Israel's political spectrum, the General Zionists were conservative, though they would be thought liberal by American standards. They opposed state economic controls and demanded curbs on the Histadrut. Paradoxically, the centrists advocated nationalization of basic industries and services, principally as a means of wresting them from the Histadrut, Israel's largest entrepreneur.

On the eve of statehood, a small left-of-center group of liberal Central European Jews (many from Germany) broke away from the General Zionists to join Aliya Hadasha (New Immigrants) in forming the Progressive party. It joined the government coalitions and closely followed Mapai leadership on most issues. The integrity of its leaders and its moderate position on most controversial matters won the Progressives such respect that one of their members was usually appointed a cabinet minister in the Labor coalitions. Generally, the Progressive program was a liberal version of General Zionism, with support for nationalization in preference to party control of the economy, education, and social services.

General Zionism's greatest achievements have been abroad, where it has had far greater influence than in Israel. The most influential Zionist groups outside Israel are affiliated with the World General Zionist Federation and it has included such personalities as Israel's first president, Chaim Weizmann, World Zionist president Nahum Goldman, and former American Supreme Court justice Louis D. Brandeis.

Until recently, the Progressive and General Zionist parties were unable to attract youth or to increase their strength substantially, relying heavily on the small number of private capitalists and on the older generation of Central European Jews who are slowly disappearing from the political scene. In 1965, when the Liberal party joined Herut to form Gahal, several former Progressives refused to go along and formed a small new party, the Independent Liberals.

Herut

Herut, a right-wing offshoot of General Zionism, outgrew the parent organization to become Israel's second largest party between 1955 and 1961, largely because it advocated an activist foreign policy and because of its forceful leadership. The founder of the Revisionists from which Herut grew, Vladimir Jabotinsky, was a romantic figure much attracted by the volatile careers of Garibaldi, Mazzini, and D'Annunzio. A member of the World Zionist executive until 1923, he resigned in protest against Weizmann's "appeasement" of Great Britain. Jabotinsky denied Churchill's right to separate Transjordan from Palestine in the 1922 White Paper and formed the Revisionist party in 1925 to restore the former frontiers. So popular was Jabotinsky's jingoism that his movement became one of the largest in the Zionist Organization. By 1935, it was strong enough to withdraw from the world movement and form its own New Zionist Organization, advocating among other things the transfer to Palestine of all Eastern European Jews within a decade.

During the 1936–1939 Arab revolt, the Revisionists opposed the policies of the Jewish Agency, which recommended Jewish use of force against the Arabs only when the Arabs attacked first. It was the Revisionists who formed the Irgun Zvai Leumi (see above) to wage more aggressive warfare against the Arab nationalist forces. Irgun leaders called a halt to hostilities against Great Britain during World War II, but renewed their terrorism after Allied victory.

Only Abraham Stern and his tiny group of followers within the Irgun refused to halt their attacks on Great Britain, continuing their sabotage even in the midst of the war. Both the Irgun and the Sternists were forced to disband after the Palestine war in 1948 and amalgamate their forces with the Israeli army. Politically, Irgun became Herut and the Sternists became the Fighters party. The latter was too bizarre to become effective and disappeared after electing a single member to the first Knesset. Herut, however, became a powerful political force, capitalizing on Jewish fears of Israel's Arab neighbors. Herut's chauvinism appealed especially to Jewish refugees from Arab countries who had been victims of Arab discrimination, although the leadership continued to be mostly Eastern European. Herut reunited with the General Zionists in view of their agreement on domestic policy, such as fewer government controls over private enterprise and more supervision by the government of Histadrut activities.

When Menachem Begin became leader of the broad Likud coalition, and in 1977, prime minister, he considerably modified Herut's expansive territorial aims. The party's aspiration to unite all of mandatory Palestine and the Hashemite Kingdom of Jordan under Jewish rule was scaled down. Instead Begin spoke of the historic unity of Israel in the West Bank, even hinting that he would make territorial concessions in the Sinai as part of a complete peace settlement. Under Begin's leadership Israel did sign a peace treaty with Egypt in 1979, returning all of Sinai as part of the agreement. However, Begin vowed that territory which was part of historic *Erez Israel* in the West Bank and Gaza would never be returned. His adamant stand on territory became an obstacle to extending the 1979 peace treaty.

Religious Parties

Because Israel's Jewish religious parties are made up of a hard core of some 15 percent of the population, one or more of them have been included in several coalitions. The parent organization, Mizrachi (from *Mercaz Ruhani*, meaning Spiritual Center), became one of the first Zionist political factions in 1902, and a party in 1918. When established, the *raison d'être* for Mizrachi was to support religious, rather than secular, education in Palestine. To divorce Jewish religion and nationalism was to these Orthodox theoreticians a distortion of the true faith. Zionism was rooted in the Jewish religion and was merely fulfillment of the Talmudic injunction to dwell in the Holy Land. Only in their own country could the Jews fully realize their religion. In exile, they would be too subject to the influences of non-Jewish culture.

In 1922, the Hapoel Hamizrachi (Mizrachi Worker) party was formed to offset the growing pressures of secular socialism in the Yishuv. It aspired to create a society based on labor and the law of Moses. Physical work, the party preached, must be revered as an ethical function of man. While Hapoel Hamizrachi was socialist, it differed from the other leftist parties in opposing secularism and attracted many more youths than its nonlabor counterpart. When the two Mizrachi groups fused in 1956 to form the National Religious party, it became one of the three or four strongest political groups and, thereby, an important partner in any balanced coalition.

Two smaller fundamentalist groups developed from the Aguda movement, established during 1911 in Germany. Originally, the Aguda was opposed to any Jewish political activity, including Zionism, and was formed to combat the drift of Jewish youth to secular ideologies. Reunion in the Holy Land would occur, but only if led by a new Messiah, not a political movement like Zionism. Throughout the mandate, Aguda was the only significant group in the country refraining from identification with Knesset Israel and with the world Jewish organizations.

After 1948, the Aguda parties made a complete about face. Not only did they call off their campaign of protest against a Jewish state, they also joined the new government. They are still more insistent than Mizrachi on the supremacy of the Torah (the five books of Moses), insisting that it is adequate as a constitution. Poalei Aguda Israel, the labor wing established in 1922, joined Aguda parties in the Torah Religious Front during some elections. At various times, the four religious groups have cooperated, even forming a United Religious Front during the first Knesset. Later, the religious groups split into separate parties, although they often supported each other in the Knesset, especially on religious matters.

Until 1977 when the DMC became the third largest Knesset group, the religious bloc held the balance of power between Labor and non-Labor parties. With their combined strength of between fifteen to eighteen Knesset seats, they were in a position to either block or assist the various Labor governments in parliament. Most prime ministers considered it more helpful to have the orthodox parties in the government coalition rather than in the opposition. In exchange for their support, they demanded and received control over many aspects of Israeli life and important ministries such as social welfare from which they could extend their influence. By bringing the religious parties into government and compromising on questions of personal status (marriage, divorce, inheritance) internal conflict over religion was avoided. Furthermore, not all orthodox Jews voted for the religious parties. Many supported Labor or Likud. Some estimates were that only half the orthodox Jews voted for religious parties; the other half distributed their votes among secular lists.

The NRP lost half its Knesset seats in 1981 when many of its former voters shifted to a new Oriental Jewish party, Tami (movement for Israel's tradition), established by several politicians of Oriental origin who were dissatisfied with their representation in the major parties—Likud, Labor, NRP. After winning 3 Knesset seats they joined Begin's new coalition government.

FACTIONAL PARTIES

The Labor, Center-Right, and Religious blocs controlled 90 to 110 of the votes in parliament until the DMC appeared in 1977 creating a fourth large bloc. Smaller parties competed for the remaining seats. Usually twice as many parties ran in elections as were voted into the Knesset. To be seated in parliament a party had to receive at least 1 percent of the total votes. Thus in each election there were several lists with less than 1 percent that were not represented despite the system of proportional representation. In 1977 13 of the 22 parties running in the election won places in the ninth Knesset and in 1981, only 10 of 31 parties won seats. Smaller parties served a useful function in expressing views of minority groups, either ethnic, political, or economic.

Several were left of center, advocates of radical social doctrines, greater concessions in peace negotiations, or more emphasis on individual rights of citizens. Before the 1981 election several right wing or nationalist factions were also formed.

Communists

At the far left was the Israeli Communist party, originally established during the 1920s by Russian Jews who broke with Paole Zion Smole because of its "nationalist orientation." Prior to 1948, the Communists concentrated their attacks on anticolonialism, with the hope of winning over Palestine's Arabs. Zionism was called a tool of British imperialism, a counterrevolutionary movement of the Jewish upper bourgeoisie. After fragmenting into dissident factions during the 1920s, the party reformed in 1948, bringing together a Jewish segment and part of the Arab League of National Liberation. Until the split in 1965 Communist policy unflinchingly supported nearly all Soviet and Arab attacks on Israel and international Zionism. Since there is no indigenous Arab nationalist party in Israel, many Arabs support the Communists as their only alternative. Communist strength has never been more than 5 percent of the total Israel electorate, but it has captured as much as half of the Arab vote (see discussion of Arab community below). During the year of political splits in 1965, the Israel Communist party also fragmented into two groups—the New Communists, Rakah, who were mostly, but not all, Arabs, supporting Arab policy in the Middle East; and the parent Israel Communist party, Maki, led by Israeli Jews who were critical of Soviet policy in the Middle East. In the seventh parliamentary elections the New Communists won three seats, whereas the parent Israel Communist party received only one. By 1973 the largely Jewish sector of the Communist party was absorbed in other groups and no longer appeared on the ballot. However, growing Arab dissatisfaction with their status in Israel and the rise of a new nationalist sentiment among the younger generation of Arab citizens greatly increased the vote for the New Communists in 1977, increasing the party's strength from four to five seats. Unrest among Israeli Arabs was also evident in local elections where Communist candidates won many offices, the most important of which was the mayoralty in Nazareth, Israel's largest Arab city.

The shift to the left of Israeli Arab political sentiment was indicated by the steady decline of support for Arab groups affiliated with the Labor party. In all elections there had been one or more such lists with as many as five seats. In 1977 a United Arab list affiliated with the Labor Alignment obtained only one seat, which it lost in 1981. In the past Arabs had also been elected as members of Mapam or the Alignment. Three Druses were also elected in 1977 on non-Labor lists, two representing the DMC and one Likud. In 1981 five Arabs were elected, two in the Labor Alignment, two in Rakah, and one in Likud.

Other than members of the New Communist party, no really independent Arab candidates were elected to parliament. The Israeli military government in Arab-populated areas stymied growth of an indigenous Arab political movement for many years after the 1948 War of Liberation. Until 1977 Labor-affiliated Arab parties usually received the most Arab votes because they were organized along traditional family lines and because Arab voters feared the consequences of not supporting the government. On the other hand villages which supported the Labor lists were often rewarded with new services, jobs, or other government-provided amenities. Arabs chosen for leadership of the Labor-affiliated lists usually represented regional and traditional interest groups headed by wealthy or influential families. They seldom took independent positions, following the Labor party leadership in the Knesset on most questions.

As a result of the numerous splits, reunions, and factionalization of Israeli politics, many small political groups in the Knesset were offshoots of larger parent parties. Six such factions were represented in the ninth Knesset chosen during 1977. They included the Independent Liberals (IL), the last remnant of Liberal party members who refused to join Gahal. When it had four or five Knesset members the IL had been a useful member of the Labor coalition, but in 1977 when it declined to one seat it was no longer eligible for cabinet status.

Shelli, whose Hebrew letters represented the double party slogan, "Peace for Israel," and "Equality in Israel," obtained two seats in 1977. It was led by a former secretary general of the Labor party who disagreed with Labor's peace platform. It also included several splinters of the former Jewish Communist party, Mapam, independent socialists and peace advocates, and part of the Israel Black Panthers, a group formed in 1968 to support the demands of Oriental Jews.

Two other Knesset lists headed by colorful personalities also won seats. Shalomzion headed by ex-general Ariel Sharon was close to Likud in its ideology. Indeed, Sharon had been a principal founder of Likud but broke with it because of personality clashes. After the 1977 election, he returned to Likud. Flatto-Sharon was a one-person list headed by a man wanted for extortion in France. Many observers asserted that he ran for the Knesset to escape extradition. With the shift in votes to the two large parties, Likud and Labor, in 1981, the number of small parties declined when six of the tiny factions represented in the ninth Knesset lost their seats.

GOVERNMENT BY COALITION

The first Knesset or single-chamber parliament was intended as a constitutional assembly, but no written constitution could be agreed upon.

Ben Gurion opposed adoption of a permanent constitution until the country had experimented with various forms of administration and a general political trend had emerged. Since the country was in such flux, constitutional principles adopted today, he argued, might soon be outmoded.

Instead of a permanent written constitution, a Transition Law, called by some the "small constitution," was passed by the Knesset and became the legal basis of government operations. A republican form of government was adopted, combining the features of a multiparty system similar to that in the French Fourth Republic, with a parliamentary system in which the executive branch is strongest. The prime minister became the dominant figure of government because of Ben Gurion's forceful personality, while the presidency faded into the background, the ailing Dr. Weizmann being physically incapable of playing an active role. The Knesset, which approves all legislation, controls finance, and can remove the prime minister by a simple majority, is in theory the supreme political factor. But because of Israel's multiparty politics, parliamentary influence and prestige has been considerably weakened.

The operative fact in Israeli politics is that none of the various parties has had a majority in parliament. Between 1949 and 1965 Mapai, then Israel's largest party, usually commanded a little over one-third of the votes. Its nearest competitor and the principal opposition group, the Freedom-Liberal Bloc, was able to win just over a fifth of the vote. Since no political party was able to win a majority, all governments were coalitions with the Mapai wing of the labor movement forming the basis of all cabinets. Until his retirement Ben Gurion, who dominated Mapai, exercised great influence, even during his temporary retirement from the post of prime minister in 1954–1955.

The Mapai core of the labor movement formed coalition governments, with parties ranging from the Marxist left (Mapam) to right-wing religious fundamentalists. Consequently most governments have usually had a strong center orientation, veering at times to the left and at times to the right. Mapai-labor governments followed a policy of moderate welfare statism resembling somewhat the socialist governments of Great Britain, Belgium, or France whereas Begin's Likud-led coalitions have resembled more the free enterprise conservative regimes of Western Europe.

Because of the narrow base of the labor-dominated governments, cabinet coalitions usually required one or more of the religious parties, and on occasion center parties such as the Liberals. The Liberals and the religious groups acted as a check on more radical socialist programs demanded by Marxists within the Labor party. Although the religious parties commanded little more than 15 percent of the vote, the necessity of including them within the cabinet has required acceptance by the coalition of religious restrictions ordered by the Orthodox Jewish rabbinate. For example, international air traffic and commerce through Israel's ports are banned on the Sabbath; there was a ban on public transport between the major cities of Israel on Saturday; and marriage, divorce, and other personal-status matters are under the control of the religious hierarchy rather than the civil courts. Cabinet crises have been caused by splits in the government between the religious parties and the labor groups over issues such as religious education in public schools, military service for women, and the legal definition of a Jew. However, major issues of national security, foreign policy, and domestic affairs were determined by the Mapai group within the Labor party until 1973, and by Ben Gurion when he was prime minister.

One consequence of coalition government is the subsequent apportionment of the government's administrative apparatus among the various political parties in the coalition. On occasion, the prime minister has even split a department into two or more ministries to create added cabinet posts needed to reward coalition partners. Ministries that have been transferred from one party to another have experienced considerable changes in administrative practices as well as in top personnel, changes in techniques and in ideological emphasis. During Israel's first years, when Orthodox members of the coalition controlled the Social Welfare Ministry, they established a pattern of administration based on Eastern European charity concepts rather than on modern social work techniques. Later, when the Orthodox lost the post, more modern policy was adopted. At the same time, there was great consistency in the policies of the vital Ministries of Defense, Foreign Affairs, and Finance, which Labor refused to surrender to any other group.

Before the civil service was modernized by a series of laws introduced between 1949 and 1959, party allegiance was the most important factor in the selection of new officials. Since new civil service legislation was adopted only gradually, many less qualified and competent officials became ensconced in important positions. Government personnel was recruited in the meantime from a variety of sources. Jews who were ex-mandatory officials were usually relegated to technical and professional posts, rather than placed in policy positions, because they were often suspected of having too close ties with the British. Personal relationships of former officials in the quasi government, the army, and the Haganah underground brought many of these men into senior posts, regardless of their qualifications. By 1955, still only 17 percent of the civil servants were Israeli born, and 40 percent had arrived after the state was created in 1948.

In May 1967, on the eve of the Six-Day War with Egypt, Jordan, and Syria, a wall-to-wall coalition government was formed including all political parties except the Communists, the Arab parties, and other small factions representing fewer than a sixth of the 120 Knesset seats. The cabinet included Gahal and its leader, Menachem Begin, for the first time in the country's history. Since questions of national security, foreign policy, and Israel's relations with Arabs in the areas occupied during the war dominated political life, there was relatively little disagreement within the "National Unity" coalition. The new government was a wide-ranging combination of Marxian socialists, right-wing nationalists, and Orthodox Jewish rabbis, as well as middle-of-the-road liberals and moderate socialists. Because of the war, bread-and-butter domestic issues were of little importance in the campaign for the seventh Knesset and in the policies of the newly formed wall-to-wall coalition government created after the 1969 elections.

The national coalition government lasted three years, until the cease-fire agreement of July 1970. Through the initiative of the United States, supported by Russia, the governments of Israel, the UAR, and Jordan agreed to halt fighting for a ninety-day period during which efforts would be renewed to end the conflict by diplomacy. Begin opposed Israel's acceptance of the cease-fire as a danger to the country's security, and withdrew from the government in order to contest its policies. After taking over the government in 1977 with only 33.4 percent of the votes, Begin's Likud Bloc was also forced into rule by coalition, although its association with the religious parties was far more congenial than had been the Labor-religious coalitions between 1948 and 1977.

ISRAEL—A WESTERN TRANSPLANT

Since the state was created in 1948, Israeli society has been in constant flux. Population figures and the ratios among national origins are constantly changing at a rapid pace, perhaps more than in most other modern nations. Changes in Israeli society within a single year often outpace those that previously took a decade to accomplish. During the first three years, nearly as many immigrants poured into Israel as its total Jewish population on the day the state was founded. The first waves of immigration that came in after statehood emptied the European Displaced Persons camps and enlarged the country's European majority. After 1951, the rate of Western immigration declined, and an influx of non-Europeans began.

The earlier immigrants, who came during the mandatory era from Russia, Poland, and Germany, had brought with them Western political institutions, economic organization, customs, mores, and attitudes. Today they still dominate government, industry, commerce, and cultural, intellectual, and social life. The prime minister, most cabinet ministers, the majority of Knesset members, many senior officials, and the greater part of middle- and lower-echelon officials are European Jews. Only in the army is there a relatively high percentage of native-born leadership, and even most of these were the children of Europeans.

Despite increasing numbers of Israelis who have become wealthy, social and economic differences between the upper and lower strata of society were not great in the early years. The highest paid government officials, the president, a general, or a director of a ministry, received a basic salary only about three to four times that of the lowest clerk, army private, or truck driver. Social status had little to do with income. Until the 1960s, the most influential Israelis lived and worked as farm laborers in agricultural cooperatives. Leadership of Israel's strongest political party, Mapai, for example, came from rural cooperatives and collectives.

By the late 1960s, especially after the 1967 war, the country experienced major economic and social changes. An economic and social gap widened between Jews from Asia-Africa (Orientals) and those from Europe-America (Ashkenazi). In the era of national prosperity between 1967 and 1973, a new crop of millionaires appeared whose social position and international contacts gave them political influence, even in the Labor movement. Foreign financial interests and multinational corporations invested heavily in Israel. The massive inflow of capital created a new elite parallel to the old establishment. Alongside the Labor establishment, the Histadrut, the Jewish Agency, and the collective settlements, prosperous "captains of industry" acquired wide influence and were involved in decision making.

> The new Zionist elite was in the upper economic brackets or in an equivalent managerial rank. Pioneering had moved from the land to industry, defense, and finance. In the past, the Zionist elite had often been a largely bureaucratic body without real connections with the masses; but in the years after the June war, the new Zionist elite was almost totally cut off from the mass of Israelis by a difference in outlook and wealth, by altogether different social aspirations and interests, and by an altogether different assessment of Israel's role in the life of the Jew. In place of the balanced society of classical Zionism came the concept of the efficient state derived from models which owed more of their concepts to the modern supermarket and merchant bankers than to the ideologies of Herzl and Weizmann.[3]

The bubble of prosperity broke after the 1973 war. Israel's own special problems caused by its huge war expenses converged with the world recession. Inflation was more intensified in Israel reaching over 130 percent by 1980, strikes were widespread, and corruption reached into the highest echelons of government. These problems rose to the surface against the background of other deeply rooted and continuing dilemmas such as the Oriental Jews and the Arab minority.

The Oriental Majority
After 1950, Israel's planners turned to non-Western sources of Jewish immigration. The principal sources of the new immigration were the Jewish minorities in the surrounding Arab world. These Eastern, or Oriental, immigrants, often called Sephardi (because of the Spanish origin of many),

have included Jews from Morocco, Tunisia, Libya, Algeria, Egypt, Yemen, Syria, Iraq, Iran, Turkey, and the Balkans. When Israel was established, they constituted only 11 percent of the Jewish population. By 1960, through this immigration, they had become the majority, creating in fact two separate Jewish communities. Oriental Jews differed radically from their Western coreligionists. Even physically, the Orientals resembled the populations among whom they had lived for generations. Arabic was the native tongue of most and their customs, practices, and attitudes toward life were those of the East, not the West.

The Arab Jews, as they were often derisively called by the European Jews, were unprepared for life in a dynamic Western state, not only for the extraordinary but even for the day-to-day demands that a modern nation makes upon its citizens. Concepts of loyalty and responsibility often did not transcend the immediate family. Oriental suspicion of government and all its ramifications was great. There was resistance to taxation, rationing, and similar controls. More often than not, the Orientals became a public responsibility rather than a responsible public.

Because of their lack of education and experience, few Orientals received responsible government posts. A large number continued to live in slums while the living conditions of their Western coreligionists were constantly improving. The Orientals were at the bottom of the wage scale, constituting the largest groups seeking relief. Only a small number were registered in the leading universities. The government has made special efforts to improve the conditions of these underprivileged citizens. At first large-scale and rapid integration aimed at destroying Oriental cultural patterns by replacing them with modern ones. Orientals were given European food, clothing, houses, sent to European-type schools, and taught European ways of daily life. But government anthropologists realized that the Orientals were only learning the superficial aspects of Western life without really grasping the reasons for learning these new ways. They understood well the way of life from which they had come, but while learning new Western ways, they did not really understand them. Too often the result was a cultural and emotional vacuum ending in demoralization. Intellectuals among the Orientals charged that the European-dominated elite was attempting to superimpose Western culture and ways of life upon the Jews from Asia and Africa, without taking into consideration contributions that their different life styles and outlook could contribute to Israel's development, especially to its absorption in the Middle East.

Oriental Jewish disenchantment with the establishment was a major factor in the defeat of Labor in the 1977 and 1981 elections when many shifted their votes to Likud. After Ben Gurion disappeared from the political scene, he was increasingly replaced by Begin as father figure and fiery-tongued hero of the Orientals. Between 1969 and 1981 the percentage of Oriental Jewish votes for Labor declined from 51 to 25 percent, with an increase from 32 to 60 percent for Likud. As the Orientals became more politically conscious and integrated into Israeli society, their demands on the establishment, which they perceived as European and Labor, increased; with frustration of their demands, they turned against the European establishment. Despite frustrations in achieving more rapid equality with the Ashkenazis and their perceptions of delayed achievement in upward economic and social mobility, larger numbers of Orientals were integrated into the political leadership of all groups. Yitzhak Navon, a native of Jerusalem, became the first Oriental President in 1978; many Jews from Asia-Africa became mayors and leaders of local governments and the Histadrut; and in the army the number of Sephardi generals increased. Both electoral politics and the upward thrust of their ambitions seemed to be changing the political status of the country's non-European Jewish communities by the 1980s.

The Arab Minority

Only 20 percent of the 850,000 Arabs who once lived in the parts of Palestine held by Israel remained after the first Palestine war. During that struggle, their economic and political organization was destroyed and most of their towns, villages, farms, and property were demolished or taken over by Israeli military forces. Palestine Arab intellectual, political, and religious leadership fled; nearly all remaining symbols of communal identity were now in what had become enemy territory. The Arab remnant in Israel was left in confusion and uncertainty.

Although according to the U.N. partition plan for Palestine, Arabs were to have comprised nearly half the population, no specific plans, but only general principles of equal treatment, had been established by Israel's leaders for dealing with them. The U.N. resolution and Israel's declaration of independence and first laws guaranteed Arab citizenship rights. But by the end of May 1948, these rights had been a victim of the war. Jewish authorities regarded the Arab minority problem primarily as one of security, and most areas where Arabs lived were placed under military controls. During Israel's first years of independence, Arabs, while citizens with full legal equality, were subjected to military-government controls. They were required to obtain passes for travel within and beyond certain points and subjected to army searches and seizures, arbitrary arrest without due legal process, expulsion from the country, and banishment to other villages in Israel. As security conditions improved and evidence grew that Israeli Arabs were not disloyal, more and more Jews pressed, first for relaxation, then for total abolition, of military restrictions. Only Mapai, under the watchful eye of Ben Gurion in his capacity as defense minister, urged continued military government. Public pressure did force the government gradually to modify its restrictions until they were abolished in 1966.

More pressing in the long run than the bothersome security restrictions have been problems of social integration. While Israeli Arabs vote, sit in the Knesset, serve in lower government offices, and prosper materially more than ever before, they, like the Oriental Jews, are an Eastern people finding it difficult to adjust to a modern Western society, a society that has suddenly been superimposed upon their Middle Eastern way of life. Many Arab villagers still wear the traditional headcloth and flowing gowns, still live in modest one-room houses, and still follow the tempo of life set by the agricultural seasons. While superficially life seems the same, however, the tremors caused by Israel's egalitarian socialist society have shaken the foundations of the Arab patriarchal structure, and it has begun to disintegrate. Leadership in the Israeli Arab community is no longer an exclusive prerogative of a relatively small landowning group. By 1950, over 65 percent of the approximately 15,000 Israeli Arab farms were fully owner operated, over 30 percent partly owned and partly rented, and less than 5 percent operated on totally rented land. Nearly 80 percent of the 250,000 acres of Arab farm land was owner operated.

The increased value and greater income represented by Arab produce in Israel's agricultural economy made Arab villages in Israel prosper as never before. Improved living standards are evident in new school buildings, roads, running water, radios, and clothing. Mechanization, irrigation, and new agricultural techniques have been brought to the rural sector by the Israeli Agricultural Ministry, substantially increasing productivity and partially compensating for government confiscation of Arab lands.

The dichotomous position of the minority—resulting, on the one hand, from the army-imposed security restrictions and, on the other, from the improvement in village living standards—intensified their conflict of emotions. As the minority acquire increasing knowledge of Westernized ways of life, unrest and discontent with second-class citizenship inevitably grow.

Israeli Arabs and the Six-Day War
The disastrous defeat in June 1967 had a serious impact on Arab-Jewish relationships in Israel. Surveys among Israeli Arabs after the war indicated great intensification of nationalist feelings and militant attitudes against Israel. According to one survey: "A feeling of uncertainty and marginality is... one of the 'Leitmotifs' in the identity of the Israeli Arab, or in the phrasing of one... respondent[s]: 'I sometimes think that we are neither real Arabs nor real Israelis because the Arab countries they call us *traitors* and in Israel—*spies*.'"[4] After the June defeat there was a startling increase in the number of Israeli Arab school children who thought it would be necessary to wage a fourth war against Israel, despite defeat in the previous three. Also after the war the numbers of Israeli Arab youth arrested for collaborating with Palestine Arab commando and terrorist organizations reached a figure within

two years that exceeded the number arrested during two previous decades. After the 1973 war this trend accelerated as larger numbers of Israeli Arabs supported the Communist party and the PLO. Election of Communists to posts in Arab villages, especially in Nazareth, demonstrated this trend dramatically.

Even if Israel's position in the Middle East becomes secure and the Arab minority attains economic and political equality, the more basic culture and ethnic chasm will still separate Western Jews and Arabs. It remains a question whether Israel's Arabs will ever identify with those intangible aspects of Israeli nationalism that are so much a part of an exclusively Jewish milieu. Similarly, will the Jewish state, established as a refuge for Jews, ever have meaning to or command the full loyalty of an Israeli Arab? The crux of the matter is whether the Jewish heritage and culture, developed through centuries of life in Eastern Europe, can ever become an Arab heritage.

Though there is little love lost between Israeli Arabs and Oriental Jews, they have many problems in common. Both regard themselves as second-class citizens excluded from positions of power and influence. The degree to which Western patterns of life remain dominant will depend on the outcome of the race between Oriental Jewish immigration and the speed with which Arabs and Oriental Jews are really integrated into the mainstream of Israeli life. By 1977 intermarriage was doing little to hasten the process. Between Jews and Arabs, instances were few; between Western and Oriental Jews, they were increasing, but still also not common.

JEWS AND ZIONISM

The establishment of Israel has considerably altered the basis of the relationship between the Yishuv and world Jewry. Until 1948, Zionism represented, in the words of Theodor Herzl, "the Jewish people on the way." The Yishuv in Palestine and the Zionists abroad were copartners in the endeavor to create a Jewish state. Once that state arrived, the relationship between it and world Jewry, which was largely responsible for its existence, became unclear. In particular, the new legal situation has made the relationship ambiguous, and since 1948, it has been the subject of various interpretations.

Former Prime Minister Ben Gurion, representing classic Zionist ideology, maintained that world Jewry constitutes a people or nation bound in common loyalty to Israel. The state "was not established for its citizens alone. It is the foremost bulwark for the survival of the Jewish people in our generation." Israel, according to this view, is important because only within its borders can an individual live a full Jewish life.

In Israel there are not two spheres, a special Jewish one for matters of tradition and religion and a general human sphere covering economic life, science, labor, and cultural affairs.

Here everybody is both Jewish and universal: the soil we walk upon, the trees whose fruit we eat, the roads on which we travel, the houses we live in, the factories where we work, the schools where our children are educated, the army in which they are trained, the ships we sail in and the planes in which we fly, the language we speak and the air we breathe, the landscape we see and the vegetation that surrounds us—all of it is Jewish.

[The Jew in the diaspora, on the other hand, is] subordinate to a non-Jewish authority in all his material and political life.

As a citizen and a resident he depends on the resources of another people; he is surrounded by a non-Jewish environment.... Specifically Jewish life, insofar as it exists, is compressed into a small corner, without roots in the reality surrounding it.... An all pervasive duality is created in the lives of those Jews who try to maintain their Jewishness because of the tremendous gulf between the Jewish sphere and the civic one.[5]

Most American Zionists differ, maintaining that all Jews need not be gathered within the walls of Israel, that they can continue to live full Jewish lives in their own native lands, and that their ties to Israel are cultural and historic, based on a common peoplehood, and not of a political nature.

The relationship between Israel and the world Zionist movement was legally defined by the Knesset in the 1952 World Zionist Organization-Jewish Agency for Palestine Law, and agreed to in a covenant signed between the Israeli government and that organization in 1954. While the state obviously can make only a moral claim to world Jewish political backing, it has contracted with the Zionist movement to receive other services, such as fiscal and informational support.

Under the existing arrangement, Jews in other countries, including non-Zionist supporters of Israel, continue their responsibility for assisting immigration and building up the nation through the Jewish Agency and its subsidiary organizations, such as the American United Jewish Appeal. New immigrants, who require assistance, are theoretically a world Jewish responsibility, not Israel's alone. Only after they have been more or less integrated into the state do these newcomers become its exclusive obligation. Indeed, had it not been for the massive financial assistance received from world Jewry during Israel's first years, the high immigration rate achieved would never have been possible.

The Law of Return and other nationality legislation, conferring automatic citizenship upon any Jew who desires it, imply a special relationship between Israel and world Jewry by giving preferential rights to Jews everywhere. The reparations agreement between the West German Federal Republic and the Israeli government implicitly recognized Israel as the moral and, to some extent, legal inheritor of European Jewry by paying some 750 million dollars to the Jewish state in partial compensation for Nazi crimes against the Jewish people.

The war in June 1967 had a traumatic effect on Jewish communities throughout the world. On the eve of the war many Jews believed that Israel was in dire peril and faced the danger of extinction. In Western countries the fate of Israel was linked by many Jewish communal leaders with relationships between Jews and Christians. Many maintained that defeat of Israel by the Arab nations would result in another massacre equal in proportions to the German liquidation of European Jewish communities during World War II. This supposed peril followed by victory did much to rally a strong Jewish consciousness in most Western countries and to make support for the state of Israel a touchstone of sympathy for the Jewish people. There were even a number of prominent religious leaders who viewed Israel's victory as a "miracle" and one of the highlights in the history of the Jewish people.

Israel's "miraculous" victory also seemed to affect the pattern of immigration. During the fifteen years prior to the war the majority of immigrants had come from Asia and Africa. In the three years after June 1967 the immigration patterns changed with most new settlers coming from the West. American Jews were the largest group of immigrants totaling over 6000 in 1970—a great increase over the 600 to 1200 a year maximum before the war. While this was but a tiny fraction of the 5,870,000 American Jews, it was an increase from 1 to 20 percent of Jewish immigrants. The new Western immigrants contributed to the already rapid development of Israel's techno-logical and scientific resources which made it possible for the country to outdistance its Arab neighbors in the rate of military, industrial, and other development.

After the 1973 war there was a spurt of renewed Jewish immigration from the Soviet Union reaching 50,000 a year. But the number quickly declined for two reasons. The Russian government made it increasingly difficult for emigrants to depart, especially those with high technical and professional skills. And many Russian Jews who reached Israel found living conditions there difficult, especially after the economic recession following the 1973 war. By 1977 nearly half the approximately 30,000 Jews leaving the Soviet Union for Israel went to other countries before reaching the promised land.

Contributions, loans, and political influence of Western Jewry in their home countries made possible the large allocation of Israeli resources to national security. But after the 1973 war when Israel had to compete in its military expenditures with Arab oil money, the relative importance of private assistance greatly declined. Military expenditures reaching 40 percent of government expenditure and 30 percent of GNP could only be financed by the United States government. In the years immediately after the war, Israel became the largest recipient of American government assistance. This assistance, in the billions of dollars, at times comprised up to a third of all American annual foreign aid.

By the 1970s, economic conditions, political restiveness, and the continued Arab pressure on Israel also caused a substantial emigration *from* Israel. Many Zionists were concerned that the number of Jews leaving was nearly as great as immigration into the country in some years. Emigration was a serious problem, less because of the number of people leaving than because of their quality. A high proportion of the Jewish *yordim* (descenders in contrast to olim—those going to Israel) were physicians, engineers, professors, scientists, and others with valuable technical skills. By 1977 there were estimates of 300,000 Israeli *yordim* in the United States alone.

ISRAEL AND THE ARAB WORLD

The ambiguities of Israel's relationships with world Jewry have contributed in no small measure to the difficulties of its integration into the Middle East. Israel's Arab neighbors do not view it as a tiny nation of 8000 square miles and some three or four million inhabitants. Theirs is the traditional Zionist image of the Jewish state, embracing the loyalty and full political, material, and moral support of world Jewry. In Arab eyes, Israel is a powerful colossus, influential in the hierarchies of the world's great powers. Thus World Zionism, with its invaluable assistance to Israel, is a specter constantly raised by the Arabs in answer to Israeli descriptions of their apparent physical limitations. To the Arabs, World Zionism seems as menacing a threat as communism.

The repeated assertions of responsible Zionist leaders that Israel has no territorial demands beyond its present borders have done little to assuage Arab mistrust. The vigorous internal development and aggressive foreign policies of the new state, the unrealized aspiration of some Israelis to double, triple, or even multiply by five the present population, and the growth of Zionist ambitions from a cultural homeland to political statehood are cited by Arabs as evidence that Jewish claims to more than its present territory have not really been abandoned, merely suspended.

The military defeat of Arab armies in 1948 was a severe blow to Arab national pride and greatly intensified Arab fears and resentment of Israel. To most Arab Middle Easterners, Israel is the epitome of Western imperialism. To the most extreme, it is a blot on the map of the Arab East that must be removed. In the large influx of Europeans and creation of a Western state on the ruins of Arab Palestine, they see parallels to Boer policy in South Africa toward the country's black majority. Proof of Israel's imperialism was, they say, its collusion with France and Great Britain in the attack on Egypt during 1956.

With the increased number of Arab states in the United Nations and the concentration of oil wealth in several, Arab international influence, especially in the Third World, greatly increased to Israel's disadvantage. In 1973 nearly all African nations, including several with which Israel had cordial relations, broke their diplomatic ties. Arab efforts to successfully link it with racist regimes in Rhodesia and South Africa isolated Israel, separating it even more from the Third World. A series of United Nations resolutions were passed condemning Israel, culminating in one which linked it with the white racist regimes in Africa and condemning Zionism as a "racist" ideology.

The presence of Palestine Arab refugees in the surrounding Middle Eastern countries was also a constant visible reminder of the Israeli danger and of the ignominious defeat in the first three Palestine wars. The Arabs continually point out that it was the loss by the refugees of their fields, orchards, vineyards, homes, shops, factories, and businesses that facilitated the incipient rapid growth of Israel. Of the first 370 Jewish settlements established after 1948, 350 were on former Arab property. Whole Arab cities—such as Jaffa, Acre, Lydda, Ramle, Baysan, and Majdal—388 towns and villages, and large parts of others, containing nearly a quarter of all buildings standing in Israel during 1948, were abandoned by the refugees. Ten thousand shops, businesses, and stores were left in Jewish hands, as well as some 30,000 acres of citrus groves that supplied at least a quarter of the new state's foreign-currency earnings. This acquisition of Palestine Arab property greatly helped to make the Jewish state economically viable.

Israeli fears of the Arab world are no less intense, although their military victories have given them far more self-confidence. To justify their anxiety about Arab threats, the Israelis have only to quote the daily broadcasts from Tripoli, Damascus, or Baghdad with their unceasing flow of venomous warnings that the Palestinian Arabs will be avenged.

The blockade of the Suez Canal to Israeli ships, the Arab League boycott of Israeli goods, and refusals to negotiate peace on the basis of the *status quo* seemed clear indication to the average Israeli that the Arabs intended to undermine his country. Arab demands for surrender of all territory seized by Israel in 1967 and insistence on the acceptance of U.N. resolutions concerning refugee repatriation were considered mere window dressing for obstinate refusal to negotiate.

Arab-Israel relations were dealt their most severe blow by the June 1967 war resulting from a series of miscalculations by both Arabs and Israelis. In reality it was a sudden escalation of the hostilities that had continued through the previous two decades. Constant border incidents between Israel and its Arab neighbors led to threats and acts of retaliation by Israel with subsequent large-scale military buildups and full mobilization of forces on both sides of the frontiers. After Egypt's President Nasser declared a blockade of the strategic Tiran Straits and ordered withdrawal of U.N. forces from Egyptian territory, Israelis were convinced that he intended to attack them. Early on June 5 Israel launched a preventive air strike against Egypt, Jordan, Syria, and Iraq, destroying most of their air forces. This was followed by six days of battle between large armies along all the frontiers, by defeat of the Arab armies, and by Israel's invasion and occupation of the Egyptian-held Gaza strip and Sinai peninsula, the West Bank of the Hashemite Kingdom, and the Golan Heights of Syria. Israel refused to withdraw from the occupied territory without direct negotiation of a full-scale peace settlement with the Arab states. The latter accused Israel of aggression and refused to negotiate, to recognize Israel, or to conclude peace treaties until late in 1970 when Egypt offered to terminate the war on equitable terms.

Not only did the war create large numbers of new refugees but it inflamed Arab nationalist passions more than ever before. On the one hand, the Arab states were determined to recoup their losses; on the other, Israel was determined to prevent the Arab states from ever again threatening its destruction.

Israel's strategic position was greatly strengthened, and for all practical purposes it became the most powerful Middle Eastern state. The paradox in this situation was that while Arab capacity to destroy Israel was less than it had ever been, Arab determination to wipe out the Jewish state was greater than ever before.

Israel's vulnerability was demonstrated in October 1973 when Egypt and Syria staged a surprise attack, at first driving Israeli forces back into Sinai and the Golan Heights. After the initial onslaught, Israel regained the initiative, establishing defensive positions and staging counterattacks deep into Arab territory. The 3,000 lives and billions of dollars in military equipment expended in the war were too great a loss for Israel to sustain without help from abroad. Without massive American aid to Israel and Russian assistance to the Arabs, neither side would have been able to continue the battle throughout October.

Israelis neither acclaimed the war as a victory, nor did they acknowledge defeat. The Arabs, however, regarded the war as their first victory over Israel. The "Crossing" of the Suez Canal by Egyptian troops and their ability to remain on the east bank of the canal, became an event of historical significance from the Arab perspective. Despite the monumental costs of the war to Egypt and Syria, financed by Saudi Arabia and Kuwait, the Arab "victory" helped redress the political balance in their favor. Through the disengagement agreements negotiated between Israel and Syria and Egypt with American assistance after the war, both Arab countries succeeded in regaining small, but psychologically significant areas which they lost in 1967. By 1977 it was clear that many Arab attitudes toward Israel had changed. In Egypt especially there was indication of willingness to seek a compromise peace settlement. While Israel was disliked and feared as much as ever, many

Arab leaders had come to accept the reality of Israel's existence and the need to coexist with the Jewish State. The mood for compromise was strongest in those Arab states immediately adjoining Israel, the "confrontation states"— Egypt, Syria, Jordan—which had borne the brunt of battle.

Changing Arab attitudes were dramatically illustrated by Egyptian President Anwar Sadat's surprise visit to Israel in 1977, where he addressed the Knesset and opened a peace dialogue with the country's leaders. After returning to Cairo Sadat continued his peace offensive, inviting Israel and the confrontation states to negotiate in Egypt. However, the most militant states still opposed any compromise. The "rejection front," Libya, Iraq, Algeria, the People's Democratic Republic of South Yemen, and the PLO excoriated Sadat for his efforts, turning down any negotiations with the Jewish state.

After Sadat signed a peace treaty, the first between any Arab state and Israel, in March 1979, Egypt's membership in the Arab League was suspended and the organization moved its headquarters from Cairo to Tunis. Egypt was also banned from participation in other inter-Arab and pan-Islamic meetings as punishment for breaking the barriers to peace with Israel. As a result of the treaty, Egypt recovered its territory in Sinai, with total evacuation from the peninsula by Israel during 1982. Progress was made in normalizing relations between the two countries, including exchange of ambassadors; opening the borders to tourism, trade, and commerce; and the first authorized passage of Israeli ships through the Suez Canal.

After Sadat's assassination in 1981 and the succession of President Mubarak, relations between Egypt and the nonrejectionist Arab states such as Saudi Arabia and Jordan, began to improve; but with Israel's invasion of Lebanon in 1982, relations between Cairo and Jerusalem deteriorated. After Israel's attack on Beirut and the massacre of refugees in a Palestinian camp by Phalangist militias allied with Israel, Egypt withdrew its ambassador to Israel. It seemed that the peace process would be put in deep freeze until Israel withdrew totally from Lebanon and became more compromising in its negotiations on autonomy for the Palestinian inhabitants of the West Bank and Gaza.

A new development after June 1967 was the rise of a Palestine Arab nationalist movement whose objective was not peace, but total destruction of the Jewish state and of its Zionist manifestations. The movement was formed around several guerrilla or commando organizations which conducted forays into occupied territory and undertook terrorist acts against Israeli civilians. The commando phenomenon only intensified hatred, weakened moderates among both Jews and Arabs, and lessened the possibilities of a peaceful solution.

Initially the official Israeli response to the revised Palestinian national movement was Prime Minister Golda Meir's statement—there are no Palestinians! Within the government, however, there were differing perspectives.

Although no government official was willing to recognize the Palestinian Liberation Organization because of its intractable rejection of the Jewish State, there were some Israelis who conceded that the Palestinians also had national rights. The difficulty was in achieving mutual recognition of the two national movements, both with claims to the same territory. Israel had the upper hand because all of Palestine was under its control. The situation was complicated by the 1977 election results which placed the Likud in power and made Menachem Begin prime minister. His party's forceful rejection of any territorial compromise over territory in Israel-Palestine made the prospects for settlement rather dim, until the Sadat visit.

Not until basic attitudes have changed on both sides of the Arab-Israeli frontier will it be possible to stabilize the relationship between these antagonists. There are indications of change. Several Arab leaders including some in the PLO have accepted the concept of two states, Palestinian Arab and Israeli Jewish as the basis for a solution, demonstrating recognition of Israel's existence. And in Israel a substantial number of Labor Alignment members have been willing to accept Palestinian and Israeli coexistence.

In the meantime, Israel's very existence depends upon close ties with the West. This in itself creates a dilemma. It is Arab hostility that forces Israel to seek ever closer ties with the West and with world Jewry, yet it is this very quest for a broad security base that exacerbates Arab fears of the Jewish state.

NOTES

1.   Chaim Weizmann, *Trial and Error,* London, 1950, pp. 537–538.

2.   Gerda Luft, "The Party that Shapes Policy," *The Jerusalem Post,* July 11, 1955, cited in Marver H. Bernstein, *The Politics of Israel,* Princeton, 1957, p. 61.

3.   Jon Kimche, *There Could Have Been Peace,* Dial Press, New York, 1973, p. 276.

4.   Yochanan Peres, *Some Problems of Educating a National Minority (A Study of Israeli Education for Arabs),* U.S. Dept. of Health, Education and Welfare, Washington, D.C., 1969, p. 14.

5.   From the text of Ben Gurion's speech to the Twenty-Fifth Zionist Congress in Jerusalem, December 28, 1960, reprinted in *The New York Times,* January 8, 1961, pp. 52–53.

12   The Hashemite Kingdom of Jordan

ORIGIN

Prior to its creation after World War I, the concept of a state of Jordan existed in no one's mind. In Ottoman times the territory now known as Jordan was subdivided among various administrative districts. The north was regarded as part of Syria and the south as part of Arabia.

At the war's end, Amir Faisal controlled the area, hoping to include it in his short-lived Arab kingdom established at Damascus in 1919 and 1920 (see chapter 6). After the French drove Faisal from his Syrian throne in 1920, there was no clear-cut authority in the region now known as Jordan, and anarchy prevailed while various Arab chiefs tried to establish their own conflicting regimes, some of them advised by British officers.

In 1920, the San Remo conference assigned the area east of the Jordan River, called Transjordan, to Great Britain as part of the Palestine mandate. When Sir Herbert Samuel, the first high commissioner for Palestine and Transjordan arrived, he set up four autonomous governments or republics in Transjordan, each based on tribal identification and each with a council of notables and a British political adviser. Despite British guidance, these governments quarreled among themselves. In one border dispute between the Moabite and Ammonite republics, their modern English advisers determined the outcome on the basis of ancient Biblical boundaries.

After the collapse of Faisal's Syrian kingdom in 1920, these autonomous Arab republics became the base of operations against France for political exiles from Damascus. Frequent raids and sabotage by the Damascus exiles

The Middle East Today

across the frontier into Syria drew a French threat to invade Transjordan. Since the area was supposedly under British supervision, British embarrassment deepened. When Faisal's brother Abdullah began to organize the vengeful Arab forces in Transjordan against France, further difficulties arose. The Arab National Congress, which had met at Damascus during 1920, had chosen Abdullah for the throne of Iraq. He had been a Hashemite wartime ally and had, furthermore, rallied an effective military force against the Turks during World War I. Not knowing how to cope with Abdullah, Alec Kirkbride, the English head of the Moabite national council, turned to Sir Herbert Samuel for orders and was advised that Abdullah's activities would not create difficulties for Great Britain. Since the young Kirkbride had only 50 policemen to thwart Abdullah's 2000 Bedouin, he welcomed the amir to Transjordan and quietly allowed the Moab government to disappear.

Abdullah, however, was quite serious about his intention to attack the French in Syria. The British were in no mood to go to war against Abdullah, nor did they want France to send troops into Transjordan against him. The dilemma was resolved by a compromise put forward by Colonial Secretary Winston Churchill, Sir Herbert Samuel, and Colonel T.E. Lawrence. If Abdullah would forego his vendetta against France and prevent the country from becoming a hostile base, if he would renounce his claims to the throne of Iraq, and if he would agree that Transjordan should become part of the British Palestine mandate, then an Arab government under Abdullah, with British subsidies and advisers, would be set up, and at some future time it would become independent. The agreement was confirmed in the mandate, which exempted the territories east of the Jordan River from the terms that governed the creation of a future Jewish national home. Had the British not needed to appease Abdullah, Transjordan might have been included within the full terms of the mandate for a Jewish homeland.

No census had ever been taken in Transjordan, but Great Britain reported to the League of Nations Council in 1924 that there were about 200,000 inhabitants of whom some 90 percent were Muslim Arabs. Minorities included about 10,000 Circassians and Chechens and 15,000 Christian Arabs. The Circassians and Chechens are Muslim groups speaking their own distinctive languages. They immigrated into this region from Russia at the invitation of Sultan Abdul Hamid during the late 1870s. More than half of the population was nomadic or seminomadic. While Transjordan's total area was large (34,550 square miles) relative to its population, only a thin strip along the Jordan River—comprising less than 3 percent of the whole—was fertile. Only small amounts of wheat and barley were grown, barely enough to sustain the small population. Amman, the capital and largest town, was an oversized village of a few thousand inhabitants. Roads, schools, police, and other government services hardly existed.

Abdullah, Lawrence, and Churchill had summoned it [Transjordan] into existence and restored it to an eminence it has lost since the great days of its antiquity, when a flow of exotic luxuries passed through the marts of Aqaba, when Jerash had its threatres and its scholars of renown, when the Nabataeans plundered the passing caravans from their rose-red Petra, or when Renoud de Châtillon, in the doomed heyday of the Crusaders, lorded it gorgeously in the castle-city of Kerak.[2]

Transjordan's Government

At first the British interfered little with Abdullah's rule, but he proved unable to cope with the turbulent Syrian exiles who flocked across the border. Not only did the exiles persist in ambushing French troops in clandestine forays, they even subsidized rebel groups inside Syria with funds they received from Abdullah's British-supplied exchequer. Many of Transjordan's officials lined their own pockets, causing H. St. John Philby, the amir's British adviser, to complain that Abdullah and his associates indulged in an orgy of maladministration and that they robbed the Treasury right and left.

After a few years of this extravagance, the British government imposed much stricter financial controls. The amir had no alternative but to comply, since British gold was his principal source of income, the *sine qua non* preventing the collapse of his government. Thus the nationalist exiles from Damascus, who had regarded the British subsidy as booty to be distributed among themselves, were removed, and their key posts were turned over to British administrators. By 1924, Transjordan was governed like a colonial protectorate under a British resident, who made all important decisions. The resident, Colonel C.H.F. Cox, who had been a Palestine district governor, began to overhaul completely the Transjordanian government. Strict economic controls were imposed and a tax system introduced. Because of the scarcity of trained local talent, new departments were staffed by many Arabs schooled in the offices of the Palestine government by British administrators. By 1929, Englishmen filled the posts of judicial and financial advisers, customs director, chief of the lands and survey department, and commander and second in command of the Arab Legion, in addition to various secondary positions.

A major British contribution was reorganization of the archaic Ottoman land system. For the first time, property was surveyed and mapped. The new Department of Lands and Surveys fixed permanent title to parcels of agricultural area, ending its yearly redistribution among the tribes. Land was no longer fragmented into such small fractions that a single owner might cultivate a dozen or more widely scattered plots, but was instead realloted in farms large enough to provide farmers with an incentive to develop the permanent cultivation and improvement of their property.

Abdullah was not particularly grateful for British reforms in government administration. He realized that as more authority was given to Arab officials, the demand for representative government would grow and, consequently, the powers of this patriarchal despotism would suffer. Under his regime, until 1924, there was no distinction between the acts of the amir and those of the government, between the public purse and the Treasury.

British obligations under the League mandate and popular opinion forced the mandatory authorities to create a more representative system. As government operations became more complicated with the introduction of more detailed administrative procedures, the Transjordanian regime became increasingly remote from the people. Abdullah was no longer the benevolent patriarchal Arab prince, accessible to all, but was protected from contact with his subjects by the cabinet, the administration, and the growing corps of officials.

Opposition to Abdullah increased, on the one hand, because he was too autocratic and, on the other, because he was a British puppet. In a partial effort to appease the spirit of nationalism, Abdullah convened an Assembly of Notables in 1926 to draft a constitution. It did not go far enough to suit the demands of those who wanted a representative council in full control of finance, government, and administration. The nationalists insisted that English officials be ousted and all ties with Great Britain, including the subsidy, be cut.

The result was an agreement with Great Britain in 1928 that regulated relations until after World War II. Under this treaty, a British resident, representing the Palestine high commissioner, was to handle all communications with other powers, that is, external policy. Internally, Great Britain was to turn over the legislative and administrative authority entrusted to it in the mandate to the amir, who was to act through a constitutional government. Thus British controls remained over foreign affairs, finance and fiscal policy, and matters affecting foreigners. Ties with the Arab world were acknowledged in a provision authorizing the association of Transjordan with its neighbors for the regulation of customs and similar purposes.

The continuation of British control over a substantial segment of Transjordanian policy offended nationalistic sensibilities. Again the nationalists accused Abdullah of being the British tool, of sacrificing national rights for his own advantage, while the British were charged with appearing to make concessions while actually strengthening their hold on the area. Ignoring the nationalists, British advisers drafted an organic law that became Transjordan's first constitution. The law presented the facade of democracy, but in fact it enabled Abdullah to retain his dominant role over government. He was authorized to appoint and dismiss all six members of the new Executive Council, as well as most other high officials. The amir also was able to exert influence in the twenty-two–member Legislative Council, six of whose members were his Executive Council. The legislature could only discuss and delay laws, and even that power was limited since Abdullah could dismiss parliament at will and rule by martial law.

Three months after Abdullah had promulgated this organic law, a national congress of those who opposed the amir and the British convened in Amman to protest. The congress adopted a national pact proclaiming their country a sovereign, independent, constitutional Arab state and repudiating the mandate and Great Britain. When the nationalists boycotted the first elections in September 1928, Abdullah declared martial law and arrested the congress president and some of its members.

The elections only strengthened the hands of a small oligarchy. During the first decade of independence, some 31 politicians held 155 posts and of these, 15 controlled 96 cabinet offices. Not more than one or two ministers ascended the ladder of power from outside the small group of local landowners, Circassians in league with the palace, and Muslim religious leaders close to the Hashemite family. But even this oligarchy was jealous of Abdullah's great power and his close ties with Great Britain.

Under the impact of this mounting opposition, the British agreed in 1934 to grant the government of Transjordan more authority, in appearance if not in substance. Abdullah was authorized by a new agreement to appoint consular authorities to the neighboring Arab countries, and Transjordanian officials were given more authority over certain financial and customs regulations. Also, Palestinian Arabs in the administration were to be replaced by Transjordanians when possible. But local administrators qualified for government employment were so few that by 1937 more than a third of the 927 non-British officials came from Palestine, Lebanon, Syria, Turkey, Hijaz, Tripolitania, and Egypt. The presence of so many foreigners in the government as well as the continuation of British controls did much to cause local dissatisfaction with Abdullah's government.

THE ARAB LEGION AND BEDOUIN CONTROL

Until well after World War I, brigandage was a chief occupation of the desert nomads east of the Jordan River. The Ottomans had unsuccessfully tried to suppress this continuous plundering, frequently sending expeditions to quell the unruly Bedouin who roamed the area. The Circassian and Chechan Muslim refugees from tsarist Russia were settled near Amman and Jerusalem during the 1870s in the hope of creating some stability in the region. It was believed that their military prowess would deter the Bedouin from attacking their wealthier neighbors. But the Bedouin considered the non-Arabic-speaking interlopers with disdain and cheerfully raided them also. Later, between 1900 and 1908, the sultan laid a railroad from Istanbul through

Damascus, Amman, and Medina, ostensibly as a boon to the pilgrim traffic, but really as a means of wresting the old caravan route along the desert fringe from the Bedouin.

Now Abdullah and the British put their hands to the task of quelling these nomadic tribesmen. The Bedouin were a "charming, violently individualist people, at once squalid and superior. They were bred to the traditions of tribal warfare, and they lived for the raid, the loot, and the glory." Their leaders were "chieftains of medieval temperament and outlook, as sharp as icicles, as predatory as hawks. Left largely unprotected by the Turks, the settled people lay flacid and irresolute at their mercy; and all too often a Bedouin commando would fall upon a settlement at dead of night, seize it, loot it, and be back in the wilderness by morning...."[2]

At first, Captain F.G. Peake organized a small security force in 1920 to keep order in Amman and along the road to Palestine. Realizing that development of Transjordan depended on securing the settled farmers from Bedouin attack, Peake initially tried to recruit his police force from villagers, but their memories of forceful recruiting by the Ottomans still rankled and they were reluctant to join him. Instead of Transjordanians, a Reserve Force was recruited from Egyptians, Sudanese, Palestinians, and others. In 1923, the force was merged with the police to form the famous Arab Legion (which became primarily Transjordanian by World War II), with some 1000 British-officered troops. It faced the immediate danger of attacks by Saudi Arabian Bedouin raiders. The Wahabi tribes from Arabia were not only plunderers but also religious zealots who sought to destroy the infidel Hashemites. A force of 5000 camel-riding Saudi Arabians nearly reached the capital of Transjordan in 1924, but they were finally repulsed by British Royal Air Force planes.

By 1930 the Bedouin had become a greater menace than ever, but now a new tactic was planned by the legion's second in command, Major John Bagot Glubb, who organized a desert patrol of the very Bedouin he was seeking to control. He had been unusually successful in pacifying nomadic tribes in Iraq and was highly informed concerning Bedouin ways and lore. By the simple device of employing the tribesmen to police their own deserts, he succeeded in putting an end to raiding, almost without firing a shot or making an arrest. At the same time, a Bedouin Control Board was established to take over jurisdiction of tribal courts in matters of "blood and honor," to fix Bedouin camping sites, and to investigate raids and other nomad breaches of the peace. A tripartite authority representing the Hashemite family, the British Arab Legion commander, and local Bedouins presided over the control board.

Until the problem of land ownership was settled, property disputes had frequently created intertribal wars. When individual plots were allocated, however, tribes began to obtain government lands and settle them as permanent settlers. On the one hand, the government sought to punish raiding severely; on the other, it sought to facilitate permanent individual settlement, with the hope that the nomad would find farming more profitable than plundering.

By 1933 Great Britain could report that tribal raiding had virtually ceased and peace and security prevailed in the country. The tribes had not fully become cultivators and they still bred stock, but many of them had taken on a semisettled status. Farming broadened the base of their economy and gave them a fixed stake in the country, providing them with a kind of economic insurance and a social anchor. By the eve of World War II, every tribe owned some cultivated land; Glubb reported that scarcely a Bedouin family did not own its patch of grain in addition to its flocks.

When Major Glubb was promoted from leader of the Desert Patrol to Arab Legion commander on the eve of World War II, he changed the former into the Desert Mechanized Force. During the war, the legion proved to be Great Britain's only loyal Arab fighting force. Even after the Dunkirk defeat, Abdullah stood by, offering to send his Arab troops anywhere in the world—a vigorous stand in view of both the German and Italian propaganda onslaughts throughout the Arab East and the prevailing anti-Western sentiment. When Rashid Ali al-Gailani and his anti-British generals seized the Iraqi government, Abdullah's Desert Mechanized Force was sent to help British troops quell the uprising (see chapter 15). In Syria, the Arab Legion also joined the Allies to drive out the pro-Vichy French authorities. Later, Glubb looked back upon these campaigns as investing the Arab Legion with a "halo of glory." Most British officers had been surprised, since they had not considered the legion a fighting force. By the end of the war, the Arab Legion was the most expensive item in Transjordan's budget, but one the British considered well worth subsidizing, for it had become a major asset to them in the Middle East.

INDEPENDENCE

What had Great Britain accomplished in Transjordan in nearly three decades? The population had grown from about 200,000 to nearly 450,000, half of which was still nomadic. About 20 percent of the population were Bedouin who did no farming, but ever growing numbers of nomads were gradually becoming permanent settlers. Although there were modest improvements in education, more than 90 percent of the population was still illiterate. Health had been improved somewhat, but it had never really been a serious problem. Transjordan was still economically dependent upon Great Britain, which supplied two-thirds of the total government revenue. Imports were three to four times as large as exports, and there seemed little possibility of implementing any extensive development programs.

By the end of the war, Great Britain was ready to grant independence to the amirate. Abdullah had been a loyal ally and local pressures were demanding freedom; the Legislative Council called on Transjordan's prime minister to declare immediate self-rule. If the country did not become independent, it would have to be placed under authority of the U.N. Trusteeship Council because it was a former League mandate.

In 1946, Great Britain granted Transjordan independence, but reserved rights, like those reserved in Iraq and Egypt before the war, that permitted the British ambassador to retain direction of foreign affairs and certain financial and military matters. The amirate became the Kingdom of Transjordan and Amir Abdullah became a king, like his grandnephew in Iraq. Anglo-Transjordanian relationships continued much as before. The Arab Legion was still commanded by British officers "on leave" from the British army. The legion's size and equipment were determined by the British ambassador (formerly the resident), and the legion continued to be financed by the British Treasury to the sum of over two million pounds sterling a year.

So transparent was continued British control that Abdullah was openly criticized by his fellow Arab League members (see chapter 6). When Transjordan sought United Nations membership, Soviet Russia twice vetoed the application, in 1946 and again in 1947, charging that the country was really a British puppet. Later, in 1955, as part of a package deal in which the Western powers agreed to admit to the United Nations a number of Soviet-sponsored applicants, Jordan (see below for change of name) and several other Western-backed applicants were also permitted to join.

Mounting Transjordanian and Arab opposition compelled Great Britain to renegotiate the 1946 treaty within two years. In the 1948 agreements, British controls were less apparent. The agreement permitted Great Britain to assist in defending the country as long as world conditions warranted it. Defense matters would now be coordinated by an Anglo-Transjordanian Joint Defense Board, and Great Britain would continue economic and social assistance.

A constitution, adopted in 1946, divided the Legislative Council into a House of Deputies and House of Notables. The king still controlled the reins of power. He appointed both the upper house and his cabinet, and the latter, not parliament, initiated all legislation. The lack of democracy was evident in the first postwar elections in 1947 when opposition leaders were forced to flee to Damascus. With only the government-sponsored Revival party participating in elections, Abdullah continued to control the government.

THE FIRST PALESTINE WAR

Transjordan's viability was jeopardized more than ever before by the results of the Palestine war in 1948, from which Abdullah had really hoped to profit. According to a scheme observers believed to have been tacitly agreed upon with Great Britain, Transjordan was to occupy those parts of Palestine not under Jewish control. Both Great Britain and Abdullah would benefit from such a scheme, which would cut the ground from under Haj Amin al-Husayni. The former Jerusalem mufti was presumed to be the most logical candidate for Palestine Arab leadership, a prospect which both Great Britain and the Hashemites disliked because the mufti was noted for his intense hatred of both. If the British-officered Arab Legion were to occupy Arab Palestine, the mufti's plans would be thwarted and British influence would continue over part of Palestine.

Recognizing the potential power of the Jewish forces, Abdullah was one of the few Arab leaders reluctant to engage them in a full-scale military campaign. He attempted to avoid the conflict through secret negotiations with the Jewish Agency's representative, Mrs. Golda Myerson (who later became Foreign Minister and Prime Minister Meir). However, the majority of the states in the Arab League (see chapter 6), of which Transjordan was a member, schemed for a quick victory and overrode Abdullah's warnings about Jewish strength. The Arab League majority opposed division of Palestine and planned to turn the country into an independent state under the former mufti.

While Abdullah, at his own request, acquired the title of commander of the Arab League's military forces, there never was any effective coordination of its forces. Each league member sent its own armies against the new Jewish state, hoping to seize as much territory as it could and to gain an advantage over its allies. The ludicrous situation was described by Alec Kirkbride in *A Crackle of Thorns*. At the Arab war council for the Palestine rescue, Syrian Premier Jamil Mardam Bey promised a whole division which, "of course," never materialized. The Egyptians took no initiative until attacked and defeated by Israel in Southern Palestine. King Abdullah continued as the commander-in-chief from whom no force except his own Arab Legion accepted orders. The Arab press wrote with glowing pride of the great victories which never occurred.[3]

Only the British-commanded, trained, and equipped Arab Legion made a creditable combat record against the Israelies. Throughout the crucial early weeks of the war, thirty-seven British officers continued in command. British medical, workshop, ordnance, and ammunition supplies saved the day. Later, many of the higher ranking Englishmen were withdrawn from Transjordan's army. Several legion units had to be withdrawn from combat against Israel and were redeployed within Transjordan to suppress uprisings of Palestinians who were protesting against Abdullah. By the end of the war, most of Palestine was seized by the Israelis. Only the tiny Gaza strip remained in Egyptian hands and the barren hill regions of central Palestine were retained by the Arab Legion.

Transjordan's territorial gains were confirmed by the Transjordan-Israeli Armistice Agreement, signed at Rhodes during April 1949. Although the document was not to prejudice the ultimate designation of frontiers, it validated Abdullah's subsequent annexation of central Palestine. An ineffective government, set up under Egyptian auspices in Gaza, disputed the annexation in the name of the mufti. While this so-called All Palestine government never exercised any authority, it was recognized by all Arab League members except Transjordan. The real purpose of the All Palestine government was to block seizure of Palestine by any league member and was intended as a rebuke to Abdullah for having annexed part of the country.

Abdullah convened his own Palestine refugee conference of some 5000 notables at Amman in October 1948 to counteract the effect of the Gaza Palestine government. The Amman refugee conference and, later, an Arab Congress convened by the mayor of Hebron called upon Abdullah to annex immediately the west bank of the Jordan River. A week later Transjordan's cabinet asked parliament to approve the merger. Civil rule replaced military government in Transjordanian-held Palestine during March 1949 (held by Transjordan since May 1948), and four Palestinians were added to the cabinet, one of whom was made refugee minister and deputy governor of Arab Palestine. A year later, the Palestinians in Jordan were invited to vote in the country's national elections, resulting in a new eleven-member cabinet including five Palestinians. When the Arab League passed a resolution opposing the growing trend toward annexation in March 1950, Abdullah boycotted the meetings and ignored the warnings.

Arab League threats did force Abdullah to abandon secret peace parleys with Israel, but he intensified his measures of incorporation. Seats in Transjordan's House of Notables were doubled and redistributed so that seven of the twenty members were Palestine Arabs. The formal union of Transjordanian-occupied Palestine and Transjordan occurred during April 1950 at a joint session of parliament. The newly enlarged state became the Hashemite Kingdom of Jordan.

Postannexation Dilemmas

Added territory and population converted Jordan from a desert principality into a full-fledged kingdom, but had its national prospects materially improved? As a result of the war, there were now nearly half a million Palestine Arab refugees in the country, in addition to the more than 400,000 west-bank Palestinian Arabs. While two-thirds of the population was Palestinian, 94 percent of the territory was on the east (Transjordanian) side of the Jordan River. Trade and commerce between the cities, towns, and villages of Arab Palestine with the Mediterranean coast had been severed. Access to the port at Haifa was lost. Much of the land and employment sources of the Palestine population lay across the frontier, in enemy territory.

Great economic and social differences separated the Palestinian majority from the indigenous Jordanians. Nearly twice as many school-aged Palestinian children (52 percent) had been receiving education before the war. Twice as many Palestine Arabs (between 30 and 40 percent) were urbanized. On the other hand, Jordan's four towns with a population of over 10,000 hardly seemed more than a number of adjoining villages. Many of the Palestinians were formerly employed in industry. Over 25,000 had been organized in more than thirty unions. At least half had some contact with nonagricultural occupations. Only the handful of Jordanians who worked for the Iraq Petroleum Company or in British military camps did not live from agriculture. The Palestinians were a volatile and politically conscious people, but their fellow Jordanians, except for a few wealthy landowners and merchants, had no political sophistication at all. The nomads on the east side of the Jordan River were quite ignorant of the world beyond and regarded Amman as the ultimate symbol of progress. The Jordanians had become a relatively manageable population as a result of the efforts of the Arab Legion; the Palestinians were a bitter, impoverished, seething body politic, awaiting vengeance for the loss of their homes and land.

Could the new Jordan sustain a population that had tripled in size? There was no industry, and nearly all income was derived from the soil, but even here primitive methods of agriculture and water shortages confined full use of the land to the narrow strip of the Jordan Valley. After the Palestine war, more than half the population was crowded into the 6 percent of the country's territory on the west bank, where population density was 580 per square kilometer, compared to a density of 107 on the east bank.

The 120,000 refugees on the east bank of the Jordan River and the 340,000 on the west bank relied entirely on United Nations relief supplies. One in three occupants of Jordan was receiving food, education, and medical and social welfare services from the international community. About a third of the refugees lived in U.N. camps. The others lived in mosques, caves, or improvised shelters. By 1960, refugee living conditions were, in general, far better than those of non-refugees. About half the school-aged refugee children were receiving free education. The refugees had lower death rates, less sickness, and an expanding population. Statistics, however, told little of the reality of their plight. The self-reliance and initiative of the former Palestinian tradesmen and farmers had been dissipated by frustration and boredom after years as refugees. Many, after a decade of living from United Nations handouts, had become professional refugees. By 1962, however, a new generation of Palestine refugee children who had never been in their parents' homeland was on the threshold of maturity. They constituted nearly 40 percent of the total refugee population and within a year or two would become the majority. Although they were as determined as their parents to "return" to their homeland, they were also eager to lead normal lives, to obtain an education, to earn a living, to marry and raise a family. Consequently, the United Nations began a new program of vocational education to train them for a productive life, one which would give them greater opportunities than those of their refugee parents.

The nonrefugee Palestinians with homes on Jordan's west bank also suffered economically. Many were worse off than the refugees. As a result of the Jordan-Israeli Armistice agreement, nearly a quarter of the Palestinian nonrefugees were deprived of their land, which was now in Israel. Other Palestinians who, before the war, had lived off the tourist trade, commerce with towns now on the Israeli side of the border, the Palestine railway, or employment in the mandatory government, had all now lost their incomes. They were not only cut off from their livelihood, but they were also ineligible to receive U.N. relief.

As a result of the annexation, Jordan's urban population grew from 10 percent to more than one-third of the total. The problems created in the cities and towns are illustrated by the situation in Amman, the capital. From a town of 30,000 in 1947, it grew to a city of over 650,000 by 1980, mostly Palestinian in origin.

Attempts to make Jordanians of the Palestinians often backfired. Abdullah's offer of citizenship to all Palestinians, whether from the east or west bank, was regarded by many as an attempt to enhance the king's power and prestige, as an act of political opportunism rather than humanitarianism. By acquiring additional territory and population, King Abdullah gave his successors a country large enough to have some influence in international affairs. Without the added territory and population, Jordan would have remained a small desert principality.

Relationships between the Palestinians and Jordanians were shaped by a struggle to determine which group would predominate. Would Jordan's Hashemite rulers inherit the patrimony of Palestine or would the Palestinians displace the Hashemites? Initially, the principal contenders in the struggle for control of the country were the Palestinian followers of the former mufti and the Jordanian partisans of Abdullah. Between the two groups stood the Nashashibis, who were willing to share power with Abdullah. The mufti's supporters nearly toppled the Hashemite regime when one of their henchmen tried to spark a revolt by assassinating King Abdullah in Jerusalem in July 1951. However, the Arab Legion crushed the incipient uprising and forestalled the clash between Palestinians and Jordanians for several more years.

Abdullah's successor, his son King Talal, attempted to appease the growing demand by the Palestinians for a more active governmental role by effecting constitutional changes, in January 1952, giving greater powers to parliament and limiting somewhat the king's prerogatives. The changes were not really effective, however, since the king and his cabinet could suspend all laws passed by parliament and place the country under military rule at any time. Since 1952, Jordan has been governed more by emergency legislation than by parliament on the grounds that Israel has constituted a continued threat to the country.

The 1952 constitution recognized a growing prosocialist sentiment, which was affecting Jordan as much as the rest of the Arab world, by including among its provisions guarantees to the right of employment, protection of labor by fair wages, hours, and unemployment compensation, rules concerning health, women's welfare, and child labor. No actual reform program emerged from these liberal promises, however, and few of the provisions were ever implemented.

Following promulgation of the 1952 constitution, top government posts and parliamentary seats were divided equally between Palestinians and east-bank Jordanians. Instead of mollifying opinion, the division only intensified hostility. In the first place, the Palestinians were still underrepresented, since they constituted far more than half the population. Continual rifts, quarrels, and jealousies weakened the government. The Palestinians were far more ardent Arab nationalists than the conservative Jordanians and ceaselessly demanded the end of all ties with Great Britain. Many were inspired by the example of the 1952 Egyptian revolution and pro-Nasser sentiment increased; his revolution became a symbol for those who sought to end the Hashemite dynasty. Increasing numbers of politicians demanded that Jordan emulate the successful Egyptian revolutionaries.

BRITISH DEPARTURE

As in other Arab countries, younger army officers became the leaders of an intense nationalism which was antagonistic to the monarchy and its conservative supporters. In Jordan, the villain was General Glubb, who was blamed for defeat in the Palestine war and was accused of influencing the army and royal family in favor of British imperialism.

Increasing economic problems and the political opposition of the Palestinians resulted in larger and more frequent street demonstrations and periodic cabinet crises. Against this background, in December 1955 the British government sent Sir Gerald Templer, chief of the Imperial General Staff, to pressure the king and his advisers into joining the Baghdad Pact (see chapter 5). Overwhelmingly, public sentiment opposed identification with any of the Western powers. The Palestinian majority was especially bitter, holding the West accountable for the creation of Israel and the subsequent Arab refugee problem.

Templer's visit sparked the rumor that young King Husain, who had ascended the throne on his eighteenth birthday in 1953—his father Talal having abdicated due to ill health the previous year—was about to sell out to the British. Early in January 1956, riots protesting the Baghdad Pact swept through Jordan, resulting in millions of dollars worth of damage to Western diplomatic and educational institutions. Only several days later, after the king and prime minister ordered new elections to determine whether or not Jordan should join the pact, did the uprisings subside.

Egypt, Syria, and Saudi Arabia—then allied in an Arab bloc—joined the fray with blasts of propaganda and promises of financial assistance to replace the British subsidy. Great Britain countered with offers of still more aid and interest-free loans to help develop the economy.

Popular opposition to Great Britain was so great that the king postponed elections lest an anti-Western government be swept into power. The government attempted to appease the opposition by announcing that Jordan would stay out of the Baghdad pact and that it would not identify with any bloc. The announcement still did not lessen the great opposition to the king and his supporters. Opponents of Jordan's pro-Western foreign policy needed proof that Jordan was not a Western vassal.

The scapegoat chosen by a group of younger army officers close to King Husain was General Glubb, most visible symbol of Jordan's subservience to British interests. On March 1, 1956, he was ordered to leave the country within hours and to take his British aides along with him. The expulsion produced the hoped-for effect. Jubilant crowds milled through the streets, cheering the king's announcement that this was "a holy day on which we have succeeded in our movement by God's will." Because of Glubb's important role in Jordan for twenty-six years, his departure meant to many Jordanians the end of British influence.

By the end of 1956, tensions between Jordan and Israel over border troubles and between Egypt and the West over the Suez Canal were at the boiling point. As a result of an election held in October 1956, the National Socialists, a pro-Nasser and anti-Western party, led by Sulaiman Nabulsi, won thirteen of the twenty parliamentary seats. Immediately after becoming prime minister, Nabulsi signed an agreement with Egypt and Syria placing Jordan's armed forces under an Egyptian major general. The British, French, and Israeli attack on Egypt late in October, soon after the Jordanian election, precipitated a final break with Great Britain, cancellation of the Anglo-Jordanian Treaty, and termination of the British subsidy.

Nabulsi's continued trend toward the left, his diplomatic negotiations with the Soviet Union, and knowledge of his intent to terminate the monarchy caused Husain and his advisers to have second thoughts about cooperation with the National Socialists and their allies. When, in April 1957, an antimonarchial army plot was exposed, the king imposed rigid security controls on the country, his loyal Bedouin units were alerted in strategic positions, and the Nabulsi government was dismissed. The king now abolished all political parties, dissolved parliament, suspended the constitution, imposed martial law, and put a government of Hashemite friends into office. By the end of April, 500 political leftists had been arrested for trial by military courts. All opposition was crushed and Jordan became a police state.

Early in 1957, the United States government began to take over the position once filled by Great Britain, lest Jordan's pro-Western government crumble from lack of support. American naval units were sent to the eastern Mediterranean in accord with the Eisenhower Doctrine and, within hours of making the request, on April 29, Jordan received ten million dollars, which were, according to the United States government, "in recognition of the steps taken by His Majesty King Husain and the Government and people of Jordan to maintain the integrity and independence of the nation."

Jordan's position was hardly improved. Instead of having to rely upon British subsidies, it now depended on American aid. Beneath the surface of a calm imposed by police controls, resentment against Husain and his government continued to seethe. The king had not gained popularity by his policies, but Egypt's President Nasser was becoming a popular figure. This was evident in February 1958 after the United Arab Republic had been formed. The enthusiasm for the new Arab republic was so strong through the Arab world that ten days later Jordan and Iraq, upon American advice, federated in an Arab Union with Iraq's King Faisal as its head. The Hashemite Arab Union aroused none of the enthusiasm that had greeted the UAR. Most nationalists considered it merely a device by reactionary monarchs to stem the republican-reformist tide. The Arab Union never really had an opportunity to function. Within five months, in July 1958, revolution had terminated Iraq's Hashemite dynasty, Iraq had become a republic, and it had severed its ties with Jordan (see chapter 15).

To forestall a similar revolution against King Husain in Jordan, 2000 British troops were flown in at his request in July 1958 to maintain the pro-Western regime. At the United Nations, Jordan charged the UAR with a plot to sabotage its Hashemite government and take over the country. By the end of 1958, the king had received enough American military equipment to ward off revolution and dispense with the British forces. Since 1958, King Husain's popularity has waxed and waned according to his relations with Egypt or with other Arab nationalists.

With American assistance Jordan increased its growth to a level which inspired expectations of its survival as an independent state. The rate, approximately 10 percent a year, was greater than that in any of the neighboring Arab countries, except Saudi Arabia. Much investment was in infrastructure such as roads, education, port expansion, and improved communications. Between 1950 and 1965 school attendance rose from over 100,000 to more than 300,000, with a corresponding decline in illiteracy from 69 percent to 15 percent among children between six and fourteen years old. By 1966 per capita income in Jordan was higher than in Syria and Egypt and nearly half that of Lebanon. After a new national university was opened in the capital, Amman, improved education made possible expansion of an active and well-trained civil service. The new network of roads linked most of the inhabited parts of the country and opened access to the modern new port at Aqaba. A major source of foreign currency was the expanded tourist industry built up around Jerusalem and Bethlehem. In the Jordan Valley, irrigation projects were initiated utilizing waters of the Jordan and Yarmuk rivers, opening more than 40,000 acres on the East Bank, providing employment for nearly 100,000 people, most of whom were Palestinian refugees. Another source of invisible income was remittances sent to families living in Jordan by about 100,000 Palestinians employed in various parts of the Arabian peninsula. All these sources of new income had reduced the unemployment rate from nearly one-third of the employable male population at the beginning of the 1950s to about a sixth by the end of the 1960s.

IMPACT OF THE JUNE 1967 WAR

Much progress achieved during the 1960s was dissipated nearly overnight as a result of the June 1967 war with Israel. Relations between Jordan and its neighbors had been deteriorating ever since the zealous Arab nationalists had called into question the kingdom's role in inter-Arab politics. Because of Jordan's close ties with the United States, Great Britain, and the conservative Saudi Arabia monarchy, both Syria and the United Arab Republic charged that King Husain was a tool of "Western imperialism." Radio broadcasts from Damascus and Cairo frequently incited the population against the "dwarf king." With the aid of Syria, Palestinians were illegally organized in commando attacks on Israel, exposing Jordan to massive retaliatory action by the Israeli army. The Israeli raids on West Bank Arab towns further antagonized the Palestinians, intensifying their resentment of the already unpopular monarchy.

Attempts by King Husain to display loyalty to the Arab cause through recognition of the new revolutionary republic of Yemen, offers of cooperation with an Arab joint command headed by an Egyptian general, and periodical juggling of cabinets to include Palestinians who would remain loyal to the government yet display sufficient patriotism to the Arab cause, were insufficient to rally most of the population behind him.

After outbreak of the war between Israel and the UAR in June 1967, King Husain sought to show his loyalty to "Arabism" by rejecting Israel's offer to remain neutral, and the country was plunged into the all-out conflict. Within three days Israel occupied all of the West Bank. Although the area comprised only some 2000 square miles, a relatively small part of Jordanian territory, it contained nearly half the population. According to a U.N. study,

The magnitude of the loss in Jordan's economic potential because of the Israeli occupation of the West Bank accounted for 38 percent of Jordan's total gross domestic product, with particularly high percentages for services (55 percent), transportation (47 percent) and wholesale and retail trade (43 percent). The contribution of the West Bank to Jordan's output of some agricultural products was even higher (e.g., over 60 to 65 percent for fruits and vegetables and 80 percent for olives) and, although the share of the West Bank in total industrial output amounted only to about 20 percent, the number of industrial establishments there represented about 48 percent of the total for the Kingdom...employing 37 percent of the Jordanian labour force engaged in industry. Income from tourism and remittances from Jordanians working abroad—two major sources of foreign exchange earnings—have declined about 85 percent and 50 percent respectively.... Implementation of the "Seven-Year Programme for Economic Development of Jordan, 1964–1970" has suffered a major blow. Several major projects have had to be suspended and others reexamined in the light of the new circumstances, special emphasis being placed on labour intensive projects which can alleviate the increasing unemployment.[4]

Israel occupied the principal towns and cities of the West Bank Hashemite Kingdom including the important Jerusalem-Bethlehem tourist center which had been developed into a mainstay of the Jordanian economy, providing about 25 percent of the country's foreign-currency earnings.

Simultaneously with the loss of West Bank productivity there was an influx of nearly 400,000 Palestinian refugees from the West Bank and Gaza, increasing the East Bank population by about one-third, and greatly expanding demands for food, shelter, and basic services. Since most of the newly added refugee population was poor and unskilled, it would take several years before it could become a productive asset on the East Bank of the diminished Kingdom. Not only was work on the major East Ghor irrigation canal halted, but parts of the vital project were severed in frequent artillery duels fought between Israeli and Jordanian forces in the months following the 1967 war. With escalation of artillery duels, air attacks, and military incursions along the river, nearly all inhabitants of the Jordan Valley had to be evacuated, endangering progress that had been made in farming the region before June 1967. Jordan's economy was saved from total collapse by financial assistance pledged by Kuwait, Libya, and Saudi Arabia at the 1967 Arab Summit Conference in Khartoum, Sudan.

Growing political uncertainty within Jordan also jeopardized stability and undermined much of the progress that had been accomplished during the 1960s. A new phenomenon was rapid growth of the Palestine commando movements. Efforts by the Jordanian government to curtail their activities, either through negotiations or through police and military force, were futile. Attacks by the commandos across the river against Israeli installations mounted rapidly. With increased militancy by the Palestinians, the severity of Israeli retaliatory action escalated to a point just short of all-out war.

The repeated Israeli blows on the one hand, and commando activities within the country on the other, seriously threatened the monarchy. The most militant commando organizations aimed not only at the destruction of Israel but also sought to overthrow all conservative Arab governments including the Hashemite Kingdom. For all practical purposes the commando organizations seized effective control of refugee camps, and won the support of Jordanian youth generally. Many refugee camps became commando training centers, and in some parts of the country were bases for their operations against Israel.

When the government attempted to exercise control over commando groups after the latter had hijacked three European airliners and their passengers to an abandoned airfield in Jordan during September 1970, a full-scale civil war erupted. After several days King Husain's loyal Bedouin forces suppressed the Palestinians and regained control of most, but not all the country. While this episode further seriously undermined Palestinian Arab confidence in the Hashemite dynasty, it culminated in large-scale military assistance from the United States government to replace the losses incurred during the civil war.

JORDAN AND THE PALESTINIANS

Jordan's internal politics and its foreign relations have been increasingly determined by its relations with the Palestinians since 1967. The civil war in 1970 and 1971, resulting in thousands of Palestinian deaths, created serious strains with the rest of the Arab world. Because more than half of Jordan's population is Palestinian, the government had to use repressive measures to prevent further uprisings, especially after seven Palestinian commando organizations called for overthrow of King Husain in 1971.

By the summer of 1971 the king announced that the guerilla problem in Jordan was "solved." Their bases were destroyed and 2,500 of them captured. The guerrillas, however, defeated in Jordan, continued their war against Husain abroad. In September they assassinated his prime minister and defense minister Wafsi al-Tal in Cairo. The action was carried out by a new commando group called Black September which was to become notorious for its terror activities elsewhere in the Middle East and in Europe.

The king attempted to balance the popularity of the commandos in Jordan with a series of political maneuvers. First, in August 1971 he appointed a tribal council of sheikhs and other notables chaired by crown prince Hassan. Since all political parties had been banned after 1963, he formed a Jordanian National Union in September 1971 to take the place of parties. Advocates of "imported ideologies" (Communists, Ba'athists, Nasserists, and Palestinian nationalists) were barred from membership. The king appointed himself president and his brother, the crown prince, vice-president. The organization was renamed the Arab National Union in 1972 and finally abolished in 1976.

Not only parties, but the parliament and the 1952 constitution were also manipulated by the king. In 1974 parliament revised the constitution to permit the king to rule without parliament for a year, in effect nullifying itself. Husain was also authorized to reorganize the kingdom, lessening the number of Palestinians in parliament and in government. During 1975 parliamentary elections were postponed. Parliament was briefly convened in 1976 to pass a constitutional amendment suspending elections indefinitely. During 1978 the king established a new quasi-parliamentary National Consultative Council of 60 members. Chosen for 2-year terms, the members were supposed to advise the monarch on all matters of importance to Jordan's citizens, but the body was little more than a decorative institution.

To counteract the growing popularity of the PLO and the wide support it commanded among Palestinians and other Arabs, Husain floated a new plan for a United Arab Kingdom in 1972. The kingdom would federate a Jordanian regime with one in Palestine or the West Bank. Jerusalem would be the Palestinian capital; Amman, capital of the Jordanian region and the Federal Capital. Although the king would rule both regions, there would be autonomy for both and a federal council of ministers.

The plan drew fire from all sides. Israel opposed it because it envisaged Jerusalem as an Arab capital and also gave political recognition to the Palestinians. The Palestinians regarded it as a device by Husain to keep control over them. Other Arab states suspected that the king wanted to use the federation to strengthen his role in the region.

A turning point in relations with the Palestinians came after the Rabat Arab Summit Conference in 1974 where the twenty Arab heads of state unanimously recognized the PLO as the "sole legitimate representative of the Palestinians." This formulation was also used in United Nations resolutions recognizing the international status of the PLO. Following the Rabat conference King Husain seemed more or less reconciled to loss of the West Bank and its establishment as a Palestinian state. Only Israel continued to insist that there could not be two Arab states "between the Mediterranean and the desert," meaning between Israel and the borders of Iraq. Israel's official policy indicated that the Palestinians would have to recognize their national aspirations within East Bank Jordan.

After the 1967 war, the 650,000 Palestinians in the West Bank and the 350,000 in Gaza lived under Israeli occupation. While permitted to manage their local and municipal affairs under supervision of the Israeli Military Government, they could not form any nationwide political bodies. General policy was to continue the local status quo existing in the West Bank under

Jordan, and the authority of local notables in Gaza. Both Jordanian and Israeli currency circulated in the West Bank, there was free trade and movement across the borders into Israel, and an "open bridges" policy permitted occupied Arabs free access to Jordan and the rest of the Arab world. Movement was in both directions, with students, merchants, and families from the West Bank and Gaza moving back and forth into the Arab world. Arab visitors were also encouraged to cross the bridges into the occupied areas and into Israel itself.

Israelis considered their occupation benign, an iron fist in a velvet glove, claiming that it even brought economic and social benefits to the West Bank and Gaza. Statistics did show that unemployment decreased and living standards improved as some 70,000 Arabs from the occupied areas found employment in Israeli agriculture, construction, and unskilled jobs. However, the occupation intensified Palestinian national consciousness. Frequent curfews, arrests without warrants, and expulsions of Palestinian leaders by Israel's occupation forces undermined positive feelings that might have emerged because of "good works." In a 1976 West Bank municipal election, the growing nationalist sentiment was revealed when most of the traditional municipal mayors and council members were displaced by younger men who supported the PLO.

Events in the region after 1977 greatly complicated questions concerning the future of the West Bank and Gaza. The new Israeli prime minister, Menachem Begin, leader of the Herut party, was determined that Judea and Samaria, as he called the West Bank, and Gaza, would become integral parts of Israel, in accord with his belief that they belonged to the Jewish people based on biblical interpretation. Therefore, he pursued a policy of suppressing political dissidence and support for the PLO by Palestinians in the occupied territories. He interpreted those parts of the 1979 Egyptian-Israeli peace settlement calling for autonomy in the territories to mean strictly local self-government for the Arab inhabitants. Consequently there was wide opposition to the peace settlement among the Palestinians as well as by Jordan. However in 1982 after the PLO defeat in Lebanon by Israel, U.S. president Ronald Reagan proposed a peaceful resolution of the conflict based on an arrangement in which Palestinian self-determination would be achieved "in association with Jordan." These events led to a reconciliation between King Husain and PLO leader Yassir Arafat and a visit by the latter to Amman where the two men negotiated possible cooperative arrangements between Jordan and the Palestinians.

By the 1980s the future of West Bank Jordan was in doubt. The possibilities were reincorporation into Jordan, annexation by Israel, establishment of a separate Palestinian state in the West Bank and Gaza, a Palestinian entity identified with Jordan, or one associated with Israel. In any event it was certain that the military occupation would continue until a peace settlement was negotiated between Israel and the Arab states.

NOTES

1. James Morris, *The Hashemite Kings,* New York, 1959, p. 93.
2. *Ibid.,* pp. 96–97.
3. Kirkbride, *A Crackle of Thorns,* London, 1956, pp. 159–163.
4. *Studies on Selected Development Problems in Various Countries in the Middle East,* UN, Ecosoc, E/4511 (Summary), 15 May 1968, pp. 14–15.

13   The Republic of Lebanon

RELIGIOUS DIVERSITY VS. ARAB UNITY

Lebanon's diversity of religious sects, more than any other factor, endows the country with a special character. It is the only Middle Eastern nation that has no single sectarian majority. Every Lebanese is a member of a religious minority. The Christian Maronites, permitted by Rome to practice their own Eastern Uniate rites, comprise about a sixth of the country's more than three million inhabitants and for many decades, until recently, were the largest religious group. In recent years the Shi'ites, because of their large population growth have become the largest group.* After them are the Sunnis, Greek Orthodox, Druses, Greek Catholics, Armenian Gregorian, Protestants of various denominations, Armenian Catholics, Syrian Catholics, Syrian Orthodox, and a few others. Preservation of the Christian political and social position against the pressures of Islam had been the *raison d'être* for Lebanese independence and was a major cause of the civil war which disrupted the traditional patterns of life after 1975. Until the war Lebanon had one of the highest standards of living in the Arab world, the highest literacy rate (less than a third of the population was illiterate), the greatest number of educated women, the lowest percentage of people economically tied to agriculture (about 40 percent), an urban population of some 60 percent, and the greatest per capita national income among non-oil producers. A relatively advanced economy had begun to develop from extensive commercial contacts

*During the last census in 1932 Maronites were 28.8 percent of the population and Shi'ites 19.6. By 1980 the Maronite percentage declined to 22 percent and the Shi'ite increased to nearly 30 percent.

with Europe in the seventeenth and eighteenth centuries. By the late nineteenth century, some 60,000 Lebanese had emigrated to Western countries and many then established businesses with close ties in the Levant. Thousands of emigrants have returned in the twentieth century with skills and capital they could profitably invest in the home country. The large Christian population has learned a great many modern techniques and skills in the Western educational institutions that have been set up in Lebanon (see below). Consequently, the educated Lebanese middle class has become far larger than any in the neighboring Arab countries. Even agriculture became organized more along European than Middle Eastern lines, and about half the rural population was made up of freeholding peasants who owned small, compact farms rather than scattered strips of land, as is the prevailing Middle Eastern pattern. Lebanese farmers produced more diversified crops and obtained a greater yield per acre. The most important contribution to the country's relative prosperity has been its advantageous commercial position, achieved through the development of the widespread commercial service transactions that Lebanese merchants undertake on behalf of foreign markets. Transshipments through the well-equipped Beirut port to neighboring countries, gold brokerage fees, exchange and commodity negotiations, all contributed to Lebanon's prosperity. A United Nations report in 1949 stated:

> Lebanon's financial capacity is remarkable, relatively, although it has not operated hitherto so much to the advantage of the State as to that of private individuals. The Lebanese have proved their ability to turn their little country into an active and efficient centre for exchange, gold dealings, brokerage, and trade involving many currencies besides their own, and the movement of goods which may never touch Lebanese territory.[1]

Independence has enabled Lebanon to maintain a free economy without import, export, and currency restrictions. More than half the country's income was from invisible imports such as tourism, foreign remittances, and business conducted through numerous relatives in various parts of the world. The desire to maintain this unique economic position has been a major consideration in keeping the country independent. Even many Muslim businessmen preferred the political *status quo* to amalgamation within a larger Arab state.

While its population was approximately half Christian, half Muslim, modern Lebanon is Arab by virtue of the language, culture, and national sentiment of its Muslims and many of its Christians. But there is an ambivalence about Lebanon's Arabism. Some leaders are so intent upon preserving the country's Christian identity that they deny Arab influences and orientation and seek to identify completely with the Christian West. Unlike its Arab neighbors, which also fell before the Arab invasion during the seventh century, the Lebanon region did not become Islamized, although it was integrated into the Arab cultural world. Isolation within natural mountain fortifications helped the diverse Christian sects retain their distinctive ways of life.

Throughout the Ottoman era, geographic isolation has also been responsible for a wide measure of autonomy, for Ottoman authority and troops were unable to conquer many areas high in the mountains. When Sultan Selim I occupied the country in 1516, he recognized the difficulties of wresting control of their land from many leaders. He even bestowed upon a Druse chieftain, who ruled the isolated, mountainous Druse region, the title "Lord of the Mountain." Druses and other local princes governed independently of Istanbul for long periods of time, maintaining only sketchy ties with the Ottoman capital. One Druse amir (prince), Fakhr ud-Din, nearly severed connections entirely with the sultan between 1590 and 1635, signing treaties with European powers and attempting to create a greater Lebanon. He was, however, ultimately defeated by the sultan.

EARLY FRENCH INFLUENCES

During the seventeenth and eighteenth centuries, several local chiefs encouraged Christian missionaries, primarily French Catholic, to expand their educational activities in the country. At the end of the sixteenth century, Pope Gregory XIII founded a special seminary in Rome where Lebanese Maronite students were trained to become clerics. The Western ideas with which many of the Roman seminary graduates returned to their native land were spread among Lebanese Maronites in an era when there were few intellectual contacts between the Ottoman Empire and Western Europe. As a result of the sultan's decree in 1649, permitting France's Louis XIV to "adopt" the Maronites, France became their special guardian. Concomitant with protection came numerous French Catholic religious, educational, and welfare establishments operated by clergymen who also began to influence Lebanese political events. French influences in the Maronite community continued to grow until, in the nineteenth century, the Maronites, because of their support from France, felt themselves strong enough to challenge the neighboring Muslims and Druses. French predominance was recognized by both the Berlin Treaty of 1878 and by the Vatican, which notified Catholic authorities that their dealings with local officials should be conducted through French diplomatic representatives. All French governments, even anticlerical ones, continued to maintain strong ties with these Eastern Christians as a way of preserving French influence in the Levant. The Maronites, especially, looked to France for assurances that they would not be engulfed in the great Muslim sea and for help in fighting the missionary endeavors of other Eastern (Orthodox) churches.

After the clash between French Maronite clients and the Druses in 1860 (see chapter 4 and, for a discussion of the Druses, chapter 14), the sultan established the independent *sanjak* (province) of Lebanon under an Osmanli Christian governor nominated by Istanbul in consultation with the Western powers. A Central Administrative Council, or *Majlis,* elected on the basis of religion, was established in 1861 to govern the mountain region that later became the heartland of the modern Lebanese republic. Representation in the council was equally distributed among Maronites, Greek Catholics, Greek Orthodox, Druses, Metawilas (a large Muslim sect), and other Muslims. The principle of religious representation adopted in 1861 still prevails today.

Most educated Lebanese Christians spoke French by World War II. Many were more at home in this language than in Arabic. French literature, rather than Arabic or Turkish, was widely read. French education also instilled in the Lebanese Christians a deep attachment for French social customs and manners. Many wealthy familes sent their sons to universities in France after they had completed their French elementary education in Lebanon. The French Université de St. Joseph, founded by the Jesuits in 1875, is one of the notable higher educational institutions of the region (see chapter 6). The wide establishment of European and American educational institutions has been responsible for Lebanon's exceptionally high literacy rate. As a result, too, there were many university graduates in the country and a large number of inhabitants who traveled to Europe.

Within the half century following the 1860 uprising, almost as many Lebanese (mostly Christian) left the country as remained there. Some went to escape Ottoman military service and taxation. Others left to seek the business and commercial opportunities open to them elsewhere as a result of their Western education. Most emigrants maintained close ties with their relatives who remained, however, and Lebanon became a bridge between the Arab East and the Occident, a country whose population was aware of Western techniques and social forces long before they were introduced to their Arab neighbors.

Although many Lebanese Muslims also attended European schools, they never were as closely identified with the West as were the Christians. Despite their Western education, frequent visits to Europe, and considerable exposure to French culture, the Muslim leaders always maintained a level of reserve. For them, the West was, after all, Christian and therefore alien. Even the most Westernized Muslim was separated from complete identification with the Occident by his deep mistrust of Christian ways of life. Unlike the Lebanese Christians, the Lebanese Muslims were part of an overwhelming majority within the larger geographical region of the Middle East and, hence, did not seek close foreign connections for protection. While Lebanon was part of the Ottoman Empire, the Muslim more readily identified with his Osmanli overlord than with the representatives of Christian Europe in the area. Despite the participation of some Christian intellectuals in the early nationalist movement (see chapter 6), mutual distrust between Christians and

Muslims was intensified after World War I when Arab nationalism began to struggle against Western domination.

When the American King-Crane Commission visited Lebanon during 1919, only the Maronites and other Uniates associated with the Vatican expressed any desire for close ties with France, largely because they feared the predominantly Muslim control of the Arab nationalist movement. Most Arabs, however, the commission found, opposed separating Lebanon from the greater region of Syria. In their recommendations, the commissioners urged a compromise in which Lebanon would retain a certain measure of independence as an autonomous government within the greater Syrian state. They recognized the reasons for Christian anxieties, but believed that there would be a four-fold safeguard against Muslim excesses: (1) the presence of a strong European mandatory force; (2) the guardianship of the League of Nations; (3) the "certainty" that the Arab government would, itself, realize that there was the need for such an autonomous government; and (4) the substantial contribution Christian Lebanon could make to greater Syria's development. Therefore the Commissioners urged unity: "For the sake of the larger interests, both of Lebanon and Syria...."[2]

FRENCH MANDATORY POLICY AND ADMINISTRATION

From the time France assumed *de facto* sovereignty of Lebanon and Syria, in 1919, until World War II, both areas were linked administratively. The League of Nations assigned them both to France in 1922 in a single mandate with the condition that they be governed as separate parts of one political entity. Instead, France subdivided the area into several autonomous states. Lebanon was not created along the lines of the autonomous Ottoman province established in 1861, however. A number of considerations motivated this decision. First, within a reconstituted Lebanon, French influence could expect to be strong because of the cultural and educational ties already established. Second, because of its large Christian population, Lebanon could act as a bulwark against the rising Arab nationalism for which the colonial administrators had no sympathy—even then they feared that Arab nationalism would incite the millions of Arabs in French North Africa. Third, many officials suspected that the British were conspiring to acquire as much of the Levant as possible and felt that French power should be firmly entrenched.

Yet France did not want to create a really independent state. Lebanon was therefore enlarged to include enough Christians to justify setting up a separate government, but also a sufficient number of Muslims to assure the need for continued French protection of their political hegemony. The heartland was Mount Lebanon where some 340,000 Maronites lived. It included the area of the former autonomous Ottoman province created in 1861. This area was tripled in size in 1920 by adding the predominantly

Muslim city of Beirut; Muslim Tripoli in the north; Sidon in the south; southern Lebanon up to the Palestine border, with a predominantly Shi'ite population; and the fertile Biqa Valley, occupied by a mixture of Muslim and Greek Orthodox residents. Maronites, who had constituted the majority of the Ottoman Lebanese province, became the largest minority in the new French-controlled Lebanon. They and other Christian groups constituted just a little more than half the population. Sunni, Shi'ite, and other Muslim sects and the Druses made up the rest. Emigration was at first forbidden lest the Christian-Muslim balance be disturbed.

Until the end of World War II France kept tight control of the Levant through a high commissioner for Syria and Lebanon, usually a French army general who held absolute power. A number of native governments were also established in Syria and one in Lebanon, each with its own constitution. Dual government was theoretically a provisional system designed to enable peoples who "politically speaking, are still minors to educate themselves so as to arrive one day at full self-government."[3] As long as these provisional native governments properly carried out their duties, French intervention was considered unnecessary. Should the native system prove deficient, the mandatory power was to use its own administration to correct native mistakes and make up for inadequacies. When a Lebanese or Syrian native government did not satisfy the French administrators, the French could impose martial law and press censorship.

The native government was staffed by Lebanese, while the high commissioner's organization was manned by French colonial officials responsible for both Syria and Lebanon. At his Beirut headquarters, the high commissioner was assisted by a French political and military cabinet who took charge of departments of security, education, public works, and antiquities and an organization for Bedouin affairs.

A staff of so-called information officers (*services spéciaux*) from the French army, operating in every district, kept the high commissioner informed of political sentiment throughout the region. These officers were considered the tutors who would prepare the Levant for future independence, and they exercised great influence over local administration and political life.

Common administrative functions—including customs, posts and telegraphs, currency, railways, and public utilities—which serviced all of Lebanon and Syria as a unit, were entirely under the high commissioner's jurisdiction. If he were a military man, the high commissioner also commanded the Syrian and Lebanese armed forces, composed mostly of French and African colonial troops, but including some local levies (the *Troupes Spéciales du Levant*). Civilian high commissioners were not field commanders, but the highest military authority was responsible to them.

Because of their favored position, French businessmen easily acquired financial control of the railroads, public utilities, and banks. Since education was French, not Arabic, oriented, and the language of the government administration was French, that language became much more useful in official and intellectual circles than Arabic. Economic policy favored France. On the one hand, tariffs were inadequate to protect local enterprise from cheap imports. On the other, French companies received the most important economic concessions. Currency instability resulted from linking the Lebanese pound to the fluctuating French franc.

Mandatory officials were often corrupt, avaricious, and arbitrary. Local employees were not chosen wisely, properly trained, or given an appropriate measure of responsibility. Consequently, development of Syrian and Lebanese public services lagged behind those in the British Palestine mandate. Too often, the Lebanese charged, they were treated like an African colony and regarded by colonial officials with contempt. Basic civil rights were violated and political suspects were frequently imprisoned without trial. Security agents even instigated disorder in their attempts to discredit native governments.

The Syrian and Lebanese native governments also had little opportunity to develop the powers they did have, for the high commissioner's representatives traveled throughout the region and kept close watch over all their activities. Furthermore, a corps of French administrative *conseillers* and technical advisers, hired separately rather than from the high commissioner's staff, were attached to the various native government departments with status as Lebanese government officials. Whenever a native government threatened to exercise too much independence, the high commissioner merely suspended its constitution and took over its administration.

However, during the mandatory era law and order was enforced, especially in the mountainous hinterland that in the past had managed to remain free from Ottoman control. Roads were built to link urban areas with the countryside and to help develop it. Better communications also facilitated the suppression of Bedouin incursions. Expansion of the school system raised the already high literacy rate. Development of health services and easier access to medical care considerably improved health standards. Beirut expanded into a metropolis and became a leading Mediterranean port. As a consequence of French material improvements, food and clothing became more plentiful and desire for emigration declined.

French policy originally satisfied the Maronites, although some Christians and most Muslims objected to being cut off from the Syrian hinterland. Because of the favored Maronite position, French control was considerably milder in Lebanon than in neighboring Syria, where several uprisings were harshly suppressed.

Material progress without more rapid development of local government only created the inevitable colonial dilemma. The more sophisticated and familiar with Western ways the population became, as a result of its higher living standards, the greater its dissatisfaction with the slow attainment of self-determination. Even many formerly pro-French Maronites became impatient with the delays in developing self-government. Thus Lebanese Christians also began to demand full independence and to identify with neighboring Arab nationalist movements.

Lebanese Native Government

The first native government was established by France in Lebanon in 1919 when the old Central Administrative Council or Majlis was restored. It was soon abolished and replaced by a more pliable appointed Administrative Commission when members of the elected body became too nationalistic. Of the fifteen commission members, there were six Maronites, three Greek Orthodox, two Sunnis, two Shi'ites, one Druse, and one Greek Catholic. When the appointed commission was itself replaced in 1922 by an elected Representative Council, this religious proportionment was preserved.

Under the terms of the mandate, a constitution was adopted in 1926 with the establishment of a Lebanese republic. The constitution, with various amendments, remains to the present day. The model followed was that of the French Third Republic, in which a president and cabinet are responsible to a bicameral legislature. After 1927, the Senate was joined with the lower house to form a unicameral Chamber of Deputies.

The 1926 constitution established a system of checks and balances between executive and legislative branches of the Lebanese native government. The president was given more power than he had in the French system, for he could appoint and dismiss all cabinet members, including the prime minister, and he could adjourn or dismiss parliament under certain circumstances. On the other hand, parliament chose the president and controlled finances. Both executive and legislature could initiate legislation and each could delay the proposals of the other, although parliament had the final word. The electoral law, providing for distribution of parliamentary seats on the basis of religion, assured that no single religious group could impose its will on the nation unless it could obtain substantial backing from other groups. According to what became unwritten tradition, Lebanon's president has ever since been a Maronite, the prime minister a Sunni, and the president of the Chamber of Deputies a Shi'ite. Foreign Affairs were for many years a Christian preserve, while defense was usually in the hands of a Muslim or Druse chief.

As a result of nationalist agitation and demonstrations against Paris in 1932, the high commissioner suspended the 1926 constitution. A new, revised constitution was promulgated in 1934 by the high commissioner, restricting the power of the Chamber of Deputies and ignoring the religious proportionment that had characterized elections and parliamentary representation. An uneasy truce prevailed between the nationalists and France until 1936, when outbreaks in Damascus forced Paris to reopen negotiations with both Syria and Lebanon.

By 1936, French policy in the Levant was also influenced by Socialist premier Leon Blum's Popular Front government. Socialist ideology opposed colonialism and Blum's government was sympathetic to nationalist aspirations. Syria was first to obtain greater self-determination in 1936. Lebanese nationalists then demanded and received similar concessions in a twenty-five year treaty. France reserved control over defense and foreign affairs, but a common policy regarding other administrative powers was agreed upon.

While Blum's reform policy led to restoration of the 1926 Lebanese constitution in January 1937, neither the Lebanese nor many Frenchmen were satisfied. Some Lebanese felt that the country had not gained enough freedom. Others, mostly Muslims, regarded their hopes for reunion with Syria as threatened because the 1936 treaty confirmed Lebanon's separate political existence. French leftists were enthusiastic, but ardent French nationalists felt that their country had been dealt a blow from which it could not recover, that both Syria and Lebanon were now "lost."

The 1937 election for the Lebanese Chamber of Deputies following restoration of the 1926 constitution was marked by widespread corruption and violence. The newly elected chamber accomplished little of positive value; it was completely bogged down in a morass of pointless and bitter discussions. Even many Lebanese became disillusioned. Those represented in parliament were mostly landlords and lawyers with little popular following or interest in public welfare. To many Lebanese, the old Ottoman system of government seemed superior to the newly won right of self-determination.

Dissatisfaction in Lebanon, as well as in France, prevented further progress toward self-government after Blum's Popular Front lost office in 1937. In Paris, a government opposed to self-determination for Syria and Lebanon returned to power and blocked the still-pending ratification of the 1936 Franco-Lebanese and Syrian treaties. Conservative French nationalists persuaded the new Paris government to denounce the documents as premature and incompatible with national interests and to take over again direct administration of the mandates in 1937.

LEBANON AND WORLD WAR II

One of the first French war measures in 1939 was to dissolve the Syrian and Lebanese Chamber of Deputies, dismiss their cabinets, suspend their constitutions, and turn both native governments over to French-appointed authorities. Even the Maronites resented these arbitrary moves. Consequently the Allied cause found little sympathy in the Levant.

After France fell in 1940, the Axis powers sent an Italian commission to supervise the armistice and prepare the way for the German and Italian occupation of the Levant. In a countermove, Great Britain extended its blockade of the French Vichy government to the Levant. The situation aroused Arab fears that they would be caught in the crossfire and that at best the British blockade would cause a famine like that suffered during World War I. Some extremists worked for a Nazi victory as retaliation against Great Britain and France for their colonial roles. But the majority were less pro-German than pro-Arab. Syrians, as usual, took the lead in forcing a showdown with the Vichy authorities. After a series of strikes and demonstrations early in 1941, new governments were formed in both countries and the Vichy-appointed authorities in Syria and Lebanon were replaced by Lebanese politicians acceptable as a compromise to both the Vichy authorities and the nationalists. Lebanon's new government was headed by a Maronite judge who had played no previous political role.

Both Syria and Lebanon became directly involved in military action in June 1941 when British and Free French troops overran the Vichy forces in the area. Allied occupation of the Levant restored the whole region to Allied control. The Free French commander immediately proclaimed that the Allied armies had come to end the mandates and to proclaim the Levant free and independent. He promised that the population would be free to chose between forming separate states or a single unified nation.

Free French attitudes soon proved to be little better than those of the Vichy government. General de Gaulle was no more eager than previous French governments to surrender France's position in the Levant. Hostility flared up, not only between the Gaullists and Arab nationalists, but with the British as well. To overcome ingrained French suspicions about their motives in the area, the British issued a statement freely admitting that France should have the predominant position in Syria and Lebanon, but stating that Great Britain was also committed to assist Syria and Lebanon to attain independence.

When the Free French commander General Georges Catroux proclaimed Lebanese and Syrian independence at the end of 1941, his statement made no reference to constitutional changes or surrender of French control. It therefore aroused no popular enthusiasm. Government posts were filled with Gaullist puppets, and even many Vichy-appointed officials were permitted to remain because of the small number of Free French personnel in the Levant. Catroux's policies worried London because they antagonized Arab leaders throughout the Middle East.

A combination of Arab nationalist and British pressures forced the Gaullists to permit the first free elections for the Syrian and Lebanese parliaments during 1943, resulting in a total defeat for French-supported candidates. Both newly elected Lebanese and Syrian governments demanded complete control of all government administration as well as the French-dominated monopolies over railroads, ports, tobacco, and municipal water and power companies.

De Gaulle asserted that his government had legally inherited mandatory obligations from the French Republic and could not repudiate them without authority from the League of Nations or its successor. Nor was he willing to terminate French control unless the Levant states signed preferential treaties with France. Since the nationalists had never recognized the validity of the mandates, they refused to accept de Gaulle's conditions. Furthermore, the Arab nationalists asserted, General Catroux's declaration had set up no conditions for independence. The Syrian and Lebanese governments would decide for themselves whether or not to sign treaties with France. Arab nationalists felt that it was absolutely necessary to acquire immediate independence in order to prevent France from attempting to reassert its position by force after the war.

The Lebanese government staged the first showdown with de Gaulle when it voted to purge the constitution of all remaining restrictions on sovereignty in November 1943. The French commander Catroux responded immediately by suspending the constitution, dissolving parliament, arresting the president and most of his cabinet, and appointing Émile Edde, known for his pro-French attitudes, as chief of state. Edde was unable to form an effective cabinet in the face of opposition from all groups, including most Maronites, and the outbreak of a general strike.

Again Great Britain intervened on behalf of the nationalists because it feared that de Gaulle's policies would antagonize the entire Arab world. In addition, Syria's and Lebanon's vital importance as Allied operational bases and communications centers would be jeopardized by revolution and the breakdown of law and order. Upon British insistence, the Free French released and reinstated the Syrian and Lebanese presidents and their cabinets and turned over several government and quasi-government services to the nationalists by the end of 1944. Only a special security force of locally recruited personnel, the *Troupes Spéciales,* remained under French control.

Still determined to retain some vestige of glory in the Levant after Germany was defeated in May 1945, de Gaulle again insisted that preferential treaties be signed before France left the area. He demanded exclusive military rights, the linkage of local currency with the franc, the hiring only of Frenchmen as foreign advisers or employees, influence over the educational system, and specific restrictions on foreign affairs. At the very least de Gaulle hoped to preserve French cultural and economic interests and to save his country's prestige from falling in the eyes of North African Muslims. He also suspected that Great Britain would fill the vacuum if France left the Levant after the war, since British troops already controlled most of the region. De Gaulle's demands were far too much for the Syrian and Lebanese governments. They would only concede friendship treaties, which gave no preference to any nation, and promised to guarantee safety for existing French educational institutions.

As the war drew to a close, British efforts to maintain a balance between nationalist aspirations and French prerogatives failed. Unresponsive to the increasing clamor for evacuation of foreign troops, France began to build up its forces in the Levant. When de Gaulle's troops were disembarked in Beirut immediately after V-E Day in May 1945, rumors spread that this was the beginning of French reoccupation. De Gaulle obstinately rejected British pleas for caution, and insurrection broke out in the principal Syrian cities. When French air and artillery bombardment of Damascus threatened this air link with the Far East, where the war still continued, Great Britain ordered the French to cease fire and withdraw or face open conflict with British troops. To prevent this conflict, France backed down.

Early in 1946, after the fighting was halted, both Syria and Lebanon appealed to the U.N. Security Council for the immediate withdrawal of all foreign troops. Although the Soviet Union vetoed an American proposal for direct negotiations leading to withdrawal of British and French troops "as soon as practicable," the spirit of the proposal was carried out in an accord reached by the four governments, leading to evacuation from Syria by April and from Lebanon by December 1946. By 1947, both nations were free and independent, ready to begin attempts to shape their own destinies.

DEMOCRATIC DEVELOPMENT

Lebanon's multiethnic society, rather than imported French institutions, has had the greatest influence on that country's political development. Frequently, when the European parliamentary system broke down, the country remained essentially democratic as a result of the fundamental compromises that governed relations among the various religious groups. Since no ethnic, religious, or social group has a majority, each must protect the rights of all the others or face the danger of a threat to its own existence. Oppression of a neighbor may lead to oppression of one's own group sooner or later. A pertinent example is the position held by Lebanon's tiny Jewish minority of some 5000 to 8000. While the position of Jewish minorities in other Arab states had become quite insecure by the late 1960s as a result of the clash between Arab and Zionist nationalisms, Lebanese Jewry continued to prosper. Jews remained prominent in social life, business and commerce, the press, and in intellectual pursuits. When local extremists did try to badger the Jewish community, there were always political groups and leaders who came to its defense. Caught in the crossfire of the 1975–1977 Revolution, many Jews left Lebanon. Today only a handful remain.

Until 1975 the variety of ethnoreligious groups enabled the country to remain, by comparison, politically the freest in the Arab East. There are fewer restrictions on the press than in other Arab countries, and there is great political variety. The widest range of organizations, from right to left, flourish. Unlike the situation in many neighboring Arab states, the most diverse opinions can be heard fervently expressed in public cafés.

The first political groups began to form around leading families in various parts of Lebanon during the mandatory era. Except for the Communists, however, no significantly large party with a real political platform developed until the 1950s. Until then, development of political consciousness and responsibility had more to do with religion than social or economic matters. Political power came from the successful manipulation of various religious minorities.

During the mandate, any group of citizens could form an electoral list, although they were nearly always organized by leaders of important families. Often the strength of a list was related to the amount of land controlled by the list leader, usually the chief of the strongest religious group in each area. Since in some regions more than one religion was represented, list leaders attempted to attract members of other faiths within their districts. In return for pledges of support from groups representing a faith other than his own, a leader might make some political compromise or payment. Influential and wealthy families also used threats and violence to obtain backing and votes. There is a saying that though a Lebanese does not have to carry a gun to the polls, it helps. List control by landed aristocrats, called *Zuama* (singular—*Zaim*), allied with less powerful minorities on the basis of services and obligations exchanged created a semifeudal system. It differed from other Middle East electoral systems, in which a single large landowner usually controlled his whole district, and resembled more that of medieval Europe, where feudal lords subdivided their authority among several lesser aristocrats who provided troops in exchange for protection and other services. This network of local controls through confessional politics has been known as the "*Zaim* System."

The cornerstone of the whole system, allocation of parliamentary seats on the basis of the ratio fixed by a census taken before World War II, remained until 1977. While the number of deputies in the Chamber of Deputies has varied (between 1947 and 1953 it was altered at every election, changing from 55 to 77 to 44; in 1960 was raised from 66 to 99), it was always a multiple of eleven, that is, a ratio of six Christians for every five Muslims. Even when Christians were emigrating at the rate of 100 a month during the 1950s and the Muslim birth rate was known to be far higher, the ratio was maintained.

By the 1930s, several of these feudal alliances had become more or less constant, and these groups began to be called political parties. Fealty to such "parties" had nothing to do with any ideology or doctrine, but was based upon personal, family, or religious ties. From time to time, special parliamentary groupings would form when coteries of deputies joined forces around some issue of common interest. Thus another form of "party" took shape. Merchants, for example, would combine to promote legislation favorable to their own business affairs. But when the issue which had brought them together disappeared from the horizon, these parties quickly dissolved. Most elected deputies, however, had no commitments other than to the local lord, if he himself was not the parliamentary deputy.

The two most significant groups before 1950 were the National Bloc and the Constitutional Bloc, both formed in 1932. Leaders of both were primarily Maronite, although the blocs did include other religions. The Constitutional Bloc was the more powerful, influential, and independent, tending to identify with moderate nationalist aspirations. Its leader, Bishara al-Khuri, urged national independence to free the country from restrictive French policies. After the 1930s, members sought to create a working relationship with Syrian nationalist leaders, believing that sooner or later Arab nationalism would win over the French.

Francophile National Bloc leader Émile Edde was made president of Lebanon with French backing between 1936 and 1941. Because Free French support made him appear a colonial puppet, he failed to win a second term after 1943. The National Bloc favored independence, but it resisted closer ties with the Arab nationalist movement, seeking to preserve Lebanon as a cultural bridge between Christian Europe and the Arab East. These differences meant little to the rank and file party membership who were guided more by their family or clan ties than by stated programs. Bishara al-Khuri's group frequently obtained endorsement from mountain villages only because his rivals backed Edde's political machine. Edde then seriously undermined his position by becoming identified with the colonialists, while al-Khuri emerged as a national hero who had stood up to France and subsequently led the first truly independent government in 1943.

His newly won prestige gave Bishara al-Khuri such influence that he successfully reconciled several religious communities by bringing about the National Pact of 1943 (see below), temporarily leading them to a unified national movement. He even won the cooperation of Riyad al-Sulh, the Sunni prime minister who had close associations with Syrian nationalists (see chapter 14) and had been a founder of the Istiqlal, the Arab secret society formed in 1919 to support the creation of a greater Arab state (see chapter 10).

Relations between Christians and Muslims were based on the unwritten National Pact agreed upon in 1943. Christians promised to abandon their traditional dependence on France, and Muslims agreed to forego their ambitions for union with Syria or a larger Arab state. Although no census had been taken since 1932, Lebanon was assumed to have a Christian majority and its existence was to be confirmed by law. The larger Muslim birth rate was to be ignored in the interest of bringing about a compromise among the seven leading communities. The legally established population ratio, based on the 1932· census, was Maronite, 29 percent; Sunni, 21 percent; Shi'ite, 18.5 percent; Greek Orthodox, 9.7 percent; and so on down to the Chaldeans with about 0.1 percent. Constitutional provisions for opening all public employment to qualified applicants were circumvented to establish "justice and concord." Communities were now to be equitably represented in government employment; after 1943 posts from clerkships up to director generals of ministries were distributed among the religious communities according to an agreed ratio. In return for an unchallenged Christian majority, Bishara al-Khuri agreed to identify with, but not become part of the Arab world. This National Pact remained a fundamental part of Lebanon's unwritten constitution for the next fifteen years. It provided a key to political organization and a reason for remaining independent from Syria. It translated "politics by religious confession" into "politics by concession."

The Rose Water Revolution

By 1952, the good will and popular support earned by Bishara al-Khuri during the struggle for national liberation had been dissipated. He seemed to ignore completely Lebanon's pressing internal problems and treated with indifference the need for fundamental social reform. Nearly all political activity was concerned with the private affairs and interrelationships of Lebanon's small elite of wealthy families. The old conservatives were oblivious to the growing desire for social change beginning to stir beneath the surface of political life. Political corruption may not have been as pervasive as it had been in prerevolutionary Egypt, but there was enough to arouse popular feeling when scandal after scandal broke into the press.

Despite declining popularity, al-Khuri retained political control through manipulation of electoral lists, bribery, threats, the buying off or beating up of journalists, and the paying off of the judiciary. A rigged election in 1947 provided a parliament of al-Khuri's supporters who adopted a constitutional amendment permitting the president to succeed himself.

Although he kept the reins of parliament tightly in hand, al-Khuri was still unable to dominate public opinion. When the economy took a sharp dip in 1952, the result was an outburst of press criticism; in June, nine newspapers were suspended for demanding expulsion of the president.

Nine parliamentary deputies, who had resisted al-Khuri's blandishments or threats, decided to act, relying on public discontent with the president rather than on the Chamber of Deputies for their support. The nine—who represented a variety of religious, political, and social backgrounds—formed the Social National Front (SNF). The new party was led by Kemal Jumblatt, hereditary leader of a large Druse faction, and Camille Chamoun, at this time a progressive independent Maronite. They were joined by the activist right wing Syrian National party in organizing an unlawful public rally demanding the ouster of the president. When both army and police disobeyed government orders to break up the demonstration, Bishara al-Khuri recognized his defeat. With "encouragement" from army chief of staff General Fuad Shehab, he resigned on September 18, 1952. His followers in parliament, realizing the consequences of continued support for so unpopular a figure, quickly defected to elect Camille Chamoun as independent Lebanon's second president.

Once initial victory in this Rose Water Revolution, so called because of its mild effects, was achieved, the SNF began to disintegrate. Jumblatt's demands for moderate social and constitutional reforms were ignored by Chamoun, who concentrated instead on administrative changes and building up his own political machine to replace al-Khuri's. Now only half a dozen or so deputies called for land reform, electoral change, readjustment of the tax system, and labor and social welfare legislation. The Muslims who had supported Chamoun were not interested in fundamentally altering the nation's economy or social organization, but only in ridding the government of al-Khuri's predominantly Christian old guard.

After the 1952 Rose Water Revolution, there were few fundamental changes in government because the religiopolitical compromise continued to reinforce the *status quo* of the political system. Voting was made compulsory for men, but not really enforced. Women also received the ballot. The power of the influential landowners was somewhat modified by increasing electoral districts from five to thirty-three. This necessitated thirty-three, instead of five, electoral lists; hence political power was divided among a larger number of list readers.

Despite this threat to the "*Zaim* System," control of local politics still remained in the hands of confessional leaders who had acquired their positions through traditional family networks creating notables who inherited political leadership. As the country became more urbanized, power of the rural *Zuama* was at times diluted. With enlargement of the urban professional class —lawyers, physicians, journalists, pharmacists, businessmen—many individuals without traditional ties entered politics, but still within an urbanized version of the "*Zuama* System." Politicians from larger towns and cities formed their own confessional ties which resembled the once all-powerful rural political network. Some formed political parties which ostensibly were nonconfessional, although in fact most of the new parties had a strong confessional bias. At the top of the political pyramid, the same traditional Christian, Muslim, and Druse family names reappeared again and again in Lebanese cabinets, the parliament, and at the head of the country.

LEBANON AND THE ARAB WORLD

Lebanon's special character as the only Christian nation in the Arab world, as agreed to in the unwritten National Pact of 1943, was also recognized by her Arab neighbors at the founding conference of the Arab League in Alexandria late in 1944. A special resolution emphasized that Arab League nations "respect[ed]...the independence and sovereignty of Lebanon...[in consequence of Lebanon's adoption of] a policy of independence...unanimously approved by the Lebanese Chamber of Deputies on October 7th, 1943."[4]

Two extreme views of Lebanon's role, as well as various moderate ones, had emerged during the mandate. One was held by many in the Sunni Muslim districts, which had identified with Faisal's abortive Damascus government in 1920; they hoped for eventual integration into Greater Syria as one of its several Arab provinces. The other was held by a Maronite element which came to regard Lebanon as part of Europe, totally independent of the Arab hinterland. Many Maronites who feared the Islamic influences in Arab nationalism embraced Phoenicianism, a concept that conceived of the Lebanese as a Mediterranean racial and cultural group distinct from the Arab world, but willing to cooperate with it on matters of mutual interest. The Phoenicianists felt themselves culturally superior to the Muslims.

The views of the Christian community also reflected internal divisions. Many members of the second largest Christian group, the Greek Orthodox, were more sympathetic to the Arab East than to the West, regarding themselves as Arabs first and Lebanese second. Their antipathy to the West derived from centuries of religious competition between the Western Catholic and Eastern Orthodox churches.

A few Muslim, and an even smaller number of Christian, Arab nationalists believed that the Arab nationalist movement could remain secular. Until popular opinion could be educated to the advantages of complete union with the Arab world, however, these secularists were willing to acknowledge Lebanon's special character and differences. Recognizing the deep fears of the Maronites concerning their position in a Muslim world, they were prepared to maintain the country's independence. In the interim, Lebanon, with an Arab character and a Western orientation, must strive to bridge the gap between Occident and Orient, between Muslim and Christian worlds.

With the growth of Arab nationalism after World War I, the Christians became increasingly aware of the dilemma they faced in belonging to the Arab East. Although they, too, were Arabs, the Christians recalled that under the Ottomans they had been accorded dhimmi status (see chapter 3) and treated as second-class subjects. Culturally, the Christians were closely tied to the West; politically, their fate was tied with the Arab East.

The Lebanese Muslim never faced the same conflict of loyalties. He was an integral part of the greater Arab world surrounding him. To him, the Christian West was imperialist and offered little emotional attraction. In classic Islamic tradition, he could view the non-Muslim world as perpetually hostile to Islam and react accordingly.

The problem of Lebanon's identity was greatly complicated after 1967 by divisions in the country over support for the Palestinians. Although Lebanon had supported all Arab League resolutions on the Palestine problem, had participated in the first Arab-Israel war in 1948, and had refused to recognize the Jewish State, the border between the two countries was relatively quiet from 1949 to 1968. Thereafter, pressures increased from Palestinian commandos and their nationalist supporters in Lebanon, to provide bases and support for attacks against Israel. This led to serious rifts within Lebanon over the question of its identity as an Arab nation in support of the Palestine Arab cause.

THE 1958 LEBANESE REVOLUTION

Bishara al-Khuri's attempt to patch up Muslim-Christian differences in the 1943 National Pact began to wear thin after a decade. New republican, socialist, and nationalist ideologies were influencing the country, and Nasser's revolution also began to acquire Lebanese supporters. By 1956, when Nasser had become not merely an Egyptian, but an Arab hero, larger numbers of Lebanese began to advocate unity with the Arab world with Nasser as its leader. In Muslim areas, it became increasingly commonplace to find homes, public places, and vehicles adorned with pictures of the new Arab leader.

Muslim grievances, which had not been expressed for a decade because of the National Pact, now came to the surface. Demands for a new census, which would obviously indicate a Muslim majority, were put forward. Centers of discontent with "second-class citizenship" sprang up in Beirut, Sidon, Tripoli, Baalbek, and other largely Muslim towns. Every Muslim in Lebanon was suffering, wrote a parliamentary deputy from Tripoli, using his own town as an example. In Ottoman days, when the town of Tripoli was the capital of Tripoli province, its leaders "enjoyed prestige and its learned men respect before sultans and ministers and governors." Its commerce, agriculture, and industry then made it one of the richest Syrian provinces. "Its markets, hotels, restaurants, clinics, hospitals, and courts were crowded with thousands of fellow Arabs, just as Beirut, the capital, today is full of the inhabitants of the outlying regions of the Republic and the neighboring countries."

After the French occupation in 1920, when Tripoli was separated from Syria and Christians became the majority in Lebanon, the Muslims began to suffer, he asserted. The town of Tripoli remained prosperous at first, but its inhabitants did not relish the loss of their connections with Syria. Throughout the mandatory era, the Muslims sustained their loyalty to Syria. In 1945 when Lebanon became independent, many Muslims believed that they would acquire full equality. However, continued the Tripoli deputy, independence brought no real change, for authority "in its entirety" was controlled by non-Muslims. Muslims, who held positions, "became a 'pliant tool' in the hands of the [Christian] President of the Republic who disposed of everything, large and small, according to whim and fancy." Muslims began to feel discriminated against by the Christian majority. Even illiteracy was widespread, ran the complaint, because the government failed to open adequate schools or enforce compulsory education. The government also practiced economic discrimination and failed to assist Tripoli's rural population "as though there were a planned policy to impoverish the Muslims."

When high customs or duties were placed on the articles of commerce that passed between Syria and Lebanon after 1950, following collapse of the French-established customs and currency union, Tripoli lost its markets, "its trade stagnated, its industries came to a standstill, and its agriculture deteriorated." The Muslim deputy acknowledged that President Chamoun attempted to "soften the harshness of economic neglect" after 1952 by expanding Tripoli's port, but it was too late to save the town from economic ruin. While the state was spending hundreds of millions of pounds on roads leading to the Maronite heartland, Mount Lebanon, he declared, those in "every other Muslim region" were neglected.[5]

Muslims also attacked President Chamoun's failure to take a more forceful stand against England and France during the Anglo-French-Israeli attack on Egypt during 1956. By the time the UAR was formed in February 1958, Lebanon was divided into pro- and anti-Nasser camps.

Christian, especially Maronite, reaction to the increased intensity of Arab nationalism was also vehement. The near deification of Nasser, the trend of Muslim opinion toward Arab unity, and the demands for equality seemed a threat to Lebanon's independence and, consequently, to the non-Muslim minorities. Identification with Nasser might cost the country Western support and leave the Christians isolated during a crisis. For the Christians a new census (the last had been taken in 1932) was, of course, out of the question, for it would reveal that Lebanon now had a Muslim majority, destroying the political fiction of a Christian majority. Altering the ratio of government posts in favor of the Muslims would be a step in that direction and, therefore, could not be countenanced. Precarious as it was, the only guarantee of Maronite security was continuation of the *status quo*.

After Nasser's first visit to Damascus in 1958, it became impossible to contain Muslim enthusiasm, and hundreds of thousands flocked across the border to welcome him. The Chamoun government's reaction, however, wrote Muslim Deputy al-Jisr, "can best be described as lukewarm. This attitude implied a serious deviation towards Western imperialist policies."[6] Each side now openly charged the other with violating the National Pact. Muslims felt that Chamoun's failure to break relations with Great Britain and France in 1956 had betrayed the Arab cause and implied support for the West against the Arab nationalists. Chamoun's backers saw in the enthusiastic support that Muslim politicians urged for Egypt an invitation to abandon Lebanon's neutral position between Arab nationalism and the West.

Added to the rancor caused by Arab nationalist resentments were the inept administrative policies and abrupt personal attitudes of Chamoun. Lebanese objections were not directed at the president's use of violence and bribery at the polls, but rather at the scale to which he used them. After his election in 1958, Chamoun failed to distribute the spoils of office among the politicians who supported him, as was the usual practice. When rumors then spread that Chamoun intended to have the constitution amended so that he could serve another term, the Muslims decided to rebel.

The uprising was sparked by assassination of a left-wing pro-Nasser editor in May 1958, followed by nationwide sympathy demonstrations and a general strike. Individual incidents flared into violent clashes between the government and opposition, until each side had seized whole areas of the country. Armed bands, opposed to the government, soon had the upper hand as a result of military supplies they received from Syria and the Lebanese army's decision to remain neutral. Government charges in the spring of 1958 that the rebellion was instigated and aided by the UAR brought the problem to the Arab League, where no action was taken, and to the U.N. Security Council, which decided to send a group of observers (UNOGIL) to investigate. UNOGIL found no evidence of foreign intervention or support of any consequence.

In the opposition were several non-Muslims who, although not Arab nationalists, supported the struggle against Chamoun for their own political reasons. They included Druse chieftain Kemal Jumblatt and the Maronite patriarch, who believed that Chamoun's extreme pro-Westernism jeopardized the position of all Christians in the East. By July, the struggle had become truly partisan and threatened to throw Lebanon completely into the Nasser camp. When this possibility seemed greatest, after destruction of the Hashemite regime in Iraq on July 14, Chamoun requested the United States to land troops under the Eisenhower Doctrine "to preserve order and to [help Lebanon] defend itself against indirect aggression."

While American troops became involved in no military incidents in Lebanon, their presence helped to neutralize both sides and the civil war gradually began to subside. Hopes for a solution were encouraged by the parliamentary election on July 31 of the army chief of staff, General Fuad Shehab, to succeed Chamoun. But the Phalangists violently objected to his choice of a cabinet headed by Rashid Karami, former opposition leader in Tripoli. This, they charged, was rewarding the ex-rebel, instead of punishing him. Fighting again flared up for several more weeks between the Phalangists, now assisted by former President Chamoun's backers, and the pro-Nasserites.

During the civil war, Lebanon's economy was seriously affected. Beirut port was forced to close, and almost all commerce, banking, industry, transport, the tourist trade, and other economic activities from which the country lived were halted. In the capital alone, there were nearly 30,000 unemployed. By mid-October, labor syndicates and businessmen had become desperate and pleaded with all factions to save the remnants of the country's economic life.

Both sides were persuaded, in October, to form a "salvation cabinet" of four leaders representing the opposing groups. Rashid Karami and Hussein Oueini represented the Muslims, and Raymond Edde and Phalange chief Pierre Jemayel, the Christians. This was an unprecedented constitutional change since the cabinet now had an equal number of Muslims and Christians. Another innovation was the appointment of a Muslim, Hussein Oueini, as foreign minister. The "salvation" government was initially granted extraordinary powers by the Chamber of Deputies to rule by decree for six months.

By the end of 1958, all American troops had been withdrawn and life returned to normal throughout the country. Transport to Syria was restored along the main artery, which had been in rebel hands; the 30,000 unemployed in Beirut began to filter back to their jobs; factories reopened; and the port renewed operations. No fundamental changes had resulted from the revolution. Religion continued to be the basis of political life. Parliamentary seats were still based on the ratio of six Christians for five Muslims. And the republic had devised no fundamentally new economic or social programs to meet the country's growing needs.

LEBANESE POLITICAL FACTIONS

Following the 1958 revolution several interlocking dilemmas faced the country. Foremost was increasing tension between representatives of the old *Zaim* System and the growing numbers of younger politicians eager to break out of the confines of traditional politics. The tensions were reflected in increased competition between two principal political groupings representing the chief antagonists in 1958.

The *status quo* in the country's political system, in its socio-economic policies, in its foreign relations, and in its Arab world role was supported by the tripartite, or triple, alliance, a grouping of political leaders also known as Chamounists because of the leadership position of former President Chamoun. Three pro-Western right-of-center groupings belonged to the triple alliance. Although they adopted political party labels, they were in reality part of the *Zaim* System. The National Liberal party headed by Chamoun represented former followers of the ex-president concentrated in the area of Lebanon, which he considered home. The National Bloc party, led by Raymond Edde, followed the traditional leadership of the Edde family. The only real national party in the alliance was the Phalangist, led by Pierre Jemayel, a largely Christian group dominated by Maronites. During the 1960s the Chamounists attempted to achieve, through political means, goals they had failed to attain in the 1958 revolution. Lebanon was to remain free of entangling alliances with other Arab countries and to maintain a peaceful frontier with Israel. The free-enterprise system, which had given the country one of the highest living standards in the Arab world, was to be maintained, and government was to interfere as little as possible in matters such as resource allocation, stabilizing the economy, or the confessional system.

The chief political rivals of the Chamounists were a coalition of groups representing both Muslims and Christians who were willing to change the *status quo* and who were therefore regarded as representative of the "new generation" and of "progressivism." This Democratic Bloc chose as its leader Chamoun's successor, the Christian former commander in chief of the army, General Fuad Shehab. They were therefore known as Shehabists. Since Shehabist leaders were more responsive to growing pressures for Lebanon's identification with the Arab world, they were also regarded as "pro-Arab" and left-of-center. When in power, the Shehabists did little to alter the country's social or political structure. Among these leaders were former Prime Minister Rashid Karami, who headed a regional group from Tripoli known as the Democratic Front, and a loose alliance of deputies in the parliament known as the National Struggle Front, who at times followed Kemal Jumblatt of the PPS. Since neither group could command a parliamentary majority, they competed for support of uncommitted deputies who held the majority of votes. Leaders of the two groups interexchanged cabinet posts, maintaining a delicate balance, at first under the presidency of Shehab and between 1964 and 1970, under President Charles Helou. While Shehab was sympathetic to the so-called radicals, Helou was regarded as more favorable toward the traditional Lebanese political stance of neutralism and *status quo*.

The close election of a new president, Suleiman Franjieh, in 1970 portended a sharp turn toward Lebanon's traditional position of neutrality. Franjieh, a traditionalist Maronite Zaim from northern Lebanon, had his own private army, which, prior to his election as president by the parliament, he had not hesitated to use against agitators who had threatened to involve the country in clashes with Israel. While still a member of parliament, Franjieh, who associated with the Chamounists, had charged that his predecessor, President Helou, had failed to protect Lebanon's sovereignty from intrusions by Palestinian guerrillas.

Competition for power between the old and new orders was played out within parliament on the one hand, and between parliament and the president on the other. Although the president was chosen by the chamber of deputies, once installed for his six-year term there was little that parliament could do to topple him. Since the president appointed the prime minister and his cabinet, and had power to dissolve the parliament and to appoint public officials, a strong chief executive could seize the upper hand in the political process. President Shehab played a strong role, attempting to improve conditions that had led to Muslim unrest in 1958. At the same time he attempted to maintain the political balance by selecting representatives from both Chamounists and Shehabists for his various cabinets.

President Helou played the role in a different style. He was more the mediator between various factions, concentrating on administrative reform rather than attempting to alter the social and economic structure. A severe blow was dealt the Helou administration by collapse, in October 1966, of the Intra Bank, one of the country's principal money institutions. The resulting crisis seriously undermined business confidence in Lebanon, where banking activities are of the highest importance.

Political life in Lebanon has tended to galvanize around loosely organized factions rather than in parties organized and structured as in Europe. The factions often are based on a leader's personality or the communal interests of his followers instead of on political principles. Political combinations sometimes were created from apparently contradictory ideologies or emerged from groups with unrelated principles. Only a few could even be called political parties in the normative sense. During the 1975–1976 civil war they divided into two main coalitions: the Front of Lebanese Forces versus the Front of National and Leftist Forces.

The Lebanese Front was a more cohesive, compact, and homogeneous coalition. Its largest group led by one of Lebanon's older statesmen, Pierre Jemayel, was the *Phalanges Libanaises*. Founded as a patriotic youth movement in 1936, within two generations it became the country's largest political party with nearly 150,000 estimated members. Its founders included Pierre Jemayel, then a pharmacist, and Charles Helou, a future president. Goals were to foster Lebanese consciousness, a civic sense, and a spirit of discipline. During the 1930s Phalange leaders were much impressed by the patriotism and discipline of European Fascism. Later the emphasis was placed on Lebanese Christian values. More than 80 percent of Phalange members were middle-class Maronites, with a sprinkling of other Christians and a small minority of Shi'ite Muslims.

In reaction to Arab nationalism the movement became politicized during the 1930s in support of Lebanon's distinctive identity. One of its unique doctrines has been that all Lebanese, both at home and abroad, are an integral part of the nation. Because only a few of the country's hundreds of thousands of emigrants have been Muslim, this doctrine strengthened the idea of a Christian majority by favoring citizenship for overseas Lebanese. The Phalangist slogan, "Lebanon above all," expressed Christian reaction against incorporation of the country into the larger Arab world. The roots of Lebanon's distinctive identity go back to ancient Phoenicia, according to the Phalange. Therefore the country's true heritage was not Arab or Islamic, but went back to ancient times. However, Lebanon should cooperate with the Arab countries in economic matters, but its political relations with other Arab League members should be those of a sovereign state.

Its doctrine of "social democratism" emphasized private initiative as the basis of the country's prosperity. The state is obligated to improve infrastructure, to rationalize management of the public sector, and to develop social policy as a way of encouraging and supporting private enterprise. In religious matters it advocated a "civil secular legislation which respects religion while excluding subjection to any canon law whether Christian or Muslim." This does not imply opposition to the confessional system. Rather, the system would be modified in time as the country evolved. The party motto, "God, Country, Family," showed its attachment to traditional religious values.

Phalangist values and programs have naturally placed it in conflict with groups advocating radical economic and social ideologies and with militant pan-Arabism. Its leaders have been in the vanguard of anti-Communist movements and oppose closer Lebanese collaboration with the Palestinians. While playing a lead role in achievement of independence from France, the Phalangists have been strong opponents of Nasserist, Ba'athist, Communist, and Palestinian influences in Lebanon.

The party's pyramidal organizational structure, with authority descending from above into sections organized in hundreds of villages and neighborhoods, has made it a formidable political and paramilitary force. Its paramilitary formations were at the core of the Lebanese Front and often led the fighting. Their deep resentment against the Palestinians for interfering in Lebanese life and compromising the country's sovereignty was a major cause of the civil war. Initially the Phalange supported Syrian intervention as a way of terminating Palestinian interference, but when it became apparent that the Syrians would remain for a long time, its leaders had second thoughts.

Groups in the Lebanese Front such as the National Liberal Party grouped around Chamoun and his family, and the Zogharta Liberation Army organized by Franjieh, were both family and regional associations, with no doctrine as developed as that of the Phalange. Guardians of the Cedars, the Order of Lebanese Monks, and the Front of the Cedar were small organizations of fervent Maronites who regard the struggle as a crusade to preserve Lebanon's Christian character. After 1978 the Phalange attempted to subsume these groups into a larger Maronite Front under Phalange control.

The Front of National and Leftist Forces was a much more heterogeneous coalition including a spectrum of groups ranging from conservative Muslim to Communist. Only two of its members could be classified as significant political factors in the Lebanese context: the Progressive Socialist party (PSP) and the Syrian Social Nationalist party (PPS). The Ba'athists, both the Syrian and Iraqi factions, and Communists also have clear political objectives, but they were not influential in Lebanese politics.

The Front of Nationalists and Leftists was led by Kemal Jumblatt, founder and leader of the PSP. A unique personality, his charisma succeeded in keeping the coalition of nationalists, leftists, Muslims, and Palestinians intact through the civil war. After his assassination in 1977, the Left Nationalist Front tended to lose its cohesiveness. Its most charismatic leader, the only one who had been able to overcome ideological, sectarian, and personal feuds was gone.

Jumblatt's son succeeded as titular leader of the PSP although he had not been active in politics before. The older Jumblatt acquired his political base as the scion of a family long recognized for its leadership of an important Druse faction (see chapter 14). Kemal Jumblatt entered parliament in 1943 as representative of his clan, not as a socialist. Most support continued to come from fellow Druses and retainers of the Jumblatt family. As he acquired a reputation for radical politics, Jumblatt's support broadened to include many non-Druses. His ideology was a synthesis of European socialist doctrines, learned while a student at the Sorbonne, and mystic teachings inspired by Gandhi during visits to India. Even while commanding leftist groups during the 1975–1976 civil war, Jumblatt continued to call himself a pacifist. After 1949, when the PSP was officially organized, many Christian intellectuals, both Arab nationalists and those with socialist inclinations, were attracted by the leader's personality and his relatively radical program. He advocated such startling innovations as unemployment insurance, universal free education on all levels, health insurance, free medical care, national housing, liberalization of press controls, and nationalization of public utilities. Initially a "neutralist" or "Third Worlder" in foreign policy, Jumblatt moved toward the left. Strong opposition to Western imperialism created close ties with Egypt's President Nasser after the 1956 war. When the Palestine issue flared up again in 1967 Jumblatt became one of the strongest supporters of the commando organizations and the PLO, insisting that they be given free rein to conduct operations from Lebanon against Israel.

The PPS, established in 1932, was also largely a one-man creation. He was Antun Saadeh, son of a Lebanese Greek Orthodox physician. Saadeh came to the Levant in the early 1930s from Brazil, where his family had settled, and became a German tutor at the American University of Beirut. Not until 1936 did Saadeh's secret group emerge in public with its platform favoring unity among "natural Syrians," originally including the population of the

Levant, Palestine, and Transjordan. Later, Iraq, Cyprus, and Kuwait were added to the area of "natural Syria." Saadeh's concept of what constituted a Syrian was drawn from a broader base than just Arab nationalism: it included all the religious, ethnic, linguistic, and national groups of the region except the Jews. The idea was to create a homogeneous Syrian society by destroying communal barriers and the traditional feudal land system and ending the relationship between church and state. Rigid discipline and strict adherence to Saadeh's so-called scientific philosophy were required of all members. His advocacy of active combat and conspiratorial tactics caused the PPS to be banned periodically by the Lebanese and Syrian authorities. When an ambush that the PPS charged was arranged by the Lebanese government killed Antun Saadeh in July 1949, party members retaliated with the assassination of the former prime minister Riyad al-Sulh. In 1953, the PPS added "Social" to its name (Syrian National Social party) to meet the growing sentiment for reform. PPS antipathy to Arab nationalism has generally alienated Muslims, and most of its members are Greek Orthodox. Emphasis on greater Syria has led the party to establish branches in the surrounding countries and among Christian émigrés in South America and in Africa.

During the civil war the PPS found itself among strange allies. Instead of joining forces with the so-called "rightist" parties, it became part of Jumblatt's Front. The organization's relatively conservative social doctrines might have placed it closer ideologically to the Phalange; however, its national credo aligned it with the groups opposed to sectarianism, partition, and further intensification of Lebanese separatism. The civil war terminated the long feud between the PPS and the Lebanese left.

The war also legitimized the Lebanese Communist party, for many decades on the fringes of political life. First established in 1924, the party has since been merged, remerged, and reorganized with other leftist groups. One of its first problems was "Arabization," that is, expanding the membership beyond a small circle of Christian intellectuals. When the party espoused the goal of Arab unity in 1930 it became known as the Syrian Communist party, and among its early leaders was Khaled Bakdash, later to become the leader of the Syrian Communist movement. After the Popular Front became the government of France in 1936, the Communist party was legalized in Lebanon, but had to go underground four years later when the Popular Front fell. During and after the war the party played an active role in the independence movement against France. At the first Syro-Lebanese Communist party Congress in 1944 separate Communist parties were formed because both Syria and Lebanon were now independent.

The Communist movement in Lebanon was active among organized labor, where it won the support of seven of fifteen unions in a national federation of workers' and employees' groups. Soon after independence the new government again declared the Communist party illegal and it was forced to go underground. Support for the Soviet position on Palestine further isolated the party. Not until the late 1950s was it able to join the mainstream by identifying with Arab nationalist groups opposed to the Baghdad Pact, the Eisenhower Doctrine, and other Western policies.

Initially the Communists were hostile to the Palestinian resistance movement and the PLO because of their "adventurist policy." After the 1973 war when the Soviet Union began to reevaluate the PLO, the Lebanese Communists also became less hostile. During the civil war the Lebanese Communist party was drawn into armed combat for the first time. Jumblatt's PSP, the Lebanese Communist Party, and another small radical Marxist group, the Lebanese Communist Action Organization, formed the nucleus of the "National and Progressive Movements." By 1977 the party had stabilized at some 15,000 members, more than half Shi'ites; about 15 or 20 percent Sunnis and Druse; Christians were about 30 percent.

The Muslim parties in Jumblatt's Front represented a mixture ranging from conservative Sunni to pan-Arab Nasserist groups. Some incorporated the membership of Muslim organizations, such as *al-Najada* (Helpers), and the National Appeal party, both established in 1936 to counteract the influence of the Phalange. They and the Sunni National Organization had been active in the 1950s but much of their support was channeled into groups considering themselves followers of the Nasserist ideal. In the Front of National and Leftist forces during 1976 there were at least four such groups, the Independent Nasserist Movement, the Popular Nasserist Organization, the Nasserist Organization—Corrective Movement, and the Nasserist Organization—Union of Popular Labor Forces. In addition there were the Arab Socialist Union and the Movement of the Deprived. The latter, headed by the Shi'ite leader of south Lebanon, Musa Sadr, was one of the first Shi'ite political manifestations of discontent with social and economic conditions. The Front also included two Ba'athist groups, one affiliated with Syria, another with Iraq.

This improbable coalition of diverse groups, with little in common other than opposition to the *status quo*, demonstrated how difficult it would be to restore stability in Lebanon. While Jumblatt was alive, he held them together. After his death, they disagreed among themselves over their relations with Syria, over which aspect of the *status quo* should be changed, and even over the kind of support to give the Palestinians. Some were conservative in their approach to economic and social policy, others militant advocates of change. A clear distinction between the Left-Nationalist Front and the large Christian Lebanese Front was that few traditional leaders were active in the former. Leaders of the Christian groups were men who had been in command since the state was established, although their sons increasingly played the surrogate role until they took charge in the 1980s. Family status continued to be important among the conservative Christians more than among their opponents.

THE GREAT CIVIL WAR

While free-enterprise Lebanon was better off than her neighbors because of income acquired from the invisible exports produced by trade, finance, and commerce, beneath the surface of apparent prosperity there were hidden social and economic problems. Population was growing at a rapid rate, having doubled since independence. As a result, Lebanon was becoming one of the most densely settled countries. After 1950, industrial production doubled through private initiative, concentrating mostly in consumer goods. However, industry contributed only a small share (15 percent) of national income. Although agriculture continued to provide nearly half the country's employment, those working on the land received a mere 15 percent of the gross national product. Trade, commerce, and tourism continued to dominate the economy, and the minority of people employed in these pursuits consumed by far the largest proportion of the GNP—well over half. Reluctant to intervene in sectors of the economy that had been traditionally in private hands and had flourished with private management, the government attempted to improve agriculture through investing in projects, such as the Litani River dam, rural electrification, and extending irrigated areas.

The most serious dilemma, by far, facing Lebanon has been the role that it is to play within its Arab context. The country's position has been complicated by divisiveness within its own population, and by the presence of about 300,000 refugees—largely, Muslim—from Israel-held territory. Because of the delicate balance between Lebanese Christians and Muslims, the country has refused to grant citizenship to most of the Palestinian refugees who have lived there since 1948. In large concentrations, often living at subsistence level under care of the United Nations, the refugees have constituted a disruptive and politically unstable element. The government has refused to grant them citizenship for fear of diluting the *de facto* Christian "majority" of the population.

With the rise of an intense nationalist sentiment among Palestinians after the 1967 war, and organization of many refugees in commando groups whose purpose was to strike at Israel, the refugee role has become even more disruptive. Public opinion in the country divided, to some extent along religious lines, but more accurately, between those identified with the triple alliance favoring the *status quo*, opposed by more militant Arab nationalists who favored support for the Palestine liberation movement. The question became more than one of ideology. Lebanon was faced with the dilemma of whether or not to expose itself to attack by Israel if it permitted the commandos to operate within its frontiers. The situation turned critical in December 1968 after Israeli commandos raided the Beirut airport, destroying thirteen aircraft belonging to Lebanese lines, in retaliation for an attack by Arab guerrillas at the Athens airport. The Israelis charged that the Palestine commandos had departed from Beirut with full knowledge of the Lebanese government in preparation for their Athens attack. The incident polarized opinion in Lebanon between those who advocated imposition of restrictions on the Palestinians, and those who favored all-out support in their struggle against Israel. The differences led to collapse of the government and to administration without a cabinet for nearly one year.

Clashes between Palestinians and Lebanese threatened to split the country politically, and to undermine its internal security. The crisis was compounded by differences between president Helou who spoke out against the "fait accompli" of the Palestine resistance, and the prime minister, Rashid Karameh, a Muslim leader who differed with the chief of state. After many incidents of fighting between Lebanese security forces and Palestinian guerrillas, the government requested Egyptian president Nasser's mediation in October 1969. A secret accord was hammered out, known as the "Cairo Agreements" signed in November by the commander-in-chief of the Lebanese army, and the president of the Palestine Liberation Organization (PLO), Yassir Arafat. The agreements authorized Palestinians to live and work in Lebanon and to establish local committees cooperating with Lebanese authorities to look after Palestinian interests. The Palestinian Armed Struggle Command (PASC) was given authority inside the country's Palestinian Arab refugee camps. While Palestinian guerrilla forces were permitted free movement in Lebanon, Lebanese civil and military authorities were to have full responsibility and authority in all parts of the country.

The Cairo Agreements were a victory for the guerrilla organizations. For the first time they were given official authority to carry out operations against Israel from Lebanese territory and control of refugee camps. Their major concession was surrender of a base in northern Lebanon and submission of activities on the Israeli border to coordination with the army, a provision that remained largely theoretical. Failure to implement it caused increasing tension between Palestinians and Lebanese.

The Agreements stirred opposition among several Christian political groups. Raymond Edde, leader of the National Bloc party, complained that it gave Israel a pretext for attacking Lebanon. However implementation was supervised by the new Minister of the Interior, Kemal Jumblatt, leader of the Progressive Socialist party known for its close ties with and sympathy for the Palestinian resistance. The result was an increase in Israeli attacks on towns in southern Lebanon and more hostility between Christian villagers and Palestinian commandos.

Defeat of Palestinian forces in Jordan and the exodus of many guerrilla leaders to Lebanon during 1970 and 1971 at first diminished their activity. But after treading softly for a few months, the Palestinian fedayeen moved their main activities to southern Lebanon. Their attacks on Israel led to large-scale retaliations and occupation of Lebanese villages by Israeli forces. When the Israelis withdrew, the Lebanese army took over in an unsuccessful attempt to prevent renewed hostilities. Raymond Edde asked parliament to repeal the Cairo Agreements, but the PLO and its Lebanese Muslim supporters refused. Through the mediation efforts of Saudi Arabia, in June 1972 the PLO agreed to temporarily suspend military activities in southern Lebanon and to withdraw from towns, cities, and agricultural areas.

The June 1972 agreements failed to neutralize southern Lebanon. In reprisal for terrorist acts in Europe by a Palestinian group called Black September (named to commemorate the events in Jordan during September 1970), Israel again invaded parts of southern Lebanon, occupying several towns for two days. The intent was to drive a wedge between the Palestinians and Lebanese, forcing the latter to disown the Cairo Agreements and to terminate relations with the PLO.

Escalating tensions with the Palestinians converged with a series of internal crises. Strikes, demonstrations against unemployment and inflation, student unrest, and fighting between Lebanese rightists and leftists showed how unstable the situation was. Government incapacity to deal with these events and the growing number of Israeli attacks undermined confidence in the new president, Suleiman Franjieh. In February 1973, after Israeli commandos attacked Palestinian guerrilla bases more than one hundred miles north of the border and shot three PLO leaders at their homes in Beirut, the government resigned. Three governments within two months failed to restore order or confidence.

Attempts to carry out civil service reforms intended to diminish the allocation of government posts by religious affiliation were regarded as insufficiently reformist by Muslims and radicals. Militant rightists in the National Liberal Party, the Phalange, and the National Bloc condemned the proposals because they conceded too much. In the meantime both Christian and Muslim groups were forming their own militias and acquiring large stocks of arms in the international market.

Although Lebanon was not directly involved in the 1973 October war, the southern part of the country was the continued target of Israel reprisal raids by land, sea, and air. During 1973 and 1974 hundreds of Lebanese were killed and wounded in the incessant spiral of guerrilla terrorist attacks and Israeli reprisals. Differing perceptions of these episodes by pro-Palestinian and anti-Palestinian Lebanese drove a deep rift through the society. Christian groups on the right, like the Phalangists and National Liberals, regarded the Palestinians as intruders who were arrogating to themselves authority that belonged to the Lebanese government. While they were willing to give verbal backing to the Palestinian cause, they opposed surrender of the country's sovereignty to the non-Lebanese "intruders." Supporters of the Palestinians included a much broader range of Lebanese, from Muslim conservatives to militant leftists, many of whom were also Christian. They regarded the Palestinians as patriots fighting the cause of all Arabs. They were led by

Kemal Jumblatt whose views became increasingly supportive of Arab nationalism and radical social change in Lebanon.

Open conflict escalated into a full-scale civil war in 1975. When the civil war ended after nineteen months of the most savage fighting the country and the region had seen in nearly a century, an estimated 60,000 lives were lost; many times that number wounded; a million people, nearly a third of the country's population displaced; and several billion dollars worth of damage done to the country. Much of Beirut lay in ruins. There was great uncertainty that it would regain its role as the center of trade and commerce for the Arab world.

Two incidents, one a clash between Palestinians and Phalangists, the other a Lebanese labor dispute, precipitated the civil war. In the first, on April 13, 1975, a prominent Phalangist was assassinated by shots from a passing automobile in a Christian neighborhood. Later in the day, Phalangists "revenged" his death by killing 27 Palestinians who were passing a church dedication in a Christian neighborhood. The Labor dispute started in February 1975 with a fisherman's strike in the southern Lebanese town of Sidon. The fishermen, mostly Muslim, opposed attempts of a large, private corporation owned by Christians who were relatives of Chamoun, to take over fishing in the area. A popular politician who supported the rights of small fishermen was shot, leading to clashes between the army and civilian demonstrators. These two incidents dramatized the differences between Lebanese who were pro-Palestinian (i.e., supported the country's stronger affiliation with Arab causes) and the militant pro-Lebanese nationalists; and between the privileged elites (perceived as Christian) and the largely Muslim working classs. Although religious affiliation at first was only incidental, it acquired increasing significance as the civil war raged on. While only a few Muslims were associated with the "Christian" side, many Christians supported the radical or Muslim factions, led by the non-Muslim Druse, Kemal Jumblatt.

The Muslim prime minister resigned after the April clash because after a week's time he was unable to stop the fighting. "To restore order," President Franjieh appointed a new government of seven military officers and one civilian. For this "military cabinet," the first since independence, he was strongly criticized by leftists, Muslims, and several Christian leaders. After three days, the military government resigned, and the president turned again to Rashid Karami, one of the traditional Muslim leaders who had been prime minister many times before.

In a short truce during the summer of 1975 several Arab countries, especially Syria, attempted to intervene. Karami took this opportunity to propose a series of reforms intended to improve the lot of workers, such as construction of 5,000 low-income homes and establishment of a housing bank. He also prepared new laws to reorganize the army and resolve the problem of naturalization. Critics on the left regarded his reform proposals as tokenism and betrayal of their support. Their "programme for the democratic reform of the Lebanese System" included more far-reaching changes such as abolition of political confessionalism, a new electoral law, and reorganization of the army.

By the end of August the "Great Truce" became frayed. Although Christians and Muslims were intermingled throughout the country, there were areas where each religious sect dominated. Frequently there were clashes when a majority in an area attempted to drive out or overpower a smaller town or village of differing ethnic background to "purify" the region.

Through Syrian intervention a National Committee for Dialogue was formed late in 1975. It included traditional representatives of all the major religious sects and political trends: conservative Christians, the moderate Muslim and Christian right, Sunni and Shi'ite Muslim traditionaliasts, and the left. Little heed was paid to its resolutions condemning violence and reaffirming attachment to coexistence among the communities. By October fighting spread again despite proclamation of dozens of cease fire announcements.

Arabization of the crisis was proposed by several Muslim and Christian leaders to end the fighting. By the end of 1975 most leaders had traveled to Damascus to discuss with the Syrians ways of halting the civil war. The Arab League, the Vatican, and France also sent emissaries to still the troubled waters. In November, French foreign minister Maurice Couve de Murville arrived in Beirut on a mission to "safeguard the independence, unity and sovereignty of Lebanon."

The Lebanese army refrained from intervention until January 1976. The precedent of nonintervention was established during the 1958 revolution when General Chehab maintained scrupulous neutrality. Because most of its top officers were Christian, the army feared that it would be accused of bias if it intervened in a sectarian struggle. In January army neutrality began to disintegrate. First, the air force intervened to relieve a military convoy blocked at the entrance to Beirut. Muslim leaders violently protested and relations between the Muslim prime minister and Christian president were embittered. Division in the army was deepened a few days later when a Sunni Muslim lieutenant, Ahmed Khatib, formed a rebel unit called the Lebanese Arab Army to join forces with the leftist-Muslim coalition. Within a few weeks it expanded to several thousand soldiers from the Lebanese army. Lieutenant Khatib demanded reorganization of the military with reform to end privileges that he claimed Christians enjoyed in recruitment, training, and allocation of choice command posts.

The inter-Arab dimensions of the conflict became more urgent by 1976. Conflict in Lebanon threatened to spread across the borders drawing in Israel, involving Syria, and upsetting the balance of power among the Arab states. In

January Syrian president Hafez el-Assad sent units of the Army for the Liberation of Palestine to restore the balance between Christian and Muslim forces. With assistance from other Palestinian groups, another short truce was imposed. During the truce President Franjieh visited Damascus, returning with another "programme for national action." These seventeen points offered a combination of reforms and reaffirmations of existing precedents. Division of the three highest offices in the republic among Maronites, Sunnis, and Shi'as was to continue. But seats in parliament were divided equally between Christians and Muslims. Presidential power would be curbed by requiring a two-thirds parliamentary majority to ratify all decisions. The prime minister, hitherto designated by the president, would be elected by the chamber of deputies. Other major changes included creation of a special court to determine the constitutionality of laws, and a Higher Planning and Development Council.

Among Christian groups, Chamoun's National Liberals accepted the reforms, but the militant Front of the Guardians of the Cedar opposed them. Jumblatt complained that they did not go far enough, while Muslim leaders were divided.

As casualties escalated, larger areas were devastated, and international implications of the civil war became more complex. Animosities among the Lebanese polarized around prominent personalities. Franjieh, Chamoun, and Jemayel became villains to the left, and the Christians regarded Jumblatt and the Palestinian leaders as the major enemy. Hoping to de-escalate the personal animosity, the Syrians called the Lebanese parliament to amend the constitution, permitting election of a new, less controversial president.

With protection of Palestinian forces from Syria, the chamber of deputies met on May 8 to elect Elias Sarkis president. Sarkis, a Maronite who had formerly served in high government posts, was considered a moderate unaffiliated with any of the controversial political factions. His election, however, split the Muslim-leftist forces into pro-Syrian and anti-Syrian factions.

After Jumblatt proclaimed his intent to press for "full military victory" against the Christian-rightist coalition, Syria, which until then had maintained the role of neutral intermediary, sent thousands of its troops across the border. Syrian intervention was advantageous to the Christians because it turned the military balance in their favor. France also proposed to send a military force to Lebanon in May. The Syrian phase of intervention changed the international dynamics of the situation by arousing anxiety in other Arab states, worsening relations between Damascus and Moscow, and sparking a threat of Israeli intervention if Syrian forces crossed an unspecified "red line" in southern Lebanon. Iraq also sent troops to support Muslim forces beleaguered by the Syrians in Sidon. Relations between the presidents of

Syria and Egypt worsened as each accused the other of betraying the Arabs. Squabbles also erupted within the small Arab League peacekeeping force sent in 1975. It seemed that nearly every inter-Arab quarrel converged in Lebanon.

Growing dangers of inter-Arab conflict and Israeli intervention aroused Saudi Arabia to action. During June 1976 its leaders summoned the prime ministers of Egypt and Syria for "friendly" talks "in a spirit of brotherhood." Saudi leverage was the massive financial aid extended to the two other Arab countries since their defeat in the 1967 war with Israel. But the feuds between Cairo and Damascus continued and the war in Lebanon raged on into October. Again Saudi Arabia seized the initiative, this time calling the presidents of Egypt, Syria, Lebanon, and the head of the PLO to a mini-summit in Riyadh. The ruler of Kuwait was also invited because of his financial support to Egypt and Syria.

The six Arab chiefs of state signed a peace plan calling for a cease fire and creation of a 30,000-member Arab "deterrent" force to supervise the pact. The 1969 Cairo agreement was reactivated and the rift between presidents Sadat and Assad was temporarily healed. These Riyadh agreements were confirmed at the eighth Arab summit conference a few days later in Cairo.

Although the newly elected President Sarkis was official chief of the "deterrent" force, about two-thirds of its members were Syrian troops, now operating under a "joint" command. By 1977 hostilities had greatly diminished. The Syrians extended their control to most of Lebanon up to the Litani River in the south, considered vital to Israel's security, and efforts were begun to restore normal life. It would be a long time before the ruins of Beirut could be restored and the city regain its role as a center of trade and commerce. In many parts of the country there was *de facto* partition where sectarian groups organized their own local governments. In the Christian enclave northwest of Beirut the small port of Jonieh was expanded and the Phalangist party constructed its own airport to compete with Beirut. Determined to give the Christians an independent economic and transport system as well as independent political life, the Maronites set up their own telecommunications system linked with Cyprus. The most adamant proponent of regionalization was Chamoun. He attacked president Sarkis as a "unitarian" who with Syrian support was trying to impose unity. As an alternative, the Lebanese Front (National Liberals, Phalangists, and followers of ex-president Franjieh) devised a scheme to divide the country into four cantons: the Shi'ites would be dominant in the south, with Sidon as their port; Beirut would be mixed but predominantly Christian; the long northern coastal strip between Beirut and Tripoli would be Maronite; and Tripoli with an arch of land reaching from the north to eastern Lebanon would be Sunni. Each state or canton would have its own police and army units, the right to collect and spend taxes, and a local elected legislative assembly and cabinet.

ISRAELI INTERVENTION

Israeli intervention in Lebanon intensified during the late 1970s with the Begin government's efforts to undermine the political influence of the PLO and to eliminate guerrilla activity, especially against Jewish settlements in northern Israel. However, the increase of PLO influence and power within Lebanon corresponded to diminishing authority of the Lebanese government, until many regions of the country, mainly in the south, were totally controlled by the Palestinians. Attempts by other Arab League members to find an accommodation between the Lebanese government and the PLO calling for withdrawal of PLO forces or curtailment of its military activities were stymied by the reluctance of many moderate and left wing Lebanese leaders to agree on such terms in the face of growing Israeli involvement. Consequently the Palestinian power base expanded, and guerrilla actions against northern Israel increased in number.

In March 1978 after a particularly serious attack by Palestinians on the main road between Haifa and Tel-Aviv resulting in several Jewish deaths, Israel invaded Lebanon in force. Its 25,000 troops occupied the region south of the Litani River for three months, until a United Nations force, the U.N. Interim Force in Lebanon (UNIFIL), replaced the Israelis during their phased withdrawal. But the relationship between Israel and UNIFIL was acrimonious. Israel greatly distrusted the U.N. force because several of its units were from countries sympathetic to the PLO; Begin's government charged that UNIFIL was an ineffective deterrent to terrorist attacks on the northern Jewish settlements.

Continued incidents in the north motivated the Begin government to establish an alliance with friendly forces inside Lebanon to share responsibility in fighting the PLO. A renegade Lebanese army officer, Major Saad Haddad, filled the role, and in 1979 he established an autonomous "Free Lebanon" in some 500 square miles of Lebanon along the border with Israel. Inhabited by about 100,000 Christians and Shi'ites, "Free Lebanon" became, in effect, a state within a state, an Israeli protectorate whose security forces were armed, uniformed, fed, and trained by the Israeli military. A "Good Fence" on the border permitted entry to privileged Lebanese from Haddad-land, and thousands of them were employed, went to schools and hospitals, and conducted trade in Israel.

In the meantime, President Sarkis continued his efforts to curtail PLO forces, but he only worsened relations with the Palestinians and further polarized the diverse Lebanese ethno-political factions between pro- and anti-Palestinians. The political system continued to factionalize; some estimates were that by 1980 there were more than 40 groups, most of them with their own armed bands. Within each of the two main divisions, the Front of Lebanese Forces and the Front of National and Leftist Forces, internecine quarrels reflected the fundamental disagreements of Lebanese society and the wider disputes of the Middle East.

In the Maronite camp Phalangist leader Bashir Jemayel, son of Pierre, sought to consolidate all the Maronites under his command, using force if necessary, "to liberate Lebanon from Palestinian occupation." During 1980 the younger Jemayel emerged as the dominant Maronite figure after his Phalangist militia defeated the Tiger militia of ex-president Chamoun's National Liberal party and Chamoun's son, Dany, leader of the Tigers, announced that he would abandon politics in disgust. This gave the Phalange nearly total control of east Beirut and its large hinterland to the north and east. Jemayel was less successful in his attempt to destroy the Marada force of ex-president Franjieh near Tripoli in northern Lebanon. The death of Franjieh's son in the intra-Maronite fighting so alienated the former president that he broke with the Maronite front and allied himself with the Syrians and some of the Muslim nationalist factions.

The Phalangists were greatly strengthened by their tacit alliance with Israel, cemented by common animosity to the PLO. The Israelis provided the Phalangists with arms, ammunition, military training, and later, after Israel's 1982 invasion, with political support.

During 1979–1980 emerging Shi'ite cohesion resulted in greatly increased Shi'ite political power, especially as it became clear that the group had grown from the third to the largest Lebanese community with more than one million members, constituting nearly a third of the population. From a formerly politically inarticulate, economically and socially underdeveloped minority, the Shi'ites were becoming a force of major consequence, with their own military wing, Amal, and political leaders capable of astute bargaining. Until the 1980s Shi'ite villages in the south were often under PLO control, but with the increase of Israeli intervention and fighting between the PLO and Israel, which overran and destroyed many of their settlements, many Shi'ites demanded control of their own areas. This caused increased violence between Amal and the Palestinians. Shi'ites were also politicized by the disappearance of their spiritual leader, Imam Mousa Sadr, who was believed to have been kidnapped by Libya during a visit to that country. After the rise of the militant Shi'ite regime in Iran and the war between Iran and Iraq begining in 1980, there were clashes between Amal and Palestinian factions in Lebanon supported by Iraq.

With much of Lebanon torn by communal warfare; with Sarkis's failure to reorganize the army or an effective security force; with escalating Israeli intervention renewed in the south, Syrian control of the Bekka Valley, and continued battles between Israel and the PLO, the writ of the government was limited to parts of Beirut and its environs. The 1978 ceasefire and the work of UNIFIL in the south seemed increasingly ineffective. The result was open war between Israel and PLO soon again. Israel staged massive air, sea, and land attacks on Palestinian bases in all parts of the country resulting in many casualities among Lebanese civilians. As Israel escalated its attacks on the Palestinians and its military aid to the Phalange, Syrian attempts to contain the Phalangist militia sparked a growing number of Israeli-Syrian confrontations. These came to a head in 1981 after Israel shot down two Syrian planes and Damascus responded by deploying antiaircraft missiles in Lebanon. It seemed that the two countries were again on the verge of war until the U.S. arranged a ceasefire covering all the major combatants—Israel, Syria and the PLO.

But the new ceasefire lasted hardly a year. The Begin government was still determined to eject the PLO from Lebanon lest it accumulate forces there to step up border attacks on Israel. Israel used the occasion of a Palestinian terrorist attack on its ambassador to London for renewing the campaign against the PLO. In June 1982 it retaliated with a large air raid on Palestinian quarters in Beirut. When the Palestinians responded with missile attacks on Jewish settlements, Israel initiated its sixth war, with another large-scale invasion of Lebanon. This time Israeli forces penetrated into Beirut, seizing nearly all of the southern third of the country.

The fighting ended after nearly three months with the seige of Beirut, with thousands of casualties on all sides, and with extensive destruction in the capital. By the end of 1982 Israel remained in Lebanon awaiting fulfillment of demands for total Syrian and PLO departure from the country before evacuating its own troops.

The war once again completely altered Lebanon's internal political balance. The PLO was driven from Beirut and the south, and its wings were clipped as a political force. Syrian influence was seriously undermined in Lebanon. Not only were Syrian forces driven from several vantage points, but Israel replaced Syria as the most influential outside factor in Lebanese politics. By virtue of its close alliance with and extensive military resources provided by Israel, the Phalange became the dominant internal force. Because of its loss of PLO support and its many internal squabbles, the Front of National and Leftist Forces became weak and ineffectual, leaving the Phalange in control of the government. This was underscored when the parliament chose, first, Phalangist militia leader Bashir Jemayel, and, after his assassination, his brother Amin, to succeed President Sarkis at the end of his six-year term in 1982. Although parliament chose the Jemayel brothers in war conditions, literally under the guns of Israel, Amin later attempted to reconcile intercommunal differences and to win non-Maronite confidence. He sought to achieve this by appointing Shafiq al-Wazzan as prime minister (he was the Muslim appointee of Sarkis) and by resisting Israeli pressures to sign a peace treaty or to make other compromises regarded as unsavory by the Muslim and nationalist factions.

The major problems facing President Amin Jemayel in his new office were to remove all foreign military forces from Lebanon, to rebuild the Lebanese army and security forces, to extend the writ of the government through all the country, and to devise political and social policies that could lead toward a longer lasting reconciliation than those attempted by his recent predecessors.

NOTES

1.   U.N. Conciliation Commission for Palestine, *Final Report of the United Nations Economic Survey Mission for the Middle East,* part I, New York, 1949, p. 49.
2.   Cited in J.C. Hurewitz, *Diplomatic History of the Middle East,* vol. II, p. 68.
3.   A.H. Hourani, *Syria and Lebanon,* London, 1946, p. 169.
4.   *Ibid.,* p. 304.
5.   From a translation by Prof. Nabih Faris of an article by Nadim al-Jisr, parliamentary representative of Tripoli. The article appeared in the Beirut daily, *al-Jaridah,* Sunday, May 18, 1958.
6.   *Ibid.*

14   The Republic of Syria

A FRAGMENTED SOCIETY

Syria is a country of political paradox. Though it is the heartland of intense Arab nationalism, the individualism of its inhabitants, the particularism of its varied regions, and the extreme partisanship of its numerous religious, ethnic, and social groups have prevented the ardent nationalist spirit from every unifying the country for more than a short period. Only months after Syria was united with Egypt in 1958, the central government in Cairo was beset with the traditional problems faced by all administrators in Syria's long history—the problems of a fragmented society.

Although 85 percent of the population is Muslim, every fifth Muslim belongs to a schismatic sect, such as the Alawis (Nusayris), Druses, Ismailis, Shi'ites, or Yezidis. Even more fragmented are the eleven Christian denominations, including Greek Orthodox, Syrian Orthodox, Armenian Gregorians, Greek Catholics, Syrian Catholics, Chaldean Catholics, Armenian Catholics, Maronites, Nestorians, and various Protestants. There are also non-Arabic speaking subminorities, such as the Sunni Muslim Kurds, the Turcomans, and the Circassians, each with its own language, culture, and distinctive social, and often political, orientation. They constitute nearly 10 percent of the population. Nearly half a million Bedouin and seminomads roam the vast desert in the eastern two-thirds of Syria. Although less than 10 percent of the total population, they are a major divisive factor. Sectionalism is still another centrifugal force weakening the State's central authority. Competing social, economic, and political interests have grouped around each of the four major cities—Damascus, Homs, Hama, and Aleppo.

National Sentiment

There is, nevertheless, an overriding Syrian sentiment distinguishing the country from its neighbors. This national sentiment began with the Umayyad Caliphate between 661 and 750 when Damascus reached the zenith of its splendor. Modern Syrians still glory in that era as in no other. From it, they draw much inspiration for revival of modern Arab literature, culture, and nationalism. Contemporary political groups also borrow its symbolism and panoply. Mu'awiyah, founder of the Umayyad dynasty, and his successors remain popular heroes. The tomb of Salah al-Din (Saladin), the Kurdish victor over the Crusaders, is still a national shrine. Even the late Egyptian President Nasser rededicated himself at Salah al-Din's grave when he visited Damascus for the first time in 1958.

Like the other Osmanli Arab provinces, Syria passed into obscurity after 1516. But Damascus remained an important trade and administrative center where caravans met passing through the Levant, northward to Anatolia, east to Iraq and Iran, west to the Mediterranean, and south to the Holy Land or to Islam's birthplace, Mecca. Syrian mosques were important religious centers whose clerics provided the Ottoman administration with many prominent military and religious leaders. A latent Arab consciousness was preserved, however, and the concept of a "Syria" (including present day Lebanon, Israel, and Jordan) remained in men's minds. Damascus was both the heart and brain of Syria. To be a Shami (from Damascus) was a matter of pride, and all Syrians boasted of their association with this ancient city.

After conquering the country in 1831 (see chapter 8), Muhammad 'Ali's son, Ibrahim, encouraged the concept of Syrian nationalism. He opened the country to modern European influences when he invited Christian missionaries to establish educational institutions in the Levant. Syrian students, both Christian and Muslim, took advantage of the educational opportunities offered by these missionaries, and many learned about the Western concept of nationalism from them. Between 1840 and World War I, Damascus and Aleppo became centers for the Arab literary revival and the nationalist movement. In the prewar era, Syrians were active participants in the Arab nationalist secret societies (see chapter 6).

By the end of World War I, with the occupation of Syria by Allied troops, the nationalist movement had acquired a wide following—both as a result of the wartime measures of the Osmanli directed against the local population and because of Allied promises of self-determination. The British controlled most of the region. A small French force occupied the Mediterranean coast, and Amir Faisal's Arab army occupied the interior, having set up bases for Arab governmental control in Damascus, Homs, Hama, and Aleppo. Most officials in Faisal's government were Syrian veterans of the Osmanli civil and military services. A small number were Iraqi officers, some of whom had served either the Osmanlis or the British. Immediately after the October 1918 armistice in the Middle East, Faisal attempted to extend his rule to Beirut and the coast, but he was thwarted by General Allenby; by a secret wartime agreement Great Britain had already recognized the French aim to occupy that region.

France, basing her claims on the Sykes-Picot Agreement (see chapter 5), regarded all northern Syria within her jurisdiction, whereas the Arabs demanded it on the basis of the Husein-McMahon correspondence. Conflict between Faisal and the French was inevitable, since each had such vastly differing concepts of their rights in the area.

Amir Faisal, as the formal head of the Hijaz delegation, presented Arab nationalist claims for self-determination at the Versailles Peace Conference; he claimed to speak for all Muslim-Arab Asia. He asserted that 99 percent of the inhabitants in the area south of Anatolia to the Arabian Sea and Persian Gulf and from the Mediterranean coast to the borders of Iran were Arabs, whom he defined as people of closely related Semitic stocks, all speaking one language, Arabic. He acknowledged that the various former provinces of Syria, Iraq, Jezira, Hijaz, Nejd, and Yemen differed greatly economically and socially and that it would be impossible to constrain them into one frame of government. Syria, however, was sufficiently advanced politically to manage her own internal affairs, needing only technical assistance, for which he offered to pay in cash.

While Great Britain and France were negotiating the division of the Osmanli provinces, President Wilson's King-Crane Commission visited the area and, in its report, revealed the existence of deep Muslim-Arab animosity to France, both because of her traditional support of the Lebanese Christians and because of the Arab nationalist determination to achieve independence. The commission's recommendations on behalf of Arab nationalism, however, were totally ignored. In the meantime, in 1919, Faisal's Arab force had begun to clash with French troops. In March 1920, the General Syrian Congress in Damascus directly challenged France by proclaiming Syria—including Lebanon, Palestine, and Transjordan—independent and offering Faisal the crown. Neither Great Britain nor France recognized the Damascus declaration of independence, making their own plans for the region; the following month the San Remo agreement allocated Syria and Lebanon as mandates to France and Palestine and Transjordan, similarly, to Great Britain.

Both sides immediately began to prepare for war. In July, French general Gouraud sent Faisal an ultimatum demanding unconditional recognition by the amir of the French mandate over Syria and Lebanon, reduction of the Syrian army, abolition of conscription, acceptance of a Franco-Syrian currency system, French military occupation of Aleppo and the railroad leading to it, and punishment of those who attacked French troops. Faisal, realizing the odds against him, agreed to accept, but, charged the French, his answer was received after the prescribed time limit. Taking advantage of this formal technicality, the French commander attacked and occupied Damascus and then all of Syria, forcing Faisal to flee.

DIVISIONS UNDER THE FRENCH MANDATE

In the previous chapter we examined the purposeful French division of the mandate for Syria and Lebanon into separate administrations under a single high commissioner. The policy was more successful in Lebanon because of the extensive Maronite support for French policies. In Syria, two-thirds of the population were Sunni Muslim Arabs who opposed foreign and Christian rule. The existence of various minorities in Syria, however, offered opportunity for divide-and-rule tactics. Lebanon was made a separate state in 1920, and Syria was cut into four states on the basis of ethnic and religious differences— Jebel Druse, Damascus, Aleppo, and Latakia. Parts of traditionally Muslim areas, like Tripoli, were also sliced away in 1920 and attached to Lebanon. Later, in 1925, Aleppo and Damascus were formed into the state of Syria. Jebel Druse and Latakia, however, remained separate, with their own governments and constitutions until, under the 1936 Franco-Syrian Treaty, they were again merged back into Syria. During World War II, from 1939 to 1942, the French once more divided the country, restoring administrative autonomy to Jebel Druse and Latakia, but both were finally reintegrated into the Syrian state in 1942.

Within the state of Aleppo, Iskenderun received a separate administration as part of the Franklin-Bouillon Agreement of 1921, ending hostilities between Ataturk's regime and France. In 1939, Iskenderun was turned over to Turkey. Jezira province in Aleppo also received its own separate administration. In each instance, the French officials announced that the separatist sentiments of these various groups, as well as their different levels of development, necessitated their separate administration.

The Alawis

Latakia became a separate state because 60 percent of its population were Alawis or Nusayris. Other small groups of the sect were scattered around Homs, Hama, Damascus, and Aleppo, but not in large enough numbers to form politically separate entities. Animosity between Sunni Muslims and Alawis served to justify French establishment of a separate state for the latter, which led to a continuation of their isolation, their feudal organization, and their economic underdevelopment.

When the French established the Alawite Republic of Latakia, the sect formed a majority in the province as a whole, but the republic also included such coastal towns as the port of Latakia in which the Alawis were a minority, occupying socially and economically inferior positions relative to the Sunnis. Many Alawis worked as sharecroppers for the Sunnis who owned the best lands along the coast. French intervention in Latakia was aimed at preventing possible violence between the two groups, whose animosity stemmed from their religious differences and the economic disparity between them.

The mountain range at the center of the Alawi area had enabled the sect to resist complete conquest by an outside power and thus to preserve its distinctive characteristics, "like an encysted foreign body in the successive empires, participating neither in their life nor in their death."[1] Within the Alawi group, there were a number of rival subsects, each ruled by a great family. At the apex of a confederation of families or tribes were the so-called "Masters of the Mountain," a leading family recognized by the French and the Osmanlis before them (see chapter 4).

The sect of the Alawis was an offshoot of Shi'ism, deriving their name from Muhammad's son-in-law 'Ali, whom the sect deifies. Nusayri, the sect's alternate name, comes from an early sect theologian, Ibn-Nusayr. The Alawi religion is a strange blend of various Islamic and non-Islamic practices and beliefs. Secret teachings, to be hidden from the masses, come from the Ismailis, another Shi'ite offshoot (see chapter 2). The Alawi liturgy appears to be of Christian origin, including the observance of Christmas and the use of ceremonial wine. Certain Iranian practices are also observed, including celebration of the Iranian New Year.

Because of their general backwardness, the Alawi masses have too often fallen prey to false prophets and miracle workers, such as Sulaiman Murshid, a shepherd turned religious mystic who founded a new subsect around 1925. Within twenty years, this subsect had a large enough following to elect Murshid to parliament, where at times he worked with the French and at times with the nationalists. Murshid and a number of his followers were assassinated in 1946, but this fate has not ended the sect, which remains strong in remote regions of the north.

During the French mandate, the social level of the Alawis was raised to that of the Sunni and Christian minorities, to which the Alawis had always been subservient. Roads were built, education facilities increased, and medical and agricultural services extended. By the end of the mandate, increasing numbers of Alawis were becoming educated as lawyers, physicians, and in technical professions. Many had cut their tribal ties and were supporting the Arab nationalist movement. Today, the Alawis are no longer a threat to Syrian unity, although as a group they have not yet totally identified with the concept of Arab nationalism. Because of opportunities available to them for free education and upward social mobility, Alawis joined the army and rose in the officer corps in larger numbers than their percentage of Syria's population. Thus, during the series of military coups during the 1960s many Alawis rose to political leadership of Syria, espousing the most radical doctrines of Arab nationalism and socialism. However, there is no evidence to indicate that they used their new found political power to show religious favoritism to their regional home areas, although preference seems to have been shown for Alawis in army promotions during this period.

The Druses

Because of their larger number of educated followers and higher level of social development, the Druses have been far more politically effective than the Alawis, although they are a smaller group. Indeed, their geographical concentration in a single area was even greater justification for separatism. Some 80 percent of Syria's more than 150,000 Druses lived in Jebel Druse (Mountain of the Druses) where they made up 90 percent of the population. Another 100,000 or so lived in Lebanon, some 30,000 in Israel, and over 30,000 outside the Middle East. In contrast to the Alawis, they are newcomers to the region, having settled there after 1860, when many of them were forced from Lebanon by French and Osmanli troops (see chapter 4). Many retreated to the mountain fastness of Hauran, renaming it Jebel Druse, to avoid Ottoman taxes and military service, to escape from increasing European influences in Lebanon, and to preserve their traditional customs and practices. Because of their physical isolation, they were able to remain autonomous and to maintain their own feudal organization. Their strongly centralized community has been headed by the Atrash family, which rose to dominate the whole region after 1860.

Warriorlike bearing and desire for military service have made Druses respected and feared and have given them the feeling of superiority over their neighbors. The Druse chieftain Sultan al-Atrash led a rebellion against France in 1925 because the community opposed attempts to impose French authority in their region. The Druses were equally stubborn in resisting pressures from the central Syrian government after World War II, and they led the revolt against the military dictatorship of Adib Shishakli in 1954.

The Druse religion is an heretical offshoot of the Shi'ite Ismailis and originated in the eleventh century. One of the early leaders, Drazi, converted the Egyptian Fatamid caliph and declared that the Egyptian ruler was directly in the line of succession from Adam through Muhammad, 'Ali, and Ismail. When the Druses began to compete with the Ismailis in Egypt, the latter forced them to flee to Lebanon. Because their theology drew heavily upon esoteric Ismaili doctrines, the sect remained small; it refused to accept converts or to permit its followers to abandon their identity, for they believe the number of Druses is fixed for eternity.

Since 1945, as a result of education in Westernized Beirut and in Europe, the Druses have mixed more readily with the rest of the population. Many have been active in the Arab nationalist movement and in Syrian and Lebanese political leadership (see chapter 13). The isolation that produced a distinctive Druse Arabic dialect, literature, and way of life has broken down. The Druses are no longer considered an esoteric, non-Arab sect. After the defeat of Syria by Israel in the 1967 war, Israel attempted to capitalize on its victory by creating divisions among Syrians through special preference for the few thousand Syrian Druses who remained in the occupied Golan Heights. For a few months there was even discussion of establishing in this area an autonomous Druse state whose subjects would be from Syria, Lebanon, and Israel, but the idea was abandoned after Israel took steps to integrate the captured territory into its own borders.

FRENCH MINORITY POLICIES

French policy in the Druse and Alawite states encouraged communal differences by nurturing the already existing germ of an idea that neither group was really Syrian Arab. What each group required, the French colonial administration argued, was a firm and enlightened government that would attempt to uplift and modernize them while respecting their attachment to their traditions and special ways of life. This policy was to be accomplished by using officials recruited from their own leading families, but men who would be guided by Europeans. The French warned that attempts to achieve premature assimilation or modernization of the Druse and Alawi social systems might prove disastrous.

Arab nationalists, however, insisted that the two minority groups were merely Arabs with distinctive customs and that to encourage separatism would only perpetuate Syrian disunity. What was needed, they said, was to give the Druses and Alawis an awareness of their common interests with other Arabs. Indeed, from the begining of the mandate there were many Druses and Alawis who identified with the Arab nationalists. As these groups became convinced that they were being used by France for her own selfish purposes, large numbers who had originally sought European protection attached themselves to the Arab nationalist cause.

While France had little difficulty in dealing with the Alawis, the Druses were far less tractable. They insisted on maintaining their own leadership, and a Druse administration was established with a member of the al-Atrash family as its governor. When he died in 1923, Druse notables chose a popular French army captain whom they believed to be exceptional to succeed him. The Frenchman's innovations to improve social conditions, his use of compulsory labor, and his lack of tact in dealing with the opposition finally turned the entire community against him, leading to the 1925 revolt. After Sultan al-Atrash defeated a large French unit, the Druses joined forces with other Syrian rebels in Damascus. By the end of the year, the rebellion had spread through the districts of Damascus, Homs, Jebel Druse, and the Druse regions of southern Lebanon. It was largely suppressed by 1926; only small scattered bands of rebels remained and they fled from the country in 1927. A general amnesty was proclaimed by the French by 1928 and Sultan al-Atrash was reinstated as a conciliatory measure to pacify the region. The revolt taught the French administrators to keep out of Druse communal affairs and to let them administer their own local government, although all important acts had to be approved by the French high commissioner in Beirut. The intensity of the situation had already been suggested in 1922 when France created a Syrian federation of Damascus, Aleppo, and Latakia without the Druses because of the vigor with which they expressed their separatist feelings. The federation itself failed within a few months of its creation because the Alawis also wanted their own separate state.

Both Latakia and Jebel Druse were incorporated within the Syrian republic after the 1936 Franco-Syrian Treaty (see chapter 13), but the two minority groups were permitted a special status until 1941. French troops were to remain, and their special administrative and financial setups were to continue. Both Druse and Alawi leaders accepted union with Syria, but they deeply resented the new government's appointment of local officials who came from outside their areas. After another Druse rebellion in 1937, Hasan al-Atrash was made governor. Even this concession did not satisfy the more militant Druses and they again rebelled against the Syrian government in 1939, expelling all Syrian officials from the province and declaring Jebel Druse independent under French protection.

The Alawis also expelled Syrian officials in 1939, giving the French an excuse to subdivide Syria again into autonomous regions as a foil against Arab nationalism. The division lasted until Free French forces occupied the Levant in 1942 and once again brought all these districts together within the Syrian republic.

Jezira Autonomy

France adopted similar policies in Aleppo, granting the Jezira and Iskenderun districts separate regimes, but not giving them the status of states like Latakia and Jebel Druse. In recently settled Jezira, the principal groups were Sunni Muslim Kurds and a number of Christian sects. Until after World War I, Jezira had been an empty expanse with only a few Kurdish villages and roaming Bedouin. French suppression of nomad raiders and brigands made possible the settlement of these rich lands by Christians and Kurds who had fled from Anatolia and from predominantly Arab Muslim areas in Syria. Thousands of Armenians, Jacobites (a Syrian Monophysite sect), Syrian Catholics, and Iraqi Assyrian Christian refugees moved in, creating new towns and villages. Thus between the two world wars Jezira became settled by immigrants, many of whom were not Arabic-speaking. Within the province could be found in microcosm the fundamental minority problems of the

Middle East, Christian versus Muslim, Arab versus Kurd, Bedouin nomad versus settled farmer. French policy here was identical to that in the rest of Syria: encouragement of each group to maintain its distinctive identity.

The Kurds. More than half Jezira's population were Kurds. Although their language, culture, and customs differ, they, like the majority of Syrian Arabs, are Sunni Muslims. The problems they created for Syria were similar to those they had presented in Turkey immediately after World War I (see chapter 7). Foremost was their refusal to recognize any but their own tribal leadership. The nearly quarter of a million Syrian Kurds (about half of whom lived in Jezira) were also imbued with strong irredentist sentiments, seeking to unite with their compatriots in Turkey, Iran, Iraq, and Soviet Armenia. In 1928, Syrian Kurdish chiefs demanded recognition of Kurdish as an official language in regions where they were predominant and more extensive employment of Kurdish officials in the government. A number of Kurdish intellectuals stimulated the nationalism of their compatriots during the 1930s, exercising great influence through their own Hoybun party and Kurdish-language publication.

When Syrian administrators took over from the French in the Jezira after the 1936 Franco-Syrian Treaty, many Kurds demanded that their own people be given government posts. Intense Kurdish nationalists, encouraged by France, insisted that the region be completely severed from Syria. A serious uprising broke out in 1937, when Kurds revolted against appointment of Arab nationalist officials in the Jezira, and only French intervention succeeded in quelling them. Arab nationalists charged that their rule would have been accepted had it not been for French instigation of the minorities.

France had never given the same degree of autonomy to the Jezira province as it accorded Latakia or Jebel Druse because the various Christian and Muslim groups in the district could agree on nothing except their opposition to Arab rule.

Since World War II, the Kurds have begun to adopt Arab customs and clothing and to learn Arabic. And, like other minorities, their demands for separate treatment have greatly abated. Many have even become integrated into the Arab nationalist movement. However, successful integration of Kurds in Syria has not been an obstacle to development of a strong Kurdish separatist movement in Iraq (see chapter 15).

Iskenderun

The old Osmanli sanjak of Iskenderun (Alexandretta), also within Aleppo, received a special regime in 1920 because of its large Turkish population. While considered part of the state of Aleppo until 1939, Iskenderun had administrative autonomy and a special budget. Turkish, French, and Arabic were recognized as the official languages.

Iskenderun's separate administration operated satisfactorily until the 1936 Franco-Syrian Treaty. Turkey feared that once the province became part of an independent Syrian republic, Ankara would lose its claims. The Turkish population of this last bit of Turkey irredentia, argued Ankara, could not be abandoned by France to the mercy of inexperienced Arab nationalists. Rebuffed by Paris on their request for a special agreement concerning Iskenderun's status, the Turkish government brought the dispute before the League of Nations, which appointed a commission to investigate. The League recommended full autonomy for Iskenderun in internal affairs, but Syrian control of foreign relations. In 1937, the French provided autonomy for the province along the general lines recommended by the League, but the Syrian government refused to recognize it. France, Turkey, and Syria continued to bicker over the province until, to win Turkish support in a military alliance France permitted Turkish troops to join French forces in patrolling the region during 1939. The province received increased autonomy until it became the Republic of Hatay, which joined Turkey during 1939 after only a few weeks of independence (see chapter 7).

Arab nationalists have never accepted Turkish annexation of Iskenderun, and it is still included within Syria on locally published maps. The region has thus changed from Turkey irredentia to Syria irredentia. Some Arab nationalists have proclaimed that Turkey intends to use Iskenderun as a bridgehead into the rest of Aleppo, although Turkey has given no justification for such fears. To the present day, the population figures of Iskenderun are in dispute. Turkey, of course, claims that the majority is of Turkish origin, while the Arab states insist that it is Arab.

Aleppo and Damascus

Not even the province of Damascus, Syria's most solidly Sunni Muslim Arab region is without minorities. France therefore also established a separate administration for it. By separating the provinces of Damascus and Aleppo, the French hoped to facilitate their handling of each area. Rivalry between the two leading towns, Damascus and Aleppo—from which the provinces derive their names—also furthered the French policy of creating separate states. But by 1925, Syrian nationalist pressures had persuaded France to combine the two provinces into the state of Syria with a single administration. In 1930, the high commissioner proclaimed Syria a republic with its own constitution. Although a native Syrian government was set up, it had little authority, all real power remaining concentrated in the hands of the high commissioner.

France had far greater problems with nationalists in Syria than in Lebanon. In all Syrian states, the native governments were more intractable than those in Lebanon, and there were frequent insurrections. The struggle in Syria was complicated, on the one hand, by the clashes of such groups as the Alawis, Druses, Kurds, and Arab nationalists against the French and, on the other—particularly after the whole region (except Lebanon) was declared the Syrian Republic in 1936—by frequent clashes between the various minority groups and the Arab nationalists.

Because Syria and Lebanon were under a single French authority vested in the high commissioner, whose headquarters were in Beirut, events leading to independence of the two nations were closely interrelated and have already been outlined in chapter 13.

SYRIAN DEMOCRACY

Fragmentation of Syrian society has produced one of the most volatile political systems in the Middle East. Since attaining independence in 1946, the country has passed through a dozen *coups d'état* and has been governed by more than six different constitutions. Although Syrians learned to stand together in the face of foreign attack, they have never attained any degree of cooperation in building a strong and cohesive government.

Organized political life in Syria is a recent phenomenon, growing out of the seeds planted by the Arab secret societies formed shortly before World War I (see chapter 6). Only one major political party of importance emerged from these groups during the French mandatory regime, the National Bloc. But the party lacked real cohesiveness and was hardly more than a working alliance of local family chieftains representing the landowning elite. Ibrahim Hananu, the founder, was an Aleppo resident who had led an insurrection against the French in 1925. Faris al-Khuri, a Protestant lawyer, teacher, and financier (and prime minister during 1944–1945) was another noted National Bloc leader. A number of groups within the party—like the Istiqlal descended from prewar secret societies—preserved a large degree of independence. The Istiqlal included not only Syrians, but also other Arabs such as Riyad al-Sulh, who became Lebanon's prime minister. A quasi-military organization, the Nationalist Youth, was an offshoot of the National Bloc, but it never acquired the influence of the parent body despite its militant stand against France in 1935 and 1936.

The National Bloc suffered from the same weaknesses that characterized most Arab nationalist organizations: its middle and upper classes had little contact with the Syrian masses and were not concerned with any of the social or economic problems plaguing their society. All nationalist efforts were concentrated on ridding Syria and the Arab world of foreign domination.

There was little effective Syrian opposition to the National Bloc. In fact, only a handful of parliamentary deputies were not National Bloc members before 1950. One small opposition group of extreme nationalists refused to recognize the mandate altogether and regarded cooperation with France as treason. Representatives of the Alawi, Druse, and Jezira separatist movements also opposed the National Bloc, but they never cooperated with one another. The only genuine party organized during the mandate was the clandestine Syrian National (PPS) party (see chapter 13). When it was uncovered by Syrian authorities in 1935, its leading members were imprisoned and the party outlawed in the country. Because of its antagonism to Arab nationalism, National Bloc members regarded the PPS as another separatist movement.

During the first nationwide free elections in 1943, the National Bloc had so little opposition that it won most of the seats in parliament. Shukri al-Kuwatli became independent Syria's first president, choosing his cabinet from the ranks of the National Bloc. After French evacuation, the Bloc lost its chief *raison d'être* and split into several groups. Like the Wafd in Egypt and the Republican People's party in Turkey, the National Bloc was the fountainhead of nearly all subsequent parliamentary political life. For several years, every new party represented in the chamber was one of its offshoots. Differences usually had little to do with ideology, but resulted from squabbles over influence, prestige, and patronage. Among these offshoots were the National (*Watani*) party and the Constitutional Bloc, which became the Peoples'(*Shaab*) party in 1947. The latter represented great estate holders and merchants from Aleppo and tended to favor closer ties with Iraq because of extensive commerce and business connections there.

MILITARY COUPS

Free political institutions were short-lived in Syria. The whole republican parliamentary structure collapsed within three years of independence. By 1949, defeat in the Palestine war, increasing dissension among its leaders, rising living costs, and dissatisfaction throughout the country led to an army coup and military domination of politics for the next five years. Syria's army, unlike the Turkish military under Ataturk, was torn by conflicting factions, reflecting in large measure the variety of Syrian religious, ethnic, social, and economic differences. There were not only Arab officers, but also Kurdish and Circassian ones, Christians and Muslims, Shi'ites and Sunnis, leftists and rightists, those who favored closer ties with the Hashemites, and those who were Egypt oriented.

The first of these military dictatorships was established by Colonel Husni Zaim in March 1949. After expelling President Kuwatli, closing parliament, and abolishing all political parties, Zaim made himself first prime minister, then marshall, then president of the Republic. Initially, he aroused the enthusiasm of younger nationalists, who regarded him as a Syrian Ataturk. Within several weeks, however, he had so antagonized his own following and Syria's Hashemite neighbors, Iraq and Jordan, that another military plot was hatched to overthrow him. In less than five months after his own coup, in August, Zaim was shot by a fellow officer, Colonel Sami Hinnawi, ostensibly for the purpose of re-establishing the parliamentary regime. The army, however, continued to manipulate political life from behind the scene.

Hinnawi was pro-Iraqi, and soon after seizing power he began to negotiate with Baghdad for a common regime to include a single army, a supreme cabinet, and a customs and monetary union. However, Hinnawi's anti-Hashemite opponents, led by Colonel Adib Shishakli, undermined the new regime within four months and arrested Hinnawi on charges of conspiring with the Iraqi monarchy. Shishakli also operated initially within a parliamentary facade, using as his front man a close civilian associate, Akram Hourani, leader of the Republican Bloc. Hourani induced Shishakli to approve a number of social reforms and made his influence felt in drafting a new constitution. Unfortunately, there were no provisions for the enforcement of the progressive principles embodied in the 1950 Syrian constitution, which replaced the 1930 constitution fashioned by the French. Implementation of these principles was left to the laws that were to be adopted by parliament. The form of government established actually differed very little from that of the 1930 constitution. A popularly elected unicameral Chamber of Deputies chose the president of the republic, who in turn appointed the prime minister. The cabinet was responsible to the chamber.

Hourani's contribution to the new constitution was inclusion of several relatively radical social reforms. For example, the constitution declared that prison was to be not only a place of punishment, but also "a mean s to reform the criminal and to educate him properly." The outlines of a welfare state were laid down, a government that was "to liberate citizens from the miseries of poverty, disease, ignorance, and fear by establishing a sound economic and social system which achieves social justice, protects worker and peasant, offers security to the weak and fearful and enables every citizen to have free access to the benefits of the country." The constitution promised progressive taxation "to ensure equality and social justice." Culture and education were to be diffused throughout the land. Work, the "most important of the basic factors of social life," was declared the right of all. Fair hours and wages, holidays, sanitary housing, health, unemployment insurance, and the right to form unions were promised the workers. The state would provide hospitals, maternity homes, and care for pregnant and nursing mothers and their children. While private property was guaranteed, its purpose was to be directed toward fulfilling "its social function." Land reform was proposed to assist tenant farmers and create cooperatives and model farms. Natural wealth, such as minerals, forests, and water power, was declared state property. A permanent council was to be established "to secure a high living standard for the people," and to implement this extensive program. A council on education was also to be set up, with the goal of eliminating illiteracy within a decade.[2]

Shishakli initiated the reform program with a flood of legislation on land policy, agricultural credit, industrial development, and rural rehabilitation. If they had been implemented, the hundreds of decrees that poured out of the dictator's office would have transformed the face of Syria. Most of them remained mere paper orders, however, measures that were never followed through. Many laws were only show pieces or quixotic flights of the imagination, such as the scheme to employ a Spanish musician to elevate Syrian musical tastes. Hourani's plans to distribute the state domain among landless peasants, to confiscate areas held illegally by powerful landlords, to impose progressive income taxes, and to organize agricultural credit threatened Syrian vested interests and aroused the fear of the wealthy that they would soon lose their privileged position.

In their attempts to create a regime like that of Kemalist Turkey, neither Shishakli nor Hourani understood that Turkey had not been transformed overnight, or that Ataturk had launched his reforms only after spending endless hours trying to persuade his opponents to accept them. Shishakli took no such pains, nor did he strive to create a popular image of himself. He only approached the public when surrounded by the panoply of his military establishment. Instead of friendly persuasion, he extended his control over Syria's political apparatus through the use of force. When attempts by the old conservative politicians to curb his power were revealed, he staged a second coup, in November 1951, dissolving parliament and appointing a military associate, Colonel Fawsi Silu, chief-of-state. By early 1952, all political parties, student organizations, trade unions, and other such activities were outlawed and replaced by an Arab Liberation Movement. In the meantime, Shishakli had broken with the one moderating influence of his regime, Akram Hourani. The suspended 1950 constitution was replaced in June 1953 with another model, this one concentrating power in the president's hands. A referendum in July elected Shishakli president and prime minister for a five-year term and approved his June constitution. Although parties other than the Liberation Movement were authorized to participate in a subsequent election, the ban on them being lifted a month before the balloting, all but the PPS boycotted the election. So complete was Shishakli's control over the country that his Liberation Movement won all but 10 of the 82 seats in parliament.

Shishakli's extensive use of police spies and informers created an atmosphere of tense fear in the capital. Students, civil servants, and others who failed to benefit from the promised reforms, formed secret organizations to overthrow the dictatorship. In February 1954, less than one year after becoming president, Shishakli was overthrown by a coalition of all the dissatisfied elements—students, leftists, the old conservative politicians, civil servants, and the Druses. A few years later the former Syrian strong man was assassinated by a political foe in Latin America, where Shishakli had taken refuge in the local Arab community.

THE BA'ATH

The strongest elements in the Syrian regime immediately replacing Shishakli's were the old conservatives, who attempted to turn the clock back to the 1949 prereform era. However, in the first free elections in 1954, the old guard returned less than half the candidates for parliament. The largest group to emerge were independents unidentified with any party, neutralist in foreign policy, and programless in domestic affairs. The most significant trend was represented by the 15 Ba'athists (Arab Socialist Resurrection party) elected to the 142-member parliament. Although they had obtained only 10 percent of the seats, they were the third largest group in parliament. The Ba'ath's influence was in fact far greater than its numbers indicated, for it was a better organized and more cohesive force than any other group except the Communists and the PPS. Aside from the Communists, only the Ba'ath could organize effective workers' demonstrations and arouse mass enthusiasm. It had gained wide influence among young intellectuals and army officers, a success indicative of its growing leftism.

The Ba'ath party had been created in 1953 from a fusion of Akram Hourani's Arab Socialists and the Arab Resurrection party. Hourani's followers had been organized in 1939 as the Youth party in Hama, where he had extensive family contacts and a personal following. During Husni Zaim's regime, Hourani began to emphasize socialism, with a program appealing to impoverished peasants in his home district. The Arab Resurrection party had been organized in 1941 as a pan-Arab student movement striving for the renaissance of a unified Arab world. Michel Aflaq, its founder and leader, had been strongly influenced by leftist ideology while a student in France. Fusion of the Aflaq and Hourani groups brought intellectuals and dissatisfied middle-class elements together with Hourani's urban labor and peasant following. Hourani's extensive influence among the younger army officers with whom he had fought in Palestine tremendously enhanced Ba'athist importance.

Party ideology looked both to the past and to the future. Aflaq's theory was to recreate in modern form the ancient glories of the Islamic Arab world. Present-day divisions and dissensions in the Arab East were considered only superficial and it was believed that they would disappear with a revival of national consciousness and re-establishment of an indivisible unity. Ba'athist socialist doctrine advocated nationalization of large industry, distribution of government lands to sharecroppers, and the creation of extensive social services such as those outlined in the 1950 Syrian constitution. All Arab countries would be asked to pool their resources for the common good. Progress and unity were indivisible, according to Aflaq. Without progress, the unified Arab world would be unable to survive against the great powers. Democracy would be threatened without the material well being of the citizen and the economic independence of the state. Therefore, a socialist economy was necessary if the free Arab state was to survive.

Between 1954 and 1958, Ba'athist political influence was at its zenith. Two of its leaders were influential members of the cabinet, one the foreign minister, the other, the minister of economics. Akram Hourani became president of the Chamber of Deputies and a leading candidate for president of the republic. Ba'athist success in Syria attracted the attention of Arab intellectuals elsewhere and the party established branches in Lebanon, Jordan, and Iraq. In Lebanon, several of Kemal Jumblatt's followers left the PSP to form a Ba'athist group. In Jordan, a Ba'athist leader obtained a cabinet post in the 1957 Nabulsi government (see chapter 12). Damascus was headquarters for these various branches, and the Syrian leaders were the most influential in determining policy for all the groups until the party was banned by President Nasser in 1959–1960, while Syria was part of the UAR (see below).

Initially, the Ba'athists viewed Nasser with suspicion, regarding him as an unenlightened military dictator who would sooner or later submit to imperialist blandishments. During the early 1950s, Ba'athist leaders cooperated with Syrian Communists in mutually opposing Western colonialism, which was used as a rallying cry and magnified into Arabdom's greatest danger and the main cause for lack of sympathetic contact with European socialists.

After 1955, when Nasser had become the symbol of Arab emancipation from the bonds of the West, the Ba'ath changed its attitude toward him, now giving him their "frank but conditional" support in the struggle against Great Britain, France, and the United States. By then the party had begun to quarrel with the Communists over the degree of cooperation that Syria should attempt to pursue with the Soviet Union. At the same time, the party had begun to meet with opposition to its reform program from the conservative majority in parliament. When Communist infiltration began to undermine the Ba'ath, Communists and Ba'athists became so estranged that they waged bloody battles in some Syrian cities. Ba'athist leaders now believed that only Syrian unity with Nasser's revolutionary Egypt could save their country from chaos or a Communist coup.

THE COMMUNISTS

After Shishakli was overthrown in 1954, Syria's Communist party became the first such party in the Arab world to operate publicly. Its 10,000 to 20,000 followers, drawn largely from Armenian, Kurdish, and other minorities could boast the largest Communist membership in the Arab East. When organized in 1933, a single organization served both Syrian and Lebanese Communists. After independence in 1945, two separate parties were formed, although they maintained close contact through joint meetings of their central committees.

Although the party ran candidates in twenty-one districts throughout the country in 1954, only one, Khalid Bakdash from Damascus, was elected. Despite paucity in numbers, the Communists were politically effective because of their excellent organization and their influence on labor, student, and army circles.

Syrian Communist leader Khalid Bakdash was one of the most forceful members elected to the 1954 parliament. Born and raised in Damascus, and later Moscow trained, he was favored by many minorities because of his own minority—Kurdish—origin. His strong attacks on Western imperialism and vehement denunciation of the West attracted many army officers and intellectuals who, as Communists, began to fill the important positions in government, in labor unions, and in other organizations.

SOCIAL CHANGES

Throughout modern Syrian history, many individuals descended from the Ottoman landowning and official aristocracy continually reappeared as the country's leaders. By the 1950s, however, the new Syrian middle class of lawyers, teachers, doctors, government bureaucrats, and army officers was becoming an effective political force. Many of the latter resented the concentration of political power in the hands of the old ruling aristocracy. The personal dissatisfactions and nationalist grievances of this rising middle class proved an explosive mixture that threatened to destroy Syria's existing political organization and to disable completely the already ineffective parliament based on an imported French model.

A third group, a new class of merchants, also began to emerge in northern Syria. Many of these men had invested their World War II profits in land development, mostly in the Jezira, and had become wealthy. Their attitudes towards the state were the *laissez-faire* views of Victorian days; they objected to government intervention in the economy and to high government expenditures. Like the nineteenth-century British merchant-liberal, they were little concerned with improving general living standards.

The Syrian peasants, constituting about three-quarters of the population, were not directly involved in the clash between the old regime and the rising middle class. Peasant conditions varied from region to region in the 1950s, but most peasants still lived at a subsistence level. Two-thirds of them owned no land, living from sharecropping. After paying for the use of their land, water, tractors, and the like, the peasant was often left with as little as 20 percent of his produce.

An Agricultural Revolution

Compared with Egypt, Syria has twenty times as much arable land per person in agriculture. Between 1943 and 1953, northern Syria underwent an agricultural revolution. Grain output doubled, while population increased only by a third.

Chiefly responsible for this development were Syrian merchants, mostly from Aleppo, who financed the rapid expansion of cotton and grain production in the north. Most of these merchants did not own land, merely renting it and investing their wartime commercial profits in pumps, tractors, and seed. Few had known anything at all about agriculture before embarking on this new venture, relying on hired experts to help them—such as Egyptian cotton specialists or foreign tractor agents who ran their machine repair shops. Many were selfmade men, including Christians whose families had immigrated from Anatolia after World War I. Their activity has been described as "an interesting example of how capital has been accumulated and invested outside the ranks of the established landowning class, by people who twenty years ago were neither wealthy nor influential."[3]

Aleppo, a town which formerly took everything from the surrounding villages and gave nothing in return, now began to invest large sums of money in land cultivation. The chief method of expansion was by means of tractors, which made northern Syrian agriculture as fully mechanized as that of any country, according to Doreen Warriner. All investment was made by private Syrian sources, without assistance from foreign capital, extensive public services, long-term planning, or agrarian reform. The various postwar governments did little to promote this economic development. The only significant measure of any aid was Shishakli's establishment of a Cotton Bureau staffed by Egyptians and Food and Agricultural Organization (FAO) experts. No railways had been built since Ottoman days and many northern regions were roadless.

Some experts warned that such hasty cultivation without simultaneous land improvement might create soil erosion and that mechanization might turn the huge Jezira expanse into a dust bowl. Not until after 1955 did the government take a hand in supervising the work and in developing cultivation on its own through state-established land-development companies. However, government intervention was too late to prevent deterioration of the land, and continued dry farming in the Jezira was no longer possible because the limit of dry crop production had been reached. Only if the area was extensively irrigated could production continue to increase, and that would be possible only with major economic development.

During the 1960s a major plan was developed to construct a huge dam on the Euphrates River in northern Syria. The project would increase the country's electricity supply by several times and would double the cultivable area by increasing irrigated land by a million and a half acres. The cost of the dam was estimated at over a third of a billion dollars, one-third in foreign currency. In 1953 West Germany entered negotiations with Syria to finance the dam, but as relations between the two countries deteriorated, West Germany backed out. As part of its effort to form closer ties with Syria, the Soviet Union undertook in 1966 to supply equipment and technicians to initiate the project. Still to be settled, however, were agreements for a division of the water with Turkey and Iraq, the other two riparian states. By the late 1970s several phases of the project were completed, greatly extending agricultural production in Syria.

Land Reform

The postwar agricultural expansion did very little to improve the general living conditions of the Syrian peasantry. In the north, where land development was greatest, those who benefited were the merchant operators and the tribal sheikhs from whom they rented the land. The sheikhs had acquired the land during the latter years of the mandate as a result of French efforts to pacify the region. French policy was to turn over state areas formerly used in common by various tribes to individual sheikhs, who became the legal owners. These lands were later leased to the new tractor farmers at high rates that enriched the tribal leaders but left their tribesmen bereft of their traditional grazing areas.

A paradox of Syria's landholding system is the existence of population scarcity and labor shortages in developing areas like the Jezira and Euphrates provinces, where land is available, at the same time that old established regions, such as the Hauran, Jebel Druse, and Latakia are overpopulated and good farm land is scarce. Resettlement of population from the overcrowded regions to the northern provinces and in state irrigation schemes could alleviate the situation.

Since there is no overall land shortage in Syria, the need is not to limit the size of individual holdings—as in Egypt where there is insufficient land to sustain the existing population—but to provide state areas for landless peasants and to enact legislation curbing the control exercised by the great landowners over their sharecroppers' income. Until the union with Egypt in 1958, sharecropping was the principal cause of peasant poverty; landlords received as much as 75 or 80 percent of the crop, leaving the peasants with barely a subsistence income.

Although the 1950 Syrian constitution laid down liberal principles for agrarian reform, such as setting the maximum area an individual might own, and the creation of cooperatives and model farms, almost nothing was done to implement them. Shishakli's 1952 Decree for Distribution of State Lands voided all possession by feudal lords and other "influential" persons of unregistered state land, but since state-owned lands had never been surveyed or defined, it was impossible to determine who was in possession of them. The only action actually carried out was state confirmation of individual ownership in certain Jezira districts that had been held collectively by Bedouin tribes. In practice, such confirmation meant that individual tribesmen, instead of their sheikh, who until 1952 had taken all the rent for himself, now received the rent paid by the urban merchants who leased the land.

THE UNITED ARAB REPUBLIC

Both the failure of the rising Syrian middle class and the old conservatives to compromise on control of the political system and the growing demands of the leftists for a share in determining national policies helped undermine national political stability. Because of their frustration in domestic politics, all of these groups turned their attention to foreign affairs. Many Syrians, including the conservatives, turned to Egypt for salvation. There was unanimity of opposition to the "imperialist West," reflected in the refusal to accept American economic assistance. Syrian experience as a mandated territory had been far more unpleasant than that of other Arab states, and Syrian bitterness after the Palestine defeat was extreme. Syrian nationalists were therefore far more vehement in their opposition to the West than were other Arabs. Syria was the only Middle Eastern nation not to accept some form of American assistance in the postwar era. The Syrian attitude toward strong leadership was ambivalent. On the one hand, individualistic tendencies had divided Syrian society into numerous competing political groups, but on the other hand, there was great yearning for a single strong leader who would again lead the nation to the glories of the Umayyad days.

In 1956, Syrian politicians began to seek closer ties with Egypt because of that country's apparent strength under Nasser's leadership. By July, the Syrian parliament had set up a committee to negotiate a federal union with Egypt, and the two countries exchanged parliamentary delegations. When in 1957 Turkish troops were moved to the Syrian frontier during a period of Syrian government instability, the Syrians invited Egyptian troops to help defend the country. By the end of the year, many Syrian politicians were seeking not only close ties, but total union with Egypt. Popular enthusiasm for the idea of unity was so great that no Arab leader could overtly disavow it. Support for Arab union, like hatred of Israel, became a *sine qua non* in Arab political life.

When it became evident by the end of 1957 that no group or individual in the country could bring about political stability, a direct appeal for union was made to Nasser. Within the leftist camp, there was a split between the Communists, favoring much closer ties with the Soviet Union, and the Ba'athists, who urged a complete merger with Egypt. Although the Communists were not strong in numbers, they had acquired several influential allies in the army and the support of a few conservatives who favored close ties with the Soviet Union because of that country's power. General Afif Bizri, who became chief of staff of the Syrian army during 1957, and Khaled al-Azm, the "Red millionaire," represented the pro-Soviet group. Al-Azm was a Syrian Talleyrand who had served both the French colonial and the independent Syrian governments. After independence, he became an ardent nationalist and was responsible for ending the Syrian-Lebanese customs union. By 1956 he came to favor full cooperation with Soviet Russia.

The Ba'athists were the most ardent proponents of the immediate and complete fusion of Egypt and Syria. The union would be the first step toward the union of all Arab states and would hasten socialization of the Arab world by extending the influence of Nasser's revolutionary government. Immediate union, they argued, would speed development of the north by making land available for settlement of tens of thousands of Egyptian fellahin. By early 1958 the Ba'athists feared that a pro-Communist coup in Syria would underine their own power, whereas union with Egypt would enhance it. They had already quarreled with the Communists, but the Ba'athists believed Nasser was accepting their ideas. Khaled al-Azm had induced Syria to break its standing refusal of all foreign aid, and military and economic assistance from the Soviet Union, totaling over a half-billion dollars, had been arranged. Syrian President Shukri al-Kuwatli paid a visit to Moscow, and many Syrians, including the Ba'athists, feared that they were about to become a Soviet satellite.

To avert the catastrophe, the Ba'athist representatives made a hasty visit to Cairo in January 1958, appealing to Nasser for immediate union to save Syria from Communism. Nasser was convinced of the feasibility of union and, in February, both Egypt and Syria announced formation of the UAR. Within three weeks, a hastily arranged plebiscite held simultaneously in Syria and Egypt approved the union and Nasser as its president.

Although Nasser was quite willing to direct Syria's foreign and military affairs, he had been somewhat reluctant to accept complete unity because he realized the great economic and social differences that existed between the countries and the complicated problems of internal management that union would create—problems of merging the civil and military forces, creating a common currency and economic system, and imposing on the individualistic Syrians the strong central authority that was traditional in Egypt. To Syrians, the union seemed like a marriage of great romance; to the Egyptians, it was more one of convenience.

Problems immediately arose. Syrian businessmen, accustomed to low taxes, few currency controls, and scarcely any restrictions on imports and exports, resented Cairo's imposition of rigid government supervision of the economy. Large landowners in Syria objected to Egyptian-imposed agrarian reforms, limiting the size of their holdings and fixing minimum incomes for agricultural laborers, although Syrian owners were actually permitted to retain much larger estates than were left to owners in Egypt.

During 1958 the Syrian Ba'athists and their allies received high government posts. Akram Hourani became one of the four UAR vice-presidents. Another Syrian nationalist, Sabri al-Assali, was also made a UAR vice-president, but he was purged soon after union. Ba'athist leader and former Syrian foreign minister Salah al-Bitar became UAR information minister and several other Ba'athists became ministers in the cabinet of the Northern Region, as Syria was now called. The warm relations between Ba'athists and Egyptians soon cooled as the former found that the Egyptians were really not interested in accepting Ba'athist ideology. The first Ba'athist setback was Nasser's ban on Syrian political parties and seizure of the Syrian press. Although intended to crush the Communists, these restrictions seriously undermined all other parties, including the Ba'ath. The Communist threat to Syria was broken (Bizri and Azm both fled), but there seemed little hope for political democracy in Syria under the Nasser regime.

The new UAR constitution (see chapter 9) was also a disappointment to the Ba'athists, since it made no mention of reforms such as those that Hourani had injected in the 1950 Syrian constitution. When Syrian political parties were replaced by the Cairo-directed National Union, Nasser refused to permit the Ba'ath to play a major role in its organization. For a while, the Ba'athists continued to operate in secret, until Nasser placed Abdal Hamid Serraj, former chief of Syrian army intelligence, in charge of the Syrian government. Although he had once been a close ally of the Ba'athists, Serraj was no ideologist and now used his influence to undermine the party and weed its members from all influential government positions.

In Syria's first National Union elections in 1959, the Ba'ath suffered a major defeat because it was held accountable for the union and the subsequent imposition of unpopular measures by Cairo. The results showed that Hourani and his followers had won only 2.5 percent of the 10,000 local National Union committee offices, compared to the 12.5 percent of the Syrian parliament seats they had held in 1957. To keep Syria under his watchful eye, President Nasser appointed his close friend, UAR vice-president and army chief Hakim Amer, as general controller of the Northern Region. In protest against the imposition of Egyptian controls in Syria, five Ba'athist ministers in the central government, including UAR vice-president Hourani, resigned in December 1959.

Ba'athist discontent with the Cairo central government was indicative of growing unrest throughout Syria. Not only the leftists but all organized Syrian groups resented Nasser's measures to integrate the two countries. Businessmen, merchants, landowners, intellectuals, and army officers feared the growing authority of Egyptians in all phases of Syrian life. Even the military were now subject to Egyptian officers, who were placed in key positions.

In July and August 1961, Nasser announced measures which were to place even more authority in the hands of Cairo. Decrees were proclaimed placing most UAR industry and commerce under central government control and further limiting large landholdings (see chapter 9). In August, Syria's separate regional cabinet was abolished and a central UAR cabinet system was established, eliminating the last vestige of what might be called a separate Syrian government. Even the power of Colonel Serraj was clipped in September when he was ordered from his commanding position in Damascus to an honorary UAR vice-presidency in Cairo. Two days after Serraj resigned in protest against the limitation on his authority, the Syrian army rebelled against Egypt.

THE SYRIAN ARAB REPUBLIC

On September 28, 1961, Syrian officers captured Egyptian Marshall Amer and other Egyptian officers, ordering them to leave the country. At first, there were reports of an attempt to prevent the revolution by Egyptian paratroopers, but they received orders from Nasser to surrender peacefully. A few days later, Nasser announced that he would accept the separation of Syria from the UAR and would do nothing to prevent its re-establishment as an independent country.

A right-of-center Syrian government was then established under Mahmun al-Kuzbari, a political figure who had served as a representative of various large Syrian industrial firms and had held office in the pre-UAR right-of-center Syrian cabinets. The new regime gradually abolished the Cairo reforms limiting the amount of landholdings and distribution of land to peasants. It also denationalized large industry, which had been taken over by the government, including the "Golden Five," a complex of textile industries in which families associated with the new government held shares. To indicate its loyalty to the Arab cause, al-Kuzbari's government renamed the country the Syrian Arab Republic and proposed a pan-Arab federation to be called the United Arab States with a pan-Arab legislature and supreme executive council, a joint army, and a constitutional court. While the proposal went far beyond anything the Arab League had ever considered (see chapter 6), it was to be a voluntary association in which members would retain individual sovereignty and their own legislative and executive systems.

Elections for candidates to a re-established Syrian parliament were called for December 1961. In preparation for the elections, some sixty politicians, representing most of the factions in the 1957 Syrian parliament, signed a

National Unity Charter early in November. The document referred to development of a "healthy socialism" that would increase productivity, ensure social justice, and an equitable distribution of income. It said that the state would combat monopolies and exploitation and would "intervene" in matters of supply and price control, but that it would also protect private initiative and ownership. Workers' rights were to be protected, and they were to be represented on boards of directors in companies for which they worked. The charter also called for the creation of a voluntary Arab Union on the basis of constitutional decentralization to include all the Arab areas from the Persion Gulf to the Indian Ocean and from the Taurus Mountains to the depths of Arab Africa.

Although Communists were banned from participation in the December parliamentary election and no other parties were permitted to be reestablished, the electoral lists and the results of the election closely resembled those in 1954, following the overthrow of the Shishakli dictatorship. Two groups of conservatives won the majority of votes. The largest was a list made up mostly of members of the former People's (Shaab) party. It won 32 of the 172 parliamentary seats. The second group represented the Nationalist (Watani) party, with 20 seats. Former Ba'athists, led by Akram Hourani, won 18 seats. So many of the former Syrian political leaders, such as Sabri al-Assali, Khaled al-Azm, and Akram Hourani, returned to the scene that a prominent Beirut newspaper commented, "Syria has not changed fundamentally; she is today the same as she was twelve years ago." It added, "If this proves anything, it is that three years of Nasserism and the dictatorships preceding it have scratched only her surface."[4]

The "sameness" of Syrian instability was indicated by still another coup that took place in March 1962; a group of army officers and civilian supporters took over the government, asserting that the group which had come to power in September was too right wing. The members of the March coup and their supporters now reinstated many of the socialist reforms that had come into effect during the UAR period. Large industry was again nationalized, and the land reform was reinstituted. Many observers believed that a strong pro-Nasser body of opinion still existed in Syria, and that the socialist reforms introduced by the Egyptian president achieved wide popularity among both workers and peasants.

The divisiveness of Syrian society was evident in the numerous civil disturbances, military coups, and political upheavals of the next few years. Clashes erupted over several key issues, including Arab unity, socialism, and economic reform, the role of Islam in Syrian society, and the continuing battle against Israel. While there was basic agreement that Syria should be identified with the greater Arab world, there was division between pro- and anti-Nasser groups which periodically erupted in student demonstrations and riots in the main cities. On social reform there was continued disagreement over the extent to which government should take over, manage, and operate various sectors of the economy. Among progressives there was an undercurrent of animosity against conservative Islamic leaders while among the latter there was a resurgence of opposition to the "Godless" socialistic government manifested in periodical demonstrations by the suppressed Muslim Brotherhood. Few, if any, Syrians objected to a strong stance against Israel. However, there was disagreement about the extent to which Syrian militancy should manifest itself in military adventures against the strong Jewish state.

In 1963 a military junta led by Ba'athists seized control of the government and established a National Council of the Revolutionary Command (NCRC). The new Ba'athist junta reopened the whole question of Arab unity, enlarging the concept to include Syria, Egypt, and Iraq. Negotiations among the three potential members of the new United Arab Republic were conducted in Cairo, and a tentative agreement was reached. However, within the Ba'athist regime, there were considerable differences of opinion, ranging from those who demanded an immediate and unqualified union to those who favored a loose association with Egypt rather than a unified state. In an attempt to gain complete control of the government, the Ba'athists, who favored loose ties with Egypt, attempted to purge the armed forces and the administration of all elements considered too pro-Nasser. Groups such as the Socialist Union, the United Arab Front, the Arab Nationalist Movement, and the Arab Socialist Front were driven underground. Feelings became so inflamed that the government executed many prominent figures among the pro-Nasserists. As a result, Egypt's President Nasser insisted that he would refuse to implement the Cairo Unity agreement of April 1963 until the Ba'athists were removed from power in Damascus.

For the next three years, until 1966, the Ba'athist government tottered between control by two principal factions, the so-called progressives versus "moderates." The progressives favored a one-party democracy guided by neo-Marxist ideology, placing emphasis on radical reconstruction of Syrian society. Although ostensibly neutralist in foreign policy orientation, the progressives strove for closer ties with the Soviet Union and placed less emphasis on the concept of Arab unity than did their principal antagonists within the party. The moderates, on the other hand, while favoring social reform were less keen to enact radical legislation which would alienate large sections of the population. They advocated closer ties with Syria's Arab neighbors and were more favorable toward allowing the military to strengthen Syria's position against Israel. The moderates controlled the National Ba'ath party, which was in effect its international wing, comprising representatives from several Arab states and including the party's founders, Michel Aflaq and Salah Bitar. They were opposed by the Regional party, comprising membership of the Syrian branches of the Ba'ath. The latter tended to be more radical and militant in domestic policies, thus endangering the party's position with the population at large. In addition to these two principal divisions, there were various other rifts. For example, Akram Hourani, another of the principal leaders and founders of the Ba'ath, broke with his colleagues in 1963, followed by still other factions which broke away over policy or personal differences.

An attempt to reconcile these various disagreements was made at an international conference of the Ba'ath party in Damascus during October 1963. The conference called for unity between Syria and Iraq in the near future, and envisioned eventual adherence to Egypt on condition that the union would not be dominated by its largest partner. Resolutions were also passed calling for nationalization of the means of production, establishment of agricultural collectives, and management of industry by committees chosen from among the workers. But attempts at reconciliation failed, and unrest continued. At one point in 1964, Salah Bitar, one of the party founders, was expelled, only to be returned to power a few days later. Attempts to implement the socialization measures, such as turning over textile factories to workers' committees, nationalization of banks, and transfer of land to peasants without adequate assistance in farming it, culminated in serious economic difficulties causing more widespread opposition. Disturbances reached such a pitch in 1964 that government troops bombarded the principal mosque in Hama and demolished the old quarter of the city in an attempt to put down defiance. The several hundred deaths resulting from the repressive measures only created additional demonstrations and strikes against the Ba'ath by ardent Muslims and conservatives in the principal towns. With threats of additional repressive measures, such as confiscation of businesses, the uprising was put down in the spring of 1964.

A so-called democratization of Syria took place with promulgation in April 1964 of a new constitution which defined Syria as a Democratic Socialist Republic, forming an integral part of the Arab nation. The sensitivities of religious conservatives were noted in the document, which stated that Islam was the official state religion and that Muslim religious law would be respected in enacting new legislation. The NCRS, as the military junta had styled itself, was replaced by a large National Revolutionary Council (NRC) in which military officers continued to be represented but only as a minority of less than one-fifth. The actual focal point of power was a Presidential Council named in theory by the NRC from its own members, which shared executive power with the cabinet of the Presidential Council's choice. Both of these executive branches were theoretically responsible to the parliament. In fact, however, the government was dominated by Lt. General Amin Hafiz until the next major upheaval in February 1966.

During this period political power shifted back and forth between the progressives and moderates, with Bitar in and out of power, and continued measures of nationalization intended to implement Ba'athist socialist doctrines. Nationalization evoked more demonstrations, strikes, and student upheavels, with continued undercurrents of opposition from the Muslim clergy. A unique innovation in government was abolition by the Presidency Council in 1965 of the offices of Commander-in-Chief, and Deputy Commander of the Syrian armed forces. Their responsibilities were transferred to the Minister of Defense, the implication being that civilians were now to control the armed forces, and military affairs were to play a less important role. Since these reforms satisfied no one, they only intensifed differences between the moderates, representing the older, more experienced politicians and founders of the party, and the progressives, mostly younger elements, extreme, left-wing, and doctrinaire in their attitudes.

The latter were represented in large measure by army officers, a large number of whom were from minorities, especially the Alawis. It was not unusual that the more radical elements in the Ba'ath were represented by minority groups. As noted earlier, the officer corps was one path to upward social mobility in Syria, a path chosen by many Alawis, resulting in their ascent to respectability in positions of influence and power. Since they had come from a group which was not only socially but economically depressed, and at times repressed, with little if any vested interest in large industrial or landholdings, it was quite natural that the most radical doctrines of Ba'athist socialism should appeal to them. It was therefore not surprising when Alawi officers took the lead in attempts to create an even more revolutionary Syrian society.

The ideological clash between the "progressives" and "moderates" erupted in a bloody coup during February 1966, bringing to power the group of young radical Alawi army officers. Among their objectives was final elimination from power of "moderates," comprising the international leadership of the organization including Aflaq and Bitar, old party leaders who were accused of betraying the basic principles of the party and of the March 1963 Ba'athist revolution. The new radical regime now further intensified nationalization measures, taking over the import-export industry, nationalizing oil companies, and establishing a state monopoly of agricultural produce, especially cotton, a major foreign currency earner. Shortly after the coup, in September 1966, Bitar and Aflaq were accused of conspiring with the United States CIA, Saudi Arabia, and Jordan to oust the radicals. Both founders of the party had to flee to neighboring Lebanon.

The radical turn to the left was symbolized by permission granted to Syria's former Communist leader, Khalid Bakdash, to return after eight years of exile, and by increasingly closer ties with the Soviet Union. The new Russian ties resulted in a substantial increase in economic assistance and military aid from the USSR.

Continually worsening relations between Syria and Israel resulted in rapprochement between Syria and Egypt in November 1966. Diplomatic relations were resumed, and agreements undertaken to coordinate political and military actions. As border clashes increased with Israel, the new radical Ba'athist regime was forced to increase its inter-Arab ties. The escalating border clashes and the supposed threat of Israel military mobilization against Syria sparked the disastrous Six-Day War in June 1967. Although Syria did not actively enter the fighting until the end of the war, it suffered humiliating defeat resulting in occupation of the Golan Heights by Israel, and flight of nearly all of the approximately 100,000 Syrians from the area. Reaction to defeat was an even more militant stance, with refusal by the Syrian government to attend the Arab Summit Conference at Khartoum in Sudan, intended to forge a common policy against Israel.

Despite supposed concentration on internal matters by the progressives, continued border incidents forced the government into a more nationalistic position similar to the pan-Arab Ba'athists. Still another attempt to unify the country was made in April 1969, when the progressives agreed to permit all factions of the Ba'ath to be represented in the government, although the progressives insisted on maintaining a predominant position. The attempt at forging national unity was symbolized by still another constitution drafted in May 1969. The new document fortified the one-party doctrine of the radicals, with the Ba'ath as the only legal party.

The struggle between the two factions of the Ba'ath was resolved in 1970 when General Hafiz al-Assad seized power. He too was an Alawi from a peasant family who rose through the ranks to top command in the army and in the party. Since consolidating power, his policies have blended those of both radical and moderate Ba'athists. By 1977 his regime had lasted longer than any since Syria attained independence and seemed less unstable than those of his predecessors.

After his 1970 coup Assad deposed most leaders of the militant progressives and was less enthusiastic in support for the Palestinians. In contrast to his immediate predecessors who invaded Jordan to assist the Palestinian guerrillas during the Jordan civil war, Assad followed a cautious path, to avoid provoking intervention by Israel. He clamped down on the guerrilla organizations operating in Syria, forbidding them to initiate any attacks on Israel from his country. In an attempt to break out of Syria's isolation in the Arab world, he joined the new Federation of Arab Republics (Egypt, Libya, and Syria) in 1971, although the Federation had practically no political significance.

Internally he consolidated power through a new constitution proposed in 1971 and approved in a 1973 national referendum. It legitimized his ascent from prime minister to president of Syria in 1971 for a seven-year term; in 1978 he was elected for a second seven-year term. To broaden the regime's political base, a People's Assembly was formed in 1971 to replace the parliament. It was the country's first legislative body to function since 1966. Attempts to liberalize and secularize the political system were strongly opposed by conservative Sunni Muslim groups. Thus President Assad asked the Assembly to insert in their new 1973 constitution an article requiring the chief-of-state to be Muslim.

The People's Assembly received broad powers in the new constitution: to designate the president of the republic, issue laws, debate government policy, and approve state budgets and development plans. Theoretically the Assembly could overthrow a government or oust a minister by withdrawing its confidence, but after 1971 it was dominated by coalitions which followed the president's directives. The constitution linked the Ba'ath party and the People's Assembly by requiring that the Assembly's choice of a candidate for president (who is then approved by popular national vote) be made on recommendation of the party. Presidential power was almost unlimited. He could dissolve the Assembly in which case he held the legislative power also. In practice, the Assembly's powers were limited by other decision-making bodies which the president controlled such as the Regional Command of the Ba'ath (Syrian party command) and the National Progressive Front of parties in the government coalition.

The National Progressive Front, the Ba'ath, Arab Socialist Union, Movement of Unionist Socialists, Movement of Arab Socialists, and Communists, emerged from the 1973 elections, the first held in Syria in over a decade. Because most opposition parties or factions boycotted the elections, the Front won two-thirds of the 186 seats in the new Assembly. Of these, the Ba'ath dominated by far with 104. Its allies in the Front won a total of 20, and the remainder went to independents, most of whom have been supporters of the Assad regime. The three noncommunist Front members were Nasserist parties whose differences were difficult to discern. Although all had "socialist" in their party names, members were mostly from the middle and managerial class. Even the Communist party split into two factions, both pro-Soviet, one inside, the other outside the Front. Any political activity outside the Front was outlawed but two underground movements remained active. They were the Muslim Brotherhood and the Arab Socialist Union of Mohamed el Jarrah (pro-Libyan). The Front remained intact through the 1981 elections to the legislative assembly with the Ba'ath as the dominant member. During the 1977 election the NPF won 159 of the 195 seats (they were increased after 1973), and in 1981 it captured them all with 60 percent going to the Ba'ath. However, the Communist members of the NPF were all defeated and lost their eight seats in parliament.

The multiparty character of the Syrian system has meant that all governments between 1972 and 1981, although dominated by Assad, were in theory coalitions. Distribution of ministries reflected the balance; for example, in 1976 a coalition was formed with 36 cabinet posts, half of them Ba'athist, 2 Communists, 2 Arab Socialist Union, 3 Unionist Socialist Movement, 2 Arab Socialist Movement, and 9 independents; each successive cabinet also reflected this trend.

Syria's initial thrust into the Golan Heights during October 1973 and the diplomatic victories resulting from the war strengthened President Assad's position since these events were perceived as a great Arab victory—the first against Israel. Reoccupation of Kuneitra, the largest city in the Golan area, as a result of the disengagement agreement with Israel in 1974 was considered a major accomplishment.

Intervention in the Lebanese civil war during 1975–1977 had both advantages and disadvantages. By sending over 30,000 Syrian troops into Lebanon, then attaining the dominant position in the Arab League "Deterent" force there, Assad extended his country's influence, and helped to break out of diplomatic isolation. On the other hand, so large a Syrian force in Lebanon raised apprehensions among several Arab states and in Israel. The Arab states feared that Syria would gain a diplomatic advantage, and Israel was anxious about any military assets that Syria would acquire. Inside the country conservative Sunni Muslims and militant Arab nationalists regarded the move with suspicion, especially after Syrian troops began to put pressure on the Palestine guerrillas in Lebanon to the advantage of Lebanese Christian forces. By the end of 1982 it appeared that influence in Lebanon was greatly curtailed as a result of the setback suffered during the Israeli invasion of 1982 (see chapter 13).

Assad's foreign ventures, the 1973 war with Israel and the intervention in Lebanon, were at the expense of economic development and socialization of the economy. War damage in 1973 was estimated at nearly two billion dollars. Most of the country's port facilities, oil refining capacity, and many of its power plants were shut down after Israeli air raids. The cost of military supplies was a continuing drain, absorbing nearly a quarter of the country's GNP.

Efforts to recoup these costs have been only partially successful. After the 1973 war, Assad introduced liberalization measures to encourage return of both foreign and Syrian capital. The liberalization, like that advocated by President Sadat in Egypt after the 1973 war, included new guarantees against confiscation and nationalization of property, and inducements to wealthy Arab oil producers to extend large loans. Following the disengagement agreements with Israel, Syria renewed diplomatic relations with the United States and modified its opposition to a peace settlement. In return, Syria became one of the largest recipients of American economic assistance for a short period.

The relative political stability during Assad's regime has been accompanied by an economic and social paradox. Syria's population is growing rapidly, from 4.5 million in 1960 to over 9 million by 1981. Potentially it is one of the richest agricultural lands, but there is a constant move from village to town. The cities are becoming larger, although the quality of urban life is declining. From 1960 to 1975 the population in Damascus increased threefold, to a million and a half, with one in five of the country's citizens living there. Contrasts of poverty and wealth abound in the capital. Streets of luxury villas are not far from shanty towns on the outskirts. Chronic housing shortages were exacerbated during 1975–1976 by the influx of nearly 500,000 refugees from Lebanon, many of them Syrians who had been unskilled laborers in the neighboring country. The inflation caused by the wars and spiraling military expenses and the "liberalization" of the economy after 1973 helped create a new affluent class, many still part of the public sector. Ba'athist slogans of Arab socialism and Arab unity were still verbalized in the party ideology, but Syria's growing dependence on economic assistance from the United States, Saudi Arabia, and Kuwait created dilemmas not only for the doctrinaire ideologues of the National Progressive Front, but for government policy makers who had to deal with questions such as war or peace with Israel, the permanency of the occupation in Lebanon, relations with "sister" socialist regimes in Egypt and Iraq, and the continually nagging problem of the Palestinians.

A major dilemma facing the regime was its growing isolation, both within the country and in the Arab world. The fact that president Assad and his most trusted aides represented either a political minority (the Ba'ath) or a sect considered heretical by Syria's Sunni majority led to increased tension between him and dissidents throughout the country, as well as with Arab neighbors. It became increasingly necessary for the president to use his special internal security forces which were headed by his brother and staffed largely by Alawites, as a chief supporting institution of his administration.

Economic recession and growing evidence of graft, nepotism, and corruption in the administration also caused a serious decline in Assad's popularity. By 1978 the growth rate declined to zero from 14 percent in 1975, and 60 percent of industrial capacity was unused because of inefficient management and poor planning. Although outlawed, a coalition of the Muslim Brotherhood, other Sunni conservatives, and dissident Ba'athists organized widespread protests against the regime, which retaliated with martial law in several major cities. Violent clashes between the civil population and the security forces was the result. During 1979 more than 60 Alawite cadets were massacred by Sunnis in an uprising at the artillery officers academy in Aleppo and fighting between Sunnis and Alawites in Latakia also led to military intervention. By 1980–1981 anti-Assad demonstrations spread to all major towns, often reflecting inter-Arab quarrels as when pro-Assad Alawites, who backed Iran in the Gulf War, fought with pro-Iraqi Sunnis. The largest uprising occurred during 1981 in Hama, the fifth largest city, when the army killed thousands of residents, drove most of the rest from their homes, and destroyed most of the buildings during artillery barrages after sealing off the region from outside contact.

Internal unrest failed to cool Ba'athist ardor for Arab unity. Between 1958 and 1976 Syria signed unification pacts with Egypt, Iraq, Jordan, and

Libya, all of them aborted by disagreements over implementation or by the pressures of inter-Arab quarrels. The 1975 agreement with Jordan to form a Supreme Command Council failed because Jordan was too moderate in its relations with the West and because Assad suspected King Husain of harboring Muslim Brother dissidents. The 1978 Charter for Joint Action with Iraq collapsed when Iraq accused Syria of plotting to kill its president and when Syria sided with Iran in the Gulf War. The 1980 merger with Libya to form a joint "Revolutionary Leadership," one Revolutionary Council, a single national congress and executive as the base for "the Arab revolutionary movement" never got beyond the Tripoli Declaration announcing the union.

Syria's closest allies in the Steadfastness and Confrontation Front, designed to subvert the Egyptian-Israeli peace settlement, were far from its borders—Algeria, Libya, South Yemen—and unable to assist in carrying out practical plans for common action to say nothing of implementing Arab unity. By the 1980s even much of the assistance from Saudi Arabia and Kuwait initiated after the 1967 war began to dissipate.

The only ally providing extensive and substantive aid was the Soviet Union, which rearmed Syria after its defeats in the 1973 and 1982 wars with Israel. Following Syrian support for Soviet invasion of Afghanistan during 1979, presidents Assad and Brezhnev of the USSR signed a 20 year treaty of friendship and cooperation, which helped to decrease Syrian isolation in the international arena. But Syrian support for Iran in the Gulf War only widened the gap between Damascus and the closet Arab capitals, Amman, Baghdad and Beirut.

NOTES

1. Raphael Patal, ed., *The Republic of Syria*, unpublished study by the Human Relations Area Files, New Haven, 1956, p. 101.
2. *Ibid.*, pp. 657–661.
3. Warriner, *Land Reform and Development in the Middle East*, p. 90.
4. From *L'Orient*, Beirut; quoted in *New York Times*, December 10, 1961.

15

Iraq

Iraq, like Jordan was one of the new states created at the end of World War I to suit the needs of the British Empire. Its strategic location at the head of the Persian Gulf and its extensive oil fields made the nation one of Great Britain's most prized Middle Eastern holdings. Between 1920 and the 1958 revolution, which changed Iraq from a monarchy to a republic, the British attempted to build it up as a political counterweight to Egypt, the strongest Arab nation. But the British, as has been the case for those who governed the country before and after them, were unable to create a strong unified nation from the conglomeration of tribal, religious, and ethnic groups that populate it. To understand the setting of modern Iraq, it is necessary to examine the diversity of groups in the country and to trace the development of British interests in the Tigris-Euphrates Valley and in the Persian Gulf.

DIVERSITY OF INTEREST GROUPS

When Iraq became independent in the early 1930s, about half the population were nomadic or seminomadic tribesmen, less than a third were settled farmers, and only 12 percent were city dwellers—concentrated mostly in Mosul, Baghdad, and Basra. Land was owned by only a few large owners. The landholding system was archaic, favoring the propertied class. Until the end of the Ottoman era, much of the land in the south was held by tribes who owned and farmed it communally under the management of their leaders. Around

1900, the nomadic tribal system began to break down as large numbers of tribesmen settled permanently.

To encourage permanent settlement, and thereby increase political stability, first the British during the 1920s and later the successive Hashemite governments encouraged legislation that turned the tribal land rights over to the sheikhs. Larger and larger areas fell into the hands of the sheikhs, who now became the legal landowners, while the former communal owners, the tribesmen, were reduced to sharecroppers. Laws were passed forbidding the sharecroppers to leave their farms if they were in debt to the new landowner. If they did flee, the families they left were driven from their farms and their homes destroyed. In effect, by 1958, the former tribesmen had become serfs with no security or freedom of action. Poverty was caused less by land shortages (as in Egypt) than by the exorbitant rents, varying according to the extent of facilities such as water and seed provided by the landlord. On pump-irrigated land, sharecroppers might have to pay five-sevenths or more of their crop to the owner. Although the sheikhs held great power within this system, based on their former status as tribal leaders, they undertook none of the traditional responsibilities or obligations for care of tribal members. They had acquired not only economic control but political power as well, since they were now chosen to represent their districts in parliament.

The size of the land holdings differed north and south. In the south, estates were usually inherited by the eldest son, according to Shi'ite inheritance law, and kept intact. In the north, where the Ottoman code prevailed, property was subdivided among usually numerous heirs. Many northern landowners were urban merchants who had accumulated their wealth through inheritance, as money lenders, or by confiscating the land of the peasants who failed to pay their debts. Throughout Iraq the scale of land ownership was larger than in either Eygpt or Syria. There were several estates of over 100,000 acres, and the two largest were estimated at 250,000 acres each.

In the north, the Kurds, constituting about 15 to 20 percent of Iraq's population, constantly refused to submit to centralized authority, to pay taxes, or to acknowledge any but their own leaders. The Kurds of Iraq were more troublesome to their central government than those of the neighboring countries because they constituted a larger proportion of the population, were better organized, and were geographically concentrated in mountainous terrain to which access was difficult. Although Kurds were usually elected to parliament and served in the government, Kurdish areas in the north were the scene of numerous uprisings and consequently subjected to frequent punitive expeditions by the Iraqi army during the 1920s and 1930s. Although the Kurds are Sunni Muslims, they do not identify either nationalistically or culturally with the Sunni Muslim Arabs, but have their own Kurdish language and customs. Until today they are a major problem for the Iraqi government because of their demands for a greater amount of autonomy than any central government has been willing to grant them (see p. 428, following).

Approximately 25,000 Yezidis (a Kurdish-speaking sect whose religion comprises both Christian and Islamic elements), who also lived in the north, demanded exemption from military service because of their religious objection to war. When the Iraqi government refused to recognize their claim in 1935, the Yezidis defied the central authorities. The Iraqi army thereupon invaded their villages, arrested, court martialled, and hanged several resistance leaders.

There were also rifts between Sunni and Shi'ite Muslim Arabs (see chapter 2), who constituted about 75 percent of the population. Although the Shi'ites constituted a slight majority over the Sunni Muslims, the latter had been the traditional leaders of the country and formed the majority of the economic, political, social, and intellectual elite. Sunnis regarded themselves as superior to the rest of the population. In the early postwar years, especially during the 1920 insurrection againt Great Britain, the two religious groups had managed to get along fairly well. Many Shi'ites even believed that King Faisal was a secret member of their sect. After Faisal's death, Iraqi Shi'ites were stirred to opposition against the Sunni-controlled government by the jeremiads of zealous preachers who crossed back and forth over the border with Iran. They naturally resented control of the government by members of a religious group to which they were antagonistic, especially since it was they who comprised the majority of the population.

The gulf between urban and rural society was yet another source of friction. The nonurban population believed that the city dwellers discriminated against them, since the urbanites held most government offices. Many tribal leaders formed close ties with the British against the socially conservative Baghdad nationalists. Only after General Bakr Sidki (see below) crushed a major uprising in the south during 1953, did the central authorities succeed in imposing some measure of authority over the tribes. Even then Baghdad's authority remained shadowy, for most tribes refused to recognize any but their own leaders. Among the more remote tribes were the Marsh Arabs (Madans) of the deep south. The most remote, who lived in permanently flooded swamps, were a group apart living from fishing and water buffaloes. Many spent most of their lives in boats and rafts, having almost no contact with the government or other Iraqi communities.

Christians and Jews have been a tiny minority which in the past wielded more influence than their numbers would indicate. Both minorities took more readily to Westernization than Muslims, discarding traditional dress, accepting innovations learned in Western schools, and playing significant roles in the country's economic, commercial, and technological development. Nearly half the approximately quarter of a million Christians belonged to the Chaldean church, headed by the Patriarch of Babylon, whose seat is in Mosul.

Other indigenous Iraqi Christian groups included the Jacobites and the Assyrians, or Nestorians. The latter suffered from severe clashes with the Iraqi government in the 1930s.

Before the departure of most Iraqi Jews for Israel in 1949–1950 they too constituted a small but influential minority of some 150,000. Active in the country's economic life and development, Jews ascended to the highest political and social positions. One became minister of finance under King Faisal. However, Jewish communal life collapsed after outbreak of the first Palestine War in 1947–1948, and most left the country.

BRITISH INTERESTS

In chapters 4 and 5 the development of British interests in the area that is today Iraq, beginning with seventeenth-century trading posts, was described. With its expanding commerce and military might, Great Britain kept the peace, suppressed piracy, charted the rivers and the Persian Gulf, and attempted to restrict the slave trade. Although the region was legally part of the Ottoman Empire, British power was supreme.

During the nineteenth century, Great Britain consolidated its hold on the Iraqi-Persian Gulf region to fend off the danger that the advancing Russians and Germans would establish bases in the Persian Gulf. In 1810 a British diplomatic mission (residency) was established in Baghdad to supplement the British residency at Basra, established during the seventeenth century as a trading post. Baghdad, because of its central location, became Great Britain's chief outpost in the eastern part of the Ottoman Empire, and one that exercised considerable influence over the sultan's representatives. On several occasions, the Ottoman government appealed to and received help from Great Britain against Iranian and Bedouin incursions. Protectorates were established all along the Persian Gulf from the seventeenth through the nineteenth centuries, and plans were made to build a railroad from the Euphrates Valley to the gulf. But these plans were never carried out because of the British fear that a railroad would make penetration by Russia and Germany that much easier. Plans were also laid out for developing Iraqi rivers and canals. In Basra and Baghdad, British residents (diplomatic officials) extended their protection to Indian traders and pilgrims on their way to the holy cities in Iraq and Arabia. Both Basra and Baghdad were given use of the Indian Postal System in 1868, and British officials were sent out to help improve sanitary conditions in the region.

Before World War I Basra was an important Anglo-Indian shipping center, and Baghdad was important because of its location in the heart of a strategic tribal area. So vital had Iraq become to British India that Lord

Curzon told the House of Lords in 1911 that Baghdad must be included in the sphere of "indisputable" British supremacy. Russia had been considered the chief threat until Kaiser Wilhelm II began his push to the East in a scheme to make Iraq and the Persian Gulf the termini of a German railroad system (see chapter 4).

British officials induced the Ottoman and German governments to give British companies part interest in the kaiser's projected Iraqi projects. Two British subjects were to be appointed to the board of the Berlin-Baghdad railroad, and there was to be British participation in developing Basra port. A new British navigation cmpany secured exclusive navigation rights there, and the sultan recognized British police authority in the Ottoman-controlled parts of the Shatt el-Arab and Persian Gulf region. Already British hegemony on the Persian side of the Shatt el-Arab and the gulf was acknowledged.

The British resident at Baghdad warned his superiors in 1913 that His Majesty's government should "preserve every kind of priority which they already possessed in Iraq, their natural sphere in the Ottoman Empire," and proposed that they expand the irrigation system as an additional means of exercising influence. "To gain cotrol of this system and create an *imperium imperio* is important. Control of water will give control of revenue assessment, perhaps control of collection,"[1] he advised. By 1914, even Kaiser Wilhelm II was ready to recognize British supremacy in the area and ordered his government to initial treaties recognizing southern Iraq and the Persian Gulf as regions of primary British influence. The agreement was suddenly aborted by the outbreak of war during the summer.

World War I

During the course of the war, Great Britain took over first southern and then central Iraq from the Ottoman, considerably strengthening the position it had built in the area during the previous three centuries through commerce and diplomacy. Throughout the wartime British occupation of Iraq, civilian and military authorities clashed over the way Iraq should be ruled. British military officers opposed reforms giving greater authority to local Arab sheikhs, asserting that they interfered with the successful conduct of the war by limiting the freedom of action of the military. The civil officials, recruited from the British Indian administration, viewed the whole region as an appendage of the India Office, to be subordinated to British Indian policies. While the British civilian authorities were willing to use trusted sheikhs to further British ends, they opposed the Arab nationalists, fearing that revolt of the latter against the Osmanlis might antagonize Indian Muslims who were still loyal to the Ottoman Caliphate.

Use of Arab nationalist allies also threatened to complicate the future of Iraq and to undermine the India Office's policies. British Indian officials preferred to sign preferential treaties with loyal tribal sheikhs, like Ibn Saud in Arabia, rather than to encourage the creation of a strong independent Arab state. Some British officials demanded that Basra and Baghdad be annexed by British India for its use as bases. Others were jealous of the authority bestowed upon the British high commissioner for Egypt to negotiate with Sherif Husein of Mecca. The high commissioner's subordinates, known as the "Hashemi" school, were prevented from encouraging Arab nationalism in Iraq by British Indian officials there. Thus in Iraq there was no organized uprising against the Ottoman Empire such as Col. T.E. Lawrence organized in western Arabia. Arab nationalism was something to be controlled, if it could not be prevented, by Great Britain.

Other complications were created by the Sykes-Picot Agreement assigning the former Ottoman province of Mosul to the French zone of influence (see chapter 5). After the war, Turkey's republican government also claimed the Mosul region, which the British had entered late in 1918. In addition, Arab nationalists asserted that the Husein-McMahon correspondence made it theirs by virtue of the promise made them that an Arab state would be established in all Arab regions of the Middle East in exchange for wartime assistance.

British Postwar Policies

At the end of the war, British Indian officials were administering Iraq much like a British colony, keeping tight control over all government functions. The British Acting Civil Commissioner Sir Arnold Wilson believed that it was England's peculiar mission "to bestow its gifts of efficient administration, of impartial justice, of honest finance and of security on backward peoples who, in return for these services were to assume places in the economic and defensive system of the Empire." No standard other than the material well-being of the subject peoples was necessary to consider. "As long as administrators spent the best of their bodily and mental vigour on the people, there was no need to justify the measures which kept them in authority. Political aspirations and the desire for self-government were to be dismissed as vagaries of ungrateful extremists or to be repressed as firmly as wayward thoughts in any adolescent youth."[2]

According to Philip W. Ireland, while on the one hand these colonial officials attempted to make Iraq totally dependent on the British Empire, on the other hand they desired to establish a regime of advanced government and material progress. They therefore wished to undermine the influence of the "Sherifian" school in Whitehall, those who favored Arab self-government, and cause the British government to pause "before wrecking the established administrative machinery by handing it over to the Arabs."

The shortage of Iraqis with the education, training, and ability to replace the British and Indian personnel strengthened the position of those who opposed self-determination for Iraq. Consequently, from 1918 to 1920, Iraq's administration resembled that of British India. A British official, directly responsible to British headquarters in Baghdad, controlled each key administrative position and sent voluminous reports to his superiors on the life in his district. Even the titles developed for the British Indian situation, such as civil commissioner, political officer, and revenue and judicial officer, were brought into use.

To give the administration of Iraq an appearance of local support, the British planned to choose a native ruler to occupy a position similar to the sheikhs of the Persian Gulf. London was so indecisive about choosing a native ruler that it turned to the acting civil commissioner in 1918 to request that he sound out Iraqi opinion about the best form of government for the area. Sir Arnold arranged a plebiscite, in 1918–1919, to determine whether or not the population favored a single Iraqi Arab state under British tutelage and, if so, whom they wanted to head it.

Sir Arnold's instructions to British political officers, however, were to conduct plebiscites only when public opinion was likely to be in accord with the British desire for a single state under British control. The acting civil commissioner genuinely believed that he knew what was best for Iraq. Like Cromer in Egypt, Wilson believed that only strong British control could bring peace, stability, and prosperity to the area. He desired to combat what he believed to be the dangerous and naive idealism of those British officials, like T.E. Lawrence, in Cairo and Whitehall who encouraged Arab nationalism.

The masses, Sir Arnold believed, were too ignorant to participate in government. The Iraqi garden cultivators, date growers, shepherds, marsh dwellers, and tribesmen had no political opinions of their own, nor the ability to form them except as echoes of their religious and secular leaders; and only urban dignitaries favorable to British control were considered truly representative by the British commander. Those opposed to British rule were either deported during the plebiscite or their complaints were dismissed as unrepresentative of those who were influential. Where there was strong opposition to British desires, plebiscite results were not reported or no plebescite was held. Thus none of the tribal unrest, conservative Shi'ite demands for a theocratic Muslim state, or nationalist sentiment influenced by the nationalist movement in Syria was indicated by the plebescite. Sir Arnold manipulated the results so that they turned out to be just what he desired: a demand to make Iraq a British-controlled state headed by Arab officials sympathetic to the British government. After a British-controlled Arab puppet regime had been installed, several hundred British officials and their families moved into the country in apparent anticipation of a lengthy British tenure.

NATIONALIST FERMENT

Sir Arnold's treatment of the native population sowed intense Iraqi nationalism. He contemptuously opposed native participation in government because, he said, it would undermine effective British control. It would be a long time, he warned, before senior Arab officials could be appointed, except in an advisory capacity, without causing rapid decay of authority followed by anarchy and disorder. Several nationalist leaders were allowed to leave for Egypt in the hope that they would be lost in exile. However, their departure only permitted their agitation abroad.

The nationalist movement was sparked by the example of the 1920 Arab revolt against France in neighboring Syria (see chapter 14), and nationalist conflict between Sunnis and Shi'ites was temporarily abandoned in the interest of creating a homogeneous nationalist movement in which there would be participation of all Iraqis. A religious element was added to Iraqi nationalism by participation in the movement of the Shi'ite priesthood at Najaf, Karbala, and Kadhimain, three Iraqi Shi'ite holy cities. Their participation indicated that the nationalist movement was not exclusively Sunni.

The anti-British movement was formed by diverse currents: former Ottoman officials who resented the British-controlled regime and the loss of their offices; landlords and tenants who disliked the efficiency with which taxes were collected; and all those who disdained the introduction of Western administrative practices.

Sunni leaders, representing the Hashemi family, and Shi'ite divines stirred hope among the tribes of evading domination by a strong central government. The tribes found Iraqi independence attractive, less because of a concern for establishing a democratic or Islamic government than in the hope of evading taxes. They were becoming restive under the fiscal burdens imposed by the British. Many tribesmen also hoped that insurrection would provide an opportunity to throw off the rule of the sheikhs, whose authority had been restored by the British in an effort to control remote nomadic regions.

Soon after Sir Arnold announced that Great Britain had received the mandate for Iraq in 1920, a tribal revolt broke out in lower Iraq. By the end of the summer, the fighting had spread considerably, causing nearly 10,000 casualties and was costing the British government the equivalent of almost 100 million dollars. British troops soon quelled the rebels, but Great Britain sought to reach a compromise by establishing an Arab government and removing Sir Arnold Wilson. This, the first truly Iraqi manifestation of national unity since the Abbasid decline, came to symbolize thereafter the movement for independence: and the heroes of this War of Liberation became the first Iraqi national heroes.

THE IRAQI GOVERNMENT

Sir Percy Cox, who had served previously as the British political resident for the Persian Gulf and the British ambassador to Iran, replaced Sir Arnold. He was considered sympathetic to Arab aspirations. Many years of experience as a British diplomat working with Persian Gulf Arabs had helped him understand their ways. One of his first moves was to replace the British officials who desired to attach Iraq to India with leading British orientalists and Arab scholars who favored the development of self-determination for the area under British tutelage. Cox organized a Provisional State Council with Baghdad's *nagib* (official Sunni leader) as prime minister. Government posts were distributed among influential Iraqi families and religious sects from the various districts of the region to obtain a proper balance in the administration. Each Iraqi official, however, was to be guided by a British political officer, and the British high commissioner, Sir Percy Cox, had the final word in all matters.

Amir Abdullah, younger brother of Faisal, had been designated by the Arab nationalists meeting at Damascus in 1919–1920 as their choice for the ruler of Iraq (see chapter 6). A problem was created for Great Britain when Faisal, their wartime ally, was driven from Syria by the French in 1920 (see chapter 14). The British solved the problem by offering the throne of Iraq to Faisal and by separating Transjordan from Palestine and offering it, instead of Iraq, to Abdullah (see chapter 12). At the Cairo Conference of British diplomats for the Middle East, convened in March 1921 to settle British policy in that area, Great Britain decided that it must appear that Iraq had chosen her own ruler. By means of threats and political pressure, Sir Percy obtained a unanimous vote for Faisal from the Iraqi Provincial Council and a 96 percent vote in a controlled plebiscite. The new ruler was crowned in August 1921.

British advisers continued to manage the government during the first years. In effect, Iraq was a British vassal state, much like Transjordan and the Persian Gulf principalities. The concept of Iraq as a separate nation was in fact British inspired. There had never been an independent Arab Iraq, nor was there any great demand among the local population for an Iraqi state. Only during Sir Arnold Wilson's regime did national sentiment begin to emerge, but largely in reaction to his harsh policies rather than as a strong, positive drive to create a new nation.

Once Great Britain had created the ostensibly independent Iraqi kingdom, it withdrew its acceptance of the mandate, which had been arranged with the League of Nations in 1920. Instead, the principles of the mandate would be incorporated into a treaty of alliance. The 1922 Anglo-Iraqi Treaty of Alliance was drawn up, with a few modifications, in terms identical to the proposed British mandate. It granted Iraq limited control of foreign affairs and a larger measure of domestic autonomy. Real power remained vested in the hands of the British high commissioner and consul general, an official who was to exercise as much power in Iraq as Lord Cromer did in Egypt after 1882. Iraq could accept only British advisers and assistance, unless permission to do otherwise was granted by London. Foreign, military, financial, and judicial affairs were directly subject to British control, and subsidiary agreements authorized the establishment of British troops and bases in the country.

Iraqi points of view about the treaty differed. Many officials opposed it. A number of sheikhs who had had their power restored to them at the end of the war favored it as a guarantee of their vested interests. Faisal was torn between his gratitude to and reliance upon Great Britain for his position and his commitments to the nationalist movement, upon which he felt he dared not turn his back. The nationalists nearly succeeded in winning over the king to their anti-British point of view, but faced with an ultimatum from the British high commissioner to sever contacts with them, Faisal bowed to British pressure and appointed a prime minister to head a government that would approve the treaty.

The first draft of a new Iraqi constitution was drawn up by the British Colonial Office with the Austrian constitution as its model. Faisal ordered another constitution based on the Ottoman constitution of 1876, one that included Muslim institutions. The two drafts passed back and forth between London and Baghdad until the constitutional assembly convened in 1923. It accomplished three tasks: approving a constitution based on both Faisal's draft and that of the Colonial Office; passing an electoral law; and ratifying the 1922 treaty with Great Britain. Nationalist opposition to the treaty was so great that it was approved by parliament only after the high commissioner brought pressure to bear upon its members. Despite his threats of reprisals against those who refused to vote for the treaty, however, there was a large number of abstentions and absentees when the vote was taken.

The final version of the constitution was based on the 1831 Belgian constitution—instead of the Austrian one—with British and Ottoman refinements. It established a limited constitutional monarchy with a bicameral legislature. The king's powers, however, were extensive. He was authorized to promulgate all laws; convene, adjourn, and dissolve the legislature; appoint senate members; act as commander-in-chief; and approve all government appointments, including the prime minister and the cabinet, through which the king could initiate legislation. During the absence of parliament, the king was authorized to proclaim laws by royal decree, although they then had to be approved at the next legislative session.

In the bicameral legislature, all senators were to be appointed by the king, but deputies were to be popularly elected. All legislation had to pass both houses. Civil rights were guaranteed, and all Iraqis were to be equal before the law. Islam was declared the official state religion, and Arabic the official language. The civil, religious, and special courts retained many aspects of the old Ottoman millet system. Both Christian and Jewish communities were permitted to continue their own religious councils. The Muslim legal system was divided between Sunni and Shi'ite religious courts.

Voting was not directly representative. In the first of the two-stage electoral process, male subjects over twenty-one who paid taxes were entitled to vote for district electors who, in turn, chose representatives to the national Chamber of Deputies. In addition, Jewish and Christian minorities in Mosul, Baghdad, and Basra were given special representation. The electoral system in effect made it possible for the leading Sunni families, the Shi'ite religious leaders from the holy cities, and the tribal sheikhs to control the voting in their areas and to place their own hand-picked candidates in parliament.

In actual practice, there were three principal influences exercised in the government. The authority of the British civil servants representing London was the strongest. It was countered by nationalist leaders, who constantly sought in every way to lessen that influence. In between the two groups stood King Faisal, who sought to keep a delicate balance between the nationalists and the British. Due largely to his warm and winning personality, the king won the confidence of many tribes and urban centers. His moderating influence on both the British and the nationalists induced these opposing elements to reach a compromise, preventing another insurrection.

THE MOSUL QUESTION

Dispute over the status of the former Ottoman province of Mosul continued during the early years of the mandate between Great Britain, supporting Iraq's claims, and Turkey. The Turks refused to recognize the province as part of British-controlled Iraq and demanded its return. Knowledge that the region contained extensive oil resources made the struggle intense. Originally, according to the Sykes-Picot Agreement, Mosul was to have been controlled by France (see Chapter 5). It was attached to Iraq at the San Remo Conference in 1920, in exchange for which France was to receive Germany's share in the Turkish (later the Iraq) Petroleum Company. The new Turkish government under Ataturk, however, refused to concede this loss: Mosul's future, according to the 1923 Lausanne Treaty, was therefore to be decided by negotiation. Since neither the Turks nor the British would surrender their "rights," Great Britain brought the matter before the League of Nations.

Great Britain and Iraq claimed that the majority of Mosul's diverse population was Arab, while Turkey claimed that it was inhabited by "mountain" Turks, that is, ethnically related Turks (Kurds) although with a culture somewhat different from their own. When a commission of inquiry appointed by the League of Nations favored the British position, Turkey challenged the League's authority; the dispute was then referred to the Permanent Court of

International Justice, which took a position similar to that of the commission. The dispute was suspended in December 1925 when the League Council awarded Mosul to Iraq on condition that the British continue to guarantee protection for minority (Kurdish) rights until 1950.

THE 1930 ANGLO-IRAQI TREATY

The Mosul question stimulated Great Britain and Iraq to renew negotiations on the independent status of the latter. Once agreement on Iraq's future was determined, the incorporation of Mosul in Iraq would be considerably easier. Iraqis were demanding much greater freedom from British controls than that power was willing to grant. Not until a British Labour government, sympathetic and responsive to Iraqi nationalist aspirations, came to power during 1929 did the negotiations make any progress. Agreement was reached in the 1930 Anglo-Iraqi Treaty of Alliance, making Iraq the first Middle Eastern mandated territory to attain full legal independence. The 1930 Anglo-Iraqi Treaty resembled the 1930 draft agreement between Great Britain and Egypt, which the latter had refused to ratify (see chapter 5). The treaty became the basis for Iraq's admission to the League of Nations, but sovereignty was still greatly limited, Great Britain retaining indirect control of foreign and military affairs. Iraq was pledged to "full and frank consultations" in matters of foreign policy and "not to adopt in foreign countries an attitude which is inconsistent with the alliance." In time of international emergency, Iraq was obligated to provide Great Britain with "all facilities and assistance" required, including railways, ports, airfields, and the like. British lines of communication were to be protected in all circumstances, and air bases were to be maintained by the British to secure their route to India. Only British officers were to be used to train the Iraqi forces, and Iraqi officers were to be trained in Great Britain. The twenty-five year treaty became operative when Iraq was admitted to the League of Nations in 1932.

Although upon admission to the League, Iraq ostensibly became an independent nation, in fact the British ambassador (formerly the high commissioner) retained an influence there tantamount to that of a viceroy in India. British troops still occupied strategic areas, and many government policies were determined in London rather than in Baghdad.

DEMOCRACY

Even though Great Britain continued to play a dominant role in Iraq after 1932, Iraqis now had greater opportunities for participation in government affairs. British officials paid less attention to, and rarely interfered in, internal matters, provided only that British interests were in no way jeopardized. British officials concentrated on matters vital to the Empire, such as communications and foreign and military affairs.

The governing elite of landowners and sheikhs, absentee owners and leaders who set up residence in Baghdad, had little contact with the masses and paid no attention to Iraq's social and economic problems. There was a shortage of trained, honest, and dedicated Iraqis to replace the British officials who had held high government posts until 1932. Within the civil administration, Jews and other minority groups did not have equal opportunities for advancement. Parliament was ineffective. Most deputies considered their office a means of personal aggrandizement. Consequently, they failed to gain popular respect or confidence. Much of the legislation acted upon favored the parliament's predominantly landowning class. Although the British had expanded the facilities of the educational system, only a minority of Iraqis were able to attend schools, and more than 90 percent of the population was still illiterate.

King Faisal, supported by young Iraqi officers who had served under him during the war, formed a small dedicated group within the government that struggled to prevent further concentration of power in the hands of the wealthy landowners. Faisal's group helped to establish a Capital Development Works Project, intended to earmark oil revenues for national reconstruction, settle tribes on agricultural land, and develop public works in Baghdad. Because of his efforts to raise living standards and improve public services, Faisal was a popular figure whose reign received wide public support.

Royal influence and prestige almost disappeared after Faisal's death in 1933 and succession of his son, Ghazi, as king. The twenty-one-year-old monarch's inexperience and lack of training made him an easy prey for the landowners who congregated around the court.

Within parliament, there were as yet no recognizable political parties; power was merely concentrated in the hands of wealthy landowners and the tribal sheikhs, who represented but a fraction of the population. Political parties, none with any large following or dedication to constructive social ends, periodically emerged, flourished for a short period, and disappeared again. Each dynamic leader gathered a clique about himself, published a newspaper, and opened a party office. When his energies were finally dissipated, his followers would go on to another group. Party differences were personality conflicts, not conflicting political platforms. The only common program was the desire to end British influence in Iraq.

Many members of the three more or less significant groups formed during the 1920s belonged to earlier groups formed to attain independence during the Ottoman era. The Progressive party collapsed when its leader committed suicide in 1929. The People's party merged into the larger National Brotherhood formed in the 1930s. The National party also disappeared after its leader joined the National Reform Force and became an active participant in the 1936 military coup (see below).

In 1930 two new groups appeared. One, led by General Nuri al-Said, favored the Anglo-Iraqi Treaty; the other, an opposition group, felt that the treaty did not grant Iraq enough freedom. Nuri, a former member of the prewar secret Arab nationalist society al-Ahd (see chapter 6), organized his group into the Ahd party favoring the gradual termination of British control. His opponents, mostly from the People's and National parties, formed the National Brotherhood, which demanded an immediate end to British influence. All these groups lost their chief reason for existence when Iraq became independent and joined the League of Nations in 1932, though they did not all fade from the national political scene for that reason.

The Assyrian Massacre and Minority Problems

Although the influence of the National Brotherhood began to decline after 1932, it remained the strongest political group until 1936. Its conservative leaders attempted to distract attention from social and economic problems by constant attacks on minorities, a program that led to the Assyrian Christian massacre of 1933. Until World War I, the tiny Nestorian Christian sect (not to be confused with the ancient Assyrians) had lived in the mountains of southeastern Anatolia, about 100 miles north of the city of Mosul. After the war, the Turks forced them to leave because they had joined the tsarist forces to fight the Ottoman Empire. Most became British-protected refugees in Iraq, where they were organized into special military levies and used to help suppress Iraqi nationalist uprisings. Because of their close association with Great Britain, their participation in British military repression of the nationalists, and their request to the League of Nations for autonomous status within Iraq, the Assyrian Christians were distrusted by the Iraqis. Clashes between armed Assyrian bands and Iraqi soldiers culminated in the massacre of some 400 Assyrians in their villages and in attempts by the National Brotherhood to rally the country against the "Assyrian peril." The massacre aroused such international furor that Iraq's position in the League was endangered, since it now appeared that the government was unable to control its army and to protect its minorities. Great Britain whitewashed the whole affair, alleging that it was only a minor and unimportant incident. If the British had defended the Assyrians, British prestige would have fallen in the eyes of the Muslim population.

Other complex problems facing Iraq between 1932 and 1936 were local clashes between tribes, Kurdish discontent in the north, and jealousy between Sunnis and Shi'ites. The tribes feuded among themselves over rights to grazing lands; the Kurds rebelled against any non-Kurdish authority; and the Sunnis and Shi'ites continued their established religious vendetta.

Tribal discontent with imposition of a strong central authority was used by politicians to gain political power. National Brotherhood leaders, for example, incited the tribes against the government when the Brotherhood leaders were not in power. So successfully did the Brotherhood politicians create tribal unrest that the king was forced to call upon the party's leaders to restore order in 1935. By this time, however, the tribes could no longer be controlled by the Brotherhood. The only individual capable of handling the situation seemed to be General Bakr Sidki, who had ruthlessly crushed the Assyrians in 1933. Knowledge of the general's repression of the Assyrians intimidated the tribes into suspending their revolt against the government.

THE 1936 COUP

By the mid 1930s, no Iraqi political group seemed capable of sustaining the government. None had been able to end the conflicts between different religious groups or to make any economic and social progress. The conservative National Brotherhood party, which had gained control of the government in 1935–1936 as a result of the tribal unrest, attempted to repress all opposition to it by use of police spies and censorship. Only the army and a group of Western-educated liberals were prepared to take action against this government. The liberals advocated democracy and socialism, while the military glorified nationalism and military dictatorship. The latter were strongly influenced by the success of Ataturk, while the liberals desired to emulate British leftist socialism.

The Ahali

The liberal group, originally called Ahali (after their newspaper), became the National Democratic party. Members educated in European universities had a broader outlook than those trained in Iraq. Their newspaper, *Ahali,* became one of Iraq's most influential publications, despite its small circulation, because of its appeal to those with grievances against the government.

Members of the Ahali group began to espouse socialism in 1934, under the influence of Abd al-Fattah Ibrahim and Muhammad Hadid. The former was influenced by his knowledge of the Soviet Union learned while a graduate student at Columbia University. Muhammad Hadid became a disciple of Harold Laski, the British left-wing Socialist, while studying at the London School of Economics. Because of the hostility with which those in power viewed socialism, regarding it as extremist or subversive, the Ahali called their ideology Populism *(Shaabiya).*

Populist doctrine were spelled out in two small volumes describing Ahali's aim as "welfare for all" regardless of class, financial status, or religious background. Sweeping reforms were proposed in which members of parliament would be chosen by occupation rather than by geographical location. However, the group disavowed the class struggle, revolutionary social change, and Marxist concepts of family and religion. While they urged patriotism, nationalism was regarded as a vice, since it often led to imperialism and domination of one class by another. "The history of nationalism," stated their manifesto, "is full of blood, tyranny, and hypocrisy."[3] Patriotism, however, was not aggressive; it called for full rights for every citizen in his fatherland.

Despite their influence, Ahali leaders still felt that organization of a political party was premature in 1934. Instead, they organized a social circle, the Baghdad Club. When the group became extremely successful in organizing the educated youth, the government banned it, charging it with being a disguised form of communism, and therefore anti-Muslim.

To defend itself against charges of leftist subversion, the Ahali temporarily gave up many of its more radical proposals. A number of liberals, who had become dissatisfied with the conservatism of the National Brotherhood, subsequently joined the group despite the government's ban; among these was Kamil al-Chadirchi, who later took charge of the Ahali movement.

The Ahali opened an offensive against the Brotherhood-controlled government in 1935. To wage a more effective political battle, Ahali established an executive committee and began to contact elder politicians and nonpolitical reform groups, such as the Society to Combat Illiteracy. As a precaution against government spies, Ahali meetings were held in secret and new members were closely watched. Populism was now replaced by a reform program, although the leftists within Ahali still continued their demands for more radical doctrines. The government cracked down on the newspaper *Ahali* with stricter censorship, made a number of arrests of "Communists," and discharged all employees suspected of leftist activity. A number of elder, respected politicians petitioned the king against these stringent measures, but to no avail. Because they were unable to make any effective political progress, Ahali leaders finally concluded that they were powerless without military support and began secretly to contact sympathetic officers. Their prize catch was General Bakr Sidki, whom they persuaded to lead an army coup against the Brotherhood-controlled government.

The Military

Until the mid-1930s, the army had not actively participated in politics, although it had won acclaim from the Muslim population for its effective repression of the "Assyrian peril." General Bakr Sidki especially was regarded with awe by all sectors of the community for his role in suppressing both the

Assyrians and dissident tribes in the south. By the mid-1930s several officers had become actively interested in politics and found that the army's reputation for suppressing the Assyrians was a political asset. The most influential officers were ultra-nationalists, who inspired many of their junior officers with pan-Arabism. Why, these officers asked, should not the army undertake to end the bickering among the Baghdad politicians? They looked to the examples of neighboring Turkey and Iran, where military dictatorships were flourishing. Among the senior officers only General Sidki could command the respect of all army elements. Other general-staff officers were considered too passive or too career minded to risk failure by venturing into politics.

The army also had its own specific grievances. Military appropriations had been cut by the government, and attempts to modernize the army were not proceeding according to General Sidki's plans. In addition, many officers resented being used by the government to repress its political opponents.

The contact man between the military and Ahali was Hikmat Sulaiman, a former member of the National Brotherhood. He was the younger brother of Mahmud Shevket Pasha, who had led the Ottoman army against Abdul Hamid in 1907–1908 to establish the Committee of Union and Progress (see chapter 3). Hikmat himself had been influenced by Turkey's Kemalist reforms rather than by socialism. Because of his brother's reputation and his own friendship for Ataturk, he was admired by youth in the rising middle class and by younger army officers.

After Bakr Sidki had become acting chief of the army's general staff in the fall of 1936, he and a group of fellow officers joined forces with Ahali leaders in a National Reform Force. Under Sidki's leadership, the army seized Baghdad and took over the government. Sidki then called upon the king to form a new cabinet of "sincere men" to be led by Hikmat Sulaiman, "esteemed for his noble career." The coup had been staged, Sidki told the people, to advance their welfare and strengthen the nation. Government officials were warned to cooperate lest the army be compelled to take measures "which may cause some harm to those who do not answer our sincere appeal, materially and morally."[4]

Sidki was content at first to remain behind the scenes of government, now headed by Hikmat Sulaiman and several Ahali men. In the beginnning, the National Reform Force issued a number of proclamations releasing political prisoners, guaranteeing civil liberties and free trade union activity, promising social and economic reforms, and strengthening the army. At first Hikmat Sulaiman tried to reconcile his coalition of Ahali leftists and right-wing nationalist army officers. But, for the sake of expediency, the Ahali men were soon pushed into the background. They had served their purpose in providing the army with a reason for seizing power. The conservative officers and the liberal reformers found that they could not agree on how to run the government. The Ahali were seriously weakened in 1936 by their failure to elect more than 12 of their partisans to the 180-member Chamber of Deputies, whose other members did not hesitate to attack their "radical" proposals. Matters were brought to a head when, because of their proposed land reforms, the reformers were charged with advocating communism by a coalition of nationalists, conservatives, and tribal sheikhs.

Nationalists opposed the Ahali group because it was lukewarm toward pan-Arabism. Ahali's reform program was also ignored by Sidki, who now sought to impose a strong military dictatorship upon the country. Within a few months, Hikmat began to follow an opportunistic policy, abandoning Ahali and joining the powerful military in attacking liberals "who would try to plant communism in Iraqi soil." By the end of the year, the reform movement had collapsed. Hikmat then discharged Ahali leaders from the government, or they resigned. He became quite vindictive, perhaps to prove his new allegiance, and arrested or exiled most of his former liberal colleagues.

With the reformists out of the way, General Bakir Sidki became the most powerful influence in the government, stronger even than the opportunistic Hikmat. Sidki now directed all government affairs, turning it into a right-wing military dictatorship. He used such iron-fisted methods that a group of his own officers assassinated him in August 1937, bringing to an end the first contemporary Arab military regime. The revolution, begun on a crest of sincere liberal reform, had degenerated into merely another military coup. The country had failed to produce sufficiently strong liberal forces to effect the needed social and economic changes, and the depressed groups themselves were so fragmented that they could not organize effective political opposition to the landlord-dominated government.

The international political climate at the time was more favorable to Bakr Sidki's methods than those of Ahali. Fascism, not democratic socialism, was the vogue in Turkey and Iran, the states closest to Iraq. Bakr Sidki's type of regime became the prototype of Iraqi government during the next five years. Between 1937 and 1941, half a dozen such military coups kept the country in continual turmoil, preventing any democratic development or any of the fundamental reforms so urgently needed to advance Iraqi society from its primitive state.

THE RASHID ALI COUP

During December 1938, in the last of the pre-World War II Iraqi military coups, General Nuri al-Said seized power. Nuri, a former critic of army interference in politics, was a staunch partisan of close ties with Great Britain. Neither he nor his Ahd associates had made any constructive internal changes during the time they had been in office prior to 1936. While professing democratic principles, Nuri and his followers did not hesitate to use the identical police controls and repressive measures of their predecessors. During his first days in office, Nuri promised to abolish press restrictions and institute more democratic electoral and parliamentary procedures. But parliament remained in the hands of the same clique of conservative landowners and tribal sheikhs, providing the few dozen familiar politicians who filled first one cabinet post, then another. Nepotism and corruption continued to undermine civil administration. Rather than reconstruct the system, Nuri sought to build alliances within it among the landowners and tribal leaders.

In one respect Nuri's ideas differed from those of the usual conservative Iraqi politician. He was loyal to the British alliance and broke relations with Germany after the outbreak of World War II, in the face of public opposition to Great Britain. Many ultranationalists were attracted by Axis propaganda and saw in German victory their redemption from Anglo-French imperialism. The more moderate Iraqis, however, were not deceived by Nazi promises and refrained from sabotaging British war efforts.

Nuri used the outbreak of the war as an excuse for imposing emergency legislation upon the country and abandoning all pretense of democracy. Despite his virtually dictatorial powers, he was unable to smother all political dissent in the country at large and, in particular, opposition in the cabinet. Personal differences among the political and military cliques were the main cause of the collapse of one government after another as well as for successive army coups. Nuri continued to play an important behind-the-scenes role during this time, influencing the policies of the various governments in power. The power of the central government had now become so weak, however, that it hardly existed outside Baghdad and a few other cities: and in the cities, British influence, exercised through Nuri's appointees, was great.

Continued Nazi military successes during the early war years dazzled the ultranationalists and helped fan the smouldering fires of anti-British sentiment throughout Iraq. Anglophobia, decked out in Fascist garb, was more appealing to nationalistic-minded Iraqi youth than the less exciting socioeconomic doctrines of the Ahali.

A former National Brotherhood anti-British leader, Rashid Ali al-Gilani, became prime minister after Nuri's fall in March 1940. Rashid Ali's coalition of civilian and military ultranationalists desired a German victory as the best way of ridding their country of British domination. When faced with British demands for additional military bases after the collapse of France in 1940, Rashid Ali insisted on keeping Iraq neutral and argued that his government was not obligated to comply. While negotiating with Great Britain, the nationalists began to cultivate friendly relations with Germany and Italy, in the wake of a massive Axis Arab-propaganda campaign. The British persuaded the regent, Abdul Illah (named regent in 1939 when the death of King Ghazi left the country with a four-year-old successor, King Faisal II), to force

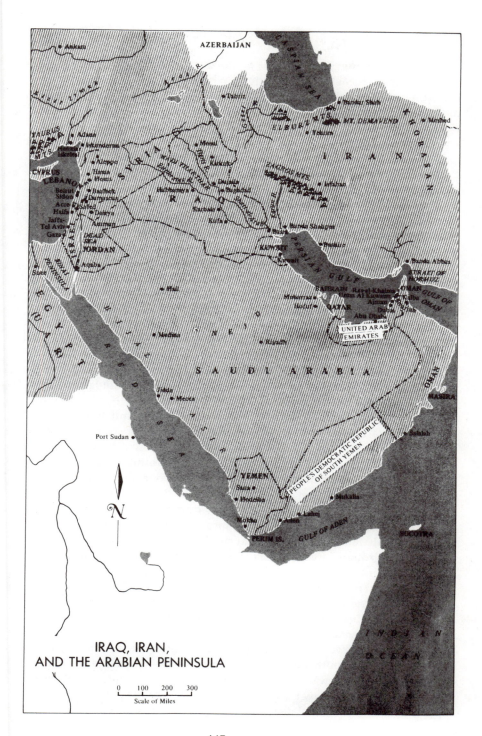

IRAQ, IRAN,
AND THE ARABIAN PENINSULA

0   100   200   300

Scale of Miles

Rashid Ali from office. Instead, the nationalists managed to turn the tables and to force the regent to flee the country. With army support, Rashid Ali now formed a National Defense government: its stated policy was wartime neutrality, but it was in fact willing to accept help from any quarter on behalf of the Arab nationalist cause.

When the neutral-nationalist government seemed about to accept Axis military assistance during 1941, British troops invaded the country to crush Rashid Ali's government (see chapter 5). Muslim religious divines proclaimed a *jihad* (holy war) and Haj Amin al-Husayni, the former mufti of Jerusalem who had fled to Iraq because of his anti-British activities, rallied the Baghdad populace to an anti-imperialist crusade. Promised Axis aid failed to materialize, however, and within a month the Rashid Ali government was overthrown by the British army. The regent returned to appoint Nuri al-Said as prime minister, and Iraq was once again under British influence.

POSTWAR PRELUDE TO REVOLUTION

From the fall of Rashid Ali's government in 1941 until the 1958 revolution, Nuri al-Said either headed or controlled most government coalitions. In April 1946, after the regent's announcement that democracy would be restored, five parties came into being: the Independence (Istiqlal), Liberal (Ahrar), National Democratic (al-Watani al-Democrati), National Union (Ittihad al-Watani), and the People's (Shaab) parties. An outlawed Communist movement also existed, but it did not emerge from its underground position until 1958.

With Germany defeated and fascism no longer in fashion, three of the five new parties adopted socialist slogans. None could boast a large following. The parties advocating socialism generally represented the younger generation of urban politicians who had fallen under Western influence. Nuri attempted to offset their influence by rallying the more conservative old guard in the Constitutional Union party formed during 1949, but his party represented only a small group of wealthy men, organized to protect their own vested interests.

The Istiqlal rightists, formed from remnants of the old National Brotherhood, had been ardent supporters of the prewar Rashid Ali regime, and many of its leaders had been interned during the war because of suspected collaboration with Axis agents.

The Liberals never succeeded in gaining any influence in the government or support from any influential group because they lacked a militant doctrine. During the Palestine war in 1948, both the National Union and People's parties were suppressed by the government on the grounds of their political radicalism. Of the three socialist groups, only the National Democrats maintained continuity, although it too was suspended during the imposition of martial law in 1948–1949.

Immediately after World War II, Nuri tried to make a long term agreement with Great Britain by means of a new Anglo-Iraqi Treaty signed at Portsmouth, England in January 1948. He agreed that England should retain special privileges in Iraq provided that the country could determine its own domestic and foreign policies. Although Great Britain agreed to surrender her bases, nationalists opposed provisions permitting the return of British troops during emergencies and the draft treaty was never ratified. So vehement were public demonstrations against it that they toppled the government that had proposed the agreement. Although he had backed the treaty, Nuri had not been premier, but only an "adviser" to the government. He could therefore now be appointed prime minister.

The Arab defeat in the Palestine war during 1948 had serious political and economic repercussions in Iraq. On the one hand, the government was discredited because of the poor showing put up by Iraqi troops fighting Jewish forces in Palestine. The defeat gave Nuri the opportunity to impose martial law on the country to protect it from the "Zionist threat." The war also led to growing tensions between Iraq's Jewish minority of some 150,000 and the Arab population. By 1949 the tensions became so great that all but about 5000 Jews left Iraq for Israel. Since the Jews had constituted a large proportion of the country's skilled government employees and urban middle class, their departure left a vacuum in government administration and in the middle-class economy—business, commerce, import-export, and the like—which it took several years to fill.

Nuri continued his traditional pro-British policy and, in 1955, aligned Iraq with the Western defense system through the Baghdad Pact, extending British military privileges in the country (see chapter 5). In theory, the pact strengthened Iraq against the threat of Communist penetration, but Nuri's pro-Western policies were so unpopular that they became a major target of the nationalists and most younger politicians.

The nationalists still resented British influence in Iraq and the suppression of Rashid Ali during the war. Many looked toward pan-Arabism and eventual federation within a greater Arab state. Even the less ultranationalististic National Democrats favored a neutralist foreign policy, free of British influence. Most political groups regarded Nuri and the Hashemite rulers as British pawns, constantly subjected to the insidious manipulations of the British ambassador. The United States, because of its close alliance with Great Britain and its active role in the Baghdad Pact, was also greatly disliked and mistrusted by the nationalists.

After 1955, nationalist feeling was intensified by the emergence of President Nasser to the forefront of Arab leadership. Nationalists admired his successes in forcing the British from the Suez Canal zone and in raising

Egypt's international prestige. Liberals were inspired by the destruction of the Egyptian monarchy and its conservative supporters and by Nasser's revolutionary reforms. Many opposition leaders in Baghdad were in constant touch with Cairo and they frequently visited and consulted with Egypt's revolutionary leaders. When the Arab world's major enemies, imperialist Great Britain, France, and Zionist Israel attacked Egypt late in 1956, even Nuri was forced to proclaim his support for Arabism and to break relations with Great Britain and France, although his critics charged that he had vacillated and pandered to British intrigues far too long.

Recognizing the great emotional appeal stirred up by creation of the United Arab Republic in January 1958, leaders of the Hashemite dynasties in Iraq and Jordan responded by forming the Arab Federation of both kingdoms in February. Although Iraq's King Faisal and Jordan's King Husain (cousins in the Hashemite family) would retain sovereignty over their respective territories, their armed forces, foreign policies, diplomatic corps, educational systems, and customs services would be unified. A Federal Legislature was to have been chosen in equal numbers from the parliaments of each nation. The Arab Federation never aroused the enthusiasm of the UAR, and the whole endeavor was aborted by the 1958 Iraqi revolution, which overthrew the Hashemite dynasty in that country. In August 1958 Jordan's King Husain declared the termination of the Federation.

Economic and Social Conditions

Nuri's unpopular foreign policy and police repression occurred against a backdrop of economic and social failures. Living conditions of the average Iraqi had hardly improved since after World War I, when British officials compared them with the conditions described in the Old Testament. The dismal poverty seemed worse than that of Egypt because of the disparity between Iraq's actual situation and her tremendous potential for development—the cultivable, but uncultivated land; the unharnessed Tigris-Euphrates system; and the vast oil resources. In Iraq there was approximately twenty times the agricultural area per person that existed in Egypt. If used for economic development, the country's resources could have provided for two to three times the existing population of some six million.

Experiments to control the environment had been initiated as early as 1903 by Sir William Willcox, British director of Egypt's reservoirs. His *Irrigation of Mesopotamia,* published in 1905, has been the basis of all subsequent surveys, including those of the Iraq Development Board created in 1950. Originally established to supervise spending of an International Bank Loan for flood control, the Development Board began to use the massive oil revenues after 1951. Seventy percent of the oil monies (nearly half the national income) was turned over to the board. By 1958, two major water control projects had been completed, the Wadi Tharthar on the Tigris and the Habbaniya on the Euphrates. They included dams that made flood control possible for the first time and increased the cultivable area by several hundred thousand acres.

Nevertheless, these and the other Development Board projects did little to affect the lives of more than a handful of the population. The land developed by the new irrigation projects belonged to a small group of owners who did not share the profits of the additional agricultural productivity with the peasants. A mere 2 percent of the landowners owned more than two-thirds of all agricultural land. Ninety percent of the peasants were landless, working as sharecroppers and forced to pay up to two-thirds of their crops to landlords for land use, irrigation water, seed, and tools. Agricultural production was not greatly increased, industry was not greatly expanded, nor was the abysmally low living standard raised. Critics charged that there was too little long-term economic planning, that too much was being invested in gigantic schemes with little attention to immediate needs. Only a few thousand propertyless farmers resettled on state lands and a few small housing projects were completed.

Unoccupied state lands were to have been distributed to peasants and reclaimed with government assistance under a 1951 law. But by 1958, only a small amount of land had been given out. In the largest project at Dujaila, irrigation waters were not properly drained and the soil became salt-encrusted and lost its fertility. The engineering planning had paid scant attention to the social and economic needs of the area. The only agricultural cooperative at Dujaila soon collapsed because of mismanagement. No organization had been established to supervise such things as crop rotation or use of improved agricultural methods.

When word of the 1952 Egyptian land reform spread through Iraq's rural areas, unrest grew among the landless peasants. By 1952 conditions in the south had become so bad that thousands had begun to flee to the northern towns, especially to Baghdad, where they hoped to find employment opportunities. In the decade before the 1958 revolution, Baghdad's population more than doubled to three-quarters of a million. The city (where nothing survived of the ancient splendor of the times of Harun al-Rashid) was totally unprepared for such an influx. Huge nightmarish slums spread, acre upon acre, around the capital. In the winter, the slum inhabitants were swamped in mud from the Tigris overflow; during the dry season, they were choked with dust storms. After a visit, Doreen Warriner described these conditions:

> There is much trachoma and dysentery, but no bilharzia or malaria, because the water is too polluted for snails and mosquitoes. The infant mortality rate is 250. A woman has a 50:50 chance of raising a child to the age of ten. There are no social services of any kind.... On the adjacent dumps dogs with rabies

dig in the sewage, and the slum-dwellers pack it for resale as garden manure.[5]

THE JULY 1958 REVOLUTION

By July 1958 the army had again become the focal point of unrest. Again it collaborated, under the leadership of General Abd al-Karim Kassim, with several nationalist and leftist civilian groups to overthrow the government. This revolution, however, was far more drastic than the 1936 one. Not only was the monarchy destroyed and Iraq made a republic, but the power of the landowners was threatened. The upheaval also differed significantly from the 1952 Eqyptian revolution. Egypt's "Blessed Event" was concocted, executed, and managed entirely by junior army officers. In Iraq, the revolution was a joint endeavor of military and civilian groups. There were less than a dozen casualties in Egypt, but scores were slaughtered in Baghdad, including King Faisal II, his uncle, the former regent, Crown Prince Abdul Illah, and Prime Minister Nuri al-Said. In Egypt, the army had controlled the street mobs; they ran amok in Baghdad, pillaging and burning at will.

Communists, Ba'athist (see p. 333, chapter 14), the Istiqlal, and National Democrats supplied the civilian component of the Iraqi revolution. After Nuri's ban on political parties in 1954, all parties had gone underground. The Istiqlal and National Democrats have already been described. The Ba'athists were junior partners of their Syrian counterpart and followed the lead of the Damascus Ba'ath leaders, Michel Aflaq, Akram Hourani, and Salah Bitar. The Communists had always been an underground movement, having been regarded by Nuri's regime as a subversive organization, like the Zionists, working against the national interest.

One of the first acts of the revolutionary government, after overthrowing the Hashemite kingdom, was to secede from the 1958 Arab federation with Jordan (see chapter 12). Iraqi independence in the realm of foreign policy was immediately flaunted by recognition of both Soviet Russia and Red China. By early 1959, all ties with the Baghdad Pact Organization had been severed, and its headquarters was forced to move from Iraq to Turkey, where it was renamed the Central Treaty Organization.

Relations with the UAR were initially so cordial that they led to negotiations for either union or federation. Both nations seemed to have much in common: they had overthrown unpopular monarchies and deprived the land-owning conservative politicians of their power; they had ended imperialistic Western influence in their internal affairs and were pursuing independent, neutralist foreign policies; and they had established revolutionary regimes intended to alter the total national economic and social structure. Identity of purpose, however, was insufficient to weld the two nations into one, and the strains created by internal differences began to weaken the bonds of friendship within weeks of Iraq's revolution.

Insistence by Iraqi Ba'athists on immediate, total union with the UAR antagonized less pan-Arab elements like the National Democrats and even cooled the latter's ardor somewhat for a close nexus with Nasser. Many Iraqis desired to share neither their oil wealth nor their political sovereignty. They realized that immediate fusion with the UAR would result in only a junior partnership for Iraq. Within months, relations between the two revolutionary governments had degenerated into a propaganda war as intense as that ever waged by Nasser against the reactionary Hashemites. While the Nasser image lost much of its charisma in Iraq, the Egyptian leader retained a sufficiently wide popular backing to sponsor the organization of antigovernment forces into a counterrevolutionary movement, which General Kassim, who became the new republic's first prime minister, could then suppress only after more bloodshed and violence.

Dispute over Iraq's role in the Arab world produced a three-way split in the revolutionary regime. Pro-Nasser forces were represented by the Ba'ath and the Istiqlal groups, both of which were soon outlawed and driven underground. At the other extreme were the Communists and their supporters, who for many months became the dominant political force. Initially, General Kassim relied on them as a foil for the ultranationalists, and many Communists had thereby obtained influential government posts. The excellent organization of the Communist party, its popular base and its wide use of front groups—such as the Peace Partisans, People's Resistance Movement, Federation of Peasants Organizations, League for Defense of Women's Rights, Democratic Youth Movement, Students' Union, and many others—gave the Communists wider influence and prestige than any other group. Furthermore, only the Communists could provide large numbers of staff well enough educated to fill the offices that had been purged of their prerevolutionary personnel.

The National Democrats offered token competition to the Communists, but they did not have the organization or the following of the Communists and remained a small group of Iraq's leading independent-minded intellectuals. Within a year, the National Democrats were also divided between those who favored closer ties with the extreme left and those who were wary of too close an association with the Communists. In the early stages of the revolution, the National Democrats played a key role in the revolutionary government, having been called upon by Kassim to fill the gap created when he was forced to sever his ties with both nationalists and leftists. But by 1960, the National Democats had lost much of their previous influence and soon after split into two, then three fragments, and finally disappeared from the political scene altogether.

By 1961, General Kassim had temporarily neutralized the political factions, striving for closer ties on the one hand with Cairo and on the other with

Moscow. Through the delicate interplay of various groups, including the dissident Kurds in the north, and with the support of the army, Kassim managed to guide Iraq along a middle-of-the-road neutralist course. While accepting extensive economic assistance from the Soviet Union, he also renewed diplomatic relations with the West and with the neighboring Arab countries.

The attempt to balance such a variety of political forces, to mollify the Kurdish minority, to retain support of both the urban middle class and the smaller landowners through moderate, rather than radical, reforms, completely vitiated the first grandiose schemes for revolutionary change. By June 1961 less than 10 percent of the more than nine million acres of land promised to the peasants had been distributed. Little progress had been made in organizing country-wide cooperatives, agricultural extension services, housing projects, and similar measures. Even work on major large-scale irrigation projects had slowed down so that less progress was being made on the engineering level than in the days immediately preceding the revolution. Only in Baghdad was there evidence of progress in the construction of new public buildings, such as a university, an opera house, and various government offices.

The major obstacle to achieving internal stability necessary for economic and social reform was the periodical internecine struggle among Iraq's revolutionary leaders. While there was general agreement on the broad outlines of revolutionary objectives, squabbles over methods to realize them created continued turmoil. Differences between Communists and anti-Communists, Nasserites and anti-Nasserites, Ba'athists and anti-Ba'athists often cut across party lines, fragmenting political parties into fractions that waged not only ideological but armed warfare against each other.

After suppressing a bloody struggle between Communists and pro-Nasserites in northern Iraq during 1959, General Kassim disbanded the People's Resistance Force, suspended political parties, and purged many Communists and their supporters from the government. He attempted to hold down political opposition by restricting the number of political parties by law to the National Democrats, the Democratic party of Kurdistan, and two selected Communist factions. Neither the Ba'ath nor the Istiqlal were registered, thereby spreading opposition to the regime.

By 1963 Kassim had alienated so many of his original Free Officer collaborators by his wavering policies that he himself was executed. The officer who replaced him, Abd al-Salam Mohammed Arif, had been one of his chief associates until he was purged in 1958. Although Kassim had spared Arif's life and imprisoned him in 1958, the latter now permitted the execution of the revolutionary leader.

Arif's 1963 coup was carried out by Ba'athists, including several civilian politicians, and nationalist air force officers. The new coalition formed a

National Council of the Revolutionary Command (NCRC) to run the country, the majority of whose members were pro-Nasser Ba'athists. Although he was not a Ba'athist, Colonel Arif was named by the NCRC as its president. Tensions immediately developed within the Council between Ba'athists and Arif. While there was agreement on a purge of pro-Kassim and Communist sympathizers, there was disagreement over how far to carry out the purges, over the extent to which radical socialist policies should be attempted, and over the degree of Arab unity desirable, especially with Egypt. During their brief period of office, the Ba'athists used their national paramilitary National Guard to an excessive point, threatening to challenge supremacy of the country's armed forces. Clashes within the Ba'ath between moderates and militants led to an unsuccessful coup by the latter, with the result that President Arif cleansed the government of all Ba'athists and outlawed their National Guard.

After his "countercoup" in November 1964 Arif took over full power, including command of the armed forces and chairmanship of the reorganized and now wholly military NCRC. All political parties were outlawed, strict press censorship was imposed, and a military regime was installed. The NCRC was replaced by a National Revolutionary Council (NRC), which transferred its powers to President Arif. In an effort to emulate UAR President Nasser's efforts to rally mass support, Arif organized a new Iraqi Arab Socialist Union, into which all political parties would be "merged." Extensive nationalization measures were carried out as part of a new "socialist" program, in which all banks, insurance, steel, cement, tobacco, food, tanneries, and construction companies were taken over by the government.

Despite his dictatorial powers, Arif failed to cope with the most urgent problems: the Kurdish rebellion, economic stagnation and deterioration, collapse of social reform efforts, and continued quarrels among pro- and anti-Nasserites and Ba'athists.

Some of the country's military junta favored full military and political cooperation with Egypt; others were more reserved. Arif attempted to placate both groups, supporting efforts to cooperate with Cairo in summit conferences and formulating blueprints for union with Egypt, but at the same time keeping close watch on officers who were pro-Egyptian and who on at least three occasions attempted to overthrow his regime.

After the death of President Arif in a helicopter accident in April 1966, he was succeeded as president by his older brother, Major General Abd al-Rahman Arif, with both cabinet and army backing. The new regime now experimented with the first civilian prime minister since the 1958 revolution. He was Professor Abd al-Rahman al-Bazzaz, a moderate nationalist who headed the government for nine months before a return to total military rule. Bazzaz scored a few small successes, such as bringing to a temporary halt the fighting with the Kurds and restarting some development projects. But soon he was replaced by another general who had no more success than his predecessors.

A successful coup against President Arif was staged by General Ahmed Hassan al-Bakr in July 1968. Arif went into exile, and his prime minister was put on trial. Although Bakr was at first believed to represent moderate Ba'athist policies, within a month he dismissed his cabinet for its "reactionary tendencies," appointed himself prime minister and commander-in-chief, and chose a new cabinet of Ba'athist radicals. Bakr continued to rule without a parliament, failing to deal effectively with internal problems or to redress the disastrous wars with Israel and the Kurds. A new aspect of the political situation was hysterical suspicion of Westerners, most of whom were invited to leave the country. Numerous Western teachers, technicians, and professionals were expelled. Iraqis who had Western wives found life increasingly uncomfortable, and many were purged from government service. The purges included several former Iraqi cabinet ministers, including Dr. Bazzaz and others who were arrested as "counterrevolutionary leaders." The most notorious of the trials ended in public execution and display of the bodies of fourteen men. The fact that nine of them were Jewish drew attention to the rapidly deteriorating situation of the Jewish remnant in Iraq, although the government denied that anti-Semitism was involved. By August 1969 a total of some fifty executions of "counterrevolutionaries" and "spies," mostly Muslim Arabs, had taken place as a warning to opponents of the regime.

Following the 1968 Bakr coup it was said that the power monopoly was not only Ba'athist, but "Takrit," that is, many key positions were occupied by Bakr's relatives, who like him, were from the village of Takrit. The second in command, assistant secretary general of the Ba'ath party and vice president of the Revolutionary Command Council, was Saddam Husain al-Takriti from a Takrit peasant family. Working closely with Bakr, Saddam Husain established a paramount role for the Ba'ath which had been a minority party in 1968. The task of suppressing the regime's opponents, mostly Nasserites and Communists, was assigned to a specially organized militia, the Green Brassards.

An abortive coup led by the regime's security chief in 1973 resulted in a constitutional amendment giving the president even more power, and to the formation of a National Progressive Front. It included the Ba'ath, the Iraqi Communist party and the Kurdish Democratic party (KDP). The secretariat of the Front High Committee was dominated by Ba'athists who constituted half of its 16 members. Local committees of the Front were established after 1973 in proportions similar to those at the top. To the extent that there was a popular base to the government, it existed through the people's popular councils of the Ba'ath. The party's National Pact, which was supposedly the document serving as the model for a constitution, defined Iraq's political regime as "democratic, popular, socialist and unionist...guaranteeing democratic freedoms to the masses and to their national progressive forces." According to this document legislative power belonged to the RCC of the party, and executive power continued to be exercised by the government.

General Bakr and Saddam Husain occasionally had to compromise with other parties in the Front. Before signing the National Pact the Communists objected to the designation of the Ba'ath as "leading party," and they demanded a date when the Ba'athists would terminate exclusive control of the state apparatus to form a parliament. A vague compromise stipulated that the "Front is led by the parties which form it," but "the Ba'ath enjoys a privileged position within the front."

The Kurdish Democrats demanded a census to determine areas that would benefit from autonomy in their agreement with Baghdad as a condition for joining the Front. They also objected to "political Arabization" as government policy in Kurdish areas, and insisted that more seats be allocated to Kurds in governing institutions at the national level to reflect their numbers. When discussions between Ba'athists and the KDP collapsed, Saddam Husain sent an ultimatum to the KDP demanding a reply within two weeks. This act ignited the fighting between the Iraqi army and the Kurds once again.

By the late 1970s Saddam Husain extended his power, finally, in 1979 taking over the ruling institutions, the RCC, the Ba'ath, and the government, in name as well as in fact. General Bakr, now over 60 years old, resigned as the country's leader because of "ill health," leaving Husain in full control. A series of purges within and outside the ruling circle eliminated many potential dissidents. In 1979 after withdrawing from the RCC and NPF the Communists were purged from government altogether and many were executed. Even Ba'athists were not secure; following Bakr's retirement dozens of Ba'athist leaders were arrested and 21 officials, including three former cabinet ministers, were executed for treason.

While eliminating the opposition, Saddam Husain also laid the ground-work for rallying public support through new elections for a revived 250 member National Assembly. The elections, the first since the 1958 revolution, gave the Ba'ath three-fourths of the assembly seats and legitimized Husain's rule. Simultaneously elections were held for a legislative council in the northern Kurdish Autonomous Region.

While entrenching his internal authority Husain also sought to reclaim Iraq's role as leader of the Arab world, dominant power in the Gulf, and *primus inter pares* among third word "progressives." Following Egypt's decline as the most influential Arab state after Nasser's death, opportunities increased for Iraq. By the 1980s its oil made it one of the richest Arab states and its high birth rate one of the most populous. While not all of its massive development plans succeeded, there were areas of achievement, especially in raising urban living standards. The fall of Iran's shah during 1979 followed by internal upheaval awakened Husain's interest in assuming the shah's mantle as protector of the Gulf. As ruler of the largest Arab power in the region, Saddam Husain correctly appraised the growing concern among other Arab regimes about the religious-revolutionary zeal of the new Shi'ite authority in Tehran.

In 1980 he decided to strike and to re-establish Iraq's hegemony. The pretext for invading Iran was to cancel the "unfair" 1975 Algiers agreement (see p. 521), reclaim Iraqi domination of the Shatt el-Arab and several border areas and Gulf islands from Iran. The resulting Gulf War soon acquired an ideological overtone as Husain attacked the "Persian racists," and the war was called Saddam's Qaddassiya, commemorating an early Arab victory over Sassanian Persia (see chapter 2). Saddam's Qaddassiya also gave rise to a new personality cult, with the president's picture burgeoning in public buildings, on the front pages of all daily newspapers, and on every TV news program. It was also the occasion for further suppression of dissidence. Tens of thousands of Shi'ite zealots, including many sympathizers of the new regime in Tehran, were dumped across the border into Iran; the principal Shi'ite cleric in Iraq, Ayatollah Muhammed al-Bakr Sadr, was imprisoned; and many of his associates were executed.

An Israeli air attack on Iraq's nuclear reactor at Osirak and its destruction in 1981 aroused Arab and third world sympathy for Iraq. Both Jordan and Saudi Arabia openly supported Saddam in the Gulf War. King Husain even promised to lead a "Yarmouk Brigade" (another seventh century battle leading to Arab conquest of Persia) against the "idolatrous Persians." However, the Gulf War polarized the Arab world. It brought to a hasty end plans for union with Syria (see chapter 14) as President Assad joined Libya and other leftist regimes in support for Iran. Soviet ambiguity in the war greatly cooled relations between Baghdad and Moscow, especially after Saddam indicated that he would turn to the United States for assistance.

Although Iraq was not one of the confrontation states with borders adjoining Israel, it has been an active and militant participant in the Palestine struggle. Iraqi troops participated in the Arab-Israeli wars of 1948, 1967, and 1973. During the 1967 war their air fields and planes were immobilized on the first day of fighting by Israeli bombers. Iraq has also been among the most militant supporters of the Palestinian guerrilla organizations. One of them, the Arab Liberation Front, was sponsored by the Baghdad government. After the 1967 and 1973 wars, the Baghdad Ba'athists joined with the most militant Arab governments in the "rejection front," which refused any compromise in negotiations for a peace settlement.

Baghdad's hard line toward a Middle East peace settlement converged with its policies for use of oil as a political weapon against the West. One of the founding members of OPEC in 1960, Iraq has ever since been aware of the growing power oil gives it in international affairs. General Bakr's decision to nationalize the Iraq Petroleum Company in 1972 greatly increased his popularity at home and in the Arab world. During and after the 1973 war Iraq benefited increasingly from the fivefold increase in oil prices. The additional income financed the purchase of a large supply of weapons from the Soviet Union and helped to extend development programs at home.

The combination of massive oil revenues, two of the largest rivers in the Middle East (the Tigris and Euphrates), and one of the potentially richest land areas has endowed Iraq with the requisites for a major development program. Some economists estimate that the country has the potential to support a population twice the eleven million inhabitants who lived there in 1977. Limitations on development were both natural and social. Soil salinity and the spread of malaria were dangers resulting from large-scale irrigation projects. The river system was difficult to control and also involved international legal complications with the other riparian states, Turkey and Syria. Drainage and irrigation projects faced obstacles because of the very flat terrain that explains why so much of the country is still either desert or swampland.

Like many other developing countries, Iraq faced the paradox of labor shortages in rural areas, simultaneously with a very high birth rate and urban overpopulation. Between 1947 and 1980 the rural population declined from 64 to 28 percent of the total, while Baghdad expanded to over four million, becoming the largest Arab city after Cairo. Despite the large population increase, Iraq faced shortages of skilled personnel, scientists, engineers, and agronomists. High rates of illiteracy and a relatively low employment level account for the paradox of labor shortages and urban overpopulation. Less than a third of the population was active, mostly in agriculture where most development efforts have been concentrated.

THE KURDISH PROBLEM

There were several attempts by the various revolutionary Iraqi governments to reach an accord with the Kurds, beginning with Kassim's regime in 1958. Kassim permitted the Kurdish leader, General Mustafa al-Barazani, to return from exile in the Soviet Union, and granted the Kurds a privileged political position above other minorities. The first republican constitution described Kurds and Arabs as partners, guaranteeing the national rights of each. In the 1959 uprising in northern Iraq, Barazani, in league with Mosul Communists, assisted Kassim in putting down pro-Nasser conservatives.

By 1961, when it became evident that the constitutional guarantees of equality were unlikely to be carried out, the Kurds revolted. At first they were divided, with an antigovernment faction under Barazani, and another joining the government in the Kurdish Democratic party. However, severity of military campaigns against the Kurds united most of them against Kassim. The

Baghdad government was greatly concerned about the uprising because oil installations in the north were threatened by the Kurds.

Unable to win a decisive military victory, President Arif reopened talks in 1964, but was unwilling to grant full autonomy demanded by the Kurds. The Bazzaz government nearly negotiated a truce, but the cease-fire broke down. Finally, in March 1970 the Bakr government announced that it had come to terms with the Kurds. In a national radio and television address President Bakr promised that the Kurds would be able to exercise their national rights in a unified area of the north. One Iraqi vice-president would be a Kurd, and the minority would have proportional representation in a parliament to be established in the future. Kurdish and Arabic would become official languages in Kurdish areas, and the Kurds would be authorized to conduct their own educational system. All this was to be written into a new constitution again recognizing that Iraq is formed of two nationalities, Kurds and Arabs.

Kurdish demands for a share in oil revenues were rejected, and the question of whether the oil town of Kirkuk would be included in Kurdish areas was left open. No mention was made in the agreement of former demands for separate Kurdish executive and legislative councils, or about proportional representation in the NCRC.

From 1973 until 1975 the Kurdish question absorbed much of the government's energies, concentration, and resources. Agreements with the Kurds were made, truces signed, and broken. Even after President Bakr proclaimed the autonomy of Kurdistan in 1974 the quarrels continued. The 1974 autonomy law gave the Kurds an elected legislative council and an executive council with authority over education, public works and housing, agriculture, transport and communications, cooperatives, and similar local responsibilities. Kurdish nationalists objected to the law because it gave the Iraqi chief of state power to dismiss the president of the executive council and to dismiss the local legislature. Furthermore it failed to make any concessions on oil revenues for the Kurds, defense, or foreign affairs.

When the KDP failed to accept a two-week ultimatum to accept the autonomy law and join the National Progressive Front, fighting broke out in the north between the army and Kurdish fighters. Saddam Husain announced that the Kurdish areas in rebellion would be subject to economic blockade, and several Kurds in Baghdad were executed for sabotage. Ba'athist policy succeeded in driving a wedge between Kurdish nationalists and militants when the government proceeded with implementation of the autonomy law, simultaneously waging a bitter war between those who refused to accept it.

International implications of the Kurdish war involved Syria, the Soviet Union, the United States, Iran and Israel. Both Syria and Iran provided guerrilla bases and training camps for Kurdish guerrillas, Israel supplied weapons and the American CIA provided economic help. On the other side, the Kurds charged that Soviet officers piloted bombers in combat missions against them in northern Iraq.

The Kurdish war greatly intensified antagonism with Iran, bringing the two countries to the brink of war in 1975. Tensions between Iraq and Iran had long historic antecedents including disputes over borders, the Shatt el-Arab waterway dividing the two countries at the head of the Gulf, charges of mutual expulsions of each other's citizens, and sharp ideological differences between the radical regime in Baghdad and the shah of Iran's anti-Communist policies.

After more than a decade of threats and counterthreats the tangle of disputes was settled at an OPEC meeting during March 1975 in Algiers. Through the intercession of Algerian president Boumedienne, the shah of Iran and Iraq vice-president Saddam Husain signed an agreement on their land frontiers, a mutually acceptable border in the Shatt el-Arab, and an end to Iran's support for the Kurdish insurgency. The immediate suspension of arms deliveries to the Kurdish forces brought the uprising to a halt. Iran began to haul away its military equipment within hours after the Algiers agreement was signed and even threatened to support the Iraqi government with force to implement the pact. Within a few weeks thousands of Kurds surrendered to the Iraqi government or fled to Iran. The Iraqi army soon reached Galala, headquarters of the Kurdish revolt, and the commander of the Northern Region announced that the Kurdish rebellion was over.

But the 1975 agreement brought only temporary respite in the hostilities. Political disputes within the KDP erupted despite promises in 1977 that some 40,000 Kurds resettled in the south could return to their homes in the north. The outbreak of war with Iran in 1980 divided the Kurds when the Democratic party of Kurdistan sided with Tehran and the Kurdish Revolutionary party supported Saddam Husain. As the war continued, all the old wounds were reopened when Kurds joined Shi'ites and Ba'athists dissidents in forming an underground "Iraqi Islamic Front" with offices in Damascus, against the "atheistic regime in Baghdad."

NOTES

1.   Philip W. Ireland, *Iraq, A Study in Political Development*, London, 1937, p. 57.

2.   *Ibid.*, p. 141.

3.   Majid Khadduri, *Independent Iraq*, London, 1960, p. 71.

4.   *Ibid.*, p. 84.

5.   Doreen Warriner, *Land Reform and Development in the Middle East*, pp. 181–182.

16 The Arabian Peninsula

The Arabian peninsula is almost as large as India and a third the size of continental United States, a statistic which belies its importance. Despite the concentration in Arabia of the world's largest oil reserves, it still contains some of the most underdeveloped parts of the Middle East; and many of its inhabitants still live at the subsistence level, due largely to a lack of arable land and water. Yet the average Westerner often romantically views the whole Middle East in the light of his impression of Arabia before its oil reserves were developed—as a region peopled by nomadic Bedouin tribes roaming the vast desert expanses. Even in the Arabian heartland that image is much less true today than it was before World War II; in recent years the inhabitants have begun to settle in permanent habitations and sedentary occupations. The modern world's demand for oil and the subsequent development of modern communications in Arabia have ended the isolation that made the region a romantic land of fantasy peopled by noble horsemen and camel caravans. The great oil companies and their auxiliary industries have set in motion a trend toward Westernization that can no longer be reversed and is revolutionizing life styles.

The peninsula today is dominated by the Kingdom of Saudi Arabia, which occupies about nine-tenths of the land surface. In addition, there are Yemen, the Democratic People's Republic of Yemen, Oman, United Arab Emirates, Qatar, Kuwait, and Bahrain.

THE KINGDOM OF SAUDI ARABIA

Origins

After Islam had expanded northward in the seventh and eighth centuries, the Arabian peninsula was isolated for nearly a thousand years. The center of Islam moved to Damascus and then to Baghdad, and the birthplace of the religion lost its predominant influence. The great flowering of Arab civilization in Syria and Iraq barely affected Arabia. Only for a brief period during the tenth century when the Carmathians, an Ismaili offshoot (see chapter 2), dominated the country, was it unified under a single government. Otherwise it was governed by a myriad of tribal leaders, and the holy cities of Mecca and Medina were ruled by local aristocrats, *sherifs,* who for long periods of time submitted to the authority of Muslim leaders in Syria, Iraq, and Egypt. After the Ottoman conquest in 1517, the Persian Gulf and Red Sea coast regions, including the holy cities, became part of the Ottoman Empire. Yemen and Oman were able to retain separate identities because they were isolated from the rest of the peninsula by rings of mountains. Within the sandy and mountainous interior, there was no established order, and tribal life continued much as it had for centuries before Muhammed.

For nearly ten centuries there were no major political or social developments in Arabia until, early in the eighteenth century, the religious reformer Muhammad Ibn Abd al-Wahab (born sometime between 1691 and 1703) won over to his way of thinking and became the religious guide of Amir Muhammad Ibn Saud, chief of the small north Arabian principality of Dairya. The Wahabi religious movement developed from opposition by north Arabian fundamentalists to what they considered impure doctrines and practices. They sought to purge Islam of the infusion of interpretations, beliefs, and practices that reflected Iranian, Indian, and other non-Arabic influences, and to return to the unadulterated faith of the Prophet. Wahabis called themselves *muwahhidin* (monotheists) because they opposed pagan saint worship, Islamic mysticism (Sufism), magical beliefs, veneration of holy men and places, and what they regarded as ostentation and an exaggerated emphasis on the personality of Muhammad so prevalent among many sects. Generally they sought to purify the religion of all practices arising after the third Islamic century. Only the Koran and earliest Hadiths (traditions) were to be considered valid sources of authority. In many respects, Wahabism was a fundamental attempt to rescue Islam from the weakness and degradation so apparent to modern reformers such as Jamal el-Din al-Afgani (see chapter 6).

The amir, Muhammad Ibn-Saud, and his religious guide gathered a large zealous Bedouin following which established control over central and eastern Arabia. Fusion of religious fervor and political drive gave the Wahabi movement power to the Red Sea coast, where he encountered Ottoman opposition.

But the Wahabis drove on, invading Iraq where they sacked the "pagan" Shi'ite holy city of Karbala. They also threatened Damascus and, in 1803, captured Mecca. Because the Osmanlis alone were unable to quell the Wahabis, the sultan requested military aid from the redoubtable Muhammad 'Ali in Egypt to hold back the Bedouin tide. Muhammad 'Ali sent three expeditions against the Wahabi-Saud forces and finally crushed them in 1818, bringing to an end the first Wahabi-Saud empire.

For the next thirty years, the Wahabi-Saud movement was quiescent. Then the Saudis' opened a new offensive against the Rashids of northern Arabia, an Osmanli-backed clan which became the Saudis' powerful rivals. Fighting continued through the nineteenth century with fortune passing now to one side, now to the other. In 1902, Ibn Saud, a descendant of the Amir Muhammad Ibn Saud previously mentioned, led a group of fifty fellow tribesmen from Kuwait, where the family had found refuge after defeat, to capture the seat of Rashidi power in Riyadh.

That dramatic event marks the origin of the present kingdom and it is celebrated to this day. Because of their ability to attract fervent followers with their religious message, Sauds replaced the Rashids within the decade. Ibn Saud's father, Abd al-Rahman, made him imam of the Wahabis and governor, or amir, of Nejd territory with his capital at Riyadh. By World War I, Ibn Saud had seized the Ottoman province of al-Hasa on the Persian Gulf and had become the most powerful leader in the peninsula.

Through the Wahabi movement, Ibn Saud revived a vibrant, active Islam, which once again gave the Bedouin a higher loyalty than that only to tribes and towns. Wahabi missionaries encouraged the growth of Ikhwan (Brotherhood) communities in a religiopolitical system, much like that originally set up by the Prophet. In the Ikhwan system, state and religion were one, according to the classic Muslim theory of society. Within a few years, the movement had united central Arabia, or the Nejd, in a unity symbolized by Ibn Saud, who boasted that he, and no one else, personified the Ikhwan. In 1916, all tribes in the Nejd were ordered to join the movement and pay an alms tax to Ibn Saud. Their sheikhs were sent to an ulema school in Riyadh, and other ulema were sent to carry the Wahabi message to the tribes. Only the converted were considered true Muslims. All others were heretics. Those who attained the new status were dignified by a strip of white cloth worn around their headclothes instead of the traditional black cord.

Sheikhs who had completed their religious instruction were given houses in the capital under the watchful eye of Ibn Saud, on whose military staff they served. Through this system of direct control, it was estimated that within 96 hours 25,000 Ikhwan colonists could be rallied into an army.

British officials responsible for Arab affairs during World War I, disagreed with each other in their evaluation of the movement. Colonel T.E.

Lawrence believed that Ibn Saud was only a passing phenomenon. After Ibn Saud's death, Lawrence asserted, the same old anarchy would return and there would be a "wild reversion" to the "natural chaos" of Arabia. Lawrence believed it wiser to back the Hashemite sherifs of Mecca because of their direct descent from Muhammad and traditional association with the holy places.

Another famous British Arabist, H. St. John B. Philby, later to become one of the monarch's principal advisers, pointed out that Ibn Saud would never accept Hashemite leadership. Ibn Saud would so alter Arabia, Philby believed, that his successors would have few difficulties in keeping it unified. Through the Ikhwan, Philby pointed out, tribal jealousies and wars were being checked. Raiding had almost become a thing of the past, and prosperity was increasing. Above all, Ibn Saud had at his command a devoted and "extremely fanatical" army.

British officials compromised with each other by supporting with arms and money both Ibn Saud and the Hashemites, although the latter received the lion's share. Despite frequent clashes between Saudi and Hashemite forces, outright war was prevented by British threats to cut off their subsidies and to help crush whichever side attacked first. In 1921, Ibn Saud defeated what was left of the pro-Osmanli Rashidi amirate and occupied its capital at Hail. After killing Ibn Rashid, the last of the enemy leaders, Ibn Saud showed political acumen by magnanimity in victory. Instead of humiliating the defeated followers of Ibn Rashid, Ibn Saud married Ibn Rashid's widow, adopted his children, and brought the surviving male members of the family to Riyadh as honored guests.

With the Nejd, or central Arabia, securely in hand, Ibn Saud reopened his offensive against Husein in the Hijaz. In the meantime, after the Osmanlis had departed from Arabia at the end of World War I, Sherif Husein had proclaimed himself king of the Hijaz, which included Mecca and Medina, the Muslim holy cities. However, Husein was unpopular with his own subjects because of maladministration, and Muslims abroad protested when he adopted the title of caliph without the authorization of any Muslim group only three days after Ataturk had abolished the institution in March 1924. The moment seemed opportune to administer the *coup de grace* to the Hashemite kingdom. After a short campaign, Ibn Saud forced Husein to abdicate in favor of Husein's son 'Ali. By December 1925, 'Ali had also fled, and in January, an assembly of Mecca notables offered the crown of the Hijaz to Ibn Saud. Within a few months, inhabitants of neighboring Asir (between the Hijaz and Yemen) also sent petitions to Ibn Saud asking to become a Saudi protectorate.

Ibn Saud's father, Abd al-Rahman, titular leader of the Wahabi-Saud movement, proclaimed his son king of the Nejd in 1926. Within two decades, Saud had risen from governor to king, established a dynasty, and become a power second to none in the Arabian peninsula. In 1932, Nejd and the Hijaz became the Kingdom of Saudi Arabia. From a loose confederation of tribes, Ibn Saud had created a state with status in the community of nations.

Tribal ties were by no means eliminated, and many chiefs even emulated their king by using the Wahabi and Ikhwan movements for their own ends—such as raiding neighboring Iraq and Transjordan ostensibly to punish irreligious Muslims. The situation forced Ibn Saud to modernize his communications and transport system, so that he could conduct effective military campaigns against these unruly tribes. The core of a small regular army and air force was established, motorized transport introduced, and high-powered radio stations set up to assist the king in controlling independent chiefs who threatened to take the law into their own hands.

Royal authority was buttressed by the title of "imam," acquired through Muhammad Ibn Saud's conversion in 1742 to Wahabism. Since then, the head of the house of Saud has automatically been chief of the Wahabi religious movement. This gave the Sauds a mission: to spread the true interpretation of the true faith. Through skillful interplay of his roles as paramount sheikh and imam, Ibn Saud won over tribe after tribe, until he was finally accepted as both secular and religious leader. Between 1902, when he had made his first bid for power as a tribal sheikh, and 1932, when he was crowned monarch of the new Saudi kingdom, he made acceptable the concept of a sovereign territorial state. The first step was to become Nejd's amir, a secular office known and accepted by the Bedouin. Implied in the change from amir to king was the transfer of loyalty from the personal sheikh to the more impersonal and institutionalized king, who attained authority less because of his personal attributes than because of his title and the respect it commanded. While Ibn Saud ruled, there was no real test of the monarchy as an institution, for he automatically commanded loyalty and respect by virtue of his personal attributes. Since 1953, when his sons became king, however, loyalty to the monarchy and to the Saudi state has been put to the test.

Tribal Government

Statistics are vague; there was no census until 1974 and only estimates since. Estimates of Saudi Arabia's population range from six to ten million, including some two million foreigners. Even if the top figure were accepted, it is small relative to its vast area of approximately 800,000 to 900,000 square miles (in many areas the borders are undefined or in dispute, thus the uncertainty about Saudi Arabia's size). Although this would indicate a density of between 8 and 10 persons per square mile, the figure is meaningless in a country with such vast wastelands. In some oasis settlements, there are as many as 2000 persons per square mile.

Less than a third of the population is nomadic or seminomadic, and about two-thirds urban. Nomad birth rates are among the world's highest, but they are counterbalanced by extremely high infant, child, and maternal mortality rates. The average life span is between forty and fifty-five years and many never reach old age.

The characteristic social pattern of Saudi Arabia is tribal, with all relationships and loyalties centered on the family unit. Family obligations still take precedence over all others, and all life is organized in terms of the family. Among both villagers and nomads, the family is largely a self-contained unit. Even in a town, business enterprise is more often than not a concern of fathers, sons, brothers, uncles, and nephews. In the political realm, the basic unit to be considered is still the family and, beyond that, the tribe. Saudi Arabians take it for granted that the individual will always use his position to assist his relatives.

The typical Saudi family usually includes three generations within a household—the patriarch and his wives, their unmarried children, and married sons with their wives and children. Descent is patrilinial, and marriages between the children of brothers (first cousins) is preferable. A family's sons usually reside in, or close to, the home of their father. Thus paternal kinsmen are in close contact. All members of the family are obligated to submit to the authority of the patriarch, although his wife directs activities pertaining to the home. To marry additional wives (four are permitted according to Muslim law) is considered an infringement upon the rights of the first unless she has given her consent.

The established family pattern of social organization found in Arabia is characteristic of all the Middle East. But outside of Arabia it has been somewhat diluted by Western social organization. Throughout the Arab East, notable families, like the Husaynis of Palestine, trace their origins to the tribes of the peninsula, and many of the prevailing social customs are vestiges of those still practiced in a more pristine form throughout Arabia. The speech of the Arabian Bedouin is still regarded as "pure," whereas others speak dialects. Only in the remote interior, where relative isolation and practice of marriage among first cousins still prevails, have the Bedouin preserved their traditional physical characteristics. Along the Red Sea and Persian Gulf coastal regions, the Bedouin have mixed with Negroid, Indian, and Malayan settlers.

Among the Saudis, "Bedouin" means those nomadic Arabs who earn their living by raising camels, sheep, and goats. The camel breeders especially regarded themselves as of noble ancestry and enjoyed great prestige even though impoverished. All Bedouin families frown on intermarriage with members of lesser tribes.

Nomad tribes live and move together as semiautonomous bands. They consider themselves members of larger tribal groupings on the basis of descent from a real or fictitious common ancestor. The family patriarch owes allegiance to a related sheikh, and each tribal subdivision pledges loyalty to chiefs of successively larger tribal units with common ancestors. The tribal units are governed by family councils *(majlis)* or elders, headed by a respected sheikh chosen by council members from a family enjoying hereditary leadership rights. Tribal units move seasonally within definite areas that have been traditionally, often for centuries, under the jurisdiction of the same tribes. Since the tribal areas often cross frontiers between nations, neutral zones, as between Saudi Arabia, Iraq, and Kuwait, were established into which tribes from more than one country may move. The Saudi-Iraqi neutral zone was divided equally between the two countries in 1975, and the zone between Saudi Arabia and Kuwait was split equally in 1966. However, oil reserves in the Saudi-Kuwait Zone were shared.

Until King Ibn Saud unified the country, amirs (princes or commanders) controlled caravan routes and military strategic outposts. Their authority was supreme, and it extended as far as their military power. At that time villages and towns also maintained their political isolation and autonomy. Tribes moved freely within the areas under their jurisdiction for there they held exclusive rights to water, pasturage, hunting, and habitation.

Ibn Saud forcibly imposed a central authority on these isolated autonomous communities during the 1920s and 1930s. Since then, there have been occasional uprisings that the Saudi army has suppressed, but generally speaking, authority of the central government has been widely accepted, due largely to Ibn Saud's sagacious policies. Contrary to the Western image of Saudi Arabia's monarch, he is not an absolute autocrat. His position is subject to its acceptance by the various tribal leaders.

Tribal organization is common, not only among the nomads, but also in many villages that are governed by family councils and elected sheikhs. Even in the newer nontribal villages, tribal organization is strong, and village leadership is divided among heads of leading families. Tribes with vague ancestry often claim descent from some notable ancestor for prestige. Throughout the Arab Middle East, noble Arabian ancestry is traced back to one of two principal legendary tribal lines—one descended from a common northern Arabian called Kahtan, the other, a southerner called Adnan. In Arab countries other than Arabia, this division has little meaning. But in Arabia tribes tended to divide up an area, each section occupying different parts of a village or camp. Often they refused to intermarry, and competition between them could break into violence.

A noble sheikh's material assets differed little from those of his nomad followers. Among the Arabian tribes, social distinctions were determined by lineage and occupation, not material possessions. Social stratifications were more marked in larger towns where there was an elite of noble families, wealthy merchants, officials, and professional men, such as doctors and lawyers. This elite is now beginning to meet competition from an emerging middle class of less wealthy merchants and civil servants. The mass of town dwellers were vendors, craftsmen, beggars, ex-slaves, and nomads separated from their tribes. It should be noted that although slavery existed in this region until it was abolished in 1964, the concept of the institution is vastly different from what is considered slavery in the West. Slaves frequently became part of the family, and many attained high official posts, married the daughters of their owners, and acquired property. Slaves were thus often a well-treated element in Saudi society. Divisions between the upper, middle, and lower classes were so rigid, however, that they were distinguished by clothing, manners, choice of occupation, and choice of spouse.

Since World War II, many traditional influences have been undermined by oil wealth and accompanying Western influences. The old common cultural heritage, which bridged the gap between the classes, is now disintegrating as the upper sheikhly families, enriched by oil wealth, are influenced by Western products, innovations, customs, and tastes. Awareness of the change has created unrest among the lower classes, which cannot yet afford to live in such ostentatious style. Bedouin tribesmen, for example, uprooted from pastoral life, congregate near the towns and become increasingly sympathetic to the restive urban proletariat. The problem is exacerbated by the influx of hundreds of thousands of poor workers from other Middle Eastern and Asian countries including Yemen, Pakistan, and Korea, who form a new lower class proletariat.

The royal family still fulfills the role of Bedouin sheikhs, and elaborate genealogical charts are maintained tracing its descent from a noble tribe. As did their father Ibn Saud before them, they have maintained a royal bodyguard linked by special bonds of kinship. The king performs such traditional tasks as holding open court on the palace steps and in village mosques. These customs are extremely significant for the Sauds, for they are regarded by many tribal leaders as townsmen with tribal connections who attained their status only by conquest and as Wahabi imams. The royal family must make special efforts to display the Bedouin sheikh's attributes of courage, leadership, and generosity and must act, ostensibly, on the basis of tribal consensus. Until recent years, the king was responsible for the most insignificant decisions, since as a patriarch he was required to know and be responsible for all that occurred within his realm. However, as the government became modernized and increasingly complex, the king became more of a manager than a desert patriarch.

Constitutional Development

When the Kingdom of Saudi Arabia was formed in 1932, it lacked modern governmental institutions and a centralized administration. The duties and obligations of the governed and the institutions by which they were to be governed had still to be defined. Ibn Saud's method of obtaining acceptance of the new and previously unaccepted forms of governmental control and administration was to establish them within the framework of the customary and traditional forms of society with which his Bedouin subjects were already acquainted. Gradually the prevailing Koranic and other religious prescriptions that governed Arabia and were the accepted law of the land were elaborated in terms of new legal norms. A quasi-constitutional system began to evolve from the great number of governmental decrees issued by Ibn Saud on matters such as taxation, border control, and other affairs with which the modern state is normally concerned. However, the government still asserts that all public law is derived from the Koran, the framework within which all legislation is still made. Therefore, the Koran and the Sharia are still the basic law of Saudi Arabia.

Within Ibn Saud's domains, there were various levels of social organization. Some regions required more complicated administration than others. The Hijaz, for example, had a larger urban population and greater intercourse with foreigners as a result of its coastal trade and the yearly influx to Mecca and Medina of thousands of pilgrims from abroad. Therefore it required more elaborate legislation, reflected in a new set of Organic Instructions, adopted in 1926, that applied exclusively to the Hijaz. Since 1926, the Hijaz legal system has been greatly altered, parts of it ignored, and others abrogated. But until 1953, the province was still governed by its own special laws, subject always, of course, to the Koran and Sharia.

The Organic Instructions gave the Hijaz a viceroy, a ministerial council, and several nonelective advisory councils for cities such as Mecca, Medina, and Jidda and for districts, tribes, and villages. All the Hijaz councils are merely advisory, with no real legislative authority. Only the agent general or viceroy, who was directly responsible to the king, governed. Until 1953, when the title was no longer used, it had been held by one of the royal princes, who ruled with the aid of his consultative or advisory council. In 1953, the Hijaz advisory council and its departments were abolished. In the other provinces of Saudi Arabia, major and minor affairs were the direct responsibility of the monarch or his authorized representative.

After 1953, a Council of Ministers was set up for the whole Saudi kingdom, including the Hijaz. Since then, the Hijaz and the Nejd have no longer been considered separate parts of the kingdom. (Until 1953, Crown Prince Faisal was viceroy of the Hijaz and the king held the title of amir of the Nejd.) Since the governmental reorganization, the Council of Ministers for the kingdom as a whole has been next in importance to the king, although its functions have not been clearly defined; the relationships between Hijaz, Nejd, and the other Saudi provinces also remained undefined. The decree represented the first effort to define authority in terms other than the traditional system in which the monarch arbitrarily makes all important decisions. Now the king is more like a constitutional monarch; his decisions are based on consultation with the Council of Ministers. In effect, the new constitutional system reflects changes in the relationships within the royal family. King Saud, a relatively weak figure who did not command the same respect and authority that was accorded his father and therefore was unable to retain Ibn Saud's magnetic sway over the country's tribal and religious leaders, gradually lost his power. First, Prince Faisal became president of the Council of Ministers, or prime minister, nearly as strong as his brother King Saud, and a behind-the-scenes struggle for power ensued between the two. In 1964 the royal family deposed Saud, and Faisal was proclaimed king. Saud left Arabia and died in exile in 1964. Faisal was assassinated in 1975 by a nephew while holding court. He was succeeded by another brother, Crown Prince Khalid, who died in 1982. He was followed as monarch by Fahd, seen by many as leader of the progressive, modernizing faction within the royal family.

Ministries were organized for the whole country in 1930 following a pattern established for the Hijaz in 1926. As the central government began to construct railways, roads, schools, and postal and telecommunications services, to develop a permanent army, and to take an interest in health and agriculture, it required permanent government offices to manage these services. Foreign Affairs and Finance Ministries were the first to be established, in 1930 and 1932 respectively. After the 1953 reorganization, Ministries of Communications, Education, Agriculture, Health, Commerce, and Industries were formed. Other government departments dealt with labor, oil and mineral resources, and public relations.

Although the government appeared to be acquiring a Western organization and structure, its operations in fact would hardly be recognized as such. Saudi Arabia was unprepared to staff this relatively complex organization. Higher posts were frequently taken over by the royal family in accordance with the tradition of trusting relatives above others. Ibn Saud's former advisor, H. St. John Philby, charged that many ministers were ambitious merchants of no particular aptitude or training who viewed their posts not as a public trust but rather as a golden opportunity to enrich themselves or advance their private commercial interests. Qualified Arabians were so few that the government was forced to hire Syrians, Lebanese, and Palestinians. Philby characterized them as an official hierarchy "recruited without system from the flotsam and jetsam of such intelligentsia as the Arab world has been able to provide...."[1]

Prince Faisal attempted to end many of the worst abuses in May 1958 when he enacted a decree centralizing responsibility and specifying the jurisdiction of each minister. Until then, the council of ministers had been only advisory. Now the council was empowered to draw up policies on all affairs, foreign and domestic, and was charged with implementing them. The decree declared that the council was to be the final authority for financial and all other matters of concern to the ministries, and charged the ministries with approving international agreements and concessions. All council members were to sever any direct or indirect business relationships with the government and all were required to be Saudi Arabian citizens. Faisal's power was considerably increased, since all council members were to be responsible to the president (the prime minister, who was Prince Faisal). Furthermore, if the king failed to act on a council order within thirty days, the prime minister (council president) could use his own initiative. After 1964, when Faisal became king, executive power was concentrated in his hands and he abolished the post of prime minister, becoming directly responsible, as king, for national policy.

The importance of this 1953 decree for Saudi Arabia is as great as the Magna Charta was for England because it undercut and greatly limited the royal prerogative. The king was no longer an oriental potentate, but a constitutional monarch. Real power was shifting to the royal council of notables, representing a variety of national interests—tribal sheikhs, religious leaders, and modern merchants. Saudi Arabia is still a long way from democracy (there are no political parties or parliament), but an initial step toward diffusion of political power had been taken. There are indications that the trend toward subdivision of power will continue until larger numbers of Saudis participate in political life. This will be a lengthy process, for Saudi Arabians have a long road to travel before they will be prepared to understand and use effectively such democratic institutions as a parliament and elections. Illiteracy is still high, and power remains vested in the royal family and tribal or clan chief. For the time being, the new constitutional changes have merely shifted authority from one man to a small group. But implicit in the shift is denial of absolute monarchy and its replacement by a modern managerial decision-making process.

A draft constitution drawn up in 1960 provided for a National Assembly of between 90 and 120 members, two-thirds to be elected, and one-third appointed from the royal family and tribal chiefs. It made provision for a ministry of justice based on Islamic law. The conservative nature of the document was reflected in its stipulation that, "Islam is the state religion, the Sharia, the source of its laws," and that "private property and capital are the fundamental values of the national wealth." But even this document was too liberal for the king who insisted that "the Koran is the oldest and most efficient of the world's constitutions," thus it was never enacted.

Faisal's reign ended suddenly in March 1975 when he was assassinated by one of his nephews. At first there were suspicions of an antigovernment plot, but the assassin was found to be mentally deranged and beheaded. The new king, Khalid, was Faisal's half brother. Power was shared between King Khalid and his brother, Prince Fahd, the new crown prince and first deputy prime minister. King Khalid's illness and frequent trips abroad for medical treatments greatly increased the power held by Prince Fahd, and raised the influence of the prime minister, in contrast to the royal throne. When Khalid died in 1982, Fahd succeeded him.

The new regime continued to allow social change to proceed at a slow pace, investing billions of dollars in development of the national infrastructure. King Faisal Medical City was opened in 1975 on the outskirts of Riyadh. It contained some of the most up-to-date facilities and was considered to be among the best equipped institutions in the world. Well over a billion dollars was earmarked for the country's new Western style Riyadh University, as part of a long-term 142 billion dollar development program. A third five-year plan, 1980–1985, increased development expenditures to $250 billion with emphasis on social infrastructure, agricultural, and petrochemicals for export. Under these development schemes billions of dollars have been invested in creating the new industrial cities, Yanbu on the west coast and Jubail in the east.

However the country generally remains conservative and traditional, and restrictions on smoking, alcohol, dress, and activities of women remain. They were still prohibited from driving automobiles in 1980.

The greatest changes under the new regime were in foreign policy. For the first time Saudi Arabia conceded Israel's right to exist within its pre-1967 frontiers in exchange for total Israeli withdrawal from Arab lands occupied in 1967 and for establishment of a Palestinian state on the West Bank of Jordan.

The Petroleum Impact

Until the discovery of oil in the 1930s, Arabia's economy had been based on the oasis, the village, and the tribe, each small unit functioning independently of the next. Extreme poverty, disease, illiteracy, and primitive agricultural or handicraft techniques were its traditional characteristics. The country was on the verge of a serious financial crisis because of the declining markets for its staple products—camels, horses, donekys, and dates. Pearling and other maritime trades were no longer profitable. Most seriously affected were the nomadic two thirds of the population who lived by animal husbandry. They had already been forced by King Ibn Saud to abandon raiding and the extortion of tribute from villagers. Some attempts were being made to resettle the tribes on farmland, but agriculture was held to be a lowly and undesirable occupation. Even if the Bedouin could be persuaded to settle, arable land was so limited that it could support no more than a small part of the population.

Fortunately, Ibn Saud, who was consolidating his kingdom, was rescued from financial disaster by the oil companies who had already started their explorations. Their findings were so successful that within a decade Saudi Arabia had changed from a poverty-ridden desert principality to an oil-rich state. Since 1933, when the California Arabian Standard Oil Company (predecessor of Aramco) received its first concession, oil has become the dominant feature of the economy, providing some 85 percent of gross domestic product and 90 percent of the foreign exchange. First millions, then tens, scores, hundreds of millions and billions of dollars a year poured into the royal treasury. The situation was as though the Saudis had suddenly broken centuries of fasting to indulge their every conceivable appetite.

Without the momentous royalties reaped from oil, Saudi Arabia would probably have remained a primitive tribal society for generations. But petroleum income has created revolutionary changes. The hundreds of millions of dollars have enabled the country to acquire many Western technological innovations, to use them more or less productively, and to develop a Western type of governmental apparatus. Around the oil camps and management centers, temporary villages grew into towns, now dependent on imports. Wells, pipelines, and water purification installations had to be brought into the country. In new urban centers, government-initiated public works established educational and medical services; and in rural areas, experimental farms were set up with the most modern equipment. Railroads connected towns that before had been accessible only by camel caravan.

On the other hand, the sudden influx of wealth, concentrated in the coffers of the all-powerful Saud family, also produced corruption, nepotism, and gross financial irresponsibility. Much of the oil income was wastefully dissipated. The royal family became a principal beneficiary. This large, extended group included not only the king and his children, but also their spouses, children, and relatives by marriage, totaling hundreds, all of whom received direct grants. No longer were the Sauds austere Wahabi desert sheikhs. They now lived in oriental splendor surrounded by every conceivable luxury. Scores of royal princes purchased several high-priced American automobiles each and went on sprees of building palaces equipped with such modern amenities as air conditioning and swimming pools.

Subsidies exacted by tribal leaders and allies throughout the peninsula drained off much of the oil income. These payments helped lessen the complaints against the high style of living and strengthened ties with the central authorities. They were necessary if the Sauds were to retain the loyalty of the numerous tribal leaders.

The zealotry with which the Wahabi tribesmen once defended fundamental Islam, with their emphasis on simplicity, has been entirely dissipated. No longer are there threatening protests against foreign luxuries. Today they are not only accepted, but all levels of society strive to attain them. Tribes that formerly lived as puritanical Wahabis have abandoned the desert for the new oil centers, where they have settled down and become accustomed to the use of Western innovations purchased with their high pay as Aramco employees.

After a decade of astounding prosperity, the Saudi government was left with no reserve fund, while carrying a public debt of millions of dollars. The root of the trouble, according to Philby, was

> unquestionably to be sought in the wave of extravagance which swept over the country on the rising tide of royalties from oil: seeping irresistibly into every stratum of society, and flattening all the defenses of its economy, and

the inevitable reaction of steeply rising prices for all the necessities and luxuries of life. The saturated soil could only breed the brine of corruption, which permeated every branch of the public life of the land: turning to ashes 'the earthly hopes men set their hearts upon,' when the new era of Wahabi rule dawned on the Hijaz but two decades back.[2]

Until 1958 the Saudi Arabian government's financial affairs had been controlled by a single individual. Now it was placed under regular administrative operation with auditing and accounting procedures. The first finance minister, who served from 1932 until 1954, had been subject only to the king's authority. Only he knew the details of state finances, recording them in a fashion that only he understood. Although an American technical assistance mission suggested establishment of a monetary agency in 1952 to supervise and stabilize currency and finances, no determined efforts were made to end past abuses until 1958, when the Council of Ministers suddenly became aware of the government's great indebtedness. As part of his governmental shake-up, Prince Faisal ordered publication of an annual budget and attempted to balance expenditures and revenue. Strict currency and import regulations were adopted, including a six-month ban on imports of all cars and luxury items. A new Office of Comptroller General of State Accounts was authorized to audit government finances and all foreign currency transactions were to take place through banks. After Faisal's assertion of power, financial restraints became an accepted part of the government system.

A man still enjoys prestige by being able to afford leisure, but increasing numbers of Saudis now work to acquire savings for the future. A middle class is emerging from the trades, occupations, and professions that have grown up around the oil towns. Many wealthy middle-class Saudis are investing their savings in overseas real estate or in foreign banks. (In 1935, a Saudi private bank was established, and many foreign banks have branches in the country, but most large deposits are made abroad.) Saudi investment of tens of billions abroad made the country into a major economic power recognized by the International Monetary Fund with a Saudi seat on the IMF Executive Board.

The thousands of Saudi tribesmen trained as skilled laborers by Aramco have become a major economic and social asset. In the early 1930s, there were no native auto mechanics, electricians, or repairmen. Since 1935, the oil companies have trained thousands in these skills, providing a nucleus of technicians for development programs that may be implemented in the future. The government has become the country's second largest employer after Aramco, which was gradually nationalized until by 1980, it was totally owned by the Saudi government's Petromin oil company.

The oil price boom after 1973 intensified the influx of Bedouin to the cities and of foreign immigrants. By 1977 over two-thirds of the population had become urban while the rural sector had declined and only a few nomads remained. Spectacular profits of 15 to 20 percent in basic industries were much higher than in other developing countries. They attracted thousands of businessmen from the West and the Arab world. Development failed to keep up with the rapid urbanization. Cities were becoming overcrowded without the infrastructure—water, electricity, housing, transportation—to sustain their multiplying numbers. Often it seemed that money was spent without rhyme or reason. Hundreds of ships clogged the ports. Unloaded cargoes frequently lay on the docks for months resulting in rusting machinery, spoiled food supplies, and deteriorating equipment. The boon further intensified the paradox of poverty in the midst of wealth in which hundreds of thousands of imported unskilled laborers with low wages lived in one of the world's most affluent societies.

As was to be expected, development of a middle and working class produced the first tremors of discontent with the monarchy, especially since the death of King Ibn Saud in 1953 and the subsequent weakening of the strong personal ties he had developed with the towns, villages, and tribes. Even though there was no strong devotion to the nation of Saudi Arabia, loyalty to the larger concept of Arab nationalism was developing within the middle and working classes. The new wealthy middle class, enriched by recent developments, resented being excluded from political power and expressed its resentment in attacks on royal extravagance and inefficiency. Although labor unions were still forbidden, the new working class was also developing political awareness, particularly the oil, construction, and transportation workers. The life of the Americans, for whom they worked, inspired desires for higher living standards, higher even than those they attained, which already placed them far above their former status or that of their compatriots in other occupations. The widespread diffusion of radios made most Arabians aware of the revolutionary changes in Egypt, Syria, and Iraq, and many who lived in towns admired Egyptian President Nasser and were drawn to the "Arab nation" concept. Discontent with the monarchy was evident in growing demands for political and social reform and in several attempted, but unsuccessful, coups by young army officers who came from the new middle class, receiving education outside the country.

After the 1979 revolution in Iran there were more overt challenges to the Saudi regime. In the Eastern Province, location of important oil installations, serious protest demonstrations erupted against the government by the Shi'ite minority. Although only 15 percent of the country's population, they were concentrated in the province where many of them held important jobs in the petroleum fields. Even more threatening was seizure of the Grand Mosque in Mecca by over 700 fundamentalist zealots, eighty percent of them Saudis: the rest included Egyptians, Pakistanis, and Yeminis. The rebels accused the Saud dynasty of betraying Islam through its pro-Western and modernization policies. It took government forces, aided by French security specialists, two weeks with hundreds of casualties to retake the mosque and to put down the uprising. In 1980, 63 of the rebel zealots were beheaded for their participation in the revolt.

During the 1960s and 1970s, several thousand students a year, including a few girls, studied abroad, mostly in the United States, creating a new class of discontented graduates. Although classified as middle class, many of them had difficulty in finding adequate positions after return to Arabia. Those who succeeded in finding government employment were often blocked in their advancement for the top positions in government and the armed forces, which were reserved for between 3,000 and 7,000 relatives of the royal family, especially the elite, that is, offspring of the forty-seven sons of former King Ibn Saud.

Since there are no legal political parties, and the local press was government controlled, underground politics was rife. Government attempts to deal with underground reformers have included major modifications in much of the severely restrictive Islamic legislation. For example, the government radio, which was once monopolized by male religious commentators, now has music and women's voices, and television has been introduced. The greatly expanded educational system now includes schools of commerce, industry, and agriculture with modern laboratories and instruction in English. Since 1960 there has been a great increase in the number of schools for girls. The increase in technical training is evident in the higher standards required by the oil industry. Twenty years ago the oil company had to hire only illiterate Bedouin locally.

King Faisal attempted to build up his prestige by assuming the role of an international Islamic leader, compared to President Nasser's role of Arab revolutionary. Despite growing discontent stemming from rapid growth and breakdown of the country's isolation, Faisal attracted attention by convening conferences of Islamic conservatives, by his own staunch anti-Israel position, by support to the monarchy of Yemen during the civil war in that country, and by contributing from Saudi Arabia's oil revenues a major share of the subsidy to the UAR and Jordan after their defeat by Israel in June 1967. However, this "international" role and promises of a forthcoming constitution to replace Sharia have not prevented hundreds of political arrests or attempted coups in the armed forces.

Saudi financing of the 1967 and 1973 wars, its predominant role in OPEC as the world's largest petroleum exporter, the huge investments in Western capital markets, and its moderate position on oil pricing, made the country one of the most influential in the Third World by the late 1970s. According to some, Saudi Arabia had replaced Egypt as the strongest Arab country. Even after investing in the 142 million dollar five year plan, there were tens of billions left to invest abroad, which placed Saudi Arabia in a powerful international position.

The centrality of the Saudi position became clear after the 1973 war when U.S. secretary of state Hernry Kissinger visited the kingdom in several rounds of negotiations for disengagement agreements between Israel and Egypt and Syria. In the subsequent parlays for peace negotiations, Saudi Arabia was also consulted. Whereas Cairo had been the focal point to restore inter-Arab quarrels during the 1960s and early 1970s, Riyadh became the new meeting ground where such disputes were settled. The 1975–1976 civil war in Lebanon was halted after King Khalid summoned the leaders of the warring factions and the presidents of Egypt and Syria to Riyadh where they signed an agreement to suspend hostilities. The kingdom's role as leader of the Arab world was evident by its intercession in several inter-Arab quarrels, including those between Algeria and Morocco and Egypt and Libya, and in the Fahd peace plan to settle the Palestine conflict.

Saudi Arabia's rising influence made it Iran's chief competitor in the region. While both monarchies were conservative in social and economic outlook, their differences over oil pricing in the late 1970s created tensions between them. Iran demanded much higher prices, but Saudi Arabia advocated moderation. This tension increased greatly after the shah was overthrown in 1979 and the Shi'ite radicals in Teheran threatened to diffuse their revolutionary doctrine throughout the region. It also led to Saudi support for Iraq in the Gulf war and establishment of close military ties with the U.S. in which Saudi Arabia became the largest customer of American arms, reaching over $8 billion in sales during 1980.

YEMEN

Until the 1950s, Yemen, located in the southwest corner of the Arabian peninsula, was one of the world's least known, most obscure, isolated nations. Few Westerners had ever penetrated its mountainous frontiers and so little was known of that country that even estimates of its population have ranged as much as from four to eight million.

In pre-Islamic times, the Yemen area had been a prosperous center of trade and commerce. According to some mythological interpretations, it was the homeland of the Queen of Sheba (Saba). Various nations, including Ethiopia and Iran, conquered it at one time or another, and its pre-Islamic rulers included both Christians and Jews.

During the seventh-century Arab conquests, Yemen became Muslim, and within the next century, the country became a Shi'ite stronghold, remaining until today one of the few nations with a Shi'ite majority (another being Iran). The recently deposed Rassid dynasty descended from the ninth-century Zaidi (see chapter 2) imam 'Ali Kasim al-Rassi, who was a direct lineal descendant of the Prophet through 'Ali's son Hasan.

Between 1517 and 1917, Yemen was nominally part of the Ottoman Empire, although Portuguese, Dutch, French, British, Danes, and Swedes all contested for control of its strategic location on the Mediterranean-Red Sea route. Only the Osmanlis succeeded in maintaining a few precarious permanent coastal outposts. High mountains were an obstacle to penetration of the hinterlands.

During the nineteenth century, Wahabi-Saud forces attacked but could not conquer or convert the Yemenis. Ibrahim's Egyptian troops finally drove the Wahabi tribesmen out in 1818, and the Zaidi imam was restored in exchange for a subsidy to the Ottoman sultan. Egyptian garrisons remained in the three chief port towns until 1840 as guardians of Ottoman authority.

Ottoman policy fluctuated between appeasement and ruthless suppression of the ruling families until a 1911 Yemeni revolution against the Porte. Led by Imam Yahya (who ruled until he was deposed in 1948), the insurrection ended in a truce between the Osmanlis and Yemenis, confirming Ottoman suzerainty but agreeing that the Ottomans and the imam were to share administrative control. The Osmanlis retained their coastal outposts and the highlands were given over to the imam's jurisdiction. Ottoman troops were evacuated after World War I, and Yemen attained freedom in fact as well as name.

British troops took over at several points in 1919, however, including Yemen's chief port, Hodeiba, in order to support the Idrisi tribes, their wartime allies, in Asir to the north. When the British departed, they turned the coastal plain over to the Idrisi, who held it for five years until Asir was conquered by Ibn Saud. The imam took advantage of Saudi Arabia's attack on Asir by seizing the coastal ports that had been in British hands. Asir was then divided between Saudi Arabia and Yemen.

The relative strengths of Saudi Arabia and Yemen were still untested, and each nation aspired to rule southwest Arabia. Ibn Saud hoped to incorporate the region in his still expanding kingdom. The imam of Yemen desired Asir, the British Aden colony, and the Aden protectorate.

A test came in 1934 when a border war broke out betwen Saudi Arabia and Yemen over the fact that the imam of Yemen had given refuge to the Idrisi chief, Ibn Saud's enemy. The Asir Idrisi chief had at first acknowledged Saudi hegemony, but he had fled to Yemen where he established a base for continued attacks on Saudi Arabia. The border war ended in a smashing Saudi victory after only three months. Imam Yahya received generous terms, however, and no territorial changes or reparations were demanded. Thereafter relations were cordial.

Conflict with Great Britain over Aden has frequently led Yemen into agreements with other nations as a safeguard against British aggression. Mussolini's government was thus one of the few to establish close ties with the imam, and during World War II the latter showed decided pro-Axis sympathies. After the war, Yemen also sought out ties with the Soviet Union and Communist China, both of which sent it military, economic, and technical assistance. The Aden dispute developed into a small war in 1957–1958, and the issue came before the United Nations. Yemen claimed all of Aden colony and the protectorate as integral parts of its territory. Yemen's bargaining position was strengthened by the growth of Arab nationalism and the country's close identification with the UAR in 1958 as part of the United Arab States. After the 1962 revolution in Yemen, the country became for the next five years a testing ground in the inter-Arab struggle between the revolutionary governments led by UAR President Nasser and the conservatives represented by the Saudi Arabian monarchy (see below).

Government and Society

Growth of contacts with the outside world has had little effect on the average Yemeni. Only a handful of the country's inhabitants had traveled abroad, and those mostly on diplomatic missions. The few who received any foreign education usually studied in Cairo.

There were almost no occupations other than agriculture in Yemen. Coffee was the principal export, and its sale abroad supplied the country's major foreign earnings. Recently, Western oil companies have begun to explore the region, but as yet, they have begun no large-scale operations. During the late 1970s, the country was classified as among the dozen most impoverished by the United Nations.

About half the population dwelling in highland villages are mainly Zaidi Shi'ites, who regarded the imam as both a religious and a political leader. The remainder, who live in the Tihama (Red Sea coastal strip), are mostly Sunni Muslims of the conservative Shafi'ite sect. Some 50,000 Jews lived in Yemen until 1949–1950, when almost 90 percent of them emigrated to Israel (see chapter 11), both because of Zionist propaganda from abroad and because of deterioration in their economic and political status in Yemen.

Yemen's geographical situation and its policy of avoiding foreign contacts helped preserve an archaic society, organized much like that existing during the ninth century when the Rassid dynasty began. Until recently there has been no distinction between civil and religious affairs, and the ruler was both imam and king, chosen from the Sayyids, descendents of 'Ali who comprised between 2 and 3 percent of the population, supplying most of the country's officials and administrators. The imam's direct, absolute hegemony permitted no representative institutions, elections, or popular participation in government. Ministers who headed government departments came from an appointed Advisory Council, but the imam's word was final in all matters. In effect, the ministries were little more than offices of secretaries. Regional officials, called residents, judges, and tax collectors throughout the country were under constant supervision from the capital. Most minister-secretaries and many other officials were either members of the royal family or related to it by marriage.

Tribal areas were controlled by taking hostages to prisons in the capital. As many as a third of the male population, including small boys, were taken from some regions, although the most important hostages, of course, were sons of the local ruler. Besides seizing hostages to maintain order, the government's principal function was to collect a tithe directly from local farmers, usually either in money or crops.

Although Imam Yahya freed Yemen from the Osmanlis, his despotic rule and the royal family's monopoly of trade and government posts stirred much opposition from wealthy merchants. Centers of discontent formed in Aden and in Cairo, where the Free Yemenis and Greater Yemeni Society were formed. In Aden, there were some 15,000 Yemeni merchants and businessmen who wanted to throw off the ruling family's medieval rule. Some 80,000 Yemenis were active in the labor movement in Aden and became ardent antimonarchists. Opposition groups had the sympathy of the al-Wazir family, large landowners related to the imam by marriage, and of Prince Saif al-Islam Ibrahim, one of the imam's young sons who believed in reforming the government.

In February 1948, the opposition formed a plot to seize the government and assassinated Imam Yahya. Abdullah al-Wazir, who replaced him, appointed a reform cabinet and chose a sixty-member legislative assembly. Because the new government aroused much controversy as a result of its seizure of power by force and assassination of the imam, the Arab League sent an investigation commission to determine the regime's legality. But due to King Ibn Saud's opposition, the commission was cancelled before it reached Yemen. Within a few weeks, the late Imam Yahya's eldest son, Crown Prince Ahmad, attacked the capital, Sana, and captured and executed the new imam, Abdullah, and his followers. The counterrevolutionaries ostensibly adopted some reforms, but they were completely ineffective.

Yemen's ancient regime had not been unaware of Arab nationalist appeals for unity and reform. It attempted to meet the challenge in 1958 by forming a political tie with the UAR. The country's rulers hoped that this gesture would help to meet the growing demands among the middle-class and educated youth for greater identification with other Arab states. They also hoped that it would strengthen Yemen's position in quarrels with Great Britain over Aden. Shortly after the UAR was formed, President Nasser and the imam proclaimed a federal union of both countries in the United Arab States. Each nation (the UAR and Yemen) was to retain its independence and international status. Only foreign and military affairs were to be integrated, while domestic matters were to remain completely within the jurisdiction of each. The pact called for a Supreme Federal Council with defense, economic, and cultural subsidiary bodies. A Federal Council in each nation was to assist the Supreme Federal Council. However, the United Arab States was only a paper organization. Indeed, relations between revolutionary UAR and feudal Yemen actually deteriorated because of the great difference between Egypt's radical government and the reactionary government of Yemen. In 1961, President Nasser terminated the United Arab States because the imam had criticized Nasser's socialist policies.

THE 1962 REVOLUTION AND CIVIL WAR

Unrest among Zaidi officers who wanted to modernize the armed forces, backed by sophisticated Shafi merchants, culminated in a plot to overthrow the monarchy in September 1962. Led by Army Chief of Staff Abdullah Sallal, a five-man revolutionary council was established to form a republic "based on social justice."

At the time of the revolution, the new imam, who had ascended the throne only a week earlier, was presumed to have been killed. However, the imam and others in his family escaped, to lead a tribal force of loyal Zaidi followers against the new republic.

With support and assistance from the UAR, President Sallal proceeded to organize his revolutionary government in areas, mostly urban, under his control. One of the first actions was to abolish slavery. The Yemen Republic was so short of technicians and administrators that large numbers of Egyptians were imported to manage and operate essential services. By 1965 enough Yemeni republicans had been trained to run routine matters under Egyptian supervision, but key ministries such as defense, foreign affairs, and finance remained under UAR control. Unable to put down the tribal forces which continued to back the imam, the republicans were forced to rely on increasing numbers of Egyptian troops to protect them. Despite a massive buildup to between 60,000 and 80,000 Egyptians, the combined revolutionary forces had difficulty, not only in extending areas of republican control, but in holding their more remote tribal areas.

To counter Egyptian support for the republicans, Saudi Arbia also intervened with large-scale military aid to the imam, fearing that the Yemen revolution might spread within the borders of the Saudi kingdom. The struggle between Yemeni revolutionaries and conservatives soon became a war by proxy between radical and conservative Arab regimes. International aspects of the civil war were also reflected in Great Britain's refusal to recognize the republic, while the United States took an opposite position.

The search for a settlement also involved the United Nations and several special emissaries from various countries sent to Yemen. An agreement signed between President Nasser and King Faisal at Jiddah in Saudi Arabia in 1965 was supposed to bring republican and royalist forces to the conference table.

Since neither side would accept the delegates of the other, the parleys collapsed, and the war continued on a larger scale than before.

Matters were further complicated by internecine factional disputes within both republican and royalist camps. As Egyptian influences spread through the republican administation, many Yemenis became concerned about the country's independence. Pro- and anti-Nasser groups formed, each attempting to outmaneuver the other. In an effort to keep control, the Egyptians at one time detained most of the republican cabinet under house arrest in Cairo.

After Egypt's defeat in the June 1967 war with Israel, Egypt withdrew its military forces and discontinued most of its large-scale assistance to the Yemeni republic. The royalist forces opened an offensive which threatened the republic capital at Sana, but cleavages among the royalists weakened their effectiveness, and the war again came to a stalemate.

Attempts at compromise envisaged joining moderate republicans and monarchists in a coalition government. By late 1968 war-weary republicans had discharged from their government the most extreme leftists; they had compromised the religious issue by including both Shi'ite Zaidis and Sunni Shafites in the administration and army; many tribal disputes had been resolved when a number of royalists came to the republican side; the pro- versus anti-Nasser problem was temporarily resolved with departure of most Egyptians and adoption of an independent "neutralist" position.

Following Egyptian withdrawal from North Yemen, there were several coups and countercoups, beginning with the overthrow of the republic's first president, Abdullah Sallal. Clashes continued between the tribes, generally well predisposed toward Saudi Arabia and the army, most of whose leaders were republican oriented. But even within the army there were coups and countercoups as one faction tried to displace another. There were at least two constitutional changes, establishment of a parliament and its discharge. Theoretically the government was run by a military-dominated Command Council whose number varied. Its president was also the army commander-in-chief, and responsible for safeguarding the revolution and the republican regime.

After the revolution and the establishment of the People's Democratic Republic in South Yemen during 1967, thousands of refugees and exiles belonging to opposition groups flocked to North Yemen. Some estimates were as high as 150,000. Banding together, they formed the United National Front which with the pro-Saudi tribes, were a strong pressure on the government to invade the south. The tribes accused the Aden government in the south of liquidating 65 of their chiefs during February 1972. According to the North Yemenis, the chiefs were invited to a reconciliation feast in the south, then killed when their tent was blown up.

The betrayal precipitated a war between North and South Yemen, stopped by mediation of the Arab League after a few days. In October 1972 the two Yemens signed a cease-fire and unification pact in Cairo. The agreement was confirmed a month later in Tripoli, Libya. It called for the establishment of a single Yemeni Republic with the capital at Sana. Islam would be the state religion and Arabic its official language. Its objective would be implementation of socialism (rooted in Islam), but private property was guaranteed. Eight mixed technical commissions were to implement the union, but it was never realized. Instead opposition from pro-Saudi tribesmen and clashes between advocates of union with the radical south continued to disrupt the government. Still another foreign intervention complicated the situation when a pro-Iraqi Ba'athist group tried to take over the government in 1974. By the late 1970s military struggles and political tensions between conservative pro-Saudi tribes, leftists who desired union with the radical republic in the south, and Ba'athists who advocated Arab unification kept the country in continuous unrest. Within the country leftist dissidents in the National Democratic Front collaborated with efforts by the Marxist regime in South Yemen to subvert the north. During 1977 and again in 1978 northern leaders were assassinated in plots organized by the south; and in 1979 South Yemen invaded again, again the Arab League intervened. NDF continued to receive arms from the south and the cycle of hostility, brotherly plans for unification, and more hostility continued. Government circles in Sana seemed ambivalent in their political orientation. At times the leaders welcomed military assistance from the United States financed by Saudi Arabia, then they suddenly turned to the Soviet Union for aid and made friendly gestures toward Marxist South Yemen. It seemed that the country was an unstable buffer between royalist and conservative Saudi Arabia in the north and the left alliance of South Yemen, Ethiopia and Libya to the south and west. There was little reason to hope for progress in facing economic problems. Yemen would remain a poor country dependent on aid from Arab and Western countries for survival, where a sizable part of the population estimated at nearly two million in 1980, worked abroad (nearly half of them in Saudi Arabia).

DEMOCRATIC PEOPLE'S REPUBLIC OF YEMEN

Until the 1960s, the Crown Colony of Aden was Great Britain's southern Arabian Gibraltar. The importance of this base, the last British Middle East possession, and its hinterland, Aden protectorate, was emphasized by the 1958 decision to establish an integrated command there, directly responsible to London. Aden, it was hoped, would replace the British base in Cyprus, which was about to become independent.

Since the sixteenth century, England had used Aden, its hinterland, and its offshore islands as strategic outposts on the Mediterranean-Far East trade routes. Fear of Napoleon's designs on India induced the British to seize tiny

Perim Island in the Red Sea, off the Aden coast. But lack of water forced the British to abandon the craggy offshore spot and withdraw to Aden proper, then part of the sultanate of Lahej (see chapter 4). Great Britain then forced the sultan of Lahej to cede Aden and to become a British vassal. For nearly a century after its capture in 1839, Aden was administered by the British India government. Finally, in 1937, it became a crown colony, ruled by a governor directly responsible to the Colonial Office in London. From then until the early 1960s Aden's British governor was the final governmental authority, responsible only to London. A Legislative Council, with advisory powers only, was established in 1947. British rule brought such material benefits as roads, schools, and health facilities. Nevertheless, Arab nationalism was strong and anti-British riots were frequent.

The British made Aden into a commercial and trading city of over 100,000 people. Within Aden's crowded eighty square miles, more than three-quarters of the population were Arabs, including several thousand from Yemen. The relatively high living standards created by employment opportunities in British naval and other installations and by the town's trade also attracted several thousand Indians, Pakistanis, and Somalis.

Aden colony was only a small enclave on the tip of Aden protectorate, a long arid belt stretching along the southern Arabian seacoast of the peninsula. Its approximately 112,000 square miles were divided into eastern and western protectorates, containing some twenty-three Arab sultanates, amirates, sheikhdoms, and minor tribal units varying in size from a few hundred people and a dozen square miles to large stretches of several hundred miles square populated by thousands. The extent of British authority exercised in each area differed, although all were subject to the governor in Aden, who appointed the local British agents. The *de jure* relationship with Great Britain was usually a treaty granting protection to the local state and giving Britain control of its foreign affairs. Most of the approximately 800,000 people of the region were Bedouin tribesmen whom even the local chiefs found difficulty in governing. The whole region was policed by the Aden Protectorate Levies, local Arab troops with British officers. The most important principality was the sultanate of Lahej, whose ruler was given the title "His Highness" by the British and was authorized to maintain a small regular army commanded by British officers.

Great Britain invited five, then ten, local rulers to form a federation, the United Arab Sultanates, renamed the Federation of South Arabia in 1962, as a device to counteract growing Arab nationalist fervor. When a third of the Lahej regular army deserted to Yemen in June 1958, in protest against British domination, Great Britain removed the sultan, who then requested help from President Nasser. A Southern Arabian League led by several Lahej officials was formed to oppose the federation formed by Great Britain. Its purpose was to create a new South Arabian state, including Aden colony and the protectorates, which then was to join Yemen and the UAR in the United Arab States.

When British officials attempted in 1962 to associate Aden colony with the South Arabian Federation, there were riots and demonstrations against the union because it was dominated by old-style sheikhs. Britain's hold over the region became increasingly precarious. Disputes were no longer merely petty inter-tribal skirmishes, but international in scope because of their involvement in the Arab nationalist movement.

The Republic of Yemen renewed traditional claims to all of southern Yemen, and border warfare broke out between the republic and British forces along the frontiers. In Aden militant nationalist groups supported by the UAR opened guerrilla warfare against the British, demanding immediate independence and rejecting authority of the "reactionary" South Arabian sheikhs. Despite stepped-up measures to grant Aden self-government, natinalist groups such as the Front for the Liberation of South Yemen (FLOSY) and the National Liberation Front (NLF) continued their attacks on British forces. After several conferences between the British and nationalist groups and after investigation by a United Nations mission, the London government in 1967 declared its intention of withdrawing from all South Arabia. Authority of the sultans also began to crumble until the whole South Arabian Federation collapsed, leaving FLOSY and NLF face to face. After several months of fighting, the two groups tried unsuccessfully to resolve their differences at a conference in Cairo. When the high command of the South Arabian army threw in its lot with the NLF, FLOSY withdrew from competition for control of the area. The NLF, supported by the army, now opened negotiations with the British to take over Aden and South Arabia. As the last British troops were leaving in November 1967, the NLF proclaimed the People's Republic of South Yemen.

Independence left the country with a depleted treasury, loss of much income from the British Base in Aden, continued internal strife, and a severe shortage of technicians and administrators to continue normal government operations. Within the fifteen-member high command of the NLF, the only political party, moderates and leftists clashed. The latter purged the armed forces and police, demanding political commissars for all military units, and establishment of a militia of "popular guards."

In two of the republic's six governorates, leftists seized control in 1968, establishing popular councils of their own choice, ignoring central government authority, ousting the police and armed forces, and taking over oil installations. Similar rebellions also threatened in other areas. In addition to internal instability, there were attacks across the border by units of FLOSY from Yemen, by deposed sheikhs and sultans from Saudi Arabia, and by neighboring sheikhs in Muscat and Oman.

Unable to cope with the situation, the leftist president resigned in June 1969, turning the government over to an even more leftist five-man presidential council headed by a former guerrilla leader. Extensive nationalization of banks, industry, and other business in November 1969 failed to improve the rapidly deteriorating economic situation, leaving the country, especially Aden, with large unemployment and many economic problems.

Since independence political stability in South Yemen was tenuous because the country lacked an integrated state structure. The 23 states or sheikdoms that existed under the British were never really unified. In addition to sectional differences, war with North Yemen, continued forays across the border by FLOSY, and clashes between nationalists and leftists in the NLF have been disruptive. The basic ideological cleavage divided NLF into two groups. The Nasserites wanted a traditional government with political and adminstrative institutions, rather than the party apparatus control of the country. The Radicals wanted the NLF apparatus, its people's organizations and trade unions to be supreme. They were zealous Marxists who called for appointment of political commissars in all army units, strengthening the people's militia, and creation of "popular guards." At times the leftists controlled parts of the east while the Nasserites ruled in Aden. In the 1975 Congress of the NLF statutes were adopted unifying activities of three organizations, the NLF, the People's Avant Garde Party of former Ba'athists, and the Communist oriented Popular Democratic Union. Rhetoric of the republic was Marxist oriented, with goals of the NLF providing for establishment of an "alliance embracing the working class, peasants, intellectuals, and petite bourgeoisie with a view to implementing the democratic and national tasks indispensable for the transformation into a socialist state." Leftist orientation was emphasized in 1970 when the new constitution changed the country's name to the People's Democratic Republic of Yemen. In 1978 the NLF was replaced by the Yemen Socialist Party, modeled on the Communist Party of the USSR. The sole legal party, it proclaimed itself a Marxist-Leninist "vanguard party" headed by a Central Committee, Secretariat, and Politburo. Since the 1970s, most of the economy was government controlled and much of its agricultural output was produced by state farms and cooperatives.

The country's many foreign involvements have been obstacles to deep social change or implementation of Marxist programs. The war with North Yemen in 1972 and participation in the Dhofar rebellion against the sultan of Oman have absorbed much of the Arab Marxist republic's resources and energies.

KUWAIT

Kuwait's strategic location, at the head of the Persian Gulf, attracted British road builders in 1850, but their plans were never carried out. When Kaiser Wilhelm II sought to use Kuwait as a terminus for his Middle Eastern railroad schemes in the 1890s, Great Britain intervened and established a protectorate over the sheikhdom. From 1899 until 1961, the protective treaty authorized British control over all Kuwait's foreign affairs and the country's sheikhs took no important action without first consulting the local British resident.

Nearly all Kuwait's 6000 square miles are waterless, barren desert. Consequently, most of the 500,000 inhabitants live in the old fortress town, also called Kuwait. (The name may be derived from the *kut* (fort) built by the Portuguese during the sixteenth century.) Before oil was discovered, the sparse population lived from pearling, sailing, boat building, and trading. Water was so scarce that it was brought in barrels on boats from the Shatt el-Arab sixty miles away. Thus agriculture was impossible and the population was severely limited in its economic activities.

Because of its great oil revenues and small population, Kuwait has one of the highest per capita incomes in the world (over $18,000 by 1980). Its oil reserves then represented about 10 percent of the Middle Eastern total. By 1961, Kuwait had become the world's fourth largest oil producer, with revenues estimated at 450 million dollars per year and nearly ten billion dollars in 1977.

Until oil was discovered in 1932 by the Kuwait Oil Company (half British Petroleum and half American Gulf Oil), Kuwait was an impoverished sand lot. After World War II, Sheikh Sir Abdullah al-Salim al-Sabah undertook major public works and economic development programs, attracting thousands of outsiders. Now the principal problem was to find something to develop. Until recently, the largest project was a plant to purify water. When operation of the plant became successful, Kuwait was freed from its continued dependence on outside water sources. Large free public hospitals have been built; public education and health programs have been expanded; and electric power plants have been constructed. And roads, airports, a sewage system, and new harbors have been laid out. In effect, Sheikh Abdullah converted his desert patrimony into a welfare sheikhdom.

The principal obstacle to continued economic development has been shortage of technical, administrative, and supervisory personnel. Consequently, many non-Kuwaitis, a total larger than the local population, have been attracted to the country to work as technicians. The sheikh had such a large surplus of money that he was unable to use most of it at home. Instead, he invested hundreds of millions of pounds on the London stock market, becoming the market's largest individual investor during the 1970s.

Kuwait has also been swept into the Arab nationalist movement and, in 1961, Great Britain decided to terminate its protectorate status. Immediately after the British government announced its decision to give Kuwait full freedom, Iraq's Prime Minister Kassim claimed the territory as an integral part of his country. The Iraqi claim was based on an assertion that the 1899 treaty with Great Britain had been forged and that Kuwait, in recent history, had been part of the Ottoman administrative region which included Iraq. No other Arab state supported Iraq's claims, and in July 1961, the Arab League voted to admit Kuwait as a full member state. However, when Kuwait applied for admission to the United Nations late in 1961, its application was vetoed by the Soviet Union, although all Arab states, except Iraq, supported Kuwait's application. Two years later Iraq gave up its claims, and the amirate, as Kuwait was now called, joined the U.N.

The influence of nationalism was evident in the constitutional crisis between the paternalistic royal family and the independent-minded National Assembly during 1965. Arab unity nationalists opposed the amir's government because of its domination by wealthy "reactionary" merchants. The amir responded by opening his cabinet for the first time to the new middle class. However, the constitutional changes were in reality more of a facade since real power remained in the hands of the royal family, which filled all principal cabinet posts including the prime ministry.

The large influx of foreigners also was beginning to create concern, since their number had increased to over half the population. Indeed, by the 1970s the country's population had increased nearly sixfold from about 206,000 in 1968 to 1,600,000 by 1982. Although many outsiders prospered in Kuwait, achieving high living standards, they were barred from high office, from suffrage, and from free use of the many welfare services available to Kuwaitis. Among the most activist were the more than 250,000 Palestinians who provided much of the support for the Arab guerrilla movements fighting Israel.

Kuwait maintained its Arab credentials through the extensive economic assistance it provided to other Arab states. In 1961 it established the Kuwait Fund for Arab Economic Development to provide capital to other developing Arab states. It also became a principal contributor to the fund established for defeated Egypt and Jordan at the 1967 Khartoum Conference. With ever-increasing wealth and so small a population base, Kuwait's material wellbeing was assured, although, as in other revolutionary situations, material wellbeing was no guarantee against political instability. This became clear in 1976 when the ruling family dissolved the National Assembly, suspended civil rights, and imposed press censorship. Until then Kuwait had been, with Lebanon, the only Arab country enjoying relative press freedom. These acts were taken to still opposition to the government because of its support for Syrian intervention in the Lebanese civil war. The royal family feared that the quarrels in Lebanon might spill over into Kuwait where Palestinians constituted nearly one in four of the inhabitants. On the other hand, Kuwait strongly supported the Palestinians in international forums such as the United Nations, the Arab League, and in Third World conferences. Along with Saudi Arabia, Kuwait was the principal financier of the 1967 and 1973 wars against

Israel and of conservative factions among the Palestine guerrilla organizations. In 1981 the regime felt secure enough to permit new elections for the
assembly. Fewer than 10 of the 50 members elected represented leftist or
Islamic radicalism despite growing apprehension that the religious fervor
from Iran would infect Kuwait's own Shi'ite minority. As a precaution to
ensure Gulf stability, Kuwait joined other Arab Gulf states to form the Gulf
Cooperation Council in 1981. The dilemma facing Kuwait was how to tread
the narrow line between support for militant Arab causes and maintenance of
its own distinctive identity based chiefly on its immense oil reserves and its
traditional sheikly families.

BAHRAIN

The Bahrain archipelago, a small Persian Gulf group of 35 largely desert
islands (213 square miles) with some 280,000 people, off the Saudi Arabian
coast, would also be totally unknown were it not for its oil resources. Bahrain
has been a naval base for powers desiring to dominate the gulf since the
fifteenth century. Portugal controlled it during that century, until it was seized
by Iran. Arabs drove the Iranians out at the end of the eighteenth century and
used Bahrain for gun running, the slave trade, and piracy. In 1820, Great
Britain imposed a treaty on the ruling sheikh in an attempt to ban slavery and
piracy. Later treaties, in 1880 and 1892, forced the island's rulers to permit
British control of its relations with other countries. Because Bahrain was the
headquarters of British Persian Gulf activities, the reins were tightly held. The
British Royal Navy Persian Gulf headquarters was until recently in Bahrain,
and British political agents, who advised other coastal sheikhs, were
responsible to the British political resident at Bahrain. The ruling al-Khalifa
family made no important decision without consulting its British adviser.
After independence in 1971, a United States small base replaced the British
naval presence.

Great Britain developed a competent civil administration for the islands,
despite the preoil poverty. After the Bahrain Petroleum Company (a
subsidiary of the California Standard and Texas Oil Companies) began to
produce in 1932, the economy was so revolutionized that the island could offer
its inhabitants free medical care and education. Because of closer British
supervision, workers there had a higher standard of living than in Kuwait.

Iran claimed Bahrain until 1969. In November 1957 the shah's government declared the islands his fourteenth province. However, in 1969 the shah
declared his willingness to recognize an independent Bahrain, provided there
was a U.N.-sponsored plebiscite. During the 1950s, proposals were put
forward for a union of Saudi Arabia, Kuwait, and Bahrain, but no action was
taken to implement them.

After Great Britain announced its intention of ending its military role in all areas east of Suez after 1971, plans were proposed to include Bahrain in a Persian Gulf Federation. However, other potential members of the proposed Federation objected because of Bahrain's considerably greater wealth, population, and consequent influence. Iran also objected to incorporation of the island in a larger Arab political entity. A U.N. mission sent to the island reported that "The overwhelming majority... wish to gain recognition of their identity in a fully independent and sovereign state."[3]

Treaty arrangements with Great Britain were terminated and full independence was proclaimed in 1971. Sheikh Isa of the Khalifa family took the title of Amir. In 1972–1973 an elected Constituent Assembly drafted a constitution which established a National Assembly. Since independence political life on the island has centered on the struggle for the Assembly's 42 seats (30 elected and 12 appointed) between the Popular List and the Religious List. Victory for the leftist popular list created contentious relations with the Amir's government. Delay in granting permission for organization of trade unions also sparked unrest. Leftist trends were represented by the Popular Front, an offshoot of the Popular Front for the Liberation of Oman and the Arab Gulf, and the Bahraini National Liberation Organization. Their demands for nationalization of large companies and for termination of the American presence in Bahrain precipitated a showdown in 1974. The Emir promulgated a new state security law authorizing him to arrest and detain opponents of the regime. The arrests were followed by a decree in 1975 dissolving the National Assembly and suspending the constitution. The 1979 revolution in Iran intensified political unrest in Bahrain where more than half the population is Shi'ite, many of whom sympathized with the Shi'ite revolutionaries in Teheran. This, and the fact that there were nearly twice as many foreign as Bahrain workers, many of them associated with the poorer Shi'ites, led Bahrain's rulers to join in the formation of the Gulf Cooperation Council as a way to combat subversion of the Gulf.

Like the other Gulf states undergoing rapid political and social change, Bahrain was faced with the dilemma of extending popular participation which would lead to intensified clashes between right and left, or imposing strict controls on the political system which would concentrate power in the hands of the royal family.

QATAR, UNITED ARAB EMIRATES, AND OMAN

Qatar, Trucial Oman, and Oman were all until recently small British-controlled desert principalities with sparse population, almost no natural resources except oil, and no effectively organized systems of government. The population of all consisted mostly of Bedouin who lived at subsistence level from grazing and camel raising. There are no large cities among them, and the few small towns are concentrated along the Persian Gulf coast where the Arab population lived from pearling, fishing, or trading.

After the British decision to leave the area by the end of 1971, Qatar Bahrain and the seven Trucial Oman states decided to form the Federation of Gulf Emirates for protection against the rivalries of Saudi Arabia and Iran, and against the revolutionary aspirations of the Arab left. The Federation was launched in October 1969, when it elected the Sheikh of Abu Dhabi as its first president. All states would have equal membership in the Federation's Assembly: thus tiny Fujaira, with only 3000 inhabitants would have equal representation with Bahrain's 200,000 inhabitants. Later, Bahrain and Oman left the Federation after its government decided in favor of independence. With the proclamation of independence in 1971 the Federation became the United Arab Emirates.

Qatar

Qatar is a remote peninsula whose only land frontier, shared with Saudi Arabia, has never been clearly demarcated, a fact that has led to frequent disputes. England controlled the territory's 4000 square miles through a political officer residing in Doha, the capital, after it signed a treaty with Qatar's sheikh in 1882. Before World War II, Qatar was a poor and desolate outpost whose 20,000 inhabitants scratched a meagre living from goat grazing or the Gulf seafaring trades—pearling, fishing, and trading.

With the beginning of oil production during and after World War II, the country began an economic upswing. The population doubled as some 20,000 immigrants, including many Palestine refugees, Indians, Pakistanis, Iranians, and Somalis, were attracted by new employment opportunities. Doha grew from a double row of mud huts strung along the shore to a large city with shops full of imported goods, large and luxurious homes, and a modern free hospital. In the prewar era, there were only a half dozen automobiles. By the 1970s more than 150,000 of Qatar's 200,000 residents lived in Doha.

When wealth first came to Qatar, both the ruling family and the people were austere Wahabi tribesmen. But as oil royalties grew, reaching fifty million dollars per year by 1960, royal spending became wasteful. The ruler disbursed about a quarter of the income among his 400 relatives who squandered it on high-priced Western commodities, such as automobiles, and other mechanical devices. The government began to clamp down, insisting that a third of the royalties be used for economic development. Some eighty million dollars was spent on sixty schools, a 120-bed hospital, roads, and other public services. When public services reached the saturation point, the usual problem arose of how to spend the surpluses.

Like its other Arab neighbors, Qatar has been troubled by growing internal unrest and the threat of external subversion (about half the population is foreign, attracted by the oil boom). The royal family has been reluctant to give up any of its authority, although a provisional constitution in 1970 did establish an advisory council. Since becoming independent it has kept close ties with Saudi Arabia and generally follows the Saudi foreign policy line.

United Arab Emirates

The U.A.E., formerly Trucial Oman, once known as the Pirate Coast, has a long and colorful history, although today its seven sheikhdoms—Abu Dhabi, Dubai, Sharjah, Fujaira, Ras al-Khaima, Umm al-Kuwain, and Ajman—are relatively tame. Until the British quelled the coastal brigands early in the nineteenth century, it was infamous as a pirate-infested refuge (see chapter 4). The Roman historian Pliny and the Italian merchant Marco Polo both wrote of the dangers. Buccaneering was so profitable that pirates were attracted from the world over, including the famous Captain Kidd. Raids on ships sailing out of India convinced Great Britain of the need to end piracy. In 1820, the British imposed a treaty on the local sheikhs forbidding them to raid ships from outside the area. A Treaty of Peace in Perpetuity, or Permanent Truce (thus Trucial states), outlawing all piracy was signed with Great Britain in 1853.

Until recently, Bedouin, who lived in the sheikhdoms, were a law unto themselves. Their love of fighting led them to hire out to feuding sheikhs. Thus the principalities were in constant turmoil. In 1951, the British organized the Trucial Oman Scouts to impose order. When two or more sheikhs threatened to fight each other, a few dozen Arab scouts under a British officer would arrive, buy a sheep, and invite the hostile sheikhs to camp for a friendly feast. All parted friends—until the next time.

After establishment of the Federation of United Arab Emirates (UAE) in 1971, oil development greatly increased its importance. Abu Dhabi, by far the most populous and richest of the seven emirates dominated by the UAE. It contained nearly a third of the more than 650,000 inhabitants, and its ruler was designated president of the UAE Supreme Council. Each of the seven ruling sheikhs retain control over internal policy and local administration in his emirate, but foreign affairs, defense, education, and development policies are decided by the Council. Cabinet seats are allocated according to the size and strength of the members. The 40 seats in the National Federal Assembly are similarly allocated. A Union Defense Force created in 1971 replaced the British-officered Trucial Oman Scouts. There are no political parties or elections and the authorities maintain a tight rein on illegal immigration lest the country become swamped with foreign laborers like many of its neighbors. The UAE also maintains a cautiously conservative foreign policy close to that of Saudi Arabia and its associates in the Gulf Cooperation Council.

Sparse population and immense oil revenues gave the UAE the world's highest per capita income in 1977, about $14,000 per person. It also added prestige and international influence. The Abu Dhabi Fund for Arab Economic Development has extended loans totaling billions of dollars for development to several Arab and other Third World countries. After the oil boom, UAE played a prominent role in financing the 1973 war and in inter-Arab parleys about the postwar situation.

Oman

The sultanate of Oman recently attracted world attention because of the dispute with Saudi Arabia over the Buraimi oasis on the border between the two countries. During the first half of the nineteenth century, the sultanate was powerful enough to possess overseas colonies. The ruling al-Abu Said dynasty then moved its headquarters to Zanzibar island, off the East African coast. After the patriarch Sultan Said Ibn Sultan died, his kingdom was divided between two sons. One established the dynasty that ruled Zanzibar island until it was overthrown and Zanzibar united with Tanzania in 1964, and the other became sultan of Muscat. The British established control in 1891, through a treaty similar to those with the other Persian Gulf Sheikhdoms. However, in 1913 Bedouin tribes in the interior rebelled and elected their own chief, called imam. Ever since, the British have supported the sultan's authority, but it was limited to the coastal regions where order was maintained by the British-officered Muscat and Oman Field Force. After 1953, when there began to be speculation about the oil potential of the Buraimi oasis, the imam and sultan disputed its ownership. Great Britain backed the sultan with troops and military equipment, while Saudi Arabia and the Arab nationalists supported the imam. Claims of a third party, the Trucial Oman sheikh of Abu Dhabi, made the dispute even more complicated, and he, too, was supported against Saudi Arabia by the British. Ten Arab countries pressed the cause of the imam against the sultan in the U.N., charging that the British controlled the sultanate and that it was therefore under colonial domination. After establishment of the People's Republic of South Yemen, hostilities broke out between the two neighboring states. The People's Republic became a base for the insurgent "Popular Front for the Liberation of the Arabian Gulf," an organization established to undermine the royal emirates. With large-scale oil production beginning in the 1960s the sultan promised to initiate several development projects. However he, like other traditional royal chiefs of state in the area, faced the prospect of growing nationalism, along with the benefits of increasing oil revenues and therefore attempted to cut off all contact by his subjects with the outside world. He forbade them to leave the country or even to own agricultural machinery. His feeble efforts at development failed to prevent his overthrow in August 1970 by a "progressive"-minded son who had been educated in England. The new young sultan promised to abolish many of the restrictions imposed by his father to prevent contact with the outside world. One of his first acts was to change the country's name to the Sultanate of Oman as a step to emphasize unity of all the country. He also formally incorporated the Dhofar region into his kingdom. Formerly it had been a separate sultanate joined to Muscat through the person of the ruler.

The new sultan at first asked the Dhofar rebels to cooperate in his development efforts, but only the Dhofar Liberation Front accepted. The Popular Front for the Liberation of the Occupied Arabian Gulf, a leftist group which controlled much of Dhofar continued its efforts to overthrow the monarchy or at least to liberate Dhofar. The Dhofar rebellion became a focal point of the struggle between traditional conservative forces and nationalist "progressives" for control of the Gulf and of South Arabia. Because he perceived the war in Dhofar as crucial, the shah of Iran sent several thousand troops to the aid of the sultan. PFLOAG claimed that there was a secret agreement between the shah and the sultan to repress leftist movements in south Arabia. Iran's large air force received its first combat experience in Dhofar. Jordan also began to assist the Sultan in 1972 with troops and aircraft and by training Omani pilots at the Jordanian Royal Air Academy. PFLOAG has also received foreign aid through the Yemen People's Democratic Republic, including equipment from Communist China. The sultan claimed a complete victory over the rebels late in 1975 and a cease-fire with South Yemen was negotiated by Saudi Arabia. However, reports continued to come from the area indicating that the rebellion continued. By 1982 there were still no representative political institutions and the sultan ruled with total authority under Koranic law.

Oman figured prominently in U.S. plans for establishment of a rapid deployment force in the region during 1982. A special strategic relationship was developed with Oman, and it, along with Somalia and Egypt, participated in military exercises within the new American military command organized to protect U.S. interests in the Gulf.

NOTES

1. Cited in George Lipsky, ed., *Saudi Arabia,* New Haven, 1959, p. 120.
2. H. St. John Philby, *Sa'udi Arabia,* London, 1955, p. 343.
3. *New York Times,* May 3, 1970.

17

Iran

Although the history of Iran (Persia) dates back to the sixth century before Christ and its continuity is longer than any other Middle Eastern nation, it is still not a nation-state in the modern sense. While 90 percent of the people are Shi'ite Muslims who share a history whose roots reach back into the pre-Islamic era, among them still flouishes a variety of ethnic, racial, and linguistic groups who live in relative isolation from each other, hindering unification of the country.

SOCIAL STRATA

Until the massive economic and social changes of the 1960s, the 80 to 85 percent of Iran's population that constituted the peasantry lived in some 50,000 villages similar to those of their Arab and Turkish neighbors; their conditions had changed little over the past 2000 years. Iranian village organization also resembled that of Arab lands where, until recent revolutions, powerful landlords owned not only the soil, but the villages and, for all practical purposes, the peasants. Until the recent land reform in Iran only 15 percent of most of the cultivated land was peasant owned. At least half the land was owned by absentee landlords, another quarter by wakf or religious endowments—such as schools, mosques, and other Muslim institutions—and about 10 percent was state domain. Because of Iran's extensive mountains and deserts, agricultural land is scarce, only 10 percent being truly arable.

Village headmen, who were feared by the peasants, usually were the estate managers of the richest landlords. Since the headmen carried out the landlord's will, collected taxes, and controlled the gendarmerie, they were regarded with deep suspicion. A common Iranian saying was: "First see the headman—then fleece the village." In a few regions where there were peasant proprietors, headmen were selected by the villagers from their own wealthier members. Other important village figures included the religious leader (*mullah*), schoolteacher, and elders. The latter, representing heads of leading families, could or could not form a council that the headman consulted should he want to. Some mullahs were politically active and organized the peasants; others were themselves illiterate and ignorant of life beyond the village. The Shi'ite clergy, led by the Ayatollah Ruhollah Khomeini, were the group which galvanized opposition to the shah during the 1960s and 1970s; they led the 1979 Revolution which overthrew the monarchy and established the Islamic Republic which followed. Teachers, many under the influence of the Communist Tudeh party, were government appointed and paid. Hence, as state officials, they also had much influence.

In larger villages along the main roads, the teahouse was the center of social life. Remote from the main thoroughfares, where there was no teahouse, villagers congregated at the home of the headman or schoolteacher, where they heard of national events from the radio or from recent visitors to the large towns. The public bath and mosque were other village institutions where the latest gossip and public events were discussed.

Social organization in the towns was patriarchal, like that in village and tribe. Life was little better for the townsman than for the villager. Both lived in dire poverty. The real distinction between Iranian towns and villages was the existence of bazaars in the former. Most bazaar towns seemed to fit a pattern: they averaged about 40,000 inhabitants; were situated along main highways; and contained quite varied social and ethnic groups and numerous minorities, such as Jews, Arabs, Assyrians, and Armenians. Since nearly all social contact took place within the family circle, the various ethnic and social groups had little contact with each other.

Within the towns resided the small but powerful group of between 200 and 1000 landowning families who occupied or controlled all key positions in the army, police, judiciary, higher clergy, and government. Mobility upward into this class was unusual, although it was possible by accumulation and manipulation of wealth, or the right connections. Because of Iran's strong tradition of a socially graded society, there was much less social mobility than in other Middle Eastern societies. Although considered equal before Allah, all Iranians were not considered equal before man. So great was the reverence for social prestige that any title indicating some kind of upward differentiation was clung to.

Another peculiarly Iranian phenomenon was the bazaar merchant. His social rank was immediately below the landowner, but he was not nearly so powerful. The bazaar merchant (including artisans, shopkeepers, and small traders) was more influential than his counterpart in other Middle Eastern Muslim lands. The bazaar in Iran was much more than a place to exchange goods; it was also a market place for ideas and opinions to which the country's rulers were especially attentive. Before modern communications, the bazaar provided the quickest means of sending news, and it was there that public reaction to the government could be most readily observed. Even Reza Shah slowed down some of his plans when he discovered opposition in the bazaar. The revolution in 1906, discussed below, was a direct result of a bazaar uprising in Tehran. With the growing influence of other institutions such as the bureaucracy, the university, and the working class, the relative influence of the bazaar declined.

Small industrialists, bankers, and businessmen, who came recently into contact with the West and were learning its techniques of operation and management, belonged to the upper-middle class. Many of the *nouveau riche* invested their money in land, hoping thereby to become members of the governing elite. In Tehran and a few other large towns, there was also a new intellectual middle class of doctors, lawyers, engineers, and government employees.

The lower-middle class were generally skilled factory laborers and white-collar workers. They too were becoming acquainted with Western ideas, tastes, and ideologies. The wide social range between the upper- and lower-middle class prevented formation of any strong middle-class consciousness. Some Iranians of this group favored more rapid progress toward reform and Westernization. Others regarded moderate ideas and methods as evil and irreligious, and strenuously opposed them. Generally speaking, however, the middle classes, collaborating with some of the more progressive landed aristocrats and clergy, gave great impetus to social change in Iran.

At the bottom of the social scale were the peasant laborers, servants, and menials. They lacked the initiative to form an effective political force, although they could be rather readily instigated into becoming violent mobs by politicians. They were often organized into a striking force, trained and paid by the politically conscious bazaar merchants, and could be induced to demonstrate for or against any issue.

THE TRIBES

Even among the 90 percent of the Iranians who are Shi'ites (8 percent are Sunnis), there is no common language spoken by a majority. Less than a third of the population speak the Persian dialect of the capital (Pahlavi), and more than two-thirds speak some other Persian tongue. In the densely settled northwestern province of Azerbaijan, where a fifth of the people live, the language is a Turkish dialect called Azari. In addition, there are a number of tribal languages and dialects spoken by the Kurds, Lurs, Bakhtiari, Kashkai, Khamseh, Shahsevans, Arabs, and Baluchis.

An important tribe is the Bakhtiaris, concentrated in their Zagors mountain homeland. They speak a dialect of Persian, although many have also absorbed Arabic or Turkish elements into their speech. Until 1924 they were politically autonomous, fostering their unity on legends of common ancestry. According to one legend, their origin can be traced to a Mongol noble, Bakhtiar, whose descendants were conquered by the Sassanids. Many ruling Bakhtiari families were wealthy landowners who lived in the capital, sent their children to American and European universities, and participated fully in Iranian national life. The second wife of Shah Muhammad Reza Pahlavi was a daughter of a leading Bakhtiari whom he married to strengthen relations with this powerful group. But he divorced her because she bore him no son.

The Kurds are more numerous than the Bakhtiari, but they have never been as influential in Tehran. They tended to remain outside the mainstream of national life, preferring to maintain their own customs and traditions free from contact with other groups. Like Persian, Kurdish is one of the Indo-European family of languages. The Kurds comprise most of the country's Sunni Muslims. Thus they are both an ethnic and a religious minority. After World War II, pro-Communist Kurdish leaders established the Republic of Mahabad with Soviet support (see chapter 5). But their revolt was crushed when Iranian troops overran the region and hanged some twenty leaders in 1947. Kurdish nationalism is still a strong centrifugal force, and the tight kinship uniting hundreds of families constantly undermines Tehran's authority in Kurdish regions.

The Lurs, who resemble the Bakhtiari, live south of the Kurds. Most Lurs still maintain a tribal organization and have a reputation for being a wild, proud people.

The Persian-speaking Kashgai occupy the southwestern province of Fars, in which they established virtual autonomy for several months after World War II. Periodical military expeditions against them failed to suppress their resistance to the central government, and they continued their independent ways with little chance of, or desire for, integration with the rest of the country.

Other tribes, like the Arabs and Baluchi, are politically less significant and have created fewer problems for the central government. A principal dilemma for Tehran is how to create among them a feeling of national identity.

Although they would probably help to defend the country from a foreign invasion, there were few ardent supporters of the central government among them.

Iranian tribes, like those of the Arabs, were organized in federations subdivided into clans and family groups. Reza Shah (see below) used the Iranian army in attempts to impose Tehran's authority on these tribes, but the army's ruthlessness only alienated them further from the government, and strengthened their allegiance to their own tribal leaders, or khans. Even today they remain a law unto themselves, often raiding caravans passing through their territory. A principal activity of the Iranian army was to control these tribes and to subdue those whose independence offered too much threat.

IRANIAN ATTITUDES TOWARD GOVERNMENT

Traditional Iranian attitudes have been unfavorable to development of democratic institutions because all society is organized in an authoritarian fashion. Sons expect to be severely punished if they disobey their fathers. The authoritarian attitudes learned in the family are applied to other areas of society, with the result that little individual initiative develops. Unless ordered to do so by a superior, the individual is usually reluctant to take action on matters which have not been charged to his direct responsibility. Power, rank, and age have been the attributes of traditionally accepted authority. The orientation upward of Iranians leads them to respect the strong leader, who is both feared and obeyed. These attitudes are reflected in Persian literature and in the practice of Shi'ite Islam in the country.

Iranians generally viewed government with fear and suspicion. They regarded it as an agent of the landlord, represented by the army, police, and tax collectors. Government was often considered an institution to be protected from, rather than as the protector of the citizen. Even the idea of popular participation in government was unknown until 1906. Until then, few disputed the shah's role as an absolute despot, responsible only to the religious hierarchy that kept an eye on the morality of his actions. Iranian tradition established the shah's position as "the shadow of God upon earth," the ultimate authority subject only to Shi'ite principles. According to pre-Islamic tradition, the land and all its subjects were his property and any rights of the shah's subjects were received only by good grace, not by divine or natural law.

NATIONAL ORIGINS

Ancient Iran

Since Iran's pre-Islamic origins play such an important role in shaping the contemporary era, it is necessary to examine them, if only briefly. The ancient Aryans gave Iran its name (meaning, land of the Aryans). They include the Medes, Persians, Parthians, Scythians, and the Achaemenid clan, closely related to and vassals of the Medes. Iran's first great ancient empire was established by the Achaemenid clan, descended from Indo-European-speaking peoples who invaded the region about 2000 B.C., possibly from the plains of what today is south central Russia. The most illustrious Achaemenian was Cyrus the Great, who established his empire 500 years before Christ. Under his leadership the ancient Iranians crushed the rival Babylonians and swept through the Levant, and his successors extended the kingdom from what today is Asia Minor and Central Asia southward to the Red and Arabian seas and from North Africa to the Punjab in northern India.

The Achaemenid Empire (500–331 B.C.) developed a noteworthy system of public works, a distinctive architecture, and an excellent governmental administration. After two centuries of domination, the empire was conquered by Alexander the Great of Macedonia. Seleucus, a successor to Alexander, introduced Greek culture to Iran, and the term "Hellenistic" is used to indicate the blend of these two civilizations. Under Hellenistic influence, Iran had become a cosmopolitan center of arts, literature, and science by the time another northern Aryan tribe, the Parthians, ended the Seleucid regime in 129 B.C.

The Parthians had nothing notable to add to Hellenistic civilization, but they did defend Iran from incursion by the Roman Empire. Some scholars suggest, however, that there success was not so much a result of their military prowess, but rather a result of Roman diversions elsewhere. By A.D. 224, Parthian strength had been dissipated, and they were unable to fight off another Aryan group, the Sassanids (from *sassan,* the ancient Iranian for "commander..), who were descendants of the Achaemenids. A dynasty of some forty Sassanid kings revived a strong, prosperous Iran modeled on that of Cyrus the Great. While dominating the regions immediately neighboring on Iran, they were unable to wrest the bulk of the Middle East from the Eastern Roman (or Byzantine) Empire, although they seriously challenged it. The Sassanids failed to expand their empire or rival the accomplishments of Cyrus the Great because, even then, it lacked the strength of unity. Imperial authority was at times divided among six or seven great noble families who provided imperial governors, generals, and other officials, but who competed with each other for the ultimate power. The religious establishment of Zoroastrianism and the punishment of heretical groups that resulted also weakened the country.

Zoroastrianism

A major religion founded by the ancient Iranians was the Zoroastrianism, which prevailed—more or less—from early Achaemenid times until the Islamic conquest in 641. The founder of this religion, Zarathustra (Zoroaster), was born sometime in either the seventh or sixth century B.C. in northwestern

Iran. His tenets emerged as a dominant influence during the rule of the
Achaemenids. Central to Zoroastrianism was the concept of continuous
struggle between the powers of good—led by Ahura Mazda (Ormazd)—and
those of evil—led by Ahriman. Religious rites, defined in the holy book *Zend
Avesta,* concerned not only the fate of the human soul, but such agricultural
matters as the proper cultivation of crops and care of domestic animals. Earth,
air, fire, and water in their pure form were considered representations of
Ahura Mazda, and their care in Zoroastrian ritual was the responsibility of
the priests. A man's fate was determined by the balance between his good and
bad deeds recorded in the *Book of Life.* After death, he was to pass over a
bridge no wider than a thread. If his good outweighed his evil, his path
widened and he reached the realm of light; otherwise, he tumbled into the dark
realm of Ahriman. The Sassanids gave new impetus to the religion as part of
their efforts to revive the ancient Achaemenid culture.

THE ISLAMIC ERA

After the Islamic conquest of 641, Zoroastrian influence in Iran was such
that many practices of Islam in Iran today differ from those of other countries.
Many ancient Iranian concepts connected with Zoroastrianism were adopted
by Shi'ite Islam in Iran. The Iranian conception of life as a continuous struggle
between good and evil is evidence of Zoroastrian influence. Because of their
contribution to the Abbasid victory over the Ummayads in 750 (see chapter 2),
Iranians acquired great influence in the eastern Muslim empire. Their higher
level of cultural development and administrative experience led to the
adoption of Iranian dress and manners in the Abbasid caliph's Baghdad court.
Persian art motifs (royal hunts, royal audiences, and battle scenes) were later
adopted by the Arabs. Persian language and literature played an important
role in the development of Arabic culture and to be truly cultivated, the Arab
was expected to know the Iranian classics. Later, in the tenth century, when
the Islamic empire began to dissolve, local Iranian Samanid and Buwayhid
kingdoms arose. Although both were Muslim, they emphasized their claim to
descent from the Sassanids; in both, Persian culture was revived and
developed. Iran's great poet, Firdausi (c. 940—c. 1020), composed the great
epic *Shahnama (Book of Kings),* a saga of 60,000 rhyming couplets about four
ancient dynasties. Two of them were legendary, drawn from the *Avesta,* and
the other two were the Parthian and Sassanid lines of kings. The *Shahnama*
became Iran's folk literature, memorized to the present day by the peasants,
even those who cannot read. During this era, many Iranian authors wrote in
Arabic script, far simpler than the complicated ancient Pahlavi lettering,
which was unrelated to Arabic. While Iranians used the Arabic script, many
Iranian words were absorbed into the Arabic language and vice versa.

Iran's independent existence was brought to an end by two more great invasions from Central Asia. About 1050, Seljuk Turkish tribes invaded, and two centuries later, the great Mongol waves swept over the land (see chapter 3). The former not only permitted but even encouraged Iranian culture. Poetry, philosophy, religion, and architecture continued to develop under Seljuk rule. But the thirteenth-century Mongol invasion, led by Genghiz Khan, was wholly destructive. His deeds and those of his grandson Hulagu are still blamed for the decline of civilization in both Iran and Iraq. No less destructive were later invasions led by Timur the Lame (Tamerlane), a Central Asian Turk who sacked, plundered, and terrorized his way to victory. Yet it would be unfair to lay only death and destruction to the Mongols and Timurids, for they began to patronize the arts after consolidating their conquests.

THE MODERN ERA

The Safavids (c. 1500–1736), who took Iran from the Timurids in the sixteenth century, are usually thought of as initiating the modern era. Shah Ismail, their founder and first ruler, led seven Turkish Shi'ite tribes into Azerbaijan, attempting to prove the legitimacy of his power by claims of direct descent from the Sassanids through marriage of 'Ali's son Husain to the last Sassanid princess after the Arab conquest. His dynasty thus claimed to have inherited both the divine right of Sassanid rulers descended from Cyrus the Great and the mantle of Islam through Muhammad's son-in-law 'Ali.

For the first time in eight centuries, under the Safavids Iran was unified and a measure of national consciousness aroused. Success lay in an appeal to Iranians on both the levels of ancient Aryan folklore and a distinctively Iranian form of Shi'ite Islam. Iranian shahs claimed to be the descendants of Cyrus and the offspring of the seventh imam, one of the eleven sinless descendants of 'Ali (see chapter 2). Shah Ismail tried to unify the conglomeration of loosely united tribes scattered through the land by their conversion to Shi'ism as the state religion. During this era theologians laid the basis of Shi'ite theology as now accepted in Iran.

The dominant Safavid figure, whose importance to Iran is second to none, was Shah Abbas (1587–1628). He replaced the haphazard tribal levies with a regular army organized by two hired Englishmen. Unruly tribes were either suppressed or moved to areas where they could be controlled. At Isfahan, a new capital—considered one of the architectural wonders of the world—was built. Roads, canals, and caravansaries were extended throughout the country, making possible the growth of trade and commerce. The Portuguese were driven from the Persian Gulf and extensive commercial alliances were signed with England and Holland.

Renewed conflict among rival tribes toppled the Safavid dynasty in 1722 when an Afghan army captured the capital at Isfahan. They in turn were defeated in 1736, when a Turkish officer who had served under the Safavids established his rule. After a partially successful attempt to expand east and north, he too was overthrown by his own amry. The government of his successor lasted only his own lifetime; at his death, the Kajars (1794–1925), a Turkish tribe, asserted its authority. Unity of a more stable kind was re-established, and from their new capital at Tehran, the Kajars ruled until they were ousted by Reza Shah in 1925. This period in Iranian history constituted a century and a quarter of foreign machinations, wars, and occupations and an internal factional struggle. After Napoleon unsuccessfully attempted to win over the Kajars, Russia began its push down to the Caspian Sea, seizing one northern province after another (see chapter 4). British fear of tsarist ambitions in the Persian Gulf and India kept Iran from being totally overrun by Russia, for Great Britain made it her policy to maintain Iran as a buffer state between the two contending empires. After they reached a compromise of their differences in an entente in 1907, the British and tsarist empires divided up the country north and south into spheres of influences, leaving a "neutral" strip between them.

During the Kajar regime in the nineteenth century, increasing contact with the West made Persia aware of its relatively backward position in the world; and there began an awakening to the need for change. In the 1860s and 1870s the first telegraph lines were set up with British assistance, establishing direct communications with foreign countries and ending Persia's virtual isolation. Under Russian direction a military unit called the Cossack Brigade was organized to keep law and order in and around the capital. Concessions were granted to foreigners to build railroads and to develop the country's rivers and its raw materials. The first modern banks were opened, again by foreign capitalists. However, the Kajar shahs often overextended the country's budget in their attempts to modernize, soon leading to foreign indebtedness and outright intervention, principally by Russia and Great Britain.

As a result of foreign pressures and the collapse of strong central authority within the country, a modern nationalist movement brought about the 1906 revolution. The movement had been growing with the increase of knowledge among Iranian intellectuals, students, merchants, and religious leaders about such Western concepts as the rights of man, self-determination, and popular government. Shi'ite *mujtahids* (doctors of divine law), mullahs, dervishes, and Tehran bazaar merchants had become disenchanted with corruption in the royal court, with the shah's inability to maintain order, with his surrender to Russian influence, and above all, with his confiscation of much clerical property. Under direction of the Shi'ite clergy, protesting masses demonstrated in the capital and bazaar merchants closed their shops, paralyzing economic life. When threatened by the shah's troops, some ten thousand Iranians, including many prominent merchants, sought sanctuary in the British legation grounds. After mediation by the British ambassador, who was sympathetic to the aims of the demonstrators, the shah was forced to convene a constituent assembly. Within a year the assembly issued Iran's first constitution.

Until the 1906 revolution, there was no separation between civil and religious institutions. Sharia law administered by the Shi'ite divines covered all problems. The shah's private purse and the national treasury were one and the same. No division separated executive, judicial, and legislative power. Laws were simply enacted by imperial decree. In effect, religion, philosophy, government, and law—as in the pre-nineteenth-century Ottoman Empire—were part of a single institution.

The 1906 constitution was inspired by the French 1875 model. It established a National Consultative Assembly, or Majlis, and a Senate. Majlis members were to be elected by constituencies divided roughly according to population, although minorities such as Armenians, Zoroastrians, Assyrian Christians, and Jews were granted special representatives. Numbers of members and their terms of office have varied. Originally, there were 162 members elected for two-year terms. The number was raised to 200, 198 elected and 2 designated as minority representatives. Because of parliamentary immunity, the Majlis became another place where opponents of the government found sanctuary.

Neither the constitution nor the resulting parliament fared well. The National Assembly (*Majlis*) represented only the nobility, the merchants, and the religious leaders, men who lived primarily in Tehran and who had little concern for the welfare of the country's nomads and peasants. Because it challenged his exclusive authority, parliament was suppressed by the shah in 1908 with Russian help. Later that year nationalists, with the aid of Bakhtiari tribesmen, rose in defense of the constitution, deposed the shah, and placed his young son on the throne. Russia, however, was determined to keep the country from becoming unified. Continued tsarist intervention in Tehran and Russian control of northern Iran blocked any further nationalist progress.

When World War I broke out, Russia and Great Britain occupied the country and divided it between them. After the Bolshevik revolution in 1917, however, Iran was left completely in British hands. The British attempt to turn the country into a virtual protectorate, the continued corruption of the Iranian government, and the young shah's incompetence stimulated another nationalist uprising in Tehran in 1921. It was led by Sayyid Zia ed-Din Tabatabay, a newspaper editor turned political reformer. Tabatabay relied on the Russian-founded Cossack Brigade to back his authority. Making himself prime minister he named the brigade's commander, Reza, minister of war.

REZA SHAH

For the next two decades, Iran's history is the story of Reza Shah. After being invited to occupy the capital, he ousted Zia ed-Din, seized power, became prime minister in 1923, and was crowned shah in 1925. In some respects, Reza's life resembled Ataturk's. Of a military family, he had distinguished himself in the Cossack Brigade, rising through the ranks despite lack of any formal education. Like Ataturk, too, he was infatuated with the material aspects of Western civilization and sought to introduce them into his country. Factories, railroads, and hospitals were set up with little concern about the availability of natural resources or markets and with very little understanding of the long process required to develop the techniques for operating modern institutions.

Reza Shah attempted to create a united national sentiment by emphasizing Iran's pre-Islamic glories. The lion and the sun, symbols of the Achaemenid and Sassanid empires, came into use; and in an unsuccessful attempt to counteract Muslim clerical influence, Zoroastrianism was reestablished together with Shi'ism as a state religion, although there were few who practiced the pre-Islamic faith. The new dyansty was called Pahlavi, a Sassanian name borrowed from the Parthians. Streets and public places were renamed, honoring pre-Islamic folk heroes, and a new Iranian calendar was adopted based on the Gregorian one of Europe. Reza Shah frequently reminded the Iranians of the glories of their past and especially of Cyrus the Great.

Much was hoped for from this renaissance; only some of it was realized. New schools, including the University of Tehran, and a national conscript army were created. Communications were improved by extending the country's roads and telegraph lines and installing wireless stations. A trans-Iranian railroad, from the Persian Gulf to the Caspian Sea, was begun, financed by the state monopolies of the country's business and industry. State industries were built for refining sugar, manufacturing textiles, and processing food and chemicals.

Reza Shah attempted to modernize the major towns by physical reconstruction. Between 1925 and 1940, he cut wide avenues through many old residential quarters, built branches of the National Bank of Iran, hospitals, and government offices. A 1929 law required Iranians to replace their traditional costumes with more Western clothing. After 1935, European hats were required; after 1936, the veil was to be discarded and the head left uncovered. Since Reza Shah's demise, there has been a reversion to the traditional woman's *chadar* (veil), a length of black cloth covering the whole figure, including the head and face except for the eyes, so that modern and traditional dress now exist side by side.

The dictator's ruthless tactics, however, undermined much of the effectiveness of his program. He did not engender the great *élan* that Ataturk inspired in Turkey. By the mid-1930s, it had become evident that Reza Shah too often surrendered to his own passion for power, wealth, and absolute domination, and his opponents were too often murdered. The aristocracy was victimized by a reign of terror. Reza seized their fortunes, villages, and lands, adding them to his own estates.

While Ataturk sought to encourage individual initiative, Reza Shah so intimidated his subordinates that they avoided any direct responsibility and gave only optimistic, but often false, reports of their activities. With no freedom of speech or press, and without strong or capable administrative and political leaders, there was complete absence of self-criticism. Moral degeneration and a sense of hopeless resignation and helplessness began to pervade the regime.

It is true that Iran was historically much less prepared for extensive reforms than Turkey. Fewer Iranians had been trained in Western educational institutions or attuned to European thought and outlook, and the country had had relatively much less contact with the West than was the case in Turkey on the eve of Ataturk's revolution. Nor was Iran as unified as Turkey, the latter being a much more homogeneous nation in which 90 percent of the population were religiously, linguistically, and ethnically related.

With Hitler's rise to power after 1933, Reza Shah saw in the German dictator a potential ally. Nazi efficiency and regimentation appealed to the Iranian, and he invited the German government to send experts and advisers to assist him. In part, his motivation was to find in Germany a strong ally against the Soviet Union. Reza Shah's commitments to the Nazis finally ensnared him in the web of the great power conflict that led to World War II and ended in the Russian and British reoccupation of Iran in August 1941. Reza Shah was forced to abdicate and leave Iran (see chapter 5).

EVENTS DURING WORLD WAR II

The sudden loosening of Reza Shah's grip on political life resulted in a succession of weak prime ministers, each of whom resigned after finding that he could do nothing about the serious inflation and shortage of goods. Both right- and left-wing extremist movements suddenly emerged, and the tribes began to demand autonomy.

During the first four years of the reign of Reza Shah's son, Shah Muhammad Reza Pahlavi, Iran was occupied by British, American, and Russian troops. Independence was lost; the allies took over or otherwise controlled most governmental functions. In the Russian-controlled northern part of Iran, the Communist Tudeh party was encouraged. To counteract its effect, the British supported a nationalist party, the National Will, led by former Prime Minister Zia ed-Din, who had returned from exile.

Only the 1942 agreement between Iran, Great Britain, and the Soviet Union calling for a withdrawal of foreign troops six months after the war prevented complete partition of the country. And even that agreement was implemented with great difficulty, for Russia was reluctant to leave. During 1945, a separatist pro-Soviet regime was set up in Azerbaijan, headed by a seasoned Communist leader of the Tudeh party. Under Russian auspices, the Kurds also established an "independent" republic in the north. Only after pressure was exerted by the U.N. Security Council and President Truman did Russia evacuate the area (see chapter 5).

MOSADDEQ

Both Russia and Great Britain showed great interest in controlling Iran's rich oil deposits after the war. When the Russians finally left the northern provinces, they did so on condition that favorable consideration be given to a Soviet oil concession. When the bill establishing a joint Soviet-Iranian Oil Company was presented to the Iranian parliament in October 1947, however, it was defeated 100 to 2. At the same time, parliament banned new concessions to any foreigner or to companies in which foreigners held shares and called for re-examination of the Anglo-Iranian Oil Company concession in the south. Between 1908, when Iranian oil was first produced in commercial quantities, and the late 1940s, Iran had become one of the world's largest oil producers and the principal source of Great Britain's oil. During these forty years, the British-owned Anglo-Persian (later Iranian) Oil Company had become a power within Iran, influencing the course of and the conduct of many of the tribes in the oil-producing areas of the country. Iranian nationalists consequently resented the foreign company's presence, and the government which protected it.

A rising storm of anti-British sentiment forced the government to approve a bill nationalizing the Anglo-Iranian Oil Company in March 1951 (see chapter 5). The leader of the new nationalist wave was Dr. Muhammad Mosaddeq, next to Reza Shah and his son Muhammad Pahlavi one of the most forceful individuals who shaped Iran's contemporary history.

In the prewar years, Mosaddeq, who had been a conservative but not an important political figure, was arrested by Reza Shah and exiled to a quiet out-of-the-way village for his criticism of the shah's dictatorship. Mosaddeq now returned to politics as a government official, parliamentary deputy, and cabinet minister. In parliament, he continually hammered away at the theme that Iran must free itself from foreign domination and influences. In a notable speech, lasting over two days in October 1944, he led the attack against the Anglo-Iranian Oil Company. The debate culminated in rejection of the Soviet demand for a concession and instigated the investigation that led up to the 1951 nationalization of that company.

Mosaddeq rallied supporters from half a dozen parliamentary splinter groups into a National Front. With its backing, he became chairman of the strategic parliamentary oil committee that drafted the 1951 nationalization law. After the bill passed, his political influence could no longer be curbed and he was made prime minister. To Iran's masses, intellectuals, middle class, and youth, he had become a messianic leader of the forces of "good" against the evil of foreign domination.

During the period in which Dr. Mosaddeq was prime minister between 1951 and 1953, rumors of a British invasion were frequent. When the oil issue was brought to the United Nations and the World Court, Dr. Mosaddeq personally presented Iran's case. President Truman sent a personal representative to Iran but he too failed to effect any compromise. Mosaddeq and his coalition of religious zealots and fervent nationalists were adamant. They would not surrender Iran's rights to its oil.

Between 1951 and 1953, Great Britain and the West boycotted Iran's oil and the industry was forced to shut down. Since the oil revenues were Iran's principal source of income, the boycott created an economic crisis and discontent in the country. By June 1953, Mosaddeq's coalition had disintegrated. The Tehran press and businessmen complained of deteriorating economic conditions caused by continued lack of oil revenues. Taking advantage of disruption in the nationalist camp, the shah attempted to dismiss Mosaddeq in August. When Mosaddeq refused to leave, street mobs turned out to support him and the shah fled from the country. It looked as though Iran might become a republic: even the capital street names were being changed from "Reza Shah" to "Republic" and from "Pahlavi" to "People."

Mosaddeq, however, had failed to win support from the army. Troops supporting the shah took over the capital, and by the end of August an army general had deposed Mosaddeq and had made himself prime minister. Involvement of the U.S. Central Intelligence Agency in overthrowing Mosaddeq alienated nationalists and the left in the country. When the shah returned from his six-day exile, he was greeted with a tumultuous welcome by the same Teheran street mobs, now paid by pro-shah supporters and organized with C.I.A. help, that only a few days earlier had demanded a republic.

The Mosaddeq phenomenon was of more than passing significance, however. He was one of the few individuals who could rally mass support for a national cause. He symbolized the nation for all classes and for all ethnic and social groups.

EARLY POLITICAL PARTIES

Until World War I, there were no political parties because there was no organized political life. The interwar era was dominated by Reza Shah's dictatorship. Thus until 1941 the constitution and the institutions of parliamentary democracy were ineffective for all practical purposes. Immediately after Reza Shah's forced abdication in 1941, several political groups sprang up, of which only two had a genuine program, a stable organization, and a permanent mass following. The Communist-supported Tudeh party was one, and will be examined below. The other was the National Will, encouraged by Great Britain and led by Zia ed-Din. Despite his program for social and economic reform, he and his followers were attacked by the left as Fascist British agents. Within three years, Zia ed-Din was arrested and disappeared from the political scene, although several of his supporters remained politically active and gave their backing to reforms later proposed by the shah.

Prime Minister Ahmad Qavam attempted to counteract the National Will party by forming the Iranian Democrats in 1946 with government financial support. After winning a parliamentary majority in 1946, Qavam's party was torn by internal dissension and disappeared. Various other so-called parties suffered similar fates in the postwar decades, and the only truly effective group other than the Tudeh was the National Front gathered around Dr. Muhammad Mosaddeq.

When Mosaddeq became prime minister in 1951, he received unprecedented popular support because of his reputation for honest and sincere patriotism. During the preceding two years, the National Front coalition formed groups representing every political viewpoint. Mosaddeq's followers included liberal-minded intellectuals, professionals, merchants, a significant number of landowners, prominent religious divines, some labor leaders, and a few tribal chiefs. Several already existing political groups identified with the National Front. They included the Iran party, a mildly nondoctrinaire group of socialist professionals and intellectuals; the Toilers party, which had made not overly successful attempts at organizing industrial workers under the leadership of Dr. Mozaffar Bakai; Pan-Iranism, an extreme nationalist body; and a band of Shi'ite zealots called Warriors of Islam (*Fidayan-i Islam*) led by Mullah Kashani. Kashani's followers threw their support from group to group, at times backing the Tudeh party, Mosaddeq, or the shah. The Warriors threatened death to all who followed Western customs and assassinated several politicians, including Prime Minister Razmara in 1951. They supported Mosaddeq during the oil crisis because of his determined and forceful opposition to foreign control of and or intervention in the country's internal affairs.

The National Front fell apart after the oil crisis created serious economic dislocations, for which Mosaddeq was blamed. Many conservatives also felt that he had overreached himself when he attempted to place himself above the shah, thus violating Iranian tradition of the shah's supremacy. Within two years, the great nationalist enthusiasm that Mosaddeq had personified had been dissipated, and politics returned to the hands of the court and the landowners. Some Mosaddeq followers organized a small but ineffective National Resistance Movement. He himself could no longer participate in politics, having been exiled to a remote village after serving a three-year prison term for high treason. Mullah Kashani, the second brightest star in the Mosaddeq constellation, also faded into obscurity as merely another Shi'ite cleric. Both men died during the 1960s, leaving behind only memories of their once powerful political influence.

The leaders of the National Front supported constitutionalism, avowed loyalty to the throne, emphasized freedom, promised honest administration, and denounced communism. But these admirable principles were not accompanied by much evidence of political realism or practicality, or by any specific program that would give thoughtful people, in or out of government, a basis for confidence in supporting the organization. As a coalition, the National Front apparently could not agree on such a program, arguing that this is the task of individual parties. Although, according to T. Cuyler Young, there was little doubt that the overwhelming majority of the politically concerned and aware among the people were back of the National Front, the masses, peasants, tribesmen, and laborers were not included. "[T]hey damn the régime, but blame the Shah's advisers and entourage. In a negative sense, the wide support of the National Front is underlined by the fact that recent governments have had to maintain stability and themselves in power by force...."[1]

Officially sponsored "parties" were organized in 1957 and 1958 to give the country a façade of democracy. An experimental "loyal opposition" was chosen by the shah to become the People's party in 1957, and a few months later a progovernment majority, the Nation party, was organized to create a synthetic two-party system. Both groups were formed by friends of the shah who were high-ranking loyal officials. Neither the Nation nor People's parties nor the subsequently organized Independents offered the country more than the same traditional coalitions of landowners, merchants, and tribal leaders. None acquired a popular following and none could offer a program that could arouse popular enthusiasm.

Even this facade of parliamentary democracy was too much for the shah. In 1975 both the government Nation party and the loyal opposition, the People's party, were dissolved. In their place a single party system was decreed. A new Iran National Resurgence party (*Rastakhiz*) was formed to weld together all those who supported the shah's White Revolution with Iran's prime minister as secretary general.

The Tudeh. Although banned from overt political activity in 1949, the Tudeh (Masses) party formed in 1942 remains a potent political force. It was established by the leaders of the old Iranian Communist party whom Reza Shah had imprisoned. When released after the Allied occupation in 1941, they again seized the opportunity to participate in political life. Since northern Iran was occupied by the Soviet Union during the war, it was easy for the party to function there. Its strongly centralized organization and discipline gave the Tudeh a decided advantage over all other political groups. To avoid the impression of foreign control or revolutionary aims, Tudeh couched its official platform in liberal, rather than Communist, terms. Party influence reached the working class, clergy, minorities, and intelligentsia through numerous front groups disguised to serve the special interests of each. For a short period, most newspapers were controlled by the Tudeh through the Freedom Front, a coalition of periodicals created in 1943 that advocated liberal reform and support for the Soviet Union.

The Tudeh party was responsible for reviving the small remnants of the labor movement, which Reza Shah had banned, and in 1942 it united all labor unions. By 1945, the Tudeh-controlled Central United Council of Trade Unions claimed over a quarter of a million members and was able to organize the first effective petroleum strikes. Successful manipulation of several unions and front groups enabled the Tudeh to obtain three cabinet posts in 1946, but when Soviet attempts to seize Azerbaijan failed, the Tudeh party was discredited. After being implicated in a plot to assassinate the shah in 1949, the party and all its organs were banned—although Dr. Mosaddeq quietly continued to cooperate with its members. In 1954, investigations revealed that Communists were placed in several government departments and that 400 military officers were organized in a clandestine, Communist-led network. The Tudeh's greatest weakness is close affinity with the Soviet Union, a country most Iranians regard with more fear than respect because of repeated attempts during the past two centuries, under tsar and Communists alike, to take over all or parts of Iran.

After 1962 Iran became less of a constitutional monarchy and more of a one-man government under the shah. The Majlis was theoretically the people's voice, since any individual could submit to its special Petition Department criticism or complaints that had to be answered. However, with creation of the *Rastakhiz* in 1975, the Majlis lost even the token powers it had before.

Although the 1906 constitution authorized a Senate, it was never convened until 1950, when it became a device to strengthen the shah by weighting parliamentary influence in his favor. Half the 60-member Senate was elected by popular vote and the other half appointed by the shah from the "well-informed, discerning, pious, and respected persons of the realm." Tehran, the capital, supplied half the total number of senators, thus receiving a higher proportion of representatives than actually warranted by its population.

There were constitutional provisions limiting the shah's powers, but little question about his predominant position. He controlled the armed forces, selected half the Senate, and chose the prime minister. His friends and relatives occupied high positions throughout the administration. In national emergencies, the shah suspended the constitutional guarantees of individual rights and freedom of the press and information, or as was frequently the case, he merely ignored them. In constitutional theory, the shah reigned, but did not rule. After 1956, however, he chose to rule. Freedom was curtailed by the shah's secret police, the State Organization for Intelligence and Security (SAVAK), and government decisions were often personal and arbitrary.

SAVAK's activities became of major importance in consolidating the Shah's powers and in the decline of any seriously competitive political or social institutions. The Organization even operated abroad, against dissidents considered a threat to the regime. Its extensive arrests and use of torture aroused international concern. In 1974–75 Amnesty International estimated that there were between 25,000 and 100,000 political pironers in Iran. The secretary general of Amnesty International observed that: "The Shah of Iran retains his benevolent image despite the highest rate of death penalities in the world, no valid system of civilian courts and a history of torture which is beyond belief."

Even though the constitution has had little effect on the life of the average Iranian, it was constantly referred to in public speeches and in bazaar debates as a symbol of Westernization, and Constitution Day became one of the important national holidays. Its influence, however, was limited to the Westernized landowning aristocracy, the bazaar merchants, the urban intelligentsia, and a handful of religious leaders. The illiterate 90 percent of the population had not even a theoretical knowledge of their "rights." Peasant contact with the political process was the vote they cast for their landlord, the only candidate they ever knew of. While members of large tribes were in a somewhat better position, their vote also automatically went to the chief or his representative.

Political power was divided among the royal court, the landed aristocracy, the wealthy merchants, the religious leaders, and the army, with the shah as keystone in the whole structure. He became virtually omnipotent over potential rivals. Each group was a check to the others and each constantly shifted its support to suit its own convenience. The landed aristocrats, for example, successfully managed to block effective implementation of modest land reform legislation by controlling two thirds of the Majlis and virtually all of the Senate until the 1960s. After World War II, the growing middle class became considerably more influential on the political scene and was in large measure responsible for the modest reforms that were made.

ISLAM IN MODERN IRAN

Late in the nineteenth century, the Shi'ite hierarchy led opposition to the shah's money-raising scheme to turn Iran's tobacco industry over to European capitalists, and a boycott organized by the most revered Shi'ite leader forced thousands to give up smoking. The boycott demonstrated to Iranians the effectiveness of passive resistance as a political weapon. It is also noteworthy that without clerical backing, the 1906 constitutional movement would probably not have succeeded.

As a result of their role in the 1906 revolution, the clergy received special parliamentary representation and the constitution authorized the ulema to determine whether or not legislation was in accord with Islamic principles. A special committee of *mujtahids* (Shi'ite clergy) and theologians was appointed to consider all matters brought before the Majlis.

Reza Shah curtailed their authority during the 1920s and 1930s, although he was not antireligious, merely anticlerical. His aim was to curb their political power rather than to end the practice and social institutions of Islam. At one time, Reza Shah was reported to be considering establishment of a republic, but he abandoned the idea in deference to the Shi'ite divines. At the same time, however, Reza Shah permitted no outright clerical interference and forcefully resisted religious opposition to many of his measures, such as universal military training.

Nonetheless Reza Shah was compelled to pay deference to many of the mystical aspects of Shi'ism, a religion in which: "The natural union between religious mysticism and ritual—natural because everything irrational asks for expression in sign, symbol, and ceremony—throws down quite different roots into the souls of men than a faith consisting of a rationalistic conviction practiced only in the inner forum."[2] Although Reza Shah did not desire to destroy religion, he did not hesitate to attack systematically its forms of expression and symbolism in an effort to undermine clerical influence. For example, Dervishes (Muslim monks, see chapter 2), for centuries part of Iranian life, were ordered from the streets and country roads. Pilgrimages to Najaf and Karbala in Iraq, Shi'ism's two most holy shrines, were discouraged. Pressure was brought to bear on the mullahs, the Shi'ite religious teachers, to change to European dress. The flagellations accompanying the fanatic Shi'ite demonstration commemorating Husain's ('Ali's son) death were first banned, then outlawed. The demonstrations were at first replaced by public recitals of the tragedy, but a year later, recitals too were forbidden. All that remained was the custom of *rosekhaneh,* in which a black flag is hung from a home announcing that inside a priest will recite the "Passion of 'Ali and His House."

An indication of Shi'ism's changing status was the initial marriage between Crown Prince Muhammad Pahlavi and the Sunni sister of Egypt's King Farouk (although they were later divorced). Fifteen years earlier, the marriage would have been unthinkable, for it conflicted with a strict interpretation of the constitutional requirement demanding that the shah "must profess and propagate this [Shi'ite] faith." Some interpreted the marriage as a demonstration that the ancient barrier which cut off Shi'ite Iran from the Sunni world was being removed.

A blow to clerical power was confiscation of all pious foundations (awkaf), which were turned over to the Ministry of Education. (Shah Nadir, 1736–1760, had attempted to secularize ecclesiastical property, but the measures were reversed after his death.) Reza Shah used the confiscated revenue to create a new school system and to improve other public services. Depriving the clerics of their wakf possessions limited their political power and means of influencing the population, for they now had no income except that which they received from the government as state functionaries. The state also took from the mullahs the task of educating the clergy, and a government theological school was established at Tehran University, and modern studies and teaching methods were adopted.

A more fundamental change was the adoption of the French legal system in 1927. The trend toward secular law had begun after the 1906 constitutional reform, but there still existed a judicial dualism, dividing legal matters between secular and religious authorities. Initially, the constitution turned jurisdiction over family matters and religious property to the Sharia courts. But Reza Shah restricted the religious courts to a mere advisory role. Clerical judges were to have authority only in cases referred to them by civil courts. While Iranian law no longer required a citizen to be a Muslim, Shi'ism was in actual practice, still the "law of the land," and to be acceptable for high public office, it was necessary to be a member of that faith.

Reza Shah also removed ordinary education from clerical control and used the school system to undermine clerical influence by teaching secularism. Despite the influence of French and British military missions and Christian missionaries during the nineteenth century, clerical influence was still the strongest force in the school system. Neither the French, British, American, German, nor Russian educational institutions opened before World War I, nor the information collected by Iranian military missions in Europe, nor the military school opened at Tehran in 1852 greatly affected the tenor of the educational system. Most Iranians never received the opportunity to attend school, and those who did were taught in institutions where only religious subjects were taught.

Religious nationalism, linking loyalty to Iran with loyalty to Shi'ite Islam, was expressed in the zealotry of Mullah Kashani's partisans and was briefly revived during the Mosaddeq era from 1951 to 1953. Kashani forced the prime minister to authorize Muslim divines to scrutinize all bills according to a constitutional requirement. Finally Kashani's demands became so overbearing that Mosaddeq broke with him. No popular uprising followed and soon after Kashani passed into political obscurity.

To help balance off the strong undercurrents of Islamic influence and tradition, the shah played up the theme of Iran's pre-Islamic greatness. In 1971 (supposedly the 2,500th anniversary of the Persian monarchy), an international festival of sumptuous dimensions was staged. Costs of the celebrations were estimated between $50 million and $300 million. A statement of the kingdom's Persianness was made in 1975 when Iran's calendar was changed from the Muslim date based on the flight of Muhammad from Mecca, to the time when Cyrus the Great established the first Persian empire 1,180 years earlier. Thus the year became 2535 instead of 1355. All of these measures so alienated the Shi'ite clergy and popular consciousness that opinion rapidly rose against the shah, and he in turn intensified repression of dissidence, bringing matters to a head in 1979 (see following).

THE PROBLEMS OF ECONOMIC DEVELOPMENT

Agriculture

Iran, like its neighboring countries in the Middle East, is still today and will remain for decades an underdeveloped country. The prevailing poverty is a product of both natural and social forces. Except for the vast oil reserves, Iran has few natural resources. (In 1967 Iran was the second largest producer of oil in the Middle East and the fourth largest in the world.) Despite the country's great income from oil, however, little has changed in the life of the average Iranian.

The most serious problem is the inadequate supply of arable land and water, the two requirements for building a basic economy. Only a tenth of the area (the total being about a fifth that of the continental United States) is arable. Seven-tenths is mountain or desert and two-tenths forest and grazing land. Mountain ranges, with peaks reaching over 18,000 feet, crisscross the country, making communications and transport difficult.

There are no great rivers. Water shortages and poor soil result in up to two thirds of the cultivable land lying fallow each year. Water is so scarce that it is a source of capital and often considered more important property than soil. Since most land is useless unless irrigated, ownership usually means control of the water supply and frequently farmers have fought over its use. There are also the problems of land tenure, insects and pests, primitive methods and implements, poor health undermining the population's vitality, and the heavy hand of tradition that binds the peasant to outmoded and unscientific farming techniques. The net result is low productivity, a high rate of rural underemployment and the massive influx of peasants to the cities.

Between 1960 and 1980 urban population increased from about a third to more than half, and agricultural production decreased so that Iran had to import much of its food.

Of the 40 percent of the population remaining in agriculture by 1979, less than half owned their own farms. The rest were tenant sharecroppers who lived in perpetual debt at a subsistence level. In theory, agricultural income was divided into five parts: land, water, seed, animals or power, and labor. The supplier of each part received a fifth of the crop. Since most peasants could supply only labor, they received but a fifth of the crop and borrowed at usurious rates to pay for the other four-fifths. Few landlords took direct responsibility for managing their estates and villages. Frequently they sold rent-collecting rights to the highest bidder, who then took as much as he could from tenants. Peasant insecurity discouraged any long-term agricultural investments or major efforts to improve land.

Industry

Since oil has been discovered, there has been a shift of rural population to urban centers. But only about a third of the population is employed in industry. Half these work in small shops and homecrafts, such as carpet-making and handloom weaving. Reza Shah began an all-out effort to industrialize the country's economy in 1930. He called upon the Majlis to make the 1930 session renowned in history as the "economic parliament." A National Economy Ministry was established to direct the drive and regulate national economic life. Since no private capital was readily available, most of it being invested in land, the government itself capitalized various projects, such as textile industries, sugar-refining plants, and monopolies on the import and export of products ranging from matches and animal products to motor vehicles. By the late 1930s, the government controlled a third of all imports and 44 percent of all exports, investing its profits in new plant construction.

Reza Shah's economic schemes were undermined by the world depression and by the failure of Iranian society to cope successfully with modern industry. Nepotism, overstaffing, reluctance to take responsibility or to show initiative, and lack of administrative and technical competence led to collapse of the modernization efforts.

The prevailing tax and administrative system actually discouraged private initiative. Subordinate clerks mismanaged the Finance Ministry despite the honesty of higher officials, and graft and tax evasion were commonplace. The amount government received from a taxpayer depended less on ability to pay then upon bargaining powers with the collector who could assess property at 100 to 200 percent of the actual value. Some rich merchants kept three sets of books, one each for the tax collector, business acquaintances, and themselves. Family connections and political influence often exempted the aristocracy from payment. A list of tax delinquents, including members of the royal family, cabinet, and Senate, was published in

1949 but then totally ignored, becoming a national joke. This system not only discouraged foreign investment but drove local capital out of the country.

Reform

Attempts to reform and develop the economy and to utilize the great oil revenues lagged far behind national requirements. A major obstacle was the reluctance of the landed aristocracy to make the required sacrifices. Until the 1962 land reform the shah had made only a modest beginning by selling royal lands at a fifth of their value to peasant occupants. Even this minimum program required no great sacrifice, since the imperial estates, estimated to cover 750,000 acres, including over 1670 villages with nearly a million occupants, were seized by Reza Shah from the aristocracy. After World War II, when the courts began to examine the legality of ownership, hearings proved so embarassing to the royal family that they were suspended.

The strongest advocates of reform were the landless middle class and the bazaar merchants. Despite extensive parliamentary discussion, the many new resolutions, regulations, and statutes were not enforced and there was no serious land-reform legislation until 1962. Since landlords controlled parliament, they blocked even token projects, fearing that once the door was opened a crack, it would be forced all the way. In January 1962, a land reform law termed "revolutionary," was adopted by the cabinet. It restricted the ownership of each landlord to only one village. The rest was to be sold to landless peasants on long-term installments, and the landlord was to be "equitably" compensated by the government. At first, the government announced, the law would be applied to landlords who owned more than five villages. This would affect some 10,000 of Iran's 45,000 to 50,000 villages. Later the law would apply to the 7000 villages belonging to landlords with more than one or less than five villages.

To achieve the reforms proposed in his "White Revolution," the shah appointed as prime minister one of his chief critics, Dr. Ali Amini. Because many of the envisaged policies were calculated to arouse the conservatives' wrath, the country was placed under martial law, and parliament was dissolved in 1961, so that royal decrees became law backed only by the shah's signature and enforced by the security establishment.

In broad outline the reforms, or "White Revolution," emphasized twelve points for economic and social development of the country: 1) land reform, 2) nationalization of forests and pastures, 3) public sale of state-owned factories to finance land reform, 4) profit sharing in industry, 5) revision of the electoral law to include women, 6) establishment of a literacy corps, 7) a health corps, 8) and a reconstruction and development corps, 9) rural courts of justice, 10) nationalization of the waterways, 11) national reconstruction, 12) educational and administrative revolution.

The new prime minister took stern measures against the widespread political corruption and economic chaos in the country. Several former high government officials and top army officers were brought to trial to account for their mismanagement or misuse of funds. Restrictions were placed on government expenditures and on import of luxury goods.

The body of measures known as the "White Revolution" was systematized in 1963 to "become the creed of the Shah and the Iranian political elite. By 1970 it stood as an important ideology against which the Shah justified his activities and his rule. It is anathema and dangerous to criticize or question the principles of the White Revolution; the most serious accusation that can be made against someone, other than portraying him as an enemy of the Shah, is to present him as an enemy of the White Revolution. This situation has seriously impeded detailed and objective analysis of the implementation of the reform."[3]

The land reform measures aroused the most opposition among the traditionalist estate owners, and the conservative clergy who feared loss of wakf lands. By 1964 it was estimated that about a fifth of the rural population had received some land which was allocated from 12,000 to 13,000 villages (out of some 50,000) that had been redistributed. A second phase of the reform permitted owners to retain a maximum of 30 to 150 hectares of nonmechanized lands. The rest could be disposed of by renting, selling, forming joint stock companies with peasants, or by other means prescribed in the law. Because of the great variety of ways in which the reform was carried out and the diverse quality of land distributed, it was difficult to estimate the effect of the land reform on the peasants. According to a United Nations survey, probably not more than 15 percent of the country's peasants got enough land to support themselves or to increase their living standards substantially. Only a third of these became actual owners. The others became leaseholders or share-owners.

Accompanying the land reform were other measures intended to raise peasant living standards. A Literacy Corps, later renamed the Education Corps, of several thousands students was organized to work with villagers. Its goal was to cut the rate of illiteracy from 80 to 50 percent within the decade. Since nearly half the country's children were receiving no schooling, this was a major priority. The corpsmen were recruited from students of military draft age, and those eligible for the army were released from army service to work in the villages. Likewise, a Health Corps and a Rural Extension Development Corps were sent to rural areas to assist in achieving development goals. In Khuzistan province several experimental programs were planned, including establishment of agro-businesses based on huge irrigated farms, petrochemical industries to utilize the country's oil, and steel plants based on coal and iron deposits believed to exist in the country.

A new innovation, intended to compete with agricultural cooperatives, was the farm-corporation, in which the farmer became a shareholder but lost management rights. In Khuzistan the agricultural corporations met resistance from conservative farmers who were reluctant to sell their traditional family plots to an agrobusiness.

Division of the shah's estates was not very successful. Peasants who acquired shares of the former royal estates knew little about the most fundamental agricultural techniques, such as crop rotation or planting times. Without extensive government programs for education, credit, and cooperative development, surrender of large estates did little to improve the peasant lot. The village moneylender and others who controlled village life continued to do so.

The Iranian Plan Organization was established to utilize 60 percent of oil revenues for national development in 1948. But its seven- and five-year plans concentrated more on great engineering schemes than on social change. It successfully completed dams, hydroelectric plants, irrigation systems in arid regions, and drainage in swamp areas. West German and American experts also lent assistance, and a five-year contract was signed in March 1956 with the American Development and Resources Corporation (Clapp-Lilienthal) to develop Khuzistan in southern Iran.

Long before the 1979 Revolution Coyler Young observed that the aristocracy, the top stratum of society, was still reluctant to share power with the urban middle class, which was becoming increasingly frustrated and angered by what they considered to be betrayal of Iran to the traditional vested interests. In short, the aristocracy feared that partnership with the middle class

> might involve its own "toppling"—that to share its prestige and power might endanger the nation's stability and security. In short, society's top does not trust the bottom, and even less the awakened and aware middle. The heart of Iran's problem is the need for revolutionary *and* responsible leadership; how to traverse the distance from a traditional paternalism to modern industrialism, how to bridge the gulf of mistrust that has developed between modern tinkerers with tradition and rebels against that tradition, how to transmit power from the small, habitual élite to the substantial, untested middle sector of society, and how to effect this in a disturbed and dynamic world in which the country's integrity and independence are ever in peril.[4]

IRAN AS A REGIONAL POWER

At the root of Iranian politics, both domestic and foreign, was the Shah's overriding ambition to make his country the dominant regional power. This required not only the position of primacy in the Gulf, but in areas beyond—by sea into the Indian Ocean and by land into the Middle East and southwest Asia. On more than one occasion he spoke of his goal to achieve status, both economic and political, equal to that of France and Germany by the 1980s and perhaps equal to the world's most advanced powers by the end of the century. In one statement he described two nations as the most important for the "Free World" in Asia—Japan in the Far East and Iran in the Middle East.

He shaped the country's internal economic development and its political institutions with these ambitions in mind. Iran's major resources, including a substantial part of oil revenues, were devoted to these aspirations. Through the "White Revolution," the "Great Iranian Civilization" would be revived. The shah's far-reaching foreign policies reflected his belief that he was "chosen by God" to perform the task of replacing European empires that once dominated the region.

Grandiose ambitions led the shah into a semialliance with Israel involving exchange of technical information, military equipment and training, with Iranian oil shipped directly to the Jewish state. The shah perceived Israel as an obstacle to Soviet subversion and expansion in the Middle East and to the militant leftist Arab regimes with which Iran has feuded.

Relations with the Arab states varied from the brink of war with Iraq, to a cool friendship with Saudi Arabia. The more radical an Arab regime, the more it was perceived as a threat. Thus Saudi Arabia, with its conservative monarchy was an acceptable junior partner in policing the Gulf and its approaches. But in OPEC meetings during the 1970s Iran strongly urged a rapid escalation in prices whereas Saudi Arabia urged only modest increases.

Iran's policies in the Gulf caused apprehension for even the conservative Arab regimes. Threats to take over Bahrain based on nineteenth-century claims were dissipated in 1970 when the shah announced that he would accept a United Nations report stating that the overwhelming majority of Bahrainis favored independence. But all the region's Arab states were incensed when Iran occupied three tiny strategic islands in the Straits of Hormuz between the Persian Gulf and the Gulf of Oman during 1970. Fears of leftist engulfment led to direct intervention by Iranian troops in Oman where they assisted the monarch to suppress the Dhofar rebellion by leftist tribal groups.

The most serious confrontation was with Iraq, the only Arab country with which Iran has a common border. After nearly erupting into war, the series of territorial, water, boundary, and ideological disputes were resolved or suspended in an agreement signed by the shah and Iraq during an OPEC meeting held in Algiers during 1975. The Algiers agreement lasted only five years, until after overthrow of the shah, when Iraq's leader, Saddain Husain, decided to renew the historic conflict. Taking advantage of turmoil in Iran, he invaded in 1980 with the intent to establish Iraqi supremacy in the Gulf, but his plans were thwarted by Iran's military resistance.

By 1975 Iran had become the largest single purchaser of U.S. military equipment with sales totaling over $15 billion between 1972 and 1978. The purchases were made possible by the fivefold increase in oil prices after 1973. The oil boom also extended the shah's global outreach by facilitating major arms and economic deals with the large countries of Western Europe, including acquisition by Iran of a 25 percent interest in Krupp, Germany's largest steel plant.

These foreign relationships and their domestic effects often created the illusion that Iran had already become a power. However, according to a study by the U.S. Senate in 1976, the appearance was deceptive. Iran had not become more independent or powerful, rather, it had increased its long term dependence on the United States. The Senate report observed that Iran "lacks the technical, educational, and industrial base to provide the necessary trained personnel and management capabilities to operate such...[military] establishment effectively."[5]

THE 1979 REVOLUTION

By the late 1970s it was becoming increasingly evident to the shah and his entourage that neither the reforms of the "White Revolution" nor the repression of SAVAK could stem the rising tide of discontent. A first overt acknowledgement of the situation was the shah's replacement during 1977 of Prime Minister Amir Abbas Hoveida, who had held the post since 1965. However, events were moving more rapidly than superficial change could cope with. Labor troubles were spreading, student protests erupted at the universities, and the clergy was more openly flouting the authorities. By 1978 the strikes and unrest slashed oil production and crippled the economy causing sharp cutbacks in government expenditures. Although the shah had already decreased his military budget to make money available to increase the salaries of civil servants and to expand public housing, the oil shutdown undermined these plans. In a desperate effort to save the regime, the shah changed prime ministers four times between mid-1977 and the end of 1978, to no avail.

Opposition to the regime broke out in mass urban demonstrations during 1978 leading to frequent clashes between security forces and protesters with thousands of casualties. Diverse groups openly showed their disapproval of the government. Workers in the cities and oil fields, although better off than a decade earlier, resented the growing gap between their living standards and the ostentatious luxury of the upper class, especially of the royal family whose imperial life style was flaunted openly. The shah's ban on labor unions only intensified hostility and resentment. Students and intellectuals objected to suppression of the press and scholarly journals; to the exile or imprisonment of many prominent Iranian writers, artists, and film makers; and to control of the universities by SAVAK. Remnants of the old nationalist movement felt humiliated by Iran's growing dependence on tens of thousands of foreign technicians and advisors and to their growing visibility in major urban centers. To many it seemed that, despite the shah's grandiose schemes for regional supremacy, Iran was becoming a satellite of the United States. The middle class bazaar merchants suffered both economic decline and psychological trauma because of the so-called reforms. Many were undermined by competition from the new state enterprises created to "modernize" the economy. Furthermore, as traditionalists, many in the bazaar felt disgraced by the influx of Westerners and their life styles introduced by the country's leaders. Their opposition was stimulated by nationalist and religious, as well as by economic resentments. The old aristocracy, whose lands were seized by the shah's father, Reza Shah, still waited for revenge against the Pahlavis, and many would eagerly support opposition to the upstart regime.

The most important center of unrest was the Shi'ite clergy, which became the focal point of opposition; its leader, the Ayatollah Khomeini, living in exile since 1963, became the symbol of opposition and the chief instigator of the movement that toppled the shah in 1979. Although the Pahlavis had successfully undercut the power of the clergy, they had failed to destroy its links to the rural and urban masses or to end the moral and financial support it received from traditionalists in the middle and lower middle classes. Despite Khomeini's exile and repression of many other leading clerics, their influence remained strong (Khomeini's leadership continued from abroad through taped sermons and politico-religious discourses smuggled into the country). He, like most of the clerical leadership was perceived as a personality of great learning, integrity, and simply life style in contrast to the irreligious, spendthrift, cruel shah. The clergy represented the grass roots while the shah personified foreign corruption. Within the religious establishment there was an extensive social welfare system providing for the needy; its managers were regarded as the guardians of social justice and morality. This network provided the informal organizations for opposition to the shah; its prayer meetings in mosques and private homes were the centers of subversion, attended, not only by the pious, but by ever-increasing numbers of other politically disaffected.

Clerical leadership against the regime was not a new phenomenon. In modern times the Shi'ite clergy was known for opposition to secular tyranny. It had played a leading role in opposition to foreign economic concessions during the Kajar dynasty in the nineteenth century and in the constitutional movement at the beginning of the twentieth. During the 1960s it was Khomeini's open denunciation of the shah's economic agreements with the

U.S. that led to his exile. By 1978 when the shah began to retreat in his war against the clergy it was too late; too many clerics had been tortured, exiled, and killed for its establishment to compromise.

By the beginning of 1979 even Shahpur Bakhtiar, a former National Front leader and longtime foe of the monarch appointed prime minister by the shah as a major concession to his opponents, was unacceptable to the clergy. The fact that he was an appointee of the hated monarch was enough to disqualify Bakhtiar in the eyes of the mullahs and their allies. At this juncture, in January 1979, the Shah decided to leave Iran for an extended "vacation." Although not a formal abdication, his departure brought to an end 37 years of his rule and for all practical purposes ended the Pahlavi dynasty in Iran.

Several days after the shah's departure, Ayatollah Khomeini returned from exile in France where he had formed the Council of the Islamic Revolution. Khomeini was received with wild enthusiasm and quickly established his personal absolute authority in the capital and in many other parts of the country. A first political act was to appoint Mehdi Bazargan as a provisional prime minister, parallel to the official Bakhtiar government which Khomeini refused to recognize. Bakhtiar resigned in less than a week, leaving Khomeini and his associates in full command of the government. On April 1, Khomeini formally proclaimed the Islamic Republic of Iran under jurisdiction of his Islamic Council for the Revolution. For the next half-year Bazargan's government was forced to share power with the Revolutionary Council, but as the clerics arrogated increasing authority, the anti-shah coalition began to fall apart. Tension increased between the civil government and the clerical Revolutionary Council until Bazargan's government fell in November and the Council assumed full command.

Even before the civil government collapsed in November, the Revolutionary Council had established a Revolutionary Tribunal in Tehran to conduct secret trials and executions of former officials, military officers, and SAVAK agents in the shah's regime. Elsewhere in the country Revolutionary Guards organized *Komitehs* (local security organizations) to carry out local purges and to impose authority of the new regime. Many harsh measures taken against those who contravened Islamic law and the severity and precipitousness of the revolutionary trials aroused wide opposition among many former Khomeini supporters. One minister in Bazargan's cabinet resigned in protest against the Revolutionary Council's "despotism," and a leading Ayatollah charged Khomeini with "dictatorship." Opposition groups, formerly allies of Khomeini, organized underground death squads to assassinate members of the Revolutionary Council. In the more distant parts of Iran there was a resurgence of ethnic rebellion among the Kurds, Turkomen, and Azerbaijanis. Although Khomeini's authority was entrenched in Tehran and in several other large cities, much of the country was in turmoil and unresponsive to the new Islamic regime.

A major change was introduction of a new Islamic constitution, approved by a 60 to 1 margin in a December 1979 referendum. The constitution emphasized Iran's Islamic character and gave priority to Shi'ite law and institutions. It established a 12-member Council of Guardians, or Leadership Council, headed by a religious leader with supreme authority over all branches of government to assure that all legislation comply with Shi'ite Islamic principles. The supreme leader, called *Faghi* (trustee or guardian) was to act in place of the twelfth Shi'ite imam who disappeared 1,100 years ago and who Shi'ites believe will return one day. According to the new constitution: "During the absence of the Glorious Lord of the Age, the twelfth imam...he will be represented in the Islamic Republic of Iran as religious leader and imam of the people by an honest, virtuous, well-informed, courageous, efficient administrator and religious jurist, enjoying the confidence of the majority of the people as a leader." The first Faghi under the republic was Ayatollah Khomeini, already in his eighties.

The Faghi was endowed with almost absolute powers, above the president or any of the legislative and judicial authorities; he was to command the armed forces, appoint and dismiss heads of the army and Islamic Revolutionary Guards Corps; he had power to declare war and mobilize the armed forces, to improve all presidential candidates, to formalize the president's election, and to dismiss the president at will.

The army, according to the constitution "...must be an Islamic army. It must be a popular and religiously educated army and it must accept worthy people who will be faithful to the goals of the Islamic Revolution and will be self-sacrificing in the attainment of these goals."

Emphasizing the Koranic injunction that followers of the Prophet conduct communal business by "consultation among themselves," the new Majlis was called the National Consultative Assembly or *Majlis ash-shura,* to carry out Islamic law. However the document did reserve several seats for non-Muslim minorities including Zoroastrians, Jews, and Assyrian, Chaldean, and Armenian Christians. Bahais, considered a heretical sect, were given no representation. Instead they were ruthlessly persecuted; many were executed and hundreds imprisoned.

Elections were held for Iran's first president and the new Majlis during 1980 to further legitimize the new regime and its Islamic constitution. However, the results only caused more political fragmentation and intensified the civil war between pro- and anti-Khomeini forces. Abdol Hasan Bani-Sadr, an intellectual who had been close to Khomeini in exile, was elected with more than 75 percent of the vote, but his rather broad world-views and liberal interpretation of Islamic doctrines soon led to confrontation with the conservative Shi'ite clerics, now organized in the Islamic Republican Party (IRP) established in 1979. Bani-Sadr represented the educated civil servants, university faculties, and army officers in contrast to the IRP, which rallied the hard line traditionalists, the bazaar establishment, the lower-middle-class and the poorest, formerly disenfranchised sectors of society.

Tensions developed between Bani-Sadr and the traditionalists over internal and foreign policy, symbolized by disagreements concerning seizure of the U.S. embassy in Tehran by a throng of zealous young students during November 1979. Although not officially approved, the event became a touchstone of Iran's new-won "independence from American imperialism." Moderates in the regime represented by Bani-Sadr finally negotiated release of the 66 American hostages after 444 days, but the affair helped to undermine his status as a staunch supporter of Khomeini.

Bani-Sadr was a disciple of Ali Shariati, considered by many to be the major influence on young intellectuals in the revolutionary movement. Shariati was both an ardent Shi'ite and a modernist who blended traditionalism with progressive economic and social concepts. He believed that Iran's culture was subverted by Western ideas—the malady of "Westoxication." Neither capitalist liberalism nor Marxist or socialist doctrines, but Muhammad's ideal society should serve as the model for Iran. Shi'ite influence was manifest in his belief that the Ummayads began the decadance of Islam. Shariati distinguished between "Alid Shi'ism" (from Muhammad's son-in-law Ali, the first Imam) and "Safavid Shi'ism." The Islam of Ali, the original Islam, represented progress and revolution; it was the Islam of the people. The Safavids who made Shi'ism the state religion politicized and degraded the religion (the latter day heir of "Safavid Shi'ism" was "Pahlavi Shi'ism"). Western democracy, he asserted, was rotten and decadent, divested of humanism, therefore no model for Islamic peoples. Only "Alid Shi'ism" and the ideal community of Muhammad could save Iran.

Bani-Sadr attempted to introduce his own refinements in the form of an Islamic economic system emphasizing social justice, but the short period of his presidency was so full of turmoil and chaos that he lost power before implementing his program. The showdown came in a constitutional crisis during 1981 when Bani-Sadr refused to sign legislation passed by the Majlis. Although at first neutral in the confrontation, Khomeini finally sided with the zealots in parliament against Bani-Sadr whom he denounced as a "corrupt person on earth." The president was first deprived of his authority over the armed forces, a post in which he gained popularity as a result of the war with Iraq. Then in July 1981 after parliament declared Bani-Sadr politically incompetent, Khomeini dismissed him from the presidency. Already in hiding, Bani-Sadr soon reappeared in Paris where he became a leader of the new anti-Kohomeini and anti-IRP coalition of republican, royalist, and other groups.

The fall of Bani-Sadr further polarized Iran's revolutionary movements between the IRP and its supporters versus several of the old anti-shah nationalists and socialist-oriented Islamic factions. Despite propagation of the most fundamentalist Shi'ite radical doctrines, the IRP maintained a working relationship with the Tudeh until 1980, although hundreds of leftists were purged from government because of their "atheism." During the 1979 Majlis elections, only the IRP, Tudeh, Fedayeen al-Khalq, and Mujaheddin al-Khalq participated while the National Front, National Democratic Front, Muslim People's Republican Party, and Arab and Kurdish parties boycotted the balloting. By 1982 the new regime had replaced SAVAK with its own security apparatus, SAVAMA, and was cited by Amnesty International for more official executions during the preceeding three years than in all other countries combined.

There was little economic progress during the first years of the revolution because of cutbacks in oil production to about a tenth of that during the peak years under the shah. Revolutionary ideology strongly militated against the import of foreign machines, luxuries, technicians, and advisors. Rather, the ideal was to strive for self-sufficiency, to cut Iran's dependence on Western goods, methods, and personnel, even if it meant a sharp decline in living standards for the few who had benefited under the shah. After all, only a relatively small number of Iranians had profited from the "White Revolution" and the shah's modernization programs. Whereas the aristocracy and the old elites under the shah were shorn of power and affluence after 1979, a whole new substratum that had been invisible before the revolution emerged from the hovels on the outskirts of Tehran, Shiraz, Izfahan, and other urban centers. Both in large cities and in many rural areas this formerly disenfranchised "non-class," so poor that it was not even called "working-class," emerged as *vox populi,* the backbone of IRP support, of Khomeini zealotry, and of revolutionary Shi'ite folk Islam.

The importance of this phenomenon reached beyond Iran, for Khomeini's message appealed not only to Shi'ites but to Muslim lower classes throughout the area. It appealed especially to the imported workers in oil rich neighbors like Saudi Arabia, Kuwait, and Bahrain. The Ayatollah's call in 1979 to "all oppressed Muslim peoples" to "overthrow the corrupt and tyrannical governments in the Islamic world" and for Islam "to rise against the great powers to annihilate their agents" was worrisome to the conservative neighboring regimes. Thus Jordan's King Husain and the Saud dynasty gave eager support to Iraq in its war with Iran after 1980. Furthermore, the war split the Arab world between the conservatives who backed Iraq, despite its secular-socialist orientations, and the Arab radicals like Syria, Libya, and South Yemen who supported fundamentalist Shi'ite Iran. Khomeini and the IRP replaced the grandiose vision of the shah for a secular empire in the region with the vision of an Islamic revival that would destroy the "corrupt and wicked" and lift up the "poor and oppressed."

NOTES

1.   Cuyler Young, "Iran in Continuing Crisis," *Foreign Affairs,* vol. 40, no. 2 (January 1962), pp. 286–287.

2.   William S. Haas, *Iran,* New York, 1946, p. 154.

3.   James A. Bill & Carl Leiden,. *The Middle East Politics and Power,* Allyn and Bacon, Boston, 1974, p. 138.

4.   Young, *op. cit.,* pp. 284–285.

5.   *U.S. Military Sales to Iran,* 1976, U.S. Senate, 94th Congress, 2nd session, U.S. Government Printing Office, Washington, D.C.

18   Epilogue

Throughout the preceding chapters we have seen that within the Middle East there are many unifying factors that have shaped its historical and political development; yet there is a diversity within the area, a diversity of geography, languages, religions, cultures, and racial and ethnic groups, which also has greatly influenced the area's contemporary image. While the unifying factors, principally the Islamic and Iranian-Ottoman past, have been responsible for many common characteristics of these countries, the diversity within the region has created quite distinctive characteristics that separate them from each other.

Since the end of the nineteenth century, all of these countries have been strongly influenced by the Western world, yet few have successfully adapted themselves to Western political and social systems, and today several are moving away from development of Western institutions. The reasons for this trend and the factors that are significant in the Middle East today should be explored.

The common Islamic heritage of all Middle Eastern countries remains the most influential factor in contemporary society. Even in the most Western and certainly least Muslim nation, Israel, matters of family status (divorce, marriage, inheritance) are still strongly influenced by Muslim institutions inherited by the new state from the Ottoman past and preserved for the most part by the British mandate. Strangely enough, other, no-so-Westernized nations such as Egypt and Turkey have abandoned religious controls over these matters; but in these nations Islam pervades the consciousness and attitudes of their citizenry.

The centuries-old rift beteen Sunni and Shi'ite Muslims still affects political life in the region. In Iraq, Lebanon, and Syria, this antagonism is a strong divisive force.

When Napoleon appeared in Egypt at the beginning of the nineteenth century, Islam was the dominant political and social force throughout the Middle East. The concept of separation between church and state was still unknown in the region, and all governmental institutions were Islamic institutions at one and the same time. With the exception of Iran and the remoter areas of Arabia, all of the countries with which this book has dealt were formally governed by the Ottoman sultan-caliph, although the extent of his authority varied from region to region. Iran was also governed by a Shi'ite Islamic hierarchy headed by a shah, the titular descendant of 'Ali. In central Arabia, the Wahabi religious revival was stirring the Sauds to re-establish a purified Islamic fundamentalist society.

In the more advanced Iranian and Ottoman territories there were superimposed upon and blended with the Islamic society, Ottoman and Persian administrative institutions, many of which still remain. For example, many of the territorial administrative boundaries within the Middle East today are vestiges of the former Ottoman hegemony. Remnants of Ottoman millet law still prevail in Lebanon, Israel, and Iraq. Ottoman legal terminology is still characteristic of the codes of many Middle Eastern nations that were at one time under Ottoman rule.

When Napoleon established his military administration in Egypt, he introduced modifications and revisions into the prevailing Islamic-Iranian-Ottoman system that were to prove of long-term significance. His innovations were followed by increasing Western contacts and gradual adoption of European law, constitutions, parliamentary institutions, and administrative apparatus throughout the area. Motivation for the changes reflected both internal and external situations. To begin with, the Muslim Middle East gradually lost its former self-confidence and sense of superiority toward the "effete" Christian West, for the area found it increasingly difficult to ward off Western intrusions. In fact, many Middle Easterns came to believe the continued existence of their traditional ways of life depended upon the good graces of those Western nations they had formerly regarded with contempt. In their search for an answer to this dilemma, Middle Eastern leaders thought that they found the solution in the adoption of Western governmental institutions, in the introduction of Western administration, and in the use of Western military equipment and organization. Perhaps, it was thought, if they too could make use of these innovations by which the West had overcome and defeated Islamic society, that society could save itself from further disintegration and degradation.

Initial attempts to use Western military devices and tactics soon led the ruling elite to discover that the effective use of Western military apparatus required the adoption of many elements of Western civil organization. Thus, adoption of Western education, hospitals, health services, fiscal reforms, and administrative systems, soon followed, replacing bit by bit aspects of the old Islamic-Iranian-Ottoman society. In Turkey, the Tanzimat era blossomed from initial attempts to reform the army, resulting in extensive legal, administrative, and parliamentary changes. Similarly, the schemes of Muhammad 'Ali and later Ismail the Magnificent to revolutionize Egypt grew from seeds already planted by early military reforms.

External pressures also played a prominent role in changing Middle Eastern society, especially in the Ottoman Empire. Western European nations, seeking to keep the tottering empire intact, also sponsored administrative and parliamentary changes, hoping to revitalize the foundering Ottoman regime. It was believed that Westernizing the government would curtail, if not eliminate, the traditional corruption, nepotism, and intrigue that had sapped the strength of Eastern governments. Therefore, during the mid-nineteenth century the West put increasing pressures upon the Ottoman sultans to "modernize." In this way pressure from within, on the part of indigenous liberals, and from without, fostered by the West, brought about the adoption of various reforms. These measures included laws equalizing the status of Muslims and non-Muslims, financial and legal changes, and new tax systems.

By the beginning of the twentieth century, a superficial kind of Westernization was well on the way. In the more advanced countries of the region, like Egypt, Turkey, and Lebanon, there already were liberal infusions of Western-type laws and administrative practices. However, the effects of these reforms reached only a handful of people, and traditional Oriental society remained unchanged at its roots. The sultan-caliph and age-old Sunni-Ottoman institutions were still supreme in Turkey, and the shah and Shi'ite ulema still dominated Iran.

Changes that occurred as a result of attempts at Westernization did little to alter the relationships between the landowning class and the peasant masses, or to increase the distribution of profits from the nation's resources. Those who ruled Middle Eastern society had never intended that the nineteenth- and early twentieth-century reforms should alter these relationships. Indeed their motivation in introducing such reforms had been to help them preserve their society and the basic relationship between those at the top and the masses below. At most, the power concentrated in the hands of the chief-of-state was to be shared with the elite, not extended to the middle and lower classes. Until the end of World War I, only the elite were represented in the growing government bureaucracies, parliaments, and cabinets of the Westernizing regimes, and they consciously used their new governmental systems to help preserve the existing social system. Tenant-landowner relationships were not disturbed: education was retricted to the well-to-do (extending learning to the peasants would only cultivate insurrection); and the religious organization of the village remained as it had been for centuries. Throughout the Middle East, village life—the life of some four out of five of its population—continued at its traditional pace and in its traditional forms, unaffected by Westernization in the larger towns and cities.

Concentration of the Western reform movement at the top of society meant that much of the reform was rootless, even artificial. Of what value could parliamentary systems be with no effective political parties or meaningful electoral laws? Often Western legal codes were adopted without lawyers or judges to administer them, and courts were opened to which the vast majority had no access. Progress was most genuine and effective in the use of modern administrative techniques and in government reorganization. In Egypt, for example, the British built up an extensive and relatively efficient civil service.

Even reforms that affected only the top level of society were not accepted without a struggle. Many fought each new innovation as though it was a matter of life and death. Conservatives often sabotaged what they could of the new measures; they wished to continue their traditional rule in their traditional way.

However, the greatest obstacle to Westernization was not created in a calculated effort by a specific group. The greatest obstacle was Oriental society itself. There did not as yet exist in the Middle East a national consciousness as had developed in the various European nations. There was yet no strong Egyptian, Iranian, Turkish, or Arab national feeling. The ideas of modern nationalism and the nation-state were familiar only to a handful of Western-educated intellectuals. For most Middle Easterners the basis of society was the family, and family or clan loyalty was the highest ideal. Nepotism, bribery, and intrigue were accepted forms of behavior in government. Traditional authority, centralized in the family, was the basis of discipline, not the state or society at large.

Beyond the settled regions, which at the beginning of this century comprised only a fraction of the Middle East, law and order were little known. Cutting across the pattern of family loyalties were intergroup hostilities such as those between Muslim and Christian, Shi'ite and Sunni, nomad tribes and urban areas.

The incipient national movements that emerged by the end of World War I in Egypt, Iran, Turkey, and the Arab countries represented only a tiny urban minority, composed primarily of those who came from the upper strata of society. Their chief aim was to rid their countries or districts of foreigners and to share power among themselves. Few showed any concern for the economic and social ills that burdened the countryside and the city slums.

After World War I the newly developing middle classes often became an important element in the burgeoning national movements, for they felt that only by ridding themselves of foreign economic domination could they prosper. Those army officers and civil servants who were frustrated by the lack of opportunity for advancement under foreign rule or students aroused by promises of a better life under their own leaders also became active nationalists.

Few leaders had any well-worked-out program for achieving national status or for developing indigenous political institutions. Most of them hoped to superimpose upon their governments copies of institutions with which they had become familiar as students in Western schools. They gave little consideration to whether or not these institutions were indeed serviceable in the Middle East.

During the interwar era, clashes developed between the new generation of Western-educated, middle-class nationalists and their conservative elders. The younger generation was more eager to emulate "modern" techniques and to abandon traditional forms of society. Few of the post-World War I nationalist leaders had intimate ties with the old religious hierarchy. The new nationalism tended to be secular, although it frequently used old Islamic symbols to rally mass approval. The Wafd party in Egypt and the People's Republican party (PRP) in Turkey avoided religious appeals, the former because it desired to include Egyptian Christians and the latter because of a conviction that Islamic institutions were "reactionary."

Although the new nationalist leaders were eager to use Western political forms—often perhaps because they indicated a "modern" approach—few desired to alter fundamental social relationships. Thus Western-type parliaments, political parties, and other institutions were adopted not only to increase the power of the rising middle class, but also to keep political power from the hands of the peasantry and urban proletariat.

In the French and British mandated territories (French Syria and Lebanon; British Iraq, Palestine, and Transjordan) constitutional and administrative forms were introduced in accord with the League of Nations requirement that self-government be extended to native peoples, and because of the growing demands of the nationalists. In Syria and Lebanon, France introduced French systems of government and administration; and in Iraq and Transjordan, Great Britain set up systems modeled on those of England or of British colonies.

Great Britain and France were concerned less with extending democracy, however, than with preserving their respective spheres of influence. Prevailing opinion among both French and British mandatory officials was that preservation of society's *status quo* would best preserve French and British influence. To alter the *status quo,* by substantially enlarging the electorate or by depriving those who were at the top of society of their authority, might create upheaval and jeopardize foreign influence. France and Great Britain carefully avoided that danger: special provisions were introduced in the Syrian, Lebanese, and Iraqi constitutions ensuring continued non-Muslim and tribal representation in parliament; and land legislation introduced in Syria and Iraq gave great power to tribal leaders to ensure their continued support for the foreign powers.

In Iraq, Transjordan, and Egypt, constitutional systems divided power among a strong monarch, the nationalist middle class, and the British. In Syria and Lebanon, France fragmented political power among diverse ethnic, religious, and linguistic groups. French and British parliamentary and constitutional forms gave the appearance, but not the substance, of democracy. To the extent that such systems adopted free speech, permitted opposition parties to exist, and allowed parliamentary discussion of legislation, they resembled Western institutions. However, they lacked those fundamentals that give life and vitality to Western democracy. Parliaments existed without an informed or literate electorate. Political parties, except the Wafd in Egypt and the PRP in Turkey, were small cliques representing minority interests. The press discussed primarily those issues that concerned the upper and middle classes. Without extending education to rural areas, there could be little increase in literacy and no informed electorate. But parliaments made little effort to provide budgets to expand educational facilities. Without an informed population there was little possibility of organizing mass movements among the peasants and urban lower classes. Existing peasant organizations and trade-union movements were regarded by those in power as subversive, and every effort was made to crush them.

Leftist attempts during the interwar era to organize mass movements all failed, usually because the organizers used terms that had no mass appeal. Most individuals who attempted to organize workers and peasants were alien to the feelings and emotions of the classes they sought to organize. Before World War II, Communists agitated for "international solidarity of the working classes," an appeal that was meaningless to most Middle Easterners. By the late 1940s the Communists had abandoned their conventional appeals and slogans and turned to nationalism as their rallying call.

Until defeat of the Axis powers in World War II, rightist ideologies rather than those of the left were popular with Middle East nationalists. The PRP in Turkey and the National Brotherhood and its successor, the Istiqlal in Iraq were more influenced by Fascist corporate-state programs than by socialist ideology. Ataturk, Bakr Sidki, and Reza Shah all found Fascist ideology more appealing because of its apparent dynamism. To these Middle Eastern leaders strongly centralized authority and an emphasis on work, discipline, and glorification of the state were all doctrines that seemed ready-made for their own national purposes. The only influential political group in the Middle East that eschewed Fascist doctrine, aside from the Jewish parties in Palestine was the Wafd party, many of whose leaders admired instead the British liberal tradition. In Iraq, the Ahali, which later became the National Democratic party, was strongly influenced by British socialism, but the group never became a potent national force.

By the end of World War II fascism was thoroughly discredited. Germany and Italy, utterly defeated, had shown that the corporate state was not invincible and that social-democratic nations were not as weak as they had appeared. By the 1950s socialism became *the* popular political ideology in the Middle East, just as it had become so elsewhere in Asia. Numerous Socialist parties flourished in the Arab East, and many political groups that were not really socialist, adopted socialist slogans to compete for popular favor. Indicative of the trend was conversion of Ahmed Husein's one-time Egyptian Fascist party to socialism, although the party never carried great weight in either guise.

After World war II the military also began to feel its political oats. Before the war, army officers had played prominent roles in Turkey, Iraq, and Iran, but they had been an effective political force only in Turkey. Even there, once they entered the political stage, they abandoned their military identity. Although both Ataturk and his successor, Inonu, were former generals, both put off their uniforms after becoming president and insisted that officers in politics surrender their army commissions and that those on active duty refrain from political activity. Reza Shah was also a former army officer who used his position to attain political power, but once he attained power he subordinated Iranian army officers to his will as shah, not as an army general. Iraq's series of military coups, beginning in 1936, soon degenerated from an idealistic reform movement into a naked power struggle among various army cliques. By the early 1940s they were thoroughly discredited and regarded as no better than the country's civilian politicians who also squabbled over personalities, not issues.

Within the Arab officer groups, the upper ranks usually represented the conservative upper levels of society, that element which desired to preserve the social *status quo*. Junior grades were more often held by men from middle- and lower-middle-class families. Many of the latter were converted to an active nationalism by their resentment of the British or French domination. Defeat of the Arab armies by a relatively small, foreign Jewish force during the Palestine war in 1947–1948 was an overwhelming blow to Arab national pride, particularly to the officer group. Many junior officers as well as younger Arab intellectuals were stirred to action by the Palestine debacle and decided that the shame must be wiped away, that the weakness in Arab society that could produce such a disaster must be removed. Initially, those who wanted reform tried the familiar approach of reforming the military machine.

The first series of post-Palestine military coups occurred in Syria. But the officers who seized power there proved to be no better than those who had ruled Iraq after 1936. After attaining power they did little to alter the country's economic, political, or social structure. So burdensome did General Shishakli's military dictatorship become that he was overthrown by a coalition of civilian forces recruited from every political faction from Communists to the conservative landowners.

But Syrian politics again degenerated into the old pattern of control by a small group of wealthy individuals, who were now pressured by the rising middle class and a new, youthful leftist group to make fundamental reforms. However, a stalemate emerged among the old guard, the middle class, and the young leftists. Although the leftists began to rally a mass following among peasants and urban labor groups, most machinery of government remained in the hands of the old guard, who used it to prevent any real social change.

The only Syrian party of consequence to put forward a program advocating fundamental socioeconomic change was the Ba'ath, a socialist group which ascended to power during the 1950s, lost power after Syria was unified with Egypt in 1958, and again in the 1960s seized control of governments in Syria and in Iraq. But the Ba'ath, like other Arab political groups, split into diverse factions, each contending with the other, with the result that no faction succeeded in accomplishing effective changes in Arab society.

The young officer group which seized power in Egypt after 1952 was far more effective. Disillusioned with their national leadership after the Palestine debacle, the group also initially sought to reform the military machine. After seizing power, the officers not only revamped the army, they also imposed fundamental reforms that altered Egypt's basic social relationships. They not only refused to collaborate with the old guard, they completely destroyed its political, economic, and social influence. All other potential sources of political competition were similarly eliminated. The Communists were driven underground, the once powerful Muslim Brotherhood was liquidated, and the Wafd party was shorn of its influence when the army seized its press and absorbed its village branches.

Egypt's revolutionary regime was the first in the Middle East not only to challenge, but drastically to alter the existing complex of social, economic, and political institutions—both those indigenous to the country's culture and those imported from the West. The criterion for accepting new political forms in revolutionary Egypt was no longer whether or not they were Western or Muslim, but how effective they were and whether the revolutionary government could use them to change society fundamentally as it desired. The first victim of the revolution was the old political machine. The European-type monarchy was abolished and the Western-style constitution discarded. At first, there were attempts to adapt the existing parliamentary system to the new regime. But when it became obvious that an effective parliamentary form of government could not work without effective political parties and an informed electorate, the attempts were abandoned. The only real political party was the Wafd, which, despite wide membership, was manipulated by a small group of politicians representing the wealthy. Neither the peasants nor the laboring class was represented in the party hierarchy, or in the governments that it formed when in office. Furthermore, the party had become thoroughly discredited because of the dishonesty of its leaders. Consequently, the revolutionary military regime that seized power in 1952 decided to abolish all political parties and resisted all attempts to reinstitute a system that would return control to the old political groups.

Because it mistrusted all who were not from the same background as themselves, Egypt's new Revolutionary Command Council turned over most responsible state positions to fellow army officers. Thus, a new officer group, representing the lower-middle class, now ascended to power. Because it had no experience in government or in administration, no clearly formulated policy, it attempted to devise new approaches, many borrowed from other political systems. The country's new leader, Gamal Abdel Nasser, had his staff systematically reviewed the programs and accomplishments of other revolutionary regimes, hoping to cull from their successes what would be of value to revolutionary Egypt.

Democratic guarantees, such as free press, free speech, and free political organization were sacrificed, since, Nasser explained, the vast majority of the population had never benefited from them anyhow. Under the old regime the depressed four-fifths of society had been unable to improve their living conditions despite the theoretical existence of democratic freedoms. Before the population could really benefit from democratic freedoms, it would have to become economically secure, literate, and free from the burdens of economic oppression. Democratic institutions imported from the West would serve no use in an Oriental society suffering from traditional Oriental poverty, disease, illiteracy, and gross inequality—so argued the young Egyptian revolutionists. Only after their country's population had attained a material standard of life resembling that in the West could it effectively use Western political institutions.

Various new political forms were tried in revolutionary Egypt to maintain contact between the new officer elite and the masses. At first a Liberation Rally, then a National Union were organized to enlist popular participation in the revolution. Both failed to sustain mass interest in the revolutionary goals; in 1962 political life was again reorganized around a congress of popular forces representing occupational groups and an Arab socialist union with the hope that they would rally the population. While national policy was formulated by the handful of army officers at the top echelon of government, attempts were made to decentralize local decisions and to give greater authority to provincial and subprovincial officials. The dilemma in Egypt, as in Ataturk's republican Turkey, was how to enlist popular support for and participation in national life while retaining control over and direction of the revolution. Nasser, like Ataturk, tried to induce participation of villagers in the national cause through extension of party organization to numerous rural centers. One difference between Ataturk and Nasser is that the Turkish president gave authority to peasants or workers only on one or two occasions, whereas the Egyptian deliberately sought to foster peasant and worker participation in the national parliament, but without great success.

Other Middle Eastern countries were still strugging with European parliamentary forms of government. None has yet found them satisfactory to meet the pressure of economic and social development, with the possible exception of "Western" Israel. In Israel, Western political forms work more or less successfully because the country's origin is European and it has a high rate of literacy, a wide divergence of political and social groups, and an unusually high percentage of popular participation in national political life. Political leaders and opinion-makers in Israel are by and large Westerners, have brought their ideologies and political system with them from Europe, or are Western educated and acculturated.

In Turkey, Iran, Lebanon, Syria, and Jordan, experiments with Western-type parliamentary institutions and constitutional systems can hardly be called successful. In none of these countries are there effective political organizations that represent peasants and laborers on a wide scale. Parliamentary life, where it exists, is controlled by the upper and upper-middle classes. The rulers of most countries so dominate the political scene that opposition is rendered totally ineffective. Lebanon's whole structure of government is distorted by the system of allocating administrative offices, parliamentary seats, and government posts according to the strength of the various religious groups in the country. In Jordan, the monarch is the pivot of political life and maintains a precarious balance between the army, landowners, merchant middle class, and nationalists, constantly fearing that some combination of these forces will topple his regime. Thus in Middle Eastern nations other than Israel, where parliamentary systems do work, such institutions are merely used by the upper stratum of society to maintain its entrenched position.

After Egypt's defeat in the 1967 war with Israel, President Nasser attempted to revitalize his country's parliamentary institutions by cutting back on the influence of the army, by allocating more responsibility to the country's single political party, the Arab Socialist Union, and by permitting greater self-criticism in parliament. Efforts were made to encourage greater and more extensive peasant and village participation in the country's elected institutions, but the low level of literacy and the great poverty inhibited effective spread of popular participation. As part of his "liberalization" measures, Nasser's successor, Anwar Sadat, permitted formation of political parties and greatly diminished the role of the ASU. These steps were seen as a return to Western type political institutions, and a move away from Nasser's revolution, although Sadat and his successor, Husni Mubarak, maintained their government control of the political system.

The Arabian peninsula has not yet been seriously affected by the impact of Western political institutions, although the first tremors of change have already been felt. Until the 1962 resolution, Yemen was ruled by an Oriental potentate, who aimed at no separation of church and state. The imam was still an absolute monarch dominating national civil and religious life, and traditional religious law determined legislation. Until the early 1950s much the same situation existed in Saudi Arabia, although there was a more extensive tribal force of democracy forcing the monarch to consider opinions of tribal chieftains with whom he was allied. Since 1950 a constitutional system has begun to emerge in Saudi Arabia. Extensive legislation has been adopted to supplement Koranic law, and the monarch's powers have been considerably trimmed as he has been forced to consult his ministers. The new oil industry has given birth to a small middle class which is rapidly expanding and insisting on greater representation in government. In other Arabian principalities the sheikhs rule, although the oil industry has awakened a new middle class not only to the material assets of the West, but also to its diverse political ideologies. However in several of these oil rich countries there is growing concern about the huge proportion of imported labor which forms a potentially restive working class.

The spread of radical nationalist ideologies was evident in establishment of the Republic of Yemen, in the new People's Republic of South Yemen, and in unrest in the Persian Gulf emirates. With impending departure of the British from the region, radical nationalist groups backed by Arab socialist regimes began to undermine the authority of traditional rulers who had governed with British support for the last century or two.

There was hope in 1950 that one-party rule in Turkey had ended when the PRP surrendered power to the Democrats, who were victorious in the country's first free elections. Although democracy, including a free press and free speech and unrestricted party activity, seemed to flourish for a year or so, the new Democratic regime soon proved to be even more authoritarian than its PRP predecessor. Parliament was converted by Democratic Prime Minister Adnan Menderes into a tool of his party, over which he held absolute control. The high-handed tactics used by Menderes soon created considerable unrest among the country's intellectuals. His regime became so oppressive that it created a popular uprising in the capital led by the army which resented the prime minister's use of its services to suppress political opponents. In rural areas, however, the many peasants who had benefited from Menderes's economic policies—especially from his protection of them against increased taxation—were not at all enthusiastic about the revolution that destroyed Menderes in 1960.

A period of coalition government followed reinstitution of the parliamentary system by the army until the Justice party won, first one majority in 1965, and then an even larger one in 1969, assuring it control of the government. Victory by the Justice party, successor to the Democratic party of Menderes, showed how strong peasant conservatism was in Turkey, but it also widened the cleavage between the urban lower class and the governing elite, since the latter was unprepared to carry out structural reforms necessary to meet the country's growing problems. Once again in 1971 the army sought to restore the balance and reinstitute a "law and order" regime when it deposed the Justice party and put a coalition government in power. By 1973 martial law was terminated and Turkey returned to multiparty democracy. The dilemma facing the country was that no party seemed able to win a majority. Thus governments were coalitions, often ineffective and unable to cope with the increasing problems. The result was the spread of political instability and tension and another army takeover in 1980.

Most of the countries of the area have resources that still await development while their peoples live in great poverty. Egypt is a notable exception, for its limited resources can not hope to provide for the expanding population under the best of conditions. Recent discovery of oil in Egypt may radically alter that country's position. A crucial problem facing contemporary Middle Eastern society is what form of government can best bring about and direct the social and economic reforms so drastically needed. The use of money and technical competence is not enough to develop national resources, as we have seen in the case of Iraq. Construction of large dams and irrigation systems and the development of land, water, and mineral reserves does not guarantee improvement in the life of the average Middle Easterner. Without extensive social and political change, the majority of the population can not really benefit from economic development. Social and political systems must be devised that can guarantee equitable distribution of the profits from national economic improvements. National resources may be exploited and expanded, but their concentration in the hands of the few individuals at the top of the social pyramid will bring little benefit to society as a whole. Under political systems today prevailing, there is little likelihood that the legislation required for a more equitable distribution of national resources is possible. Effective land reform will continue to be difficult in governments controlled by landowners or wealthy states. Nor will such governments take adequate measures to educate the peasant, organize cooperatives, and extend government services to underdeveloped rural areas.

Even political revolution is not enough. Mere confiscation of wealthy landowners' property will not guarantee an equitable social system or higher living standards. In Egypt, Syria, Yemen, and Iraq, there have been revolutions that have considerably curbed the landowners' political power. But in Egypt the rapidly expanding population still outstrips national resources, and political change alone can not alter the situation. The problem is a social one; it is a question of peasant attitudes toward the family. Technological improvements in agriculture, irrigation, the use of power, and development of industry can improve, but they can not solve the dilemma of Egypt's population explosion.

Most Middle Eastern nations are not yet ready for technological revolution. There are not enough technicians to set up and operate industrial plants, too few economic planners to determine what industries are best suited to development of available national resources, a shortage of managerial talent to direct these operations, and a lack of capital and markets required for industrial expansion. In Egypt confiscatory measures (that is, nationalization of capital) have been inadequate to develop industry, so that the country has again turned to foreign economic and technical assistance—both American and Russian. Concomitant with industrial development are the problems of social uprootedness caused when peasants flock to large cities, where, after they have lost their family and religious ties, they easily become victims of extremist agitators. The large new industrial slums add to the already existing problems of sanitation, health, educaiton, and security.

Growing impatience with the failures of Western political institutions and technolgoical innovations to improve life for the masses in the Middle East became increasingly overt by the late 1970s and early 1980s; it was manifest in the phenomenon described in the West as "Islamic resurgence," i.e., the attraction to fundamentalist Islam of many students, intellectuals, and middle class former adherents of radical secular ideologies. Many of the disenfranchised among the working classes and peasantry openly expressed their disillusionment with Western ways and techniques through their political support for Islamic zealots who entered the political arena like the Muslim Brothers in Egypt and Syria or the Ayatollah Khomeini in Iran. Toppling the shah in the 1979 Islamic Revolution was more than an Iranian happening. It stimulated interest and stirred fundamentalist fervor among the Muslim lower-middle class and proletariat throughout the region and aroused deep apprehension in established regimes.

The economic and social problems of developing nations become international problems when they are the focal points of competition in the world power struggle. Both the United States and the Soviet Union are competing to assist developing Middle Eastern, as well as other nations. Each of the great powers hopes to use influence gained through economic and technical assistance to persuade developing nations of the value of its own political, social, and economic institutions. This power struggle in the Middle Eastern context is closely related to the contest for power between the Soviet Union and the United States in the larger global context. Its effects upon each nation in the region, from an internal point of view, have yet to be resolved.

The intensity of great power competition in the area has greatly increased since the June 1967 war between Israel and Egypt, Jordan, and Syria. The disastrous Arab defeat has led to greater radicalization of politics, with the USSR giving all-out political support and military assistance to revolutionary Arab governments. On the other hand, the ties between Israel and the United States have become closer. Countries in the middle, such as Jordan and

Lebanon, are increasingly threatened by revolutionary movements, especially by the Palestinian Arab commandos. As fighting escalates and each side, the U.S. and the USSR, escalates assistance to its protégés, the danger of big power confrontation becomes greater.

Growing awareness by both superpowers of the dangers in escalating the conflict between their Middle East protégés was evident in their agreements during 1967, 1970, and 1973 to support cease-fires in the Arab-Israeli wars. However, success of the cease-fire depends on willingness of Israel and the Arab states to negotiate their differences, and on an agreement by the United States and the Soviet Union to halt the dangerous supply of even more sophisticated military equipment to the combatants. These were difficult and at times contradictory goals. Each of the wars was followed by an extended series of peace negotiations through the United Nations, bilaterally between the United States and the Soviet Union, through involvement of the middle powers such as Great Britain and France, and even through indirect talks involving Israel and some Arab states. The October 1973 war was followed by the first formal peace talks involving the combatants at Geneva. But after two meetings the Geneva Middle East Peace Conference was suspended for several more years until Egyptian President Anwar Sadat's peace initiative in 1977 which led to the Egyptian-Israeli peace treaty in 1979.

A major obstacle to an overall settlement was the Palestine problem. The Israeli government refused to attend any talks at which the PLO, the official representative body of the Palestinians, attended. The Palestinians, at first ambivalent about representation in peace talks, later insisted that the PLO be given official recognition by the United States and Israel. By 1982 issues of mutual Israeli-Palestinian recognition, Israeli occupation of the territories it had seized in the 1967 war, and doubts about formal recognition of Israel by the Arabs continued to stymie progress.

Throughout these extended parleys, the dangers of renewed war greatly intensified. All parties escalated the quantity and quality of their arms supplies to a level never imagined before. By 1977 Middle East countries, including Iran which was not involved in the Arab-Israeli conflict, were purchasing billions of dollars worth of military equipment yearly. Both in quantity and sophistication, the arms levels of Middle East countries had reached the levels of European NATO members. The world's major arms suppliers, the United States, the Soviet Union, and France, were sending the great bulk of their shipments to the Middle East. This was a threat, not only to Middle Eastern and to world peace, but a substantial drain on the area's resources undermining progress toward economic and social development. Instead of becoming secure and stable, the Middle East had become one of the most volatile regions in the international political system. Even Egyptian President Anwar Sadat's dramatic and surprise peace initiatives in 1977 raised as much apprehension about the future as it stimulated hope. His efforts to unilaterally end the thirty-year war with Israel divided the Arab world and intensified the competition in the region between the superpowers. Only a few Arab states supported his peace offensive at first; most were either reluctant to become involved in direct negotiations with the Jewish state or adamantly opposed them. The United States supported his efforts after initial reserve, but the Soviet Union condemned Sadat for acting without the other Arab states.

By the beginning of the 1980s, the inventory of Middle East problems, both internal and foreign, was far greater than the region could cope with itself, or than any single outside power could manage. No regional constellation of countries, not the U.S. nor the USSR, alone could resolve the Arab-Israeli conflict, settle the Palestinians, end the Iraq-Iran war, terminate the strife in Lebanon, bring stability to the countries torn by civil war, or improve economic and social conditions. Not only did these problems require physical resources beyond the means of any single nation, they required insight, planning, and understanding on a large scale, a scale that would require cooperation among the nations of the Middle East as well as among the powers outside the region for whom the Middle East would be an area of vital importance during decades to come.

Selected Bibliography

Bibliographical, Periodical, and Reference Works

Atiyeh, George N. *The Contemporary Middle East 1948–1973*. Boston, 1975. A massive and comprehensive bibliography of books, articles, and studies.

Bodurgil, Abraham. *Turkey, Politics and Government: A Bibliography 1938–1975*. Washington, D.C., 1978.

Grimwood-Jones, Diana; Hopwood, Derek; and Pearson, J.D. *Arab Islamic Bibliography*. Sussex, 1977. Extensive coverage.

Guclu, Meral. *Turkey*. Santa Barbara, 1981. Part of World Bibliographical Series, vol. 27. Detailed bibliography of all aspects of Turkey.

International Journal of Middle East Studies. A quarterly published by the Middle East Studies Association of North America.

Journal of Palestine Studies. Beirut. Quarterly on Palestinians and the Arab-Israel conflict published by the Institute for Palestine Studies; includes excellent bibliographic references, chronology, and documentation.

Khalidi, Walid, and Khadduri, Jill. *Palestine and the Arab-Israel Conflict*. Beirut, 1974. The most extensive bibliography on the conflict to date with 4,580 listings.

Legum, Colin, and Shaked, Haim, eds. *Middle East Contemporary Survey*. Vols. 1–4, 1976–1980. A series of essays and detailed country reviews with excellent references, diagrams, tables, etc.

MERIP Reports. Washington, D.C. Monthly periodical with Marxian analysis published by the Middle East Research and Information Project.

The Middle East and North Africa. London, latest edition. An annual survey and directory with historical, economic, and geographic background. (1st ed., 1948.)

The Middle East Journal. Washington, D.C. The Middle East Institute. Contains the best English-language bibliography on contemporary affairs, including periodical literature and recent books, with reviews of important works. It is published quarterly.

Middle East Record. Jerusalem. Annual published from 1962 by Shiloah Institute covering political and economic events of the region and its individual countries. Replaced by *Middle East Contemporary Survey* after 1970.

Middle Eastern Studies. London. Quarterly scholarly magazine with historical emphasis.

New Outlook. Monthly published in Tel Aviv, Israel. Contains articles on Israel and its neighbors directed toward Arab-Jewish rapprochement.

Partington, David, ed. *The Middle East Annual: Issues and Events.* Vol. 1, 1981. Boston, 1982. Series of scholarly articles covering principal events with excellent annotated bibliography.

Schultz, Ann. *International and Regional Politics in the Middle East and North Africa: A Guide to Information Sources.* Detroit, 1977. Major emphasis on bibliographic material related to international relations.

Sherman, John, ed. *The Arab-Israeli Conflict, 1945–1971: A Bibliography.* New York, 1978. 419 pages of items.

Atlases

Atlas of the Arab World and the Middle East. New York, 1960. A good presentation of physical characteristics, resources, population, and climate.

Atlas of Islamic History. Compiled by Harry W. Hazard and H. Lester Cooke, Jr. Princeton, N.J., 1951. Traces the history of Islam with helpful commentary.

Gilbert, Martin. *The Arab-Israeli Conflict, Its History in Maps.* 2nd ed. London, 1976.

Historical Atlas of the Muslim Peoples. Compiled by R. Roolvink, *et al.* Cambridge, Mass., 1957. A detailed historical atlas.

The Middle East and North Africa. London, 1960. An economic atlas showing resources, population, industry, and agricultural developments.

Pounds, Norman J.G., and Kingsbury, Robert C. *An Atlas of Middle Eastern Affairs.* New York, 1963. A geopolitical historical atlas from the ancient to modern periods.

Geographical Studies

Beaumont, P.; Blake, G.; and Wagstaff, J. *The Middle East: A Geographical Study.* New York, 1976. Brings up to date older studies.

Fisher, W.B. *The Middle East: A Physical, Social, and Regional Geography.* London, 1950. 7th ed., 1978. Treats the area by geographical regions and in great detail.

Collections of Writings by Middle Easterners and Interpretive Essays

Dessfosses, H., and Levesque, J. *Socialism in the Third World.* New York, 1975. A reader with essays including Syria, Iraq, Libya, and Algeria.

Gardner, George H., and Hanna, Sami A. *Arab Socialism: A Documentary Survey.* Leiden, 1969. Socialist authors and documents.

Gendzier, Irene L. *A Middle East Reader.* New York, 1969. A collection of Middle East and other authors, strongly emphasizing nationalism.

Haim, Sylvia G., ed. *Arab-Nationalism: An Anthology.* Berkeley and Los Angeles, 1976. A selection of writings by Arab authors.

Hamalian, Leo, and Yohannan, John D., eds. *New Writing from the Middle East.* New York, 1978. A collection of fiction, poetry and drama from Arabic, Armenian, Persian, Israeli and Turkish authors.

Hammond, Paul Y. and Alexander, Sidney S. *Political Dynamics in the Middle East.* New York, 1972. Extensive collection of essays on contemporary Middle East political problems including international relations.

Karpat, Kemal, ed. *Political and Social Thought in the Contemporary Middle East.* Rev. ed. New York, 1982. A collection of political writings and statements of all Middle East countries with extensive commentary.

Landen, Robert G. *The Emergence of the Modern Middle East,* New York, 1970. A collection of documents and observations from medieval to modern times.

Peretz, Don. *The Middle East: Selected Readings.* Rev. ed. Boston, 1973. A compilation of writings by Europeans and Middle Easterners from early times to the present.

Anthropological and Sociological Studies

Baer, Gabriel. *Population and Society in the Arab East.* London, 1964. An introduction to the area by an Israeli scholar.

Beck, Lois and Keddie, Nikki, eds. *Women in the Muslim World.* Cambridge, Mass., 1978. A useful series of studies on women.

Berger, Morroe. *The Arab World Today.* New York, 1962. An excellent study of contemporary Arab social organization and institutions, including an examination of attitudes, personality, relationships between men and women, and political life.

Eickelman, Dale F. *The Middle East: An Anthropological Approach.* Englewood Cliffs, N.J., 1981.

Hourani, Albert H. *Minorities in the Arab World.* London, 1947. An account of minority groups and their backgrounds in each of the Arab countries.

El-Saadawi, Nawal. *The Hidden Face of Eve: Women in the Arab World.* Boston, 1982. An account by a woman physician of taboo subjects and oppressive beliefs and practices.

Sweet, Louise E. *Peoples and Cultures of the Middle East.* 2 vols. Garden City, 1970. Collection of essays by anthropologists and sociologists on life in the desert, towns, and cities.

Van Nieuwenhuijze, Christoffel, A.O. *Sociology of the Middle East: A Stocktaking and Interpretation.* Leiden, 1971. Social structure and change in the Middle East region and by country.

———. *Commoners, Climbers and Notables: A Sampler of Studies on Social Ranking in the Middle East.* Leiden, 1977.

Economic Studies of the Region

Cooper, Charles A., and Alexander, Sidney S. *Economic Development and Population Growth in the Middle East.* New York, 1972. Studies of growth and development in several countries and in the region as a whole.

Issawi, Charles P., ed. *The Economic History of the Middle East: 1800–1914.* Chicago, 1966. A documentary collection dealing with economic life.

Lloyd, Edward M.H. *Food and Inflation in the Middle East, 1940–1945.* Stanford, 1956. Describes Middle East economics and planning during and after World War II.

Sayigh, Yusuf. *The Economics of the Arab World.* New York, 1978. Basic and comprehensive study from Morocco to Iraq.

Warriner, Doreen. *Land Reform and Development in the Middle East, A Study of Egypt, Syria, and Iraq.* London, 1957. Critically analyzes agrarian reform, private enterprise, and the flow of oil royalties into three Arab countries.

Economic Developments in the Middle East 1959–1961. Supplement to World Economic Survey, 1961. New York, 1962. Compilation of economic statistics on the region as a whole. Part of a United Nations series begun in 1949–1950.

Final Report of the United Nations Economic Survey Mission for the Middle East. 2 vols. New York, 1949. A critical analysis of economic development possibilities in Israel and the Arab East.

Middle Eastern Oil

Anderson, Irvine H. *Aramco, The United States and Saudi Arabia: A Study of the Dynamics of Foreign Oil Policy, 1933–1950.* Princeton, 1981.

Blair, John M. *The Control of Oil.* New York, 1976. A critical account of oil company policy.

Conant, Melvin A. *The Oil Factor in U.S. Foreign Policy, 1980–1990.* Lexington, Mass., 1982. An overview of the global problem.

Engler, Robert. *The Brotherhood of Oil: Energy Policy and The Public Interest.* Chicago, 1977. A critical account of the oil companies and government policy.

Issawi, Charles, and Yeganeh, Mohammed. *The Economics of Middle Eastern Oil.* New York, 1962. An account of oil investment, production, and the world market.

Lenczowski, George. *Oil and State in the Middle East.* Ithaca, 1960. Examines economic and legal aspects of relations between the oil companies and their host countries.

Longrigg, Stephen H. *Oil in the Middle East, Its Discovery and Development.* London, 1954. 3rd ed., 1968. Factual history of oil in the Middle East.

Mosley, Leonard. *Power Play—Oil in the Middle East.* New York, 1973. History of oil and politics in the Middle East.

Rustow, Dankwart A. *Oil and Turmoil: America Faces OPEC and the Middle East.* New York, 1982. A critical account.

Sampson, Anthony. *The Seven Sisters.* New York, 1975. History of the international oil cartel and its relationships with the Middle East.

Shwadran, Benjamin. *The Middle East, Oil and the Great Powers.* New York, 1955. 2d ed., 1959. A study of oil politics and maneuvers among the great powers.

Tetreault, Mary Ann. *The Organization of Arab Petroleum Exporting Countries: History, Policies, and Prospects.* Westport, Conn., 1981.

Annotated Documents

Alexander, Yonah, and Nanes, Alton, eds. *The United States and Iran: A Documentary History.* Frederick, Md, 1980. A collection of mostly U.S. documents.

Eayrs, James. *The Commonwealth and Suez: A Documentary Study, 1956–57.* New York, 1963. Documentation on the Suez crises and its background.

Fraser, T.G. *The Middle East, 1914–1979.* New York, 1980. Compendium from Husain-McMahon correspondence in 1914 to Camp David, with commentary.

Higgins, Rosalyn, ed. *United Nations Peacekeeping: Documents and Commentary. The Middle East.* Vol. 1. New York, 1969. Documents on UN Middle East forces.

Hurewitz, J.C. *The Middle East and North Africa in World Politics.* Vol. 1. *European Expansion, 1535–1914.* New Haven, 1975. Vol. 2. *British-French Supremacy, 1914–1945.* New Haven, 1979. Well annotated.

Moore, John Norton. *The Arab-Israeli Conflict: Readings and Documents.* Princeton, 1977. Includes materials from 1897 to 1975, official and unofficial.

Department of State. *Foreign Relations of the United States,* Vol. 5, part 1, *1947.* Washington, D.C., 1971; Vol. 5, part 2, *1948.* Washington, D.C., 1976; Vol. 6, *1949.* Washington, D.C., 1977. Extensive documentation on American policy making in the Middle East.

Islam and the Arabs

Of the hundreds of books on Islam and the Arabs, the following few may be particularly helpful as background works for the beginning student of the contemporary Middle East:

Ajami, Fouad. *The Arab Predicament: Arab Political Thought and Practice Since 1967.* Cambridge, 1981. A critical analysis of Arab radicals, Muslim fundamentalists, and conservatives.

Anderson, J.N.D. *Islamic Law in the Modern World.* New York, 1959. A brief study of Islamic law and modern life, including marriage, divorce, and inheritance.

Andrae, Tor. *Mohammed, the Man and His Faith.* New York, 1936. One of the best volumes on the founder of Islam.

Arberry, A.J., ed. *Religion in the Middle East.* 2 vols. Cambridge, England, 1969. Extensive treatment by various authors of Judaism, Christianity, and various Muslim groups.

Bill, James and Leiden, Carl. *Politics in the Middle East.* Boston and Toronto, 1979. A theoretical and analytical study of modernization and politics.

Cragg, Kenneth. *The Call of the Minaret.* New York, 1956. A sympathetic treatment of Islam by a Christian who attempts to understand the religion and its problems in the modern world.

Esposito, John L., ed. *Islam and Development: Religion and Sociopolitical Change.*

Syracuse, 1980. A survey of contemporary Islamic thought and practice in Egypt, Saudi Arabia, Iran, Pakistan, Nigeria, Senegal, and Malaysia.

Esposito, John L., and Donahue, John J. *Islam in Transition: Muslim Perspectives.* New York, 1982. Writings of modern Muslim thinkers; significant documents, with commentary.

Fisher, Sydney N. *The Middle East: A History.* 3rd ed. New York, 1979. Good historical background on Islam from early periods to the present.

Gibb, Hamilton A.R. *Mohammedanism, An Historical Survey.* New York, 1949. 2d ed., 1968. An excellent history of the rise of Islam, its development, and its situation in the modern world.

Gibb, H.A.R., and Kramers, J.H., eds. *Shorter Encyclopedia of Islam.* Ithaca, 1965. Extensive and detailed compilation of Islamic terminology.

Guillaume, Afred. *Islam.* Toronto, 1954. 2d ed., 1956. A brief history of Islam's rise, its sects, philosophies, and contemporary beliefs.

Von Grunebaum, G.E. *Medieval Islam.* Chicago, 1946. An interesting study of Islamic developments during the "Golden Age" of Islam.

Keddie, Nikki R., ed. *Scholars, Saints and Sufis: Muslim Religious Institutions since 1500.* Berkeley and Los Angeles, 1972. A very useful collection of studies on Islam's influence up to the present.

Khaldun, Ibn. *The Muqaddimah: An Introduction to History.* Translated by Franz Rosenthal. 3 vols. New York, 1958. An early Islamic philosophy on the rise and fall of dynasties.

Kritzeck, James, ed. *Anthology of Islamic Literature from the Rise of Islam to Modern Times.* New York, 1963. A useful compilation illustrating Islamic life.

Levy, Reuben. *The Social Structure of Islam.* Cambridge, 1957. Examines social status in the Muslim world, the status of women, children, and slaves, and the religion's fundamental institutions.

Lewis, Bernard. *The Arabs in History.* London, 1950. 3d ed., 1956. The best-written brief history of the Arabs and the rise of Islam.

Lewis, Bernard, ed. *Islam.* Vol. 1, *Politics and War;* Vol. 2, *Religion and Society.* New York, 1974. Collection of translated documents from era of Mohammed to the fall of Constantinople.

Long, David E. *The Hajj Today: A Survey of the Contemporary Pilgrimmage to Makkah.* Albany, 1979. How the Hajj works.

Mortimer, Edward. *Faith and Power: The Politics of Islam.* New York, 1982. The rise, spread, variety, and complexity of Islam in a dozen countries.

Pickthall, Mohammed Marmaduke. *The Meaning of the Glorious Koran.* New York, 1953. 7th ed., 1959. One of the better translations of the Koran with explanatory comments by an English convert to the religion.

Rahman, Fazlur. *Islam.* New York, 1966. An interpretation of Islam from a sympathetic but critical Muslim viewpoint.

Said, Edward. *Orientalism.* New York, 1978. A sharp critique by an American-Arab scholar of Western scholarship about the Middle East.

Schroeder, Eric. *Muhammad's People: A Tale by Anthology.* Portland, Maine, 1945. An anthology of early Islamic writing.

Southern, R.W.. *Western Views of Islam in the Middle Ages.* Cambridge, Mass., 1962. European misconceptions of Islam.

The Ottomans

Until recently, useful English language works on the Ottoman era were few. The following are among the best for supplying an historical background to the contemporary scene:

Brockelmann, Carl. *History of the Islamic Peoples.* New York, 1960. Contains detailed information on the Ottomans in part 3.

Creasy, Edward S. *History of the Ottoman Turks: From the Beginning of their Empire to the Present Time.* London, 1878, reprint, Beirut, 1961. One of the most extensive works tracing Ottoman history from its origins in 1876.

Davison, Roderic H. *Reform in the Ottoman Empire, 1865–1876.* Princeton, 1963. An authoritative study of the Tanzimat era.

Eliot, Charles N.E. *Turkey in Europe.* London, 1908. Reprint, London, 1965. One of the most interesting and best-written accounts of the Ottoman Empire during the nineteenth century, with historical background.

Fisher, Sydney. *The Middle East: A History.* Cited above. Has good historical survey of the rise and fall of the Ottomans.

Gibb, Hamilton A.R. and Bowen, Harold. *Islamic Society and the West, A Study of the Impact of Western Civilization on Modern Culture in the Near East.* Vol. I, *Islamic Society in the Eighteenth Century,* London, 1950 (part 1) and 1957 (part 2). A comprehensive study of Islamic political and social institutions and their evolution from early times.

Gokalp, Ziya. *Turkish Nationalism and Western Civilization.* Translated and edited, with an introduction, by Niyazi Berkes. New York, 1959. A collection of Gokalp's essays on nationalism, religion, and society.

Heyd, Uriel. *Foundations of Turkish Nationalism: The Life and Teachings of Ziya Gokalp.* London, 1950. Biography of the first modern Turkish nationalist philosopher.

Itzkowitz, Norman. *Ottoman Empire and Islamic Tradition.* New York, 1972. Useful text on history of Ottomans and their institutions.

Kushner, David. *The Rise of Turkish Nationalism, 1876–1908.* London, 1977. The era of Abdul Hamid II.

Lewis, Bernard. *Istanbul and the Civilisation of the Ottoman Empire.* Norman, Okla., 1963. A colorful account of the Ottoman capital at its glory.

Mardin, Serif. *The Genesis of Young Ottoman Thought.* Princeton, 1962. Describes the origin of modern political thought in the Ottoman Empire.

Ramsaur, Ernest E., Jr. *The Young Turks.* Princeton, N.J., 1957. The best account of the Young Turks and their era.

Shaw, Stanford H., and Shaw, Kural Ezel. *History of the Ottoman Empire and Modern Turkey.* Vol. 2, *Reform, Revolution and Republic: The Rise of Modern Turkey 1808–1975.* New York and London, 1977. Deals primarily with the era leading up to establishment of the Republic.

Stavrianos, L.S. *The Balkans Since 1453.* Parts 2 and 3. New York, 1958. Gives an excellent account of the rise and fall of the Ottoman Empire.

Vucinich, Wayne S. *The Ottoman Empire: Its Record and Legacy.* Princeton, 1965. Collection of readings with commentary.

Modern History of the Middle East and Its Relations with the West

The number of books on relations between the Middle East and the West is legion. The subject is covered in part by several of the previously mentioned volumes, particularly those dealing with the region as a whole, and it will be covered in part by books to be listed later under specific countries. Detailed bibliographies dealing with relations during the nineteenth and twentieth centuries can be found in several of the following books.

Bromberger, M. and S. *Secrets of Suez*. London, 1957. Purports to reveal secrets of the French government concerning background of the 1956 attack on Suez.

Dawisha, Karen. *Soviet Foreign Policy Towards Egypt*. New York, 1979. A discussion of Soviet policy objectives, mostly during the Nasser era.

Dekmekian, Richard Hrair. *Patterns of Political Leadership: Egypt, Israel and Lebanon*. Albany, 1975. Study of political elites in three countries.

De Novo, John A. *American Interests and Policies in the Middle East, 1900–1939*. Minneapolis, 1963. A history of American commercial and other interests in the area.

Finer, Herman. *Dulles over Suez: The Theory and Practice of His Diplomacy*. Chicago, 1964. A highly critical account of American and Egyptian policies.

Hallberg, Charles W. *The Suez Canal: Its History and Diplomatic Importance*. New York, 1931. Examines the history of the canal and Anglo-French rivalry over its control.

Halliday, Fred. *Soviet Policy in the Arc of Crisis*. Washington, D.C., 1981. Refutes theory that all problems in the region come from Soviet instigation.

Heikel, Mohammed H. *The Road to Ramadan*. Glasgow, 1976. Account of the 1973 war by an Egyptian official close to Nasser.

———. *The Sphinx and the Commissar: The Rise and Fall of Soviet Influence in the Middle East*. New York, 1978. An account by a direct participant in Egypt's negotiations with the USSR.

Hourani, Albert. *Arabic Thought in the Liberal Arts, 1798–1939*. New York and London, 1962. A history and interpretation of modern Arab thought.

Howard, Harry N. *The King-Crane Commission: An American Inquiry in the Middle East*. Beirut, 1963. A study of post World War I American Investigation Commission.

———. *The Partition of Turkey: A Diplomatic History, 1913–1923*. Norman, Okla., 1931. The best work on the postwar manipulations leading to dismemberment of the Ottoman Empire.

Kedourie, Elie. *England and the Middle East*. London, 1956. Presents a critical study of British policy during and after World War I.

Lord Kinross (Patrick Balfour). *Between Two Seas: The Creation of the Suez Canal*. London, 1968. An account by a British diplomat.

Kirk, George. *The Middle East in the War*. London, 1952.

———. *The Middle East, 1945–1950*. London, 1954. This volume, like the one that preceded it, was issued under the auspices of the Royal Institute of International Affairs as part of the Survey of International Affairs; both are very well documented, although the author's pro-British point of view is fully evident.

Lacquer, Walter. *Confrontation: The Middle East and World Politics.* New York, 1974. Account of the 1973 Arab-Israeli war and its impact on world politics, including the oil crisis.

Lenczowski, George, ed. *Political Elites in the Middle East.* Washington, D.C., 1975. Collected essays on elites in various Middle Eastern countries.

————. *The Middle East in World Affairs.* Ithaca, 1952. 4th ed., 1980. Useful diplomatic history of the area since World War I.

Lewis, Bernard. *The Middle East and the West.* Bloomington, 1964. An extensive historical essay on relations with the West.

Long, David E., and Reich, Bernard. *The Government and Politics of the Middle East and North Africa.* Boulder, 1980. A good introduction, with emphasis on the 1970s.

Love, Kennett. *Suez: The Twice Fought War.* New York, 1969. A voluminous study of the 1956 and 1967 wars.

Mangold, Peter. *Superpower Intervention in the Middle East.* New York, 1978. A compendium of superpower activities, largely since 1970.

Marriott, J.A.R. *The Eastern Question: An Historical Study in European Diplomacy.* Oxford, 1917. A classic study of diplomacy in the area during the nineteenth century.

Meade, Edward Earle. *Turkey, the Great Powers, and the Baghdad Railway: A Study in Imperialism.* New York, 1923. A standard work on the Baghdad railroad and the diplomacy surrounding it in the quarter century before World War I.

Monroe, Elizabeth. *Britain's Moment in the Middle East, 1914–1956.* Baltimore, 1963. Britain's role as a dominant power in the Middle East.

Quandt, William B. *Decade of Decisions: American Policy Toward the Arab-Israeli Conflict, 1967–1976.* Berkeley and Los Angeles, 1977. Survey by an informed ex-insider.

Rubenstein, Alvin Z. *Red Star on the Nile: The Soviet-Egyptian Relationship Since the June (1967) War.* Princeton, 1977.

Sachar, Howard M. *Europe Leaves the Middle East, 1936–1954.* New York, 1972. Comprehensive history of Western involvements in the Middle East.

Schonfield, Hugh J. *The Suez Canal in World Affairs.* New York, 1953. A useful history of the canal and the problems surrounding it.

Shotwell, James T., and Deak, Francis. *Turkey at the Straits: A Short History.* New York, 1940. A diplomatic history of the Straits question.

Sousa, Nasim. *The Capitulatory Regime of Turkey, Its History, Origin, and Nature.* Baltimore, 1933. Survey of the capitulations from the sixteenth through twentieth centuries.

Spector, Ivar. *The Soviet Union and the Muslim World, 1917–1958.* Seattle, 1959. A useful survey based on Soviet sources.

Thomas, Hugh. *The Suez Affair.* New York, 1967. A critical analysis.

Tillman, Seth P. *The United States and the Middle East.* Bloomington, 1982. U.S. policy with a focus on the Arab-Israeli problem.

Toynbee, Arnold J. *Survey of International Affairs, 1925.* Vol. I: *The Islamic World since the Peace Settlement.* A classic analysis of the post World War I Middle East.

Wilson, Arnold. *The Suez Canal.* London, 1933. A useful history.

Arab Nationalism

Books in English on Arab nationalism began to appear in large numbers only after World War II. There is an overlap between the subject of Arab nationalism and others treated in this text, and many of the above-mentioned volumes have excellent sections on the subject, as do many of those later listed under specific countries. The following are a few of the best volumes available in English devoted wholly to the subject:

Abu-Lughod, Ibrahim, ed. *The Transformation of Palestine: Essays on the Origin and Development of the Arab-Israeli Conflict.* Evanston, Illinois, 1971. Land, population and other problems in pre-Israel Palestine from an Arab perspective.

Antonius, George. *The Arab Awakening: The Story of the Arab National Movement.* Philadelphia, 1939; New York, 1965. The classic account, giving an Arab's point of view of the rise of the nationalist movement.

Be'eri, Eliezer. *Army Officers in Arab Politics and Society.* London, 1970. A history and analysis of the role of the military in modern Arab life.

Dawn, Ernest C. *From Ottomanism to Arabism: Essays on the Origins of Arab Nationalism.* Urbana, 1973.

Hassouna, Hussein A. *The League of Arab States and Regional Disputes: A Study of Middle East Conflicts.* Dobbs Ferry, New York, 1975. Covers Arab League activities related to regional disputes between 1945 and 1975.

Hudson, Michael C. *Arab Politics: The Search for Legitimacy.* New Haven and London, 1977. A discussion of political modernization and its dilemmas in the Arab world.

Kerr, Malcolm. *The Arab Cold War, 1958–1967: A Study of Ideology in Politics.* 3d ed., New York, 1971. A critical analysis of inter-Arab politics.

Khadduri, Majid. *Political Trends in the Arab World: The Role of Ideas and Ideals in Politics.* Baltimore, 1970. A critical analysis.

———. *Arab Personalities in Politics.* Washington, D.C., 1981. Case studies of monarchs in Jordan, Saudi Arabia, Oman, UAE, Sadat in Egypt, and Assad in Syria.

Khalidi, Walid, ed. *From Haven to Conquest, Readings in Zionism and the Palestine Problem Until 1948.* Beirut, 1971. An excellent collection from diverse perspectives.

Khalil, Khalid Muhamad. *From Here We Start.* Washington, D.C., 1953. A translation from the Arabic of a work stressing the social and economic aspects of nationalism.

Nuseibeh, Hazem Z. *The Ideas of Arab Nationalism.* Ithaca, 1956. A philosophic study of Arab nationalism by a man who became foreign minister of Jordan in 1961–1962.

Saab, Hassan. *The Arab Federalists of the Ottoman Empire.* Amsterdam, 1958. A detailed treatise on the philosophic origins of the Arab nationalist movement.

Sayegh, Fayez A. *Arab Unity: Hope and Fulfillment.* New York, 1958. Studies the attempts at Arab unity and gives an evaluation of their successes and failures.

Sharabi, Hisham. *Arab Intellectuals and the West: The Formative Years, 1875–1914.* Baltimore, 1970. Origins of an Arab ideology.

Zeine, Zeine N. *Arab-Turkish Relations and the Emergence of Arab Nationalism.*
Beirut, 1958. 3d ed. Delmar, N.Y., 1976. An excellent account of the origins of the
Arab nationalist movement and its early relations with Ottoman authorities from
a fresh viewpoint.

———. *The Struggle for Arab Independence.* Beirut, 1960. An account of the Arab
Nationalist movement during and immediately after World War I.

Modern Turkey and the Cyprus Conflict

Books listed above under the "Ottomans" and those dealing with Turkey
under "The West and the Middle East" provide background for the coming of
the Turkish republic. The following are only a few of the many worthwhile
volumes published on the subject since World War I:

Ahmad, Feroz. *The Turkish Experiment in Democracy—1950–1975.* London, 1977.
Comprehensive and clear study of Turkish politics since World War II.
Berkes, Niyazi. *The Development of Secularism in Turkey.* Montreal, 1964. A study of
secularism from the Ottoman to the modern era.
Crawshaw, Nancy. *The Cyprus Revolt: An Account of the Struggle for Union with
Greece.* London, 1978. A comprehensive historical account of the Cypriot-Greek
revolt against Great Britain.
Dodd, C.H. *Democracy and Development in Turkey.* North Humberside, U.K., 1979.
An examination of Turkey's history, society, and government.
Hale, William. *The Political and Economic Development of Modern Turkey.* New
York and London, 1981. A useful introduction to Turkish economic problems.
Iz, Fahir, ed. *An Anthology of Modern Turkish Short Stories.* Chicago, 1978. 37
stories published from 1900 to 1975.
Karpat, Kemal, and contributors. *Social Change and Politics in Turkey: A Structural-
Historical Analysis.* Leiden, 1973. Study of Turkish politics and society.
Karpat, Kemal. *The Gecekondu: Rural Migration and Urbanization.* New York, 1976.
Detailed study of urban slum expansion in modern Turkey.
Lord Kinross (Patrick Balfour). *Ataturk: A Biography of Mustafa Kemal, Father of
Modern Turkey.* New York, 1965. An extensive and colorful biography.
Landau, Jacob M. *Radical Politics in Modern Turkey.* Leiden, 1974. A detailed study
of both right and left political factions.
Lewis, Geoffrey L. *Turkey.* New York, 1955. 4th ed., 1974. A concise, factual, excellent
volume on present-day political and social life in Turkey and the background
leading up to developments in 1962.
Makal, Mahmut. *A Village in Anatolia.* London, 1954. An account by a teacher of life
in a traditional village.
Özbunden, Ergun. *Social Change and Political Participation in Turkey.* Princeton,
1976. An analysis of the effect of social change on Turkish politics.
Salih, Halil Ibrahim. *Cyprus: The Impact of Diverse Nationalism on a State.* Ala-
bama, 1978. A well-documented account of events leading up to the 1974 Turkish
intervention.
Stirling, Arthur P. *Turkish Village.* New York, 1966. A study of tradition and change
in a Turkish village.

Toynbee, Arnold J., and Kirkwood, Kenneth P. *Turkey.* New York, 1927. An excellent account of transformation of the Ottoman Empire to the Turkish republic.

Ward, Robert E., and Rustow, Dankwart. *Political Modernization in Japan and Turkey.* Princeton, 1968. A collection of essays by various authors on comparative modernization.

Webster, Donald E. *The Turkey of Ataturk: Social Process in the Turkish Reformation.* Philadelphia, 1939. A detailed and sympathetic survey of political and social change in Turkey up to 1938.

Weiker, Walter F. *The Turkish Revolution, 1960–1961: Aspects of Military Policies.* Washington, 1963. A study of the 1960 coup.

—— *The Modernization of Turkey: From Ataturk to the Present Day.* New York and London, 1981. An overall evaluation of political and social development.

Egypt

Since the 1952 revolution in Egypt the number of books in English on that country has greatly increased, partly as a result of its predominant role in the Arab world today. Books dealing primarily with the Suez Canal problem have been listed above. The following references deal with the country as a whole.

Ahmed, Jamal M. *Intellectual Origins of Egyptian Nationalism.* London, 1960. Contains an excellent study of philosophic origins of the nationalist movement.

Ayrout, Henri H. *The Fellaheen, Cairo, 1945.* Reissue, Boston, 1968. The best account of Egyptian peasant life by a priest who has spent most of his life among the fellaheen.

Baer, Gabriel. *A History of Landownership in Modern Egypt, 1800–1950.* London, 1962. A survey of prerevolutionary landholding.

Binder, Leonard. *In a Moment of Enthusiasm: Political Power and the Second Stratum.* Chicago, 1978. An analysis of second level or local politics in Egypt.

Cooper, Mark N. *The Transformation of Egypt.* Baltimore, 1982. An analysis of the internal problems from 1967 to 1977.

Critchfield, Richard. *Shahhati: An Egyptian.* Syracuse, 1978. A narrative account of the life of an Egyptian peasant from an anthropolgical perspective.

Cromer, Evelyn Baring, Earl. *Modern Egypt.* 2 vols. London, 1908. Presents a British ruler's account of his regime and its social background.

Dekmejian, Richard Hrair. *Egypt Under Nasser: A Study in Political Dynamics.* Albany, 1971. Analysis of the revolutionary leadership and its background.

Harris, Christina Phelps. *Nationalism and Revolution in Egypt: the Role of the Muslim Brotherhood.* The Hague, 1964. Historical account of the Brotherhood.

Holt, P.M., ed. *Political and Social Change in Modern Egypt: Historical Studies from the Ottoman Conquest to the United Arab Republic.* New York, 1967. Three-part anthology: part 1, source material; part 2, 1517–1798; part 3, nineteenth and twentieth centuries.

Hopwood, Derek. *Egypt: Politics and Society: 1945–1981.* Winchester, Mass., 1982. Survey of the Nasser and Sadat regimes.

Issawi, Charles. *Egypt at Mid-Century.* New York, 1954. A fundamental economic analysis.

———. *Egypt in Revolution: An Economic Analysis.* London, 1963. Egypt's economy since the 1952 revolution.

Lacouture, Jean and Simone. *Egypt in Transition.* New York, 1958. A translation from the French of revolutionary Egypt and its background.

Lacouture, Jean. *Nasser: A Biography.* New York, 1973. One of the best on Nasser.

Lane, E.W. *Manners and Customs of the Modern Egyptians.* New York, 1923. A good survey of rural and city life along the Nile.

Lloyd, George Ambrose. *Egypt Since Cromer.* New York, 1933–1934. A former British high commissioner's account of events after Cromer.

Marlowe, John. *A History of Modern Egypt and Anglo-Egyptian Relations, 1800–1953.* New York, 1954. A useful survey of relations with Great Britain.

el Messini, Sawsan. *Ibn Al-Balad: A Concept of Egyptian Identity.* Leiden, 1978. A sociological study of the lower middle class in Cairo.

Mitchell, Richard P. *The Society of Muslim Brothers.* London, 1969. Background, origins, structure, and ideology of the Brotherhood.

Nasser, Gamal Abdel. *Egypt's Liberation: The Philosophy of the Revolution.* Washington, D.C., 1955. The late president's early views on the revolution, which differ from his later ones.

Neguib, Mohammed. *Egypt's Destiny.* New York, 1955. An account of the revolution by the Egyptian republic's first president.

O'Brien, Patrick. *The Revolution in Egypt's Economic System: From Private Enterprise to Socialism, 1952–1965.* London and New York, 1966. Economic change since Nasser.

Richmond, John C.B. *Egypt, 1798–1952—Her Advance toward a Modern Identity.* New York, 1977. An introductory survey.

Rivlin, Helen Anne B. *The Agricultural Policy of Muhammad 'Ali in Egypt.* Cambridge, Mass., 1961. An excellent analysis of Muhammad 'Ali's attempts to create a modern economy.

Sadat, Anwar. *In Search of Identity: An Autobiography.* New York, 1978.

Safran, Nadav. *Egypt in Search of Political Community, An Analysis of the Intellectual and Political Evolution of Egypt, 1804–1952.* Cambridge, Mass., 1961. A valuable survey.

El-Shamy, Hasan M., ed. *Folktales of Egypt.* Chicago, 1980. A collection and analysis of folklore.

Vatikiotis, P.J. *The Egyptian Army in Politics, Pattern for New Nations?* Bloomington, Ind., 1961. Useful analysis of the officers' backgrounds and their attempts at reform.

———. *Nasser and His Generation.* New York, 1978. A psychopolitical portrait of Nasser and his milieu.

Waterbury, John. *Egypt: Burdens of the Past, Options for the Future.* Bloomington, 1978. A series of essays on diverse economic, social, and political problems by a long-time observer.

———. *Hydropolitics in the Nile Valley.* Syracuse, 1979. A study and analysis of political and economic development plans in Egypt and Sudan.

Israel

So great is the amount of material published on Israel and the Palestine problem that it probably exceeds that published on all the other countries covered in this book. The following are but a few of the more useful items:

Begin, Menachem. *The Revolt*. New York, 1978. Revised edition of the Israeli prime minister's early years in Palestine-Israel.

Ben-Dor, Gabriel. *The Druses in Israel, A Political Study: Political Innovation and Integration in a Middle East Minority*. Jerusalem and Boulder, 1979. A study of socio-political change from the local and national perspective.

Ben Gurion, David. *Rebirth and Destiny of Israel*. New York, 1954. Contains a collection of essays on Israel's role by its first prime minister.

Benvenisti, Meron. *Jerusalem: The Torn City*. Minneapolis, 1976. Discusses pros and cons of nearly 50 solutions for the Jerusalem problem.

Brecher, Michael. *The Foreign Policy System of Israel: Setting, Images, Process*. New Haven, 1972. Comprehensive study of organization and context of Israeli foreign policy.

El-Asmar, Fouzi. *To Be an Arab in Israel*. London, 1975. Experiences of an Israeli Arab.

Elon, Amos. *The Israelis Founders and Sons*. New York, 1971. Reissue, 1983. An Israeli's insights into the old and new generations of Israelis.

Fabian, Larry L., and Schiff, Ze'ev. *Israelis Speak: About Themselves and the Palestinians*. Washington, D.C., 1977. In-depth discussion by Israelis of diverse orientations about Arab-Israel and other problems.

Friedlander, Dov, and Goldscheider, Calvin. *The Population of Israel*. New York, 1979. A detailed and scholarly analysis.

Granott, A. *The Land System in Palestine: History and Structure*. London, 1952. History of Arab, Jewish, and government landholdings and laws before 1948.

Halabi, Rafik. *The West Bank Story: An Israeli Arab's View of a Tangled Conflict*. New York, 1982.

Halperin, Samuel. *The Political World of American Zionism*. Detroit, 1961. Contains a good account of the role played by Zionist groups in shaping American policy.

Halpern, Ben. *The Idea of the Jewish State*. Cambridge, Mass., 1961. Detailed and thorough analysis of the concept of Jewish sovereignty.

Herzl, Theodor. *The Jewish State: An Attempt at a Modern Solution of the Jewish Question*. London, 1934. Translation from the German of Herzl's original views.

Hurewitz, J.C. *The Struggle for Palestine*. New York, 1950. A good factual account of the Arab-Jewish-British conflict in Palestine.

Kanofsky, Eliahu. *The Economy of the Israeli Kibbutz*. Cambridge, 1966. A critical analysis.

Laqueur, Walter. *A History of Zionism*. New York, 1972. A comprehensive, in-depth history.

Lilienthal, Alfred. *The Zionist Connection: What Price Peace?* New York, 1978. An anti-Zionist study of Israel–U.S. relations.

Lustick, Ian. *Arabs in the Jewish State: Israel's Control of a National Minority*. Austin, 1980. Discussion of Israel's Arab minority in a new theoretical context.

Penniman, Howard R., ed. *Israel at the Polls: The Knesset Elections of 1977.* Washington, D.C., 1979. Collection of essays on many aspects of the election.

Peretz, Don. *The Government and Politics of Israel.* Boulder, 1979. Discussion of the origins and operation of Israel's government.

Perlmutter, Amos. *Military and Politics in Israel: Nation Building and Role Expansion.* London, 1969. Examines the influence of Israel's military establishment.

————. *Politics and the Military in Israel, 1967–77.* Cambridge, Mass., 1978.

Sachar, Howard M. *A History of Israel from the Rise of Zionism to Our Time.* New York, 1976. Excellent and comprehensive history of modern Israel.

Safran, Nadav. *Israel: The Embattled Ally.* Cambridge and London, 1978. A comprehensive survey of both internal and foreign developments.

Schiff, Gary S. *Tradition and Politics: The Religious Parties of Israel.* Detroit, 1977. An account of the National Religious and Aguda Israel parties.

Schnall, David J. *Radical Dissent in Contemporary Israeli Politics: Cracks in the Wall.* New York, 1979. An examination of several smaller, but important left and right factions.

Segre, Dan V. *A Crisis of Identity: Israel and Zionism.* Oxford and New York, 1980. A discussion of whether or not traditional Jewish culture can adapt to Israel.

Shimshoni, Daniel. *Israeli Democracy: The Middle of the Journey.* New York, 1982. A discussion of diverse problems in policy making.

Smooha, Sammy. *Israel: Pluralism and Conflict.* Berkeley and Los Angeles, 1978. A comprehensive survey of the situation of Israeli Arabs, Oriental and Religious Jews.

Weizmann, Chaim. *Trial and Error: The Autobiography of Chaim Weizmann.* New York, 1949. Relates the trials of Israel's first president up to the time of statehood.

Willner, Dorothy. *Nation-Building and Community in Israel.* Princeton, 1969. A study of Oriental-Jewish community life in Israel.

The Palestinians and the Arab-Israeli Conflict

Amos, John W. *Palestinian Resistance: Organization of a Nationalism Movement.* New York, 1980. An extensive study of all aspects of the Palestinian movement.

Aronson, Sholomo. *Conflict and Bargaining in the Middle East: An Israeli Perspective.* Baltimore, 1978. A heavily documented history of negotiations from Kissinger on.

Brecher, Michael. *Decisions in Crisis: Israel 1967 and 1973.* Berkeley, 1980. A detailed study of decisions by Israeli policy makers leading to the 1967 and 1973 wars.

Brown, William R. *The Last Crusade: A Negotiator's Middle East Handbook.* Chicago, 1980. An examination of the importance of mutual perceptions in negotiations.

Cohen, Aaron. *Israel and the Arab World.* New York, 1970. Excellent study of Arab-Jewish relations in Palestine. Translated from Hebrew.

Dayan, Moshe. *Breakthrough: A Personal Account of Egypt-Israel Peace Negotiations.* London and New York, 1981.

ESCO Foundation for Palestine, Inc. *Palestine: A Study of Jewish, Arab, and British Policies.* 2 vols. New Haven, 1947. A collection of articles on Palestine during the mandate era.

Flapan, Simha. *Zionism and the Palestinians.* New York, 1978. A study of some lost opportunities for peace.

Herzog, Chaim. *The Arab-Israeli Wars.* New York, 1982. A popular but professional military history.

Hirst, David. *The Gun and The Olive Branch: The Roots of Violence in the Middle East.* London, 1977. A sympathetic but not uncritical discussion of the Palestinian movement.

Kerr, Malcolm H., ed. *The Elusive Peace in the Middle East.* Albany, 1975. A collection of articles on Arab-Israel relations and efforts to attain a peace settlement.

Khouri, Fred. *The Arab Israel Dilemma.* Syracuse, 1968. 2d ed., 1976. An extensive study based mostly on UN sources.

Lesch, Ann Mosley. *Arab Politics in Palestine, 1917–1939: The Frustration of a Nationalist Movement.* Ithaca and London, 1979. A scholarly study.

Migdal, Joel S. *Palestinian Society and Politics.* Princeton, 1980. Collection of essays on history and social structure of the Palestinians.

Nakleh, Khalil, and Zureik, Elia, eds. *The Sociology of the Palestinians.* New York, 1980. A collection of articles in social structure and society.

O'Ballance, Edgar. *No Victor, No Vanquished: The Yom Kippur War.* San Rafael, California and London, 1978. An interesting and well-written account.

Polk, William R.; Stamler, D.; and Asfour, E. *Backdrop to Tragedy: The Struggle for Palestine.* Boston, 1957. The best study available of the emotions involved in the Palestine conflict.

Said, Edward. *The Question of Palestine.* New York, 1979. A forceful presentation of the Palestinian case by a Palestinian-American.

Sid-Ahmed, Mohamed. *After the Guns Fall Silent: Peace or Armageddon in the Middle East.* London and New York, 1976. A leftist analysis of the Arab-Israeli conflict and the role of the great powers.

Sykes, Christopher. *Crossroads to Israel.* New York, 1965. Story of Anglo-Jewish Arab relations, 1919–1948.

Weizmann, Ezer. *The Battle for Peace.* New York, Toronto, London, 1981. A former general and defense minister's critique of Begin's peace negotiations.

Wilson, Evan M. *Decision on Palestine: How the U.S. Came to Recognize Israel.* Stanford, 1979. A veteran diplomat's insight into American policy making.

Zurayk, Constantine N. *Palestine: The Meaning of the Disaster.* Beirut, 1956. An analysis of the Arab defeat by a noted scholar, translated from the Arabic.

Lebanon

Because Syria and Lebanon had many aspects of a single administration until their independence at the end of World War II, some authors have treated them in a single volume. The following lists contain a few more useful specific items:

Barakat, Halim. *Lebanon in Strife: Student Preludes to the Civil War.* Austin and London, 1977. A survey and analysis of Lebanese student attitudes.

Deeb, Marius. *The Lebanese Civil War*. New York, 1980. A topical account.

Gabriel, Philip Louis. *In the Ashes: A Story of Lebanon*. Ardmore, Penn., 1978. An account of the social origins of the civil war.

Gordon, David C. *Lebanon: The Fragmented Nation*. Stanford and London, 1980. A personal account of the civil war by an American.

Gulick, John. *Social Structure and Culture Change in a Lebanese Village*. New York, 1955. An anthropologist's study of changing ideas and values.

Hudson, Michael. *The Precarious Republic: Political Modernization in Lebanon*. New York, 1969. A critical political analysis.

Khalidi, Walid. *Conflict and Violence in Lebanon: Confrontation in the Middle East*. Cambridge, Mass., 1980. Background of the civil war by an informed insider.

Owen, Roger, ed. *Essays on the Crisis in Lebanon*. London, 1976. Essays by diverse authors tracing the conflict to its nineteenth century roots.

Polk, William R. *The Opening of South Lebanon, 1788–1840*. Cambridge, 1963. A study of change in nineteenth century rural Lebanon.

Salibi, Kamal S. *Crossroads to Civil War, Lebanon 1958–1976*. Delmar, N.Y., 1976. An account of the 1975–76 war explaining the diverse groups, trends, events, military faces, and personalities.

———. *The Modern History of Lebanon*. New York, 1965. Major emphasis on the nineteenth century.

Suleiman, Michael W. *Political Parties in Lebanon: The Challenge of a Fragmented Political Culture*. Ithaca, 1967. A soçio-political study.

Syria

Abu Jaber, Kamal S. *The Arab Ba'ath Socialist Party: History, Ideology, and Organization*. Syracuse, 1966. First major study of the Ba'ath party in English.

Devlin, John F. *The Ba'ath Party: A History From Its Origins to 1966*. Stanford, 1976. Origins during the French mandate to evolution in Jordan and Iraq.

Hourani, Albert H. *Syria and Lebanon*. London, 1946. The best account and analysis of the Levant up to the end of World War II.

Longrigg, Stephen H. *Syria and Lebanon Under French Mandate*. London, 1958. A scholarly history of the Levant from Ottoman times to independence.

Rabinovitch, Itamar. *Syria Under the Ba'ath 1963–1966: The Army-Party Symbiosis*. New York, 1972.

Seale, Patrick. *The Struggle for Syria: A Study of Post-War Arab Politics, 1945–1958*. New York, 1965.

Torrey, Gordon H. *Syrian Politics and the Military, 1945–1958*. Columbus, 1964. A study of the manuevers leading to union with Egypt.

Jordan

In addition to previously mentioned general works, the following books are recommended:

Abdullah Ibn Husayn. *Memoirs of King Abdullah*. New York, 1950. An autobiography, translated from Arabic by G. Khuri.

Antoun, Richard. *Low-Key Politics: Local-Level Leadership and Change in the Middle East.* Albany, 1979. An anthropologist's account of politics at the village level in Jordan.

———. *Arab Village: A Social Structural Study of a Transjordanian Peasant Community.* Bloomington, Illinois, 1972. An anthropological study.

Glubb, J.B. *A Soldier with the Arab.* New York, 1957. Glubb's account of Jordan's role in the 1948 Arab-Israeli War.

———. *The Story of the Arab Legion.* New York, 1957. Personal account of Arab Legion commander.

Harris, George L. *Jordan: Its People, Its Society, Its Culture.* New York, 1958. A composite study by several authors.

Hussein of Jordan. *My "War" With Israel.* New York, 1969. King Hussein's account of the Six-Day War.

———. *Uneasy Lies the Head: The Autobiography of His Majesty King Hussein of the Hashemite Kingdom of Jordan.* New York, 1962.

Lutfiya, Abdullah M. *Baytin: A Jordanian Village: A Study of Social Institutions and Social Change on a Folk Community.* The Hague, 1966.

Shwadran, Benjamin. *Jordan: A State of Tension.* New York, 1959. A history and background of Jordan.

Vatikiotis, Panayotis, J. *Politics and the Military in Jordan: A Study of the Arab Legion, 1921–1957.* New York, 1967.

Iraq

Arfa, Hassan. *The Kurds: An Historical and Political Study.* London, 1966. Kurdish history from early times to the present.

Birdwood, Christopher. *Nuri as-Said: A Study in Arab Leadership.* London, 1960. Eulogistic biography of the former Iraqi prime minister.

Caractacus. *Revolution in Iraq.* London, 1959. An anonymous Englishman's favorable story of the 1958 Iraqi revolution and a critique of Western Middle East policy.

Dann, Uriel. *Iraq Under Qassem: A Political History, 1958–1963.* New York, 1969. The early revolutionary period.

Foster, Henry A. *The Making of Modern Iraq.* Norman, Okla., 1953. A scholarly account of the early history of Iraq.

Gabbay, Rony. *Communism and Agrarian Reform in Iraq.* London, 1978. A historical focus.

Ghareeb, Edmund. *The Kurdish Question in Iraq.* Syracuse, 1981. The Kurds in Iraq with primary focus on the Ba'ath government's approach.

Khadduri, Majid. *Independent Iraq: A Study in Iraqi Politics from 1932 to 1958.* London, 1960. 1st ed., 1951. A thorough study of Iraqi politics and parties.

———. *Republican Iraq: A Study in Iraqi Politics Since the Revolution of 1958.* New York, 1969.

———. *Socialist Iraq: A Study in Iraqi Politics Since 1968.* Washington, D.C., 1978.

Ireland, Philip W. *Iraq: A Study in Political Development.* London, 1937. An excellent account by an American diplomat of Iraq's early history and political progress.

Longrigg, Stephen, and Stoakes, Frank. *Iraq.* New York, 1958. A comprehensive history.

O'Ballance, Edgar. *The Kurdish Revolt, 1961–1970.* London, 1973. Military account of the Kurdish war.

Shwadran, Benjamin. *The Power Struggle in Iraq.* New York, 1960. Analyzes the 1958 revolution and the subsequent political turmoil.

Arabian Peninsula

In addition to the previously mentioned books on oil, which deal primarily with the Arabian peninsula, the following were also recommended:

Anthony, John Duke. *Arab States of the Lower Gulf: People, Politics, Petroleum.* Washington, D.C., 1975. Study of the nine Gulf states.

Clements, F.A. *Oman: The Reborn Land.* New York, 1980. A laudatory account of the Qabus regime.

Doughty, Charles M. *Travels in Arabia Deserta.* New York, 1955. Represents the classic study of an English traveler through the Arabian desert.

Halliday, Fred. *Arabia Without Sultans.* New York, 1975. Survey of revolutionary change in south Arabia and the Gulf from a left perspective.

Holden, David, and Johns, Richard. *The House of Saud: The Rise and Rule of the Most Powerful Dynasty in the Arab World.* London and New York, 1981. A critical account.

Hogarth, David. *The Desert King: The Life of Ibn Saud.* London, 1968. An authoritative biography.

al-Ibrahim, Hasan A. *Kuwayt: A Political Study.* Kuwait, 1975. Covers the political development of Kuwait from 1896 through the 1960s.

Khalifa, Ali Mohammed. *The United Arab Emirates: Unity in Fragmentation.* Boulder, 1979. Treatise on formation and problems of the U.A.E.

Lackner, Helen. *A House Built on Sand: A Political Economy of Saudi Arabia.* London, 1978. A socialist critique of Saudi life and economy.

Long, David E. *The Persian Gulf: An Introduction to Its Peoples, Politics and Economies.* Boulder, Col., 1976. Good short introduction.

Morris, James. *Sultan in Oman.* New York, 1957. A British journalist's story of his adventures in Muscat and Oman.

Nakhleh, Emile. *Bahrein: Political Development in a Modernizing Society.* Lexington, Mass., 1976.

Peterson, John E. *Yemen: The Search for a Modern State.* Baltimore, 1982. The dynamic of political change in Yemen.

Philby, H. St. John, B. *Arabian Jubilee.* London, 1951. The story of the Saud dynasty by a British former close associate and advisor of the king.

———. *Saudi Arabia.* New York, 1955. Philby's history of the kingdom.

Quandt, William B. *Saudi Arabia in the 1980s.* Washington, D.C., 1981. An overview of current Saudi foreign and domestic policies with emphasis on the U.S. connection.

Salibi, Kamal. *A History of Arabia.* Delmar, N.Y., 1980. A detailed history of the Peninsula from 3000 B.C. to the present.

Shaw, John A., and Long, David E. *Saudi Arabian Modernization: The Impact of Change on Stability.* Washington, D.C., 1982. Analysis of problems and potential of economic development and its socio-political impact.

Stookey, Robert W. *Yemen: The Politics of the Yemen Arab Republic.* Boulder, Col., 1978. An insightful work on a little known country.

Thesiger, Wilfred. *Arabian Sands.* New York, 1959. Another account of a British traveler's experiences in the deserts of southern Arabia.

Townsend, John. *Oman: The Making of a Modern State.* New York, 1977. Critique of administrative development and institution building in Oman.

Van der Meulen, Daniel. *The Wells of Ibn Saud.* New York, 1957. Experiences of a Dutch diplomat who lived in Saudi Arabia over ten years.

Zahlan, Rosemarie Said. *The Origins of the United Arab Emirates: A Political and Social History of the Trucial States.* New York, 1978. A critical account of British rule.

Iran

In addition to the general works previously listed, the following are recommended:

Abrahamian, Ervand. *Iran: Between Two Revolutions.* Princeton, 1982. An account from 1905 to 1979 with focus on the Tudeh Party.

Ahmed, Eqbal, ed. *The Iranian Revolution.* London, 1979. A special issue of the British journal, *Race and Class,* vol. 21, no. 1, Summer 1979. Containing a comprehensive group of informative articles.

Akhavi, Shahrough. *Religion and Politics in Contemporary Iran: Clergy-State Relations in the Pahlavi Period.* Albany, 1980. An informed study of the religious background on the 1979 Revolution.

Bill, James A. *The Politics of Iran: Groups, Classes, and Modernization.* Columbus, Ohio, 1972. Study of elites and the power structure.

Browne, Edward G. *The Persian Revolution of 1905–1909.* Cambridge, 1910, republished London, 1966. The best account available of that revolution.

Cottam, Richard W. *Nationalism in Iran.* Pittsburgh, 1964. An analysis of various contending group interests.

Elwell-Sutton, Lawrence P. *Persian Oil: A Study in Power Politics.* London, 1955. The Persian point of view of the oil dispute with Great Britain.

Halliday, Fred. *Iran: Dictatorship and Development.* New York, 1979. A social and economic analysis.

Heikal, Mohamed. *Iran: The Untold Story: An Insider's Account of America's Iranian Adventure and Its Consequences for the Future.* New York, 1981.

Hooglund, Eric J. *Land and Revolution in Iran, 1960–1980.* Austin, 1982. A critique of the Shah's "White Revolution."

Issawi, Charles, ed. *The Economic History of Iran 1800–1914.* Chicago, 1971. Documentary economic history.

Keddie, Nikki R. *Roots of Revolution: An Interpretive History of Modern Iran.* New Haven and London, 1981. The 19th and 20th century origins of the 1979 Revolution.

Kedourie, Elie, and Haim, Sylvia, eds. *Towards a Modern Iran: Politics and Society.* London, 1980. A series of useful essays on background of the 1979 Revolution including some personality sketches.

Lambton, A.K.S. *Landlord and Peasant in Persia: A Study of Land Tenure and Land Reserve Administration.* London, 1953.

———. *Islamic Society in Persia.* London, 1954.

Ledeen, Michael, and Lewis, William. *Debacle: The American Failure in Iran.* New York, 1981. A critique of American policy.

Lenczowski, George. *Russian and the West in Iran, 1918–1948.* Ithaca, 1949. An excellent study by a former Polish diplomat in Iran.

Millspaugh, Arthur C. *Americans in Persia.* Washington, D.C., 1946. The experiences of an American adviser to the Shah.

Pahlavi, Mohammed Reza. *Answer to History.* New York, 1980. The late Shah's account for his regime and its fall.

Ramazani, Rouhollah, K. *Iran's Foreign Policy, 1941–1973: A Study of Foreign Policy in Modernizing Nations.* Charlottesville, Va., 1975.

Rubin, Barry. *Paved With Good Intentions: The American Experience in Iran.* London and New York, 1981. Post World War II relations between the U.S. and Iran.

Saikal, Amin. *The Rise and Fall of the Shah.* Princeton, 1980. History and analysis of the Pahlavi dynasty.

Shuster, Morgan W. *The Strangling of Persia.* New York, 1912. Observations of an American financial adviser to Persia before World War I.

Sykes, Percy M. *A History of Persia.* London, 1915. 3d ed., 1930. 2 vols. Lengthy and detailed history of Persia from ancient times to 1930.

Wilson, Arnold T. *Persia.* New York, 1933. Primarily a historical survey.

Zonis, Marvin. *The Political Elite of Iran.* Princeton, 1971. Relations between Shah and elite.

Index

About the Author

Don Peretz has been professor of political science at the State University of New York in Binghamton, New York since 1967. He was the director of the university's program in South West Asian and North African studies from 1967 to 1977. From 1962 to 1967 he was associate director of the Center for Comparative Programs and Services of the New York State Education Department—University of the State of New York. Other books he has written or co-authored include: *Government and Politics of Israel; Israel and the Palestine Arabs; The Middle East—Selected Readings; Middle East Foreign Policy; Islam—Legacy of the Past, Promise of the Future.* His articles have appeared in *Foreign Affairs, Orbis, Middle East Journal, Wilson Quarterly, Jewish Social Studies, Christianity and Crisis, Progressive, Commonweal, Christian Century, Annals of the Academy of Political and Social Sciences,* and others. He is a member of the Editorial Advisory Board of the *Middle East Journal* and has been a member of the Board of Directors of the Middle East Studies Association of North America.